SEAN T. SEXTON

Managerial Economics

Text, Problems, and Short Cases

Irwin Publications in Economics

Managerial Economics

Text, Problems, and Short Cases

K. K. SEO

Professor of Business Economics and Quantitative Methods
University of Hawaii, Honolulu

1984
Sixth Edition

 RICHARD D. IRWIN, INC.

Homewood, Illinois 60430

To my family
Kathy, Darius, Margaret, and Judy
and
To William A. Long, pragmatic econ-
omist and a most treasured friend.

© RICHARD D. IRWIN, INC., 1959, 1964, 1968, 1975, 1979, and 1984

ISBN 0-256-02814-1

Library of Congress Catalog Card No. 83–81172

Printed in the United States of America

1 2 3 4 5 6 7 8 9 0 D 1 0 9 8 7 6 5 4

Preface

We live in an era of rapid technological change in both public and private sectors. More often than ever before, decision makers are called upon to apply economic analysis to challenging problems. It is not enough for a decision maker to have a firm grasp of economic theory; he or she must be able to apply the theory in a practical way to real problems. The objective of this text is not only to provide the theory of the firm but also to bridge the gap between economic theory and practical application. The bridge has been constructed on a solid base of microeconomic theory, using a blend of quantitative methods, other business disciplines, and good illustrative examples.

Like the previous edition, this sixth edition is aimed at intermediate-level undergraduate and first year graduate students in business and economics. However, many changes have been made in the basic framework of the book as well as in its contents. In addition to updating textual materials to reflect the changing environment of business, some topics have been dropped or reorganized and a substantial amount of new material has been added.

After reviewing a number of very helpful critiques by instructors and students of the previous edition, the following basic approach has been achieved in the sixth edition:

1. *Appropriate level of discourse.* The sixth edition presupposes noth-

ing more than a typical introductory course in economics and one in college algebra. The writing style has been changed in favor of simplicity, and explanation of the more difficult concepts and tools has been expanded, even though it makes the book longer.

2.   *Flexibility of coverage.* Largely self-contained chapters may be covered in virtually any order, thus permitting considerable teaching flexibility. Further flexibility is provided by appendixes to certain chapters, which contain either a fuller or more rigorous explanation of basic material presented in the chapter. Still more flexibility is provided to accommodate students with differing backgrounds by separating chapters covering fundamentals from chapters containing additional rigorous material. For example, the general topic of demand analysis is now covered by five chapters. For fundamental treatment, there are the specific topics of (1) utility theory and consumer behavior, (2) elasticities of demand, and (3) elementary techniques of demand estimation. For more advanced study, there are the additional topics of (4) multiple regression analysis and (5) forecasting. Detailed suggestions for use of the text in undergraduate and graduate courses are contained in the Instructor's Manual.

3.   *Illustrative problems and short cases.* End-of-chapter problems and short cases reinforce the text by further illustration of practical applications of the economic principles discussed in the chapter.

4.   *Separate student study guide and workbook.* A study guide and workbook under separate cover is available for the first time. It consists of chapter outlines, true-false and multiple-choice questions and their answers, problems and their solutions, and glossaries of important terminology. The study guide and workbook will:

a.   Emphasize the important concepts that the student must grasp.

b.   Help the student solve the end-of-chapter problems by similar examples.

c.   Provide practice in the application of economic theory to practical problems.

d.   Help the student to prepare for course exams.

Following the approach outlined above has resulted in numerous changes from the previous edition:

1.   Of the fifth-edition material that is still appropriate, about 80 percent has been rewritten, in plain English, for a better flow and easier reading.

2.   Expanded coverage has been provided for the following subjects:

    a.   The introductory chapter has been expanded to include alternative models of the firm and an explanation of why we use the profit-maximization model.

    b.   Decision analysis has been expanded to two chapters, one entitled "Decision Analysis," the other entitled "Approaches to Decision Making." The first of these two chapters contains expanded material on risk and risk adjustment. The second contains additional material on decision making under conditions of uncertainty and (in an appendix) a discussion of probability distribution of cash flows.

c. Demand analysis and estimation now is covered by five chapters, as noted above.

d. Production is now covered by two chapters, one on analysis and one on empirical measurement.

e. Cost is also now covered by two chapters, one on analysis and one on empirical measurement.

f. The discussion of pricing is now completely revised, with one chapter on how output and prices are decided in various market structures, and one on actual pricing practices and the modern approach to pricing problems. The second chapter has an appendix on transfer pricing.

g. The chapter on government and business has been completely rewritten with a major shift in emphasis from the legal environment of business to the economic role of government and recent developments in antitrust cases.

3. About 80 percent of the end-of-chapter problems are new. The end-of-chapter problems have been coordinated with textual materials to illustrated specific sections of the text and thus reinforce student understanding with current examples.

Acknowledgments

In preparing this edition, I was fortunate to receive many helpful suggestions and comments from students and professors who have used the previous edition. Also, I have benefited from the advice and criticisms of many colleagues. I am particularly grateful to Professors Thomas J. Hailstones of Xavier University (Cincinnati), J. K. Kwon of Northern Illinois University, J. Scott Armstrong of Wharton School, University of Pennsylvania, Richard E. Peterson, Jack P. Suyderhoud, and Reginald G. Worthley of the University of Hawaii, Mr. Chang-Kyoo Kim, President of Honam Ethylene Company, for his contribution and review of a number of case materials used in the test. Also, I wish to express my deep appreciation to Dr. David H. Bess, Dean of the College of Business Administration at the University of Hawaii, for his encouragement and support.

My special thanks go to Professor William A. Long, University of Hawaii, who taught me the subtleties of the English language and was helpful at every stage of this book's development and editing. My thanks for their able assistance also go to Ben Bystrom, Steven Schoen, and Vicky Sullivan, graduate assistants at the University of Hawaii, and to Pauline Abe who patiently and cheerfully typed and retyped the many versions of the manuscript. Finally, I would like to thank the entire editorial staff at Richard D. Irwin for their assistance, advice and encouragement.

Although every effort has been made to eliminate errors in the text, some may have slipped through. If so, I accept full responsibility for the error. I would appreciate advice from anyone who detects an error, as well as suggestions for further improvement of this text.

It is my sincere hope that this text will meet the requirements of managerial economics curricula and that it will help decision makers to make better decisions.

K. K. Seo

Contents

Introduction to Managerial Economics

The application of economic theory and its stock of analytical tools to everyday activities is no easy matter, as many frustrated students of economics have found out. "The theory is very neat," they say, "and I understand the tools, but how do I apply them to real-life problems?"

This is a legitimate question and one for which there are no easy answers. However, beginning with Joel Dean's pioneering work in 1951,[1] a new branch of economic study has emerged to bridge the gap between the theory and practice of economics. It is called managerial economics, and it is studied because it contributes to better decisions about economic problems in the real world.

Managerial economics today is an integral part of both undergraduate and graduate programs in business administration. Yet the principles and techniques of managerial economics are not limited to profit-seeking organizations. That is why managerial economics is also a popular offering in the curricula of other professional schools, such as those in engineering, public administration, public health, law, and urban and regional planning.

In this introductory chapter, two main topics will be discussed:

1. The nature of managerial economics and what distinguishes it from other branches of economics.

---

[1] Joel Dean, *Managerial Economics* (Englewood Cliffs, N.J.: Prentice-Hall, 1951).

2. Alternative models of the firm and the underlying assumptions of each regarding the motivations and objectives that govern a firm's behavior.

The Nature of Managerial Economics

Scholars have offered a number of definitions for managerial economics. To some, it is the application of economic theory (particularly microeconomic theory) to problems in both the public and private sectors. Other scholars view managerial economics as applied microeconomics, an approach requiring the integration of principles and practices from other functional areas such as accounting, finance, marketing, and production. Still other scholars regard managerial economics as a link between economic theory and decision science. Its purpose in this capacity is to contribute to sound decision making not only in business but also in government agencies and nonprofit organizations. In particular, managerial economics assists in making decisions about the optimal allocation of scarce resources among competing activities. Where alternative allocation strategies are available, managerial economics helps to pinpoint the best alternative through the application of techniques from management science and operations research.

Actually, all of these views are correct, for managerial economics is all of these things. We need not choose among them, for certain common elements are readily apparent in all the definitions. These common elements are:

1. Managerial economics is an application of economic theory, particularly of microeconomic theory, to practical problem solving.
2. Managerial economics can be used to make better management decisions.
3. Managerial economics pertains to decision making about the optimal allocation of scarce resources to competing activities.
4. Managerial economics can be applied to government agencies and other nonprofit organizations as well as to business.

Economic Theory and Managerial Economics

Economic theory traditionally is divided into two broad subfields: (1) microeconomics, which deals with the economic behavior of individual consumers, firms, or resource owners, and (2) macroeconomics, which deals with the behavior of economic aggregates such as the gross national product, national income, employment, and aggregate consumption. Macroeconomics focuses on the collective results of millions of individual economic decisions, while microeconomics focuses on the behavior of individual decision makers.

Since microeconomic theory deals with topics that are more closely associated with resource allocation (namely, consumer behavior and demand theory, production and cost analysis, market structure and pricing, capital budgeting and finance), it makes a major contribution to managerial economics. However, the individual firm does not operate in a vacuum. Its environment is the general economy, which both affects and is affected by the activities of millions of individuals.

The national economic climate, over which individual firms have no control, largely influences the price and availability of the economic resources that a firm buys. These resources include labor, materials, supplies, machinery, and equipment. The national economic climate also affects the cost and availability of financing, particularly with respect to interest rates. On the revenue side, the national economic climate strongly influences the firm's ability to sell its products. Macroeconomics does make important contributions to managerial economics, therefore, even though managerial economics draws more heavily from the microeconomic side of economic theory.

Although a combination of micro- and macroeconomic theory is brought to bear on economic problem solving, effective decision making depends on more than economic theory. As illustrated in Exhibit 1–1, managerial economics also relies on economic methodology, analytical tools, and the principles of accounting, finance, marketing, personnel administration, and production.

Economic Methodology: Descriptive and Prescriptive Models

As shown in Exhibit 1–1, there are two broad approaches to economic methodology, both of which involve the use of models.[2] One approach is to use *descriptive* models to explain and predict economic behavior. The other approach is to use *prescriptive* models to prescribe decision rules for optimizing a stated objective. The two types may be used separately or in conjunction with each other.

Descriptive models are based upon empirical observations. They attempt to describe and explain economic relationships as they exist in the

---

[2] A model is a simplified representation of reality whose purpose is to explain or predict the phenomenon being modeled. We may develop *verbal* models, which use words to describe the phenomenon; *iconic* models, such as globes, which resemble their referent; *analogs*, or working models, which behave like their referents; and *symbolic* or *mathematical* models, such as regression equations, which describe relationships by means of equations and other mathematical formulae. It is common practice to use more than one model to describe a phenomenon. For example, a function may be depicted, jointly or separately, by an equation, graph, or verbal explanation.

Exhibit 1–1

The Nature of Managerial Economics

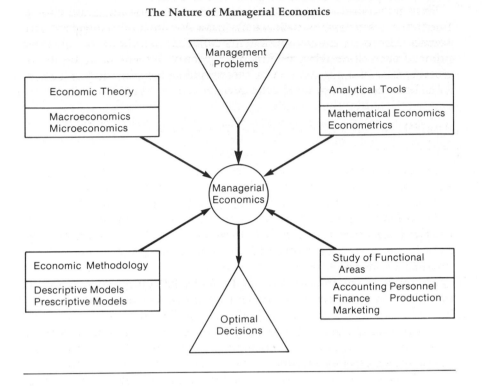

real world, but in a simplified, abstract way. Simplification is achieved through the aggregation of details, and often through necessary simplifying assumptions that do not correspond perfectly to facts in the real world. A good example of a descriptive model is the model of perfect competition (to be discussed in more detail in a later chapter). It assumes perfect knowledge of the market by all concerned, which is manifestly impossible. Nevertheless, the model has been highly successful in explaining and predicting pricing behavior in the real world. The fact that the model does not accurately describe real life in all respects does not prevent it from achieving its purposes, which are to *explain* and *predict* pricing behavior.

Prescriptive models are also called *normative* or *optimizing* models. An optimizing model enables a decision maker to find the most efficient way to reach a stated objective. An optimizing model defines an *objective function* in operational terms. It characterizes the set of *alternative strategies* that can achieve the objective within specified constraints. Finally, it prescribes the procedure(s) by which the decision maker can determine the optimal strategy given those constraints. Note that optimizing models do not attempt to specify what the objective *ought* to be; they simply accept the objective as given or assumed.

Since most business decisions are related to the optimization of some function, prescriptive models are the principal tools of managerial economics. However, descriptive models are often helpful in the development of such optimizing models. Our interest lies not so much in the classification of a model as in its descriptive and explanatory adequacy in its characterization of the phenomenon under study.

Analytical Tools: Mathematical Economics and Econometrics

In mathematical economics, economic relationships are expressed in mathematical form, thereby rendering them amenable to empirical testing or other modeling techniques. In addition to making the search for solutions easier, mathematical representations often permit insights into problems that would easily be missed in a purely descriptive approach. Moreover, mathematical modeling often defines the limits of analysis and pinpoints unfeasible alternatives.

Econometrics uses statistical techniques to test economic models that are developed to explain economic relationships. For example, the demand for a company's product is a function of many factors—the product's price, consumer tastes and preferences, the price of related products, consumer income, advertising, consumer expectations, the range of goods and services available, the number of potential consumers, and other factors. The firm controls only two of these—the product's price and the firm's advertising. It may be able to influence other factors, such as consumer tastes, preferences, and expectations by means of its promotion and advertising.

In order to make informed decisions, the firm's management must understand the relationship involved and the strength or weakness of each factor's influence upon demand. The econometric model attempts to provide such information. Its primary analytical tool is regression analysis. Since most hypotheses in economics deal with the simultaneous movements of several variables, multiple regression—which is uniquely capable of handling these multiple interactions—is used extensively by econometricians. Regression will be discussed more thoroughly in later chapters.

Theory of the Firm in Alternative Models

One of the major concerns of managerial economics is the way that profit-seeking businesses interact with the society in which they operate. To understand the firm's role in society, we might begin with the elementary proposition that raw materials are worthless until combined with labor and capital in an effective process of transformation. The role of the firm is to marshal the resources of capital and labor, allocate these scarce resources to competing activities, direct the transformation process so that useful goods and services are produced, and distribute these products to those members of society who demand them.

Society relies upon the profit-seeking firm not only to produce goods or services that it desires, but also to provide employment, pay taxes, and allocate scarce resources in an efficient manner. When the firm effectively serves society's desires for goods and services, the firm is rewarded with the profit that it seeks. This reward—*profit*—is in a certain sense the engine that drives the economic system for the benefit of all—workers, managers, investors, and consumers.

The Profit-Maximization Model

It has long been customary for economists to assume that the primary goal of any type of organization is to maximize the benefits provided by the organization's operations in relation to its costs. In the case of a business organization, the benefits it seeks are profits. Since our economic system permits the firm to earn all it can, it was originally proposed that the firm is best described by a profit-maximization model.

The profit-maximization model is derived from the theory of the firm set forth in microeconomic studies. In earlier versions of it, the model concentrated on decision making to maximize short-run profits. In later versions, the model was expanded to include the concepts of *uncertainty* and the *time value of money*. As a consequence, the assumed goal of the firm has broadened. It is now the maximization of the owners' wealth—not just short-run profits—that is the primary goal of business.

Limitations of the Profit-Maximization Model.   The profit-maximization model, like all models, is a simplified, abstract version of reality. In an ideal world, it would provide a perfect description of the way our economic system works. In the real world, however, there are a number of complexities that limit its descriptive adequacy.

1.   Economists recognize that there are legal, moral, and social constraints that limit the firm's pursuit of maximum profit. These constraints are especially strong in the legal area, where many federal and state laws inhibit actions that the firm might otherwise take in order to increase profits. In addition to antitrust laws, there are laws that bear on the hiring, firing, and wages of employees; laws that grant monopolies to labor unions; laws that impose safety standards and regulations; and laws that limit the discharge of pollutants into the environment.

2.   The firm also must consider the difference between maximizing

profits, which is basically a *short-run* concept, and maximizing *benefits,* which is a *long-run* concept. Many firms—especially large firms—have objectives other than profits that also must be satisfied. One of these objectives is to maintain good community relations. Management has learned that sacrificing some short-run profit for the sake of good community relations is good business in the long run.

3. Many firms have interests beyond their customers. Such firms take a genuine interest in the welfare of their employees and are more generous than necessary in the matters of wages, fringe benefits, and working conditions. Business is becoming more and more sensitive to the effects of its activities upon our physical and social environment. Many firms contribute large sums to charitable and civic organizations. In March 1982, a White House task force reported that both corporations and individuals now give 2 percent of their net income to worthy causes. This amounts to $3 billion annually from corporations and $43 billion from individuals.[3] The task force recommended doubling such contributions within the next four years. Regardless of whether or not this happens, it seems fair to say that most firms do appear to want to do what is right—both legally and ethically—even if it means less profit.

Clearly then, there are many legal, ethical, and social constraints that limit a firm's all-out pursuit of profit. Within this network of constraints, the firm seeks optimal profit. This means that firms do not necessarily seek maximum profits but seek instead to balance their desire for profit with other goals and objectives—short-run and long-run, economic and noneconomic. Thus maximization of benefits is not necessarily the same as maximization of profit. Recognition of this fact has led to a number of alternative theories which state that the motivation of the firm is something other than profit maximization. These theories, which are of considerable importance to the understanding of managerial economics, can be grouped into four general classes:[4]

1. *Sales maximization theories,* which argue that the firm's primary objective is to increase sales.
2. *Growth maximization theories,* which argue that the firm's primary objective is to maximize the rate of growth of some aspect of its activities.
3. *Present value maximization theories,* which argue that the firm attempts to maximize the present value of a future stream of income.

---

[3] Los Angeles Times Service dispatch datelined Washington, *Honolulu Advertiser,* March 25, 1982.

[4] There are also "realism-in-process" theories (developed by behavioral scientists) and game theories (developed by operations research analysts). For more detailed discussion, see James Koch, *Industrial Organization and Price Level,* 2d ed. (Englewood Cliffs, N.J.: Prentice-Hall, 1980), chap. 3, and other references at the end of this chapter.

4. *Managerial behavior theories,* which stress the effect of the separation between owners and managers in the corporation.

Sales-Maximization Model

The sales-maximization model is probably the best known alternative to the profit-maximization model. This is because it is easily understood and because it can be supported by intuitively appealing examples and impressionistic evidence. Rigorous empirical tests, however, have failed to support the sales-maximization hypothesis.

The classic exposition of the sales-maximization hypothesis by Baumol[5] can be explained with the aid of Exhibit 1–2 (see page 9). The upper panel shows the effects of the volume of production and sales *(Q)* on total revenue *(TR)* and total cost *(TC)*. The lower panel shows a curve representing total profit *(TP)*, which is the difference between total revenue and total cost.

At point *B* on the upper panel, *TR = TC,* and *TP* (lower panel) is zero. This corresponds to Q_s units of production and sales. Any greater volume of sales would require a lower price, which would result in lower revenue as well as higher costs of production, thus resulting in a loss. Therefore, Q_s is taken to be the maximum possible sales, and it would result from a "pure" sales-maximization policy. Of course, no such policy is ever pursued. Rather, the proponents of sales maximization recognize that some minimum level of profit is necessary for survival. This minimally satisfactory level of profit is portrayed by the line P_0, which intersects the *TP* curve at point *C.* This corresponds to the *constrained maximum sales,* Q_c, which is the goal of a sales-maximizing firm.

In contrast, a profit-maximizing firm would strive for the sales volume designated Q_p. The difference between maximum profit (at *M*) and satisfactory profit (at *C*) is what the sales-maximizing firm is willing to give up in order to increase sales. For example, a firm might be willing to keep an unprofitable outlet open or continue production of an unprofitable product in order to increase total sales. Baumol calls the difference between *M* and *C* "sacrificeable profits." Each dollar of sacrificeable profit is given up where it will generate the greatest additional sales revenue.

Baumol notes many reasons why firms might give primary consideration to sales revenues. These may be summarized as follows:

1. A change in sales will bring about larger changes in selling and production technology than an equivalent change in profits.

---

[5] William J. Baumol, *Business Behavior, Value and Growth,* rev. ed. (New York: Harcourt Brace Jovanovich, 1967).

Exhibit 1–2

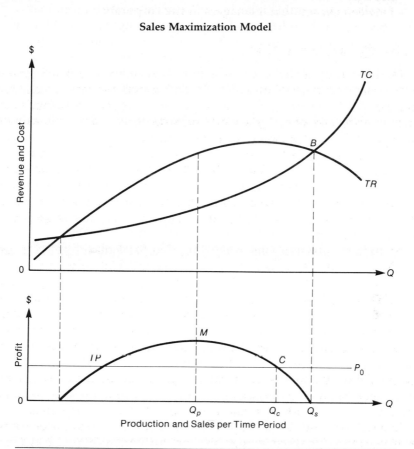

Sales Maximization Model

2. Constant or falling sales impair the company's reputation and deal-
   ings with its customers, distributors, financial institutions, and employees.
3. Constant or falling sales reduce the company's influence in the marketplace and make it more vulnerable to competitors.
4. Because of the separation of management from ownership, management performance is more apt to be judged by the level of sales than
   by the level of profits (as long as a satisfactory profit is maintained).
5. Firms that do business on a national basis cannot afford to abandon
   established outlets or products even if they prove to be unprofitable.

Proponents of the sales-maximization model do not claim that it is universally true, nor that it is always inconsistent with profit maximization. Because of the difficulty of devising meaningful tests of the profit-constrained sales-maximization hypothesis, few rigorous empirical investigations have been conducted. In general, those few tests cast doubt upon the validity of the model. The most careful test was made by Hall, who concluded that his findings lent no support to the sales revenue-maximization thesis.[6]

Despite the lack of rigorous empirical support for the sales-maximization model, it is conceivable that after reaching a satisfactory level of profit, a firm might choose to try to increase its market share rather than to maximize profit. Casual observations have been made of behavior of this type. Japanese firms, in particular, seem to be waging a continuous struggle to increase their share of the world market, and this is an important factor in international trade. However, the nature of the evidence suggests that such firms may be sacrificing some short-run profits in order to maximize profits in the long run. Sales maximization is part of their strategy to secure an advantageous competitive position.

Growth-Maximization Model

In any company, growth is apt to be the cornerstone of corporate strategy. Growth and growth potential are the yardsticks used to measure corporate success in annual reports, in the financial pages of the press, and by financial analysts and investors. Under the conventional profit-maximization model, however, once the firm finds an equilibrium level of output that will maximize its profits, output will remain constant as long as costs and demand remain constant. There is no reason for the firm to expand production and sales any further.

In reality, of course, demands and costs do not remain constant, and firms do want to grow for many of the same reasons (cited above) that motivate them to maximize sales. Growth, however, must be financed either from retained earnings or from borrowing. Although internally generated funds are not free—there is an opportunity cost—they are more desirable for financing growth than borrowed funds. Debt must be serviced, and future debt service payments might inhibit future growth capacity. The decision to maximize growth, therefore, is necessarily a decision to maximize profit.

---

[6] Marshall Hall, "Sales Revenue Maximization: An Empirical Investigation," *Journal of Industrial Economics*, April 1967, pp. 143–56. Hall tested the hypothesis that increased amounts of sacrificeable profits should lead in subsequent time periods to increased sales. He used the Fortune 500 firms for the years 1960–62 as his sample. To represent the minimum acceptable level of profit, he used the mean profit rate in the firm's industry and the mean profit rate for the entire sample.

Major theoretical contributions to the growth-maximization theory have been made by Baumol.[7] Baumol's model assumes that growth is desired primarily to increase profitability. The firm's objective is to find the optimal short-run growth rate that will contribute the most to long-run profitability. As shown in Exhibit 1–3, the model relates total reve-

Exhibit 1–3

Growth-Maximization Model

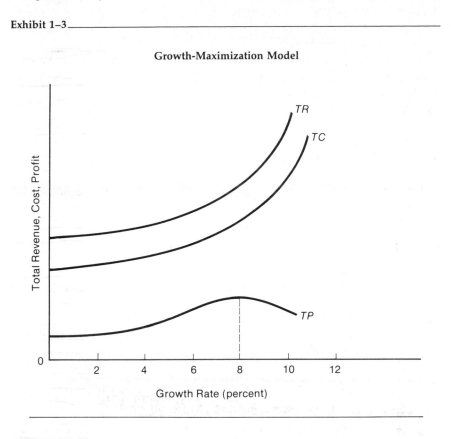

nue *(TR)*, total cost *(TC)*, and total profit *(TP)* to the growth rate of the firm.

The model shows that total cost rises faster than total revenue at higher rates of growth. Some reasons for this are imperfect capital markets, exceptionally high construction and expansion costs, decreasing returns to fixed investment, and increased risk. The higher ratio of costs to revenues causes profits to diminish after reaching a peak. The most profitable rate of growth is shown to be 8 percent.[8]

[7] Baumol, *Business Behavior, Value and Growth*, chap. 10.

[8] Koch, *Industrial Organization*, chap. 3.

Exhibit 1–3 actually is a model of profit maximization by means of growth rather than a model of growth maximization. However, it can easily be modified to illustrate the case of a firm that wants to maximize growth, subject to a minimum profit constraint, as shown in Exhibit 1–4.

Exhibit 1–4 _____

Maximization of Growth Subject to Profit Constraint

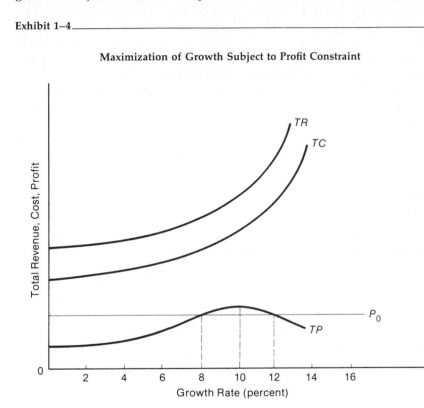

Here a growth rate anywhere between 8 and 12 percent would yield the required profit or more.

Marris has offered a variation of this theory that stresses the maximization of growth subject to the security of management in its position.[9] Marris' thesis is that executive actions are limited by the need for management to protect itself from dismissal or takeover raids in the event of failure. In order to do this:

1. The manager must walk a tightrope between a debt/asset ratio high enough to stimulate growth but not high enough to indicate an imprudent level of risk.

_____

[9] Robin Marris, "A Model of the 'Managerial' Enterprise," *Quarterly Journal of Economics,* May 1963, pp. 185–209.

2. The manager must also maintain a liquidity ratio (liquid assets/total assets) low enough to enhance earning power, but not low enough to endanger paying all obligations on time.
3. Finally, the prudent manager will want to retain as much of the firm's earnings as possible to finance growth, while still paying a satisfactory dividend to stockholders.

In both the Baumol and Marris models, the long-run growth of the firm and its ability to satisfy its constraints depend upon the continued availability of a large stream of profits. It seems clear, then, that whatever differences may exist in the short-run interests of growth-maximizing, sales-maximizing, or profit-maximizing firms, their long-run interests and decisions are virtually the same. Policies that attempt to maximize sales or assets in the long run will maximize profits.

Present Value Model (Maximization of Owners' Wealth)

An alternative to the growth-maximization model suggests that firms desire to maximize owners' wealth. Owners' wealth can be measured by valuation of the firm's expected cash flow. By its very nature, such a valuation is future-oriented, and the future introduces the element of uncertainty. In static analysis, profit maximization extends only across the time interval in which business transactions are completed. Thus, if management starts production in Year 1 with the aim of selling in Year 2, its forecasts extend only as far as Year 2. That is, management formulates plans in the current time period (t_1) in anticipation of events that will take place in future time periods $(t_2, t_3,$ and so forth). If the events that are expected to occur within future time periods can be forecast with certainty, plans can be formulated so that no further decisions beyond the initial one of establishing operations are necessary. Profit maximization then reduces itself to the problem of making the initial decisions required for arriving at maximum profits over the given (planned) time period(s).

But even in such a situation, a forecast of a $100 profit in some future time period is not the equivalent of a $100 profit in the current one. This is true because the interest obtainable on a perfectly certain investment, such as government bonds, is greater than zero. Consequently, there is a time preference that favors the present over the future. To illustrate, suppose that a government bond maturing in one year is available at a yield of 10 percent. That is to say, the risk-free interest rate is 10 percent. Suppose also that a profit of $100 from a production process involving no uncertainty will be realized one year from today. Such a profit would have a present value of $100/1.10 ($100/110 percent) or approximately $90.91.

This computation of present value is known as *discounting*, and 10 percent is the discount rate. Conversely, $90.91 invested today at 10 percent would be worth $100 one year from today through the process of *compounding* interest. Similarly, if a two-year government bond were available at 10 percent yield, then $100 obtainable two years from today from a production process with no uncertainty would have a present value of $100/(1.10)^2$, or approximately $82.64. If this same process were to produce a stream of $100 to be available at the end of one year and another $100 to be available at the end of the second year, the present value of these two payments would be the sum of their separate present values, or $173.55.

In the real, dynamic world, however, uncertainty is an ever-present element in the economic environment. Related to the discussion above, this means that future receipts must be discounted (capitalized) at a rate in excess of that available on an investment of perfect certainty. The result is that the present value of such future receipts are accordingly lowered. We may express this concept in general terms, namely:

$$I = \frac{R}{(1 + r)^n} \tag{1}$$

where I represents an investment that will produce a net cash revenue, R, available at the end of n discount periods in the future, and where the discount rate is represented by r per period, expressed in decimal form. The present value of I is what the valuation model attempts to maximize. When a stream of income is expected over a period of years, the equation can be expanded as below, where R_1, R_2, R_3, and R_n, represent flows of cash earnings in the first, second, third, and nth years:

$$I = \frac{R_1}{(1 + r)} + \frac{R_2}{(1 + r)^2} + \frac{R_3}{(1 + r)^3} + \cdots + \frac{R_n}{(1 + r)^n} = \sum_{t=1}^{n} \frac{R_t}{(1 + r)^t} \tag{2}$$

In static analysis, where the current period's profits are simply extended repetitively into the future, the problem of maximizing an earnings stream reduces simply to the problem of maximizing R. But in a dynamic situation, where fluctuating values for R are projected, the problem of maximizing is greatly complicated. However, as a practical approach to the problem, it is often useful to estimate a uniform annual profit and to project this into the future until a change in conditions (such as installation of a new plant) calls for a new projection. Where the flow of expected uniform annual profit, U, is projected for an indefinite period of time, the following equation defines the present value, I, of this income sequence into perpetuity:

$$I = \frac{U}{r} \tag{3}$$

where r is the appropriate capitalization rate.

The appropriate capitalization rate reflects the degree of business risk suffered by the firm. If I represents the firm's invested capital, r is the cost of capital (at least) as discussed in Chapter 19. If the expected annual earnings, U, is divided by the number of common stock shares outstanding, Equation (3) can be rewritten as

$$V = \frac{E}{r}$$

where E is annual earnings per share, r is the stockholder's required rate of return, and V is the firm's value per share.

This approach is employed universally in the valuation of stocks by investors who multiply estimated earnings by a factor known as the price-earnings multiplier to arrive at an estimated value for the stock in question. The price-earnings multiplier is simply the reciprocal of r, the capitalization rate. The same technique is also commonly employed in the real estate industry: estimated annual rentals are multiplied by some figure (the reciprocal of the capitalization rate) to arrive at an estimate of the value of the real estate.

To illustrate, suppose a firm's business risk is such that the owners require a 10 percent rate of return on their investment.[10] If the firm's annual earnings are $1 per share, the capitalized value of the firm is:

$$V = \frac{1.00}{.10} = \$10$$

Now suppose that the firm has an opportunity to invest in a project that will increase earnings by 20 cents per share but will also increase its business risk to the point where a prudent investor would demand a 15 percent return. The capitalized value of the common stock would then be:

$$V = \frac{1.20}{.15} = \$8$$

The lesson should be clear—the proposed project would increase "profit" by 20 percent, but the minimum acceptable rate of return has increased by 50 percent (from .10 to .15). Consequently, the owners' wealth has declined. This is why it is axiomatic in business that the higher the risk, the higher the required profit. Otherwise, riskier projects would not be undertaken. The present value model thus holds that a firm's management seeks to maximize the present value of future profits subject to a given level of risk. Since the present value of future profits represents the value of the firm at any given level of risk, maximizing the present value of profits is the same as maximizing owners' wealth.

---

[10] See Chapter 2 for discussion of the risk-adjusted discount rate.

The principles governing the present value model may tell us much about how firms would like to behave, how they would like to make decisions, and how they would prefer to time their activities. In a world in which the timing of investments is crucial to success, the present value model can give important insights into the probable behavior of firms. The major problem with this model, however, is its lack of descriptive realism. The model requires that the firm be able to predict accurately the magnitude and timing of a stream of profits to be realized in the future—something that is difficult to do under the best of circumstances and impossible under the worst.

Managerial Utility Model

In 1932, Berle and Means were the first to suggest that the separation of ownership and management in modern corporations results in economically important behavior.[11] They argued that owners (stockholders) want high dividends and are therefore interested in maximizing profits. Managers have a different set of motives, needs, and desires, however, and are more interested in satisfying these than in maximizing profits for the owners. Further, Berle and Means suggested that the lack of corporate democracy leaves owners with little or no power to change corporate policy. Further, since the corporation can generate needed capital internally by means of retained earnings, management need not venture into the capital markets, where the firm would be subject to critical scrutiny. Hence professional corporate managers are free to pursue their own interests without fear of discipline.

A more recent proponent of this model is Galbraith, who has written provocative variations on the Berle-Means theme in a trio of popular books.[12] The Berle-Means-Galbraith thesis asserts that (1) profit rates are lower in manager-controlled firms than in owner-controlled firms because management ignores the profit-maximizing interests of the owner and (2) professional managers have no personal interest in maximizing profits. Neither of these propositions has stood up under rigorous empirical investigation.

A few studies have found differences in profit rates between owner-controlled and manager-controlled firms.[13] Many other studies, how-

---

[11] A. A. Berle and G. C. Means, *The Modern Corporation and Private Property* (New York: Commerce Clearing House, 1932).

[12] J. K. Galbraith, *American Capitalism: The Concept of Countervailing Power* (Boston: Houghton Mifflin, 1952); *The Affluent Society* (Boston: Houghton Mifflin, 1958); and *The New Industrial State* (Boston: Houghton Mifflin, 1967).

[13] John P. Shelton, "Allocative Efficiency vs. 'X-Efficiency': Comments," *American Economic Review*, December 1967, pp. 1252–58; and R. J. Monsen, J. S. Chiu, and D. E. Cooley, "The Effect of Separation of Ownership and Control on the Performance of the Large Firm," *Quarterly Journal of Economics*, August 1968, pp. 435–51.

ever, could not find any such differences.[14]

The implication that professional managers have no personal interest in maximizing profits received early support when McGuire, Chiu, and Elbing found a closer relationship between executive salaries and the size of the corporation than between salaries and profitability.[15] However, separate studies by a number of scholars demonstrated that salaries were only a small part of total executive compensation.[16] For example, Masson found that salary was only one-sixth of the total package. The remainder took the form of stock options, grants, and profit sharing, all of which depend upon profits. The empirical evidence suggests, then, that professional managers do have a direct and personal interest in maximizing profits.

A more useful theory of the firm based upon managerial behavior is found in the managerial discretion model proposed by Williamson.[17] In the Williamson model, managers are free to pursue their own self-interest once they have achieved a level of profit that will pay satisfactory dividends to stockholders and still provide funds for growth. The manager's self-interest depends upon many other things besides salary. These include other forms of compensation, the number and type of people supervised, nonincome perquisites, and the amount of discretion exercisable in spending or investing the firm's money. When the firm is prospering, managers tend to extract nonessential perquisites from the firm (such as chauffeured limousines). Behaviorists call these nonessential items "management slack."

The general hypothesis of the Williamson model is that firms led by a utility-maximizing manager spend more on staff expenditures and exhibit more organizational slack than a profit-maximizing firm. The empirical evidence offered by Williamson is only mildly supportive and suffers from several deficiencies. Most notably, the measure of compensation does not give sufficient weight to compensation other than salary.

---

[14] These included Harold Demsetz, "Where Is the New Industrial State?" *Economic Inquiry*, March 1974, pp. 1–12; David R. Kamerschen, "The Influence of Ownership and Control on Profit Rates," *American Economic Review*, June 1968, pp. 432–47; John P. Palmer, "The Separation of Ownership from Control in Large U.S. Industrial Corporations," *Quarterly Review of Economics and Business*, Autumn 1972, pp. 55–62; and Peter Holl, "Control Type and the Market for Corporate Control in Large U.S. Corporations," *Journal of Industrial Economics*, June 1977, pp. 259–73.

[15] J. W. McGuire, J. S. Chiu, and A. O. Elbing, "Executive Incomes, Sales and Profits." *American Economic Review*, September 1962, pp. 753–61.

[16] Wilbur G. Lewellen and Blaine Huntsman, "Managerial Pay and Corporate Performance," *American Economic Review*, September 1970, pp. 710–20. See also Robert T. Masson, "Executive Motivations, Earnings, and Consequent Equity Performance," *Journal of Political Economy*, November 1971, pp. 1278–92.

[17] O. E. Williamson, *The Economics of Discretionary Behavior: Managerial Objectives in a Theory of the Firms* (Chicago: Markham, 1967).

Consequently, it may seriously underestimate the profit-maximizing behavior of managers in the real world.

Evaluation: Why We Use a Profit-Maximization Model

As we saw in the preceding discussion, there are many critics of the
profit-maximization model. The main arguments they offer can be summarized as follows:

1. Profit maximization is not a rational action for managers to take.
2. In the real world of uncertainty, managers do not have the knowledge of demand, costs, and future events that is necessary for profit
   maximization.
3. In the modern firm, managers pursue many goals besides profit.
4. The separation of ownership and management in a modern corporation diverts managers' interests from maximizing profits to maximizing their own welfare.
5. Policies that tend to maximize profits cause increased risk and instability, which managers fear. Therefore, risk-averse managers avoid
   a policy of profit maximization.

Defenders of the profit-maximization model respond with three major
counterarguments:

1. There is very little empirical evidence to support *any* of the proposed
   models, including the profit-maximization model.
2. Regardless of what managers may say about their motivation, if
   they act as if they are attempting to maximize profits, then the
   profit-maximization model is valid.[18]
3. When vigorous competition exists, the firm that does not maximize
   profits does not survive.

We can expand these arguments into at least five good reasons why
we should persist in using the profit-maximization model:

1. *Survival against competition requires profits.* Consider the strong
competition that a firm encounters, not only in the markets where it sells
its goods, but also in the financial markets where it must obtain its
working capital. Such competition forces management to pay close attention to profits. The larger its profits, the easier it is for the firm to
succeed in both markets. Hence, the tendency is to pursue maximum
profits.

2. *Managerial compensation is closely related to profitability.* Recent studies reveal that the gap between managers' and owners' interests is more

---

[18] Milton Friedman, *Essays in Positive Economics* (Chicago: University of Chicago Press,
1953), pp. 3–43.

apparent than real, and managers do have a strong incentive to maximize profits. Furthermore, about 40 percent of corporate stock is held by financial institutions, and this share is growing. These institutions rarely intervene in corporate management, but the potential for control is there. Top management of the affected corporations is well aware of this potential, and thus has a powerful incentive to maximize profits.

3. *The profit-maximizing model best explains and predicts the firm's behavior.* The assumption of profit-maximizing behavior by business managers may be an oversimplification of the firm's multifaceted objectives. This doesn't matter as long as the resulting model enables us to understand and predict the behavior of business firms. The profit-maximization model actually serves two additional purposes: (1) it provides a basis for extension of the model for deeper understanding, and (2) it provides a basis for evaluating alternative models.

4. *The profit-maximization model explicitly provides for necessary cost analyses.* Before management can arrive at a decision whether to maximize profits or to settle for something else, it must consider costs as well as benefits.

5. *The profit-maximization model provides an insight into the relative costs and benefits of long-range versus short-range planning.* The difference is particularly apparent when social responsibilities are considered. The pursuit of profit maximization is often tempered by the firm's social responsibilities. Most of these are imposed by government action, but in some cases the firm's management assumes social responsibilities on its own initiative. There is, however, a question: How far can a firm be expected to go in bearing the costs of social responsibility programs without receiving commensurate benefits—especially in the short run?

Some farsighted firms, without abandoning their goal of profit optimization, have already initiated programs designed to create *long-run* benefits for themselves as well as for society. Such firms are willing, *within limits*, to sacrifice a certain amount of short-run profit to obtain a long-run benefit. A good example is Control Data Corporation, which has initiated programs to teach useful skills to the unemployed, to construct plants in disadvantaged neighborhoods of inner cities, and to develop an efficient and effective work force composed almost entirely of part-time working mothers. The company reported that these programs have turned out to be good business, but it also reported that federal government subsidies were necessary to launch the endeavors.[19]

Government subsidies for the private development of such programs seems to be a reasonable approach. If society as a whole is to benefit from these programs, then society as a whole should share in the costs. It is simply unrealistic to think that private firms will abate pollution,

---

[19] *Social Responsibility Report* (Minneapolis, Minn.: Control Data Corporation, 1978).

create jobs for the unskilled and underprivileged, and raise the capital that is necessary to sustain economic growth unless and until they are assured of long-run profit.

Summary

Managerial economics is a relatively new branch of economic study that bridges the gap between economic theory and practice. It is studied largely for its contribution to sound decision making, not only in profit-seeking businesses, but also in nonprofit organizations and government agencies.

Managerial economics incorporates elements of both micro- and macroeconomics, and it uses both descriptive and prescriptive models. Managerial economics also uses the analytical tools of mathematical economics and econometrics. The principal tool of econometrics is multiple regression, used to explain economic relationships.

Managerial economics shows that the profit-seeking firm enjoys a mutually beneficial relationship with the society in which it exists. The firm provides employment, taxes, and goods or services by allocating scarce resources in an efficient manner. In exchange for these benefits, the firm is rewarded with profits. Profit, then, is the engine that powers our economic system.

The profit-maximization model will be used throughout this text to explain and predict the behavior of business organizations. There are, however, a number of models that postulate objectives other than the maximization of profits. These objectives include maximization of sales, maximization of growth, and maximization of the firm's present value. A close examination of these three models reveals some differences between them and the profit-maximization model in the short run, but they all attempt to maximize profits in the long run.

Another model stresses the effect of the separation between owners and managers, and holds that managers seek to maximize their own welfare. However, close scrutiny reveals that a manager's welfare is more closely tied to his company's profits than to anything else.

The profit-maximization model holds that a manager tries to maximize profits within the constraints imposed by limited resources, the firm's level of technology, and the laws and customs of the society in which the firm must operate.

In seeking to maximize profits, the firm must operate within legal, moral, and social constraints, and according to the economic facts of life—that is, the consumer has the last word in the marketplace and will not buy if the price is too high. In the long run, the firm seeks to maximize benefits in relation to costs. Benefits may include the satisfaction of objectives other than profit, such as the fulfillment of perceived social responsibilities. Some farsighted firms have initiated programs to benefit society as well as themselves. Such firms are willing, within limits, to sacrifice a certain amount of short-run profit in order to obtain long-run benefits. Ultimately however, these firms expect long-range benefits to be expressed as profits. Consequently, the profit-maximization model is the model best suited to explain and predict a firm's behavior in both the short run and the long run.

Problems

1.   Professor Milton Friedman (Nobel prize winner in economics) has argued in a most persuasive manner that economic models do not have to bear a resemblance to reality in order to be useful. Accordingly, Friedman believes the traditional model of pure competition should not be rejected in favor of some other approach, as long as it continues to make acceptable predictions of changes in prices and/or output. Explain whether or not you agree with Friedman. Do you feel that accuracy in prediction is the sole criterion that should be considered? Discuss.

2.   In *Time* magazine Tinnan wrote, "It is historical irony that in the United States, the stronghold of world capitalism, so few citizens understand that profits provide the basis for the prosperity on which rests the well-being of both individuals and the nation."

a.   Do present moves toward deregulation (e.g., in the airline, trucking, and banking industries) show that Americans are learning to understand the role of profit in the economy? Explain.

b.   The telephone company and electric power companies are examples of government-regulated industries. Inasmuch as profit is such a strong incentive, why does the government continue to regulate them?

3.   Johnson and Johnson, the makers of Tylenol, had its share of the pain reliever market threatened by unfortunate circumstances. Removing all Tylenol capsules from the shelves, conducting hundreds of tests, and running a costly promotional campaign resulted in a tremendous drop in profits. Because of these drastic measures, however, Johnson and Johnson may have managed to save a large portion of its market.

a.   What profit theory was Johnson and Johnson following?

b.   Why do companies focus on market share?

c.   Why didn't Johnson and Johnson simply change the Tylenol brand name?

4.   Global Inc. has a current capitalized value of $25 per share and current annual earnings of $3 per share. Global has been offered a lucrative investment that would increase earnings by 95¢ per share but that at the same time would increase the company's business risk so as to require a 15 percent return on investment.

a.   What is Global's present rate of return on investment?
b.   Should Global accept the new investment?
c.   Explain the correlation between risk and return.
d.   What is Global's major problem when making investment decisions for the future?

5.   What effect would the following situations have on the capital value of a firm's stock?

a.   Interest rates rise substantially.
b.   The firm develops a time-saving technological breakthrough.
c.   The union wins a labor dispute resulting in a 20 percent pay hike.

6.   A firm is contemplating an advertising campaign that promises to yield $115 in increased profits one year from now for every $100 spent now. Should the firm give up $100 of current profits to make $115 one year from now?

7.   A firm has three proposals under consideration. As shown below, the first proposal promises a cash inflow of $10,000 per year for 10 years. The second proposal offers a return of $75,000, all of which comes in the first four years. The third proposal offers a return of $115,000; receipts don't start until the fourth year, but they are fully realized within the following five years.

| | Timing of Cash Flow | | |
Year	Proposal 1	Proposal 2	Proposal 3
1	$ 10,000	$30,000	–0–
2	10,000	20,000	–0–
3	10,000	15,000	–0–
4	10,000	10,000	10,000
5	10,000	–0–	15,000
6	10,000	–0–	20,000
7	10,000	–0–	30,000
8	10,000	–0–	40,000
9	10,000	–0–	–0–
10	10,000	–0–	–0–
Total	$100,000	$75,000	$115,000

a.   What is the present value of each proposal at discount rates of 8 percent, 12 percent, and 18 percent?
b.   What affect does the timing of the cash flow have on the present value of the proposals?

Case Problem: Business—Public or Profit?

8.   American big-business firms, such as GM, AT&T, and IBM, are admired for their size and industrial muscle. In 1981, American Telephone and Telegraph alone employed 1 million people—over 1 percent of the entire U.S. labor force—and listed estimated assets of $183 billion.[20] Production of goods and services by such industrial giants has led to better jobs, which in turn have raised America's standard of living. The U.S. per capita disposable income in real terms has risen from $2,073 in 1934 to over $7,400 in 1982—greater than a 3.5-fold increase. Not only has business raised incomes but also, while competing for profits, it has built the United States into a consumer paradise unmatched in both the variety and price of its products and services.

Of course, the large growth of business in America has produced some undesirable side effects. For example, social costs are imposed when wastes are dumped into the air and water, or when the earth is defaced by strip mining. In addition, there is a tendency for power to become overcentralized in the hands of giant corporations. Because of the increasing number of mergers and takeovers the past few years, moreover, some people fear big business' power and are skeptical and distrustful of corporate America. These people feel that business is profit-mad and will stop at nothing in its pursuit of money. They feel that business is not working for the public good; instead, business seeks only to maximize profits.

Is profit maximization the serious problem that some think it to be? Is there another side to the story?

According to Professor Milton Friedman, "Business has one and only one social responsibility—to make profits (so long as it stays within legal and moral rules of the game established by society). Few trends could so thoroughly undermine the very foundations of our free society as acceptance by corporate officials of a social responsibility other than to make as much money for their stockholders as possible."

Why does Friedman feel that the public good is served better if a business focuses on profit maximization than if business focuses instead on social responsibility?

In order to maximize profits, business must efficiently meet the consumers' demand for goods and services. In essence it is thus the consumers, not the captains of industry, who dictate the actions of business. Consumer dollars are a signal to business to produce what society desires. In meeting this demand, profits supply the motive for business to innovate and to strive for more efficient means of production. The profit motive moves society's scarce resources to the areas of highest demand, thereby maximizing utility and benefit for all.

---

[20] "Fortune Directory of the 50 Largest Utilities," *Fortune*, July 12, 1982, pp. 144–45.

On the other hand, if business is forced to change and pursue social responsibility instead of profit, then the consumer loses his vote on the actions of business. Should business determine, for example, whether society needs a new hydroelectric project or more funds for senior citizens' health care? There are some who say yes. On the other hand, in a democracy, isn't it the job of elected government representatives to decide what society needs? Leaving decisions about the public good to business would surely increase the very corporate power that some people fear. Isn't it better for American business to be controlled by market forces and to leave decisions concerning social responsibility to a more democratic process?

Questions:
a. Does business perform a public service when it attempts to maximize profits, or should its main goal instead be some form of social responsibility?
b. Friedman stresses profit maximization, "so long as it (business) stays within legal and moral rules of the game established by society." What are the rules of the game? Where do you draw the line, for example, when a business pollutes the environment while maximizing profits?
c. What is the government's role in business? Could government, through the use of tax incentives and other measures, make profit maximization and the maximization of social good one and the same? (Consider, for example, President Reagan's inner city economic zones.)
d. Should business be allowed to make as much profit as possible? What do you think about the windfall profits tax levied on oil companies? Is it fair? Is it wise from an economic viewpoint?

Case Problem: Corporate Crime

9. "In the last decade 2,690 corporations of all sizes were convicted of federal criminal offenses. Of America's 500 largest corporations 115 have been convicted of at least one major crime or have paid civil penalties for serious misbehavior," states the September 6, 1982, issue of *U.S. News and World Report.*

The reason behind all this crime? Money! Profit maximization is the foundation of America's capitalistic system. Profit, while an excellent motivator of innovation and efficiency, can also lure corporations to fix prices, pollute the environment, and violate other laws of society. The cost of corporate criminal activity? "Approximately $200 billion a year, 60 billion in price-fixing alone."

Questions:

a. Is corporate crime increasing or decreasing? Why?

b. Should government initiate stiffer laws and penalties to curb business crime? What would be the costs of a larger government role in business activities?

c. Can awareness by consumers—for example, through Ralph Nader–style consumer protection—help keep business within the law? Why or why not?

d. Oil companies overcharged U.S. consumers by over $600 million during the OPEC oil squeeze (by charging prices higher than those fixed by the government). Why didn't the public hear more about this? What influence does big business exert on the news media (whose stability is closely tied to advertising revenues)?

e. In June, 1982, industrial spies from Mitsubishi Electric Corporation and Hitachi Ltd. of Japan were indicted for stealing technological information. Unlike price fixing, for example, this type of corporate crime is not directed at consumers. Industrial spying is instead crime between corporate competitors. Who gets hurt? What is the effect of spying on profit maximization's ability to fuel innovation?

References

Anthony, Robert N. "The Trouble with Profit Maximization." *Harvard Business Review,* November–December 1960.

Bailey, Duncan, and Stanley E. Boyle. "Sales Revenue Maximization: An Empirical Vindication." *Industrial Organization Review* 5, no. 1, 46–55 (1977).

Baumol, William J. *Business Behavior, Value and Growth.* Rev. ed. New York: Harcourt Brace Jovanovich, 1967.

_____. "What Can Economic Theory Contribute to Managerial Economics?" *American Economic Review,* May 1961, pp. 142–46.

Berle, A. A., and G. C. Means. *The Modern Corporation and Private Property.* New York: Commerce Clearing House, 1932.

Boulding, Kenneth. "Implication for General Economies of More Realistic Theories of the Firm." *American Economic Review,* May 1952, pp. 30–44.

Copeland, Thomas E., and Keith V. Smith. "An Overview of Nonprofit Organizations." *Journal of Economics and Business,* Winter 1978, pp. 117–51.

Cyert, Richard M., and James G. March. *A Behavioral Theory of the Firm.* Englewood Cliffs, N.J.: Prentice-Hall, 1963.

Dean, Joel. *Managerial Economics.* Englewood Cliffs, N.J.: Prentice-Hall, 1951.

Demsetz, Harold. "Where Is the New Industrial State?" *Economic Inquiry,* March 1974, pp. 1–12.

Elliott, J. W. "Control, Size, Growth, and Financial Performance in the Firm." *Journal of Financial and Quantitative Analysis,* January 1972, pp. 1309–20.

"Fortune Directory of the 50 Largest Utilities." *Fortune,* July 12, 1982, pp. 144–45.

Friedman, Milton. "The Methodology of Positive Economics." *Essays in Positive Economics.* Chicago: University of Chicago Press, 1953.

Galbraith, J. K., *American Capitalism: The Concept of Countervailing Power.* Boston: Houghton Mifflin, 1952. *The Affluent Society.* Boston: Houghton Mifflin, 1958. *The New Industrial State.* Boston: Houghton Mifflin, 1971.

Granger, Clive W. J. "Some Consequences of the Valuation Model when Expectations Are Taken to Be Optimum Forecasts." *Journal of Finance,* March 1975, pp. 135–45.

Hall, Marshal. "Sales Revenue Maximization: An Empirical Investigation." *Journal of Industrial Economics,* April 1967, pp. 143–56.

Holl, Peter. "Control Type and the Market for Corporate Control in Large U.S. Corporations." *Journal of Industrial Economics,* June 1977, pp. 259–73.

Kamerschen, David R. "The Influence of Ownership and Control on Profit Rates." *American Economic Review,* June 1968, pp. 432–47.

Larner, Robert J. *Management Control and the Large Corporation.* Lexington, Mass.: Lexington Books, 1970.

Lewellen, Wilbur G., and Blaine Huntsman. "Managerial Pay and Corporate Performance." *American Economic Review,* September 1970, pp. 710–20.

Mansfield, Edwin. "How Economists See R&D." *Harvard Business Review.* November–December 1981, pp. 98–106.

Marvis, Robin. "A Model of the 'Managerial' Enterprise." *Quarterly Journal of Economics,* May 1963, pp. 185–209.

Masson, Robert T. "Executive Motivations, Earnings, and Consequent Equity Performance." *Journal of Political Economy,* November 1971, pp. 1278–92. Masson's data set included the top three to five executives in 39 electronics, aerospace, and chemical firms over the 1947–66 period.

McGuire, J. W., J. S. Chiu, and A. O. Elbing. "Executive Incomes, Sales and Profits." *American Economic Review,* September 1962, pp. 753–61.

Palmer, John P. "The Separation of Ownership from Control in Large U.S. Industrial Corporations." *Quarterly Review of Economics and Business,* Autumn 1972, pp. 55–62.

Shelton, John P., R. J. Monsen, J. S.-Y. Chiu, and D. E. Cooley. "The Effect of Separation of Ownership and Control on the Performance of the Large Firm." *Quarterly Journal of Economics,* August 1968, pp. 435–51.

Simon, Henry A. *Models of Man.* New York: John Wiley & Sons, 1957.

Social Responsibility Report. Minneapolis: Control Data Corporation, 1978.

Tinnan, David B. "Profits: How Much Is Too Little?" *Time,* August 16, 1976, pp. 54–55.

Williamson, O. E. "Managerial Discretion and Business Behavior." *American Economic Review,* September 1963, pp. 1032–57.

————. *The Economics of Discretionary Behavior: Managerial Objectives in a Theory of the Firm.* Chicago: Markham, 1967.

Decision Analysis

When a patient requests medical treatment from a physician, he is asking the physician to diagnose a problem and treat it. The physician's objective is to make the patient well. His problem is to identify the illness, its cause, and its treatment. Since the physician has spent many years learning how the human body functions, he can proceed to gather information that might relate to the patient's problem. The information may be obtained from several sources: by questioning the patient, by conducting a physical examination of the patient, and by testing blood and urine samples of the patient in the laboratory. After gathering sufficient information, the physician makes his diagnosis. He considers ways of treating the problem, and ends up prescribing what in his judgment is the best treatment. Sometimes the correct diagnosis is not readily apparent. In that case the physician may order further tests. In the meantime, however, he will often treat immediate symptoms in order to give the patient some relief.

The physician's diagnosis and treatment of a patient's illness is analogous to decision making in business and government. Doctors and managers alike must make both short-range and long-range decisions. Likewise, just as the additional tests ordered by the physician can be quite expensive, as anyone who has undergone such tests is well aware, the additional business information ordered by a manager can be quite expensive, too. Similarly, medical decisions and business decisions both must be *timely*. If a physician delays treatment until all tests are completed, the patient may die. If a business manager puts off a necessary decision in order to obtain more information, the business may be seriously damaged.

Effective decision making is the art of making the best choice from all available alternatives. The decision-making procedure is the same whether it is conducted in medicine, profit-seeking business, nonprofit organizations, or government agencies. In each case, the effective decision maker must:

1. Define the problem and establish objectives.
2. Identify all pertinent factors, constraints, and relationships.
3. Collect as much relevant information as possible within constraints of time and cost.
4. Analyze the information.
5. Specify alternative solutions and evaluate them in terms of benefits versus costs.
6. Choose the best solution.

The ability to make good decisions is the key to success. Nevertheless, decision making is a human activity. It is not surprising, therefore, that it is largely subjective, depending upon the personality, temperament, and experience of the decision maker as well as the environment in which the decision must be made. Yet within the framework of subjective decision making, there are analytical tools that can be coupled with disciplined, logical thinking to provide some objectivity in the decision-making process. These tools and evaluative processes are usually discussed under the heading of decision theory or decision analysis.

Business decisions usually consist of choices between courses of action, or *strategies*. Frequently these choices must be made in an environment over which the decision maker exercises limited or even no control. We use the general term *states of nature* to designate such conditions. The decision hinges, therefore, on the decision maker's knowledge of possible states of nature and how each contemplated strategy might fare under each possible state of nature. The decision maker's state of knowledge can be classified as a state of *certainty, risk,* or *uncertainty*.

Each of these conditions calls for a different set of decision-making tools and techniques. These will be discussed in the next chapter and from time to time in later chapters when appropriate and timely. In this chapter, however, we are more concerned with the concepts that provide the foundation for the procedures and techniques to be introduced later. We begin with an examination of decision making under conditions of certainty, risk, and uncertainty. After that, a decision model called the *payoff matrix* is introduced to aid in a discussion of decision theory. This is followed by an analysis of the concepts of *utility, risk aversion,* and *risk premiums*—concepts that do much to explain the behavior of managers, investors, and entrepreneurs.

Decision Environments

The distinctions among *certainty, risk,* and *uncertainty* reflect differences in the degree of knowledge enjoyed by the decision maker. If we conceive of one's state of knowledge as a continuum, then certainty (complete knowledge) would occupy one end and uncertainty (complete lack of knowledge) would occupy the other. Risk (partial knowledge) would occupy the middle. The continuum thus would represent degrees of certainty (or uncertainty, whichever you prefer).

The Concept of Certainty

Certainty is defined as a state of knowledge in which the decision maker knows in advance the specific outcome to which each alternative will invariably lead. In other words, the decision maker has perfect knowledge of the environment and the result of whatever decision he might make.

How realistic is this concept? At first thought this state may appear to be theoretical and impractical and therefore only of academic interest. Actually, the opposite is generally the case. There are many short-run situations in which the manager has complete knowledge. Many business decisions require only a knowledge of current prices, terms, and quantities demanded, and these can be ascertained with certainty in the short run. For example, suppose a firm has borrowed $100,000 on a short-term note that still has 30 days to maturity. The interest rate on the note is 3 percent more than the yield on Treasury bills. If the firm generates $100,000 in surplus cash, management can determine with certainty that it is better off to prepay the loan than to invest in a Treasury bill.

Decision making under certainty includes most of the problems pertaining to theories of choice that arise in economics and the behavioral sciences. Certainty may be found in classical applications of calculus and algebra, and in many types of optimization models such as linear and nonlinear programming. These models are used to find the allocation of resources that yields the highest value of some index (such as profits or utility) or the lowest value of some other index (such as costs), given specified constraints.

In reality, however, few things remain certain for very long. The outcome of a long-range investment, for example, is really impossible to predict when we consider the dynamic interaction of many unknown variables, such as the general economic situation, competition, consumer tastes, the political climate, and technological advances. Thus, most *strategic* decisions are made under conditions of less than perfect knowledge. We classify such conditions as either *risk* or *uncertainty*.

The Concept of Risk

Risk is defined as a state of knowledge in which each alternative leads to one of a set of specific outcomes, each outcome occurring with a probability that is known to the decision maker. Risk may be regarded, therefore, as the quantitative measurement of an outcome, such as a loss or a gain, such that the probability of the outcome can be predicted. Under conditions of risk, the decision maker possesses some *objective* knowledge of the environment and is able to predict the probability of the known possible states of nature and the outcome or payoff of each contemplated strategy. Thus, among the central ideas in the concept of risk are measurement and prediction, which are used to estimate the likelihood of an eventuality or contingency. Let us note briefly, intuitively and conceptually, how this is accomplished.

Methods of Estimating Risk

Two approaches can be used to measure probability: one is *a priori*, by deduction; the other is *a posteriori*, by statistical analysis of empirical data. Both methods attempt to provide the information needed to make decisions.

In the *a priori* method, the decision maker is able to determine the probability of an outcome without experimentation or an analysis of past experience. Instead, probabilities are determined deductively on the basis of assumed principles, provided that the characteristics of the eventuality are known in advance. For example, we know a coin has only two sides. Because of this, a tossed coin must come up with either a head or a tail. Assuming the coin is evenly balanced, we can deduce there is an equal probability of getting a head or a tail on any one toss. Thus it is not necessary to toss a coin a large number of times to discover that the relative frequency of a head (or tail) approaches ½, or one out of every two tosses. By the same reasoning, it is not necessary to continuously draw cards from a deck containing 52 cards to conclude that the probability of drawing any particular card is ½2.

Are these probability statements intended to predict a particular outcome? No. They merely state that in a sufficiently large number of trials a particular outcome will be realized. It follows then, that the habitual gambler, entertained with organized games of chance, faces a condition of risk, not of uncertainty; the only thing that is nearly certain is that he will lose and the house will win in the long run.

The a priori method of estimating risk is appropriate whenever the decision maker can compute the probability of an outcome without relying upon experimentation, sampling, or past experience. When this is not possible, the decision maker must fall back on the a posteriori method. In the a priori method, we proceed from cause to effect. In the a posteriori method, we observe the effect by means of empirical measurement and then seek to establish the cause.

The a posteriori method assumes that past performances were typical and will continue in the future. In order to establish a probability measure, statistical theory requires that frequency data must satisfy three technical conditions: (1) the data must provide enough cases or observations to exhibit stability, (2) the observations must be repeated in the population of observations, and (3) the observations must be independent.[1]

If these conditions are satisfied, the statistical probability of an event can be computed and the likelihood of the outcome can be classified as a risk. Thus, insurance companies can predict with a high degree of accuracy the probabilities of deaths, accidents, and fire losses. These probabilities enable them to make decisions about premium levels and rates. Although they cannot establish the probability that a particular individual will die or that a particular house will burn, they can predict with small error how many people in a given age group will die next year or how many houses of a given type and general location will burn.

When faced with eventualities or outcomes that involve risks, a primary task of professional decision makers (e.g., managers) is to develop techniques that will enable them to calculate and subsequently minimize the risks inherent in a particular problem. One method used to accomplish this is to calculate the probability distribution of possible outcomes from a set of sample observations, and then compute an expected value.[2]

For example, suppose that it is now January and an automobile dealer must order the cars to be sold in June. From the historical data accumulated over several years and from estimates of the market, the dealer is able to construct a probability distribution table as illustrated in Exhibit 2–1.

---

[1] Independence means that the observations are drawn at random, and thus the magnitude of any particular random variable is not affected by the magnitude of another random variable drawn from the same population.

[2] *Expected value* is a weighted average of outcomes in which each outcome is weighted (multiplied) by its probability of occurrence and the resulting products are summed. The course of action that has the largest expected value would be chosen as the "best" strategy to adopt—best in the sense that it is the optimal course of action against the given probability distribution. Expected value is discussed in more detail in the next chapter.

Exhibit 2–1

Probability Distribution of New Car Sales in June

Number of Sales	Probability
Less than 5	.00
5–15	.10
16–25	.20
26–35	.40
36–45	.25
46–55	.05
56 or more	.00
Sum	1.00

Notice that in constructing a table such as this, the decision maker is not assigning an individual probability to each event. Rather, the decision maker is assigning a consistent and comprehensive set of probabilities to some range of possible events. For the purpose of constructing the table, it is assumed that the actual event is certain to occur within this range; therefore, the total of all probabilities must be 1.0.

When a histogram is developed from these data, as in Exhibit 2–2, the probability scale on the vertical axis must range from 0 to 1, since the proportion of outcomes can never be negative and can also never exceed 100 percent, or a relative frequency of 1.00. That is, a probability must always lie between 0 and 1. On the horizontal axis, the outcomes being analyzed are scaled off. These might be wheat yields per acre, glass breakage in restaurants, or some other variable under consideration. A frequency or probability distribution of outcomes is then plotted.

At this point perhaps a finer, more detailed probability distribution may be needed in order to determine the parameters necessary for the analysis. That is, a measure of central tendency is needed, such as the mean, median, or mode, to describe the typical size of the distribution; a measure of dispersion such as the standard deviation or variance to establish the scatter; a measure of skewness to denote the degree of symmetry; and a measure of kurtosis or degree of peakedness. In particular, therefore, a smoothing of the probability distribution in the example would be of use, as suggested by Exhibit 2–3. This smoothing process would reflect the facts that (1) distinct, and usually nonequal, probabilities are associated with numbers in the car sale intervals; and (2) the distribution empirically determined is merely an approximation of the "true" underlying probability function from which the graph was derived.

Exhibit 2–2

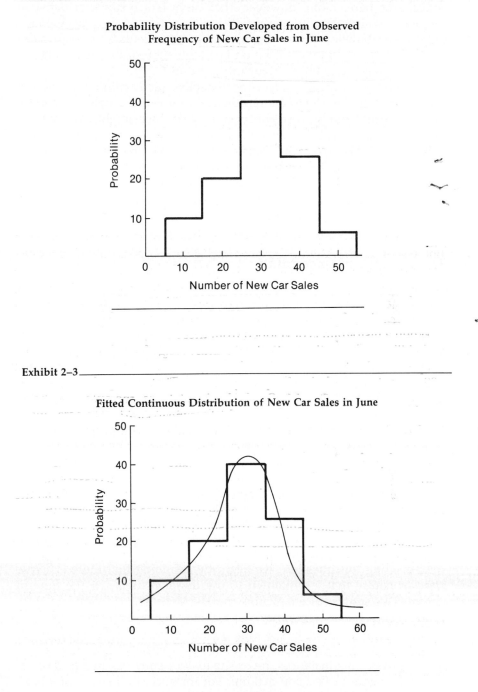

**Probability Distribution Developed from Observed
Frequency of New Car Sales in June**

Exhibit 2–3

Fitted Continuous Distribution of New Car Sales in June

Various smoothing devices are available for this purpose and need not concern us here. Note, however, that there is a distinction between frequency distribution and probability distribution. A frequency distribution is a tabulation of how many times certain events have occurred in the past. A probability distribution is a tabulation of the percentage of time that they are likely to occur in the future.

The simplest way to construct a probability distribution is to make a direct conversion of the frequency distribution. For example, if a certain event occurred during 5 of the past 10 years, we might say that the expected frequency, and hence the probability, of occurrence next year is 50 percent. However, the decision maker is not required to accept a direct conversion of the frequency distribution. The decision maker can modify the probability distribution to correct for the presence of new factors that might have important bearing upon later economic behavior, or to correct for past controls not continuing into the future.

The Concept of Uncertainty

Uncertainty is a state in which one or more alternatives result in a set of possible specific outcomes whose probabilities are either not known or not meaningful. Unlike risk, therefore, uncertainty is a subjective phenomenon: no two individuals who view the same event will necessarily formulate the same quantitative opinion because of a lack of knowledge or sufficient historical data on which to base a probability estimate. This in turn is caused by rapid changes in the structural variables or states of nature that determine each economic or social environment.

Degree of Uncertainty

Since expectations are subjective, there will be degrees of uncertainty on the part of decision makers. Two businessmen may view the same event, for example, but each will establish his own expectations with greater or less confidence than the other. What are the different ways in which decision makers might view the uncertain outcome of an event? In answering this question, we begin by assuming that there is a true state of nature that is unknown to the decision maker at the time of choice. Two sources of uncertainty may be identified: (1) complete ignorance and (2) partial ignorance.

Complete ignorance is the situation in which the decision maker makes no assumptions about the probabilities of the various states of nature. In these circumstances, he or she may use any one of a number of rational criteria for decision making. For instance, in the case of a business venture, the decision maker may adopt a pessimistic or conservative outlook. In that event he or she might examine the minimum outcome or profit expectation associated with each combined strategy and state of nature, and then choose the strategy that yields the maximum of these minimum profits. This is called the "maximin criterion." Other criteria have also been established to meet the particular needs of decision makers under conditions of uncertainty in which complete ignorance (i.e., complete lack of knowledge) is the prevailing condition. These criteria are discussed in the next chapter.

Partial ignorance is the situation in which the decision maker assumes the ability to assign a prior probability distribution to possible outcomes. When probability considerations are introduced, the theory of choice may be extended to theories of decision making under risk and uncertainty. This raises the issue of the choice of strategies, a consideration that led to the development in the early 1950s of "subjective" or "personal" probability theories.

In his monumental work, *The Foundations of Statistics*, L. J. Savage[3] developed a procedure for transforming a decision problem under uncertainty into one under risk. This was possible through the development of an *a priori, subjective* probability distribution for the possible states of nature in a given decision problem. Since a great many decisions in business and the social sciences are made on the basis of partial ignorance or incomplete knowledge of the facts, a brief intuitive sketch of the notion of subjective probability distributions should be of interest.

Subjective Probability Distributions

Degrees of uncertainty may be illustrated by the set of probability or frequency distributions of expectations shown in Exhibit 2–4. Expected outcomes, profits, sales, GNP, or other items of interest are plotted horizontally, while the subjective probability of a particular outcome is measured off vertically.

The top panel of Exhibit 2–4 has three normal distributions, but only A is of unit or standard normal form. In contrast to C, A represents greater uncertainty, owing to the greater variance or spread of its distribution.

If X is taken as the modal or most frequent outcome, the greatest variation in expectations (or greatest uncertainty) occurs in B because it has the widest spread; the least variation or uncertainty is in C because it has the least spread. Thus, as an indication of the degree of uncertainty, a measure of the *dispersion* of expectations such as the range, the standard deviation, or the variance could be used. The degree of uncertainty could be said to vary directly with the dispersion: a dispersion of zero would mean "perfect certainty," or a single-valued expectation; a larger

---

[3] L. J. Savage, *The Foundations of Statistics* (New York: John Wiley & Sons, 1954).

Exhibit 2–4

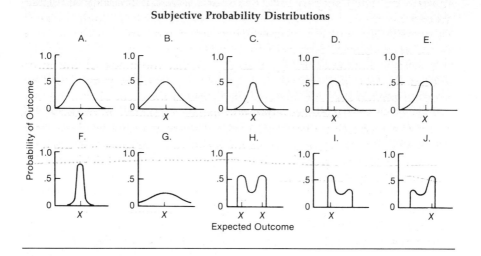

Subjective Probability Distributions

dispersion would indicate greater uncertainty or multivalued expectations.

Figures D and E illustrate the significance of *skewness*. Compare these
curves with the normal curve of A, where the expected outcomes are
arranged symmetrically about the modal outcome. In A, there is an even
chance that a deviation from the most probable (modal) outcome will
be greater or less than the mode. In D, a deviation from the mode X will
most probably occur in the direction of higher values, while in E the
most probable deviation is toward lower values. Thus, a measure of
skewness, since it describes the lopsidedness of a distribution, is a further indication of the degree of confidence or uncertainty.

A comparison of F and G reveals still further characteristics. The degree of peakedness of a distribution, called *kurtosis* in statistical terminology, is yet another indication of uncertainty. In F the probability of the
particular modal outcome X is greater than for any other distribution
shown. In G, however, where the distribution is relatively flat-topped,
the subjective probability of the modal outcome is only slightly greater
than that of outcomes higher or lower. In F, the decision maker is relatively certain of the modal outcome; in G, the expectations cover a wide
range of almost equal probabilities, and it would be difficult to formulate
plans based on the modal outcome or on outcomes higher or lower
than X.

Finally, H, I, and J represent a different pattern of distribution. The U-
shaped distribution of H implies high, equal probabilities of outcomes

whose values are either large or small, and a low probability of outcomes in between. The J-shaped curve of J shows a high probability of higher-valued outcomes, while the reverse-J curve of I implies a high probability of the lower-valued outcomes. These latter two curves have statistical connotations similar to those of E and D, respectively.

Theorists sometimes disagree as to whether the mode or the mean should be used as the expected value for prediction purposes. One group contends that the mode is preferable as the most probable value because it is more realistic: a decision maker is unlikely to calculate the mean of a probability distribution whose shape may not be clear-cut to begin with. Another group favors the mean value because it is the theoretically correct one from which to compute the standard deviation as a measure of dispersion for the distribution.

It is beyond our scope to investigate these arguments. What concerns us most is the development of a conceptual orientation—a way of thinking about the nature of uncertainty—that forms the basis for scientific decision making and planning in modern management theory.

The Payoff Matrix

The previously mentioned pioneering research by L. J. Savage on subjective probability distributions was extended subsequently by Robert Schlaifer and Howard Raiffa[4] and put into more operational form. We refer to these modern developments under the broad heading of "decision theory", a term resulting largely from the ground-breaking work of Abraham Wald (1902–50), who is chiefly responsible for conceiving statistics in a decision-making context. One of the fruits of his labors is the *payoff matrix*, which was originally developed to support the theory of games. However, it has since been adapted to general decision making under conditions of risk or uncertainty.

Under conditions of risk or uncertainty, the typical decision problem is sufficiently complex to permit a number of possible outcomes or payoffs for each strategy, depending on conditions beyond the control of the decision maker. A payoff matrix, also called a decision matrix, provides a useful tool for the presentation and analysis of these outcomes. The payoff matrix helps the decision maker to conceptualize and formalize the decision process into:

1. A statement of objectives.
2. The selection of payoffs.

---

[4] See Robert Schlaifer, *Probability and Statistics for Business Decisions* (New York: McGraw-Hill, 1959); Robert Schlaifer, *Introduction to Statistics for Business Decisions* (New York: McGraw-Hill, 1961); and Howard Raiffa and Robert Schlaifer, *Applied Statistical Decision Theory* (Boston: Division of Research, Harvard Business School, 1961).

3.   The evaluation of alternative payoffs.
4.   The selection of alternative strategies.

An example of a payoff matrix is shown in Exhibit 2–5, in which the decision maker's five alternative strategies are listed at the left as S_1 through S_5. The decision maker also envisions four possible environ-

Exhibit 2–5

Payoff Matrix

Alternative Strategies	States of Nature			
	N_1	N_2	N_3	N_4
S_1	6	6	6	4
S_2	25	7	7	−15
S_3	20	20	7	−1
S_4	19	16	9	−2
S_5	20	15	15	−3

ments or states of nature, which are marked off along the top as N_1 through N_4. The numbers in the matrix represent the resulting payoffs or outcomes for each strategy and associated state of nature.

In this example, the strategies might be different advertising campaigns, and the states of nature could be economic conditions of boom, stability, recession, or depression. The payoffs represent the decision maker's best estimate of outcomes for each combination of strategy and state of nature, expressed in the most meaningful terms. Conceptually, the most meaningful terms might be quantities, such as units of output sold, dollar volume of sales, dollars of profits, or any other number that makes sense to the decision maker. (In this illustration, the payoffs would have to represent some function of profit, since it is not possible to have negative output or sales.) Three questions always arise about the payoffs:

1.   What do they represent?
2.   How do we find them?
3.   How do we evaluate them?

The first question was answered above. A general answer to the second question is that payoffs are developed from the best sources available. For example, if estimates of production are required, consult the managers of production. For estimates of sales, consult the firm's marketing managers.

As for the question of evaluation, the matrix makes it clear that the best strategy depends upon which state of nature occurs. Unfortunately, the decision maker cannot predict what state of nature will occur. Nevertheless, he must select a strategy. Which strategy should the decision maker choose?

Under conditions of *certainty*, the decision process involves the optimization of some known objective (such as profits), given certain known constraints (such as costs). Under conditions of *risk*, the decision maker may obtain objective posterior probability estimates as previously explained. But under conditions of *uncertainty*, probability distributions and constraints are not known.

Obviously, one of the great challenges for the business executive is planning under conditions of uncertainty. Yet how can this be done? Strategically, the best first step probably is to simplify the problem by identifying structures and factors relevant to the firm and its products. This may be done, in part, by forming mental images of possible future outcomes that cannot be verified in any quantitative manner. This means that, unlike risk, uncertainty cannot be integrated into the firm's cost structure.

The parameters of an underlying subjective probability distribution cannot be established empirically because of their very subjectivity, i.e., because they are simply a function of a manager's own expectations of the future. At best, it may be possible to make arbitrary assignments of probabilities to anticipated outcomes, but the resulting distribution of expectations cannot be established with any degree of precision. Scholars of decision theory offer a number of criteria by which a decision maker operating under uncertainty may select a strategy without any knowledge of probabilities. (These criteria will be discussed in the next chapter.) Nevertheless, it does seem evident that the decision maker would have an easier time if he or she had some idea of the probability of each outcome. Consequently the decision maker may elect to make subjective estimates of relevant parameters.

In the *Bayesian* probability approach, the decision maker lists the set of outcome values that a particular parameter might take and the corresponding probability estimate that has been subjectively assigned to them by the decision maker, *a priori*. In theory, these prior probabilities express the decision maker's vision of the future, which no two individuals may see in the same way. In actual practice, however, most decision makers follow the Bayesian postulate, which says that in the absence of meaningful knowledge of probabilities, equal probability should be assigned to each outcome.

After examining the subjective probability distribution, the decision maker may either act upon the basis of this evaluation or elect to gather more information at a further cost of time and money. The additional information may be used to change prior probabilities into posterior probabilities.[5]

Where should one draw the line in the search for additional information on which to base a decision? The answer is that the decision maker should continue to search for new alternatives, or should process additional information about known alternatives, as long as the marginal expected gains of such additional efforts exceed their cost. For example, a car buyer should continue to shop around for a new automobile up to the point where the cost of the trip to the next dealer, in terms of time, transportation, and so forth, is greater than the expected gain—in terms of, say, a better discount from the sticker price. Beyond this point, further search is inadvisable: it costs more than it is worth.

Classicists have objected to the use of "personal" or "subjective" probabilities, arguing that only objective probabilities are meaningful. Bayesians, on the other hand, reply that their use of prior probabilities is logical and consistent, and classicists, if they are reasonable, will utilize this information in decision making.

Whether the probabilities are objective or subjective, they must add up to 1.0 since one of the outcomes is certain to occur. In symbols,

$$P_1 + P_2 + \cdots + P_n = 1.0 \tag{1}$$

Since the probabilities add up to 1.0, they may be used as weights to calculate the mean (or average) payoff known as the *expected value*. In symbols,

$$E(X) = P_1 X_1 + P_2 X_2 + \cdots + P_n X_n \tag{2}$$

where

$E(X)$ = The expected value or weighted mean payoff
P_i = The probability of the ith payoff
X_i = The ith payoff

---

[5] Posterior probabilities may be calculated with the aid of Bayes' Theorem:

$$P(E_i|R) = \frac{P(E_i)P(R|E_i)}{P(E_1)P(R|E_1) + P(E_2)P(R|E_2) + \cdots + P(E_n)P(R|E_n)}$$

where

R = The outcome of a test or experiment
$P(E_i)$ = The prior probability of event E_i, i.e., the probability assigned to E_i before the test or experiment takes place
$P(R|E_i)$ = The likelihood or conditional probability of R, given that E_i is true
$P(E_i|R)$ = The posterior probability of E_i, i.e., the conditional probability of E_i, given the result R

A full explanation of Bayes' Theorem with examples may be obtained from numerous textbooks on statistical analysis.

Utility, Risk Aversion, and Risk Premiums

Under conditions of risk and uncertainty, the potential outcomes of a given strategy may vary widely. Therefore, there is an element of risk that decision makers must deal with. How the decision maker elects to deal with risk may well depend upon his or her attitude. A *risk seeker* prefers a riskier investment to a safer one, even if the monetary rewards are the same. The *risk avoider*, on the other hand, is averse to risk, and is thus attracted to the safest investment. A person *indifferent to risk* overlooks risk differentials among investments that offer equal returns.

Across the vast sea of human personalities, there are undoubtedly some who seek risk and some who are indifferent to it. But both common sense and empirical observation reveal that most investors and business managers are risk avoiders. Why? A number of theories attempt to explain this fact about human behavior, but the most logical, satisfactory explanation lies in *utility theory*.

Utility and Decision Making   *Quiz 3*

Suppose two engineering firms are invited to submit design specifications for a large construction project. Company A, with assets of $50 million, is considerably larger than Company B, whose assets amount to only $1 million. However, the cost of preparing the bid, $1 million, is the same for both companies, and it cannot be recovered by the firm whose design is not accepted. On the other hand, the company that wins the competition can expect a profit of $25 million on the subsequent work.

The management of each company feels that it has an even chance of winning the competition.[6] Consequently, the probabilities are .5 for winning and .5 for losing. The alternatives are: (1) compete and (2) do not compete. If both companies compete, the expected value for each is (in millions of dollars):

$$E(\text{Profit}) = .5(-1) + .5(25) = 12$$

Despite the fact that the expected value of competing is $12 million, the smaller firm may elect not to compete. Why not?

---

[6] If the two firms have entered similar competitions in the past, management's belief might be based on experience, in which case it is applying objective probabilities under conditions of risk. But if it has no empirical data on which to base an opinion, the probabilities applied are subjective estimates formed under conditions of uncertainty (here, according to the Bayesian postulate of equal probability).

[handwritten margin note: Cash flow problem]

The reason is that $12 million is only the theoretical average return from *many* trials. In reality, however, there is only *one* trial in which the company will either win $25 million or lose $1 million. If such a loss would put the firm into bankruptcy, the firm would not risk its survival no matter how great the potential reward. On the other hand, if the company is in a position to absorb a million dollar loss, it might be more inclined to assume the risk.

The conclusion to be drawn is that a transformation of dollar payoffs into some other reward structure may be necessary before a proper analysis can be made. If dollar values do not adequately reflect the decision maker's *feelings* or *attitude* toward gain or loss, the dollar values must be converted into a more meaningful measurement.

Utility is such a measurement, and it can be expressed in conceptual units called "utils." Unfortunately, no one has been able to establish a standard util by which one can perform a cardinal measurement of utility. Nevertheless, the concept is useful. Decision makers intuitively use this concept when arranging alternatives in order of preference. In other words, an ordinal measurement of utility is quite practical even if a cardinal measurement is not actually possible.

Diminishing Marginal Utility

At this point, it is necessary to explain the relationship between risk and utility in a formal manner. To do so, profit and loss must be measured in terms of *marginal utility* rather than absolute dollar values. Marginal utility is defined as the change in total utility that takes place when one more unit of money is gained or lost. In the example above, if the company cannot afford to take a $1 million loss, it places a higher marginal utility on a $1 million loss than on a $25 million gain.

The three ways in which utility may theoretically relate to income are depicted in Exhibit 2–6.

The three panels of Exhibit 2–6 depict behavior of different types of investors when investment yield or income is increased by equal increments. The horizontal axes represent income measured in dollars. The vertical axes represent utility of dollars gained, measured in utils. Each curve represents utility as a function of income. The slope of each curve represents *marginal utility*, which is where our interest lies.

In panel A, marginal utility grows larger as income rises. This reflects the case of the compulsive gambler, who places higher utility on dollars won than on dollars lost. The rising curve thus describes the behavior of a *risk seeker*—the more he wins, the more important winning becomes.

The straight lines of panel B have constant slopes, characterizing the person indifferent to risk, for whom the marginal utility of a dollar lost is equal to that of a dollar gained. Indifference to risk, however, is not the

Exhibit 2–6

Utility of Income

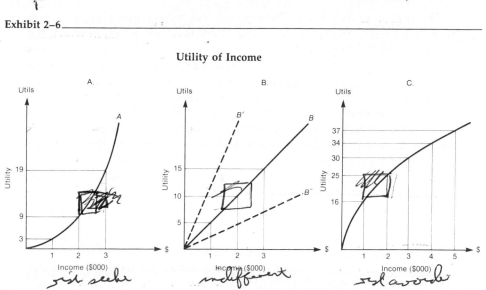

same as indifference to profit. The individual represented in B' places a higher utility value on a dollar gained or lost than does B, and B gets more utility out of a dollar than does B".

The most common investor, whose risk-return behavior is depicted in panel C, is a risk avoider. The reason for risk aversion is *diminishing marginal utility*. Panel C shows that with no investment there is, of course, no return. Upon receipt of the first $1,000, total utility increases by 16 utils as the investor satisfies his immediate needs. The second $1,000, while no doubt welcome, is not needed as badly as the first $1,000. Consequently, total utility rises by only 9 utils. That is, marginal utility for the second $1,000 is 9 utils, as compared to 16 for the first $1,000. When the third $1,000 is received, total utility rises to 30 utils, but marginal utility falls to 5 utils. Clearly, marginal utility diminishes as the return or income increases, and this has a decisive effect upon the investor's behavior.

For example, suppose that the investor has a choice between a risk-free investment in government bonds that will yield $3,000 and an investment in the stock of a new electronics firm that will yield $4,000 if all goes well, but only $1,000 if the new product fails to develop as expected. Suppose also that a thorough investigation convinces the investor that there is a probability of .75 that the new product will do well. The expected *dollar* values of the two projects are as follows:

$$E(\text{government bond}) = (1.0)\ (\$3,000) = \$3,000$$
$$E(\text{new venture}) = .75\ (\$4,000) + .25\ (\$1,000) = \$3,250$$

The expected utility values of the two projects are (from panel C, Exhibit 2–6), in utils:

$$E(\text{government bond}) = (1.0)\,(30) = 30$$
$$E(\text{new venture}) = (.75)\,(34) + (.25)\,(16) = 29.5$$

Thus we see that the expected monetary yield is greater for the new venture in the electronics firm, but the expected utility is greater for the risk-free government bond. The risk-averse investor will therefore prefer to buy the government bond.

Risk Premiums

It is conceivable that human behavior may follow any of the curves on Exhibit 2–6, or even some entirely different curve. There may be a few compulsive gamblers (panel A types) who actually succeed in business. There may also be some managers who are indifferent to risk (panel B types), perhaps because they are unaware of risk or do not understand its significance. If such managers exist, they certainly are in a minority. Most managers are panel C types, keenly aware of business risk. Hence, the utility function of most business managers exhibits diminishing marginal utility. They get more pain from losing a dollar than pleasure from gaining one.

Managers' and investors' aversion to risk is manifested in many ways. Grade AA bonds sell for more than grade B bonds. Investors diversify either by creating individual portfolios or by investing in mutual funds. People deposit their money in federally insured savings accounts at low rates of interest rather than in uninsured savings accounts that may earn twice as much. And people buy all kinds of casualty and life insurance.

Why, then, if investors are averse to risk, do they put their money into common stocks, commodities, precious metals, collectibles, and other risky investments? The answer is that they do not do so unless they receive a *risk premium.* The investor wants to be compensated not only for the use of his or her money, but also for the risk that it may be lost. In other words, the investor demands a higher rate of return when risk is involved.

To illustrate the concept of risk premium, suppose an investor has a utility function like the one in Exhibit 2–7, and is asked to bet $1,000 on the flip of a coin at even odds. Thus if he wins he gets $1,000 and if he loses he pays $1,000. Should he take the bet? To get the answer, let us look at Exhibit 2–7, which illustrates an investment without a risk premium. If the investor wins $1,000, he gains 8 utils of utility; but if he loses, he loses 12 utils. In other words, the utility of winning is 0.008 per dollar, while the disutility of losing is 0.012. Since the probability of winning or losing is the same (.5), the expected value in utils or average

Exhibit 2–7

Utility of Bet with No Risk Premium

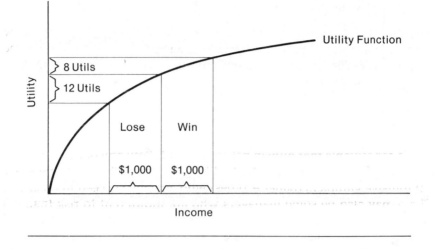

return is 0.008(.5) = 0.012(.5) = −0.002. Since the expected value is negative, it is clear that the investor should not take this bet.

Now let us suppose that the same investor is offered a premium if he will take the bet. If he loses, he loses $1,000; but if he wins, he wins $1,800. Should he take the bet? Let us look at Exhibit 2–8.

The answer depends upon the investor's utility function. As the curve is drawn in Exhibit 2–8, a loss of $1,000 will bring a disutility of 12 utils, while a win of $1,800 will provide a utility of 12 utils. The expected value of the bet then is 0.012(.5) − 0.012(.5) = 0, meaning that the investor may be indifferent to the bet. If the risk premium is increased, he will accept the bet; but if the risk premium is decreased, he will not accept.

Now let us suppose that the same investor is offered another bet for $500, again on the flip of a coin. Will he also require an $800 premium on the $500 bet? This time we look at Exhibit 2–9.

Exhibit 2–9 shows that the loss of $500 for this investor involves the loss of 5 utils. In order to win 5 utils, the investor requires a risk premium of $100. But this is only one eighth of the risk premium required for the $1,000 bet. That is to say that when the bet is increased two times, the risk premium demanded is increased eight times. How can this be?

The answer, of course, lies in the shape of the investor's utility function or curve. The risk is measured by the dispersion of possible outcomes. Since the dispersion of ±$1,000 is twice as great as the dispersion of ±$500, it would seem that the risk should be twice as great. But we

Exhibit 2–8

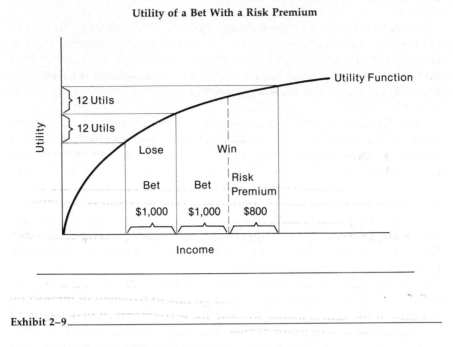

Utility of a Bet With a Risk Premium

Exhibit 2–9

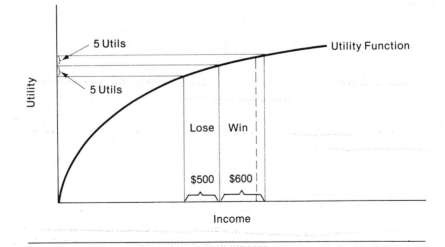

Risk Premiums for a Smaller Bet

have seen in Exhibits 2–8 and 2–9 that when a risk premium is added to the winning side of the bet, the dispersion of the possible outcomes is changed, hence the risk is also changed.

The investor's attitude toward risk depends first of all upon the shape of his or her utility curve, and second upon one's current position on the curve, which is determined by current income. If current income is low, marginal utility of income (measured by the slope of the curve) is high, and one will accept risk for a much lower premium than when income is higher.[7]

To a firm, the risk premium may be viewed as having two components, a business risk and a financial risk. Business risk is always present to some degree, since no business is guaranteed success. The degree of risk depends upon the nature of the business and the demonstrated skill of its management. Certain types of businesses are inherently more risky than others. Within any type of business, an investor would usually perceive more risk in a newly established firm than in one with a longer record of earnings. On the other hand, a long-established firm whose products or business methods have become outdated may present a high degree of risk.

Financial risk is incurred whenever the firm includes long-term debt in its capital structure. Earnings must go first to payment of interest on the debt. If the firm is unable to make these payments, it may be forced into bankruptcy. To a lesser degree, financial risk is also incurred by the sale of preferred stock, since preferred stock dividends must be paid before the equity investor can receive any return on his or her investment.

Risk Adjustment

In estimating the payoffs for a particular strategy, the decision maker must consider not only the degree of risk involved, but also the time

---

[7] Students who feel a bit uneasy with this conclusion are in the company of two well-known scholars—Milton Friedman and Leonard J. Savage—who were also troubled with the traditional marginal utility approach. Of course, we get the above outcome because of the particular form of the utility function assumed. In the above case, marginal utility is declining over the entire range of values for income. However, suppose marginal utility turned out to be a more complex function than the one we are assuming. Suppose it rises initially but then decreases: then we might reach a different conclusion from the one above. Essentially, we are describing part of the Friedman-Savage hypothesis about the relationship of utility to income. And while we cannot explore all of the points embraced in this intriguing approach, we should note that Friedman and Savage believe their hypothesis explains what, on the surface, appears to be a contradiction in human behavior—a person buys insurance (indicating an aversion toward risk) but at the same time engages in a game of chance with unfavorable odds (indicating a preference toward risk). For further insights, see Milton Friedman and Leonard J. Savage, "The Utility Analysis of Choices Involving Risk," *The Journal of Political Economy*, August 1948, pp. 279–304.

value of money. Both considerations are incorporated in the valuation model developed in Chapter 1:

$$NPV = \sum_{t=1}^{n} \frac{R_t}{(1 + r)^t} \tag{3}$$

where

NPV = The net present value of a flow of future profits
R_t = The net return or profit in time period t
r = The required rate of return considering the level of business risk involved
n = The number of time periods considered

Several ways to adjust the valuation model for risk are discussed in the literature of finance. Two of the most commonly used methods are the *risk-adjusted discount rate* and the *certainty-equivalent approach*. (A third method, the *probability distribution approach*, is discussed in Chapter 3.)

The Risk-Adjusted Discount Rate

As discussed earlier, every firm has a required rate of return reflecting its perception of business risk. In order to find the present value of a project's future payoff, the firm uses its required rate of return as the discount rate, provided the project's business risk is the same as the firm's. If the project's risk is greater than the firm's normal risk, a higher discount rate will be used to compensate for the greater risk.

For example, suppose a firm's normal business risk requires a 20 percent rate of return. The firm is considering an investment strategy that initially costs $100,000 and is expected to yield $50,000 per year for the next three years.

At a normal discount rate of 20 percent, the net present value equals:

$$NPV = -\$100,000 + \frac{\$50,000}{(1.20)} + \frac{\$50,000}{(1.20)^2} + \frac{\$50,000}{(1.20)^3} = \$5,324$$

Since the net present value is positive, the project is acceptable. But suppose the risk were such that management feels it should get a 25 percent return. Then the net present value equals:

$$NPV = -\$100,000 + \frac{\$50,000}{(1.25)} + \frac{\$50,000}{(1.25)^2} + \frac{\$50,000}{(1.25)^3} = -\$2,400$$

Now the net present value is negative, so the proposal should be rejected. Thus in the risk-adjusted discount rate approach, risk is wholly reflected by the discount rate and discounting process. There are, however, at least three limitations to this approach.

First, how do we determine the appropriate discount rate? Clearly, the introduction of a new product is riskier than buying government bonds—but how much riskier? It is very difficult to resolve this question consistently and objectively, particularly when there is no historical evidence on which to base an estimate.

Second, this method ignores the probability distribution of future cash flows—information that could be of great value. It is possible that management may consider such probabilities in determining what discount rate to use, but there are better ways of evaluating and incorporating such information.

Third, the risk-adjusted discount rate does not offer any consistent method for incorporating the decision maker's attitude toward risk; however, this objection may be overcome by the *certainty-equivalent approach*.

The Certainty-Equivalent Approach

The risk-adjusted discount rate approach discussed in the preceding subsection simply modified the discount rate in the denominator of the valuation model. In contrast, the certainty-equivalent approach uses a risk-free discount rate in the denominator and accounts for risk by modifying the numerator of the valuation model, as follows:

$$NPV = \sum_{t=0}^{n} \frac{\alpha_t R_t}{(1 + i)^t} \tag{4}$$

where

i = The risk-free interest rate, assumed to be constant for all future periods
R_t = The risky cash flow in the tth time period
α_t = The certainty-equivalent coefficient for the tth time period

The certainty-equivalent coefficient, α, is a number between 0 and 1 that reflects the decision maker's utility function. It varies inversely with the degree of risk. A value of 0 means the decision maker feels the project is too risky to offer any effective return. A value of 1 means that the decision maker sees the project as risk-free.

The decision maker's attitude toward risk is incorporated by first determining for each time period a risk-free cash flow, R_t^*, that the decision maker regards as equivalent to the risky cash flow, R_t. Then the certainty-equivalent coefficient, α_t, is calculated as the ratio of the equivalent certain cash flow to the risky cash flow:

$$\alpha_t = \frac{\text{Equivalent certain sum}}{\text{Expected risky sum}} = \frac{R_t^*}{R_t} \tag{5}$$

To illustrate, recall the firm that is considering an investment strategy having an initial cost of $100,000 and expected to yield $50,000 per year for the next three years. Suppose that the interest rate on (risk-free) Treasury bills is 12 percent.

Management believes that the longer it has to wait for a return the riskier it becomes. Consequently, it determines that $\alpha_0 = 1.0$, $\alpha_1 = .90$, $\alpha_2 = .80$, and $\alpha_3 = .70$. Then the net present value of the investment is:

$$NPV = -\$100,000 + \frac{.9(\$50,000)}{1.12} + \frac{.8(\$50,000)}{(1.12)^2} + \frac{.7(\$50,000)}{(1.12)^3}$$

$$= -\$3,021$$

The net present value of the return on the Treasury bills equals:

$$NPV = -\$100,000 + \frac{\$12,000}{1.12} + \frac{\$12,000}{(1.12)^2} + \frac{\$12,000}{(1.12)^3} + \frac{\$100,000}{(1.12)^3} = 0$$

The proposal would be rejected because the returns are not commensurate with management's perception of the risk involved.

The certainty-equivalent approach also presents practical problems when it comes to implementation, mainly with respect to the calculation of certainty-equivalent coefficients. However, it is theoretically superior to the risk-adjusted discount rate approach because it does consider the decision maker's attitude toward risk.

Summary

Good decision making follows the same general procedure whether it takes place in a profit-seeking business, a nonprofit organization, or a government agency. The decision maker must define the problem, establish objectives, identify all relevant factors, gather and evaluate relevant information, specify alternatives, and finally evaluate alternatives in order to choose the best solution to the problem.

Decisions are made within the context of a decision maker's state of knowledge, which defines the conditions of certainty, risk, or uncertainty. Each of these conditions calls for a different set of decision-making tools and techniques. Under conditions of certainty, the decision maker can calculate in advance the specific outcome to which each available strategy invariably leads. Conditions of certainty prevail in many short-run operating problems in which the decision maker needs no more than a knowledge of current prices, terms, and quantities demanded. The condition of certainty is often associated with optimizing models.

Risk is defined as a state of knowledge in which each alternative leads to one of a set of specific outcomes with objectively determined probabilities. Risk can be determined *a priori* (i.e., by deduction) or *a posteriori* (i.e., by statistical analysis of data obtained by experimentation or sampling).

Uncertainty is defined as a state of knowledge in which one or more alternatives result in a set of possible outcomes whose probabilities are either unknown or meaningless. All decisions under uncertainty are made subjectively because of a lack of objective knowledge.

If sufficient knowledge is not available to assign probabilities, there are still certain criteria by which a decision can be reached. (These criteria and methods are discussed in the next chapter.) If possible, however, the decision maker may assume that he or she possesses sufficient knowledge to assign subjective probabilities to each possible state of nature, thereby converting the situation to one of risk.

Under conditions of risk or uncertainty, a payoff matrix provides a useful decision model, showing possible states of nature, available strategies, and the payoffs associated with each strategy and state of nature. Payoffs are developed from the best sources available, and may be expressed as quantities, dollars, utility values, or any number that makes sense to the decision maker.

How the decision maker chooses to deal with risk depends upon his or her attitude. Some may seek risk, some may be indifferent toward it, but most business people try to avoid risk. Their attitude is based upon a utility function in which increasing increments of income (profits) bring decreasing increments of satisfaction (utility); the decision maker will accept risk only if there is a commensurate risk premium.

Every business firm and individual investor has in mind some required rate of return that reflects the perceived risk. As the degree of risk increases, the required rate of return also increases along a market indifference curve that depicts the investor's risk-return trade-off function.

The profit-maximization model can be simultaneously adjusted for both risk and the true value of money by several techniques. Two of the most common are the risk-adjusted discount rate and the certainty-equivalent approach. In the risk-adjusted discount method, the discount rate r, in the model,

$$NPV = \sum_{t=1}^{n} \frac{R_t}{(1 + r)^t}$$

is adjusted to reflect perceived risk.

In the certainty-equivalent approach, the discount rate of the model is set at the risk-free interest rate. The numerator of the model is multiplied by the certainty-equivalent coefficient. This is a number between 0 (too risky to consider) and 1 (risk-free). The certainty-equivalent coefficient enables the decision maker to quantify his or her attitude toward risk. For this reason it is considered to be theoretically superior to the risk-adjusted discount rate.

Problems

1. Define the concept of risk. Explain the a priori and the a posteriori methods of estimating risk.

2. Suppose that you have before you an urn containing nine red balls, eight white balls, and seven green balls. If you shake the urn in such a way that the balls are thoroughly mixed and then draw out one ball, what is the probability that it will be green? Is this an a priori or an a posteriori probability? Why?

3. What is the difference between a frequency distribution and a probability distribution?

4. Of what value are the measures of dispersion such as the range, variance, and standard deviation in indicating the degree of uncertainty in decision making?

5. Classify each of the following situations as decision making under certainty, risk, or uncertainty, and explain your answers.

a. A farmer in Illinois must decide how many acres to plant in corn and how many in soybeans.

b. In very hot weather at the baseball stadium, ice cream is the big seller with hot dogs a poor second; but if the weather is moderate or cool, the opposite occurs. Sanitary regulations do not permit the concessionaire to store either hot dogs or ice cream for more than two days. Because the concessionaire's orders are so large, suppliers require orders seven days in advance or else they cannot guarantee delivery. Therefore the concessionaire must decide now what to order for next week's big game.

c. Quality standards used by a maker of animal feeds set minimum percentages of protein, fat, and carbohydrate and a maximum percentage of inert ingredients in the final mixture. Three basic ingredients are available for mixing, each with different proportions of protein, fat, carbohydrate, and inert matter, and each with a different cost. The feed maker desires to meet or improve the quality standards at minimum cost and must decide what proportions of the basic ingredients to use in the final mixture.

6. A data processing firm is considering mailing 1,000 announcements of a new service. Interested parties will need to write for more information. The firm believes that one of every two replies will come from one of its present customers. From past experience, it is estimated

that the probability of a reply from noncustomers is .40. Assuming the mailing list includes the names of 300 present customers, how many replies can be expected? Suppose clerical costs are $2 to mail a letter and $10 to respond to each reply. Assuming the profit margin on the new service is $100 and that only one out of five replies actually results in the purchase of the new service, should the company mail the announcements?

7. Suppose that a firm's utility function is as shown below. Find the expected utility if the company's profits for one product line are $50,000, $80,000, and $100,000. Their respective probabilities are .4, .3, and .3. What concept does this exercise describe?

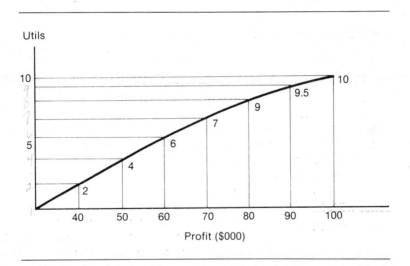

8. Smith has recently purchased a new house for $70,000. Fire insurance for the house can be bought for an annual premium of $200. Smith is uncertain whether or not the insurance should be purchased, however, since a friend who is an actuary has indicated that the probability of a fire destroying Smith's house is only .002. Should Smith purchase the insurance? Assuming you were Smith, would *you* purchase the insurance?

Suppose Smith is a real estate investor with a thousand $70,000 houses located throughout the United States. Should each house be insured assuming the same conditions given above?

9. After reviewing all aspects of a certain business investment, the board of directors decides that the deal seems too risky. The investment initially costs $150,000. It is believed that it will yield $40,000 per year for the next four years. The board recommends that more analysis should

be pursued using the risk-adjusted discount rate approach. Using this method, the board feels that a risk premium of 10 percent above the normal cost of capital of 15 percent is needed to cover the added risk encountered in the investment. Find the net present value using this risk-adjusted discount rate. Should the firm make the investment?

10.   Suppose a firm requires a 20 percent rate of return to cover normal business risks. The firm is considering an investment that costs $500,000 initially, and is expected to yield $150,000 per year for the next three years. Calculate the net present value, using the required discount rate. Should the firm engage in the investment? Explain. How does the certainty-equivalent coefficient, α, vary with the degree of risk involved in decision making?

Case Problem: Trans-Atlantic Corporation

11.   The Trans-Atlantic Corporation has recently completed productions of its new model of telex machine. The company has already conducted various market studies to choose the best strategy by which to promote its new product. After the field of possible marketing strategies was narrowed down, two alternatives remained. Management must now decide between these alternatives, called Strategy A and Strategy B. Strategy A calls for promoting the telex machine among final consumers. The emphasis in this approach is placed on advertising in the media. Strategy B is oriented toward distributors to persuade them to carry the telex machine. Vigorous sales calls by Trans-Atlantic sales executives will form a large part of this strategy.

The following table lists estimated sales volumes for each strategy. Included also is the probability for each sales volume under each approach. These probabilities were determined subjectively and represent management's best guesses about the future.

Strategy A (Consumer Emphasis)		Strategy B (Distribution)	
Probability	Outcome (Sales)	Probability	Outcome (Sales)
.2	$100,000	.3	$200,000
.3	250,000	.3	250,000
.3	300,000	.4	300,000
.2	450,000		

Questions:
a.   Assume that Trans-Atlantic has a 40 percent profit margin on sales. What are the expected profits under each strategy?

b. Construct a bar graph of possible profits for each strategy. By visual inspection of the two graphs, which strategy appears riskier?
c. Calculate the standard deviation of the profit distribution for each strategy. Which appears to involve more risk?
d. Suppose that the company's utility function is as shown below. Which strategy should the marketing manager recommend to the company?

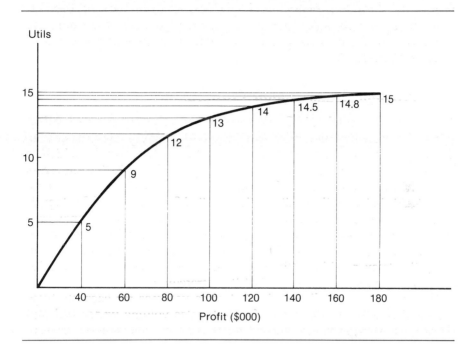

References

Bierman, Harold, Jr., and Warren H. Hausman. "The Resolution of Investment Uncertainty through Time." *Management Science*, August 1972, pp. 654–62.

Blume, M. E. "On the Assessment of Risk." *Journal of Finance*, March 1971, pp. 95–117.

Friedman, Milton, and Leonard J. Savage. "The Utility Analysis of Choices Involving Risk." *Journal of Political Economy*, August 1948, pp. 279–304.

Gale, B. T., and B. Branch. "Cash Flow Analysis: More Important Than Ever." *Harvard Business Review*, July–August 1981, pp. 131–36.

Hakansson, Nils H. "Friedman-Savage Utility Functions Consistent with Risk Aversion." *Quarterly Journal of Economics*, August 1970, pp. 472–87.

Hull, J., P. G. Moore, and H. Thomas. "Utility and Its Measurement." *Royal Statistical Society Journal* 136, part 2, 226–47 (1973).

Kihlstrom, Richard E., and Leonard J. Mirman. "Constant, Increasing and Decreasing Risk Aversion with Many Commodities." *Review of Economic Studies,* April 1981, pp. 271–80.

Page, Alfred N. *Utility Theory.* New York: John Wiley & Sons, 1968.

Swalm, Ralph O. "Utility Theory—Insights into Risk Taking." *Harvard Business Review,* November–December 1966, pp. 123–36.

Approaches to Decision Making

The preceding chapter introduced concepts pertinent to decision making by business firms, nonprofit institutions, and government agencies. This chapter discusses the methods and approaches by which those concepts can be applied to decision making under conditions of certainty, risk, and uncertainty.

This chapter is organized into three sections. The first section deals with decision making under certainty. It introduces the important tools of marginal analysis and linear programming.

The second section deals with decision making under risk. This section includes discussion of risk measurement, risk-return trade-offs, and payoffs. It also introduces the decision tree, a useful tool in sequential decision analysis.

The last section deals with methods of decision making under conditions of uncertainty. This discussion includes, among other things, four major criteria for evaluating a decision matrix under conditions of uncertainty.

At the end of the chapter are two appendixes that provide a closer examination of marginal analysis and the probability distribution of cash flows.

For expository purposes, we shall continue to use the payoff matrix introduced in Exhibit 2–4 in Chapter 2. For convenience, it is reproduced here as Exhibit 3–1.

Exhibit 3–1_____

Payoff Matrix

	States of Nature			
Alternative Strategies	N_1	N_2	N_3	N_4
S_1	6	6	6	4
S_2	25	7	7	−15
S_3	20	20	7	−1
S_4	19	16	9	−2
S_5	20	15	15	−3

Decision Making under Certainty

Under conditions of certainty, the decision maker has complete knowledge of the various states of nature that are relevant to the decision and
knows which one will occur. This effectively reduces the decision matrix
to one column. The decision maker simply chooses the strategy, course
of action, or project that yields the greatest payoff. In our example (see
Exhibit 3–1), the decision depends upon which state of nature the decision maker is sure will occur. The possibilities are shown in Exhibit
3–2.

Exhibit 3–2_____

Possible Decisions under Condition of Certainty

Certain State of Nature	Best Strategy	Payoff
N_1	S_2	25
N_2	S_3	20
N_3	S_5	15
N_4	S_1	4

In general, decision making under certainty requires that we find the
largest payoff either by maximizing benefits (such as revenue, profit, or
utility) or by minimizing costs. Powerful tools available to the decision
maker for this purpose are *marginal analysis, linear programming,* and
incremental profit analysis.

Marginal Analysis

Marginal analysis utilizes the concepts of marginal utility and marginal cost. Marginal utility is defined as the additional (incremental) satisfaction or value to be gained from acquiring one more unit of some good or service, while marginal cost is defined as the additional (incremental) cost of acquiring or producing one more unit. Economic theory and common sense both tell us that if marginal utility exceeds marginal cost, it would pay to acquire one more unit; otherwise it would not.

Fortunately for people in business, utility can usually be equated with revenue, and both revenues and costs can be quantified in the common denominator of money. All other things being equal, the correct decision is then indicated by the relationship between marginal revenue and marginal costs, as illustrated in Exhibit 3–3.

Exhibit 3–3

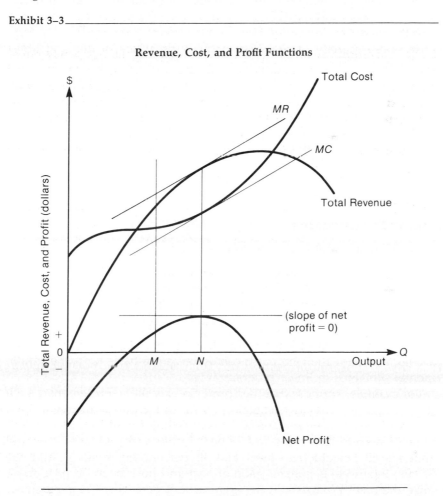

Revenue, Cost, and Profit Functions

Exhibit 3–3 shows a typical net profit curve of microeconomic theory, with profit scaled on the vertical axis and output (quantity produced and sold) scaled on the horizontal. Marginal analysis finds the most profitable output to be N units. This is indicated in three different ways: (1) at this level of output, the slope of the profit function, or marginal profit, is zero; (2) at this level of output, the vertical distance between total cost and total revenue $(TR - TC)$ is at a maximum; and (3) at this level of output, the slope of the total revenue curve (marginal revenue) equals the slope of the total cost curve (marginal cost). Hence we say that *profit is maximized when marginal revenue equals marginal cost*. Thus, in the marginal analysis type of problem, the precise extent to which resources are utilized is specified, and the decision maker needs only to select the unique output level that maximizes profit.

Instead of specifying the precise degree of resource utilization necessary for profit maximization, we can build some realistic complexities into the model by indicating that certain resource limitations exist. Suppose that a scarcity of resources or perhaps a lack of demand limits production to M units. The decision maker must then find out whether the output that maximizes profit under limited production is M units, or whether it is some other output to the left of (less than) M. This becomes a difficult problem with a general solution involving any number of dimensions and variables. Constrained optimization techniques using the Lagrangian multiplier can be used, as illustrated in Appendix 3A. However, if certain conditions exist, as explained below, *linear programming* offers a powerful alternative procedure.

Linear Programming

Consider the well-known nursery rhyme:

> Jack Sprat could eat no fat,
> His wife could eat no lean,
> And so you see between the two
> They licked the platter clean.

Although most people learned this ditty in their childhood, how many are familiar with the fact that it can serve as the basis for some fundamental problems in linear programming?

For example, suppose that the Sprats' weekly diet requirement is such that Mr. Sprat needs at least eight pounds of lean meat and Mrs. Sprat needs at least two pounds of fat. If beef selling for $4.50 a pound contains 75 percent lean meat and 25 percent fat, and pork at $2 a pound contains 60 percent lean meat and 40 percent fat, what should the Sprats' total weekly consumption of beef and pork be in order to minimize the cost? What would the answer be if pork costs $4 per pound?

Questions of this nature are typical of some types of problems that are encountered in linear programming.

What is linear programming? It is a form of mathematical modeling that deals with the optimal allocation of scarce resources among competing activities. In terms of actual application, it is perhaps the most successful and widely used approach for resource allocation problems. Its usage closely parallels growth in computer technology, because a complicated linear programming problem has enormous computational requirements that only a computer can handle efficiently. The student who wants to learn more about linear programming should consult an operations research text. For most business managers, it is enough to be able to recognize a linear programming problem, then set it up for computer input.

Linear programming is applicable only to problems that display all four of the following characteristics:

1. A set of nonnegative, independent variables critical to the problem.
2. One and only one objective that is a function of the variables, such as cost minimization or profit maximization.
3. Constraints that limit the attainment of the objective. These usually take the form of upper or lower limits on combinations of the variables.
4. Linearity of all quantitative relationships.

Any economic problem that is concerned with maximizing or minimizing (i.e., optimizing) a linear objective function (e.g., total cost, net profit, or a similar economic quantity) and that is subject to a set of linear inequalities in the form of constraints (e.g., limitations of men, materials, capital, or other resources) is a linear programming problem. Techniques of nonlinear programming also exist. Programming techniques, both linear and nonlinear, have been used with enormous success to solve a variety of business problems, such as:

1. *Determining a product mix that meets certain established specifications at minimum cost.* Examples are found in the blending of gasolines and in obtaining feed mixes that satisfy specified nutritional requirements.
2. *Determining optimal product lines and production processes.* Examples are found wherever capacity limitations exist (e.g., factory size, warehouse space, machine time, and the like) and where decisions must be made as to which products to produce, given such scarce resources.
3. *Determining optimal transportation routes.* Examples occur in the case of a firm whose plants and warehouses are scattered and whose objective is to minimize transportation costs from factories to warehouses.

These are a few of the common types of problems that are routinely handled by linear and nonlinear programming methods.

Example. Suppose that a chemical plant receives an order for 5,000 pounds of a special mixture of three ingredients, the composition of which is constrained as follows:

Ingredient 1, costing $5 per pound, not to exceed 1,500 pounds.
Ingredient 2, costing $6 per pound, not less than 750 pounds.
Ingredient 3, costing $7 per pound, not less than 1,000 pounds.

How much of each ingredient should be used in order to minimize the cost?

The problem is set up as follows:

Let

$$x_1 = \text{pounds of Ingredient 1} \tag{1}$$
$$x_2 = \text{pounds of Ingredient 2} \tag{2}$$
$$x_3 = \text{pounds of Ingredient 3} \tag{3}$$

Objective:

$$\text{Minimize } Z = 5x_1 + 6x_2 + 7x_3 \tag{4}$$

subject to

$$x_1 + x_2 + x_3 \geq 5{,}000 \tag{5}$$
$$x_1 \leq 1{,}500 \tag{6}$$
$$x_2 \geq 750 \tag{7}$$
$$x_3 \geq 1{,}000 \tag{8}$$
$$x_1, x_2, x_3 \geq 0 \tag{9}$$

The first three equations simply identify variables x_1, x_2, and x_3 in terms of quantities of Ingredients 1, 2, and 3, respectively. These quantities, of course, cannot be less than zero.

Equation (4) states the objective to be the minimization of the total cost of the ingredients. (The cost of an ingredient is calculated by multiplying the quantity of that ingredient by its respective unit cost. Summing the costs of all the ingredients produces the total cost.)

Equation (5) says that the total mixture must weigh at least 5,000 pounds. Equation (6) says that no more than 1,500 pounds of Ingredient 1 may be used. Equation (7) says that at least 750 pounds of Ingredient 2 must be used. Equation (8) says that at least 1,000 pounds of Ingredient 3 must be used. Equation (9) formally states that the variables are nonnegative.

The problem setup as illustrated above conforms to the format required by computer packages for linear programming. When the data are entered, they are processed by the package, and the solution to the problem appears in the output: $x_1 = 1,500$, $x_2 = 2,500$, $x_3 = 1,000$. This means that the objective of cost minimization is satisfied if one uses 1,500 pounds of Ingredient 1, 2,500 pounds of Ingredient 2, and 1,000 pounds of Ingredient 3. Note that these values also satisfy each of the constraints, as they must.

Incremental Profit Analysis

Marginal analysis, it will be recalled, is concerned with changing values of related but unchanging functions. In the real world, however, demand, revenue, production, and cost functions cannot be known with much precision and are subject to change. Nevertheless, these problems can be largely overcome by the broader concept of *incremental profit analysis,* a practical application of the marginal analysis concept.

Incremental profit analysis is concerned with *any* change in revenues, costs, and consequent profits that results from a particular decision. Thus, the concept of incremental analysis includes changes in the functions themselves as well as changes in their values. The basic decision rule is to accept any proposal that will increase profits and reject any proposal that will not.

Since incremental decision making is concerned only with variables that can change, fixed costs are irrelevant to the decision. Hence, incremental decision making is a short-run concept. Unfortunately, many managers do not think in incremental terms; rather, they make decisions based on average values. Almost invariably, short-run decisions based on average cost, for example, will be wrong if the firm's objective is to maximize profit.

Example. Suppose a tire manufacturer is currently producing and selling 100,000 tires per month at a price of $24 each. Variable cost is $14 per tire, and fixed cost is $600,000; hence the fully absorbed cost is $20 per tire.

Now suppose that a large discount store (not a current customer) offers to contract for 25,000 tires per month at a price of $18 each. In order to make the additional 25,000 tires, the manufacturer would have to work overtime, which would add $2 to the variable cost of the additional 25,000 tires. The average cost per tire would be:

Variable cost of first 100,000 tires at $14	$1,400,000
Variable cost of next 25,000 tires at $16	400,000
Fixed cost	600,000
Total cost of 125,000 tires	$2,400,000
Average cost per tire	$19.20

If the firm based its decision on average cost, the order would be rejected on the grounds that the cost is greater than the offered price.

But if incremental costs are calculated, the incremental cost of the last 25,000 tires is $16 each, while the incremental revenue offered is $18 each. Thus the proposed contract would bring in profits of $50,000 that the firm would not earn otherwise.

Does incremental profit analysis provide the last word in this decision? Not necessarily, since other (nonquantifiable) considerations might outweigh the results of the incremental profit analysis (e.g., reactions of current customers if they find out about this deal, or even the legality of this type of price discrimination). Nevertheless, incremental profit analysis provides a powerful and relatively easy-to-use tool for the decision maker.

Decision Making under Risk

As noted in Chapter 2, risk exists when the decision maker does not know in advance the specific outcome of a decision but is able to establish an objective probability distribution of payoffs, either a priori (i.e., by deduction) or a posteriori (i.e., by empirical measurement). Under conditions of risk, the primary decision criterion is *expected value*, which is computed as:

$$E(X) = P_1X_1 + P_2X_2 + \cdots + P_nX_n = \sum_{i=1}^{n} P_iX_i \qquad (10)$$

where

X_i = value of the ith payoff
P_i = probability of the ith payoff (which is equal to the probability of the ith state of nature)

To make a decision, the expected value is computed for each strategy and the one with the highest expected value is chosen. Taking the example portrayed in Exhibit 3–1, let us suppose that the decision maker assumes a 20 percent chance of boom (N_1), a 65 percent chance of stability (N_2), a 10 percent chance of recession (N_3), and a 5 percent chance of depression (N_4). (Note that these probabilities add up to 100 percent.) The expected value of each strategy is calculated as follows:

$$
\begin{aligned}
S_1&: .2(6) \;+ .65(6) \;+ .10(6) \;+ .05(4) \;\;= \;\;5.90 \\
S_2&: .2(25) + .65(7) \;+ .10(7) \;+ .05(-15) = \;\;9.50 \\
S_3&: .2(20) + .65(20) + .10(7) \;+ .05(-1) \;= 17.65 \\
S_4&: .2(19) + .65(16) + .10(9) \;+ .05(-2) \;= 15.00 \\
S_5&: .2(20) + .65(15) + .10(15) + .05(-3) \;= 15.10
\end{aligned}
$$

These results are depicted in Exhibit 3–4.

Exhibit 3–4_____

Expected Value Calculation

Alternative Strategies	States of Nature				Expected Value $E(S_i)$
	N_1	N_2	N_3	N_4	
S_1	6	6	6	4	5.90
S_2	25	7	7	−15	9.50
S_3	20	20	7	−1	17.65*
S_4	19	16	9	−2	15.00
S_5	20	15	15	−3	15.10

* Best strategy.

If Exhibit 3–4 represented an experiment in which each strategy was repeated many, many times, the payoffs would average out to the expected value. Like any average, the expected value need not be contained in the set of values from which it is derived, although it may be contained therein by sheer coincidence. In the exhibit, notice that none of the expected values is contained in the respective sets of payoffs. For example, if S_4 is pursued, the payoff will be 19 or 16 or 9 or −2, never 15.00.

If the expected value does not represent an actual event, what good is it? It is valuable as a yardstick for comparison with other alternatives. *Indeed, this is its only purpose.* Considering only one strategy, a positive expected value will tell us that executing the strategy is better than not executing it. When comparing two or more strategies, the one with the highest expected value is best. Thus in the preceding example, there was a clear decision in favor of strategy S_3 because it had the highest expected value. But suppose that the expected values of alternative strategies are the same, as illustrated in Exhibit 3–5—then what?

Exhibit 3–5_____

Expected Value of Three Projects

Alternative Strategies	States of Nature			Expected Value $E(S_i)$
	N_1 $(P = .25)$	N_2 $(P = .50)$	N_3 $(P = .25)$	
S_1	20	10	20	15
S_2	40	10	0	15
S_3	10	10	10	10

Exhibit 3–5 shows a decision matrix with a probability of .25 for N_1, .50 for N_2, and .25 for N_3. Included also are the payoffs for three different strategies or projects. Their expected values are calculated as follows:

$$E(S_1) = .25(20) + .50(10) + .25(20) = 15.0$$
$$E(S_2) = .25(40) + .50(10) + .25(0) = 15.0$$
$$E(S_3) = .25(10) + .50(10) + .25(10) = 10.0$$

Clearly either S_1 or S_2 is preferable to S_3. But in order to choose between S_1 and S_2, which have the same expected value, we must use some other yardstick. The yardstick is *degree of risk,* which is considered a secondary or auxiliary measure of expected value.

Measurement of Risk: Standard Deviation

Intuitively, we sense that the degree of risk is indicated by the degree to which the actual outcome or payoff of a strategy or project deviates from its expected (mean) value. This is indicated by the spread or *variation* in the probability distribution of possible outcomes for each proposal.

One way of measuring variation is to calculate the *range,* which is the difference between the most extreme payoff values. In our example (refer to Exhibit 3–5), the range of S_1 is 10 (from a low of 10 to a high of 20) while the range of S_2 is 40 (from a low of 0 to a high of 40). While the range may be a useful preliminary evaluation, it considers only the most extreme values and gives no weight to values in between. A more common and more accurate measurement of variation is the statistic called the *standard deviation,* σ (sigma). Calculation of the standard deviation may proceed in four steps, as follows:

Step 1. Calculate the expected value (arithmetic mean) of the distribution:

$$E(X) = \sum_{i=1}^{n} X_i P_i \tag{11}$$

where

X_i = The *i*th payoff or outcome
P_i = The probability of the *i*th payoff
$E(X)$ = The expected value, or weighted mean outcome, with probabilities as the weights

Step 2. Subtract the expected value from each outcome to obtain a set of deviations from the expected value, i.e.,

$$d_i = X_i - E(X) \tag{12}$$

Step 3. Square each deviation, then multiply the squared deviation by the probability of its related outcome. Then sum those products to obtain the *variance*, σ^2, of the probability distribution:

$$\sigma^2 = \sum_{i=1}^{n} [X_i - E(X)]^2 P_i \tag{13}$$

Step 4. Take the square root of the variance to obtain the *standard deviation*:

$$\sigma = \sqrt{\sum_{i=1}^{n} [X_i - E(X)]^2 P_i} \tag{14}$$

Equation (14) may also be written as

$$\sigma = \sqrt{\sum_{i} (X_i - \mu_X)^2 P_i} \tag{15}$$

since the arithmetic mean of the distribution, μ_X (read mu of X), is the expected value. The notation in Equation (15) is less cumbersome than that in Equation (14). Applied to Exhibit 3–5, the calculations are as shown in Exhibit 3–6:

Exhibit 3–6

Calculation of Standard Deviation

Strategy S_i	$(X_i - \mu)$	$(X_i - \mu)^2$	P_i	$(X_i - \mu)^2 P_i$	
S_1	5	25	.25	6.25	
	−5	25	.50	12.50	
	5	25	.25	6.25	
				$\sigma_1^2 = $ 25.00	$\sigma_1 = 5$
S_2	25	625	.25	156.25	
	−5	25	.50	12.50	
	−15	225	.25	56.25	
				$\sigma_2^2 = 225.00$	$\sigma_2 = 15$
S_3	0	0	.25	0.0	
	0	0	.50	0.0	
	0	0	.25	0.0	
				$\sigma_3^2 = $ 0.0	$\sigma_3 = 0$

Exhibit 3–7 illustrates the range of probabilities for any normal distribution. The figure is drawn to the *standard* or *Z-scale*, which has a mean of zero and a standard deviation of 1. For any normal distribution, the probability distribution curve is symmetrical about the mean. The area under the curve represents a total probability of 1, divided into two

Exhibit 3–7

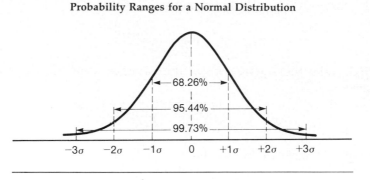

Probability Ranges for a Normal Distribution

equal parts. Thus the probability to the left of the mean is .5 and to the right is .5.

If we consult a table of normal distribution (such as Table E in the appendix at the end of this book), we find that a Z-value of 1.0 (meaning 1 standard deviation away from the mean) corresponds to an area of .3413. Hence, the area between $Z = 1.0$ and $Z = -1.0$ is .6826. In other words, there is a 68.26 percent probability that the actual outcome will lie within 1 standard deviation of the mean (in either direction). Using the same procedure, the area within 2 standard deviations of the mean is .9544, or 95.44 percent, and the area within ±3 standard deviations is 99.73 percent, as shown on the exhibit.

Returning to our earlier comparison of strategies S_1 and S_2, Exhibit 3–8 shows the probability distributions for each strategy, as well as the mean and standard deviation of each.

In Exhibit 3–8, the zone of 68 percent probability, i.e., $\mu \pm 1\sigma$, is shown as a shaded area. For the probability distribution of S_1, this is a narrow band between payoffs of 10 and 20. For the probability distribution of S_2, there is a much wider band ranging from 0 to 30.

Clearly, the absolute variation of possible payoffs is much greater for S_2 than for S_1. The greater variation indicates S_2 is riskier than S_1, since the two alternatives have the same expected value.

Coefficient of Variation

Suppose a firm has an opportunity to invest in two different projects. One has an expected value of $500,000 with a standard deviation of $5,000. The other has an expected value of $100,000 with a standard deviation of $2,000. Which is riskier? If we use standard deviation as a measure of risk, we would have to conclude that the larger project is

Exhibit 3–8

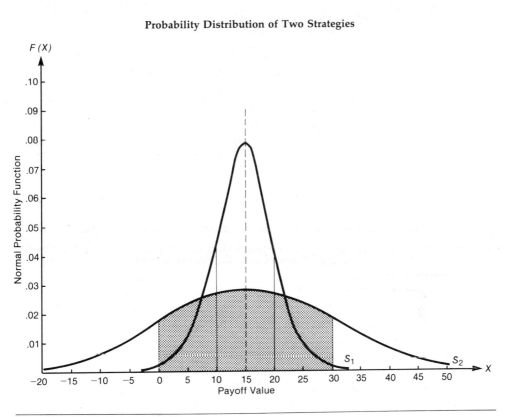

Probability Distribution of Two Strategies

riskier. But considering the standard deviation in relation to the size of project, the relative risk is smaller for the larger project. Clearly, in order to compare the riskiness of projects with widely differing magnitudes of investments, payoffs, and expected values, a *relative* rather than an absolute measurement is necessary. *Relative standard deviation* is such a measurement, more commonly (but less accurately) called the *coefficient of variation*.

The coefficient of variation is the ratio of the standard deviation to the expected value, or mean. When calculated as a percentage, it provides an index of the risk per dollar of return, and thus makes possible a comparison of strategies or projects of widely differing magnitude. The formula is

$$C = \frac{\sigma}{\mu} (100)$$

where

σ = the standard deviation,
μ = the expected, or mean, value.

In continuing the example outlined in Exhibit 3–6, the calculations for the coefficient of variation for each strategy are as follows:

$$\text{For } S_1: C_1 = (5/15)(100) = 33$$
$$\text{For } S_2: C_2 = (15/15)(100) = 100$$
$$\text{For } S_3: C_3 = (0/10)(100) = 0$$

In this case, using the coefficient of variation leads to the conclusion arrived at when the standard deviation was used to measure risk. But, this does not happen when expected values are different. For example, suppose we are contemplating two projects and there are three possible states of nature, namely, N_1, N_2, and N_3, with probabilities of .20, .70, and .10, respectively. Two projects, S_4 and S_5, offer the payoffs shown in Exhibit 3–9, which also shows the expected value, $E(S_i)$, standard deviation, σ, and coefficient of variation, C, for each project.

Exhibit 3–9 _____

Analysis of Risk for Two Projects

Project	N_1 $(P = .20)$	N_2 $(P = .70)$	N_3 $(P = .10)$	$E(S_i)$	σ_{S_i}	C_{S_i}
S_4	20	10	5	11.5	4.5	39
S_5	150	100	75	107.5	22.5	21

In Exhibit 3–9, we see that S_5 has a larger standard deviation than S_4, indicating greater absolute risk. But the relative risk per dollar return, as measured by the coefficient of variation, is much less for S_5 than for S_4. Since the expected value of S_5 is also greater than that for S_4, we can conclude S_5 is a more desirable project.

Risk-Return Trade-Offs

What a decision maker decides depends on his or her attitude toward risk as well as on other considerations. To illustrate, in Exhibit 3–10 are plotted the expected return and relative risk for S_1, S_2, and S_3, presented earlier in Exhibit 3–6.

The horizontal axis of Exhibit 3–10 represents absolute risk, which is measured by the standard deviation, σ, and the relative risk, which is measured by the coefficient of variation, C. The vertical axis represents

Exhibit 3–10

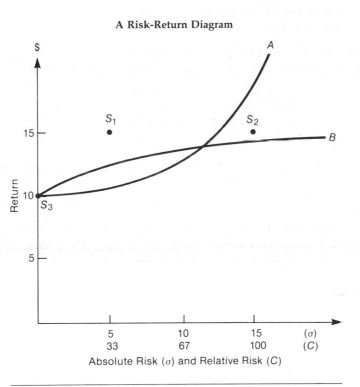

A Risk-Return Diagram

Absolute Risk (σ) and Relative Risk (C)

the expected mean payoff of a strategy or a project, in dollars. The intersections of return and risk for the three strategies of our example are plotted as the points S_1, S_2, S_3.

Curves A and B represent *risk-return functions* of Decision Maker A and Decision Maker B, respectively. (They are also called *market indifference curves*.) They are plots of required return as a function of risk. Curve A reflects risk aversion because as risk increases the required return increases at an increasing rate. Curve B reflects the attitude of a risk seeker. As risk increases, the required return also increases, but at a decreasing rate.

The desirability of an expected return is measured by its vertical distance and direction from the decision maker's risk-return tradeoff curve. Decision Maker A would not consider S_2 because it is below his curve. He would choose S_1 over S_3, even though S_3 is risk-free, because the expected return of S_1 is greater than the return he requires after due consideration of risk. Decision Maker B would consider all three strategies to be acceptable, but would also choose S_1 because it promises the greatest return in excess of requirements.

Development of Payoffs

Expected value depends on the payoffs associated with different states of nature, as well as on their probabilities. Thus the decision maker is faced with the problem of determining meaningful payoffs as well as their probabilities. The payoff may be a single value that is readily determined; more likely, however, the payoff is a stream of income to be realized in the future.

In financial literature, there are a number of ways by which decision makers adjust for risk in the process of developing payoffs. Two of these methods—the risk-adjusted discount rate and the certainty-equivalent approach—were discussed in Chapter 2. Each method views income to be realized at a later time as a fixed amount. Actually, as illustrated in Exhibit 3–11, the income to be realized at some future time is itself a mean or expected value of a probability distribution. Thus the decision maker must reduce the stream of income to a single number that is actually the mean of a set of means. Furthermore, the decision maker must recognize the *time value of money*, so the expressed payoff represents the value of a future stream of income *at the present time*, as explained in Chapter 2.

The method for dealing with this situation is called the *probability distribution approach*. A short discussion and illustration of the equations and techniques used is contained in Appendix 3B at the end of this chapter for the convenience of interested students. A full discussion, however, is beyond the scope of this text but can be found in finance texts.

Sequential Decision Analysis Using Decision Trees

A decision tree is a graphic device that shows a sequence of strategic decisions and the expected consequences under each possible set of circumstances. The construction and analysis of a decision tree is appropriate whenever a sequential series of conditional decisions must be made under conditions of risk. By conditional decision, we mean a decision that depends upon circumstances or options that will occur at a later time.

Construction of the decision tree begins with the earliest decision and proceeds forward in time through a series of subsequent events and decisions. At each decision or event the tree branches out to depict each possible course of action, until finally all logical consequences and the

Exhibit 3–11

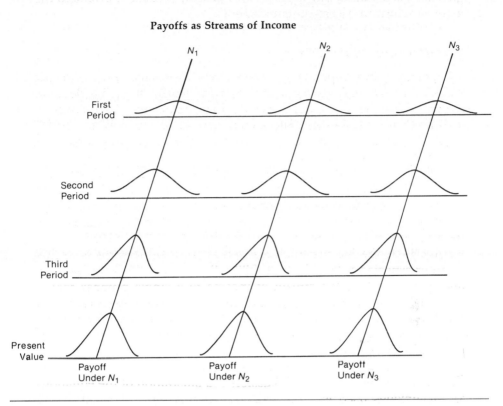

Payoffs as Streams of Income

resulting payoffs are depicted. Exhibit 3–12 is an example of a decision tree.

Exhibit 3–12 describes a problem faced by a firm that must decide whether to spend $35,000 to market a new product or to invest the money elsewhere for a 10 percent return. Taking the sequence of events from left to right, the first decision (symbolized by a square) is whether or not to market the product. If not, the payoff will be $3,500 from the alternative investment. If the firm markets the product, the next event (a noncontrollable situation, symbolized by a large circle) may be the entry of a competitor into the market. The probability of competition (.8) and the probability of no competition (.2) are entered in parentheses beside the appropriate branches.

It is important to note that in the construction of a decision tree, the branches out of squares represent strategies. Since the decision maker has full control over which strategy is chosen, these branches do not

Exhibit 3–12

A Decision Tree Depicting the Consequences of Marketing a New Product

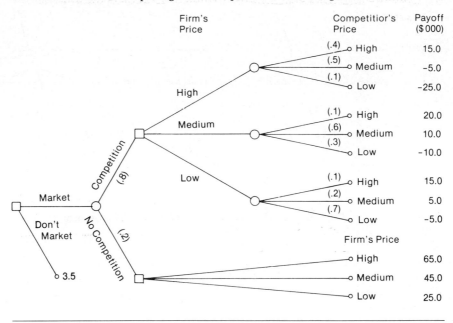

	Firm's Price		Competitior's Price	Payoff ($ 000)
		(.4)	High	15.0
	High	(.5)	Medium	-5.0
		(.1)	Low	-25.0
	Medium	(.1)	High	20.0
		(.6)	Medium	10.0
		(.3)	Low	-10.0
	Low	(.1)	High	15.0
		(.2)	Medium	5.0
		(.7)	Low	-5.0

	Firm's Price	
	High	65.0
	Medium	45.0
	Low	25.0

Market — Competition (.8)

Don't Market — 3.5

No Competition (.2)

have probabilities. Branches out of circles represent states of nature over which the decision maker has no control. Therefore, these branches have probabilities and the probabilities for all branches coming from any one circle must add up to 1. In this example, the probabilities of competition (.8) and no competition (.2) add up to 1, since one or the other must happen.

If there is no competition, the only remaining decision is whether to charge a high, medium, or low price. The three branches are drawn and labeled, and the payoff for each is noted. If there is competition, the same three branches are appropriate. However, each branch divides again into the competitor's options to price high, medium, or low. Each of these final branches is marked with a probability, and the payoff is noted at the end of each one. Once again, the probabilities add up to 1 for each circle, since the competitor is certain to charge either a high, medium, or low price. The decision tree thus depicts in graphic form the expectation that the price a competitor charges depends upon the price the firm sets and consequent profits depend upon what price the competitor charges.

Since each decision depends upon the evaluation of events that take place at a later time, the analysis of a decision tree begins at the end of the sequence and works backwards. Exhibit 3–13 depicts the analysis for our example.

Exhibit 3–13

Analysis of a Decision Tree

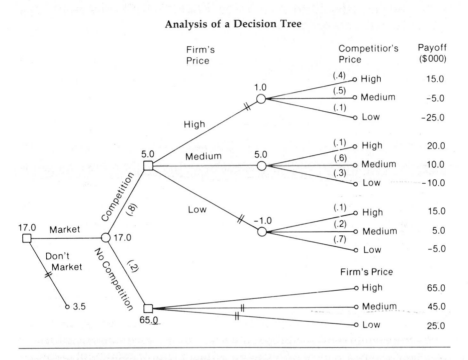

Beginning in the upper right of Exhibit 3–13, the analyst calculates the expected value if the firm's price is high and there is competition. The expected value is $(15 \times .4) + (-5 \times .5) + (-25 \times .1) = 1$. This expected value is noted in or above the event circle. The expected values of medium and low prices are computed and noted in a similar manner. Since the medium price gives the highest expected value, that value is noted in the decision box, and the other two branches are slashed to indicate they are nonoptimal. In the alternative state of no competition, the only question is whether to charge a high, medium, or low price. The payoffs indicate that a high price is optimal, and the other two branches are marked out.

At the first event point (introduction of a competitive product) the expected value is $(5 \times .8) + (65 \times .2) = 17.0$. The firm is now ready to make a decision. If it does not market, it gets $3,500. If it does market its product, there is an expected return of $17,000. Clearly, then, the firm should enter the market.

The diagram also gives a clear indication of the most profitable pricing strategy. The product should be initially marketed at a high price. If competition develops—and there is an 80 percent probability that it will—the price should then be lowered to a medium price in order to maximize the expected return.

Decision Making under Uncertainty

In Chapter 2, uncertainty was defined as the state in which one or more alternatives result in a set of possible specific outcomes whose probabilities are either unknown or meaningless. This means that decision making under uncertainty is always subjective. However, if the decision maker can identify the possible states of nature and estimate the resulting payoffs for each available strategy, then two basic approaches are available:

1. The decision maker may use the best available information and his or her own personal judgment and experience to assign subjective probabilities to the possible states of nature. (Subjective probabilities were discussed in Chapter 2). This effectively converts the condition of uncertainty to a condition of risk for which expected value is the criterion of choice.
2. The decision maker may either disregard probabilities or treat them as equal, which amounts to the same thing. When this approach is taken, four decision criteria are available for evaluation of proposed strategies:
    a. The *Wald* decision criterion, also called *maximin*.
    b. The *Hurwicz alpha* decision criterion.
    c. The *Savage* decision criterion, also called *minimax regret*.
    d. The *Laplace* decision criterion, also called the *Bayes* decision criterion.

The first three are modern developments suggested by their originators during the period 1950–54. The Laplace criterion has been used for more than 2,500 years and was formally articulated by Laplace (a mathematician) early in the 19th century.

Perhaps the most difficult task for the decision maker is choosing the one criterion most appropriate to the problem at hand. The choice of a criterion should be both logical under the circumstances and also consistent with management's philosophy and temperament. Is the current management outlook optimistic or pessimistic? Conservative or adventurous?

The Wald Decision Criterion

The Wald, or *maximin*, decision criterion is described by various authors as the criterion of pessimism, the criterion of extreme conservatism, and an attempt to maximize the security level. It envisions nature as perverse and malevolent with Murphy's law fully operational.[1] Therefore the criterion says: determine the worst possible outcome of each strategy and then pick the strategy yielding the best of the worst results.

The maximin criterion can be illustrated by applying it to the example first shown in Exhibit 3–1. Now, however, assume that the probabilities of the various states of nature are unknown. As shown in Exhibit 3–14,

Exhibit 3–14

Application of Maximin and Maximax Criteria

Strategy	States of Nature				Criterion	
	N_1	N_2	N_3	N_4	Maximin	Maximax
S_1	6	6	6	4	4*	6
S_2	25	7	7	−15	−15	25*
S_3	20	20	7	−1	−1	20
S_4	19	16	9	−2	−2	19
S_5	20	15	15	−3	−3	20

* Best strategy under stated criterion.

the most dismal payoff from each row is chosen as the minimal security level associated with the strategy. The largest of these, a value of 4, implies that strategy S_1 is the best strategy under this criterion.

Is this a good choice? It all depends upon what you mean by "good." Note that if state of nature N_4 should occur, S_1 is the only strategy that avoids a loss. On the other hand, should any other state of nature occur, strategy S_1 repeatedly results in the poorest return. Is such a situation inconsistent with reality? Perhaps, but perhaps not. S_1 simply represents the conservative banker's strategy—it involves the smallest risks but at the same time promises the smallest returns. It is up to the firm to decide just how a minimal level of return is to be weighted in the deci-

---

[1] Murphy's law is the wry jest that if anything can go wrong, it will.

sion-making process and how much it can afford to risk if things turn for the worse. Because the criterion is fiscally conservative, it is particularly well suited to small business firms whose survival depends upon avoiding losses.

Added to Exhibit 3–14 is the antithesis of maximin, called the maximax criterion. Here the decision maker is completely optimistic and therefore chooses the maximum payoff for each strategy as his yardstick. The strategy that offers the best of the best is then chosen as optimal. This, of course, is nonsense. We have included it because maximax and maximin represent the extremes of alpha in the Hurwicz alpha decision criterion, which will be discussed next.

The Hurwicz Alpha Decision Criterion

The Hurwicz alpha decision criterion proposes to create a decision index *(d)* for each strategy, which is a weighted average of its extreme payoffs. The weighting factors are a *coefficient of optimism* (α), which is applied to the maximum payoff *(M)*, and its complement $(1 - \alpha)$, which is applied to the minimum payoff *(m)*. The value of each strategy is thus:

$$d_i = \alpha M_i + (1 - \alpha)m_i \qquad (16)$$

The strategy with the highest value for d_i is chosen as optimal.

The coefficient of optimism ranges from 0 to 1, enabling the decision maker to express his attitude toward risk-taking as a subjective degree of optimism. If the decision maker is completely pessimistic, he may decide that $\alpha = 0$. The result is the Wald or maximin criterion. If the decision maker is an incurable optimist, he may decide that $\alpha = 1$. The result would be the maximax criterion.

Actually, the Hurwicz alpha criterion was advanced to enable the decision maker to look at both the worst and the best payoffs for a particular strategy and to assign a subjective probability to each. Suppose, for example, that the decision-maker is on the optimistic side and decides that $\alpha = 0.7$. His analysis of the current decision problem would be as shown in Exhibit 3–15. It can be seen that the highest weighted average payoff results from selecting strategy S_3.

The decision indicated by the Hurwicz alpha criterion depends on the value of α, which in turn depends on the decision maker's own attitude toward risk.[2] It is suitable for use by business firms; but if the decision

---

[2] The decision will tend toward maximax as alpha increases and toward maximin as alpha decreases. You should verify this by finding the value of alpha at which the decision is changed in our example. *Hint:* One shift point occurs when $d_1 = d_3$. Perhaps another advantage of alpha is that it forces the decision maker to be consistent from one decision to another. If the decision maker believes one alpha value is appropriate for one decision while another value is used in a second decision, perhaps he knows more about the decision than was initially believed. If so, this information should be brought into the decision making.

Exhibit 3–15

Hurwicz Alpha Solution to Decision Problem

	M	α	αM	m	$1 - \alpha$	$(1 - \alpha)m$	d
S_1	6	0.7	4.2	4	0.3	1.2	5.4
S_2	25	0.7	17.5	−15	0.3	−4.5	13.0
S_3	20	0.7	14.0	−1	0.3	−0.3	13.7*
S_4	19	0.7	13.3	−2	0.3	−0.6	12.7
S_5	20	0.7	14.0	−3	0.3	−0.9	13.1

* Best strategy under stated criterion.

maker's degree of optimism proves unfounded, substantial losses are likely. Therefore, due caution is advised.

The Savage Decision Criterion

The Savage criterion, sometimes called the *minimax regret criterion*, examines "regrets," which are the opportunity costs of incorrect decisions. Regret is measured as the absolute difference between the payoff for a given strategy and the payoff for the most effective strategy within the same state of nature.

The rationale for measurement of regret is quite simple. If any particular state of nature occurs in the future, and if we have chosen the strategy that yields the maximum payoff for that state of nature, then we have no regret. But if we choose any other strategy, regret is the difference between what actually occurs and what we could have earned had we made the optimal decision. After determining the maximum regret for each strategy, the strategy with the smallest maximum regret is chosen.

A regret matrix is needed, and it is constructed by modifying the payoff matrix. Within each column (state of nature) the largest payoff is subtracted from each payoff number in the column. The absolute difference between them is the measurement of regret. From our example in Exhibit 3–1, we construct the regret matrix seen in Exhibit 3–16. This exhibit shows that when the state of nature turns out to be N_1 and the decision maker has chosen S_2, there is no regret, because the right strategy was chosen. However, if S_1 had been chosen, the regret is measured as $|6 - 25| = 19$; if S_3, regret would be $|20 - 25| = 5$; and so forth. After completing the regret matrix, the correct strategy is seen to be S_4 because it minimizes the maximum penalty for an incorrect guess about the state of nature.

Note that the decision maker who uses the Savage criterion explicitly abandons attempts to maximize payoff in favor of a strategy to achieve a

Exhibit 3–16

Construction of a Regret Matrix

| | Payoff Matrix | | | | Regret Matrix | | | | Maximum |
Strategy	N_1	N_2	N_3	N_4	N_1	N_2	N_3	N_4	Regret
S_1	6	6	6	4	19	14	9	0	19
S_2	25	7	7	−15	0	13	8	19	19
S_3	20	20	7	−1	5	0	8	5	8
S_4	19	16	9	−2	6	4	6	6	6*
S_5	20	15	15	−3	5	5	0	7	7

* Best strategy under stated criterion.

satisfactory payoff with less risk. The Savage criterion is therefore particularly useful for evaluating a series of projects over a long span of time.

The Laplace Decision Criterion

There is a Bayesian postulate that if the probabilities of occurrences
are unknown, they should be assumed equal. The Laplace criterion uses
this postulate to calculate the expected value of each strategy; hence the
Laplace criterion is also called the "Bayes criterion." The strategy selected is the one with the greatest expected value that results from the
assumed (subjective) probabilities.

For strategies S_1, S_2, S_3, S_4, and S_5 from our example, the expected
values are 22/4, 24/4, 46/4, 42/4, and 47/4, respectively, and strategy S_5
would be selected. The effect of assuming an equal probability for each
of the states of nature is to transform the decision problem under uncertainty into one under risk, so the previous discussion of the decision
criterion under risk applies.

The Laplace criterion is a criterion of rationality, completely insensi-
tive to the decision maker's attitude. It is extremely sensitive, however,
to the decision maker's definition of the states of nature. For example,
suppose the states of nature are hot, warm, and cool weather. In the
absence of any weather forecast, the Bayesian probability of cool
weather would be one third. But suppose the states of nature are warm
and cool. Now the probability of cool weather has changed to one half.
In reality, of course, equiprobability of all states of nature is unlikely,
particularly in the short run. Thus the Laplace criterion is more suitable
to long-run forecasts by larger firms.

To conclude, the process of decision making under uncertainty is
essentially one of choosing a criterion and then performing the calcula-

tions necessary to establish a choice within that criterion. We have also seen that the four decision criteria discussed, when applied to the same decision matrix, can lead to four different strategy selections.

Which criterion is "best"? There is no universally correct answer. Each of the criteria is logically defensible under particular circumstances, and each can be criticized on one ground or another. The choice will often depend on personal considerations. In view of this, of what use is the notion of a payoff matrix? Perhaps the best answer is that it provides a useful tool for conceptualizing and formalizing the decision process into (1) a statement of objectives, (2) a selection of payoffs, (3) an evaluation of alternative payoffs, and (4) a selection of alternative strategies. At this point it should be noted that there are other, nonquantitative methods of dealing with uncertainty. Before discussing these other methods, however, let us first examine a case that illustrates some of the decision-making methods and principles that have been discussed in this chapter and Chapter 2.

Illustrative Case.   Tropical Products, Inc., with headquarters in Hawaii, is one of the world's largest producers of canned and fresh pineapple. In recent years, the company has also moved into the production of macadamia nuts, which are native to Australia but do well in Hawaii. Up to now, Tropical Products has sold its macadamia nuts in the local market. The product, because of its high quality, has been popular among tourists. This has led the company to believe that a national, and perhaps international, market exists for its product. Having enlarged its plantations to support its envisioned market expansion, additional production will soon be available for national marketing.

The firm's marketing division has proposed two alternative strategies for its national promotion of macadamia nuts, each of which will cost $3 million:

1. Strategy 1 (S_1): National television promotion consisting of sixteen 15-second prime-time spots on a nationwide network over a period of four weeks.
2. Strategy 2 (S_2): Distribution of samples to Hawaii-bound passengers on all flights of United, American, and Pan-American airlines for one year.

The marketing division proposes to price the product to yield a gross profit of 30 percent on the sales dollar, out of which the promotional expenses will be paid. At that price, marketing has estimated revenues for each strategy under highly successful, moderately successful, and unsuccessful sales campaigns, using subjective probabilities, as shown in Exhibit 3–17.

Exhibit 3–17

Estimated Sales ($ millions)

Strategy	Highly Successful (P = .30)	Moderately Successful (P = .40)	Not Successful (P = .30)
S_1	80	45	15
S_2	45	35	30

The company's financial vice president believes that the firm's utility function with respect to profit is as shown on Exhibit 3–18.

Exhibit 3–18

Assumed Utility Function

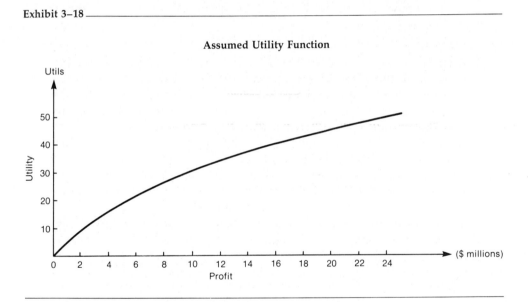

The financial vice president also notes that:

1. The current yield on government bonds is 10 percent.
2. The company's cost of capital is 15 percent.
3. The riskiness of S_1 and S_2 is such that risk premiums of 20 percent for S_1 and 8 percent for S_2 are required.

All of the foregoing information is turned over to a financial analyst, who is instructed to prepare a briefing, complete with charts, from which top management may be able to choose between the two proposed strategies, S_1 and S_2. The analyst proceeds as follows:

1. Convert the matrix of expected sales into a matrix of expected net profits after deducting the cost of promotion, as shown in Exhibit 3–19.

Exhibit 3–19———————————————————————————————————————

Estimated Gross Profits ($ millions)

	N_1	N_2	N_3
S_1	$21.0	$10.5	$1.5
S_2	10.5	7.5	6.0

2. For each strategy, calculate the expected value of gross profits discounted by the firm's cost of capital (15 percent), the standard deviation of the profit distribution, and the coefficient of variation, as shown in Exhibit 3–20.

Exhibit 3–20———————————————————————————————————————

Estimated Gross Profits ($ millions) Discounted by Firm's Cost of Capital

Strategy	N_1 $(P = .3)$	N_2 $(P = .4)$	N_3 $(P = .3)$	$E(S_i)$	σ_{S_i}	C_{S_i}
S_1	18.261	9.130	1.304	9.522	6.575	69.1
S_2	9.130	6.522	5.217	6.913	1.549	22.4

3. For each strategy, calculate the expected value, standard deviation, and coefficient of variation for gross profits discounted by the risk-adjusted discount rate. First, note that S_1 requires a risk premium of 20 percent in addition to the cost of capital (15 percent), for a total required return of 35 percent. For S_2, the risk premium is 8 percent in addition to the cost of capital, for a total required return of 23 percent. The risk-adjusted payoffs are as shown in Exhibit 3–21.

Exhibit 3–21———————————————————————————————————————

Estimated Gross Profits ($ millions) Discounted by Risk-Adjusted Discount Rates

Strategy	N_1 $(P = .3)$	N_2 $(P = .4)$	N_3 $(P = .3)$	$E(S_i)$	σ_{S_i}	C_{S_i}
S_1	15.556	7.778	1.111	8.111	5.601	69.1
S_2	8.537	6.098	4.878	6.464	1.448	22.4

4. For each strategy, calculate the payoffs, expected value, standard deviation, and coefficient of variation using the certainty-equivalent approach.

To calculate the certainty-equivalent coefficient, α, for each strategy, note that the current yield on government bonds is 10 percent, which may be taken as the risk-free interest rate, i. For a present value of $1, $1.10 would be needed at the end of the year. For S_1, the required return is 35 percent, as noted above. Therefore, a present value of $1 would require $1.35 at the end of the year. The certainty-equivalent coefficient therefore is

$$\alpha_{S_1} = \frac{\text{Certain cash flow}}{\text{Risky cash flow}} = \frac{1.10}{1.35} = .815$$

For S_2, the required return is 23 percent, hence a present value of $1 would require $1.23 at the end of the year. The certainty-equivalent coefficient is

$$\alpha_{S_2} = \frac{1.10}{1.23} = .894$$

Each payoff in Exhibit 3–22 below is calculated as $\alpha_{S_i}A$, where A is the amount shown in Exhibit 3–19 and α_{S_i} is the appropriate certainty-equivalent coefficient.

Exhibit 3–22 _____

Estimated Gross Profits ($ millions) Calculated by the Certainty-Equivalent Approach

Strategy	N_1 $(P = .3)$	N_2 $(P = .4)$	N_3 $(P = .3)$	$E(S_i)$	σ_{S_i}	C_{S_i}
S_1	17.115	8.558	1.223	8.925	6.162	69.1
S_2	9.387	6.705	5.364	7.107	1.592	22.4

5. After examining Exhibits 3–20 through 3–22, it seems clear that S_1 promises a greater return even after adjustment for risk, but it remains about three times as risky as S_2. One task remains, and that is to evaluate the payoffs in terms of utility rather than dollars. Although it is very difficult to make a precise measurement (from Exhibit 3–18), the approximate utility values are shown in Exhibit 3–23, which shows that S_1 and S_2 are very close in terms of expected utility of profits. However, S_1 is four times as risky, with a range of utility values of $41.0 - 1.0 = 40$. While S_2 promises a slightly smaller return, it is much less risky with a range of values of $29.0 - 19.0 = 10.0$.

Exhibit 3–23

Utility Values of Estimated Gross Profits Calculated by the Certainty-Equivalent Approach

Strategy	N_1 $(P = .3)$	N_2 $(P = .4)$	N_3 $(P = .3)$	$E(S_i)$	σ_{S_i}	C_{S_i}
S_1	41.0	28.5	1.0	24.0	15.92	66.3
S_2	29.0	23.5	19.0	23.8	3.881	16.3

Other Methods of Dealing with Uncertainty

It was noted in Chapter 2 that it is rarely possible to insure against uncertainty or to incorporate uncertainty into a firm's cost structures and forecasts. There are, however, a number of approaches that knowledgeable business executives commonly use to reduce the perils of uncertainty. Among these are: referral to authority for guidance, attempts to control the environment, hedging, introduction of flexibility into investments, diversification of the firm's interests, modification of goals, and acquisition of additional information.

Referral to Authority for Guidance.   Perhaps the most pragmatic approach to the reduction of uncertainty, and unquestionably a very common one, is to let an authority make the decision. In some cases, there is a literal authority, such as the Civil Aeronautics Board, the Securities and Exchange Commission, or the Labor Relations Board, which dictates the choice of behavior whether the business executive wants it or not. But there are also figurative authorities, such as tradition, rule of thumb, convention, peer group pressure, professional ethics, or simply what others are doing.

The trouble with this approach is that the decision maker shifts the decision to others who may have even less knowledge of the firm's situation. For example, a fixed markup percentage ignores the rate of turnover, so for fast-moving items the price is too high to meet the competition, while on some slow-moving items the price may be too low. Referral to authority may yield satisfactory temporary solutions to short-run problems, but in the long run this approach cannot cope with a constantly changing environment.

Control of the Environment.   A more sophisticated approach to the reduction of uncertainty is the attempt to gain some control over the business environment. This approach usually takes the form of attempts to gain a monopoly by means of patents, copyrights, exclusive dealerships, or just by being the first to "fill a hole" in the market. As with referral to authority, this approach only works, if at all, in the short run. Government casts a jaundiced eye on any reduction of competition, to say nothing of outright monopoly. In addition, if the market is profitable, competitors may be quick to enter despite patents or copyrights.

Hedging.   Hedging is one of the most widespread methods by which business executives can replace future uncertainty with the security of a present contract. Hedging takes many forms, but it emerges most commonly in the writing of contracts for goods and services and in the trading of futures at commodity exchanges. Contracts for the supply of goods and services, especially in the construction industry, usually contain protective clauses for both the buyer and the contractor. The buyer is protected by clauses that spell out penalties against the contractor for late delivery or nondelivery. The contractor is protected by escape clauses that excuse late delivery or nondelivery caused by conditions beyond his control, such as labor disputes, natural disaster, or civil disorder.

In the commodity exchange, futures market trading is predicated on a series of spot (current) prices and a series of future (forward) prices for various commodities. These markets perform two vital functions besides facilitating actual exchanges of commodities: (1) they provide an opportunity for both buyers and sellers to guarantee the future market price of the goods they are exchanging, and (2) they provide an opportunity for speculators to enter the market.

The speculator may either buy or sell futures. When buying, he bets the spot price will be higher upon delivery so he can immediately sell at a profit. If he sells, the speculator hopes the spot price will be lower at the time of delivery so he can buy and deliver at a profit. If the speculator guesses wrong, he loses. But win or lose, speculators provide the financial liquidity necessary for suppliers and users of commodities to complete their transactions.

Flexible Investments.   The wise manager knows change is inevitable and thus doesn't get locked into investments in specialized capital assets unless it is clear that the requirement for such specialized assets will exist over the life of the investment. For example, a general-purpose machine costs more than a specialized machine, but the general-purpose machine permits rapid changeover from one line of goods to another. Flexibility is particularly important for long-term investments such as land and buildings. While it may cost more to erect a general-purpose building than one tailored to the firm's current business, this flexibility will pay off if conditions change and the building must be sold or leased to another business.

Diversification of the Firm's Interests. Diversification is closely related to flexibility. This approach is summed up by the old adage, "Don't put all your eggs in one basket." Diversification stresses stability and a long-run point of view. In the short run, maximum profit would result from concentration on the most profitable product. However, such a policy might well lead to a firm's demise if the market for that one product diminishes or disappears. Diversification of the product line may dampen fluctuations in the firm's profit function by stabilizing production and earnings. It helps insure survival of the firm, and may even maximize profits in the long run. The manufacturer who produces a varied line of products, the investor who buys a diversified portfolio or stock in a mutual fund, and the conglomerate corporation all are examples of investors who diversify to reduce uncertainty.

Modification of Goals. In the face of complete uncertainty, an optimal decision might be impossible. However, if the decision maker is willing to settle for something less than the maximum, the problem is reduced to more manageable proportions. For example, break-even analysis can be used to establish a sales goal that will provide a satisfactory return on investment. Although some uncertainty remains as to whether or not the goal can be met, the higher degree of uncertainty (with reference to maximization) becomes less relevant to the decision. Thus, pricing objectives are commonly established to achieve a target return on investment, to stabilize prices and outputs, to realize a target market share, or to meet competition.

Acquisition of Additional Information.   Reliable, relevant information is the key to successful decision making. Obviously, the more information gathered about the future, the less uncertain it will be. This is only true up to a point, however, after which the law of diminishing returns takes over. The collection of information is a costly business, and the benefits to be derived from additional information must be weighed against the additional cost of obtaining it. Moreover, time is of the essence in most decisions. Hasty decisions made before sufficient information is gathered can be very costly. On the other hand, a decision delayed too long in the pursuit of information may put the firm in the position of "too little, too late." Both the timing of the decision and the amount of information to be gathered are important concerns for the decision maker.

Summary

This chapter has dealt with methods and approaches to decision making that decision makers may use under conditions of certainty, risk, and uncertainty. Under conditions of certainty, the decision maker's task is to select the strategy that maximizes the payoff. Two powerful methods are available for this task: (1) marginal analysis, which utilizes the optimizing techniques of differential calculus; and (2) linear programming, which is a form of mathematical modeling that seeks to maximize or minimize (whichever is desirable) a unique objective function, subject to linear constraints.

Under the condition of risk, the decision criterion for selecting the optimum strategy is expected value. Expected value is defined as the weighted mean or average outcome, using probabilities for weights. The degree of risk is indicated by the spread or variation of the probability distribution for each strategy or proposal. An accurate measurement of risk is provided by the *standard deviation;* however, the standard deviation cannot be used to compare risk when expected values are different. Such comparisons require the *relative standard deviation,* commonly called the *coefficient of variation,* which is simply the ratio of the standard deviation to the mean, expressed as a percentage. When a sequential series of conditional decisions are to be made under risk, a *decision tree* enables the decision maker to visualize and evaluate all possible options for action.

What a decision maker under risk actually decides depends largely upon his or her attitude toward risk. This may be expressed by a *risk-return function* or *market indifference curve.* The net present value of the payoff must lie on or above the decision maker's market indifference curve for it to be acceptable. It may be that a payoff is a single value that is readily determined. It is more likely, however, that the payoff represents the net present value of a stream of income to be realized in the future.

Under conditions of uncertainty, the decision maker is faced with a state in which one or more alternatives result in a set of outcomes whose probabilities are unknown or meaningless. Four criteria for decision making under uncertainty were discussed:

1. The *Wald* or *maximin* criterion, by which the strategy that yields the best of the worst results is chosen.
2. The *Hurwicz alpha* criterion, which allows the decision maker to inject optimism or pessimism into the decision process.
3. The *Savage* or *minimax regret* criterion, which seeks to minimize the opportunity cost of incorrect decisions.
4. The *Laplace* or *Bayes* criterion, which gives equal probability to each state of nature.

There are also methods for dealing with uncertainty in a nonquantitative way. These include referral to authority for guidance, attempts to control the environment, hedging, flexible investments, diversification, modification of goals, and the acquisition of additional information.

Whatever method of dealing with uncertainty the decision maker may choose, he or she should strive for as much objectivity as possible. Poor decisions result when decision makers allow their emotions and personal prejudices to overrule good judgment and common sense. Good decision makers temper subjectivity with education, knowledge, experience, and stable temperaments.

Problems

1. In researching a new product, a marketing consultant has come up with four alternative brand names, five package designs, and three advertising campaigns.

a. How many strategies must management consider?

b. What states of nature might affect management's choice? Give examples.

c. How can management take into account the reaction of competitors?

2. The Fleetwood Sporting Goods Company manufactures three types of racquetball racquets. Previous sales data indicate the Economy model priced at $10 accounts for 50 percent of total sales, the Junior Champion model at $15 accounts for 20 percent, and the Elite model at $25 accounts for the remaining 30 percent. The company's profit margin is 20 percent on the Economy, 25 percent on the Junior Champion, and 30 percent on the Elite. Fleetwood's manufacturing capacity is 80,000 racquets a year. What is its profit at peak capacity if all production is sold?

3. Refer to Problem 2. Management at Fleetwood estimates that it would cost $30,000 to double the capacity for manufacturing the Elite line and would require an advertising campaign costing $35,000 to sell the increased production. Given these conditions, should production capacity for the Elite line be increased?

4. You are traffic manager of a firm that makes computer-controlled robots for manufacturing operations. Late one afternoon, the director of customer services informs you that the failure of a certain component has caused a good customer to shut down his assembly line. An emergency shipment of a replacement is required, and the customer has offered a bonus of $15,000 if the shipment reaches his plant by 6 A.M. tomorrow. After considering ground transportation times at both ends of the route, you conclude that there is no chance of making the 6 A.M. delivery using scheduled flights. A local air freight line has two types of small cargo planes available for charter: jet and turboprop. The cost of chartering the jet is $10,000, while chartering the turboprop aircraft will cost $7,000. Because of the difference in flying time, you estimate the probability of making the delivery on time is .8 for the jet, and .3 for the turboprop.

a. Construct a decision tree that includes all pertinent data relative to the decision to be made.

b. What is the expected return for shipment by jet? By turboprop?

c. Which alternative would you choose? Why?

5. A firm has the opportunity to invest $6,000 in one of two projects. For Project A, the probability of a return with a net present value of $3,000 is .20, of $5,000 is .10, and of $7,000 is .70. For Project B, the probability of a return with net present value of $4,000 is .35, of $6,500 is .40, and of $8,000 is .25.

a. What are the expected present values for each investment?

b. Find the standard deviation for each investment. Which investment should be chosen?

c. Which investment should be chosen if the firm's marginal utility of income function is $U = 15 + 3X$, where X is in thousands of dollars of present value? Why?

6. The coefficient of variation and the standard deviation are methods of measuring risk. Under what conditions is each appropriate?

7. Suppose a firm has an opportunity to invest in two different projects. Using the matrix below, find the expected values of both investments, and their standard deviations. By using the coefficient of variation, indicate which investment is riskier, and explain why.

		Probabilities	
Project	1/3	1/3	1/3
#1	80	60	20
#2	75	65	30

8. Given the accompanying payoff matrix, which alternative would be selected by applying the five criteria we have discussed (Laplace/Bayes, Hurwicz, Savage, Wald, and maximax)? Assume that the coefficient of optimism is 3/5.

	States of Nature			
Strategy	N_1	N_2	N_3	N_4
A	11	15	9	6
B	13	4	14	7
C	10	10	10	10
D	9	11	15	13
E	8	3	7	5

9. A stock market advisory service offers three investment portfolios for its clients. Portfolio A contains speculative stocks, which aim for

capital gains through price appreciation; portfolio B's stocks emphasize stable dividend yields over the long run; portfolio C contains stocks with a moderate potential for growth as well as stable dividend yields.

You are considering investing in one of these portfolios for a period of one year, but you know that the return on your investment will depend on whether the economy (i.e., state of nature) during that period is in inflation, recession, or depression. Accordingly, you estimate your potential gains and losses after all taxes in the accompanying payoff table, with your subjective probability estimate P for each state of nature as shown.

	States of Nature		
Portfolio	Inflation $P = .7$	Recession $P = .2$	Depression $P = .1$
A	100	50	−60
B	50	45	40
C	70	50	−10

a. If your sole objective is to maximize the return on your investment, which portfolio should you choose?
b. If you could not tolerate a loss, which portfolio should you select?
c. Suppose that you had no knowledge of the various states of nature and hence were unable to assign any probabilities to them. What would be your maximin strategy? Explain.

10. The Grand Slalom Ski Company is contemplating three new lines of downhill racing skis. The cost schedule for the three designs is shown below:

Skis	Fixed Costs	Variable Cost per Pair
A	$50,000	$75
B	75,000	60
C	90,000	30

Three probable levels of sales are estimated to be 2,000 pairs, 4,000 pairs, and 6,000 pairs, with probabilities of .30, .45, and .25, respectively. The selling price will be $400 per pair.
a. Construct an appropriate payoff matrix. Which design should be chosen?
Now suppose that the firm has no knowledge of probabilities of the three sales levels.
b. Which line would be chosen under the Bayes criterion?
c. Construct a regret matrix and determine which line would be chosen under the Savage criterion.

11. A prospector has contacted a diamond merchant in New York with evidence of a diamond deposit in a remote area in Canada. He offers the merchant, who has very large financial resources, half interest in his claim in exchange for $500,000 to develop it. If diamonds are found in commercial grades and quantities, the claim will be worth at least $2 million; otherwise, it will be worthless. Should the diamond merchant accept the prospector's proposition?

12. A firm has produced a new product that has been unusually successful, and in order to meet the unexpectedly high demand it will be necessary to add additional production facilities. The troubling question is whether the high demand will continue, increase, or decrease. An eight-year marketing study has yielded the results in the following table.

Demand, First Three Years	Demand Last Five Years	Probability
High	High	.4
High	Low	.2
Low	High	.3
Low	Low	.1

Three plans are under consideration. Plan A provides a permanent increase in capacity at a cost of $100,000 and will yield a cash inflow of $40,000 per year if demand is high, $5,000 per year if demand is low.

Plan B is a stopgap measure that can be converted to a permanent capacity by a supplementary investment B' after three years when the demand pattern is better known. If demand is high, plan B will yield $30,000 per year for the first three years, and $20,000 per year thereafter without the supplement B'. With B' and high demand, the last five years will yield $40,000 per year. If demand is low, plan B will yield $20,000 per year for the first three years, and $10,000 per year thereafter without the supplement. With the supplement and low demand, Plan B will yield $20,000 per year during the last five years. Plan B will cost $70,000 initially, and the supplement, if added, will cost $45,000.

Use a decision tree to determine which plan or combination of plans appears most attractive. (Ignore time values of money.)

13. A small foundry is having trouble with its old arc furnace, which has been completely depreciated for accounting purposes but can be sold for $6,000. The immediate decision is whether to modify the old machine or to buy a current model, which has many desirable features that cannot be included in modification of the old machine. The decision is complicated by the general opinion in the industry that a break-through in furnace technology is coming within three years.

The best estimates the owners can get are that there is a 40 percent chance of a radically improved furnace in about three years. If the new furnace actually appears, the probability that it will make all current models noncompetitive is .9 and that it will amount to no more than a minor improvement is .1.

The cost of modifying the old furnace is $8,000, and the cost of a current model is $25,000. In either case, the furnace will be used for eight years and then sold. The accompanying table gives the expected annual savings and the salvage value under three conditions (states of nature):

N_1: No technological breakthrough
N_2: New furnace developed that makes all current furnaces obsolete
N_3: New furnace developed that provides only minor savings

	Buy New Furnace		Modify Old Furnace	
State	Annual Savings	Salvage Value	Annual Savings	Salvage Value
N_1	$6,000	$8,000	$2,000	$4,000
N_2	2,000	2,000	1,000	2,000
N_3	3,000	4,000	1,000	3,000

The table is based on a study period and life of eight years for both furnaces. The sharp decrease in savings and salvage value in states N_2 and N_3 occurs because the development of a radically different or even an improved furnace would probably cut into the foundry's demand and its general competitive position.

Another alternative exists for the foundry. If the new type of furnace is developed in three years, the modified old furnace could be sold at that time for $9,000 and the radical new furnace purchased for an estimated $45,000. There is a .9 probability of state N_2, in which case the new furnace would save $13,000 annually and be worth $20,000 at the end of five years; and a .1 probability of state N_3, in which case the new furnace would save only $8,000 a year and would be worth only $15,000 after five years. If a new furnace is purchased now, it will be used for eight years, regardless of new developments.

Use a decision tree to determine whether the old furnace should be modified or a new, current model should be purchased. (Ignore the time value of money.)

Case Problem: Pan-Pacific Corporation

14. Pan-Pacific Corporation is a major producer of athletic equipment for schools, professional athletes, and the Olympic games. The

corporation was quite successful from 1950 to 1970, reaching a sales volume near $300 million with profits of about $15 million annually. In recent years, however, the market has been flooded with cheap imports, causing Pan-Pacific to suffer severe losses, first from falling sales, then from a profit squeeze as it cut prices to meet the competition. Losses the past three years amounted to $40 million:

	1983	1982	1981
Sales ($ millions)	300	270	250
Loss	(20)	(10)	(10)

In an effort to deal with the problem, Pan-Pacific has researched the possibility of entering new market segments or of producing other products that would be more profitable. After evaluating the staff's research, the Board of Directors has decided that Pan-Pacific should follow a strategy of producing and marketing one of the following new products:

S_1:   CB radios, selling for $100 each.

S_2:   Telecommunications systems (specifically teletype machines), selling for $800 each.

S_3:   Personal computers, selling for $1,000 each.

The firm estimates that the needed initial investment in plant and equipment will be $10 million, whichever product they decide to produce. Sales volume will depend upon which of three states of the economy occurs: boom, stability, or recession. Fully allocated unit cost will vary with sales volume, as shown in Table 1.

Table 1 _____

Estimated Average Annual Unit Sales and Costs,
1985–1987

Product	State of Economy	Unit Sales	Unit Cost of Production
S_1: CB Radios	Boom	950,000	$ 94.56
	Stability	900,000	94.57
	Recession	860,000	94.75
S_2: Teletypes	Boom	280,000	729.75
	Stability	240,000	746.30
	Recession	200,000	753.80
S_3: Computers	Boom	120,000	820.40
	Stability	90,000	925.75
	Recession	75,000	967.80

The estimated annual cash flow is shown in Table 2.

Table 2

Estimated Annual Cash Flow, 1985–1987

Product	State of Economy	Unit Sales (000)	Gross Revenue ($ millions)	Production Costs ($ millions)	Net Cash Inflow ($ millions)
S_1: CB Radios	Boom	950	95	89.832	5.168
	Stability	900	90	85.113	4.887
	Recession	860	86	81.485	4.515
S_2: Teletypes	Boom	280	224	204.330	19.670
	Stability	240	192	179.112	12.888
	Recession	200	160	150.760	9.240
S_3: Computers	Boom	120	120	98.448	21.552
	Stability	90	90	83.318	6.683
	Recession	75	75	72.585	2.415

If the net cash inflows shown in Table 2 are realized in each of the three years 1985, 1986, and 1987, the present value of the net cash inflows, discounted at 10 percent, would be those shown in Table 3:

Table 3

Present Value of Three-Year Cash Inflow Discounted at 10 Percent

Product	State of Economy	Average Annual Cash Inflow ($ millions)	Present Value of Three-Year Cash Inflow ($ millions)	Initial Outlay ($ millions)	Present Value of Net Profit ($ millions)
S_1: CB Radios	Boom	5.168	12.852	10.0	2.852
	Stability	4.887	12.153	10.0	2.153
	Recession	4.515	11.228	10.0	1.228
S_2: Teletypes	Boom	19.670	48.916	10.0	38.916
	Stability	12.888	32.051	10.0	22.051
	Recession	9.240	22.979	10.0	12.979
S_3: Computers	Boom	21.552	53.597	10.0	43.597
	Stability	6.683	16.620	10.0	6.620
	Recession	2.415	6.006	10.0	(3.994)

Pan-Pacific's management is uncertain about which state of the economy will prevail over the next three years. Therefore, it has constructed a payoff matrix using present values of the three-year cash inflows as payoffs. The decision criteria for decision making under uncertainty are then applied, as shown in Tables 4, 5, and 6.

Table 4———————————————————————————————————————

Application of Maximin, Maximax, and Hurwicz Alpha Criteria

| | State of Economy | | | Criteria | | |
Product	Boom	Stability	Recession	Maximin	Maximax	Hurwicz $\alpha = .5$
S_1: CB Radios	2.852	2.153	1.228	1.228	2.852	2.049
S_2: Teletypes	38.916	22.051	12.979	12.979*	38.916	25.948*
S_3: Computers	43.597	6.620	−3.994	−3.994	43.597*	23.796

* Best choice under stated criterion.

Table 5———————————————————————————————————————

Application of the Minimax Regret Criterion

| | State of Economy | | | Regret Matrix | | | Maximum Regret |
Product	Boom	Stability	Recession	Boom	Stable	Recession	
S_1: CB Radios	2.852	2.153	1.228	40.745	19.989	11.751	40.745
S_2: Teletypes	38.916	22.051	12.979	4.681	0	0	4.681*
S_3: Computers	43.597	6.620	−3.994	0	15.431	16.973	16.973

* Best choice under stated criterion.

Table 6———————————————————————————————————————

Application of the Laplace Criterion

| | State of Economy | | | | | |
Product	Boom $P = \frac{1}{3}$	Stability $P = \frac{1}{3}$	Recession $P = \frac{1}{3}$	Expected Value	Standard Deviation	Coefficient of Variation
S_1: CB Radios	2.852	2.153	1.228	2.078	0.665	32.0
S_2: Teletypes	38.916	22.051	12.979	24.649*	10.747	43.6
S_3: Computers	43.597	6.620	−3.994	15.408	20.398	132.4

* Best choice under stated criterion.

The coefficients of variation in Table 6 show that the three proposals have different degrees of risk. Pan-Pacific's management believes, therefore, that the discount rate should be adjusted to reflect the different degrees of risk, as follows:

Product	Risk-Adjusted Discount Rate
CB Radios	12%
Teletypes	15
Computers	20

This will change the present value of the net cash flows, as shown in Table 7.

Table 7_____

Annual Cash Flows Adjusted for Different Degrees of Risk

Product	State of Economy	Average Annual Cash Inflow ($ millions)	Present Value of Three-Year Cash Inflow ($ millions)	Initial Outlay ($ millions)	Present Value of Net Profit ($ millions)
S_1: CB Radios	Boom	5.168	12.413	10.0	2.413
	Stability	4.887	11.738	10.0	1.738
	Recession	4.515	10.844	10.0	0.844
S_2: Teletypes	Boom	19.670	44.911	10.0	34.911
	Stability	12.888	29.426	10.0	19.426
	Recession	9.240	21.097	10.0	11.097
S_3: Computers	Boom	21.552	45.399	10.0	35.399
	Stability	6.683	14.078	10.0	4.078
	Recession	2.415	5.087	10.0	(4.913)

Questions:
a. Which product should management choose? Why?
b. Evaluate the estimation of sales and profits. What are the assumptions in computing the present values of net profits?
c. How may you improve decisions involving various risk analysis criteria?
d. Do you think Pan-Pacific should stop producing athletic equipment? Why?

References

Brunk, Gregory G. "A Test of the Friedman-Savage Gambling Model." *Quarterly Journal of Economics,* May 1981, pp. 341–48.

Dorfman, Robert; Paul A. Samuelson; and Robert M. Solow. *Linear Programming and Economic Analysis.* New York: McGraw-Hill, 1958.

Gay, Gerald D., and Steven Manaster. "Hedging Against Commodity Price Inflation: Stocks and Bills as Substitutes for Futures Contracts." *Journal of Business,* July 1982, pp. 317–44.

Graham, Daniel. "Cost-Benefit Analysis Under Uncertainty." *American Economic Review,* September 1981, pp. 715–27.

Hespos, Richard F., and Paul A. Strassman. "Stochastic Decision Trees for the Analysis of Investment Decisions." *Management Science,* August 1965, pp. 244–59.

Knight, Frank H. *Risk, Uncertainty, and Profit.* Boston: Houghton Mifflin, 1921.

Magee, J. F. "Decision Trees for Decision-Making." *Harvard Business Review,* July–August 1964, pp. 126–36.

————. "How to Use Decision Trees in Capital Investment." *Harvard Business Review,* September–October 1964, pp. 79–96.

Margolis, Julius. "Sequential Decision Making in the Firm." *American Economic Review,* May 1960, pp. 526–33.

Parsons, James A. "Decision-Making under Uncertainty." *Journal of Systems Management,* August 1972, pp. 43–44.

Peterson, Richard, and K. K. Seo. "Public Administration Planning in Developing Countries: A Bayesian Decision Theory Approach." *Policy Sciences,* September 1972, pp. 371–78.

Pratt, John W., Howard Raiffa, and Robert Schlaifer. "The Foundations of Decision under Certainty: An Elementary Exposition." *Journal of the American Statistical Association 59,* 353–75 (1964).

Riddell, Craig W. "Bargaining Under Uncertainty." *American Economic Review,* September 1981, pp. 579–91.

Van Horne, James C. *Financial Management and Policy,* 2d ed. Englewood Cliffs, N.J.: Prentice-Hall, 1971.

Woods, Donald H. "Improving Estimates That Involve Uncertainties." *Harvard Business Review,* July–August 1966, pp. 91–98.

Appendix 3A | Case Illustration of Marginal Analysis

Two methods may be used to find the marginal value of a function. One is the *tabular method,* which can be used whether or not the function is known. The other is *differential calculus,* which can be used only when the function is known and continuous.

The marginal value of a function is rigorously defined as the change in the dependent variable that is caused by a one-unit change in a single independent variable while all other independent variables (if any) are held constant. This definition explicitly specifies that the selected values of the independent variable must be discrete numbers in increments of 1.0. By this strict definition, the marginal value is the slope, $\Delta Y / \Delta X$, of the secant line between the two points P_1 and P_2, as shown in Exhibit 3A–1.

Exhibit 3A–1

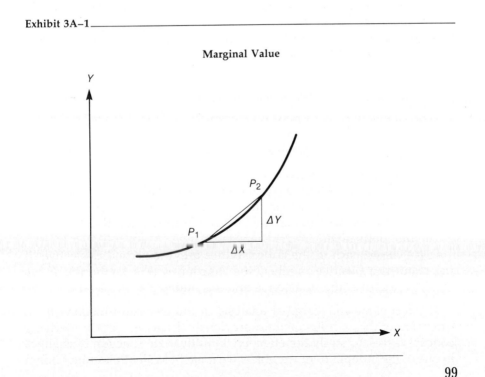

Marginal Value

When the tabular method is used in actual practice (usually because the function is unknown), discrete values of the independent variable are used, but the requirement that $\Delta X = 1$ is relaxed. The marginal value is taken to be $\Delta Y/\Delta X$, whatever ΔX may be. If the function is linear, this causes no problem, since the slope of the line is constant. But if the function is not linear, large values of ΔX will introduce error. The amount of error will depend upon the slope of the curve as well as the magnitude of ΔX.

If the function is known and continuous, common practice is to approximate the marginal value by taking the first derivative. This means that the marginal value is measured as the slope of a line tangent to the curve precisely at P_1 in Exhibit 3A–1. This is not equal to the slope of the secant between P_1 and P_2 unless the function is linear. Consequently, some error is introduced when the derivative is used as the marginal value of a nonlinear function. But the error is inconsequential and therefore ignored in actual practice.

Of course, to find the marginal value as the slope of a curve, one must be able to take a derivative (i.e., differentiate the function). This requires no more than becoming familiar with standard notation and memorizing a few simple rules, which are provided in Table I of the Appendix at the end of this book. As for notation, if we have the function $Y = f(X)$, the first derivative may be written as $f'(X)$ (read "f-prime of X") or dY/dX (read "the derivative of Y with respect to X"). The first derivative is also a function of X and can be differentiated to obtain the second derivative, which is written as $f''(X)$ or d^2Y/dX^2.

Optimization of a Function

When a function is at a maximum or minimum the slope of its curve is zero; therefore, the first derivative is zero at that point. The maximum or minimum points on the curve can be located by the following procedure:

Step 1. Find the first derivative of the function and set it equal to zero.

Step 2. Solve the resulting equation for the *critical value or values* of X, i.e., the value(s) of X at which the function is maximum or minimum.

Step 3. Find the second derivative of the function; i.e., the derivative of the first derivative.

Step 4. Insert each of the critical values into the second derivative. If the result is a positive number, the function is at a minimum. If the result is negative, the function is at a maximum.

The technique for marginal analysis of multivariate functions is an extension of the calculus method previously discussed. The underlying concept is this: to study the effect on a multivariate function of changes in one of the independent variables, we must hold all other independent variables constant. We carry this concept into calculus when we take a partial derivative. The same rules of differentiation are followed to take the derivative with respect to one variable while all other variables are treated as constants.[1]

A Case Illustration

Suppose that a firm has developed a new product and during its first year on the market has sold 500 units at a price of $300 per unit. Variable costs of production are $100 per unit, and fixed overhead allocated to the product is $40,000. These costs are not expected to change during the coming year.

The firm has engaged an advertising agency to promote the product. The agency recommends an advertising campaign featuring full-page ads in two nationally circulated magazines, *Medium One* and *Medium Two*. A full-page ad in *Medium One* costs $6,000. *Medium Two*, which has a smaller circulation, charges $4,000 for a full page.

After conducting appropriate market research, the advertising agency advises the firm that the effectiveness of the campaign will depend upon the number of ads run, according to the demand equation

$$Q = 500 + 100A - 5A^2$$

where Q represents the number of units that will be sold at a price of $300 if A units of advertising are used. A unit of advertising consists of one page in *Medium One* and one page in *Medium Two*, at a total cost of $10,000.

The firm has a choice between two marketing strategies—one that will maximize profits (in the short run) and one that will maximize sales (which may improve profits in the long run). The question facing management is how much to budget for advertising under each of the two strategies.

The first step in solving this problem is to identify all of the variables that pertain to it. These are:

A = Number of units of advertising at $10,000 each.
P = Price of the product ($300).
Q = Number of units of the product.
VCP = Variable cost of production ($100).
TVC = Total variable cost at a given level of advertising, calculated as the cost of production plus the cost of advertising.

---

[1] The scope of this discussion of optimization is necessarily limited. Students who desire a more comprehensive explanation should consult a standard text on differential calculus.

FC = Fixed cost ($40,000).
TC = Total cost $(FC + TVC)$.
TR = Total revenue from the sale of Q units.
CP = Contribution profit per unit $(P - VCP = \$200)$.
TCP = Total contribution profit $(TR - TVC)$.
π = Operating income.

The next step is to express the relationships among the variables in a set of equations.

$$Q = 500 + 100A - 5A^2 \qquad (1)$$
$$TR = PQ = 300(500 + 100A - 5A^2)$$
$$= 150,000 + 30,000A - 1,500A^2 \qquad (2)$$
$$TVC = Q(VCP) + 10,000A = 100(500 + 100A - 5A^2) + 10,000A$$
$$= 50,000 + 20,000A - 500A^2 \qquad (3)$$
$$TCP = TR - TVC = 100,000 + 10,000A - 1,000A^2 \qquad (4)$$
$$TC = TVC + FC = 90,000 + 20,000A - 500A^2 \qquad (5)$$
$$\pi = TR - TC = 60,000 + 10,000A - 1,000A^2 \qquad (6)$$

At this stage, two methods are available for solving the problem. One is to construct a table as shown in Exhibit 3A–2, in which the crucial relationships are revealed. The other method is to use the maximization technique of calculus. Using calculus is faster and easier, but the tabular method perhaps gives more insight into the true relationships of the variables and the concept of marginal analysis. We shall demonstrate both methods.

Tabular Method

The tabular method of marginal analysis requires the construction of a table like that in Exhibit 3A–2. The first step in constructing the table is to select the desired values of the independent variable, in this case, advertising purchased. Note that the selected values of the independent variable must be *discrete* numbers in increments of 1.0. This is because marginal value is defined as the change in the function that results from a one-unit change in the independent variable.

Each of the selected values of the independent variable is then substituted into the appropriate equation to obtain corresponding functional values. In this case, Equations (2), (3), and (4) are used to obtain total revenue, variable costs, and contribution profit, respectively, for each selected number of units of advertising purchased.

Exhibit 3A–3 presents the histograms of the functional values shown on Exhibit 3A–2. We shall use these histograms to gain a better understanding of the concepts of marginality.

Exhibit 3A–2_____

Revenues, Variable Costs, and Contribution Profits as Functions of Advertising

(1) Advertising Purchased (units)	(2) Total Revenue ($000)	(3) Marginal Revenue ($000)	(4) Variable Costs ($000)	(5) Marginal Costs ($000)	(6) Contribution Profit ($000)	(7) Marginal Profit ($000)
0	150.0		50.0		100.0	
		28.5		19.5		9.0
1	178.5		69.5		109.0	
		25.5		18.5		7.0
2	204.0		88.0		116.0	
		22.5		17.5		5.0
3	226.5		105.5		121.0	
		19.5		16.5		3.0
4	246.0		122.0		124.0	
		16.5		15.5		1.0
5	262.5		137.5		125.0	
		13.5		14.5		−1.0
6	276.0		152.0		124.0	
		10.5		13.5		−3.0
7	286.5		165.5		121.0	
		7.5		12.5		−5.0
8	294.0		178.0		116.0	
		4.5		11.5		−7.0
9	298.5		189.5		109.0	
		1.5		10.5		−9.0
10	300.0		200.0		100.0	
		−1.5		9.5		−11.0
11	298.5		209.5		89.0	
		−4.5		8.5		−13.0
12	294.0		218.0		76.0	

Note in Exhibit 3A–3 that the columns are centered on the discrete values of the independent variable, and that the *margins* or boundaries of the columns have been extended upward to aid our visualization. Note also that the midpoints of the upper ends of adjacent columns have been joined by straight lines. For ease of reference, we will call these lines of change.

When the independent variable changes from one value to the next, we travel to the new functional value along the line of change. In mak ing this movement, we are traveling ΔX units in a horizontal direction and ΔY units in a vertical direction. The *slope* of the line of change is the ratio $\Delta Y / \Delta X$. Since the line of change is a straight line, its slope is everywhere the same, including at the point where it crosses the margin between $f(X_1)$ and $f(X_2)$. Since we have restricted ΔX to a value of 1.0, the marginal value by definition is equal to ΔY.

Exhibit 3A–3

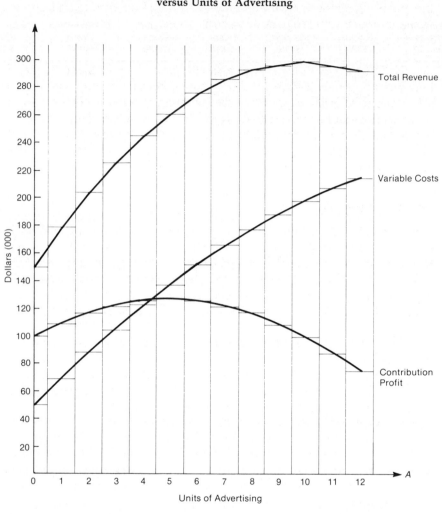

**Histograms of Total Revenue, Variable Costs, and Contribution Profit
versus Units of Advertising**

Taking total revenue on Exhibit 3A–2 as an example, we see that at the margin between 0 and 1 unit of advertising, the marginal revenue is 178.5 − 150.0 = 28.5; between 1 and 2 units, marginal revenue is 204.0 − 178.5 = 25.5; and so on.

When we examine all of the data in the total revenue column, we find that total revenue is at a maximum when 10 units of advertising are purchased. We note that the marginal revenue at the left-hand margin is +1.5, while at the right-hand margin it is −1.5. Looking at Exhibit 3A–3, we see that the change of slope from positive to negative takes place at the top of the histogram column for 10 units of advertising. Similarly, we note that maximum contribution profit occurs when 5 units of advertising are purchased. Marginal profit on the left is +1.0 and on the right is −1.0.

Note that in developing marginal profit data, fixed costs and the resultant operating income are ignored. This is because fixed costs do not affect marginal profits, as we can see by referring again to Exhibit 3A–3. If we were to deduct fixed costs from the contribution profit data, we would merely reduce the height of each column by the same amount. The slopes of the lines of change would be exactly the same as before, hence the marginal profit would be the same.

The Calculus Method

Referring again to Exhibit 3A–3, we see that although the lines of change are straight lines, when joined together they come very close to forming the smooth curve that we associate with a continuous function. This is the basis for using differential calculus to find marginal values. We assume that the function is continuous even if it is not, so that instead of many lines of change, we have just one smooth, continuous curve.

The calculus method is far more powerful than the tabular method for two reasons:

1.   Because we know that a function is optimal[2] when the slope of its graph is zero, we can find the optimal value of the independent variable simply by taking the first derivative of the function, setting it equal to zero, and solving for X. For example, Equation (2) says:

$$TR = 150,000 + 30,000A - 1,500A^2$$

If $d(TR)/dA = 30,000 - 3,000A = 0$, then $A = 10$, as we have seen before.

2.   Calculus enables us to handle multivariate functions that would be very difficult, perhaps impossible, to handle by the tabular method. The technique for the marginal analysis of multivariate functions is an extension of the calculus method previously discussed. A partial derivative is taken for each independent variable, holding all other independent variables constant. All partial derivatives are then set equal to zero. The result is a system of equations in which the number of variables is

---

[2] Of course, optimization also covers minimization. In order to determine whether the function is at a maximum or a minimum, certain conditions concerning *second* derivatives must be met, as previously noted.

equal to the number of equations, and hence can be solved for the value of each variable. We shall demonstrate the technique by continuing with our case illustration.

Marginal Analysis of Multivariate Functions

Suppose after some experience with the firm's advertising campaign, the advertising agency acquires new information that reveals the specific impact of ads in each of the two magazines. It now says that the demand equation is:

$$Q = 500 + 66M_1 - 3M_1^2 + 34M_2 - 2M_2^2 \qquad (7)$$

where M_1 represents the number of full-page ads placed in *Medium One* and M_2 represents the number of full-page ads in *Medium Two*.

In the light of this additional information, what should the advertising budget be for each of the two magazines? To answer this question, we take the partial derivatives of Equation (7):

$$\frac{\partial Q}{\partial M_1} = 66 - 6M_1 \qquad (8)$$

$$\frac{\partial Q}{\partial M_2} = 34 - 4M_2 \qquad (9)$$

Optimal Input Factors.   Equation (8) says that demand (output) for the product will change by $(66 - 6M_1)$ units per unit change in M_1 when M_2 is held constant. Equation (9) says that demand will change by $(34 - 4M_2)$ units per unit change in M_2 when M_1 is held constant. These functions are called the *marginal products* of M_1 and M_2, respectively.

We can now apply the theory of marginal productivity to determine the optimal mix of M_1 and M_2. Marginal productivity theory says that the optimal allocation of the factors of production occurs when the ratio of the marginal product *MP* of the factor to its price *P* is the same for all input factors; that is, when

$$\frac{MP_A}{P_A} = \frac{MP_B}{P_B} = \cdots = \frac{MP_N}{P_N}$$

Applying this rule, we have

$$\frac{66 - 6M_1}{\$6,000} = \frac{34 - 4M_2}{\$4,000}$$

when allocation is optimal. Upon solving this equation, we find that $M_1 = M_2 + 2.5$; that is to say, we should always place 2.5 more ads in *Medium One* than in *Medium Two*. This does not tell us how many ads are optimal—it simply says that *at any level* of output, we will get the most output for our money by following the indicated allocation.

Optimal Output.   If by "optimal" we mean a maximum of sales, we can get our answer simply by setting Equations (8) and (9) equal to zero. We learn from this that M_1 should be 11 and M_2 should be 8.5. Although this agrees with our conclusion regarding the optimal mix of ads in *Medium One* and *Medium Two*, it requires us to buy one half-page ad in *Medium Two*. This is contrary to the stated condition that we would run full-page ads only. Can it be that our assumption of continuity of the demand function has led us astray?

Technically, the answer is yes, but as a practical matter the error is inconsequential. If we substitute the values $M_1 = 11$ and $M_2 = 8.0$, 8.5, or 9.0, we get the following results:

M_1	M_2	Q
11	8.0	1,007.0
11	8.5	1,007.5
11	9.0	1,007.0

Buying a half-page ad could have unpredictable results, and making and selling half a product may be impossible (depending on the product), so it does not take long to decide to run 11 full-page ads in *Medium One* and 8 full-page ads in *Medium Two*. Does this advertising budget improve our performance? Under the previous 1:1 allocation, our optimum production was 1,000 units worth $300,000 in sales at an advertising cost of $100,000. With the new allocation, our optimum production is 1,007 units with a sales value of $302,100 at an advertising cost of $98,000. This improves our profit by $4,100.

Optimal Profits.   If by "optimal" we mean maximum profits, we must first use Equation (7) to develop new equations for total revenue, total variable cost, and contribution profit. The new functions are:

$$Q = 500 + 66M_1 - 3M_1^2 + 34M_2 - 2M_2^2 \tag{7}$$

$$\begin{aligned} TR = 300Q &= 150,000 + 19,800M_1 \\ &\quad - 900M_1^2 + 10,200M_2 - 600M_2^2 \end{aligned} \tag{10}$$

$$\begin{aligned} TVC = 100Q &+ 6,000M_1 + 4,000M_2 \\ &= 50,000 + 12,600M_1 - 300M_1^2 + 7,400M_2 - 200M_2^2 \end{aligned} \tag{11}$$

$$\begin{aligned} TCP = TR - TVC &= 100,000 + 7,200M_1 \\ &\quad - 600M_1^2 + 2,800M_2 - 400M_2^2 \end{aligned} \tag{12}$$

To determine the allocation of advertising to secure maximum profits, we take the partial derivatives of Equation (12) and set them equal to zero:

$$\frac{\partial(TCP)}{\partial M_1} = 7,200 - 1,200M_1 = 0; \ M_1 = 6 \tag{13}$$

$$\frac{\partial(TCP)}{\partial M_2} = 2,800 - 800M_2 = 0; \ M_2 = 3.5 \tag{14}$$

Constrained Optima

In the preceding discussions, we made the implicit assumption that unlimited resources were available. No limits were placed on plant capacity or the amount of working capital that could be spent on advertising. In real life, however, planners are not able to work under such blissful conditions. All planners must make trade-offs in the allocation of scarce resources in order to do the best they can within the limitations imposed by management decisions or simply the hard facts of business life. Fortunately, marginal analysis via differential calculus can come to the rescue.

Once again, we shall use our case to illustrate the point. We have shown that sales will be maximized if we place 11 ads in *Medium One* and 8 ads in *Medium Two* at a total cost of $98,000. But suppose we can spend only $80,000 on advertising—how shall we spend it to maximize sales?

Application of Marginal Productivity.   From our previous maximization of sales without any constraint on advertising, we obtained the optimal mix equation,

$$M_1 = M_2 + 2.5 \tag{15}$$

If we can spend only $80,000 on advertising, we know that

$$\$6,000M_1 + \$4,000M_2 = \$80,000 \tag{16}$$

Substituting Equation (15) into Equation (16), we get

$$6,000(M_2 + 2.5) + 4,000M_2 = 80,000$$
$$10,000M_2 + 15,000 = 80,000$$
$$M_1 = 9.0$$
$$M_2 = 6.5$$

The conclusion is that we should buy nine ads in *Medium One* for $54,000 and six ads in *Medium Two* for $24,000, a total expenditure of $78,000. At this level of advertising, sales should be

$$Q = 500 + 66(9) - 3(81) + 34(6) - 2(36) = 983 \text{ units}$$

The contribution profit would be

$$TCP = 200(983) - 78,000 = \$118,600$$

Lagrangian Multiplier.   An even more powerful tool for optimizing any multivariate function subject to one or more constraints is the Lagrangian multiplier. A Lagrangian multiplier is an artificial variable usually symbolized by the Greek letter lambda (λ). It can be more easily explained by use of the same example.

We have the demand function

$$Q = f(M_1, M_2) = 500 + 66M_1 - 3M_1^2 + 34M_2 - 2M_2^2 \qquad (17)$$

and the constraint equation

$$6,000M_1 + 4,000M_2 = 80,000 \qquad (18)$$

The demand function will be maximized when we set both the constraint Equation (18) and the partial derivatives of Equation (17) to zero and solve for M_1 and M_2. We can set the constraint equation to zero by rewriting it as

$$6,000M_1 + 4,000M_2 - 80,000 = 0 \qquad (19)$$

but when we take the partial derivatives of Equation (17), we end up with a system of *three* equations with only *two* variables, for which there is no solution.

The way out of our dilemma is to multiply Equation (19) by the artificial variable and add it to Equation (17). Now we have a function of three variables:

$$f(M_1, M_2, \lambda) = 500 + 66M_1 - 3M_1^2 + 34M_2$$
$$- 2M_2^2 + 6,000\lambda M_1 + 4,000\lambda M_2 - 80,000\lambda$$

When we take the partial derivatives of this function, we obtain three equations in three variables, which we can solve:

$$\frac{\partial f}{\partial M_1} = 66 - 6M_1 + 6,000\lambda = 0$$

$$\frac{\partial f}{\partial M_2} = 34 - 4M_2 + 4,000\lambda = 0$$

$$\frac{\partial f}{\partial \lambda} = 6,000M_1 + 4,000M_2 - 80,000 = 0$$

Notice that the partial derivative with respect to λ is just the constraint equation, *as it always is*. When we solve the system, we get:

$$M_1 = 9.0; \quad M_2 = 6.5; \quad \lambda = -0.002$$

Observe that the values of M_1 and M_2 are the same as we got from the application of the theory of marginal productivity. *The value of lambda, however, gives us information that we can get in no other way.* The negative sign tells us that the value of the function will be increased if we reduce the restraining effect of the constraint equation. How much will it be improved? In this instance, by approximately 0.002 unit for each dollar added to the advertising budget.

We already know that the advertising budget at optimum would be $98,000 and 1,007 units would be sold. From $80,000 to $98,000 is an increase of $18,000; multiplied by 0.002, we get an approximate increase of 36, which would bring sales up to 1,019 units, which is a good rough estimate.

Of course, in real life we often have a multivariate function with multiple constraints. The Lagrangian multiplier method will still work. We merely introduce one additional artificial variable for each additional constraint equation.

Probability Distribution of Cash Flows

In adjusting the profit-maximization model for risk, the risk-adjusted discount rate approach and the certainty-equivalent approach view the income received at future times as given sums.[1] In reality these sums are more apt to be expected values of probability distributions. Hence the net present value will be the present value of a series of expected values. The elements of the series may or may not be independent; that is to say, the outcome in time period t may or may not depend upon what the outcome was in time period $t - 1$. If the outcomes are independent, then the net present value is

$$NPV = \sum_{t=0}^{n} \frac{E_t}{(1 + i)^t} \tag{1}$$

where E_t is the expected value of the outcome in time period t, and i is the risk-free interest rate.[2] The standard deviation of the probability distribution of possible net present values is

$$\sigma = \sqrt{\sum_{t=0}^{n} \frac{\sigma_t^2}{(1 + i)^{2t}}} \tag{2}$$

where σ_t^2 is the variance of the probability distribution of net cash flows in time period t, calculated as:

$$\sigma_t^2 = \sum_{t=1}^{n} (A_{xt} - A_t)^2 P_{xt} \tag{3}$$

where A_{xt} is the xth possible net cash flow in time period t and P_{xt} is the probability of its occurrence. To illustrate this method, suppose that the risk-free interest rate is 12 percent, and we have possible cash flows for the next three years as shown in Exhibit 3B–1.[3]

---

[1] As discussed in Chapter 2.

[2] Since we are using the dispersion of the probability distribution of possible net present values to measure risk, we must use the risk-free interest rate to avoid accounting twice for the same risk.

[3] Note that the decision maker has developed more-or-less objective probabilities for Periods 1 and 2. For the third period, however, he apparently has resorted to Bayesian analysis under uncertainty, giving all payoffs the same probability.

Exhibit 3B–1

Probability Distribution of Possible Cash Flows

Period 1		Period 2		Period 3	
Net Cash Flow ($000)	Probability	Net Cash Flow ($000)	Probability	Net Cash Flow ($000)	Probability
10	.05	10	.10	10	.20
20	.15	20	.20	20	.20
30	.40	30	.30	30	.20
40	.25	40	.25	40	.20
50	.15	50	.15	50	.20

For this example, the first step is to calculate the expected value and variance for each time period, as follows:

Period 1:

$$E_1(X) = .05(10) + .15(20) + .40(30) + .25(40) + .15(50) = 33$$
$$\sigma^2 = (10 - 33)^2(.05) + (20 - 33)^2(.15) + (30 - 33)^2(.40)$$
$$+ (40 - 33)^2(.25) + (50 - 33)^2(.15) = 111$$

Period 2:

$$E_2(X) = .10(10) + .20(20) + .30(30) + .25(40) + .15(50) = 31.5$$
$$\sigma_2^2 = (10 - 31.5)^2(.10) + (20 - 31.5)^2(.20) + (30 - 31.5)^2(.30)$$
$$+ (40 - 31.5)^2(.25) + (50 - 31.5)^2(.15) = 142.75$$

Period 3:

$$E_3(X) = .20(10) + .20(20) + .20(30) + .20(40) + .20(50) = 30$$
$$\sigma_3^2 = (10 - 30)^2(.20) + (20 - 30)^2(.20) + (30 - 30)^2(.20)$$
$$+ (40 - 30)^2(.20) + (50 - 30)^2(.20) = 200$$

The net present value and standard deviation for the three periods are:

$$NPV = \frac{33.0}{1.12} + \frac{31.5}{(1.12)^2} + \frac{30.0}{(1.12)^3} = 75.929$$

$$\sigma = \sqrt{\frac{111.0}{(1.12)^2} + \frac{142.75}{(1.12)^4} + \frac{200.0}{(1.12)^6}} = \sqrt{280.53} = 16.749$$

Evaluation of the Probability Distribution.   If the distribution of possible net present values is normal (which it usually will be), the normal distribution table in the Appendix at the back of this book (or in any statistics text) can be used to determine the probability that the actual net present value is greater or less than any given amount.

For example, suppose we want to know the probability that the net present value of the cash flows of Exhibit 3B-1 will be less than zero. The first step is to determine the number of standard deviations that zero is away from the mean. This can be determined by computing the Z-value for zero, using the formula:

$$Z = \frac{X - \mu}{\sigma} \qquad (4)$$

In our example, $Z = (0 - 75.929)/16.749 = -4.53$. In a table of normal distribution areas[4] we find that for a Z-value that large, the corresponding area is in excess of .49997. The area remaining to the left of Z therefore is too small to measure. For all practical purposes, therefore, there is no chance that our actual return will be less than zero.

Dependent Cash Flows.   The relatively simple technique discussed in the preceding section assumes independent cash flows. In reality the cash flow realized in one period usually depends on the cash flow realized in the preceding period. Under these circumstances, the calculation of the net present value of the possible cash flows is much more complicated. In some cases, it may require full-scale simulation on a computer. A full discussion of the equations and techniques used is beyond the scope of this text, but may be obtained from many finance texts.

---

[4] Table E of the Appendix at the end of this book.

Demand Analysis and Consumer Behavior

Demand analysis provides the basic information needed to guide some of the firm's most crucial activities. These include:

1. Sales forecasting.
2. Production planning.
3. Cost analysis and financial planning.
4. Pricing and the manipulation of other demand variables such as advertising and promotion.
5. Resource and inventory management.

From a managerial viewpoint the main objectives of demand analysis are the discovery and measurement of the variables that affect product sales. For a profit-seeking firm, therefore, the study of demand is an essential part of business planning. Moreover, the firm cannot be content with a purely descriptive investigation. It must understand the dynamics of the forces that affect demand, and it must determine whether and how these forces can be manipulated to improve profitability.

Since demand analysis is a prerequisite for successful business operations, a thorough discussion of demand analysis and measurement will be presented in the following four chapters:

114

The main thrust of the present chapter is to provide a framework for demand analysis. We will begin with the ultimate determinant of all demand—the consumer—because the demand function is directly related to the manner in which consumers are willing and able to act. Therefore, it is necessary to understand consumer behavior in order to understand the forces that determine demand for any commodity. (We shall use the word "commodity" to designate any economic good or service.)

In order to understand consumer behavior, we shall explain two different approaches to the construction of the model of consumer equilibrium. One is the cardinal approach, which requires cardinal measurement of utility. The other is the ordinal approach, which requires only that commodities be ranked in order of preference.

The Cardinal Approach to Consumer Equilibrium

Why do you purchase goods or services? Why do you choose to buy some goods and services, but not others? A large part of your answer must be that some goods and services provide you with more utility than others do.

The economist defines utility as the pleasure or satisfaction associated with having, using, or consuming goods or services (commodities). Utility has many sources or causes. It may have objective features (for example, any building is objectively useful as shelter), but it is mostly subjective. This is because utility is a function of individual tastes, preferences, perceptions, personality, state of mind, and background. Furthermore, utility is not an absolute value. Rather, it varies from person to person. Also, even for a single individual, it varies from time to time and from place to place. At the time of decision, however, each consumer evaluates the utility of a commodity and bases the decision to buy or not buy upon that perception.

Cardinal Measurement of Utility

Conceptually, utility can be measured in units called *utils*. The problem, however, is that nobody can define a util, so it is actually impossible to measure utility in this way. Nevertheless, it is analytically useful to pretend we can in order to establish the law of diminishing marginal utility. This law says that the consumer's marginal utility decreases as consumption increases. Marginal utility is defined as the change in total utility that results from a one-unit change in consumption, i.e.,

$$MU_X = \frac{\Delta TU_X}{\Delta Q_X} \tag{1}$$

where

MU_X = The marginal utility of commodity X
ΔTU_X = The change in total utility of commodity X
ΔQ_X = The change in the quantity of commodity X consumed per time period

In actual practice, this rigorous definition of marginal utility is relaxed a bit to permit its application to continuous functions. In this case, marginal utility is defined as the slope of the utility function's curve. It can be measured at any particular point on the curve by taking the first derivative of the function at that point, i.e.,

$$MU_X = \frac{dTU_X}{dQ_X} \tag{2}$$

To illustrate both of these concepts, suppose we let $TU = 20Q_X - 2Q_X^2$. As consumption of X increases from 0 to 6, discrete and continuous marginal utilities change, as shown in Exhibit 4–1.

Exhibit 4–1

Discrete and Continuous Marginal Utilities

Consumption (Q_x)	Total Utility (TU_x)	Discrete Marginal Utility $\Delta TU_x/\Delta Q_x$	Continuous Marginal Utility dTU_x/dQ_x
0	0		
		18	
1	18		16
		14	
2	32		12
		10	
3	42		8
		6	
4	48		4
		2	
5	50		0
		−2	
6	48		−4

These values are plotted on Exhibit 4–2, which shows the total utility function on the upper panel and the corresponding marginal utility function on the lower panel. As an aid to understanding the concept of marginal utility, a histogram of the discrete values of Q_X has been superimposed on the lower panel. The histogram shows that discrete marginal utility is measured at the boundary of each column, while continuous marginal utility is measured at the center. In other words, the marginal utility of a continuous function is measured at the point where the change of total utility begins. Hence, the saturation point is easily determined as the point where the marginal utility (the slope of the utility function) is zero.

An intuitive analysis of our own consumption patterns fits in well with the total and marginal utility functions depicted on Exhibit 4–2. For example, suppose Commodity X is a hamburger. If we are very hungry, we might get great satisfaction from eating one hamburger—18 utils worth, according to Exhibit 4–2. But if we were to eat more hamburgers, the additional pleasure from additional consumption (marginal utility) would continuously diminish. We would receive no pleasure from the fifth hamburger, and the sixth would make us sick.

This steadily decreasing marginal utility, which indicates a steadily decreasing rate of change in total utility, is called the *law of diminishing marginal utility*. Although it is an accepted principle on account of its predictive and explanatory value, it should be noted that we haven't yet discovered how to test this law since we cannot measure utility in a cardinal way. Nevertheless, this law's usefulness is not vitiated by the current lack of a definition of a util or a cardinal scale for measuring it. This assumption of diminishing marginal utility is one of the two most important cornerstones of economic theory. (The other is the similar *law of diminishing marginal returns*, which applies to input factors of production, and is discussed in Chapter 9.)

Acquiring Maximum Utility

A consumer's purchases are constrained not only by the law of diminishing marginal utility, but also by the amount of income available. Spendable income may be gotten from some combination of (1) current income (e.g., wages, salaries, dividends, interest, rents, and other receipts), (2) borrowing, (3) withdrawal from savings accounts, and (4) liquidation of assets. A consumer's income is either spent or saved (held as money). Holding money (saving) is also desirable, so we treat money as another commodity whose price is $1 per unit.

In the analysis of consumer behavior, as with many other aspects of economics, it is helpful to think of maximum utility as a position of equilibrium. A consumer in equilibrium will balance the cost of con-

Exhibit 4–2

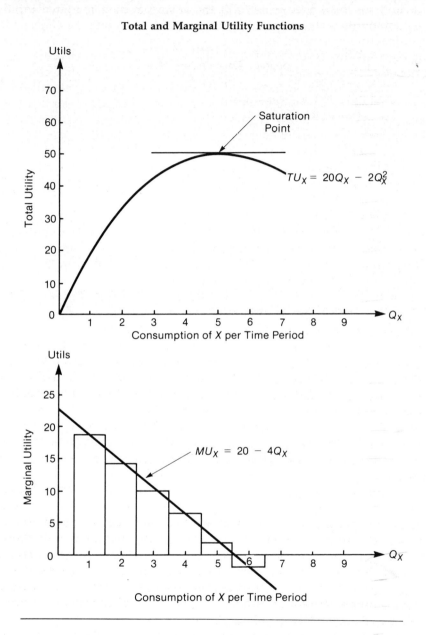

Total and Marginal Utility Functions

sumption against the utility to be gained from purchasable goods and services. In order to construct a model of such behavior, a few simplifying assumptions are necessary.

1. Consumers are free to spend their incomes as they please.
2. Consumers have perfect knowledge of all factors that may affect their decisions, such as income, prices of other commodities, and the utility of each commodity.
3. The sales units of all commodities are infinitely divisible. This assumption is necessary to establish a *continuous* function such that total utility depends upon the quantity consumed per period of time.
4. The consumer's tastes and preferences are so well established that he or she has no difficulty in choosing between one bundle of commodities and another in a consistent manner.
5. The marginal utility of each commodity diminishes for the consumer as the quantity consumed increases.
6. *More* is better than *less* (useless or nuisance items are either disregarded or redefined).
7. Finally, the consumer always attempts to maximize utility while either spending or saving his or her entire income.

In real life, of course, consumers spend their incomes on many different commodities. Each commodity provides utility that diminishes as consumption increases, and each can be purchased at a particular price. The marginal utility of each commodity is associated with the last unit purchased or the last dollar spent. If we divide the marginal utility of that transaction by the price of the commodity, the resulting ratio, MU_X/P_X, is the marginal utility per dollar. This ratio enables us to compare the relative satisfaction gained from purchasing many different commodities with widely differing prices, such as bread and automobiles.

Now suppose a consumer buys both apples and oranges. If the last dollar spent on apples yields more marginal utility than the last dollar spent on oranges, the consumer will buy more apples and fewer oranges. But as more apples are consumed, their marginal utility diminishes. As fewer oranges are consumed, their marginal utility increases. Eventually, the marginal utility per dollar equalizes for apples and oranges. At this point the consumer can no longer increase total utility by buying more or less of either. He or she is in *equilibrium*, because $MU_{apples}/P_{apples} = MU_{oranges}/P_{oranges}$.

The same procedure can be used to establish equilibrium in the consumption of other commodities. Further, by treating money as a commodity whose price is always $1 per dollar saved, we can state a general rule for consumer equilibrium:

The consumer achieves maximum total utility at the point of equilibrium where the marginal utility per last dollar spent is equal for all commodities, including savings, i.e.,

$$\frac{MU_A}{P_A} = \frac{MU_B}{P_B} = \cdots = \frac{MU_N}{P_N} \tag{3}$$

Equation (3) is the utility model for maximizing consumer satisfaction. It includes MU_M, the marginal utility of money saved.[1] How realistic is it, considering that most consumers have never heard of it? Does the model *explain* and *predict* real-world consumer behavior? Yes, if we keep in mind that utility is personal and variable, as previously mentioned. All the model really says is that most people most of the time try to get the most for their money. Failure to do so is usually due to lack of information. Some observers contend that consumers are not rational economic persons, as assumed by the model. To support such views, they cite such attributes of consumer behavior as habit, loyalty, whim, impulse, inertia, and reluctance to change. However, it can be argued that these attributes are simply aspects of each consumer's unique individual utility function. Common sense tells us that if, *at the moment of decision,* the consumer knew how to get more for the money, he or she would do so.

There are many superficial events or conditions, of course, that might influence one particular consumer's decision about a particular purchase at a given time. But underlying these superficial variations is a sustained and consistent pattern of consumer behavior in which the consumer attempts to obtain maximum utility from a limited income. The consumer does this by allocating income to expenditures on various commodities according to a personal perception of marginal utility per dollar.

Consumers' efforts to get the most for their money are reflected in market demand curves, which are simply the aggregate of all individual consumer demand curves. Since utility is based on individual taste and preferences, each market demand curve reflects market preferences. As such, a market demand curve is a powerful signal to the producer about what and how much to produce.

Effects of Advertising and Promotion

The model of consumer behavior depicted by Equation (3) shows that a consumer's purchases are regulated by the ratio of marginal utility to price. This ratio fluctuates when either marginal utility or price is

---

[1] Equation (3) can be derived mathematically by using the differential calculus procedure for constrained optimization, as shown in Appendix 4A at the end of this chapter.

changed. For example, suppose beef sales are rising at the expense of pork sales. The implication is that there is an imbalance in the equation such that

$$\frac{MU_{beef}}{P_{beef}} > \frac{MU_{pork}}{P_{pork}}$$

This inequality shows that the consumer receives more utility per dollar from beef than from pork. As a homemaker buys more beef and less pork, the marginal utility of beef will decline and the marginal utility of pork will rise until the ratios are equal.

In these circumstances, how can the producers of pork halt the decline of their sales? They have two options: (1) reduce the price of pork to equalize the ratios, or (2) change the marginal utility of pork. Since the utility of any commodity exists *only in the consumer's mind,* marginal utility may be changed by persuasive advertising and promotion. Promotion may include point-of-sale displays, distribution of recipes for pork dishes, or anything that will enhance the image of pork as a desirable food.

Marginal Utility and Demand Curves

A consumer's demand curve can be derived from marginal utility data. As we have seen, when the consumer is at equilibrium, the marginal utility per dollar for any particular commodity is equal to the marginal utility of money, i.e.,

$$\frac{MU_X}{P_X} = MU_M \tag{4}$$

Hence

$$P_X = \frac{MU_X}{MU_M} \tag{5}$$

To simplify, suppose the marginal utility of money is constant. Any number will do, but suppose we say $MU_M = 2$. Referring to the utility function on Exhibit 4–2, we can see that prices would be calculated as shown by Exhibit 4–3.

The quantity demanded, Q_X, and the price, P_X, may be graphed as the linear demand curve in Exhibit 4–4.

Marginal Utility and Consumer Surplus

The downward sloping demand curve in Exhibit 4–4 is predicated upon there being a different price for each unit consumed. But we know

Exhibit 4–3

Marginal Utility and Price

Q	MU_X	MU_M	P_X
0	20	2	10
1	16	2	8
2	12	2	6
3	8	2	4
4	4	2	2
5	0	2	0

Exhibit 4–4

Linear Demand Curve

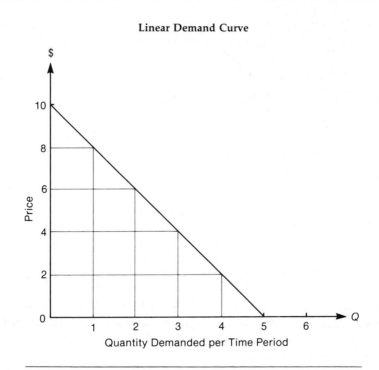

Quantity Demanded per Time Period

products are not priced this way. As shown in Exhibit 4–5, a single price is set for all units demanded at that price.

The shaded rectangular area in Exhibit 4–5 represents the total amount paid for three units of the commodity at a price of $4 per unit. The diagram shows that the consumer is willing to pay $8 for the first unit and $6 for the second unit. Thus the consumer has received a

Exhibit 4–5

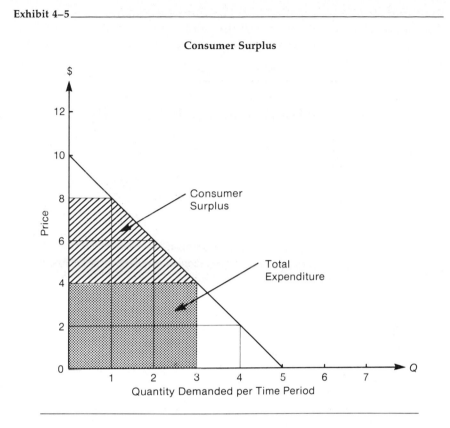

Consumer Surplus

"surplus" of utility, as represented by the area of the cross-hatched triangle, which is worth (½)(3 × $6) = $9.

The question arises: Why doesn't the seller raise the price and thus recover the consumer surplus? The answer is: Because at a higher price, the quantity now being sold would not be sold. The point is that *as long as there is a single price for a commodity, that price will be established by the marginal utility of the last or least valuable unit sold.* Thus we may define consumer surplus as the extra utility that consumers get but do not pay for because they are required to pay only the price set by the marginal utility of the least valuable unit purchased.

This principle explains why some commodities, such as gems and precious metals, are very expensive while other commodities, such as water, are low priced. In most places, water is so plentiful that the last gallon, which we are willing to pour upon the ground, is not worth much. But in the desert, where water is very scarce, the last pint of drinking water may be worth more than gold or diamonds. Thus when water is abundant, it is a product whose marginal utility becomes very low even when its total utility is very high. An even more striking example is the air we breathe. Its total utility is the value of life itself. But the supply of air is so plentiful that the price of the last cubic foot that we breathe is zero. Therefore, we pay nothing for the first precious life-sustaining breath.

The Ordinal Approach to Utility

The cardinal utility concept offers useful insights into consumer behavior, but the inability to actually measure utility in a cardinal manner limits its usefulness. In particular, it is difficult to connect consumer preferences, which are *subjective,* to changes in prices, incomes, and other *objective* variables in the marketplace. Consequently, economists have developed an alternative model. The *ordinal* approach requires only that combinations of consumed commodities be ranked in order of preference. Ordinal ranking takes the place of cardinal measurement.

The ordinal approach to demand analysis uses the same basic assumptions as those used with the cardinal approach. In addition, it is assumed that consumers are able to rank all conceivable bundles of commodities. That is, when confronted with two or more bundles of goods and services, consumers can determine an order of preference among them.

Order of preference does not require consumers to estimate how much utility will be attained from a bundle of commodities. Only the ability to rank is fundamental. For example, when a homemaker goes to the supermarket, she doesn't count utils for each commodity. She simply chooses the preferred commodities that she thinks will give her the most satisfaction for her money. Furthermore, the degree of preference is irrelevant. It is quite enough for the consumer to think, subjectively and idiosyncratically, that one commodity or bundle of commodities is better than another.

In more precise terms, we assume that the consumer's preference pattern possesses the following characteristics:

1. Given three bundles of goods (A, B, and C), if an individual prefers A to B and B to C, he must prefer A to C. Similarly, if an individual is indifferent between A and B and between B and C, he must be indifferent between A and C. Finally, if he is indifferent between A and B and prefers B to C, he must prefer A to C. This assumption obviously can be carried over to four or more different bundles.
2. If an individual can rank any pair of bundles chosen at random from all conceivable bundles, he can rank all conceivable bundles.
3. If bundle A contains at least as many units of each commodity as bundle B, and more units of at least one commodity, A must be preferred to B.

Now that we understand our basic assumptions and the consumer's preference pattern, we are ready to consider the concept of the indifference curve and the budget line, which are used to derive the consumer equilibrium model.

Indifference Curves

Consumers purchase and use varying quantities of many different commodities, a fact captured by the total utility function *TU*:

$$TU = f(X_1, X_2, \ldots, X_n) \tag{6}$$

where $(X_1, X_2, \ldots, X_n)$ represents the quantities consumed per period of time of a set of commodities. Fortunately for our analysis, we need to consider only two commodities at a time. Suppose *X* represents the quantities consumed per period of time of one commodity and *Y* the quantity consumed per period of time of another commodity or bundle of commodities. Then Equation (1) reduces to

$$TU = f(X,Y) \tag{7}$$

This equation describes the surface of a three-dimensional figure, an example of which is shown in Exhibit 4–6.

By repeatedly passing a plane through the figure in Exhibit 4–6, keeping it parallel to the base, level curves such as *AA*, *BB*, and *CC* are traced on the surface. Each curve represents the locus of all possible combinations of *X* and *Y* that yield equal utility. For example, at the left end of the curve *AA*, the combination of Y_1 units of commodity *Y* and *A'* units of commodity *X* yields *A* utils of total utility, whatever a util may be. At the right end of the line, the combination of X_1 units of *X* and *A'* units of *Y* also yields *A* utils of utility. The curve *AA* represents all other combinations of *X* and *Y* that also yield *A* utils of utility. Logically, the consumer would be indifferent as to which of these combinations is consumed. Consumers would not be indifferent, however, as to which level of utility is reached, since we assume consumers always seek the highest level of utility their incomes will allow.

When these level curves are projected onto the *X–Y* base of the figure the result is a set of indifference curves on an indifference map, such as *A'A'*, *B'B'*, and *C'C'* in Exhibit 4–6. The *X–Y* base on which the indifference map is drawn is called the *commodity space*.

Definition: An *indifference curve* is the locus of all combinations of commodities *X* and *Y* that yield the same level of total utility or satisfaction. An *indifference map* is a graph that shows a set of indifference curves.

Exhibit 4–7 shows a typical indifference map on which the curves U_1, U_2, and U_3 represent three of the many possible utility levels derived

Exhibit 4–6

Total Utility Gained from Consumption of X and Y

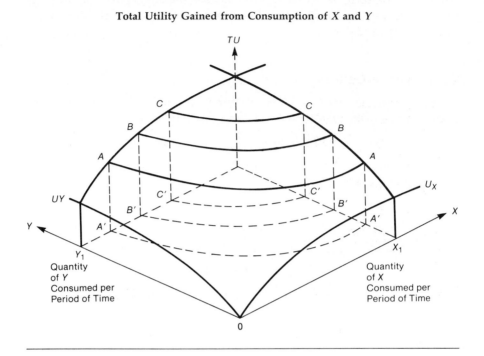

from the consumption of various combinations of X and Y during the same period of time. Since all the points along any one curve represent equal levels of satisfaction, the consumer would have no preference among positions A, B, C, or D on the figure. Any of these points, however, would be preferable to position W, which lies on a lower curve.

Characteristics of Indifference Curves. Indifference curves have five elementary properties that are important for an understanding of consumer behavior:

1. There are an infinite number of indifference curves; therefore, every point in the commodity space lies on an indifference curve.
2. Indifference curves are continuous and downward-sloping.
3. The farther away from the origin an indifference curve is, the higher the level of utility it represents.
4. Indifference curves are concave from above (convex to the origin).
5. Indifference curves cannot intersect, as illustrated in Exhibit 4–8.

Exhibit 4–7

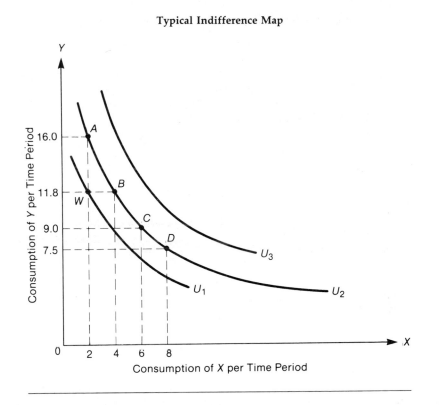

Typical Indifference Map

As shown in Exhibit 4–8, if two indifference curves intersect at point P, then to the left of P, IC_1 represents a higher level of utility than IC_2; but to the right of point P, IC_2 represents more utility than IC_1. Since each curve represents the same level of utility throughout, their intersection is logically impossible.

Curves that do not exhibit all of the properties described above are excluded from our analysis.[2]

Marginal Rate of Substitution

In the preceding discussion, it was seen that indifference curves are concave from above and downward-sloping. These characteristics arise from the assumption of diminishing marginal utility that was built into

_____

[2] Excluded curves include those for perfect substitutes, those for perfect complements, and those for situations where one commodity is good but the other is not desirable. Students may consult a standard price theory text for further explanation.

Exhibit 4-8

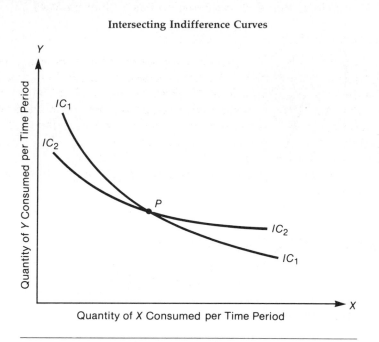

Intersecting Indifference Curves

Quantity of Y Consumed per Time Period

Quantity of X Consumed per Time Period

the utility surface from which the indifference curves were derived. Since diminishing marginal utility plays such a crucial role in the consumer behavior model, it must be thoroughly understood.

As previously noted, different combinations of commodities can provide equal levels of total utility. When a consumer remains on the same indifference curve, one commodity can be substituted for the other so that the consumer remains as well off as before. The rate at which a consumer is willing to make such a substitution is a matter of great interest and importance. We call it the marginal rate of substitution, X for Y, defined as follows:

Definition: The marginal rate of substitution, X for Y, (written MRS_{XY}) indicates the number of units of Y that must be given up to acquire one additional unit of X while satisfying the condition of constant total utility.

The MRS_{XY} is a rate of change. It is measured as the slope of the indifference curve, which is different at each point along the curve.[3]

---

[3] To find the slope at a particular point P, draw a line tangent to the curve at P. Using a segment of this line as a hypotenuse, complete a right triangle with base ΔX and

Since each point represents a different combination of commodities X and Y, it follows that each combination has a different MRS_{XY}.

Relationship between MU and MRS

Is there a relationship between marginal utility and the marginal rate of substitution? Indeed there is, since the slope of the indifference curve is the direct result of the law of diminishing marginal utility. To understand the relationship, consider what happens when we move down the indifference curve between any two points. Consumption of Y is reduced by $-\Delta Y$ units, causing a loss of utility of $-\Delta Y \cdot MU_Y$ utils. But since total utility is unchanged as we move down the curve, the loss of utility from conserving less Y is precisely offset by a gain from consuming more X, i.e.,

$$-\Delta Y \cdot MU_Y = \Delta X \cdot MU_X$$

Dividing both sides by $\Delta X \cdot MU_Y$, we get

$$\frac{-\Delta Y \cdot MU_Y}{\Delta X \cdot MU_Y} = \frac{\Delta X \cdot MU_X}{\Delta X \cdot MU_Y}$$

so that the slope of the curve is

$$\frac{\Delta Y}{\Delta X} = -\frac{MU_X}{MU_Y}$$

To illustrate, let us return to Exhibit 4–7, which is drawn so that the consumption of X increases in increments of 2 units. All points on the indifference curve U_2 yield the same level of total utility; but as we move down the curve, successively smaller increments of Y are given up in order to increase X by one increment without changing total utility.

---

height ΔY. The slope of the tangent line is $\Delta Y/\Delta X$, and this is the slope of the curve at P.

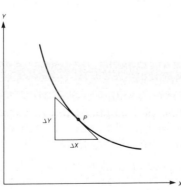

At point A, the consumer is using 16 units of Y and 2 units of X to gain a certain level of total utility represented by the indifference curve U_2. Now suppose that 4.2 units of Y are taken away, forcing the consumer to point W on the lower indifference curve, U_1. The change in utility from this move is:

$$\Delta U_Y = -\Delta Y \cdot MU_Y = -4.2 MU_Y$$

where MU_Y means the marginal utility of Y and the minus sign indicates a loss of total utility. But the lost utility can be restored by substituting 2 more units of X. This moves the consumer back onto the indifference curve U_2 at point B. The utility gained from 2 more units of X is:

$$\Delta U_X = \Delta X \cdot MU_X = 2 MU_X$$

Since total utility at point B is equal to total utility at point A, then

$$2 MU_X = -4.2 MU_Y$$

hence

$$\frac{MU_X}{MU_Y} = \frac{-4.2}{2} = -2.1$$

indicating a negative slope.

Now, as we go from point B to point C, we have

$$MRS_{XY} = \frac{MU_X}{MU_Y} = \frac{-2.8}{2} = -1.4$$

then from point C to point D we have

$$MRS_{XY} = \frac{MU_X}{MU_Y} = \frac{-1.5}{2} = -0.75$$

The pattern is clear: The more of X consumed, the less its marginal utility in relation to the marginal utility of Y; that is to say, the MRS_{XY} declines as more X is consumed. This explains why the indifference curve is concave from above. Only such a curve can satisfy the condition of a continuously declining slope.

The continuously declining MRS is the logical result of the assumption that marginal utility of a commodity decreases as we obtain more of it. It follows, then, that the more of a commodity a person has, the more willing he is to trade it for another commodity. For example, a person with ten shirts and one pair of shoes might be willing to trade three shirts for another pair of shoes. But if he had three pairs of shoes and only five shirts he might be willing to trade only one shirt for another pair of shoes.

The Budget Line

Indifference curves show what a consumer is *willing* to do. They reflect his or her personal feelings about the relative value of consumption combinations of any two commodities. They are totally independent of the consumer's income and market prices, but income and market prices determine what a consumer is *able* to do, as distinguished from what he is *willing* to do.

The consumer's ability to buy Commodities X and Y is determined by the budget constraint, which can be expressed graphically as the *budget line*, or *line of attainable combinations*. To illustrate, suppose a consumer has a limited amount of money to spend on Commodities X and Y. Let us also suppose that he will spend all of his income on X and Y. The budget equation then is:

$$B = Q_X \cdot P_X + Q_Y \cdot P_Y \tag{8}$$

where

B = Consumer budget (income) available for the purchase of X and Y

Q_X and Q_Y = Quantity of Commodity X and Commodity Y, respectively, purchased during some given period of time

P_X and P_Y = Price of Commodity X and Commodity Y, respectively

To explain the budget line, suppose a consumer has $25 to spend on X and Y, both of which cost $5 per unit. As illustrated in Exhibit 4–9, if the entire budget were spent on Y the consumer could purchase 5 units of Y. Hence the Y-intercept is at (0,5). Likewise, if the entire budget were spent on X the consumer could purchase 5 units of X. Hence the X-intercept is at (5,0). The budget line is represented by the straight line B_1 between the two intercepts.

Definition: The budget line is the locus of all combinations of commodities X and Y that can be purchased when all available income is spent on X and Y.

Exhibit 4–9 also shows a family of budget lines for three levels of income. With the price of X and Y remaining constant at $5 per unit, line B_2 represents a budget of $50, and line B_3 represents a budget of $75. The lines are parallel because the prices have not changed. Line B_4, however, has a different slope because the prices have changed to $7 per unit for X and $3 per unit for Y, applied to a $50 budget.

For any budget line, the Y intercept is at B/P_Y and the X intercept is at B/P_X. If we move down the line from the Y-intercept to the X-intercept,

Exhibit 4–9

A Family of Budget Lines

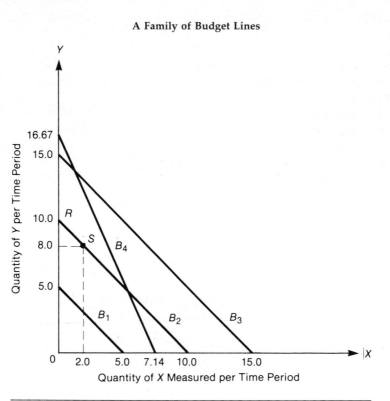

the change in Y is $-B/P_Y$ units and the change in X is B/P_X units. Therefore the slope of the line is

$$\frac{\Delta Y}{\Delta X} = \frac{-B/P_Y}{B/P_X} = -\frac{P_X}{P_Y}$$

The equation states that the slope of the budget line is the negative ratio of the price of X to the price of Y.

Consumer Equilibrium

The principal assumption upon which the theory of consumer behavior rests is that the *consumer attempts to allocate his limited money income to purchase available goods and services so as to maximize his satisfaction (utility).* In other words, the consumer must achieve an *equilibrium* between what he is *willing* to purchase and what he is *able* to purchase at the highest possible level of satisfaction.

Exhibit 4–10

Illustration of Consumer Equilibrium

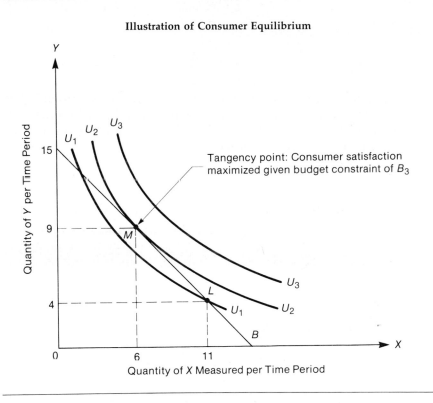

As illustrated in Exhibit 4–10, the point of equilibrium can be located by drawing the budget line on the indifference map for commodities X and Y. Since there is an infinite number of indifference curves upon the indifference map, one curve will be tangent to the budget line, regardless of where the budget line lies. The point of tangency is the point of equilibrium, representing the attainable combination of X and Y that gives the highest level of utility.

Exhibit 4–10 illustrates that budget line B is tangent to the highest possible indifference curve, U_L, at point M where the consumer acquires nine units of Y and six units of X. It should not be difficult to see why point M is preferable to any other point on B. For example, point L also exhausts the income, but it clearly offers less total utility than point M because it lies on a lower indifference curve.

At the point of tangency of the indifference curve and the budget line, the negative slope of the indifference curve, MU_X/MU_Y equals the negative slope of the budget line, P_X/P_Y, i.e.,

$$\frac{MU_X}{MU_Y} = \frac{P_X}{P_Y} \tag{9}$$

which is easily manipulated to give

$$\frac{MU_X}{P_X} = \frac{MU_Y}{P_Y} \tag{10}$$

The conclusion from this two-commodity case can be extended to cover all possible goods the consumer might purchase, including future consumption. The general equation for achieving an optimal allocation of income among all commodities is

$$\frac{MU_A}{P_A} = \frac{MU_B}{P_B} = \cdots = \frac{MU_N}{P_N} \tag{11}$$

which is the same model provided by the cardinal approach. The model states that total utility from consumption is maximized when the consumer's income is allocated in such a way that the marginal utility per dollar expenditure on each commodity is equal. As before, this model includes the marginal utility of money held in savings or otherwise unspent as a commodity with a price of $1 per dollar held.

Summary

Consumer behavior is best explained in terms of *utility*, which is defined as the satisfaction gained from having, using, or consuming goods or services. Conceptually, utility can be cardinally measured in units called utils, even though we are unable to define a util. Marginal utility is defined as the change in total utility caused by a one-unit increase in consumption of some commodity (good or service). Thinking of total utility as a function of consumption enables us to establish the law of diminishing marginal utility, which says that marginal utility decreases as consumption increases, and becomes zero at the saturation point, where total utility is maximum. Further consumption will cause disutility to set in, with marginal utility becoming negative and total utility falling. Maximum total utility occurs when the marginal utility per dollar is the same for all commodities, including money (savings), i.e.,

$$\frac{MU_A}{P_A} = \frac{MU_B}{P_B} = \cdots = \frac{MU_N}{P_N}$$

When this equation prevails, the consumer is said to be in equilibrium, receiving the most for his money. A consumer may be thrown out of equilibrium by a change in price or a change in marginal utility. Since utility exists only in the consumer's mind, advertising and promotion constitute attempts by the seller to change the consumer's perception of utility.

The consumer's demand curve for a particular commodity is directly related to marginal utility. The downward-sloping demand curve is predicated upon there being a different price for each unit demanded. In reality, however, a price is set and all units demanded at that price are purchased at that price. Since the consumer would be willing to pay more for a smaller quantity, a *consumer surplus* is said to exist. However, as long as there is a single price for a commodity, that price will be established by the marginal utility of the last, least-valuable unit to be sold.

The equation for consumer equilibrium can also be reached by an ordinal approach, which requires only that the consumer be able to rank commodities in order of preference. When such an order is established, pairs of commodities may be combined in an infinite number of quantities yielding an equal level of satisfaction. Graphing these combinations results in an *indifference curve* on an *indifference map*.

The slope of an indifference curve is called the *marginal rate of substitution, MRS_{XY}*, and is equal to MU_X/MU_Y. It represents the quantity of one commodity, Y, that must be given up in order to obtain one more unit of the other commodity, X, without changing total utility. The MRS_{XY} diminishes as we move down the curve, as a direct result of the law of diminishing marginal utility.

Indifference curves portray what a consumer is *willing* to do. What the consumer is *able* to do is portrayed by a *budget line*, or *line of attainable combinations*. The budget line is defined as the locus of all combinations of commodities X and Y that can be purchased by full expenditure of a given income, or budget. The slope of the budget line is the ratio of commodity prices, i.e., P_X/P_Y.

When the budget line is drawn upon an indifference map it is tangent to some indifference curve at a particular point or combination of X and Y. This is the maximum total utility attainable within the constraint of the budget and is the point of consumer equilibrium. At that point, the slope of the indifference curve and the slope of the budget line are the same; hence,

$$\frac{MU_X}{MU_Y} = \frac{P_X}{P_Y}$$

Therefore,

$$\frac{MU_X}{P_X} = \frac{MU_Y}{P_Y}$$

More generally, the equation for consumer equilibrium in the allocation of income among all commodities is

$$\frac{MU_A}{P_A} = \frac{MU_B}{P_B} = \cdots = \frac{MU_N}{P_N}$$

Problems

1. An indifference map and budget line are indicated below. Assume X costs $8 per unit.

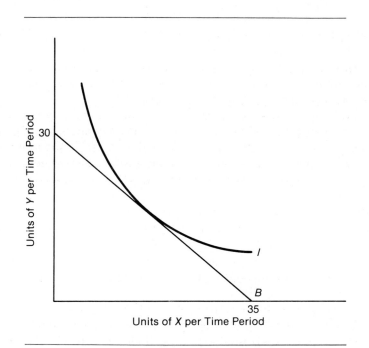

a. What is the total amount that could be spent on Y? What is the price of Y?

b. Calculate the equation for the budget line B.

c. Draw a new budget line with the cost of X increasing to $12 per unit. Using the indifference map, will this increase or decrease total utility?

d. Assume the cost of X is $8 and Y is $5. Indicate the new budget line when total expenditures are reduced to $200.

2. Construct an indifference curve for two products, X and Z. Also, construct a budget line tangent to the indifference curve at some point.

Now, assume the preferences for X increase because of a successful advertising program, while the preferences for Z decline. Construct a new equilibrium position reflecting these changes and discuss your answer.

3.   Suppose a shopper is equally satisfied by the following combinations of goods:

Oranges	Apples
3	9
5	7
7	5
9	3
11	1

a.   What is the marginal rate of substitution between oranges and apples? Does it vary?
b.   In the shopper's opinion, which has greater utility, oranges or apples?
c.   Is this a realistic situation? Explain.

4.   Two computer manufacturers both produce and use microchips Q and Z. Corporation One has a marginal rate of substitution between Q and Z equal to 6Q for 5Z; Corporation Two's MRS is 13Q for 10Z.
a.   Does it make sense for the corporations to swap microchips?
b.   If a trade were to take place, what would be traded and why?

5.   Assume:

$$\frac{MU_{savings}}{P_{savings}} < \frac{MU_{new\ car}}{P_{new\ car}}$$

a.   Assuming constant prices, what would result from this situation? Why?
b.   What would result from an increase in car prices?
c.   What would result from a jump in money market rates?

6.   If the consumer is presently in equilibrium with $P_X = \$7$ and $P_Y = \$13$, what is the slope of the indifference curve at the point of equilibrium?

7.   List at least six independent variables that will likely influence the demand for new automobiles. Indicate whether their effect is positive or negative when estimating the demand function.

8.   Business executives often receive many fringe benefits: free trips, company cars, and stock options. Considering the progressive tax system, why might fringe benefits have a greater utility than higher salaries? What would be the effect of a 20 percent flat income tax rate?

9.   Jack Miller hopes to get into the school of engineering next semester. For acceptance he must raise his grade point average by 0.15. Today

is the last day of classes so Jack has five days left in which to prepare for final exams, In desperation, Jack asks you, a distinguished economics major, to help him maximize his grade point average. Jack's final exam in chemistry represents 35 percent of his final grade; in calculus, 35 percent; and in mechanical analysis, 30 percent. Since mechanical analysis is a major requirement, the grade is twice as important as the others for admittance to the school of engineering.

If Jack plans to study for seven hours each day, how many hours should he spend in preparation for each final exam?

Case Problem: Alaskan Telephone & Telegraph

10.   The town of Skyridge, Alaska sprang up almost overnight. In 1979, a large iron ore deposit was discovered near Skyridge and in two years the town boomed from 150 to 7,700 residences. Because of the increased population, Alaskan Telephone & Telegraph, a public utility, is now required by law to make telephone service available to every residence in Skyridge. Skyridge's remote location and relatively small population make installation costs for telephone service greater than potential revenues. However, after the system is completed the cost of service is essentially independent of the number of subscribers.

To establish a pricing policy, Alaskan Telephone conducted a demand analysis in Skyridge. The staff economist estimated the demand for telephone service to be:

$$Q = 5,800 - 150P$$

where

Q = Number of customers
P = Monthly bill for service

Questions:
a.   What is the optimal monthly service change? Explain using both algebraic and graphical techniques.
b.   The town of Skyridge, seeking additional tax revenues, plans to levy a license fee on telephone service. The telephone company has two alternatives: pay a flat $3 rate per customer or 20 percent of the total dollar sales. Which alternative should Alaskan Telephone select? Again support your conclusions using both equation and graphical techniques.
c.   Alaskan Telephone is licensed to serve the public. Thus, instead of maximizing revenues, its actual goal is to maximize the total utility of telephone service. To say that Alaskan Telephone has maximized utility what assumption must be made? Is this assumption valid?

References

Alchian, A. A. "The Meaning of Utility Measurement." *American Economic Review*, March 1953, pp. 26–50.

Bernardo, John J. "A Programming Approach to Measure Attribute Utilities." *Journal of Economics and Business*, Spring/Summer 1981, pp. 239–45.

Friedman, Milton. *A Theory of the Consumption Function.* Princeton, N.J.: Princeton University Press, 1957.

Henderson, James M., and Richard E. Quandt. *Microeconomic Theory.* 2d ed. New York: McGraw-Hill, 1971.

Hicks, J. R. *A Review of Demand Theory.* London: Oxford University Press, 1959.

Hirshleifer, Jack. *Price Theory and Application.* 2d ed. Englewood Cliffs, N.J.: Prentice-Hall, 1980.

Katona, George. "Consumer Behavior: Theory and Findings on Expectations and Aspirations." *American Economic Review*, May 1968, pp. 19–30.

Lancaster, Kelvin J. *Consumer Demand: A New Approach.* New York: Columbia University Press, 1971.

Willig, R. D. "Consumer's Surplus Without Apology." *American Economic Review.* September 1976, pp. 589–97.

Appendix 4A | Mathematics of Consumer Equilibrium

The consumer will spend or save his entire income, so that

$$I = P_1X_1 + P_2X_2 + \cdots + P_nX_n \tag{1}$$

where

$$I = \text{Consumer's income}$$
$$X_1, X_2, \ldots, X_n = \text{Quantities of } n \text{ commodities, one of which is savings}$$
$$P_1, P_2, \ldots, P_n = \text{Price of each of the } n \text{ commodities, respectively}$$

The consumer wants to maximize

$$TU = f(X_1, X_2, \ldots X_n) \tag{2}$$

subject to the constraint of Equation (1) above. Equation (2) is maximized when all of its partial derivatives and the constraint equation (1) are equal to zero. However, this gives a system of $n + 1$ equations with only n variables, which we cannot solve. Therefore, an artificial variable (λ) known as the Lagrangian multiplier must be introduced.

After setting the constraint equation equal to zero, we multiply it by λ and add the result to Equation (2). This gives:

$$TU = f(X_1, X_2, \ldots X_n) \\ + \lambda(I - P_1X_1 - P_2X_2 - \cdots - P_nX_n) \tag{3}$$

The marginal utility of each commodity is its own partial derivative. Taking the partial derivatives of Equation (3), we get:

$$\frac{\partial TU}{\partial X_1} = MU_{X_1} - \lambda P_1 = 0 \tag{4}$$

$$\frac{\partial TU}{\partial X_2} = MU_{X_2} - \lambda P_2 = 0 \tag{5}$$

$$\frac{\partial TU}{\partial X_n} = MU_{X_n} - \lambda P_n = 0 \tag{6}$$

$$\frac{\partial TU}{\partial \lambda} = I - P_1X_1 - P_2X_2 - \cdots - P_nX_n \tag{7}$$

Equation (7) says that the entire income is spent (or saved) when total utility is at a maximum. Dividing Equations (4), (5), and (6) by P_1, P_2, . . . , P_n, respectively, we get

$$\frac{MU_{X_1}}{P_1} = \lambda; \quad \frac{MU_{X_2}}{P_2} = \lambda; \quad \frac{MU_{X_n}}{P_n} = \lambda$$

Things equal to the same thing are also equal to each other. Since money is one of the commodities, we conclude that total utility is at a maximum when the marginal utility of the last dollar spent or saved is the same for all commodities, i.e.,

$$\frac{MU_A}{P_A} = \frac{MU_B}{P_B} = \cdots = \frac{MU_N}{P_N} \tag{8}$$

Demand Functions and Elasticities of Demand

To a professional economist, the term *demand* has a specific meaning. It refers to the number of units of a particular commodity (good or service) that consumers are willing and able to buy under explicitly stated conditions of time, place, price, and so forth. Thus demand is a function of a number of independent variables or demand determinants, and can be expressed as an algebraic equation.

In the first section of this chapter, we examine the concept of the market demand function, which in a very real sense is the market manifestation of the variables derived from consumer behavior theory, which was discussed in the preceding chapter. Management controls some of these variables, such as the price and quality of the product, customer service, and the advertising budget. Other variables, such as consumer tastes, preferences, and expectations, cannot be controlled by the firm, but they can be influenced by skillful advertising and promotion. Still other variables, such as consumer income, prices of related products, the range of goods and services available, the number of potential consumers, and interest rates, are completely beyond management's control. Regardless of the degree of control a firm exercises over particular demand variables, however, it must be able to measure their effects on demand in order to develop a successful marketing strategy.

142

The most commonly used measurement of the sensitivity of demand to a change in any demand variable is *elasticity*, which is explained in the second section of the chapter. After that, the remainder of the chapter is devoted to discussion of four demand elasticities that are most commonly encountered in economic analysis as well as in marketing, finance, and other disciplines.

Market Demand Functions

Businessmen and economists know that the demand for most products is affected by many factors other than price. Nevertheless, it is the effect of price on demand, when all other variables are held constant, that is of most concern in the demand theory of microeconomics. In notational shorthand,

$$Q_d = f(P|X_1, X_2, \ldots, X_n)$$

where Q_d = quantity demanded, P = price, and $X_1, X_2, \ldots, X_n$ are all other demand determinants, which are held constant, as indicated by the vertical line.

Markets and market demand vary tremendously in size, arrangement, and dynamics. For example, the United States as a whole is the market for a wide range of household products, whereas only those states with heavy winter snowfalls form the domestic market for such goods as snowmobiles. Likewise, the market for collectibles, such as rare coins, paintings, and stamps, consists of only a few customers scattered all over the world. All markets are alike, however, in that they consist of buyers and sellers, with third parties such as brokers or agents occasionally providing auxiliary services to bring buyers and sellers together.

In the preceding chapter, we saw that demand is created by the behavior of individual consumers. Individual consumer demand curves show the quantity of a particular commodity purchased at a particular time and place, at each price within some range of prices. The market demand curve is the horizontal summation of all consumer demand curves in that market. That is, individual demand quantities for a given price are combined to get the market demand for the product at that price. This summation, repeated for all prices, results in the market demand curve.

Quantity Demanded versus Change in Demand

The student must be careful to distinguish changes in the quantity demanded from changes in demand. When the price changes while all other variables are held constant, the result is a change in the quantity demanded. As illustrated in panel A of Exhibit 5–1, lowering the price

Exhibit 5–1_____

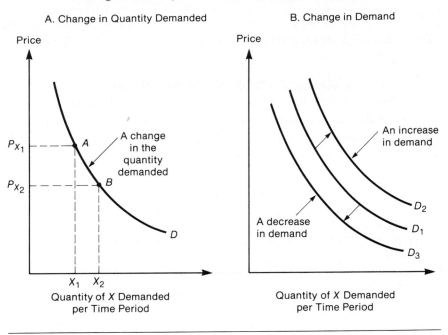

Change in Quantity Demanded versus Change in Demand

A. Change in Quantity Demanded   B. Change in Demand

from P_{X_1} to P_{X_2} causes movement along the demand curve from point A to point B. The quantity demanded changes from X_1 to X_2.

Panel B of Exhibit 5–1 illustrates the effect of changing income. For example, starting with the demand curve D_1, an increase in income causes the whole curve to shift outward to D_2. Thus a larger quantity is demanded at all price levels. Conversely, a decrease in income reduces the quantity demanded at all price levels, and the entire curve shifts to D_3. This is the meaning of the term change in demand, *which can be caused by a change in any variable other than price.*

The Nature of the Demand Function

When an economist speaks of market demand or the demand curve, these terms refer to demand as a function of price alone. However, the same analysis that leads to demand as a function of price can be used to calculate demand as a function of any other single variable, with all other variables held constant. To illustrate, suppose that a large food processor has identified the multivariate demand function for a brand of Swiss cheese that it markets on a national basis. The function is:

$$Q_X = 5.0 - 10.0P_X + 15.0P_Y - 25.0P_Z + 0.001I$$

where

Q_X = Annual consumption per family of Brand X Swiss cheese, in pounds

P_X = Price per pound of Brand X Swiss cheese

P_Y = Price per pound of competing brands of Swiss cheese

P_Z = Price index of 10-ounce packages of snack-type crackers

I = Median annual family income

The parameters of Equation (1) show the effect of each variable upon the overall demand when all other variables are held constant, as follows:

1. $-10.0P_X$ indicates that a $1 increase in the price of Brand X Swiss cheese will cause a 10-pound decrease in its annual consumption per family.

2. $15.0P_Y$ indicates that a $1 increase in the price of competing brands will cause a 15-pound increase in consumption of Brand X.

3. $-25.0P_Z$ indicates that a 100 percent increase in the price of complementary snack-type crackers will cause a 25-pound decrease in the consumption of Brand X Swiss cheese.

4. $0.001I$ indicates that a $1,000 increase in median family income will cause a 1-pound increase in consumption of Brand X Swiss cheese.

Now let us assume the following values of the variables for the upcoming year: P_X = $2.50, P_Y = $3.00, P_Z = $1.00, and I = $15,000. Exhibit 5–2 shows that expected sales next year of Brand X Swiss cheese are 15.0

Exhibit 5–2 _____

Demand Function: Estimate of the Sales of Brand X Swiss Cheese

(1) Independent Variable	(2) Expected Value of Independent Variable	(3) Value of Parameter in Demand Equation	(4) Total Effect (2) × (3)
P_X	2.50	−10.0	−25.0
P_Y	3.00	+15.0	+45.0
P_Z	1.00	−25.0	−25.0
I	15,000.00	+0.001	⎸15.0
Constant term			+ 5.0
Expected Sales			+15.0

pounds per family. The accuracy of the forecast will depend, of course, upon the reliability of the parameter values in the forecasting equation, and also upon whether or not any other factors exert any influence on Q_X.

The quantity-estimating equations for each independent variable— when all other variables are held constant—are as follows:

$$Q_X = (+45.0 - 25.0 + 15.0 + 5.0) - 10.0P_X = 40.0 - 10.0P_X$$
$$Q_X = (-25.0 - 25.0 + 15.0 + 5.0) + 15.0P_Y = 30.0 + 15.0P_Y$$
$$Q_X = (-25.0 + 45.0 + 15.0 + 5.0) - 25.0P_Z = 40.0 - 25.0P_Z$$
$$Q_X = (-25.0 + 45.0 - 25.0 + 5.0) + 0.001\ I = 0.0 + 0.0001\ I$$

For example, in the case of the variable P_X, if P_Y, P_Z, and I are held constant, then

$$Q_X = f(P_X | P_Y, P_Z, I) = 40 - 10.0P_X$$

When the expected value of each variable is inserted into its own equation, each of the four quantity-estimating equations gives the same answer:

$$Q_X = 15.0$$

Exhibit 5–3 presents the four equations in graphic form. All of the graphs on Exhibit 5–3 except panel A are in mathematically conventional form with the independent variable on the horizontal axis. Because of the way in which demand curves (as a function of price) are derived, it is customary to represent the independent variable, price, by the vertical axis. That causes no trouble here, but correct identification of the dependent and independent variables is crucial to the calculation of elasticity. This will be discussed later in the chapter, but first it is important to discuss some other factors that might affect demand.

Other Demand Determinants

There are many other determinants of demand, such as consumer tastes and preferences, advertising and promotion, the number of potential customers, consumer expectations, interest rates, and the availability of credit. Some are quantifiable, but many are not. Two nonquantifiable factors of particular interest are the differences between durable and nondurable goods, and the differences between markets for consumer goods and producer's goods.

Durable versus Nondurable Goods.   Durable goods are broadly defined as those lasting for more than 12 months of normal usage. The chief characteristics of durable goods are that they can be stored and that their purchases can be postponed. This causes the market for durable

Exhibit 5–3

Diagrams of Quantity-Estimating Equations for the Individual Variables in the Demand Function for Brand X Swiss Cheese

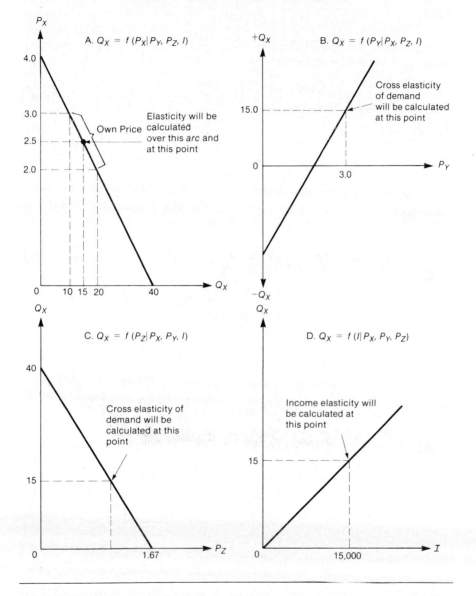

A. $Q_X = f(P_X | P_Y, P_Z, I)$

Elasticity will be
Own Price calculated
over this *arc* and
at this point

B. $Q_X = f(P_Y | P_X, P_Z, I)$

Cross elasticity
of demand
will be calculated
at this point

C. $Q_X = f(P_Z | P_X, P_Y, I)$

Cross elasticity of
demand will be
calculated at this
point

D. $Q_X = f(I | P_X, P_Y, P_Z)$

Income elasticity will
be calculated at
this point

goods to be much more volatile than the market for nondurable goods. In times of inflation, a consumer might make an early purchase of a durable good before its price goes up. In times of recession, consumers make the old car, washing machine, or lawnmower last a little longer by having it repaired rather than buying a new one. When the recession ends, however, there is a release of the pent-up demand for durable goods. Thus, the manufacturing of durable goods is characterized by a boom-and-bust demand cycle.

Demand for Producer's Goods.   If goods are created for the ultimate consumer, they are called *consumer goods,* even though they pass through a chain of distribution in which considerable buying and selling takes place. But if goods are produced because they are needed by another firm to make additional products, such goods are called *producer's goods.*

Demand for producer's goods is *derived* from demand for consumer goods. For example, automobiles are consumer goods. But in order to make automobiles, the manufacturer must buy steel, aluminum, copper, plastics, fabrics, rubber goods, paint, other materials, and thousands of fabricated parts. The producers of these goods, in turn, buy their raw materials from other producers. Ultimately, the chain goes back to the earth from which miners, oil drillers, loggers, and farmers extract or grow raw materials.

Producer's goods are input factors of production. Hence, we say derived demand creates *factor markets* for producer's goods. Since producer's goods are more homogeneous than consumer goods, factor markets are more competitive and far more sensitive to price. The buyers of producer's goods are professionals. They are much more knowledgeable about what they buy, and therefore less responsive to *persuasive* advertising or promotion. However, they welcome *informative* advertising and promotion, such as trade shows at which new products are exhibited.

Professional buyers of producer's goods are also more demanding of product quality and supplier integrity. After all, they can't afford a high percentage of rejects in their production because of poor quality of purchased components. Nor can they afford to have their production shut down because a supplier is late in delivering an order. For these reasons as well as price, buyers favor long-term contracts with reliable suppliers.

In analyzing the demand for a producer's good, remember it is a derived demand. Criteria or specifications used by the purchasing agent must be added to the basic determinants of the consumer goods for which the producer's good is an input. When this is done, analysis of demand for the producer's goods is conceptually no different from analysis of demand for consumer's goods.

The Concept of Elasticity

If we lower our product's price, we know that sales will increase, but by how much? And what will happen to our total revenue? What will happen to sales if the disposable income of our customers is increased? What will happen to sales if we increase our advertising budget? Will a change in the price of butter affect the sales of margarine? If so, by how much? These are important questions in the business world, and they all can be answered by the measurement of *elasticity*.

Elasticity is the most commonly used measurement of the sensitivity of the demand function to changes in any of its variables. Yet the concept of elasticity goes far beyond the demand function alone. Indeed, elasticity can be measured for *any* function, and there are many specific types of elasticity in the literature of economics, especially in the study of demand, production, and cost.

Measurement of Elasticity

In general, *the elasticity of any function is defined as the percentage change in the dependent variable that is caused by a one percent change in one independent variable while all other variables are held constant.* The general equation for the measurement of elasticity is:

$$\text{Elasticity} = \frac{\text{Percentage change in the dependent variable}}{\text{Percentage change in the independent variable}}$$

In symbols,

$$\varepsilon = \frac{\Delta Y/Y}{\Delta X/X} = \frac{\Delta Y}{Y} \cdot \frac{X}{\Delta X} = \frac{\Delta Y}{\Delta X} \cdot \frac{X}{Y} \tag{1}$$

where

ε = Elasticity
Y = Quantity of dependent variable
X = Quantity of independent variable
Δ = "The change in"

Thus the elasticity of a function is simply the rate of change, $\Delta Y/\Delta X$, combined with a multiplicative factor, X/Y, which makes it independent of units.

There are two types of elasticity measurement. One is *point elasticity;* the other is *arc elasticity.* Point elasticity is the elasticity of a function at a particular point on the curve, whereas arc elasticity is the average elasticity over a segment of the curve that represents some range of the function.

Point Elasticity. The general definition of elasticity previously given as Equation (1) actually refers to point elasticity, for which ε (epsilon) is the symbol. That is to say,

$$\varepsilon = \frac{\Delta Y}{\Delta X} \cdot \frac{X}{Y} \tag{2}$$

The term $\Delta Y / \Delta X$ approximates the slope of the curve in the neighborhood of point (X, Y) if ΔX is sufficiently small. If we want the precise slope at that point, we call on differential calculus and let ΔX approach its limit of zero. Hence we have the condition $\lim_{\Delta X \to 0} \frac{\Delta Y}{\Delta X}$, which is the definition of the derivative dY/dX. Consequently, we may define point elasticity

$$\varepsilon = \frac{dY}{dX} \cdot \frac{X}{Y} \tag{3}$$

To illustrate, consider the demand function $Q = 30 - 2P$, where Q represents quantity demanded and P represents price. What is the elasticity at the point on the demand curve where $P = 6$? By Equation (2) we get

$$\varepsilon = \frac{dQ}{dP} \cdot \frac{P}{Q} = (-2) \frac{6}{18} = -0.67$$

This may be interpreted to mean that when the price is $6, a 1 percent change in price will cause a 0.67 percent change in quantity demanded. The minus sign indicates that the variables move in opposite directions.

If there are a number of independent variables in a function, the point elasticity of each variable, X_i, can be found by taking partial derivatives, i.e., $\Delta Y / \Delta X_i = \partial Y / \partial X_i$.

Arc Elasticity. The definition of point elasticity in Equation (2) refers to very small incremental movements from point to point along a curve. There are many instances, however, when we are interested in measuring elasticity over a larger segment of the functional curve. If we designate the end points of the arc as (X_1, Y_1) and (X_2, Y_2), a point halfway between them would be $\left(\dfrac{X_2 + X_1}{2}, \dfrac{Y_2 + Y_1}{2}\right)$. The distance or change between the end points would be $\Delta Y = Y_2 - Y_1$ and $\Delta X = X_2 - X_1$. We can then modify Equation (1) to find the elasticity *at the midpoint* of the arc by the formula:

$$\begin{aligned}
E &= \frac{Y_2 - Y_1}{(Y_2 + Y_1)/2} \div \frac{X_2 - X_1}{(X_2 + X_1)/2} \\
&= \frac{(Y_2 - Y_1)/(Y_2 + Y_1)}{(X_2 - X_1)/(X_2 + X_1)} = \frac{(Y_2 - Y_1)(X_2 + X_1)}{(Y_2 + Y_1)(X_2 - X_1)}
\end{aligned} \tag{4}$$

Elastic versus Inelastic.   The coefficient of elasticity determined by either the point or arc formula consists of two components: sign and magnitude. The sign indicates the relative direction of movement between the two variables. If the sign is negative, they move in opposite directions. If it is positive, they move in the same direction. The magnitude (absolute value) of the coefficient indicates the degree of sensitivity of the dependent variable to change in the independent variable, i.e.,

1. If $|\varepsilon| = 1$, the function is unit elastic, meaning that a 1 percent change in the independent variable will cause a 1 percent change in the dependent variable.
2. If $|\varepsilon| > 1$, the function is elastic, meaning that a 1 percent change in the independent variable will cause greater than a 1 percent change in the dependent variable.
3. If $|\varepsilon| < 1$, the function is inelastic, meaning that a 1 percent change in the independent variable will cause less than a 1 percent change in the dependent variable.

The Elasticities of Demand

The general concepts of elasticity noted above will be given concrete meaning in the remainder of the chapter as we discuss specific measures of elasticity that are related to demand. In theory, the demand function has an elasticity for each of its many independent variables. However, we shall confine our discussion to the four demand elasticities that are most widely discussed in the literature of demand theory. These are:

1. *Price elasticity of demand,* which measures the responsiveness of sales to changes in price.
2. *Income elasticity of demand,* which measures the responsiveness of sales to changes in consumer income.
3. *Cross elasticity of demand,* which measures the responsiveness of sales of one commodity to changes in the price of another commodity.
4. *Advertising elasticity,* which measures the responsiveness of sales to changes in the amount spent on advertising and promotion.

The general elasticity formulas given in the preceding section may be adapted to estimating price elasticity by letting P and Q denote price and quantity, respectively. Then the point elasticity formula for measuring the price elasticity of demand in general is

$$\varepsilon_D = \frac{\Delta Q/Q}{\Delta P/P} = \frac{\Delta Q}{\Delta P} \cdot \frac{P}{Q} \tag{5}$$

or, if the function is known,

$$\varepsilon_D = \frac{dQ}{dP} \cdot \frac{P}{Q} \tag{6}$$

To illustrate the application of price elasticity, let's return to Exhibit 5–2, where we have the following demand function for Brand X Swiss cheese:

$$Q_X = 40.0 - 10.0P_X \tag{7}$$

Suppose we want to find the price elasticity when $P_X = \$2.50$. From Equation (7) at a price of $2.50, the quantity demanded will be:

$$Q_X = 40 - 10(2.50) = 15$$

for which the derivative is:

$$\frac{dQ_X}{dP_X} = -10 \tag{8}$$

The price elasticity from Equations (6) and (8) is:

$$\varepsilon_D = -10\left(\frac{2.5}{15}\right) = -1.667$$

meaning that an increase (decrease) of 1 percent in the price of Brand X Swiss cheese leads to 1.667 percent decrease (increase) in the quantity demanded. Similarly, a 10 percent increase (decrease) in the price leads to a 16.67 percent decrease (increase) in the quantity demanded.

Note that demand curves are almost always negatively sloped, since price and quantity demanded are normally inversely related. This means that the price elasticity of demand is almost always negative. Consequently, the negative sign is often omitted in economic discussions because it is assumed to be understood. In any case, the degree of elasticity, which is indicated by the magnitude of the elasticity coefficient, thus can range from zero to infinity.

The arc elasticity of demand (E_D) may be calculated with the formula

$$E_D = \frac{(Q_2 - Q_1)/(Q_2 + Q_1)}{(P_2 - P_1)/(P_2 + P_1)} = \frac{(Q_2 - Q_1)(P_2 + P_1)}{(Q_2 + Q_1)(P_2 - P_1)} \tag{9}$$

Again using the Swiss cheese example, suppose we select two prices: $P_2 = 2.0$ and $P_1 = 2.5$. Then $Q_2 = 20.0$ and $Q_1 = 15.0$. Making the appropriate substitutions in the formula above gives us

$$E_D = \frac{(20 - 15)}{(20 + 15)} \cdot \frac{2.5 + 2.0}{2.0 - 2.5} = -1.29$$

Graphical Measurement of Price Elasticity

Up to now, we have used formulas to calculate price elasticity. But suppose we have constructed a graph of the demand curve from a demand schedule. Is there a way to estimate price elasticity by visual inspection of the curve? The answer is yes. For example, suppose we have the linear demand curve AC, as shown in Exhibit 5–4.

The line AC in Exhibit 5–4 represents a linear demand function. Point B is located at the midpoint of this line. We want to find the elasticity at point B.

Exhibit 5–4

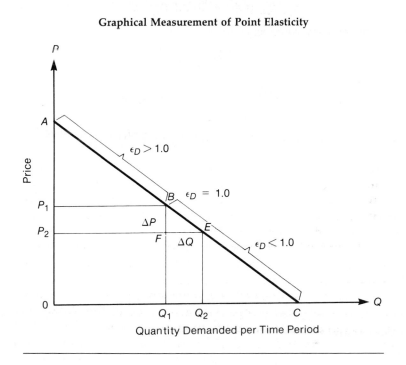

Graphical Measurement of Point Elasticity

Quantity Demanded per Time Period

First, note that the triangles AOC, AP_1B, and BQ_1C are similar, since all of their corresponding angles are the same. Therefore, their corresponding sides are proportional. Since point B is placed such that $AB = BC$ this means that $OQ_1 = Q_1C$ and $OP_1 = P_1A$.

Next, note that triangles BFE and BQ_1C are also similar. Suppose we let the price decrease a very small amount—say, from P_1 to P_2, i.e.,

$$\Delta P = p_1 P_2 = BF$$

This causes the quantity demanded to increase from Q_1 to Q_2, i.e.,

$$\Delta Q = Q_1 Q_2 = FE$$

At point B, the price, P, is OP_1 dollars, and the quantity, Q, is OQ_1 units. Therefore,

$$\varepsilon_D = \frac{\Delta Q}{\Delta P} \frac{P}{Q} = \frac{FE}{BF} \frac{OP_1}{OQ_1} \tag{10}$$

By triangular similarity,

$$\frac{\Delta Q}{\Delta P} = \frac{FE}{BF} = \frac{Q_1 C}{BQ_1}$$

Since $BQ_1 = OP_1$,

$$\frac{\Delta Q}{\Delta P} = \frac{Q_1 C}{BQ_1} = \frac{Q_1 C}{OP_1}$$

By substitution into Equation (10),

$$\varepsilon_D = \frac{\Delta Q}{\Delta P} \cdot \frac{P}{Q} = \frac{Q_1 C}{OP_1} \cdot \frac{OP_1}{OQ_1}$$

Hence,

$$\varepsilon_D = \frac{Q_1 C}{OQ_1} = \frac{BC}{BA}$$

by triangular similarity.

   Since we have located B at the midpoint of the line AC, (i.e., $BC = BA$), we conclude that the linear demand function is unit elastic at the midpoint of AC. It follows that given any point $B_{(Q,P)}$ on a linear demand curve with P-intercept at A and Q-intercept at C,

> If $AB = BC$, or $OP = PA$, or $OQ = QC$, $\varepsilon_D = 1.0$
> If $AB > BC$, or $PA > OP$, or $QC > OQ$, $\varepsilon_D < 1.0$
> If $AB < BC$, or $PA < OP$, or $QC < OQ$, $\varepsilon_D > 1.0$

Curvilinear Function.   To find price elasticity at a point, B, on the graph of a curvilinear demand function, we simply draw a line between the axes and tangent to the demand curve at point B. If we designate the Y-intercept of the straight line as A and the X-intercept as C, then elasticity is the ratio BC/BA, as shown above.

Demand, Revenue, and Price Elasticity

   Since the demand curve plays such a critical role in economic analysis and planning, it is important that we increase both our understanding of it and our ability to work with it in solving business problems. In addition to price elasticity, however, total revenue and marginal revenue are also functionally related to the demand curve. These relationships, along with price elasticity, will now be examined with the aid of the data in Exhibit 5–5, some of which are graphed on Exhibit 5–6.

The data in Exhibit 5–5 are largely self-explanatory. Nevertheless, several comments should be made. First, the demand equation may be

Exhibit 5–5 _____

Total Revenue, Marginal Revenue, and Price Elasticity of the Demand
Curve for Brand X Swiss Cheese:
$$Q_X = 40 - 10P_X$$
$$\text{or } P_X = 4 - .01Q_X$$

Price P_X	Quantity Q_X	Total Revenue TR_X	Marginal Revenue $MR_X = \dfrac{dTR_X}{dQ_X}$	Price Elasticity $\varepsilon_D = \dfrac{dQ_X}{dP_X} \cdot \dfrac{P_X}{Q_X}$	
4.0	0	0	∞	$-\infty$	
3.5	5.0	17.50	3.0	-7.00	
3.0	10.0	30.00	2.0	-3.00	Elastic
2.50	15.0	37.50	1.0	-1.67	
2.00	20.0	40.00	0.0	-1.00	Unit Elastic
1.50	25.0	37.50	-1.0	-0.60	
1.00	30.0	30.00	-2.0	-0.33	
0.50	35.0	17.50	-3.0	-0.14	Inelastic
0	40.0	0	-4.0	0	

written to show that the quantity demanded is a function of the price charged, i.e., $Q = f(P)$. However, price is often established to correspond to the most profitable level of production, i.e., $P = f(Q)$. Mathematically, it doesn't matter which way we do it. As we can see from Exhibit 5–6, rolling the graph over to reverse the axes will not change the relationships. Hence we can write this demand function as

$$Q_X = 40 - 10P_X \tag{11}$$

or as

$$P_X = 4 - 0.1Q_X \tag{12}$$

which is mathematically equivalent. Total revenue may be expressed either as

$$TR_X = P_X Q_X = P_X(40 - 10P_X) = 40P_X - 10P_X^2 \tag{13}$$

or as

$$TR_X = P_X Q_X = (4 - 0.1Q_X)Q_X = 4Q_X - 0.1Q_X^2 \tag{14}$$

Exhibit 5–6

Relationships of the Demand Curve (D_X) to Marginal Revenue (MR_X), Total Revenue (TR), and Price Elasticity (ε_D)

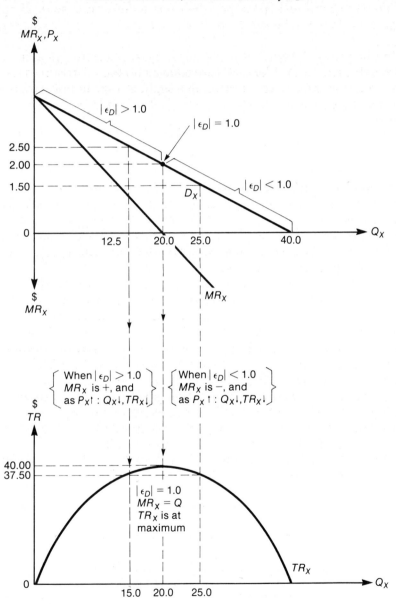

and the answer in dollars will be the same. However, the derivatives of equations (13) and (14) are *not* equivalent, since one expresses total revenue as a function of price, and the other expresses total revenue as a function of the quantity demanded. Since marginal revenue is defined as the change in total revenue when one more unit is sold, marginal revenue is taken to be the derivative of equation (14), i.e., with respect to Q_X.

In calculating the price elasticity of demand, we must remember that although equations (11) and (12) are equivalent, their derivatives are *not*. Price elasticity measures the effect of a slight change in price; therefore, we use the derivative of equation (11), *not* of equation (12), in the formula:

$$\varepsilon = \frac{dQ}{dP} \cdot \frac{P}{Q}$$

Total Revenue and Price Elasticity.   Exhibit 5–6 shows that on the upper portion of the demand curve (where price is highest), elasticity is greater than 1, hence the demand is said to be elastic. In the lower portion of the curve, elasticity is less than 1, hence the demand is said to be inelastic. At the center of the curve, where price is $2, elasticity equals 1, hence demand is said to be unit elastic.

The exhibit shows that when demand is elastic, reducing the price causes total revenue to rise. Why? Because elasticity greater than 1 means that if the price is cut, the quantity demanded will rise by a greater proportion. The increase in the number of units sold will more than make up for the smaller price, and total revenue will increase. By the same reasoning, when demand is inelastic, a price increase will cause total revenue to rise even though fewer units are sold.

Maximum revenue occurs when elasticity equals 1, as shown in Exhibit 5–6. At this point, a small change in price in either direction will cause a proportional change in quantity demanded, leaving total revenue unaffected. Hence, total revenue cannot be increased.

These relationships between price changes, elasticity, and total revenue are summarized in Exhibit 5–7.

Exhibit 5–7 _____

Price Changes, Elasticity, and Total Revenue

Change in Price	Change in Total Revenue		
	$\|\varepsilon\| > 1.0$	$\|\varepsilon\| = 1.0$	$\|\varepsilon\| < 1.0$
Fall	Rise	No change	Fall
Rise	Fall	No change	Rise

CAUTION: Do not confuse *maximum revenue* with *maximum profit.* When cost is considered, maximum profit usually, but not always, occurs at a lower level of sales than does maximum revenue. This means that, in most cases, the firm attempting to maximize profit operates in the elastic portion of its demand function.

Marginal Revenue and Price Elasticity.   As noted above, marginal revenue may be derived from Equation (14) as

$$MR_X = \frac{dTR_X}{dQ_X} = 4 - 0.2Q_X \tag{15}.$$

Going back to the demand function of Equation (12), we see that the slope of the related marginal revenue function in Equation (15) is just twice as steep. It follows that the MR_X curve will lie exactly halfway between the demand curve and the vertical axis, as shown in Exhibit 5–6. This is characteristic of all linear demand functions.

Since marginal revenue is derived from total revenue, it follows that marginal revenue is also intimately related to price elasticity of demand. This relationship is illustrated by Exhibit 5–6 and the table in Exhibit 5–5. Both show that as the price decreases, the quantity sold increases and:

1. Marginal revenue continuously decreases.
2. Marginal revenue is positive throughout the elastic range of the function, where total revenue increases as the quantity sold increases.
3. Marginal revenue is zero when the function is unit elastic and total revenue is at a maximum.
4. Marginal revenue is negative throughout the inelastic range of the function, where total revenue decreases as the quantity sold increases.

The relationships depicted in this demand curve can be generalized for all linear demand curves. Finally, there is a useful formula that links together price, price elasticity, and marginal revenue:

$$MR_X = P_X\left(1 - \frac{1}{|\varepsilon_D|}\right) \tag{16}$$

where $|\varepsilon_D|$ means the absolute value (ignore sign) of price elasticity.[1]

---

[1] To understand how the formula is derived, consider the following figure, in which we have the linear demand curve, *AC,* and the marginal revenue curve, *AM,* which everywhere lies halfway between *AC* and the vertical axis.

Factors that Affect Price Elasticity

Decision makers need to be aware not only of the relationships among price, price elasticity, total revenue, and marginal revenue, but also of the reasons why different products have different price elasticities. There are many such reasons, but they can be generally lumped into four categories:

1. *Substitutability.* The more substitutes there are for a product, the more price elastic it is apt to be. In contrast, when the price of a comple-

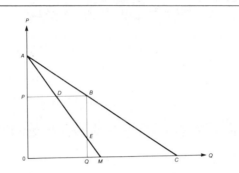

As we noted earlier with the aid of Exhibit 5–4, price elasticity of demand at point B can be expressed by any of the ratios

$$\frac{BC}{AB} = \frac{QC}{OQ} = \frac{OP}{AP}$$

Also, by triangular similarity,

$$\frac{PA}{PB} = \frac{QB}{QC}$$

and by triangular congruency,

$$PA = EB$$

since $PD = DB$. It follows, therefore that

$$\frac{EB}{PB} = \frac{QB}{QC}$$

Hence,

$$EB = PB\left[\frac{QB}{QC}\right] = QB\left[\frac{PB}{QC}\right]$$

Then, considering that $QE = QB - EB$,

$$QE = QB - QB\left[\frac{PB}{QC}\right] = QB\left[1 - \frac{PB}{QC}\right]$$

The term PB/QC is equivalent to $1/(QC/PB)$. But $PB = OQ$, and QC/OQ is one of the expressions for price elasticity. Since QE = marginal revenue and QB = price, Equation (15) follows, i.e.,

$$MR_X = P_X\left(1 - \frac{1}{|\varepsilon_D|}\right)$$

mentary good or service changes, demand is affected for both that commodity and its complement. Since complementary commodities, in effect, share the price change, they tend to be less price elastic. Closely related to the substitution effect is the effect of multiple uses of a product. If a product has only one use or a very limited number of uses, then the effect of a change in price is relatively limited. But if there are many ways in which the product can be used, then the effect of a price change is more profound. Therefore, products with many uses are apt to be more price elastic than single-use products.

2. *Relative size of expenditure.* Price elasticity is also affected by the cost of the commodity relative to the consumer's total budget, and this tends to coincide with the classification of goods as durable or nondurable. Demand for nondurable goods, unless they are luxuries, tends to be inelastic. Likewise, products such as light bulbs and motor fuel are usually purchased as the need arises, whereas the consumer would be more price-conscious about meals in a high-class restaurant. Big-ticket durable items such as large appliances, solar water-heating systems, wall-to-wall carpeting, automobiles, or houses tend to be very price elastic, not only because of the relative size of the expenditure, but also because such purchases may be postponed.

3. *Necessities versus luxuries.* One of the most important determinants of elasticity is the consumer's perception of a product as a necessity or as a luxury. Consumers will continue to buy almost the same quantity of a necessity even when the price goes up. Consequently, demand for necessities tends to be inelastic. Some examples are prescription medicines and food staples such as bread, milk, and salt. By contrast, luxuries are commodities that consumers buy when they can afford them. Since what they can afford with any given income is determined by price, demand for luxuries tends to be price elastic.

4. *Time period to which the demand curve pertains.* Given enough time, a substitute can be found for almost any product. Consequently, a prod-

Exhibit 5–8 _____

**Summary of Product Characteristics with
Respect to Price Elasticity**

Tendency of Product Characteristic

Elastic	Inelastic
Substitutes	Complementary Goods
Luxuries	Necessities
Large Outlays	Small Outlays
Durables	Nondurables
Multiple Uses	Limited Uses
Long Time Frame	Short Time Frame

uct such as natural gas may be price inelastic in the short run, but in the long run, users of natural gas will substitute some other fuel.

Although we have discussed each of the product characteristics above separately, a single product may exhibit characteristics tending toward both elasticity and inelasticity. The net effect will depend, of course, on which characteristics are the strongest. Exhibit 5–8 summarizes the way that each characteristic tends to affect elasticity.

Applications of Price Elasticity

Following are just a few examples of the many applications of price elasticity to managerial decision making:

1. *Price elasticity as a guide for setting prices.* Price elasticity is especially useful as a guide for setting prices. As we saw in Exhibit 5–6, marginal revenue is negative throughout the inelastic portion of a firm's demand curve. Therefore, a firm will never knowingly operate in the inelastic range. If it should find itself in such an unfortunate predicament, the way out is to raise prices at least until $|\varepsilon_D| = 1$.

Raising prices, however, should not be an automatic, reflex action whenever the firm is losing money. If costs are too high, maximum revenue can still result in losses. For example, many municipal transit systems operate at a loss that must be made up by taxpayer subsidy. Before raising fares, the transit authority needs to determine that it is actually in the inelastic range of its demand function. If it is in the elastic range, raising fares will only make a bad situation worse.

2. *Deregulation of oil prices.* Price elasticity of demand has been a key element in the establishment of national policy toward deregulation of oil and natural gas prices. Debates about the advisability of deregulation have often centered on the question of price elasticity. During the Arab oil embargo of 1973, for example, government officials believed that oil consumption would have to be reduced by 20 to 30 percent. To reduce the quantity demanded, officials had to decide either to raise prices or to resort to rationing. Some economists believed that the demand for gasoline was so inelastic that enormous, politically unacceptable price increases would be required to reduce demand as required. Others felt that demand was sufficiently elastic that acceptable price increases could do the job. As it turned out, when the government deregulated oil prices, supply, demand, and prices soon stabilized, and prices actually declined in 1982. The debate continues, however, over deregulation of natural gas.[2]

---

[2] Estimates of the price elasticity of demand for natural gas have ranged from 0.2 (U.S. Transportation Department), through 0.4 (Townsend Greenspan, Inc.), to 3.0 (Data Resources, Inc.). See *Business Week*, December 15, 1973, p. 23.

3.   *Deregulation of air transportation.* In the airline industry, deregulation led to widespread discounting of fares amid a shuffling of routes among the carriers. Airline managements had to decide whether to keep or drop old routes, whether or not to enter new markets, and how to price their services in the market in the face of vigorous competition. Price elasticity of demand played a key role in such decisions as airline executives tried to determine whether lower fares would increase total revenue.

4.   *Legal service fee schedules.* Mabry noted that many legal associations maintain "suggested, advisory, or minimum" fee schedules that they᛫ expect their members to honor.[3] These suggested prices are intended to raise the income of lawyers, but they may not do so. Why? Because the demand for legal services may be more price elastic than lawyers commonly think. Furthermore, the total effect of reducing fees is not immediately apparent. Reduced fees may mean that more people can afford to litigate. Litigation always takes two lawyers, one to attack and one to defend, so reduction in fees by one lawyer may well result in more work for other lawyers as well. Determining the full effect would require empirical research. Unfortunately, it can't be done as long as the suggested fee schedules are maintained.

Other Demand Elasticities

Conceptually, every factor that affects demand has an elasticity. However, the nature of some factors, such as tastes and preferences, or consumer expectations, are impossible, or at least extremely difficult, to quantify. The variables that are readily quantified are income, the prices of other products, and the level of advertising expenditures. Each of these variables thus has its own elasticity, as discussed below.

Income Elasticity of Demand

Income elasticity of demand measures the sensitivity of the quantity demanded to changes in income. The point elasticity formula for income elasticity is:

$$\varepsilon_I = \frac{\Delta Q}{\Delta I} \cdot \frac{I}{Q} \tag{17}$$

---

[3] Rodney H. Mabry, "A Note on the Elasticity of Demand for Legal Services," *Southern Business Review*, Spring 1975, pp. 8–11.

where I = income and Q = quantity demanded when price and all other variables are held constant. The arc formula is:

$$E_I = \frac{(Q_2 - Q_1)(I_2 + I_1)}{(Q_2 + Q_1)(I_2 - I_1)} \quad (18)$$

Demand with respect to income may be elastic or inelastic, depending upon whether the magnitude of the income elasticity coefficient is greater or less than 1. But unlike price elasticity, which is always negative, the sign of the income elasticity coefficient may be either plus or minus. A plus sign indicates a *normal good*, which is defined as a good whose consumption increases as income rises. A negative sign indicates an *inferior good*, that is, one whose consumption decreases when income rises. These properties are illustrated by Exhibit 5–9:

Exhibit 5–9————————————————————————————————

Estimated Income Elasticity of Demand for Selected Commodities

Commodity	Income Elasticity
Butter	0.42
Cheese	0.34
Cream	0.56
Eggs	0.37
Fruits and berries	0.70
Flour	−0.36
Liquor	1.00
Margarine	−0.20
Meat	0.35
Milk and cream	0.07
Restaurant consumption	1.48
Tobacco	1.02

Source: H. Wold, *Demand Analysis,* New York: John Wiley & Sons, 1953, p. 265.

Exhibit 5–9 shows two products with negative income elasticities: flour and margarine. In the case of flour, this presumably is because as income rises, less baking will be done at home. The negative income elasticity of demand for margarine, however, is probably attributable to its being considered inferior to butter. Butter and other foods on the list are income inelastic, however. Presumably this is because families that are adequately fed will not greatly increase expenditures on basic foods when their incomes rise. By contrast, restaurant meals, which may be considered luxuries, are in the elastic range. Liquor, with an elasticity of

+1.0, may be described as "riding the GNP curve," which means that changes in its sales evenly match changes in the overall economy. In general, higher positive elasticities may be expected of luxury items and durable goods, while necessities are essentially income inelastic and grow more inelastic as income rises.

Applications of Income Elasticity

Income elasticity of demand is applicable to a broad range of planning and strategy problems. Some examples are:

1. *Long-range planning of the firm's growth.* Over the long run, we expect consumer income to rise. Consequently, prospects for long-run growth in sales are much brighter for luxury goods because of their higher income elasticities. On the other hand, higher income elasticities mean greater sales volatility in the short run, which is not desirable. For example, the income elasticity of demand for automobiles has been estimated at values ranging from +2.5 to +3.9. No doubt this high value can partially explain why new car sales fall so drastically during recessions and then rebound so vigorously during recoveries.

Thus we see that companies whose products have high income elasticities can look forward to growth in a generally growing economy, but will be much more vulnerable to recession. On the other hand, companies whose products have low income elasticities are virtually recession-proof, but cannot expect to share fully in a growing economy when times are good. Such firms may find it necessary to diversify into different products or even a different industry in order to achieve healthy growth.

2. *Establishment of national farm policy.* In recent years, it has become painfully apparent that the incomes of farmers growing our foodstuffs (which have low income elasticities) have not kept up with urban workers' wages. Since farmers cannot usually diversify into products with high income elasticities, the nation can expect to have a "farm problem" for a long time to come. Congress may therefore find it necessary to continue or increase certain farm subsidies.

3. *Developing marketing strategies.* The income elasticity of demand influences decisions on the location and nature of sales outlets as well as the extent and focus of advertising and promotional activities. For example, vendors of luxury goods typically direct their advertising to rising young professionals whose incomes can be expected to grow substantially.

4. *Forecasting housing requirements.* A particularly interesting application of income elasticity is in the area of housing. In a study published in 1971, de Leeuw estimated income elasticity of demand to be between 0.8 and 1.0 for rental units and between 0.7 and 1.5 for owner-occupied

housing.[4] We can use these figures to forecast demand for rented and owner-occupied housing in, say, 10 years, assuming an annual growth in real income between 2 and 3 percent. If the annual growth in real income is 2 percent, the compounded growth in 10 years would be $(1.02)^{10} = 1.219$, an increase of 21.9 percent. At 3 percent, the compounded growth in 10 years would be $(1.03)^{10} = 1.344$, an increase of 34.4 percent. Forecasts of the growth of demand for rental units corresponding to income elasticities of 0.8 and 1.0 are shown on Exhibit 5–10.

Exhibit 5–10 _____

Forecasted Growth of the Demand for Rental Units in 10 Years

	Annual Increase in Incomes	
Elasticity	*2%*	*3%*
0.8	17.5%	27.5%
1.0	21.9%	34.4%

Exhibit 5–10 shows that in 10 years the growth for *rental* housing units due to growth of income could range from a low of 17.5 percent to a high of 34.4 percent. The growth of demand for *owner-occupied* units is shown in Exhibit 5–11.

Exhibit 5–11 _____

Forecasted Increases in the Demand for Owner-Occupied Housing Units in 10 Years

	Annual Increase in Incomes	
Elasticity	*2%*	*3%*
0.7	15.3%	24.1%
1.5	32.9%	51.6%

The range of the growth in demand for owner-occupied housing units is even greater than that for rental units, i.e., from a low of 15.3 percent

---

[4] Frank de Leeuw, "The Demand for Housing: A Review of Cross Section Evidence," *Review of Economics and Statistics*, February 1971, pp. 1–10.

to a high of 51.6 percent. It must be emphasized that this growth in demand is due solely to increased income. No doubt it would be offset to a greater or less extent by a decrease in demand due to higher prices.

Cross Elasticity of Demand

Several different measures of elasticity may be developed for interpreting the economic effects and interactions of substitute and complementary products. The most important of these measures is the *cross elasticity of demand.* Suppose we let P_X and P_Y denote the prices of commodity X and commodity Y, respectively, while Q_X and Q_Y denote the respective quantities demanded. The cross elasticity of demand measures the percentage change in the quantity of X demanded relative to a slight percentage change in the price of Y. The point formula is:

$$\varepsilon_C = \frac{\Delta Q_X}{\Delta P_Y} \cdot \frac{P_Y}{Q_X} \tag{19}$$

The arc formula is:

$$E_C = \frac{(Q_{X_2} - Q_{X_1})(P_{Y_2} + P_{Y_1})}{(Q_{X_2} + Q_{X_1})(P_{Y_2} - P_{Y_1})} \tag{20}$$

The cross elasticity can be positive, negative, or zero. It will be positive if the products are substitutes. Thus, other things remaining the same, if the price of butter increases, the consumption of margarine should also increase (to replace the decrease in butter consumption). On the other hand, when commodities are complementary, their cross elasticities are negative. Increases in the prices of cameras, for example, should bring decreases in the purchases of film, again assuming a constancy of other factors. Finally, a small or zero cross elasticity would indicate that the products (or the markets in which they are sold) are effectively independent, since variations in the price of one produce no appreciable changes in purchases of the other.

In his well-known study, Herman Wold estimated cross elasticities between beef and pork, and between butter and margarine; his results are shown in Exhibit 5–12.

These cross elasticities show that the sensitivity of the demand for beef to changes in pork prices is twice as great as the sensitivity of the demand for pork to changes in the price of beef. Neither demand reacts strongly, and both are cross inelastic. Cross elasticities are somewhat higher between butter and margarine, but the demands are still cross inelastic. Apparently, consumers who like butter are inclined to ignore changes in the price of margarine, while users of margarine are somewhat more sensitive to changes in the price of butter.

Exhibit 5–12 _____

Cross Elasticities of Demand for Two Pairs of Commodities

Commodity	Substitute	Cross Elasticity
Beef	Pork	+0.28
Pork	Beef	+0.14
Butter	Margarine	+0.67
Margarine	Butter	+0.81

Source: H. Wold, *Demand Analysis,* New
York: John Wiley & Sons, 1953, pp. 282, 285.

The concept of cross elasticity of demand is particularly useful in two different levels of business. At the level of the firm, cross elasticities help in the formulation of marketing strategy. The firm needs to know how the demand for its products will react to price changes in either substitute or complementary goods offered by a competitor. At the industry level, the cross elasticity of demand indicates whether or not a substitute exists for the industry's product. For example, when the price of imported oil became too high, extraction of oil from shale became economically feasible and attractive. But when OPEC prices fell in response to a worldwide glut of oil, development of shale oil extraction was halted. Demand for coal is also responding to changes in the price of oil, and demand for oil can be expected to respond to changes in the price of natural gas.

Advertising Elasticity of Demand

Advertising elasticity of demand measures the sensitivity of sales (quantity demanded) to changes in expenditure for advertising and promotion. Like the other elasticities discussed so far, formulas for advertising elasticity may be adapted from the general formulas in the first section of this chapter if we assume that sales are a function of advertising expenditure. The point formula is:

$$_A\varepsilon_S = \frac{\Delta S}{\Delta A} \cdot \frac{A}{S} \tag{21}$$

where S = the quantity sold or total revenue from sales and A = units of advertising expenditure. Arc elasticity is measured as:

$$_AE_S = \frac{(S_2 - S_1)(A_2 + A_1)}{(S_2 + S_1)(A_2 - A_1)} \tag{22}$$

In treating sales as a function of advertising expenditure, the analyst must recognize that the effect of the advertising budget is clouded by a number of factors, such as:

1. The stage of the product's market development.
2. The extent to which competitors react to the company's advertising, either with their own advertising campaigns or by increased merchandising.
3. The quality and quantity of the company's past and present advertising compared to that of competitors, since variations in qualitative factors (e.g., choice of media) obscure the effects of differences in advertising outlays.
4. The importance of nonadvertising demand determinants, such as growth trends, prices, and incomes, and the extent to which these can be filtered out of the analysis.
5. The time that elapses between advertising outlays and a sales response to those outlays, which is difficult to ascertain because such intervals depend in part on the type of product, type of advertisement, and so forth.
6. The influence of the "investment effect" of the company's past advertising and the extent to which this may affect current and future sales through delayed and cumulative buying.

All of these factors must be considered when reckoning sales as a function of advertising. In order to do this, measurement methods must be devised that will allow and compensate for the complexities just mentioned. As one might imagine, this is no easy task. Indeed, it may prove to be exceptionally difficult, but the usefulness of advertising elasticity depends on the successful accomplishment of this task.

Combined Effect of Demand Elasticities

As we said at the beginning of this section, every factor that affects demand has an elasticity. When all factors are allowed to change simultaneously, their combined influence on demand is simply the sum of their individual elasticities.

For example, suppose a firm is producing a luxury good and enjoys annual sales of 100,000 units. Currently the sales price per unit is twice the direct cost of manufacture. The firm's management estimates that the price elasticity of demand for this product, ε_D, is about -1.3 and the income elasticity of demand for it, ε_I, is about 2.0. Economic forecasters expect real disposable income to increase by 6 percent in the coming year. The company has just signed a labor contract that will increase direct manufacturing costs by 10 percent. If the company follows its current pricing policy next year, how many units can it expect to sell?

The quantity demanded next year, Q_1, will be the current demand, Q_0, plus the change caused by the price increase, plus the change caused by the rise in income, i.e.,

$$Q_1 = Q_0 + Q_0 \left(\frac{\Delta P}{P}\right) \varepsilon_D + Q_0 \left(\frac{\Delta I}{I}\right) \varepsilon_I = Q_0 \left(1 + \frac{\Delta P}{P} \varepsilon_D + \frac{\Delta I}{I} \varepsilon_I\right)$$

where

Q_0 = Quantity demanded in year 0 (this year)
Q_1 = Quantity demanded in year 1 (next year)
$\Delta P/P$ = Proportionate change in price
ε_D = Price elasticity of demand
$\Delta I/I$ = Proportionate change in income
ε_I = Income elasticity of demand

Hence,

$$Q_1 = 100{,}000[1 + (.10)(-1.3) + (.06)(2.0)] = 99{,}000$$

That is to say, the effect of the price increase will more than offset the effect of the increase in income. The net result will be a loss in sales if we assume that all other factors, such as advertising and competitor's prices, remain the same.

Summary

The market demand for a commodity is simply the aggregation of all consumer demand curves. Demand curves express the quantity demanded as a function of price. If price changes, movement takes place along the demand curve. But if income or some other factor changes, the entire demand curve shifts to a new position at all prices.

Of course, the demand for some commodity, X, is a function of (1) the price of X, (2) consumers' tastes and preferences, (3) income, (4) prices of other products, (5) consumers' expectations, (6) the range of alternative goods and services, (7) the number of potential consumers, (8) advertising and promotion, and (9) other factors.

Among other factors affecting demand are market saturation, interest rates, and the nature of the product. The demand for durable goods is more volatile than the demand for nondurables. The markets for producer's goods, which are goods used in the production of other goods, are different from those for consumer goods. Producer's goods are more homogeneous than consumer goods, and are purchased by professional buyers who have criteria and motivations different from those of private consumers.

Elasticity is the most commonly used measurement of the sensitivity of demand to any of its determinants. In general, elasticity is defined as the percentage change in a dependent variable that is attributable to a 1 percent change in an independent variable, holding other independent variables constant. Elasticity may be measured at a point on the functional curve with the *point* formula

$$\varepsilon = \frac{\Delta Y}{\Delta X} \cdot \frac{X}{Y}$$

It may also be computed as the average elasticity over a segment of the curve with the *arc* formula:

$$E = \frac{Y_2 - Y_1}{Y_2 + Y_1} \cdot \frac{X_2 + X_1}{X_2 - X_1}$$

The result of either formula is an elasticity coefficient whose sign indicates the relative direction of movement between the two variables, and whose absolute value or magnitude indicates the degree of sensitivity. If the magnitude is less than 1, the function is said to be inelastic at the point of measure. If it is greater than 1, the function is elastic, and if it is equal to 1, the function is unit elastic at the point of measure.

Elasticity is a general concept that applies to any function. When applied to demand, four elasticities are of primary interest: (1) price elasticity, (2) income elasticity, (3) cross elasticity, and (4) elasticity of advertising.

Price elasticity of demand measures the sensitivity of demand to changes in price. Its sign is always negative, indicating that an increase in price will reduce the quantity demanded, and vice versa. The demand function is unit price elastic at the point where marginal revenue is zero and total revenue is at a maximum. Below this point, demand is inelastic, marginal revenue is negative, and a price increase will increase total revenue. Above this point, demand is elastic and the firm can reduce price to increase total revenue.

Income elasticity of demand measures the sensitivity of demand to changes in consumer income. Its sign will be plus for a normal good, minus for an inferior good. Income elasticity is an important consideration in long-range planning as well as in the formulation of short-run marketing strategy.

Cross elasticity measures the sensitivity of demand to changes in the price of some other commodity. The sign is plus if the two products are substitutes and minus if they are complements. For unrelated products, the coefficient will be zero or very close to zero. Cross elasticity is important for the development of marketing strategy as well as for the evaluation of the competitive position of entire industries.

Advertising elasticity measures the responsiveness of demand to changes in advertising expenditure. This is a particularly difficult quantity to measure because of the many factors that interact with advertising.

Each factor that affects demand has its own elasticity. In reality, all of these factors act simultaneously. The total effect on demand is the sum of their individual effects.

Problems

1. The J. P. Jackson Company, a department store, conducted a study of the demand for men's ties. It found that the average daily demand Q in terms of price P is given by the equation:

$$Q = 60 - 5P$$

a. How many ties per day can the store expect to sell at a price of $3 per tie?
b. If the store wants to sell 20 ties per day, what price should it charge?
c. What would be the demand if the store offered to give the ties away?
d. What is the highest price that anyone would be willing to pay for these ties?
e. Plot the demand curve.

2. "Demand elasticity measures percentage changes in quantity demanded relative to percentage changes in price. It follows that with 10 equal demanders for a product, the elasticity will be 10 times as great as it is for one." True or false? Explain.

3. "The elasticity of demand for a product usually increases with the length of time over which a price change persists. Thus, a 1 percent decrease in price may result at first in a less than 1 percent increase in quantity demanded, but eventually the quantity may increase by 2 percent, 5 percent, or even more." True or false? Explain why.

4. The more narrowly a product is defined—"Chevrolet Camaro" versus "automobile," for example—the more elastic the demand. True or false? Explain.

5. Generally speaking, would you expect the cross elasticity of demand to be positive, negative, or zero for each of the following pairs of products? What general rule, if any, can you infer from your answers?
a. Convertibles and sedans.
b. Coca-Cola and Pepsi-Cola.
c. Textbook sales and school enrollments.
d. Desks and chairs.
e. Chinese egg rolls and children's socks.

6. Central City Meat Packers has noted that the demand Q for its smoked breakfast sausages is affected by changes in per capita personal income I in such a way that $Q = 1,000 + 0.2I$.

do extra for class

a. Calculate the quantity demanded at each $1,000 of per capita income from $2,000 to $6,000.

b. Calculate the income elasticity of demand if income changes from $3,000 to $5,000 and from $10,000 to $15,000.

c. Judging from the behavior of income elasticity, are smoked breakfast sausages a luxury or a necessity?

7. Bruce Home Products manufactures a vacuum cleaner that it sells for $100 a unit. At this price sales have been averaging about 2,000 units per month. The company, however, has recently learned that its major competitor intends to cut the price of its vacuum cleaner from $90 to $80. Management at Bruce believes the cross elasticity of demand between its product and that of the competitor is +0.8. Assuming no changes in other demand variables, calculate the sales loss in units and dollars to Bruce Home Products resulting from the competitor's price cut.

8. Consider the accompanying demand curve and assume we are interested in calculating price elasticity at a selected price, A. Price elasticity, then, is

$$\varepsilon = \frac{A}{A - M}$$

Elasticity at the price B is

$$\varepsilon = \frac{B}{B - M}$$

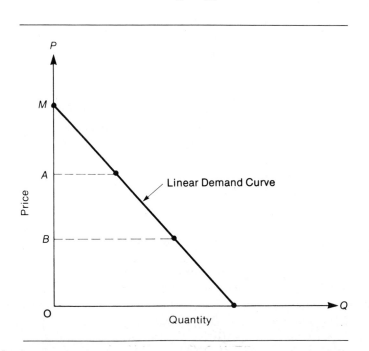

Now, use the demand curve given above along with this geometric method and the marginal revenue formula, $MR = P - (P/|\varepsilon|)$, to fill in the table.

P	Q	TR	$|\varepsilon|$	MR
12				
10				
8				
6				
4				
2				
0				

9.   Problem 8 illustrates a geometric technique for finding price elasticity and then applies it to a linear demand curve. However, the same approach can be used for estimating point price elasticities on nonlinear demand curves. For example, on the accompanying demand curve we are interested in determining price elasticity at the price A. The line MN is drawn tangent to the demand curve at price A and price elasticity is estimated as before: $\varepsilon = A/(A - M)$.

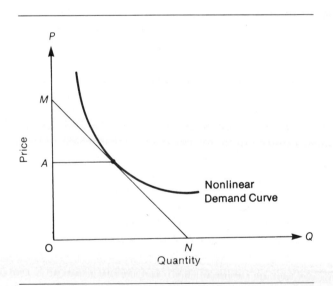

Now, consider the demand curve $P = 20/Q$ and fill in the table.

Q	P	TR	$|\varepsilon|$	MR
5				
4				
3				

10.   The Upland Sears automotive center typically sells 300 deluxe five-year auto batteries every month for a list price of $54. However, sales declined last month to 225 units. The manager of the automotive department feels the decline in sales was a result of a sale on three-year batteries, whose price was reduced from $39 to $34.

a.   Calculate the arc cross elasticity between five-year and three-year auto batteries.

b.   Calculate the sales of five-year batteries if the price of three-year batteries were set at $37.

11.   Freshbake and Dreambake both sell wedding cakes. Assume current wedding cake sales to be $Q_F = 1,650$ and $Q_D = 620$. The demand curves for the two competitors are:

$$\text{Freshbake:} \quad P_F = 750 - .3Q_F$$
$$\text{Dreambake:} \quad P_D = 700 - .5Q_D$$

a.   Calculate the point price elasticities for Freshbake and Dreambake.

b.   Freshbake reduced the price of wedding cakes, thereby increasing sales from 1,650 to 1,734 units and reducing Dreambake's sales to 610 units. What is the cross elasticity between Freshbake and Dreambake wedding cakes?

c.   What does the cross elasticity coefficient calculated in part (b) indicate about the substitutability of the two products?

d.   Does the price reduction by Freshbake make sense with regard to revenue?

12.   (Library research.) Obtain price and consumption data covering the most recent 10 or more years for any two competing or complementary products. (Suggestion: USDA, Agricultural Statistics, published annually, provides data for numerous agricultural products. Check the index of the most recent volume for price and consumption statistics for various products.) Examples of products that may be selected include meat: beef, veal, lamb, pork, ham; dairy: cheese, milk, ice cream; or citrus: oranges, lemons, and so forth. A pair of products may be selected from different product groups, such as ham and eggs or meat and cheese, if it makes economic sense to do so. Of course, you may choose nonagricultural products from any source you can find. Analyze the data for the two products you have selected by estimating the arc measures for the cross elasticity of demand, and interpret your results.

Case Problem: Sparklife Industries

13.   Sparklife Industries presently controls 4 percent of the sparkplug market. The sales manager at Sparklife is taking an aggressive position to increase the company's market share. At the last board meeting, he showed top management that after a price reduction from $1.10 to $1.00,

made in January 1976, sales climbed from 2.2 million to 2.75 million units per year.

While this is a dramatic jump, members on the board were quick to point out other factors that may have influenced the situation: (1) The consumer price index rose 11 percent. (2) Per capita disposable income rose 3 percent. (3) A well-known auto parts manufacturer entered the market. (4) A composite index of auto, truck, and motorcycle manufacturers showed a 6 percent increase in sales. (5) Other sparkplug producers exhibited stable prices. (6) The OPEC oil embargo increased gas prices during the last three months of the year by 20 percent.

Questions:
a. Calculate the price elasticity of demand with all other factors remaining constant.
b. Analyze each of the additional factors, explaining possible effects on your original measure of price elasticity.
c. Which of the additional factors are quantifiable?
d. Considering only the information given, would you advise a price reduction?

Case Problem: LRS Corporation

14. Video Magic is a retail distributor of new and used television sets. In 1972, Video Magic was purchased and became a wholly owned subsidiary of LRS Corporation, a holding company that owns several large hotels. Because of its hotel operations, LRS often makes large purchases of television sets, and this gives them increased operating leverage in the television set market. Also, Video Magic provides an excellent outlet for selling LRS's used television sets. To develop more efficient ordering and pricing policies, a company accountant organized the following data for the past 10 years of operations:

Year	Price of New Televisions	Price of Used Televisions	Number of New Televisions Sold	Average per Capita Disposable Income
73	$600	$150	2,000	$2,000
74	650	150	1,900	2,000
75	650	175	2,000	2,250
76	650	200	2,100	2,250
77	600	150	2,000	2,250
78	600	175	2,100	2,250
79	600	175	2,000	2,000
80	700	175	2,100	2,250
81	750	150	2,000	2,250
82	750	150	1,900	2,250

Questions:
a.   Economists predict further rises in disposable income; what plans should management make for future inventories?
b.   An LRS hotel is scheduled for renovation, which includes replacing 1,050 four-year-old televisions. To get rid of the old sets, management is considering a sale at reduced prices on all used sets. Will a price reduction on used televisions have an effect on new television sales?
c.   Management is also evaluating pricing policies for its new televisions; what suggestions could you make?
Hint: All these questions involve a form of elasticity. Elasticity applies only when "all other things" remain constant.

References

Addison, William, and Marc Nerlove. "Statistical Estimation of Long-run Elasticities of Supply and Demand." *Journal of Farm Economics,* November 1958, pp. 861–80.

Clark, Kim B., and Richard B. Freeman. "How Elastic Is The Demand For Labor?" *Review of Economics and Statistics,* November 1980, pp. 509–20.

Dean, J. "Estimating the Price Elasticity of Demand." In *Managerial Economics and Operations Research,* ed. E. Mansfield. 3d ed. New York: W. W. Norton, 1975.

de Leeuw, Frank. "The Demand for Housing: A Review of Cross Section Evidence." *Review of Economics and Statistics,* February 1971, pp. 1–10.

Gibson, Betty Blecha. "Estimating Demand Elasticities for Public Goods from Survey Data." *American Economic Review,* December 1980, pp. 1069–76.

Marby, Rodney H. "A Note on the Elasticity of Demand for Legal Services." *Southern Business Review,* Spring 1975, pp. 8–11.

Nelson, D. C. "A Study of the Elasticity of Demand for Electricity by Residential Consumers: Sample Markets in Nebraska." *Land Economics,* February 1965, pp. 92–96.

Reekie, W. D. "The Price Elasticity of Demand for Evening Newspapers." *Applied Economics,* March 1976, pp. 69–79.

Stevens, R. D. "Elasticity of Food Consumption," *Foreign Agricultural Economic Report* No. 23, Washington, D.C., Economic Research Service, U.S. Department of Agriculture, March 1965.

Suits, D. B. "The Elasticity of Demand for Gambling." *Quarterly Journal of Economics,* February 1979, pp. 155–62.

Taplin, John. "A Coherence Approach to Estimates of Price Elasticities in the Vacation Travel Market." *Journal of Transport Economics and Policy,* January 1980, pp. 19–35.

Taylor, L. D. "The Demand for Electricity: A Survey." *Bell Journal of Economics,* Spring 1975, pp. 74–110.

Weisskoff, Richard. "Demand Elasticities for a Developing Economy: An International Comparison of Consumption Patterns." In *Studies in Development Planning,* ed. H. B. Chenery. Cambridge, Mass.: Harvard University Press, 1971.

Wold, H. *Demand Analysis.* New York: John Wiley & Sons, 1953.

6

Demand Estimation: Elementary Techniques

The main objective of demand analysis is to discover the forces that affect sales of a product and to establish the relationships between these controlling forces and sales. To achieve this objective, management uses empirical data to discover the structural form and parameters of the demand function.

Two elementary approaches to this task are discussed in this chapter: (1) statistical analysis and (2) marketing research. Statistical analysis involves regression and correlation analysis, while marketing research involves some degree of direct contact with the consumer through observation, surveys, or marketing experiments. Which approach is used depends upon the availability and reliability of empirical data. When sufficient reliable data are available, statistical analysis is the preferred method. When reliable data are nonexistent (such as for a new product) or insufficient, consumer contact may be necessary.

Regression analysis denotes the method by which the relationship between quantity demanded and one or more independent variables, such as price and income, is estimated. It includes measurement of the errors that are inherent to the estimation process. *Correlation analysis* is the measurement of the strength of the relationship between variables.

Both regression and correlation analyses are performed in a single procedure. *Simple regression analysis* is used when the quantity demanded is estimated as a function of a single independent variable, such as price. *Multiple regression analysis* is used to estimate demand as a function of two or more independent variables that vary simultaneously. This chapter discusses simple regression analysis, while the more complex procedure of multiple regression is explained in the next chapter.

In this chapter, two methods of simple linear regression are explained. The *graphic method* is presented first because of its value as a learning device. This is followed by an explanation of the least squares method, which can be used in a hand calculation of the regression equation as well as in computer programs. The next section deals with the evaluation of the regression equation (correlation analysis). The last section discusses three marketing research techniques that are used to investigate consumer buying habits.

Statistical Analysis

When adequate data are available, statistical analysis is the preferred approach to demand analysis on the grounds of its reliability and cost. Economists commonly use two different types of data for demand estimation: (1) *time-series* data and (2) *cross-sectional* data.

Time-Series Data

Time-series data record historical changes in price, income, population, and other variables that affect demand. Since a demand relation with only certain specified independent variables is wanted, it is often necessary to eliminate the influence of other independent variables that have a significant effect. Thus, in a demand-price study where the influence of price is the only independent factor under consideration, it is generally necessary to adjust the data to eliminate the effects of population growth and monetary inflation.

Population Adjustment. To neutralize the effects of population variation on product sales, incomes and demand quantities are reduced to a per capita basis. This transformation is usually made, however, only when the data cover a number of years, since population figures do not usually show sharp fluctuations from year to year. The result of the adjustment is to leave changes in demand attributable to factors other than population change. If the product being analyzed is a family-type good, such as an automobile or washing machine, a better demand estimate is often obtained by reducing the relevant data to a per house-hold or per family basis rather than a per capita one. Such reductions do not adjust, however, for changes in the age distribution, racial composition, or other elements in the population that may affect demand over the long run.

Deflation Adjustment.   Over a number of years, the purchasing power of money decreases because of inflation. This inflation makes it impossible to make valid comparisons of nominal dollar amounts of different time periods. The solution to this problem is to divide all nominal dollar amounts by an appropriate price index. The index most commonly used in consumer demand studies is the consumer price index, since it reflects the weighted average of prices paid by consumers for most goods and services, relative to a previous base period. The result of this division is to convert the time series from nominal dollars to "constant dollars" of the base period.

In addition to population and deflation adjustments in time-series analysis, other adjustments are sometimes made, such as removal of trend, seasonal, and cyclical influences. Methods for making these adjustments are discussed in Chapter 8.

Cross-Sectional Analysis

Time-series analysis is conducted to determine how a variable changes over time. By contrast, cross-sectional analysis tries to determine how demand is affected by variables such as price, income, geographic location, and the like at some specific point in time.

For example, in establishing a sales-income relationship for measuring the income elasticity of demand, the time-series approach would use past variations in the data as a basis for measurement. In contrast, the cross-sectional approach would compare the different levels of sales among different income groups at one specific point in time, and the elasticity measure would be based on these differences. As in the time-series method, adjustments in the data might be needed to eliminate the effects of other factors (in this case, all factors other than income) on the demand for the product.

The choice between the time-series approach and the cross-sectional approach often depends upon time and expense considerations and the data already available. For these reasons, the time-series method is perhaps more commonly used in demand studies—the data being already available from published sources—with some use made of cross-sectional information when it seems appropriate.

Fitting a Curve to the Data

In curve fitting, observed data are used to estimate the parameters of a selected demand function. Once the demand function is formulated, it is used to predict the value of the dependent variable when values of the independent variables are given.

When decision makers engage in curve fitting, there are two fundamental questions that they must answer:

1. What sort of an equation should be used?
2. How well does the curve fit and how well does the estimated function predict demand?

With respect to the first question, the choice of an equation to be fitted to the data will depend upon two considerations: (1) the number of independent variables involved, and (2) the distribution of the data (i.e., is the distribution linear or nonlinear?).

If the trend of observed values of the dependent variable is approximately linear and there are multiple independent variables, then the estimating equation will be of the form

$$\hat{Q} = b_0 + b_1 X_1 + b_2 X_2 + \cdots + b_k X_k \tag{1}$$

where

$\hat{Q}$ = Estimated quantity demanded of the commodity under investigation

X_i = Quantity of the ith independent variable

b_0 = The constant term

b_j = Parameters of the demand function; i.e., coefficient of the jth independent variable, $j = 1, 2, \ldots, k$.

Mathematically, this equation describes a hyperplane of *multiple regression* (to be discussed in the next chapter). If the data can be reduced to a single independent variable (such as price) and the trend of the dependent variable is approximately linear, then a *simple regression analysis* can be used to fit the equation of a line, whose general form is:

$$Q_X = a + b P_X \tag{2}$$

where

Q_X = The quantity of commodity X demanded per time period (the dependent variable)

P_X = Price per unit of commodity X (the independent variable)

a = The constant parameter (which is the Y-intercept on the graph)

b = The regression parameter or regression coefficient for P_X (which is the slope of the line)

If the trend of the dependent variable follows the nonlinear curve of a power function, its general form will be:

$$Q_X = aP_X^b \tag{3}$$

This may be rewritten in its logarithmic form by taking the common logarithms of both sides of Equation (3):

$$\log Q_X = \log a + b \log P_X \tag{4}$$

The new logarithmic function is linear, and it can be estimated by simple regression analysis.

Graphic Method of Simple Linear Regression

Most regression work today is done by computers through packaged regression programs. Indeed, simple regression analysis can be done quickly and easily on many inexpensive hand-held electronic calculators. Nevertheless, even when these electronic helpers are used, there remains the need to understand and interpret regression results. The graphic method can be very useful for this purpose, as we shall demonstrate.

Although the basic technique for both simple and multiple regression is the method of least squares (a mathematical procedure to be discussed in the next section), there is a graphic method that can yield relatively good results. There are two reasons for presenting the graphic method:

1. It provides a systematic preliminary analysis of the data, revealing relationships between the dependent and independent variables that are not readily apparent when algebraic methods are used. For example, a graph will reveal a lead-lag relationship, if one exists, thus letting the researcher know that adjustment of the data will be necessary before a valid regression analysis can be performed.
2. The graphic method is a valuable learning device. The step-by-step approach of the graphic method makes it easier for the student to understand the basic underlying assumptions of demand estimation.

Linear Model

To demonstrate simple linear regression by the graphic method, consider, for example, the demand for beef from 1965 through 1979, as shown in Exhibit 6–1. The graphic method proceeds as follows:

Step 1. Construct the variables. Before any method can be applied, we must construct the variables to be used in the regression analysis. Our objective is to see whether or not a simple relationship can be established between beef consumption and beef prices over the time period of our analysis.

During this period, various factors affecting beef consumption, such as population and purchasing power, as well as beef prices, underwent important changes. Hence, in order to express beef consumption as a function of beef prices, the data must be adjusted to remove the influence of changes in population and purchasing power. Adjustment for population is obtained by expressing the dependent variable as *beef consumption per capita.* Adjustment of the independent variable for *both* income and population changes is obtained by using the ratio: *price of beef/ disposable income per capita.* The procedure for constructing the necessary variables is illustrated in columns (1) through (6) of Exhibit 6–1.

One of the first problems in performing studies of this sort is finding good sources of data. We are fortunate in the United States that many government agencies and private institutions are now publishing data required for this type of demand analysis. These publications are usually available in college and public libraries. The *Statistical Abstract of the United States* is a good first source to consult, since it abstracts from many other sources and gives specific references to other publications that may also be of assistance.

Other periodicals containing fairly extensive economic statistics are:

1. *The Annual Economic Report to the President,* published by the Council of Economic Advisors.
2. *The Survey of Current Business,* published monthly by the U.S. Department of Commerce.
3. *Business Statistics,* published biennially by the U.S. Department of Commerce.
4. The summary of business published weekly by *Business Week* magazine.
5. *Agricultural Statistics,* published yearly by the U.S. Department of Agriculture; this is an extremely useful general source for data relating to agriculture and the marketing of agricultural products.

Step 2. Plot the variables over time. Regardless of the method chosen for regression analysis (graphic or least squares), it is helpful first to plot the variables over time, as illustrated in Exhibit 6–2. This serves two purposes: (1) a visual comparison of their fluctuations will uncover any leads and lags between the variables and the consequent necessity for adjustment, and (2) the underlying trend will be revealed as linear or nonlinear so that an appropriate model for fitting a curve to the data

Exhibit 6–1

Beef Demand Study

Year	(1) Civilian Population (millions)	(2) Disposable Personal Income ($ billions)	(3) Disposable Income per Capita ($) (2) ÷ (1)	(4) Beef Consumption per Capita (pounds) (Q)	(5) Price of Beef ($ per 100 lbs.)	(6) Price of Beef/Disposable Income per Capita (P)	(7) Freehand Regression Estimates: Q = 187.8 −5,266.7P (4) vs (6)
1965	191.6	$ 472	$2,463	99.5	$ 40.48	.0164	101.4
1966	193.4	512	2,647	104.2	40.28	.0152	107.7
1967	195.3	546	2,796	106.5	41.01	.0147	110.4
1968	197.1	591	2,998	109.7	43.84	.0146	110.9
1969	199.1	634	3,184	110.8	47.75	.0150	108.8
1970	203.8	682	3,346	113.7	46.82	.0140	114.1
1971	206.2	740	3,589	113.0	52.39	.0146	110.9
1972	208.2	799	3,838	116.1	55.34	.0144	112.0
1973	209.9	901	4,293	109.6	67.41	.0157	105.1
1974	211.4	981	4,640	116.8	67.09	.0146	110.9
1975	213.1	1,074	5,040	120.1	73.64	.0146	110.9
1976	215.2	1,185	5,507	129.3	60.96	.0111	129.3
1977	216.9	1,305	6,017	125.9	62.66	.0104	133.0
1978	218.5	1,458	6,673	120.1	80.80	.0121	124.1
1979	220.6	1,624	7,362	107.6	101.72	.0138	115.1
Total				1,702.9		.2112	
Mean				113.5		.0141	

Sources: Columns 1 and 2: *Statistical Abstract of the United States* (annual); columns 4 and 5: USDA, *Agricultural Statistics* (annual). Other general sources such as USCD, *Business Statistics*, published biennially, carry most of these data.

Exhibit 6–2

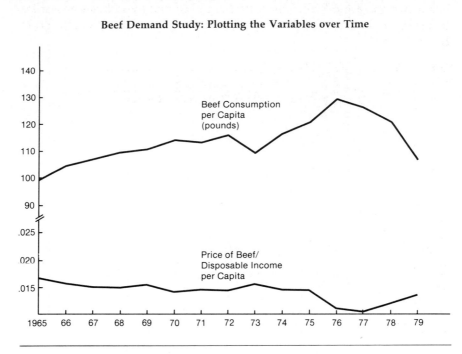

Beef Demand Study: Plotting the Variables over Time

may be chosen. In the current example, Exhibit 6–2 indicates the following:

1. There is an inverse relationship between consumption and price, as there should be on the basis of economic theory.
2. There is no apparent lead-lag relationship between the variables (nor is there reason to expect such a relationship). If a lead-lag relationship were discovered, then the data would be adjusted by moving one series or the other forward or backward through time until the lead-lag relationship disappears.
3. The underlying trend of each series appears to be linear (and there are no reasons to expect any curvilinear trend).

This information gives us a background for plotting the scatter diagram.

Step 3. Plot the scatter diagram. The data base for a simple linear regression will be the set of ordered pairs, (P_X, Q_X), which are the observed values of P_X and Q_X. In this example P_X represents the ratio of the price of beef to disposable income per capita, and Q_X represents beef consumption per capita, in pounds.

If we hypothesize that the true underlying function, $Q_X = f(P_X)$, is linear, we must first determine whether or not that hypothesis is correct. In order to do this, we plot the data on a *scatter diagram*, as shown in Exhibit 6–3.

Exhibit 6–3

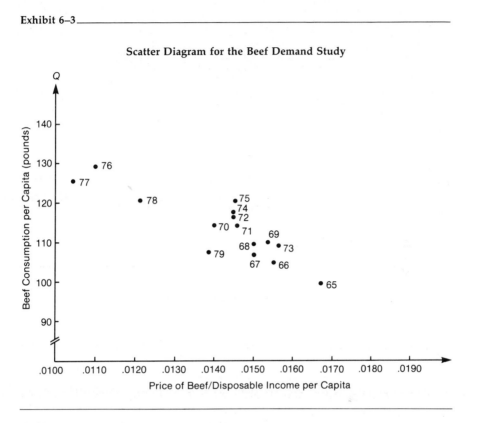

Scatter Diagram for the Beef Demand Study

Since it was determined in the previous step that there was no lead or lag relationship between the variables, we can plot each year's consumption variable against the same year's price variable, without having to shift one of the series forward or backward. Also, since it was decided that the underlying trend of each series is linear, the scatter diagram can be plotted on ordinary arithmetic scales. On the other hand, if the trends of the variables were approximately geometric, they could be plotted on logarithmic scales in order to express them more simply as linear relationships. An example of such a case will be given later.

Step 4. Fit the freehand regression line. How is a regression line fitted to a set of points? In the graphic method the regression line is approximated by sketching it freehand, as shown in Exhibit 6–4. The equation of the

Exhibit 6–4

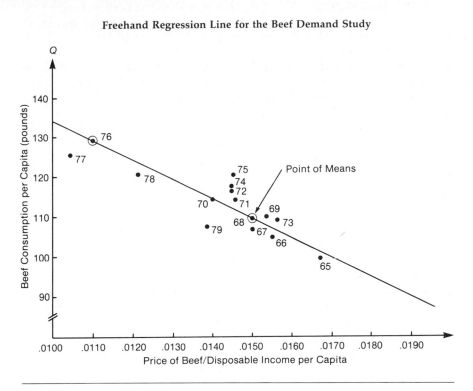

Freehand Regression Line for the Beef Demand Study

line then can be estimated directly from the graph. In attempting to locate the line on the graph, we soon learn that most of the observed data points will deviate from the regression line, either above or below it. The vertical distance between the observed data point and the regression line is called a *deviation* or *residual*. The precise placement of the regression line requires the mathematical method of *least squares*, which places the regression line in such a position that the sum of the squared deviations is minimized. (We shall discuss this method later.) Even though we are sketching freehand, we are actually attempting to locate a least-squares regression line; that is, we are attempting to place the regression line in such a way that the sum of the squared deviations from it will be less than the sum of the squared deviations from any other line. With practice, a freehand regression line can be located very close to the least squares position.

In sketching the freehand regression line, the following suggestions may be useful:

1. The direction of the line, that is, whether it slopes upward or downward, should agree with economic theory and judgment. Thus, in Exhibit 6–4 the line slopes downward, which is to be expected, since it has already been decided in Step 2 above that the price-quantity relation is an inverse one.
2. It can be shown that a least squares regression line will always pass through the point of the means $(\bar{P}, \bar{Q})$, and the positive and negative deviations from it total zero.
3. The regression line can be rotated about the point of the means until roughly half the observations are above the line and half below. It should be emphasized that this is a rough guide and not a rigid rule.

Step 5. Estimate the regression equation. The equation for the regression line can be estimated directly from the graph by utilizing the two-point formula from analytic geometry:

$$\hat{Q}_X = Q_{X_1} + \frac{Q_{X_2} - Q_{X_1}}{P_{X_2} - P_{X_1}} (P_X - P_{X_1}) \tag{5}$$

where $\hat{Q}_X$ (read "Q-hat") indicates the Q-coordinate of a point on the estimated regression line as distinguished from Q_X, which indicates an observed Q-coordinate.[1] We already have one point on the line, namely, $(\bar{P}_X, \bar{Q}_X) = (.0141, 113.5)$. To use Equation (5), we need to locate one other point on the line. Since we have drawn the regression line through the observation for 1976, we can use those coordinates, i.e.,

$$P_{X_1} = .0141, \quad Q_{X_1} = 113.5$$
$$P_{X_2} = .0111, \quad Q_{X_2} = 129.3$$

Substituting into Equation (1), we get:

$$\hat{Q}_X = 113.5 + \frac{129.3 - 113.5}{.0111 - .0142} (P_X - .0141)$$

$$= 113.5 - 5{,}266.67(P_X - .0142)$$
$$= 113.5 - 5{,}266.67\, P_X + 74.24$$
$$= 187.8 - 5{,}266.7\, P_X \tag{6}$$

Equation (6) may be interpreted as follows:

1. The Y-intercept of 187.8 provides vertical location of the line upon the graph. It has no economic significance.
2. The coefficient of $P_X(-5{,}266.7)$ indicates that the per capita consumption of beef is reduced by about five pounds for each .001 increase in the ratio of the price of beef to disposable income per capita.

---

[1] The P coordinates are the same whether we are talking about the observed or calculated values. Therefore we don't need a $\hat{P}$.

Thus Equation (6) predicts the effect of simultaneous changes in the price of beef and per capita disposable income. For example, suppose the price of beef is $75 per 100 pounds and disposable income per capita is $5,500. The demand for beef is:

$$\hat{Q} = 187.8 - 5,266.7 \left(\frac{75}{5,500}\right) = 116.0 \text{ pounds per capita.}$$

Now suppose the price of beef rises to $85 per 100 pounds and disposable income per capita increases to $6,000. Then the demand for beef declines to

$$\hat{Q} = 187.8 - 5,266.7 \left(\frac{85}{6,000}\right) = 113.2 \text{ pounds per capita.}$$

Thus the positive effect of rising income is more than offset by the negative effect of rising price. The net effect is a decrease in the per capita consumption of beef.

Step 6. Compare calculated and actual values. How close are the calculated values of the dependent variable to the actual values? In other words, how well does our regression equation predict the beef consumption variable on the basis of the price variable? A visual answer to this question is obtained by plotting the actual and calculated values over time, as shown in Exhibit 6–5.

The deviation of the calculated line from the observed line is a reflection of the fact that all of the dots in Exhibit 6–5 did not fall along the regression line. For if they had, the variation in Q_X would be completely explained or accounted for by the variations in P_X and hence Q_X would equal $\hat{Q}_X$. The fact that the dots depart from the regression line indicates that forces other than price and disposable income affect beef consumption. In a multiple regression analysis, one or more of these other forces would be incorporated into the regression equation.

Logarithmic Models

Sometimes time-series data follow a curvilinear trend when plotted on arithmetic scales, where equal distance represents equal absolute change in value. This does not prevent regression analysis if it can be hypothesized that the data approximate a geometric progression of the form

$$Y_i = a\, T_i^b \tag{7}$$

where

Y = The value of the variable in question
T = The pertinent time period

Exhibit 6–5

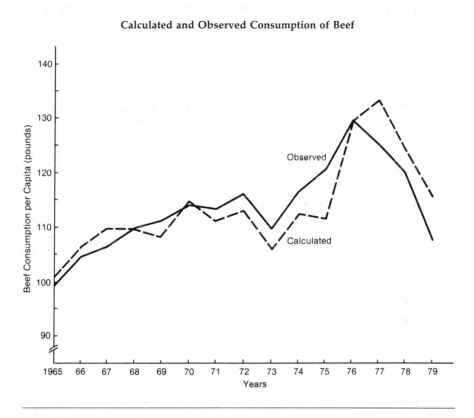

Calculated and Observed Consumption of Beef

A curve that approximates a geometric progression will tend to approximate a straight line if it is plotted on a logarithmic scale, where equal distances represent equal ratios. Algebraically, this amounts to a transformation of Equation (7) into the logarithmic form:

$$\log Y_i = \log a + b \log T_i \qquad (8)$$

Equation (8) is called a *log-log model* because it uses logarithms on both sides of the equation. It is a linear equation that assumes an exponential curve for both variables. This is not the case with the variable T_i, which is already linear. Hence we modify Equation (8) to obtain a *log-linear model*:

$$\log Y_i = a + b T_i \qquad (9)$$

This is a linear function that expresses a logarithmic distribution of the dependent variable and a linear distribution of the independent variable.

The use of the log-linear models can be illustrated by a millinery demand study based on the data in Exhibit 6–6.

The data in the price index and sales index columns of Exhibit 6–6 refer to prices and sales for a group of millinery products in a multi-

Exhibit 6–6————————————————————————————————————

Millinery Demand Study

Week	Price Index*	Sales Index*	Logarithm of Sales Index†
1	105	560	2.7482
2	102	571	2.7566
3	110	408	2.6107
4	114	466	2.6684
5	122	232	2.3655
6	113	310	2.4914
7	124	319	2.5038
8	122	200	2.3010
9	122	180	2.2553
10	126	182	2.2601
11	133	178	2.2504
12	142	175	2.2430
13	139	129	2.1106
14	149	101	2.0043
15	150	120	2.0792
Means	124.9	238	2.3766

* Previous year's corresponding 15-week period = 100.
† Common logarithms may be obtained from a calculator or from Table C in the Appendix at the end of this book.

branch department store. They are expressed as indexes, i.e., as percentages of a previous period. Logarithms of the sales indexes (column 4) have been added for purposes of regression analysis. The price and sales data were obtained from controlled experiments at the store's branches during 45 midweek shopping days (Tuesdays to Thursdays for 15 weeks). This short time period permitted wide price manipulations while other influential factors, such as income, seasonal changes, fashion variations, and competitor's price reactions, could be assumed to remain constant. This made it possible to confine the analysis to a simple correlation between demand and price.

As in the previous study of the demand for beef, one of the first steps is to plot the variables over time on arithmetic scales, as shown in Exhibit 6–7. When a freehand trend line (dashed line) is drawn through each of these series, it becomes apparent that the sales series exhibits a curved trend, while the price series exhibits a linear trend. For a linear regression, therefore, a log-linear model is appropriate.

Exhibit 6–7

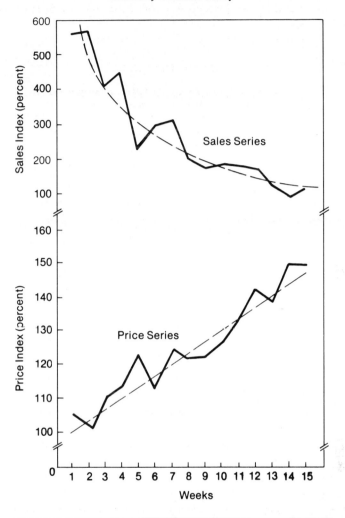

Millinery Demand Study

The log-linear model for this regression analysis is

$$\log \hat{Q}_X = a + b\,P_X \tag{10}$$

where

log Q_X = Logarithm of sales index
P_X = Price index

In order to find the regression equation by the graphic method, price and sales indexes are plotted on semilog paper, which has arithmetic scaling on the horizontal axis and logarithmic scaling on the vertical axis. As shown in Exhibit 6–8, this allows the demand function to be drawn as a straight line.

Exhibit 6–8 _____

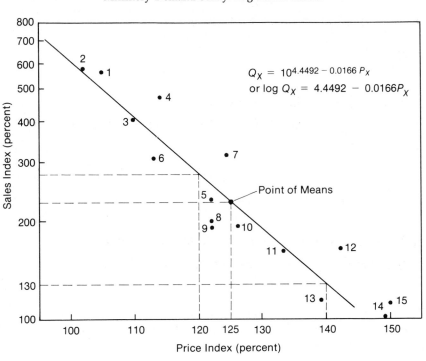

Millinery Demand Study: Log-Linear Model

$Q_X = 10^{4.4492 - 0.0166\,P_X}$

or $\log Q_X = 4.4492 - 0.0166 P_X$

The first step is to locate the point of means, through which the line must pass, no matter what its slope is. The mean value of the price index is the sum of the price index column divided by n (i.e., 15). However, the mean value of the sales variable is *not* the average sales index. It is obtained by taking the average of the *logarithms* of the sales indexes. The average logarithm is 2.3766 and this corresponds to a sales index of 238, i.e., $10^{2.3766} = 238$. Therefore, the point of means is at (P_X, Q_X), where $P = 124.9$ and $Q = 238$.

After locating the point of means, we choose any other point on the line. The appropriate two-point formula for computing the regression equation is:

$$\log \hat{Q}_X = \log Q_{X_1} + \frac{\log Q_{X_2} - \log Q_{X_1}}{P_{X_2} - P_{X_1}} (P_X - P_{X_1}) \qquad (11)$$

To illustrate, suppose we decide that the data for week 2 are on the line. Then

$$\log \hat{Q}_X = 2.3766 + \frac{2.7566 - 2.3766}{102 - 124.9} (P_X - 124.9)$$

$$\log \hat{Q}_X = 4.4492 - .0166 \, P_X$$

therefore,

$$\hat{Q}_X = 10^{4.4492 - .0166 \, P_X}$$

To check our calculation, suppose we let $P_X = 120$. Then,

$$\log \hat{Q}_X = 4.4492 - 0.0166(120) = 2.4572$$

and

$$\hat{Q}_X = 10^{2.4572} = 286.5$$

This accords with our visual inspection of Exhibit 6–8.

Estimating Elasticity with Logarithmic Models

One of the properties of a power function of the form

$$Q = aP^b \qquad (12)$$

is that its elasticity is the exponent of the independent variable. To see why this is true, recall that when a demand function is known, price elasticity is defined as

$$\varepsilon_D = \frac{dQ}{dP} \cdot \frac{P}{Q} \qquad (13)$$

When Equation (13) is applied to Equation (12), we get

$$\varepsilon_D = ba P_X^{b-1} \cdot \frac{P_X}{aP_X^b} = ba P_X^{b-1} \cdot \frac{1}{aP_X^{b-1}} = b$$

Thus, when the power function

$$\hat{Q}_X = aP_X^b \qquad (14)$$

is transformed into the log-log model

$$\log \hat{Q}_X = \log a + b \log P_X \qquad (15)$$

the exponent b of Equation (14) becomes the coefficient of the logarithm of P_X in Equation (15), but it still measures the elasticity of the function, which is everywhere the same. However, for the log-linear model,

$$\log \hat{Q}_X = a + bP_X \tag{16}$$

the left side of the equation is measured on a logarithmic scale, in which equal distances represent equal ratios or percentage changes. Hence the point elasticity formula becomes

$$\varepsilon_D = \frac{d\hat{Q}_X}{dP_X} \cdot \frac{P_X}{\hat{Q}_X} = \frac{d\hat{Q}_X / \hat{Q}_X}{dP_X / P_X} \tag{17}$$

But we recognize that $d\hat{Q}_X / \hat{Q}_X$ is the derivative of the natural logarithm of $\hat{Q}_X$. Translating into common logarithms, we get

$$d\hat{Q}_X / \hat{Q}_X = d \ln \hat{Q}_X = 2.303 \, d \log \hat{Q}_X.$$

Therefore, Equation (17) becomes

$$\varepsilon_D = 2.303 \, P_X \frac{d \log \hat{Q}_X}{dP_X} \tag{18}$$

Since

$$\log \hat{Q}_X = a + bP_X$$

we have

$$\varepsilon_D = 2.303 \frac{d(a + bP_X)}{dP_X} (P_X) = 2.303 \, bP_X \tag{19}$$

To illustrate, take the preceding example, for which

$$\log \hat{Q}_X = 4.4492 - 0.0166 \, P_X$$

If we let $P_X = 120$, the elasticity at that point is

$$\varepsilon_D = 2.303(-0.0166)(120) = -4.588$$

To find the arc elasticity of a log-linear model, we first calculate values for $\hat{Q}_{X_1}$ and $\hat{Q}_{X_2}$ for corresponding values of P_{X_1} and P_{X_2}. Then we use the standard arc formula:

$$E_D = \frac{\hat{Q}_{X_2} - \hat{Q}_{X_1}}{\hat{Q}_{X_2} + \hat{Q}_{X_1}} \cdot \frac{P_{X_2} + P_{X_1}}{P_{X_2} - P_{X_1}} \tag{20}$$

For example, suppose we want the price elasticity for the arc between $P_{X_1} = 115$ and $P_{X_2} = 125$. Then

$$\log \hat{Q}_{X_1} = 4.4492 - 0.0166(115) = 2.5402; \quad \hat{Q}_{X_1} = 346.9$$
$$\log \hat{Q}_{X_2} = 4.4492 - 0.0166(125) = 2.3742; \quad \hat{Q}_{X_2} = 236.7$$

and

$$E_D = \frac{(236.7 - 346.9)(125 + 115)}{(236.7 + 346.9)(125 - 115)} = \frac{-110.2(240)}{(583.6)10} = -4.532$$

This means that for the range in question, a 1 percent change in the price variable produces about a 4.5 percent change in the opposite direction in the demand or sales variable.

Least Squares Method of Simple Linear Regression

The least squares method is a mathematical procedure for fitting a line to a set of observed data points (X, Y) such that the sum of the squared deviations between the calculated and observed values of Y is minimized. In order to do this, the parameters a and b must be calculated for the line

$$\hat{Y}_i = a + bX_i \tag{21}$$

where

X_i = The ith value of the independent variable
$\hat{Y}_i$ = The calculated value of the dependent variable corresponding to X_i
a = The Y-intercept of the regression line
b = The slope of the regression line

If b is positive, the regression line will resemble the one shown in Exhibit 6–9.

Residuals or Deviations

Exhibit 6–9 demonstrates that wherever the regression line is drawn, it passes through the point of means $(\overline{X}, \overline{Y})$, but it is unlikely to pass through many of the observation points (X, Y). Some may lie above the line, some below, and maybe some will be right on it. The calculated value $\hat{Y}_i$ lies on the regression line. The vertical distance between the observed Y_i and the regression line is called a residual or a deviation, e_i and it is measured as:

$$e_i = Y_i - \hat{Y}_i \tag{22}$$

hence

$$Y_i = a + bX_i + e_i \tag{23}$$

Exhibit 6–9

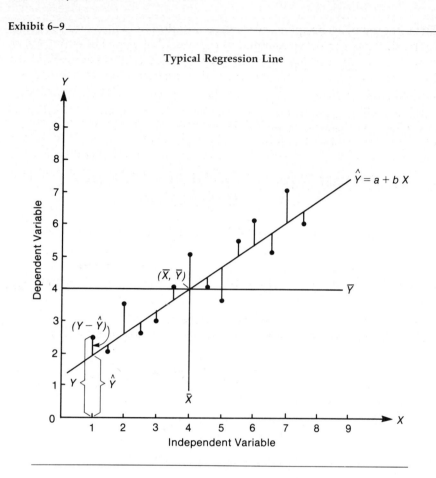

Typical Regression Line

Equation (23) states that the observed value of the dependent variable is equal to the calculated value plus the residual error term. If the observed value lies on the regression line, the residual error is zero.

The error term, e_i, exists for one or more of the following reasons:

1. Some of the factors that affect the behavior of the dependent variable probably have been omitted.
2. Errors in the measurement of economic data are to be expected.
3. Random errors are inevitable, considering the unpredictable nature of human behavior, environmental fluctuations, and so on.

Obtaining the Best Fit

If all of the residuals were zero, the regression line would be a perfect fit. That is, all observed points would lie upon the regression line. Since this rarely (if ever) happens, we need a criterion by which one particular regression line can be determined unequivocally to be a better fit than all others. It seems reasonable to expect that such a line would yield the least total error. The best fitting line is the one that minimizes the sum of the squared deviations. Such a line is called an *ordinary least squares regression line.*

As explained in Appendix 6A at the end of this chapter, differential calculus can be used to obtain equations for the calculation of the parameters *a* and *b* of the regression equation $\hat{Y}_i = a + bX_i$. Several equivalent versions of these equations can be worked out. One version is the following (*n* is the number of observed points):

$$b = \frac{n\Sigma X_i Y_i - \Sigma X_i \Sigma Y_i}{n\Sigma X_i^2 - (\Sigma X_i)^2} \tag{24}$$

and

$$a = \frac{\Sigma Y_i - b\Sigma X_i}{n} \tag{25}$$

If we let $\overline{X}$ and $\overline{Y}$ denote the mean values of X and Y respectively, then $\Sigma X_i = nX$ and $\Sigma Y_i = nY$. Hence, Equation (24) can be rewritten as:

$$b = \frac{\Sigma X_i Y_i - n\overline{X}\overline{Y}}{\Sigma X_i^2 - n\overline{X}^2} \tag{26}$$

and Equation (25) can be rewritten as

$$a = \overline{Y} - b\overline{X} \tag{27}$$

Example of Least Squares Calculation

The beef study data presented in Exhibit 6–1 will be used to illustrate the least squares calculation of a regression line. The first step is to calculate the sums and averages as shown in Exhibit 6–10.[2]

Then, by Equation (24),

$$b = \frac{n\Sigma PQ - \Sigma P\Sigma Q}{n\Sigma P^2 - (\Sigma P)^2} = \frac{15(23.82039) - (.2112)(1702.9)}{15(.0030118) - (.2112)^2}$$

$$= \frac{-2.34663}{.00057156} = -4,105.658199$$

---

[2] Since regression calculations are only *estimates* of the true situation, you may want to round off the intermediate calculations. We won't say this is wrong, but you should be aware that doing so will make a substantial difference in your final answer. Also be aware that the equivalent equations given in statistics texts for calculation of the parameters *a* and *b* are *not* equivalent when intermediate calculations are rounded off. Computer programs do not round off until final output, and even with hand-held electronic calculators, it is actually easier to store and work with unrounded numbers, as we have done throughout this chapter. However, the final answer should be rounded to avoid giving the impression of accuracy that does not actually exist.

Exhibit 6–10

Beef Demand Study Summary Data

(1) Year	(2) Beef Price/ Disposable Income Per Capita (P)	(3) Observed Consumption of Beef per Capita (Q)	(4) (PQ)	(5) (P²)	(6) Regression* Estimates $\hat{Q} = 171.3343341 - 4,105.658199P$	(7) Deviations $(Q - \hat{Q})$	(8) Deviations Squared $(Q - \hat{Q})^2$	(9) Observed Consumption of Beef per Capita Squared (Q^2)
1965	.0164	99.5	1.63180	.00026896	104.0015396	−4.501539637	20.2638591	9,900.25
1966	.0152	104.2	1.58384	.00023104	108.9283295	−4.728329476	22.35709963	10,857.64
1967	.0147	106.5	1.56555	.00021609	110.9811586	−4.481158575	20.08078217	11,342.25
1968	.0146	109.7	1.60162	.00021316	111.3917244	−1.691724395	2.861931429	12,034.09
1969	.0150	110.8	1.66200	.00022500	109.7494611	1.05053885	1.10363949	12,276.64
1970	.0140	113.7	1.59180	.00019600	113.8551193	−0.155119314	0.024062001	12,927.69
1971	.0146	113.0	1.64980	.00021316	111.3917244	1.608275605	2.586550422	12,769.00
1972	.0144	116.1	1.67184	.00020736	112.2128560	3.887143965	15.1098882	13,479.21
1973	.0157	109.6	1.72072	.00024649	106.8755004	2.724499624	7.422898201	12,012.16
1974	.0146	116.8	1.70528	.00021316	111.3917244	5.408275505	29.24944502	13,642.24
1975	.0146	120.1	1.75346	.00021316	111.3917244	8.708275605	75.83406401	14,424.01
1976	.0111	129.3	1.43523	.00012321	125.7615281	3.538471908	12.52078344	16,718.49
1977	.0104	125.9	1.30936	.00010816	128.6354888	−2.735488831	7.482899145	15,850.81
1978	.0121	120.1	1.45321	.00014641	121.6558699	−1.555869893	2.420731124	14,424.01
1979	.0138	107.6	1.48488	.00019044	114.6762510	−7.076250954	50.07332756	11,577.76
Total	.2112	1,702.9	23.82039	0.00305207			269.3919534	194,236.25
Mean	.01408	113.526667						

* See footnote 2, page 197.

and, by Equation (25),

$$a = \frac{\Sigma Q - b\Sigma P}{n} = \frac{1702.9 + 4{,}105.658199(.2112)}{15} = 171.3343341$$

Hence the least-squares regression equation is[3]

$$\hat{Q} = 171.3343341 - 4{,}105.658199\, P$$

which may be rounded off to

$$\hat{Q} = 171.3 - 4{,}105.7\, P$$

Interpretation of the Parameters

The parameter a is a constant term that establishes the Y-intercept of the line when the function is graphed. It usually has no economic meaning in the demand equation $\hat{Q} = a + bP$ because it is unlikely that $P = 0$ will ever be within the range of observed data. Whether or not it has meaning in other functions will depend upon whether or not zero is within the range of observed values of the independent variable.

The parameter b is the slope of the regression line. It represents the marginal contribution of each unit of the independent variable to the value of the dependent variable. For the demand function $Q_X = a + bP_X$, b (which commonly is negative) is the estimated change (commonly a decrease) in quantity demanded when the price is increased by one dollar.

Evaluating the Regression Equation

The primary purpose of linear regression analysis is to establish a linear equation that can be used to predict the value of the dependent variable, Y, for any given value of the independent variable X, especially when the selected value of X is not among previous observations. The question then immediately arises: How meaningful or accurate is the predicted Y? Two statistical measures are used to answer this question: (1) the standard error of estimate and (2) the coefficient of determination, r^2, and its square root, r, which is called the coefficient of correlation.

---

[3] This may be contrasted with the freehand regression line $\hat{Q} = 187.8 - 5{,}266.7\, P$ that was previously obtained from the same data.

The Standard Error of Estimate

To understand the standard error of estimate, first recall that there is a theoretically true, but unknown and unknowable regression line with the equation:

$$Y_i = \alpha + \beta X_i + \mu_i \qquad (28)$$

For each value of the independent variable, X_i, there is a theoretical population of residuals,

$$\mu_i = Y_i - (\alpha + \beta X_i) \qquad (29)$$

where α and β are parameters of the true regression line, and μ_i is the residual; i.e., the deviation of an observed value of Y from the true regression line. This population is assumed to have a normal probability distribution with a mean of zero. Further, we assume that each of these populations (one for each X_i) has the same variance and standard deviation.

Our estimate of the true regression line is:

$$\hat{Y}_i = a + bX_i + e_i \qquad (30)$$

where $a =$ the estimate of α
   $b =$ the estimate of β
   $Y_i =$ the estimate of Y_i given X_i
   $e_i =$ the estimate of μ_i for X_i.

The error term, e_i, which estimates the unknown μ_i, is calculated as:

$$e_i = Y_i - (a + bX_i) = Y_i - \hat{Y}_i \qquad (31)$$

Since the probability distribution of the theoretical residuals, μ_i, is assumed to be normal, the probability distribution of the estimated residuals, e_i, is also assumed to be normal. Hence, for small samples ($n < 30$), it follows the t-distribution depicted on Table F in the Appendix at the end of this book.

The standard error of estimate is simply the sample statistic that we use to *estimate* the standard deviation of μ. It is calculated as the standard deviation of e; i.e.,

$$S_e = \sqrt{\frac{\Sigma(Y_i - \hat{Y})^2}{n - k - 1}} \qquad (32)$$

where

   $S_e =$ Standard error of estimate for the regression equation[4]
   $Y_i =$ Observed Y-value at X_i

---

[4] The symbol S_e indicates that we are talking about the standard deviation of a sample taken from a population of residuals whose standard deviation is σ_μ. The notation may be made more specific by indicating the dependent and independent variables, in that order, as subscripts. For example, $S_{Q \cdot P}$ indicates the sampling distribution of residuals of Q as a function of P. This enables a distinction between the standard error, which refers to

$\hat{Y}_i$ = Calculated Y-value at X_i
n = Number of observations
k = Number of independent variables

Equation (32) says that the standard error of estimate is equal to the square root of the sum of the squared residuals or deviations divided by $n - k - 1$ degrees of freedom.[5] From Equation (32) it can be seen that the standard error of estimate represents the *average* error of estimate that may be expected in predicting a value for the dependent variable on the basis of a value for the independent variable in the regression equation.

To illustrate the computation of the standard error of estimate, suppose we return to our study of the demand for beef, using the regression equation

$$\hat{Q}_i = 171.3343341 - 4{,}105.658199\ P_i \qquad (33)$$

that was derived by the least-squares method. In order to use Equation (31), we must first calculate and sum the squared deviations, as shown in Exhibit 6–10. Using the data in column (8), we get:

$$S_e = \sqrt{\frac{269.3919534}{13}} = \sqrt{20.72245795} = 4.55$$

There is a short-cut formula available that avoids the tedious work of calculating and adding the squared deviations:

$$S_e = \sqrt{\frac{\Sigma Y_i^2 - a\Sigma Y_i - b\Sigma X_i Y_i}{n - k - 1}} \qquad (34)$$

Equation (34) uses the same summations that were used to calculate the regression equation, plus ΣY_i^2. For our example, the necessary data are on Exhibit 6–10.

$$
\begin{aligned}
S_{Q\cdot P} &= \sqrt{\frac{\Sigma Q^2 - a\Sigma Q - b\Sigma PQ}{n - k - 1}} \\[2mm]
&= \sqrt{\frac{194{,}236.25 - 171.3343341(1{,}702.9) + 4{,}105.658199(23.82039)}{13}} \\[2mm]
&= \sqrt{20.72245914} = 4.55
\end{aligned}
$$

This agrees with the earlier calculation.[6]

---

deviations from the regression line, and the standard deviations of the sample data from their mean values, which would be designated as S_X and S_Y.

[5] The term "degrees of freedom" refers to the fact that if we know n-1 terms of a sum, the nth term is automatically determined. To calculate the standard error of estimate for a univariate function, we lose two degrees of freedom because the Y-value requires the parameters α and β, which are estimated by a and b in the regression equation $\hat{Y}_i = a + bX_i$. It should be noted also that there is a different t-distribution for each different degree of freedom.

[6] The results of Equation (32) and Equation (34) are precisely the same only if no rounding of numbers has taken place.

The Standard Error of the Regression Coefficient

The standard error of the regression coefficient, S_b, measures the standard deviation of the distribution of the regression coefficient, b. It thus provides a measure of reliability of the regression coefficient. It is calculated as:

$$S_b = \frac{S_e}{\sqrt{\Sigma(X - \bar{X})^2}} \tag{35}$$

Confidence and Prediction Intervals

In the case of our regression model of the demand for beef, we have omitted a number of variables other than price that might influence consumption of beef. In demand models such as this, the effects of such omitted variables are assumed to be minor. It is further assumed that, being both positive and negative, they will tend on average to cancel each other out. Yet for any given year this may not be true. Hence it is useful to provide a range of values or *intervals* within which the predicted figure may be expected to fall with a given probability.

Interval estimates may be made for two types of predictions. One is for the *conditional mean* or *conditional average value* of the dependent variable, and is usually called a *confidence interval*. The other is for an *individual value of Y*, and is usually called a *prediction interval*.

Confidence Interval.   Going back to our beef demand study (Exhibit 6–10), suppose we want to predict the mean or average per capita consumption of beef if the ratio of price of beef to disposable income is stabilized over a long period of time. The conditional mean value of Q, given the condition that $P = P^*$, lies on the true regression line, which we can only estimate as

$$Q = a + bP^*$$

To create a confidence interval for Q, we need a t-value for $t_{\alpha/2}$, where $(1 - \alpha)$ is the desired level of confidence. For example, if we desire a .95 (95 percent) level of confidence, we need a value for $t_{.025}$ (in each tail) and $n - k - 1 = 13$ degrees of freedom. The t-value from Table F is 2.160. The confidence interval is then calculated as:

$$\hat{Q} \pm t_{\alpha/2}S_e \sqrt{\frac{1}{n} + \frac{(P^* - P)^2}{\sum_i P_i^2 - nP^2}} \tag{36}$$

Suppose we let $P^* = .0140$. Then

$$\hat{Q} = 171.3 - 4{,}105.7P$$
$$= 171.3 - 4{,}105.7(.0140) = 113.8$$

The .95 confidence interval is:

$$114.2 \pm (2.16)(4.15) \sqrt{\frac{1}{15} + \frac{(.0140 - .01408)^2}{.0030118 - 15(.01408)^2}} = 114.2 \pm 2.3$$

Thus, if the conditional probability distribution of Q is indeed normal, we can be 95 percent confident that the true conditional mean of Q will lie within the interval 111.9 to 116.5. It should be clear from Equation (36) that as P^* is chosen farther and farther from the mean $\bar{P}$, the confidence interval will grow wider. This makes sense when we remember that the least squares regression line always passes through $(P, \bar{Q})$. Geometrically, then, the point $(\bar{P}, \bar{Q})$ is a pivot about which the estimated regression line may be rotated as we attempt to find the proper location. The farther away from the pivot point we get, the wider will be the sweep of the line between possible positions.

Prediction Interval.   Now suppose we simply want to predict beef consumption next year if we establish a price/income ratio of .0140. Since we are asking for prediction of an individual value for Q rather than a mean value, the prediction interval will be somewhat wider than the confidence interval, according to the formula

$$\hat{Q} \pm t_{\alpha/2} S_e \sqrt{\frac{n + 1}{n} + \frac{(P^* - \bar{P})^2}{\sum_i P_i^2 - n\bar{P}^2}} \tag{37}$$

The .95 prediction interval is

$$114.2 \pm (2.16)(4.15) \sqrt{\frac{16}{15} + \frac{(.0140 - .01408)^2}{.0030118 - 15(.01408)^2}} = 114.2 \pm 9.3$$

Thus, if the conditional probability distribution of Q is indeed normal, we can be 95 percent confident that the interval 104.9 to 123.5 contains the true value of Q when $P = .0140$. Like the confidence interval, the prediction interval also grows wider as we get farther away from the point of means, $(\bar{P}, \bar{Q})$.

Testing for Fit

What proportion of the total variation in Q_X is attributable to P_X and what proportion is attributable to chance or other variables not included in the regression equation? In other words, how strong is the linear association between the variables Q_X and P_X?

This question is answered by the *coefficient of determination* and its square root, called the *coefficient of correlation*.

Coefficient of Determination.   Testing the goodness of fit of the regression line is conceived in terms of explaining or accounting for the variation in the dependent variable. A graphical presentation of the concept is shown in Exhibit 6–11.

Exhibit 6–11

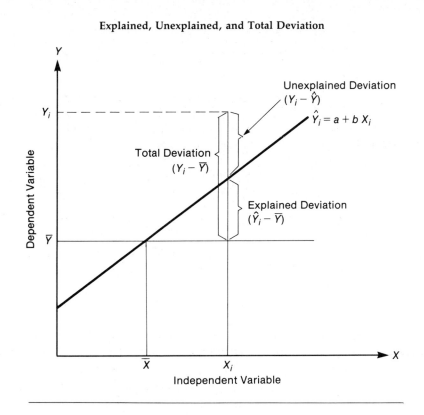

Explained, Unexplained, and Total Deviation

In Exhibit 6–11, $\bar{Y}$ is the mean of all observed Y-values on which the regression line is based, and (X_i, Y_i) is a particular observation. If $\bar{Y}$ were used to estimate Y_i, the *total deviation* would be $Y_i - \bar{Y}$. However, we can get a better estimate by using the regression line to estimate the Y-value. In so doing, we divide the total deviation $(Y - \bar{Y})$ into two parts. The deviation of the lower part, $(\hat{Y} - \bar{Y})$, is explained by the regression equation. The deviation of the upper part, $(Y - \hat{Y})$, is not explained. In a similar way, we can divide the total squared variation of the regression analysis $\Sigma(Y - \bar{Y})^2$ into two parts, so that[7]

$$\Sigma(Y_i - \bar{Y})^2 = \Sigma(\hat{Y}_i - \bar{Y})^2 + \Sigma(Y_i - \hat{Y}_i)^2 \tag{38}$$

$$\begin{pmatrix} \text{Total} \\ \text{variation} \end{pmatrix} = \begin{pmatrix} \text{Explained} \\ \text{variation} \end{pmatrix} + \begin{pmatrix} \text{Unexplained} \\ \text{variation} \end{pmatrix}$$

The coefficient of determination, r^2, measures the degree to which total variation is explained by variation in the independent variable. It is calculated as the ratio of the explained variation to total variation:

$$r^2 = \frac{\text{Explained variation}}{\text{Total variation}} = \frac{\Sigma(\hat{Y}_i - \bar{Y})^2}{\Sigma(Y_i - \bar{Y})^2} \tag{39}$$

which is equivalent to

$$r^2 = 1 - \frac{\text{Unexplained variation}}{\text{Total variation}} = 1 - \frac{\Sigma(Y_i - \hat{Y}_i)^2}{\Sigma(Y_i - \bar{Y})^2} \tag{40}$$

The form of Equation (40) leads to the following formula:

$$r^2 = 1 - \frac{\Sigma(Y_i - \hat{Y}_i)^2}{\Sigma Y_i^2 - \Sigma(Y_i)^2/n} \tag{41}$$

If we apply this formula to our example, using the data from Exhibit 6–10, we get:

$$r^2 = 1 - \frac{269.3919534}{194,236.25 - (1702.9)^2/15}$$

$$= 1 - \frac{269.39}{911.69} = 1 - .2955 = .7045$$

There is also a short-cut formula for r^2 that avoids the tedious computation of $(Y_i - \hat{Y}_i)^2$ by using the same summations as the regression equation. The formula is

$$r^2 = \frac{a\Sigma Y_i + b\Sigma X_i Y_i - (\Sigma Y_i)^2/n}{\Sigma Y_i^2 - (\Sigma Y_i)^2/n} \tag{42}$$

Applying this formula to the data on Exhibit 6–10, we get

$$r^2 = \frac{171.3343341(1702.9) - 4,105.658199(23.82039) - (1702.9)^2/15}{194,236.25 - (1702.9)^2/15}$$

$$= \frac{642.29}{911.69} = .7045$$

---

[7] Some textbooks and computer programs use the terminology: "Total sum of squares = Regression sum of squares + Error sum of squares" or SST = SSR + SSE.

This tells us that about 70 percent of the variation in per capita consumption of beef is explained by variation in the ratio of price to disposable income per capita. Since the explained and total variation (regression sum of squares and total sum of squares) are always positive numbers, values of r^2 may range from 0 to 1 (or in percentage terms, from 0 to 100 percent). A magnitude of zero indicates no relationship between the variables. A magnitude of 1 means that the regression line is a perfect fit, with all variation in Q_X being explained by the variation in P_X. That is, all observed points lie upon the regression line. This, of course, rarely (if ever) happens.[8]

Coefficient of Correlation.   The square root of the coefficient of determination is the *coefficient of correlation, r,* which is a measure of the degree of association between the variables. Since r^2 may range from 0 to 1, r will range from -1 to $+1$. In the present problem,

$$r = \sqrt{.7045} = -.839$$

The sign of r indicates the relative direction of movement between the two variables. It is chosen by the analyst according to the slope of the regression line. The degree of association between the variables is indicated by the magnitude of r. In this case, a fairly strong inverse relationship is indicated between the consumption of beef and its price.[9]

Testing the Basic Assumption

As previously shown, there is a deviation or residual between the estimated Q and the observed Q for most values of P. Regression analysis assumes that the residual for any given value of P is a random sample from an unknown population of residuals. Regression analysis makes

---

[8] A short-cut graphic device that may be used to approximate the standard error and the coefficient of determination is as follows:

1. Estimate the standard error S_e by drawing two lines parallel to the regression line so that approximately two thirds of the dots lie between them (and hence one sixth lie on the far side of each line). The vertical width of the resulting band, measured on the Y-axis, is roughly $2S_e$, so one half of this is approximately S_e.
2. Estimate the sample standard deviation s_Y by drawing two horizontal lines to include approximately two thirds of the dots (and hence exclude one sixth above and below). The vertical width of this band is roughly $2s_Y$, so one half of this is approximately s_Y.
3. The coefficient of determination r^2 is then computed from the formula

$$r^2 = 1 - \left(\frac{S_e}{s_Y}\right)^2$$

[9] The coefficient of correlation does *not* indicate *cause* and *effect*. It merely indicates the degree to which two variables move together. However, economic theory may indicate that there is a cause-and-effect relationship.

three basic assumptions about the distribution of the residuals related to each value of P:

1. They are *randomly* distributed about a mean value of zero (the Q-values are independent).
2. Their distribution is *normal*.
3. All distributions have the *same variance* and *standard deviation*.

If one or more of these assumptions are violated, the validity of the regression analysis is questionable. We will discuss such problems in more detail in the next chapter, although we cannot go deeply into this complex part of econometrics. For detailed coverage of this topic, the student may consult any standard text on econometrics.

For our purposes in this chapter, a simple graphic method can be used to get some idea of whether or not the stated assumptions are being met in a particular study. Exhibit 6–12 shows deviations for a case in which

Exhibit 6–12————————————————————————————

Deviations from a Regression Equation Exhibiting a Random Pattern

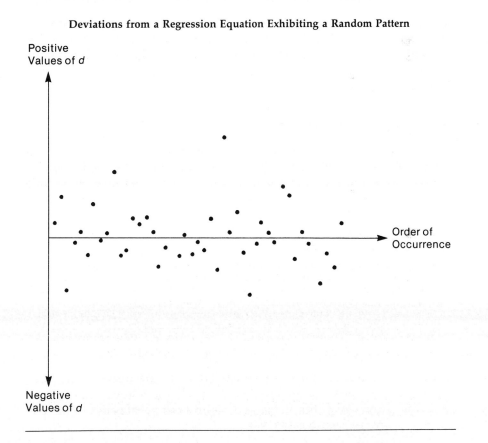

the assumptions are being met. Notice that when the deviations are plotted against their order of occurrence, there is no apparent pattern. That is, they seem to be randomly distributed about the X-axis.

A plot of the residual from the beef consumption study is shown in Exhibit 6–13. Can you detect a pattern?

Exhibit 6–13

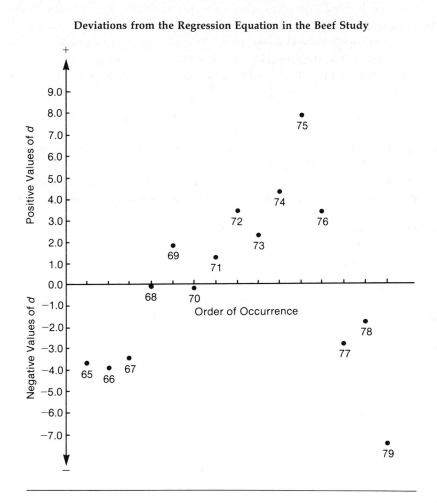

Deviations from the Regression Equation in the Beef Study

You should notice that negative deviations in the three earlier years are followed by positive or zero deviations for the following nine years in a row, after which the deviations again become negative. This pattern indicates the existence of trends in the variables[10] and serves as a warning to the analyst that it might be better to work with "detrended" data.[11]

Marketing Research Approach to Demand Estimation

When sufficient demand data for statistical analysis are not available, it may become necessary to perform marketing research in which the analyst obtains certain information directly from the consumer rather than from statistical data. Some of the reasons why direct approaches might be necessary or desirable are:

1. *A new product is being introduced:* A direct approach is necessary because no data exist for statistical analysis.
2. *Changes are suspected in qualitative variables, such as taste, preference, or consumer expectations:* Statistical data on variables such as price are analyzed on the assumption that such qualitative variables are constant. If they have changed, the statistical data are meaningless.
3. *Market experimentation is necessary:* In order to develop a pricing strategy, the firm needs to determine price elasticities in geographically separate markets.

The list above is representative rather than exhaustive. Undoubtedly there are many other reasons why marketing managers would desire a direct approach to the consumer. The direct approaches most commonly discussed in the marketing literature are *consumer surveys, consumer clinics, and market experiments.*

Consumer Surveys

Consumer surveys are conducted by asking questions of a representative sample of present or potential buyers. Consumers are asked for their reactions to hypothetical changes in demand variables such as price, income, prices of other products, advertising expenditures, and

---

[10] Other patterns in the deviations reveal other kinds of problems. For a more thorough discussion, see J. Walter Elliot, *Economic Analysis for Management Decisions* (Homewood, Ill.: Richard D. Irwin, 1973), pp. 53–55.

[11] There is a variety of techniques for trend removal; some are discussed in Chapter 8. A very easy method is to use a multiple regression model that has trend as one of the independent variables. Multiple regression is covered in the next chapter.

other demand determinants. In theory, the analyst should be able to construct a demand relationship from consumers' responses to these questions. In practice, however, consumers may be either unable or unwilling to give accurate answers to such questions. For this reason, conclusions based on direct answers may be unreliable. Nevertheless, trained interviewers using properly designed questionnaires can gain useful information, indirectly, from the answers. For example, if people seem unaware of price differentials among competing goods, it may be a good indication of price inelasticity. The effectiveness of an advertising campaign may also be measured by the consumers' awareness of the ads.

Consumer surveys can be rather expensive, with survey costs being a function of sample size and the elaborateness of the analysis. However, for at least one important demand variable, namely, consumer expectations, there is no substitute for personal interviews. Consumer expectations regarding future prices, inflation, income, and the availability of substitute goods can have a strong influence upon the demand function. The only way to find out what consumers expect is to ask them. Consumer interviews are also a good way to detect changes in tastes and preferences.

Consumer Clinics

Another method of observing consumer response to changes in demand variables is to conduct a controlled experiment called a *consumer clinic*. The participants in this experiment are given small amounts of money with which to buy certain items from the clinic. The clinic then manipulates demand variables such as producer price or the price of competing goods. The consumers' reactions to these changes are observed and recorded.

The reliability of the data gained from such an experiment is often questioned on the grounds that participants know they are being watched, and therefore do not act naturally. In spite of such shortcomings, in some circumstances a consumer clinic can provide useful information about the demand for a product, particularly when the clinic is complemented by a consumer survey. For example, consumer clinics can detect differences in consumers' reactions in different geographical areas while avoiding the risks associated with market experiments (to be discussed below).

Market Experiments

Unlike the consumer clinic, which is conducted under laboratory conditions, a market experiment is performed under actual market conditions. The markets chosen for an experiment must be similar yet seg-regated from one another. After the choice of markets has been made, the firm begins the experiment, varying one or more of the demand determinants in these markets and noting results. For example, the firm might charge different prices in different markets and com-pare results. With the help of demographic statistics developed by the U.S. Census Bureau, firms can perform experiments in several markets to determine how demand is affected by characteristics such as age, occupational classification, educational level, family size, and ethnic background.

Market experiments must be conducted on a scale sufficiently large to insure validity of the results, even though experimentation on a large scale is very expensive and can be quite risky. Consumers are unaware that they are the subjects of an experiment. If they are driven away by price increases or shifts in advertising emphasis, they may never come back.

If a controlled experiment is attempted, the cost goes even higher. If the experiment is not controlled, however, the firm is unable to distin-guish the effects of experimental manipulation from those stemming from random disturbance factors such as strikes, bad weather, or unan-ticipated actions by competitors. Because of their high cost, market ex-periments tend to be of short duration and limited scope. If an experi-ment can't be verified by other means, moreover, the firm may end up making long-run decisions on the basis of just a few short-run observa-tions.

In spite of these problems, direct market experimentation can be quite useful. For example, if the firm is introducing a new product, no statisti-cal data on it will exist. A market experiment may provide the best possible guidance for pricing the new product. A firm may also find market experiments useful for verifying the results of a statistical study before it commits itself to a particular marketing strategy.

Example of a Market Experiment

In 1962, researchers at the University of Florida chose Grand Rapids, Michigan, as the site for a market experiment to determine the effects of price competition on three varieties of Valencia oranges.[12] One variety was from California, one from the Indian River district in Florida, and one from the interior district of Florida. The city of Grand Rapids was

---

[12] Reported by Marshal B. Godwin, W. Fred Chapman, Jr., and William T. Hanley in "Competition between Florida and California Valencia Oranges in the Fruit Market," *Bulletin 704* (Gainesville, Florida: Agricultural Experiment Stations, Institute of Food and Agricultural Services, University of Florida, in cooperation with the U.S. Department of Agriculture, Florida Citrus Commission, December 1965).

chosen as the site of the experiment because it was typical of midwestern markets in size, demographic characteristics, and economic base. Nine supermarkets located in various parts of the city participated in the experiment, which lasted 31 days.

Each day the price of each variety of range was changed, and the quantity sold was recorded for each variety. The range of prices was 32 cents—16 cents above and below the going price when the study began. Recorded sales during the experiment exceeded 9,250 dozen oranges. Results of the study are summarized in the 3 × 3 matrix of Exhibit 6–14.

Exhibit 6–14_____

Price Elasticities and Cross Elasticities of Valencia Oranges

| Variety Undergoing Price Change | Relative Change in Quantity Demanded | | |
	Florida Indian River	Florida Interior	California
Florida Indian River	−3.07	+1.56	+0.01
Florida Interior	+1.16	−3.01	+0.14
California	+0.18	+0.09	−2.76

The **boldface** entries in Exhibit 6–14 show price elasticities; that is, the percentage change in the quantity demanded of each variety as its own price changed. The remaining entries are cross elasticities of demand; that is, the percentage change in the quantity demanded of the variety named in the column heading in response to a 1 percent change in the price of the variety named in the row heading. The cross elasticities are particularly revealing. Consumers apparently viewed the two varieties of Florida oranges as close substitutes and would readily switch from one to the other when prices changed. But California oranges seem to occupy a distinct market; that is, California and Florida oranges were not viewed as close substitutes. This impression of two distinct markets is reinforced by the price elasticities in boldface type. The Florida oranges are not only quite sensitive to price changes, but also exhibit almost the same price elasticity (−3.07 versus −3.01). The California oranges were also highly price elastic at −2.76, but not as sensitive as the Florida fruit.

Two conditions that were essential to the validity of this study. First, the time period was short enough to prevent changes in variables other than price, such as income, taste, population, and inflation. Second, the experimenters were able to insure an adequate supply of each variety at each experimental price.

Summary

Demand estimation is an essential part of demand analysis. It is a crucial input to managerial decision making about the short run and the long run. The method most often used for empirically measuring demand is linear regression. If the quantity demanded is considered to be a function of a single independent variable, then simple linear regression may be used. When two or more independent variables are involved, then multiple regression analysis (to be discussed in the next chapter) is called for.

When adequate records are available, statistical analysis is the best method for demand measurement. The data base for statistical analysis may be one of two types:

1. *Time-series data,* which record movements of selected variables over a fairly long span of time. These data must be adjusted for population changes and inflation (or deflation) before they can be useful. It may also be necessary to remove trend, seasonal, and cyclical influences from them.
2. *Cross-sectional data,* which provide a snapshot of many variables at one point in time. These data also require adjustment to get rid of unwanted influences.

Demand measurement is accomplished by curve fitting. This involves finding an equation, preferably linear, that explains the variation of the dependent variable in response to variation in the independent variable. The basic procedure for curve fitting is the method of least squares. In demand estimation, the method of least squares is used to fit a straight line, called a regression line, to the data. However, there is a graphic method that can be used to fit a simple regression line with good results.

The graphic method is beneficial in that it provides a valuable preliminary analysis that reveals relationships that are often not readily apparent when following the mathematical method of least squares. The graphic method also assists in the evaluation of a calculated regression line (no matter how calculated) and is a valuable learning device for both students and analysts.

Of course, regression analysis cannot be performed unless an adequate statistical data base is available. If one is not available, then the consumer must be approached directly. Direct approaches may take the form of:

1. *Consumer surveys,* in which consumers are asked for their reactions to hypothetical changes in price, income, prices of other products, advertising, and other determinants of demand.
2. *Consumer clinics,* in which demand variables are manipulated and the resulting consumer reactions are observed under controlled laboratory conditions.
3. *Market experiments,* in which prices or other variables are manipulated in single or multiple markets and the resulting consumer reactions are observed.

Problems

1.   Explain why a scatter diagram is an important first step in analyzing the relationship between dependent and independent variables.

2.   Critically evaluate the following statements:

a.   "A very large sample size in a regression analysis will always result in a useful outcome."

b.   "A high coefficient of determination (r^2) means a significant regression."

3.   The results of an empirical demand study are: regression equation: $\hat{Y} = 20 + 4X$; mean values: $\overline{Y} = 40$, $\overline{X} = 5$; standard error of the estimate: $S_e = 3.0$; standard deviation of Y: $s_Y = 6.8$; and number of data points: $n = 60$.

a.   Construct a scatter diagram of the data points as you imagine it might be.

b.   What demand variable might X represent? Explain briefly.

c.   Calculate r^2.

d.   Suppose management can control X and is planning a value of 8 in the upcoming period. Forecast $\hat{Y}$ and explain the degree of confidence you have in your estimate. (*Hint:* Consider a range of possible values for Y.)

4.   The Road Ranger Manufacturing Company makes conversion kits to transform ordinary pickups into recreational vehicles for camping. The company's management believes that sales of recreational vehicles are closely related to disposable income of the nation. The following data have been gleaned from the company's records and the *1981 Statistical Abstract of the United States.*

Year	Company Sales ($ millions)	Disposable Personal Income ($ billions)	Population (millions)	Consumer Price Index
1973	$ 83.6	$ 914	211.9	133.1
1974	101.2	998	213.9	147.7
1975	111.1	1,096	216.0	161.2
1976	126.5	1,194	218.0	170.5
1977	143.0	1,312	220.2	181.5
1978	162.8	1,463	222.6	195.4
1979	212.3	1,642	225.1	217.4
1980	224.4	1,822	227.7	246.8

a. Make appropriate adjustments to the sales and income data.
b. Plot the variables over time. Are there any leads and lags in the data? What are the underlying trends?
c. Plot the scatter diagram and fit a freehand regression line.
d. Estimate the regression equation.
e. Plot the actual and calculated values of sales.

5.   a. Plot a scatter diagram for each of the following three sets of data. What sort of curve seems to fit each set?

A		B		C	
Price P	Units Sold Q	Daily Average Temperature X	Admissions to Municipal Swimming Pool Q	Number of Employees X	Monthly Contributions to IRA Accounts ($000) Q
$2.40	12,000	80.3°	340	650	$ 82.8
3.13	5,700	69.4	210	100	5.0
2.65	8,000	83.1	410	520	59.3
3.03	6,400	85.7	480	960	148.7
2.52	8,900	82.3	400	210	15.2
2.43	11,300	79.8	320	740	100.6
3.74	4,800	76.4	280	140	8.3
2.60	9,000	73.7	250	360	34.0
2.62	9,300	80.6	330	1,050	110.1

Using the least squares method:
b. Calculate the regression equation for data set A and show that the calculated line passes through the point of means. CAUTION: Do not round off any numbers until you have completed the exercise.
c. Repeat part (b) for data set B.
6.   Develop a log-log model for data set C of Problem 5 and use the least squares method to develop the appropriate equation for IRA contributions as a function of the number of employees.

7.   A professor, hoping to encourage students to continue in higher education, assigned them a study of the relationship between income and education. His students discovered the following data at the university library.

Average Number of Years of Education X	Average Annual Income ($000) Y
4	$ 6
5	7
6	8
7	9
8	11
10	12
12	15
14	21
15	30
17	40
20	45

a.   Determine the regression equation.
b.   What percentage of the variation of annual income is explained by the average number of years of education?
c.   Critically evaluate the relationship between income and years of education. Can you suggest any other variables that should be included?

8.   The sales manager of a large furniture store is attempting to measure the effectiveness of a newspaper advertising campaign. Over the past 13 weeks, varying amounts of space have been used to advertise sales of major appliances and other big-ticket furniture items. Letting X represent column-inches of advertising space and Y the number of items sold in response to the ads, the data collected may be summarized as follows:

$$\Sigma X = 1,407 \qquad \Sigma Y = 403$$
$$\Sigma X^2 = 184,971 \qquad \Sigma Y^2 = 13,983$$
$$\Sigma XY = 48,552$$

a.   Calculate the regression equation.
b.   Calculate the standard error of estimate.
c.   Calculate the coefficient of determination.
d.   Evaluate the regression equation.

9.   A new England fuel oil company has collected the following data to determine the relationship between average daily temperature and average daily fuel oil consumption.

Average Daily Temperature (°F)	Average Daily Fuel Oil Consumption (gallons)
10	7.0
25	6.3
32	5.1
44	4.6
50	3.4
62	2.9
69	1.3
83	1.0
90	0.6

a. Calculate the estimated linear relationship and interpret the estimated intercept and slope. Do they both make sense?
b. Calculate the standard error of estimate.
c. Predict the average daily fuel oil consumption when the average daily temperature is 55° F, and construct a 95 percent confidence interval for your prediction.

10.   Since a major determinant of demand is per capita income, policy makers are always concerned about anything that will affect per capita income. Of particular concern is fertility rates in developing countries. Suppose that data from 26 countries in Latin America and 26 countries in Africa have been used to develop the regression model

$$\hat{Y} = b_0 + b_1 X$$

where

Y = Per capita income
X = Percentage of population under age 15

Computer runs have produced the following results:

Latin America:

$$b_0 = 2{,}170.7 \qquad \text{SSR} = 954{,}235$$
$$b_1 = -42.0 \qquad \text{SSE} = 33{,}402$$
$$\text{SST} = 987{,}637$$

Africa:

$$b_0 = 893.57 \qquad \text{SSR} = 153{,}785$$
$$b_1 = -17.28 \qquad \text{SSE} = 3{,}774$$
$$\text{SST} = 157{,}559$$

a. What is the meaning of the slope coefficient in each model?
b. Compute and interpret the coefficient of determination for each model. Which one has a better fit? Why?

c. A Latin American manufacturer wants to know what the per capita income of a particular country might be if its population under age 15 is reduced to 12 percent of the total population. Can you tell him?

11. An automobile dealer has performed a regression analysis of the relationship between monthly expenditures on advertising and monthly sales of automobiles. From data covering 24 months, the least squares regression equation is

$$\hat{Q} = -2.3 + .39A$$

where

$\hat{Q}$ = Estimated number of cars sold
A = Advertising expenditure in hundreds of dollars

In addition, the following calculations have been made:

$$S_e = 4.65$$
$$r^2 = .8012$$
$$S_e \sqrt{\frac{1}{n} + \frac{(A^* - \bar{A})^2}{\Sigma A^2 - n\bar{A}^2}} = 2.09 \text{ when } A^* = 110$$
$$S_e \sqrt{\frac{n + 1}{n} + \frac{(A^* - \bar{A})^2}{\Sigma A^2 - n\bar{A}^2}} = 5.10 \text{ when } A^* = 110$$

a. The automobile dealer's sales manager claims that in those months in which $11,000 is spent on advertising, 42 cars on the average will be sold. Can he be right? Hint: Construct a .95 confidence interval of $A = 110$ (hundreds of dollars) and see whether it encompasses $Q = 42$.

b. Construct a .95 prediction interval for Q if $A = 110$.

12. In an effort to determine the correct price for a new product, a company introduced the product in 10 similar markets with the same promotion but with 10 different prices. After gathering data on the first month's sales, the following regression equation was developed:

$$A = 1,812.11 - 73.91P$$

for which the coefficient of correlation, r, is $-.519$.

a. Given the value of the correlation coefficient, is there sufficient evidence to say that there is a negative linear relationship between price and the quantity demanded?

b. How strong is the relationship between price and quantity demanded? Discuss.

Case Problem: Midland State University

13.   Midland State University is a state institution dedicated to the proposition that anyone who wants should be able to get a college education. Consequently, the policy of the board of regents, with the backing of the state legislature, has been to keep tuition charges for state residents as low as possible. The last tuition increase occurred eight years ago, and the present tuition of $250 per semester is one of the lowest (if not the lowest) in the United States. However, costs have risen until the current tuition represents no more than 5 percent of the actual cost per student. It is clear that tuition must be increased; the question is: By how much?

In an effort to determine the effect of increased tuition charges on student enrollment, the chancellor of the university has presented a questionnaire to a cross section of 1,000 students. Each student was asked to choose one of six responses as to whether he or she would remain in school at five different levels of tuition charges. The six responses were: (1) definitely not, (2) probably not, (3) perhaps, (4) probably, (5) very probably, and (6) definitely. In quantitative terms, these responses are equivalent to the following probabilities of remaining in school: (1) 0.0, (2) 0.2, (3) 0.4, (4) 0.6, (5) 0.8, and (6) 1.0. The results of the survey are as follows:

Tuition per Semester	Number of Students Responding in Category					
	(1)	(2)	(3)	(4)	(5)	(6)
$400	0	25	50	225	300	400
500	50	100	100	300	250	200
600	100	150	250	250	150	100
700	300	225	175	150	100	50
800	500	300	125	50	25	0

Questions:
a.   How many students per 1,000 currently enrolled may be expected to remain in school?
b.   Plot the tuition charges and related enrollment expected and sketch the demand curve.
c.   Perform linear regression analysis to estimate the true demand curve.
d.   At what tuition charge will revenue be maximized?

Case Problem: Foodland Grocery Stores

14.   Foodland is the largest grocery chain in Honolulu, operating nine stores in various locations. Mr. Moore, the marketing director, has observed the selling price and sales volume of milk for 10 randomly selected weeks during 1983. The information has been organized and tabulated as follows:

	Milk Sales and Price	
Week	Sales (Y) (000 gallons)	Price (X) (per gallon)
1	11	$2.50
2	6	3.30
3	5	3.10
4	13	2.60
5	10	2.70
6	16	2.10
7	6	3.00
8	12	2.80
9	18	2.10
10	20	2.20

Mr. Moore wants to input the data to a computer regression program and to present the results to Mr. Kepple, who is general manager. Mr. Kepple doesn't have too much background in regression analysis, so you are assigned to run the computer program and to explain the computer output with definition of the statistical terminology. (If you do not have access to a linear regression program on a computer, the problem can be solved using a hand-held calculator.) You must include at least the following; add any other significant findings:

a.   Regression equation
b.   Intercept
c.   Regression coefficient
d.   Standard error of estimate
e.   Standard error of regression coefficient
f.   R-squared
g.   Coefficient of correlation
h.   Sum of squares deviation from regression
i.   Sum of squares total
j.   Residuals
k.   Explained variation
l.   Unexplained variation

If you have studied regression analysis in a statistics class, you may also try to explain the following:

m.   Computed t-value

n.   Analysis of variance (ANOVA) and F-statistic
o.   Finally, state your conclusion concerning the reliability of the regression equation.

References

Baumol, William J. *Economic Theory and Operations Analysis,* 4th ed. Englewood Cliffs, N.J.: Prentice-Hall, 1977.

Dean, Joel. *Managerial Economics.* Englewood Cliffs, N.J.: Prentice-Hall, 1960.

Goodwin, M. R.; W. F. Chapman, Jr.; and W. T. Manley. *Competition Between Florida and Valencia Oranges,* Bulletin 7, Economic Research Service, U.S. Department of Agriculture, Washington, D.C., December 1965.

Hanke, J. E., and A. G. Reitsch. *Business Forecasting.* Boston: Allyn & Bacon, 1981, pp. 74–110.

Lapin, L. *Statistics For Modern Business Decisions,* 3d ed. New York: Harcourt Brace Jovanovich, 1981.

Working, E. J. "What Do Statistical 'Demand Curves' Show?" *Quarterly Journal of Economics,* February 1927, pp. 212–35.

7

Demand Estimation: Multiple Regression Analysis

In the preceding chapter, we saw how simple linear regression can be used to analyze the relationship between a single independent variable and the demand for some good or service. In some cases, variations in demand are explained satisfactorily by variations in the selected independent variable. In other cases, however, we may want to examine the relationship between demand and two or more independent variables that vary more or less simultaneously. This can be done by means of *multiple regression analysis*.

Multiple regression analysis estimates the simultaneous relationship between a dependent variable (here Q, quantity demanded) and any number of independent variables, X_1, X_2, X_3, . . . , X_k (here the factors that affect demand). Therefore, multiple regression analysis is basically the estimation of the regression parameters for each variable, each parameter (or coefficient) being a measure of how much each variable influences demand while all others are held constant.

The material in this chapter covers three main topics:

1. Construction of a multivariate demand equation.
2. Evaluation and testing of the multivariate demand equation.
3. Some special problems with multiple regression.

Because it is difficult to perform a multiple regression by hand, it is best left to a digital computer. A representative computer printout will be used to illustrate multiple regression analysis.[1] However, the computer output does not explain the results of regression analysis. Therefore, this chapter will stress the interpretation, testing, and validation of the multiple regression equation.

Construction of a Multivariate Demand Function

Construction of a multivariate demand equation must meet three very important requirements: (1) it must reflect as closely as possible the true relationships among the dependent and independent variables, (2) it must be a model that is reliable and easy to interpret, and (3) it must be feasible within given constraints of time and cost.

The technical aspects of multiple regression models are explained in most standard statistics or econometrics textbooks. In addition to having a working knowledge of these technical aspects of multiple regression, a skillful multiple regression analyst requires sound economic thinking, judgment, and imagination. To gain a better understanding of how regression analysis can be applied to the study of demand, therefore, we will take a step-by-step approach, beginning with the identification of the variables involved.

Step 1: Identification of the Variables

In any empirical study of demand, we need to identify the independent variables, of course, and their relationship with demand. But we must also identify their relationships with each other. Accurate estimates of demand relationships are often difficult to obtain because of close interrelationships among demand determinants and the fact that their values change more or less simultaneously. This problem can be overcome only if we are able to *identify* interrelated variables. Hence we refer to this as the *identification problem.*

The identification problem arises when we are dealing with demand measurement. To understand the nature of the problem, let us recall that market price is established at the equilibrium point between supply and demand. That is to say, the intersection of the supply and demand curves establishes the price. As long as the supply and demand curves remain stable, the price will not change. Hence, a change in price indi-

---

[1] Computer printouts of multiple regression analysis are not standardized, but for the most part, the differences lie only in the format of the printout rather than in its contents. If you become familiar with the format in this chapter, you should have no difficulty in interpreting the output of another computer program in a different format.

cates that either the supply curve or the demand curve has shifted, or maybe both have shifted, as shown in Exhibit 7–1.

Exhibit 7–1 illustrates a situation in which statistical data indicate that at least three different equilibrium points have existed, at the demand

Exhibit 7–1_____

A Series of Equilibrium Points as Supply and Demand Curves Shift

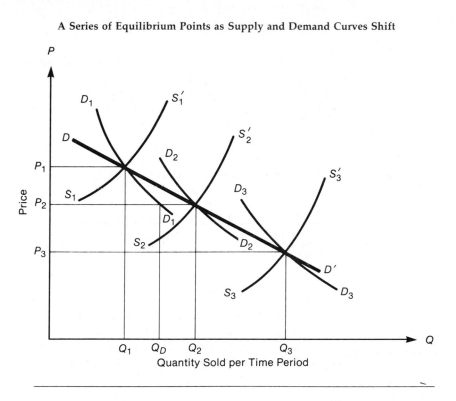

levels, Q_1, Q_2, and Q_3. All three of these equilibrium points lie on the regression line DD', which slopes downward in conformity with economic theory. But this is not enough to conclude that the regression line DD' in fact represents the demand function. The diagram clearly shows that the line DD' rests upon three different demand functions. But price-quantity plot points can trace out a single demand curve if only the supply curve has shifted, as shown in Exhibit 7–2.

A good example of the situation depicted by Exhibit 7–2 is the market for microprocessors, often called home computers or personal computers. Technological breakthroughs have rapidly lowered the cost of producing such machines. Consequently, producers have been willing

Exhibit 7-2

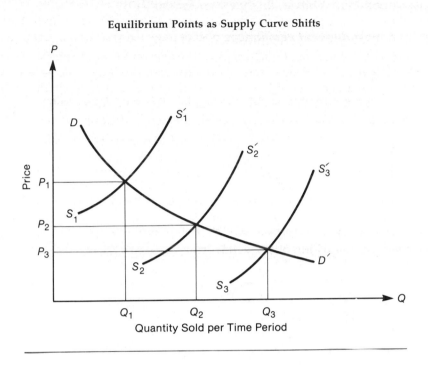

Equilibrium Points as Supply Curve Shifts

Quantity Sold per Time Period

to increase the supply at successively lower prices. This means that the supply curve has shifted successively farther to the right while the demand curve has remained relatively stable. Thus the rapid increase in quantity demanded is mostly due to dramatic reduction in price.

If it can be determined that the condition depicted by Exhibit 7-2 exists, then the demand curve can be closely approximated by a simple linear regression, as explained in the preceding chapter. But if it is determined or suspected that the condition depicted by Exhibit 7-1 exists, then variables other than price are causing the demand curve to shift. This suggests that a multiple regression analysis is appropriate.

Step 2: Data Collection and Adjustment

Once the variables have been specified, data must be obtained. Sources for such data are highly dependent, of course, upon the model's requirements. Nevertheless, as noted in Chapter 6, the *Survey of Current Business*, the *Statistical Abstract of the United States*, the *Federal Reserve Bulletin*, and the *Annual Economic Report to the President* are usually good starting points. In gathering the data, two aspects must be considered:

(1) data organization, i.e., whether to use monthly, quarterly, or annual data and (2) the number of observations needed for good results.

Data Organization and Adjustment.   The question of whether to use monthly, quarterly, or annual data is often answered simply on the basis of availability. Many data sources do not publish economic series as often as researchers would desire, leaving researchers to make do with annual data. If available, quarterly data are often highly desirable, since more data observations usually permit greater estimation efficiency.

All time-series data must be adjusted for population and inflation variations, as discussed in the preceding chapter. When using quarterly data, moreover, it is also important to account for any seasonality by making sure that seasonal fluctuations do not affect the specification of the model. Further, since many economic phenomena respond to changing conditions only after a lag, econometric models using quarterly data may be constructed with lagged, rather than current, variables on the right-hand side of the equation.

Sample Size.   The question of how many observations are needed for good results is not easily answered. Perfect results might be expected if we had a census of the population of possible demand values for all possible combinations of the independent variables. In reality, of course, it is rarely possible to work with a census. Indeed, some populations are infinite, so that a census is impossible. But even with finite populations, limitations on the time and money available for data collection force us to use a sampling method. The size of the sample is a trade-off between the rising cost of data collection and the diminishing cost of sampling error as the sample size grows larger.

If the model has been specified incorrectly, then no amount of data will yield good results. However, even a properly specified model will require at least as many observations as there are parameters to be estimated. A still better rule of thumb is to obtain at least three to four times this number to permit the least squares estimation technique to work well. After collecting and adjusting sufficient data, the next step is to choose the form of the regression equation.

Step 3: Choosing the Best Form of the Equation

There usually is no a priori reason to favor one form over another. When this is the case, it seems prudent to try several theoretically appropriate forms, then to choose the one that best explains the relationships between demand and the independent variables. Computer programs have made this very easy to do, provided the data can be fitted directly or else can be transformed to fit the linear function:

$$\hat{Q} = b_0 + b_1 X_1 + b_2 X_2 + \cdots + b_k X_k \tag{1}$$

where

$\hat{Q}$ = Estimate of quantity demanded
X_j = Value of the jth independent variable
b_j = Value of the jth regression parameter

Multiple linear regression is particularly well suited to empirical research for three reasons:

1. Many demand functions are in fact linear over the range for which empirical data are available.
2. When the data indicate that the underlying function is clearly not linear, it is still possible to use linear regression to fit either the logarithmic form of a power function or the transformation of a quadratic function. (A quadratic function may be transformed into a linear function by treating the X^2 term as an independent variable.) If we postulate a power function of the form

$$\hat{Q} = b_0 X_1^{b_1} X_2^{b_2} \cdots X_k^{b_k} \tag{2}$$

   the estimating linear regression equation would be

$$\log \hat{Q} = \log b_0 + b_1 \log X_1 + b_2 \log X_2 + \cdots + b_k \log X_k. \tag{3}$$

   Functions in the multivariate power form have the useful property that the elasticity of each variable is equal to its respective exponent. Hence, in the logarithmic form, the coefficients of the independent variables are their respective elasticities.[2]
3. In terms of analysis, multiple linear regression is an extension of the least squares method of simple linear regression that was explained in the preceding chapter. The method of least squares can be applied quickly and accurately by a computer program to estimate the parameters (regression coefficients) of the regression equation. The computer printout not only provides values for all of the parameters of the regression equation, but also provides test data by which the validity of the model may be judged.

---

[2] If all independent variables of a power function are increased simultaneously by some proportion, k, then the proportionate increase in the dependent variable will be k multiplied by the sum of the exponents of the independent variables.

There are at least three different ways that analysts might experiment with a regression model:

1. Try various unit definitions of measures of a particular variable. For example, labor can be measured by number of employees, by hours worked, or by wages paid.
2. Try both linear and nonlinear fits to the data.
3. Take out and put in various independent variables to see what happens to the regression equation.[3]

Because of the ease with which the regression equation can be manipulated by computer programs, it is extremely important that the analyst have good a priori reasons for including each of the independent variables, keeping in mind that a strong correlation between the dependent variable and a particular independent variable does *not necessarily* indicate cause and effect.[4]

The analyst must also beware of discarding a variable simply because its regression coefficient is not statistically significant. If there are strong a priori economic reasons for believing that the variable affects demand, it probably is best to leave it in. The lack of significance, or even the presence of the wrong sign, may be the result of *multicollinearity*, which we shall discuss later.

In addition to the theoretical considerations mentioned above, the analyst must also consider the availability of data. A mathematical characteristic of multiple regression is that the results can be improved by increasing the number of observations (sample size). It may or may not be improved by adding variables. Obviously, neither sample size nor the number of variables can be increased without sufficient data.

Step 4: Calculating the Regression Equation

To illustrate the calculation of a multivariate demand function, we shall use cross-sectional data for a marketing problem. Suppose that Pacific Traders (a fictitious import-export firm) imports black mush-

---

[3] In order to observe the effects of adding independent variables in a systematic way, the analyst may use a *stepwise multiple regression* program. In such a program, the analyst inputs data for a set of independent variables. The computer first selects the independent variable that results in the greatest reduction of unexplained variation and runs a simple regression. Then under operator control, it performs successive regression analyses by adding one more variable to each run. The variable added is the one that offers the greatest additional reduction of the unexplained variation. The program continues until all variables in the set have been included, or until none of the remaining variables can make a significant reduction in the unexplained variation.

[4] For example, a strong correlation can be shown between teachers' salaries and liquor sales. This does not mean that teachers are drinking—it simply means that teachers' salaries and liquor sales are both related to another variable, the general level of disposable income.

rooms from China. This oriental food specialty is then sold in 15 cities of the United States where there are concentrations of people of oriental ancestry. Since the price is the same in all 15 markets, Pacific Traders believes that the quantity sold is primarily influenced by two variables: (1) the size of the target population and (2) the per capita income in that population. The cross-sectional data are shown in Exhibit 7–3.[5]

Exhibit 7–3

Sales Data for 15 Cities

City	Average Weekly Sales (cases) Q	Target Population (000) X_1	Per Capita Income X_2
1	162	274	$2,450
2	120	180	3,254
3	223	375	3,802
4	131	205	2,838
5	67	86	2,347
6	169	265	3,782
7	81	98	3,008
8	192	330	2,450
9	116	195	2,137
10	55	53	2,560
11	252	430	4,020
12	232	372	4,427
13	144	236	2,660
14	103	157	2,088
15	212	370	2,605

The selected demand function is

$$\hat{Q} = b_0 + b_1 X_1 + b_2 X_2 \qquad (4)$$

where

$\hat{Q}$ = Estimated demand for black mushrooms, in number of cases per week

X_1 = Size of the target population (potential customers) in thousands of persons

X_2 = Per capita income of the target population, in dollars

b_0, b_1, b_2 = Parameters to be estimated by the regression analysis

[5] If we were using time-series data, we would have to examine the data for each independent variable to determine whether or not its distribution is linear. This may be done by plotting the X_i values over time. If any of the variables follow curvilinear trends, then a logarithmic or other transformation may be necessary.

Input of the data to a multiple regression computer package results in the typical output shown in Exhibit 7–4. The output format varies depending on the packaged program used, but the general content remains the same.[6]

Exhibit 7–4_____

Typical Output of a Multiple Regression Program

VARIABLE #	B	STD. ERROR	RATIO FOR THE T-TEST
0	3.45301	2.43013	1.42091
1	.496006	6.05316E-03	81.9416
2	9.19890E-03	9.67909E-04	9.50389

ANALYSIS OF VARIANCE	SUM OF SQ.	MEAN SQ.	F. VALUE
REGRESSION	53844.7	26922.4	5681.88
ERROR	56.8594	4.73828	
TOTAL	53901.6		

THE DEGREES OF FREEDOM FOR THE REGRESSION- 12

R-SQUARED= .998945   R= .999472

STANDARD ERROR OF THE ESTIMATE= 2.17676

THE DURBIN-WATSON STATISTIC= 2.70218

In addition to the more or less standard output illustrated by Exhibit 7–4, most programs will provide additional information upon request, such as the mean and standard deviations of the distribution of each variable, a correlation matrix, a variance-covariance matrix, and an analysis of the residuals. Thus, the computer program provides not only the regression equation, but also the data and test statistics necessary to evaluate the regression analysis.

_____

[6] Although the general content will be the same across regression packages, the specific content of the output may differ a bit because of the way in which rounding is handled. When there are many variables, some of which are highly correlated, rounding errors can accumulate into a serious problem. For this reason, it is wise to run a test problem, for which the answers are known, before adopting a particular package program for use.

Interpretation of the Computer Printout

In performing multiple regression analysis, we are hypothesizing a "true" regression equation, or population regression function, of

$$Q_i = \beta_0 + \beta_1 X_{1i} + \beta_2 X_{2i} + \cdots + \beta_k X_{ki} + \mu_i \tag{5}$$

In the notation of Equation (5), the independent variables have a double subscript, X_{ji}. The first subscript $(j = 1, 2, \ldots, k)$ serves as an identification of the variable by which it can be associated with its coefficient, b_j. The second subscript is the observation number. For each observation, i, there is a value for Q_i, a value for each X_{ji}, and a value for the residual μ_i.

As with simple linear regression discussed in Chapter 6, we assume that each μ_i belongs to a population that is normally distributed with a mean of zero and a variance of σ^2. Further, we assume that every probability distribution of μ_i has the same variance.

We cannot know the true regression equation, but we can estimate it to be:

$$\hat{Q} = b_0 + b_1 X_{1i} + b_2 X_{2i} + \cdots + b_k X_{ki} + e_i \tag{6}$$

where $\hat{Q}$ is an estimate of Q, and B's are estimates of the corresponding β's in Equation (5), and e_i is an estimate of μ_i. Since e_i is an estimate of μ_i, we make the same assumptions about its probability distribution; i.e., it is normal with a mean, or expected value, of zero, and has the same variance for all distributions, $s_{e_i}^2$.

When a multiple regression program is run on a computer, output values are provided to fit the equation:

$$\hat{Q} = b_0 + b_1 X_1 + b_2 X_2 + \cdots + b_k X_k \tag{7}$$

An e_i term does not appear in the output because we have assumed that its expected value is zero.

On the output of Exhibit 7–4, "VARIABLE #" is the subscript of the coefficients (b_0, b_1, b_2) on the right side of the estimating equation,

$$\hat{Q} = b_0 + b_1 X_1 + b_2 X_2 \tag{8}$$

When suitably rounded, the estimating equation is calculated to be

$$\dot{Q} = 3.5 + .5X_1 + .01X_2 \tag{9}$$

This result may be interpreted as follows:

1. The regression constant, b_0, positions the regression plane in space. Theoretically, it represents the quantity demanded if all independent variables are zero, and mathematically it can be negative. In reality, of course, it is impossible to have a negative demand, nor

will all of the variables ever be zero in the observed data. Hence, the parameter b_0 has no real economic meaning.

2. Each of the other parameters, b_j, indicates the direction and magnitude of change in the dependent variable, $\hat{Q}$, that is associated with a one-unit increase in the corresponding independent variable, X_j, when all other independent variables are held constant.[7] In this case:

   a. The addition of 1,000 people to the target population while holding per capita income constant is estimated to increase expected demand by .496 case per week.[8]

   b. An increase of $1 in per capita income while holding the population constant is estimated to increase expected demand by .0092 case per week.

Evaluating and Testing the Results

In multiple regression analysis, our objectives are to estimate reliable parameters for independent variables on the basis of a sample; to draw statistical inferences about such parameters, both individually and collectively; and to test the validity of the estimated regression equation for demand forecasting. The computer printout illustrated by Exhibit 7–4 indicates such inferences and the results of statistical tests.

Testing the Validity of the Model

The computer will accept whatever data are given to it as long as the data are in the correct format. The computer merely follows a mathematical procedure specified by the program, and will indifferently crank out a regression analysis that has the correct form, whether or not it has any valid economic substance. Thus it is up to the analyst to determine whether or not the output is valid for predicting demand. In general, the validity of the model may be judged by seeking answers to two fundamental questions:

1. Do the regression parameters bear the correct sign and are they of reasonable magnitude?

---

[7] Mathematically, the parameter b_j is the partial derivative of the function, i.e.,

$$\frac{\partial \hat{Q}}{\partial X_1} = b_1; \frac{\partial \hat{Q}}{\partial X_2} = b_2; \ldots; \frac{\partial \hat{Q}}{\partial X_n} = b_n$$

[8] In this discussion of the relationships between demand and the independent variables, we have been very careful to avoid the word "causes." At this stage, all we have is a statistical association. As we pointed out in Chapter 6, this does not necessarily indicate cause and effect.

2. How well are variations in demand explained by variations in the independent variables, both singly and collectively?

The first question calls for answers based on economic theory and the analyst's judgment. The second question requires certain statistical tests.

Sign of the Parameter.   Each regression coefficient (parameter) represents the marginal response of the demand function to a unit change in the associated independent variable. The sign of the parameter should indicate the theoretically correct relative direction of movement between the variable and the demand function. Referring to the output in Exhibit 7–4, we expect increases in X_1 and X_2 to cause an increase in $\hat{Q}$. We note that the positive signs of b_1 and b_2 accord with this theory. If a sign is wrong, it may indicate that we have specified the model incorrectly by leaving out an important variable. In some cases, the wrong sign accompanies other symptoms of the statistical problem of *multicollinearity*, which we shall discuss later.

Magnitude of the Parameter.   The test for reasonableness is clearly a test of judgment. Although there are no conventional limits, most economists have some ranges of values in mind that are associated with certain parameters. In other cases, a parameter may take a value that is clearly impossible. For example, suppose that we have modelled aggregate consumption demand in dollars as a function of price and disposable income:

$$C_d = b_0 + b_1 X_1 + b_2 X_2 \tag{10}$$

where X_1 = price and X_2 = disposable income.

Now suppose that the signs of the parameters come out right, but b_2 assumes a value of 1.3. Does this make sense? Clearly not, since b_2 represents the aggregate marginal propensity to consume or, in more familiar language, the additional consumption that could be anticipated from a unit increase in income. Hence, the estimated value of 1.3 is clearly unreasonable because it states that the average consumer will spend $1.30 of the next $1 of incremental income he or she receives.

Test Data.   The typical linear regression computer program prints out certain measures that answer the questions: "How well do variations in the independent variables explain variation in the dependent variable?" and "Are the independent variables statistically significant?" These questions are asked and answered both for the relationship between the dependent variable and the independent variables taken as a whole, and between the dependent variable and each individual independent variable.[9] For the regression as a whole, the test measures are:

1. The *coefficient of multiple determination*, R^2, and its square root, the *coefficient of multiple correlation*, R.
2. The *F-statistic* for the regression
3. The *standard error of the estimate* for the regression

For the parameters of individual variables, the test measures are:

1. The coefficient of correlation, r, of each variable with each other variable.
2. The *standard error of the coefficient* for each parameter
3. The *t-test ratio* for each parameter.

The way in which each of these measures is interpreted and used to test the validity of the model is discussed in more detail in the following subsections.

Overall Tests

1. **The Coefficient of Multiple Determination, R^2.** As we explained in the preceding chapter, the total variation in the dependent variable can be divided into two parts:

$$\Sigma(Y_i - \bar{Y})^2 = \Sigma(\hat{Y}_i - \bar{Y})^2 + \Sigma(Y_i - \hat{Y}_i)^2 \tag{11}$$

that is,

$$\left(\begin{array}{c}\text{Total} \\ \text{variation}\end{array}\right) = \left(\begin{array}{c}\text{Explained} \\ \text{variation}\end{array}\right) + \left(\begin{array}{c}\text{Unexplained} \\ \text{variation}\end{array}\right) \tag{12}$$

or

$$\text{SST} = \text{SSR} + \text{SSE} \tag{13}$$

where

SST = Total sum of squares
SSR = Regression sum of squares
SSE = Error sum of squares

The coefficient of multiple determination, R^2, measures the proportion of total variation in the dependent variable that is accounted for, or explained, by variations in the independent variables taken together in the equation of best fit, that is,

$$R^2 = \frac{\text{Total explained variation}}{\text{Total variation}} \tag{14}$$

---

[9] The Durbin-Watson d statistic is used as a test for autocorrelation, which is explained later.

This can be written as

$$R^2 = \frac{\text{Total variation} - \text{total unexplained variation}}{\text{Total variation}} \tag{15}$$

or

$$R^2 = \frac{\Sigma(\hat{Y}_i - \bar{Y})^2}{\Sigma(Y_i - \bar{Y})^2} = \frac{\text{SSR}}{\text{SST}} \tag{16}$$

On the computer printout in Exhibit 7–4, we see under the heading "Analysis of Variance" that the regression sum of squares is 53,844.7 while the total sum of squares is 53,901.6. Thus, R^2, which is printed farther down, is .9989, meaning that 99.89 percent of the variation in sales is explained by variation in the target population and per capita income acting together in the equation of best fit.

The value of R^2 may range from zero to one. A value of zero indicates that there is no relationship between demand and any of the independent variables. A value of one would mean that all of the variation in demand is explained by simultaneous variations in the independent variables.[10]

What is an acceptable value for R^2? This is largely a matter of individual judgment, and even this judgment varies according to the subject being studied. Cross-sectional analyses tend to have lower R^2 values than time-series studies. As a measure of significance, R^2 has an inherent weakness in that it does not consider either the number of observations on which the estimate was made or the number of independent variables involved in it. It is not unusual in empirical analysis to obtain a high R^2 accompanied by some regression coefficients that are statistically insignificant or that have the wrong sign. Moreover, it is a mathematical property of the least squares method of multiple linear regression that adding another variable will provide no decrease, and may provide an increase in R^2, whether or not the added variable is related to demand. Because of this characteristic, there may be a temptation to include as many variables as possible in order to achieve a high R^2. The temptation should be resisted, for not much can be said for a model that includes variables with little or no theoretical justification. We must remember that our objective is to develop reliable estimates of the true population parameters—not to develop a high R^2. In demand analysis, R^2 of .75 or more is considered to be acceptable.

2. **The F-Test for Overall Significance.**   The F-value is determined by an *analysis of variance*, as shown in Exhibit 7–4. The F-value is computed

---

[10] If *all* variation in demand is explained, this would mean that all observed points lie on the regression plane with zero deviations. Hence, SST = SSR and SSE = 0.

as the ratio of explained variance to unexplained variance, (or the ratio of the regression mean squares to the error mean squares), that is,

$$F = \frac{\text{(Total explained variation)}/(k)}{\text{(Total unexplained variation)}/(n - k - 1)}$$

$$= \frac{R^2/k}{(1 - R^2)/(n - k - 1)} \quad (17)$$

where

    k = Number of independent variables
    n = Number of observations

Equation (17) shows that the F-value is intimately related to the coefficient of multiple determination, R^2, which is the ratio of explained to total variation. However, the F-statistic overcomes an inherent weakness of R^2 by considering both the number of observations and the number of independent variables.

The numerator of Equation (17) represents the mean or average variance that is explained by the independent variables. It is calculated as the regression sum of squares (explained variation) divided by the appropriate degrees of freedom. The denominator represents the mean or average residual variance that is not explained by the independent variables. It is calculated as the residual or error sum of squares (unexplained variation) divided by the appropriate degrees of freedom.

Degrees of freedom (d.f.) refers to the number of unrestricted chances for variation in the measurement being made. For the numerator of Equation (17) there is one chance of variation for each independent variable, hence d.f. = k. In the denominator, the chances of variation depend upon the number of observations, n, reduced by the $(k + 1)$ estimated parameters, $b_0, b_1, \ldots, b_k$. Hence d.f. = $n - k - 1$. When a sum of squared deviations or residuals is divided by an appropriate d.f., the result is *variance*. Thus, the F-statistic is a variance ratio. The sampling distribution of this ratio is called the F-distribution.

The F-test for overall significance is based on the fact that for the regression equation to be statistically significant, at least one of the true regression parameters must not be zero. The F-value is used to test the null hypothesis that all of the true regression parameters are zero, that is,

$$H_0: \beta_1 = \beta_2 = \cdots = \beta_n = 0 \quad (18)$$

To test for overall significance, we compare the F-value calculated by the computer program with the corresponding upper-tail *critical value* of the F-distribution. If the computed F-value is greater, then the equation is statistically significant. Values of the F-distribution depend upon (1) the degrees of freedom in the numerator, (2) the degrees of freedom in the denominator, and (3) the level of significance.[11] Values of the F-distribution for significance levels of .05 and .01 are contained in Table G in the Appendix at the end of this book.

Example: The printout in Exhibit 7–4 reported a regression of two independent variables based on 15 observations. Therefore, the numerator has 2 degrees of freedom, while the denominator has $15 - 2 - 1 = 12$ degrees of freedom. Thus the F-value is

$$\frac{53,844.7/2}{56.8594/12} = \frac{26,922.4}{4.73828} = 5,681.89$$

This means that the explained variance is 5,681.89 times as great as the unexplained variance. The critical F-value from Table G is 3.89 at a significance level of .01. Since the computed F-value is 5,681.89 we conclude that the regression is statistically significant at both levels. This does not imply, however, that all variables are significant. The individual variables must be separately tested for significance by means of the t-test explained in the next subsection.

3.   **The Standard Error of the Estimate.**   The standard error is an estimate of the standard deviation of the probability distribution of the dependent variable when the independent variables are all held constant. Thus it measures the dispersion of observed values of Q about the estimated $\hat{Q}$. It is calculated as the square root of the mean sum of the squared deviations (error sum of squares, SSE) by the formula:

$$S_e = \sqrt{\frac{\Sigma(Q - \hat{Q})^2}{n - k - 1}} = \sqrt{\frac{SSE}{n - k - 1}} = \sqrt{MSE} \tag{19}$$

where

S_e = Standard error of the estimate
Q = Observed value of the dependent variable
$\hat{Q}$ = Estimated value of the dependent variable
n = Number of data points observed (15 in our example)
k = Number of independent variables (2 in our example)
$n - k - 1$ = Degrees of freedom (d.f.)
SSE = Error sum of squares
MSE = Error mean square

---

[11] In hypothesis testing, rejecting a null hypothesis when it is true is called a Type I error. Accepting a null hypothesis when it is false is called a Type II error. The level of significance is the maximum tolerable probability of a Type I error. There is a trade-off between Type I and Type II errors. The lower the level of significance, the higher the probability of a Type II error.

In our example, $S_e = \sqrt{4.7382} = 2.17676$, as shown. This number represents the "average" error that exists in the equation of best fit.

Testing Individual Parameters

So far we have tested for the reliability and significance of the independent variables as a group when all are allowed to vary simultaneously. It is now necessary to perform a separate test for the reliability and significance of each independent variable while all others are held constant. For these tests we use the standard error of the regression coefficient and the t-test ratio, both of which are included on the computer printout.

1.   **Standard Error of the Regression Coefficient.**   Each regression coefficient, b_j, is the sampling mean of a normal distribution of possible parameter values. The standard error of the regression coefficient measures the dispersion of parameter values about the regression coefficient in the same way that standard deviation measures the dispersion of random variables about their mean. The computer program uses a complicated formula to calculate the standard error of each regression coefficient in the regression equation, and these values are routinely printed out.

The standard error of the regression coefficient indicates the reliability of that particular parameter. If the standard error is small relative to the estimated parameter, it indicates that the estimated parameter is near the true parameter. However, it still must be determined whether or not the true parameter might be zero. For this purpose, the standard error is divided into the regression coefficient to obtain the t-test ratio, which is also printed as part of the standard output of the computer program. The t-test ratio is used to test for statistical significance of the individual variable, as explained below.

The t-Test for Individual Significance.   On a typical computer printout, such as the one illustrated in Exhibit 7–4, a t-test ratio is

$$t\text{-Test ratio} = \frac{\text{Regression coefficient}}{\text{Standard error of the regression coefficient}}$$

That is, the t-test ratio is the number of standard errors contained in the regression coefficient.[12] If an individual variable is statistically significant, the true value of its parameter cannot be zero. Therefore, we must

---

[12] Since the standard error of the regression coefficient is always positive, the t-test ratio takes its sign from the regression coefficient. The sign is not important—we are concerned only with the magnitude.

test the null hypothesis that the true parameter equals zero, i.e., $H_0: \beta_j = 0$. If we can reject this hypothesis, we can infer that the independent variable does indeed have some effect on the dependent variable. We can test the hypothesis with the aid of the t-test ratio and an appropriate t-distribution. Like normal distribution, the t-distribution is a sampling probability distribution that is symmetrical about a mean of zero, and the area under the curve represents a probability of 1.0. The exact shape of the curve depends upon the degrees of freedom,[13] calculated as:

$$\text{d.f.} = n - k - 1 \tag{20}$$

where

n = Number of observations
k = Number of independent variables

As illustrated by Exhibit 7–5, in order to test for statistical significance at the level of α, we divide the appropriate t-distribution into three

Exhibit 7–5

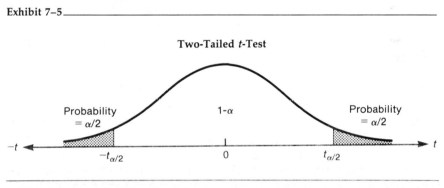

Two-Tailed t-Test

Probability
= $\alpha/2$

$1-\alpha$

Probability
= $\alpha/2$

$-t$ $-t_{\alpha/2}$ 0 $t_{\alpha/2}$ t

Note: α is the probability of type I error.

parts. Exactly in the middle (i.e., centered on the mean), we carve out (1 $- \alpha$) percent of the total probability, bounded on the left by $-t_{\alpha/2}$ and on the right by $+t_{\alpha/2}$. This leaves $\alpha/2$ percent probability in each tail.

The t-values $\pm t_{\alpha/2}$ are called *critical values of* t, and they are published in tables such as Table F in the Appendix at the end of this book. Table F is a matrix of probabilities versus degrees of freedom. The cells of the matrix contain the corresponding critical t-values.

The t-test requires only that we compare the t-test ratio with the critical t-value for our desired level of significance and the appropriate

---

[13] The t-distribution approaches the normal distribution as the sample size grows larger. For an infinite number of degrees of freedom, the t-distribution and normal distribution are precisely the same. The approach to this limit is quite rapid, and there is a widely applied rule of thumb that normal distribution is used when $n > 30$.

degrees of freedom. If the t-test ratio is larger, we can reject the null hypothesis that $\beta_j = 0$, and state that the variable X_j is statistically significant at the α level.

In our example of Exhibit 7–4, the t-test ratio for $X_1 = 81.942$ and for $X_2 = 9.504$. From Table F, we find the critical t-value for $\alpha = .01$ under a probability of $\alpha/2 = .005$. For d.f. $= 12$, the critical t-value is 3.055. Since both test ratios are many times greater, we conclude that both variables are statistically significant at the .01 level of significance.

Confidence Intervals for the Regression Coefficients

If the t-test for significance determines that the true parameter does not equal zero, we may still want to know, with some level of confidence, the interval in which the true parameter lies. This is easily determined from the regression coefficient and its standard error of estimate calculated by the computer and an appropriate t-value from Table F.

If the desired level of confidence is $(1 - \alpha)$, then the confidence interval for b_j is:

$$b_j \pm t_{\alpha/2}S_{b_j} \tag{21}$$

where

$b_j =$ The jth regression coefficient
$t_{\alpha/2} =$ The t-statistic with $\alpha/2$ in each tail
$S_{b_j} =$ Standard error of estimate for the jth regression coefficient

For example, suppose we want a 95-percent confidence interval for the regression coefficients of Exhibit 7–4. From Table F, we obtain the t-statistic for $\alpha/2 = .025$ and d.f. $= 12$. We find it is 2.179. Hence for $b_1 = .496$, the 95-percent confidence interval is

$$.496 \pm (2.179)(.00605316) = .496 \pm .013$$

For $b_2 = .009$, the 95-percent confidence interval is

$$.0091989 \pm (2.179)(.000967909) = .0091989 \pm .0027$$

Assumptions and Special Problems of Multiple Regression Analysis[14]

Multiple regression is one of the most frequently used techniques in the empirical investigation not only of demand functions, but also of pro-

---

[14] Material in this section has been extracted from Damodar Gujarati, *Basic Econometrics* (New York: McGraw-Hill, 1978), pp. 167–251.

duction functions, cost functions, and many others. It is a powerful technique, but it is also limited by its assumptions, which are quite specific. When any one of these assumptions is violated, a special problem arises. In particular, we may have the problems of multicollinearity, heteroscedasticity, or autocorrelation. A thorough discussion of these problems is beyond the scope of this text. Nevertheless, a brief explanation of the regression model's assumptions is in order, as is a brief summary of the problems that arise when these assumptions are violated.

The validity of the regression model rests upon certain statistical assumptions, which must be clearly understood. First of all, regression analysis requires that the analyst specify a set of independent variables $(X_1, X_2, \ldots X_k)$, each of which consists of a set of values. Although the X_i variables may actually be random variables, once their values have been selected (e.g., by observation), they do not change.

The observed value of the dependent variable, Q, is determined not only by the selected combination of X_j values, but also by other variables that have not been identified and by variations due to chance. Consequently, for any given combination of X_j values, many values of Q are possible. For example, suppose that we postulate

$$Q = f(X_1, X_2)$$

where

Q = Loaves of whole wheat bread
X_1 = Price of whole wheat bread
X_2 = Per capita income

If we were to ask many households with the same per capita income how much whole wheat bread they buy at a given price, we would expect to get many different answers. Of course, in actual practice, we would not attempt to limit our survey to households with the same per capita income or to the same price. Instead we observe the Q-value corresponding to many combinations of X-values, and use these data to perform a multiple regression analysis of the form:

$$Q_i = \beta_0 + \beta_1 X_{1i} + \beta_2 X_{2i} + \cdots + \beta_k X_{ki} + \mu_i \qquad (22)$$

It should be emphasized that only Q is a random variable. This means that when the regression equation

$$\hat{Q} = b_0 + b_1 X_1 + b_2 X_2 + \cdots + b_k X_k \qquad (23)$$

is used to estimate Q, values of the independent variables are known precisely, but the estimated value of Q is subject to error. The value $\hat{Q}$ in Equation (23) is the mean, or expected value, of the distribution of the random variable Q in Equation (22). The distribution of Q is reflected in the error term, μ, which is a random disturbance or variation in Q that is not related to the specific independent variables. It is with this error term that we account for the observed values of Q that lie above or below the regression plane rather than upon it. Hence it is necessary to make certain assumptions about the error term:

1. The random fluctuations in Q are normally distributed with a mean of zero. That is, their deviations are both positive and negative and they cancel each other out.
2. The error term distributions have constant variance. This is the characteristic called *homoscedasticity* ("homo" means "same", "scedasticity" means "scatter"). If it is not true, the function is said to be *heteroscedastic*.
3. The error terms are independent of the values of the independent variables, X_j, and of each other.

    These first three assumptions apply to both simple and multiple linear regression. In addition, one more assumption is necessary for multiple regression analysis.
4. There are no strong linear relationships among the independent variables.[15]

With this understanding of the assumptions underlying regression analysis, we are now ready for a brief look at what happens when any of the assumptions is violated.

Multicollinearity

Our fourth basic assumption is that the variables are independent of one another, so that no linear relationship exists between any independent variable and any other independent variable or linear combination of other independent variables. If this assumption is not true, then multicollinearity exists. The clearest sign of multicollinearity is a high R^2 with individual variables that fail the t-test for significance. One or more of the regression coefficients might also have the wrong sign. A good test for multicollinearity is to examine the correlation matrix, which is provided routinely or optionally in the computer printout. Exhibit 7–6 shows the correlation matrix for our previous example. The rows and columns of the correlation matrix pertain to variables X_1, X_2, and $\hat{Q}$, respectively. Each number in the matrix is the coefficient of correlation between variables represented by row and column. Since each variable is perfectly correlated with itself, the principal diagonal consists of 1s (or numbers very close to 1). The matrix is symmetric, so some printouts omit the coefficients above or below the principal diagonal.

---

[15] We should also note that it is necessary for the number of observations or data points to be greater than the number of variables plus one constant; that is, $n > k + 1$.

Exhibit 7–6

Typical Correlation Matrix on Computer Printout

	X_1	X_2	$\hat{Q}$
X_1	1	.56856	.995493
X_2	.56856	.999999	.639301
$\hat{Q}$	.995493	.639301	1.

In this exhibit, the coefficient of correlation between X_1 and X_2 is .56856, so there is no reason to suspect multicollinearity.

Heteroscedasticity

One of the basic assumptions of multiple linear regression is that all of the distributions of the error terms have the same variance, σ^2. If this assumption of equal variance is violated, we have the situation of *heteroscedasticity*.

The consequence of heteroscedasticity is that the usual *t*- and *F*-tests are very likely to exaggerate the statistical significance of the regression coefficients. Although it is easy to document the consequences of heteroscedasticity, it is not easy to detect. This is because we have no way of determining the variance of the error terms.

Sometimes the nature of the investigation indicates whether or not heteroscedasticity is likely. For example, if small-, medium-, and large-sized firms are sampled together in a cross-sectional analysis of investment expenditure versus sales, rates of interest, and so forth, heteroscedasticity may be expected. If the nature of the investigation does not suggest the problem, a number of ways have been devised to detect heteroscedasticity by working with the residuals or squares of the residuals, which is a routine or optional output of most multiple regression computer programs. These methods include a graphical method, the Park test, and Spearman's rank correlation test. A full explanation of these tests and of the remedial measures that may be taken is beyond the scope of this text, but may be found in textbooks on econometrics.[16]

---

[16] An especially lucid discussion is contained in Gujarati, *Basic Econometrics*, pp. 200–206.

Autocorrelation.   One of our basic assumptions is that the error terms are independent, that is, the error related to any one observation is not influenced by the error associated with any other observation. If we are dealing with time-series data, we assume that the events of the time t-1 do not influence the events of time t. If they do, then autocorrelation or serial correlation exists. If autocorrelation exists, the usual t- and F-tests are no longer valid and can cause misleading conclusions.

There are a number of reasons why autocorrelation may exist in time-series data. Among these are:

1.   *Inertia.* The movement of variables, up or down, leaves a built-in momentum that causes each successive observation to be influenced by the one before. For example, when recovery from a recession begins, increased employment in one time period leads to increased demand for goods and services, which leads to increased employment in the next period. The upward momentum continues until the supply of skilled labor is fully absorbed.

2.   *Specification bias from excluded variables.* In attempting to purify a regression analysis, the analyst may exclude variables that should be left in. For example, suppose we have the demand model,

$$Q = \beta_0 + \beta_1 X_1 + \beta_2 X_2 + \beta_3 X_3 + \mu \qquad (24)$$

where

Q = Quantity of Cadillac automobiles demanded
X_1 = Average price of Cadillacs
X_2 = Per capita income
X_3 = Average price of Lincolns

Suppose we run the regression

$$Q = \beta_0 + \beta_1 X_1 + \beta_2 X_2 + v \qquad (25)$$

If Equation (24) is correct, then by running (25) we let $v = \beta_3 X_3 + \mu$. To the extent that the price of Lincolns affects demand for Cadillacs, the term v will follow a systematic pattern, thereby creating a false autocorrelation.

3.   *Specification bias from incorrect functional form.* If a straight line is fitted to data that are actually curvilinear, autocorrelation will result. For example, suppose the quadratic curve

$$Q = \beta_0 + \beta_1 X_i + \beta_2 X_i^2 + \mu \qquad (26)$$

is fitted with the straight line

$$Q = \beta_0 + \beta_1 X_i + v_i \qquad (27)$$

In Equation (27) the term $v_i = \beta_2 X^2 + \mu$.

As X increases, X^2 also increases systematically, and a false autocorrelation is generated.

4. *Cobweb phenomenon*. The dependent variable, such as supply, reacts to the independent variable, such as price, with a lag of one time period. This phenomenon is most common in agriculture, where the farmer's decision on how much to plant is greatly influenced by the price received for last year's crop. This causes the disturbance term μ to follow a regular pattern of up, then down, as farmers overproduce one year, then decrease production the next.

5. *Other lags*. In a time-series regression of demand as a function of income, for example, the consumption expenditure in one time period often depends upon the consumption expenditure of the previous period.

6. *Manipulation of data*. In empirical analysis, raw data are often manipulated by devices such as moving averages, or by interpolation or extrapolation. These devices amount to modification of current data by data from the past, which is a direct introduction of autocorrelation.

All of these things make autocorrelation more common in time-series data, but it can also occur in cross-sectional data, where it is sometimes called spatial autocorrelation. One way to detect autocorrelation is to plot the residuals of a regression analysis to see if any regular pattern emerges, such as those shown in Exhibit 7–7.

Another method of detecting autocorrelation is to make the Durbin-Watson d-test. The Durbin-Watson d-statistic is defined as

$$d = \frac{\sum_{t=2}^{n} (e_t - e_{t-1})^2}{\sum_{t=1}^{n} e_t^2} \tag{28}$$

where e_t is the estimated residual, which is a proxy for the unknown disturbance term μ_t. Equation (28) says that the d-statistic is the ratio of the sum of squared differences in successive residuals to the residual sum of squares. It is calculated and printed out by most regression programs.

The Durbin-Watson statistic is used to test the null hypothesis that there is no first-order serial correlation in the disturbances, μ_i. As shown in Exhibit 7–8, Durbin and Watson identified the upper and lower limits of two zones of indecision as d_L and d_U and $4 - d_U$ to $4 - d_L$. The limits d_L and d_U depend only on the number of observations (which must be at least 15) and the number of explanatory variables.

To apply the Durbin-Watson test statistic, we need a table of the critical lower (d_L) and upper (d_U) values for the given sample size and

Exhibit 7–7

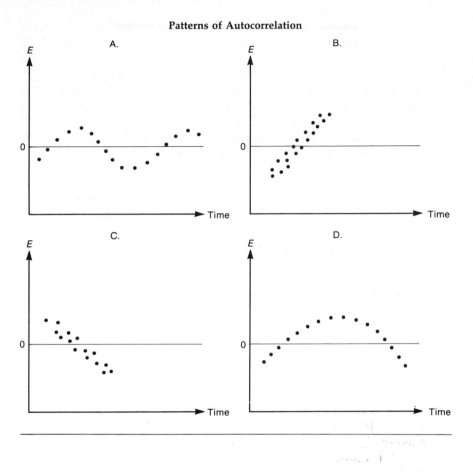

Patterns of Autocorrelation

number of variables, such as Table H in the Appendix at the end of this book. Suppose we have run a regression analysis for which the sample size is 30 and the number of independent variables is 4. At the .05 level of significance, we find that $d_L = 1.14$ and $d_U = 1.74$. Our printout shows a Durbin-Watson statistic of 0.98. How do we interpret this? Exhibit 7–8 illustrates the decision rules.

As shown in Exhibit 7–8, autocorrelation is clearly evident only when the Durbin-Watson statistic on the computer printout is less than d_L (positive autocorrelation) or greater than $4 - d_L$ (negative correlation). In the middle of the Durbin-Watson distribution is the zone of acceptance of either hypothesis:

H_0: No positive autocorrelation
H_0^*: No negative autocorrelation

Exhibit 7–8

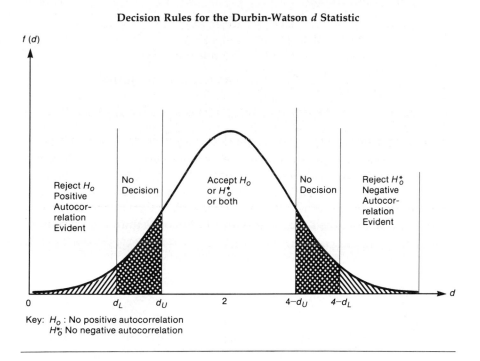

Decision Rules for the Durbin-Watson *d* Statistic

Key: H_o : No positive autocorrelation
H_o^*: No negative autocorrelation

The zone of acceptance is bounded by d_U on the left and $4 - d_U$ on the right. On either side is a zone of confusion. The left-hand zone is bounded by d_L and d_U, the right-hand zone by $4 - d_L$ and $4 - d_U$. If the computed test statistic falls in either of these zones, then no conclusions can be drawn.

To review the rules: If the null hypothesis, H_0, is that there is no *positive* serial correlation, then if

$$d < d_L: \text{Reject } H_0$$
$$d > d_U: \text{Do not reject } H_0$$
$$d_L \leq d \geq d_U: \text{The test is inconclusive}$$

If our null hypothesis, H_0^*, is that there is no *negative* serial correlation, then if

$$d > 4 - d_L: \text{Reject } H_0^*$$
$$d < 4 - d_U: \text{Do not reject } H_0^*$$
$$4 - d_U \leq d \leq 4 - d_L: \text{The test is inconclusive}$$

If the null hypothesis, H_0^{**}, is that there is neither positive nor negative serial correlation, then if

$$d < d_L: \text{ Reject } H_0^{**}$$
$$d > 4 - d_L: \text{ Reject } H_0^{**}$$
$$d_U < d < 4 - d_U: \text{ Do not reject } H_0^{**}$$
$$\left.\begin{array}{c} d_L \le d \le d_U \\ 4 - d_U \le d \le 4 - d_L \end{array}\right\} \text{ The test is inconclusive}$$

For our example, the test statistic of 0.98 is less than d_L. Therefore we have reason to believe that positive autocorrelation exists.

When autocorrelation is detected, the first step is to run a simple linear regression on each variable to determine which ones yield autocorrelation and which do not. In general, further corrective action requires transformation of the data to eliminate the spillover effects from one observation to the next. A thorough explanation of the procedure involved is beyond the scope of this text, but may be found in econometrics texts.[17]

Summary

Multiple regression analysis is a method of analyzing demand as a function of a number of independent variables acting more or less simultaneously. Because of the complexity and difficulty of the mathematical calculations in multiple regression analysis, it is best performed by digital computers. Many programs are available for this purpose.

The statistical aspects of multiple regression models are well explained in statistics and econometrics textbooks. The analyst, however, must supply the economic thinking, judgment, and imagination for constructing a regression model and for interpreting and testing its results.

The basic economic variables that affect demand include demographic factors, buying power factors, price factors, promotion factors, and qualitative factors. The regression model of demand is:

$$Q_i = \beta_0 + \beta_1 X_{1i} + \beta_2 X_{2i} + \cdots + \beta_k X_{ki} + \mu_i \tag{29}$$

where

Q = Quantity demanded
X_j = jth independent variable
β_0 = Regression constant
β_j = Regression coefficient of the jth variable
μ_i = Mean of the distribution of error terms (always assumed to be zero) of the ith observation.

---

[17] See, for example, Gujarati, *Basic Econometrics*, pp. 239–45.

The computer output *estimates* the regression equation as:

$$\hat{Q} = b_0 + b_1 X_1 + b_2 X_2 + \cdots + b_k X_k \tag{30}$$

where $\hat{Q}$ is the estimate of Q and each b_j is an estimate of the regression parameter β_j.

Data collection involves a trade-off between sampling error and sampling cost. A rough rule of thumb is that the minimum sample size should be three or four times the number of parameters. Because of the ease with which regression may be performed by the computer, the analyst must have good *a priori* reasons for including each of the independent variables.

After running a regression on a computer, the analyst must interpret and test the results. Testing the validity of the results involves two fundamental questions:

1.   Do the regression parameters bear the correct sign and are they of reasonable magnitude?
2.   How well are variations in demand explained by variations in the independent variables—both singly and collectively?

The computer program prints out certain test data to aid in the evaluation. These include the coefficient of multiple determination (R^2), the coefficient of multiple correlation (R), the standard error of estimate, the F-statistic, and the Durbin-Watson statistic for the regression as a whole. For evaluating individual variables and parameters, the printout includes the coefficient of correlation (r) of each variable with every other variable, and the standard error and t-test ratio for each regression coefficient.

The validity of the regression rests upon certain assumptions about the input data. If any assumption is violated, special problems arise.

Multicollinearity arises when two variables are not truly independent of one another. They move together so closely that the regression procedure is unable to distinguish their effects upon Q. The solution for this problem is to eliminate one of the variables from the regression.

Heteroscedasticity exists when there is a violation of the assumption that all distributions of the error terms have the same variance. The consequences are that the usual t- and F-tests will exaggerate the statistical significance of the regression coefficients. A number of methods for detecting this problem are contained in econometrics texts, along with remedial measures.

Autocorrelation. If we are dealing with time-series data, a basic assumption is that events at time $t - 1$ do not influence events at time t. If this is not true, autocorrelation, or serial correlation, exists, and the usual t- and F-tests are not valid. There are a number of reasons for autocorrelation, including inertia, specification bias, the cobweb phe-

y intercept   *R² - goodness of fit*
close to 100

nomenon, other lags, and manipulation of data in an attempt to correct other problems. Autocorrelation can be detected by the Durbin-Watson *d*-test. Correction requires transformation of the input data to eliminate the spillover effects from one time period to the next.

Durbin Watson 1.5-2.5
around 2
<1.5 >2.5 serial correlate

Problems   *t's ±2*

1. The Campus Bike Shop, located near the campus of a large university, sells and repairs bicycles of all types. The owner has been in the habit of ordering the same number of 10-speed bicycles each month, but the result has been overstockage in some months and the loss of sales because of lack of inventory in other months. As a consultant, you propose to predict monthly sales by the linear regression equation

$$\hat{Q} = b_0 + b_1 X_1 + b_2 X_2 + b_3 X_3 + b_4 X_4$$

where

$\hat{Q}$ = Estimated monthly sales
X_1 = Average selling price, in dollars
X_2 = Average price of lead-free gasoline, in dollars
X_3 = 1 if fall semester, otherwise zero
X_4 = 1 if spring semester, otherwise zero ($X_3 = 0$ and $X_4 = 0$ implies summer term)

Using the data from the past 15 months, you obtain the following results from a linear regression program on a computer:

VARIABLE	COEFF	STD ERROR	T-VALUE
1	−0.604	1.33	−0.45
2	77.44	38.91	1.99
3	42.84	16.18	2.65
4	14.83	14.39	1.03
INTERCEPT	22.64	59.59	0.38

R-SQUARED = .636
STANDARD ERROR = 4.4
F-VALUE = 8.14

Q = 22.64 - .604x₁ + 77.44x₂ + 42.84x₃ + 14.83x₄

a. Write the estimated regression equation and interpret the estimated coefficients. *-.604 monthly sales fell ... 604 for*
b. Test the regression equation for overall significance at the .05 level.
c. Interpret the coefficient of determination. *63.6 not confident enough*
2. Referring to Problem 1:
a. Next month the average price of a 10-speed bicycle is expected to be $150 and the average price of lead-free gasoline is expected to be

$1.20. How many 10-speed bicycles can the Campus Bike Shop expect to sell?

b. Calculate a 95 percent confidence interval for your answer to (a) above.

c. Construct a 95 percent confidence interval for each of the parameters of the regression equation.

3.   A land developer on the Kona coast of the Island of Hawaii has constructed a linear regression model to estimate the selling price of building lots as

$$\hat{P} = b_0 + b_1 X_1 + b_2 X_2 + b_3 X_3$$

where

$\hat{P}$ = Estimated selling price, in thousands of dollars
X_1 = Area of the lot, in hundreds of square feet
X_2 = Elevation of the lot, in feet above sea level
X_3 = Slope of the lot, in degrees

The computer printout of a multiple regression program provides the following information:

COEFFICIENTS

VARIABLE	B	STD ERROR (B)
AREA	.099	.058
ELEVATION	.029	.006
SLOPE	.086	.031
CONSTANT	-2.491	1.011

SUMMARY STATS

MULTIPLE R	R-SQUARE
.8854	.7838

ANOVA

SOURCE	SUM OF SQUARES	DF	MEAN SQUARE	F
REGRESSION	21.409	3	7.136	19.339
RESIDUAL	5.903	16	.369	

a. Write the equation for $\hat{P}$.

b. Predict the price of a lot containing 5,000 square feet, located at an elevation of 200 feet, with a slope of 8 degrees.

4.   Referring to Problem 3:

a. Interpret the regression coefficients. Are their signs correct? Do they seem reasonable in magnitude?

b. Which of the explanatory variables are statistically significant at the .05 level?

c. Interpret the coefficient of determination. Considering its value, would you drop any insignificant variables from the model to try to improve it?
d. Interpret the F-value computed by the analysis of variance (ANOVA).
e. Do you consider this model to be acceptable? Why or why not?

5. A marketing research firm has collected data for 50 sales districts on the variation in sales with respect to income per household (INCOME) and advertising expenditures (ADVERT) by their client company. All figures were recorded in thousands of dollars, then input to a multiple regression computer program. Part of the output was as follows:

COEFFICIENTS:	VARIABLE	B	STAND. ERROR
	INCOME	2.350	.622
	ADVERT	17.234	2.894
	CONSTANT	55.016	25.678

ANOVA:	SOURCE	SS
	Regression	7290.28
	Residual	606.95

a. Write the regression equation for SALES.
b. Interpret the regression coefficients.
c. Test the regression coefficients for statistical significance at the .05 level.
d. Compute and interpret the multiple coefficient of determination.
e. Calculate and interpret the F-value.

6. What makes a good salesperson? The Sun Solar Company conducted a random survey of 16 full-time solar system sales people to analyze this question. First, salespeople were interviewed and given an aptitude test developed by the Maximum Sales Training Institute in Dallas, Texas. Then, an effort index was calculated on the basis of a salesperson's observed car mileage divided by the estimated mileage required to cover the assigned region satisfactorily. (Company cars have been provided by The Sun Solar Company for salespeople.) The data have been analyzed by a newly hired young college graduate from Denton University. She reported the following regression equation:

$$S = 18.0 + 0.75T + 22.4E$$
$$(0.08) \quad (2.05)$$

where

S = Sales in thousands of dollars
T = Aptitude Test Score
E = Effort Index

and the numbers in parentheses are standard errors of the regression coefficients.

Further, she found that the standard error of the estimate was 3.82 and the standard deviation of sales was 18.2.

a. Interpret the regression coefficient of the variables.
b. Calculate and interpret R^2 and the F-statistic.
c. Estimate sales performance for Mr. Jones, who has an aptitude test score of 72 and an effort index of 0.65.

The Sun Solar Company would like to use this equation for predicting a salesperson's potential. What is the size of the 95 percent confidence interval for predicting S?

7.   Performance Auto Supplies (PAS) is a national franchise selling automotive parts and accessories. At corporate headquarters in Chicago, Illinois, top management is developing a model to estimate the annual sales of each regional area. If the regional sales can be predicted, then the total sales for PAS can be predicted. Also, a good sales model can assist regional inventory scheduling and result in more accurate production orders to PAS's contracted manufacturers. The sales manager at PAS suggested using two predictor variables: (1) the current number of retail outlets in each region; (2) the number of automobiles registered in each region as of April 30 (end of first quarter). Data are as follows:

Region	Annual Sales ($ millions) Y	Number of Retail Outlets X_1	Number of Automobiles Registered (millions) X_2
1	52.5	1,780	21.5
2	24.6	2,470	20.2
3	18.5	450	6.1
4	15.6	440	11.5
5	32.2	1,650	9.2
6	45.0	2,102	10.6
7	33.0	2,305	18.9
8	3.6	121	4.3
9	34.7	1,801	9.1
10	24.6	1,130	5.6
11	40.0	1,650	8.7

a. Estimate the prediction equation.
b. How much error is involved in the prediction for regions 1 and 3?
c. Estimate the annual sales for a new region 12, given 2,000 retail outlets and 15.5 million registered automobiles.
d. Discuss the accuracy of the estimate made in part (c).
e. Calculate the standard error of estimate.
f. Interpret the regression coefficients. Explain how good they are.
g. Suggest how this regression equation can be improved.

8. Refer to Problem 7. PAS's sales manager is dissatisfied with the regression results because fluctuations in regional economic conditions are not incorporated in the annual sales model. To account for this, personal income, a new predictor variable, is added to the regression. Data are as follows:

Region	Personal Income ($ billions)
1	97.2
2	32.5
3	34.6
4	30.2
5	65.3
6	92.7
7	62.1
8	18.6
9	65.2
10	60.5
11	82.0

a. Does the additional variable, personal income by region, make a significant contribution to the prediction of annual sales?
b. Estimate the annual sales for a new Region 12 with the assumption of $37 billion in personal income, 2,000 retail outlets, and 15.5 million registered automobiles.
c. Explain the accuracy of the sales estimate for Region 12.
d. Which variables would you include or exclude in your regression model? Why?

9. Fire Prevention Equipment Company (FPE), Cincinnati, Ohio, produces smoke-detectors and many other hardware items in the fire prevention field, which are sold through 26 retail outlets in midwestern states. Smoke-detector sales have been increasing at an annual rate of 8 percent and FPE's market share has been 22 percent in the region for the last three years. Since there is increasing competition, FPE is planning various means to compete better and thereby improve the sales of its smoke-detectors. The director of market research for FPE has performed a regression analysis of sales in the company's retail outlets with the following results:

$$Q = 12.6 - 9.2P + 2.2A + 0.6D + 0.3H$$
$$(7.2) \quad (2.1) \quad (1.2) \quad (0.24) \quad (0.12)$$
$$(R^2 = .89; \; SSE = 7.6)$$

where

    Q = Smoke-detector sales (in thousands of units)
    P = Price of smoke-detector (per unit)
    A = Advertising expenditure (in thousands of dollars)
    D = Disposable income per household (in thousands of dollars)
    H = Number of households (in hundreds)

and the numbers in parentheses are standard errors of the regression coefficients.

a. Interpret R^2 and SSE.
b. Calculate the F-statistic.
c. Do sales depend more on the price of a smoke-detector than on advertising expenditures?
d. Which independent variables have the most influence on sales of smoke-detectors?
e. Evansdale, Indiana, is a potential midwestern market with an economic environment and characteristics similar to the locations where FPE outlets are now located. In planning for the opening of a new outlet in Evansdale, the director of market research provided the following information for its first year: $A = 42$; $D = 22$; $H = 60$.
   (i) Derive the demand equation for the Evansdale outlet.
   (ii) Estimate the probability that the Evansdale outlet will generate at least \$42,000 in revenue if the price of smoke-detector is \$14 per unit.

Case Problem: Determinants of Fast Food Sales*

10. The objective of this case is to illustrate how multiple regression can be used to construct a model of aggregate sales. The subject of this study is a fast food chain in Hawaii. Because of intense competition, it is important for the chain to be able to determine what factors influence sales and to predict sales given certain scenarios of market and economic development.

Speedy Burger[1] has 13 stores located in various parts of the state. These stores are classified into three groups according to the type of clientele each serves. TOURIST stores primarily serve tourists, METROPOLITAN stores are those frequented by urban customers, and RURAL stores cater to those who live and work in rural areas of the islands.

---

* This case was prepared by Dr. Jack Suyderhoud, University of Hawaii, College of Business Administration.
[1] The name has been altered to maintain the confidentiality of the data source.

Since each type of store has a different type of customer, it is not unreasonable to expect sales at each type of store to be affected differently by the same set of independent variables.

Data were collected for 28 monthly periods of the 13 stores in the chain. The dependent variable is total monthly sales for each category of stores. The independent variables are:

a. *Consumer variables:*
   (1) HOLIDA = Number of school holidays and weekends in the month
   (2) VISITO = Tourist (visitor) count for Hawaii in that month (in thousands)
   (3) RAIN   = Average rainfall in that month (in inches)
b. *Marketing variables:*
   (4) NOST   = The number of Speedy Burger stores open for business during the month
   (5) ADV1   = Speedy Burger advertising, i.e., weighted advertising expenditures
   (6) ADV2   = Same as ADV1 except different weights
   (7) CADV   = Weighted advertising expenditures by Speedy's competitors
   (8) NEWPRO = Percentage of month during which a new product promotion takes place
   (9) GAME   = Percentage of month during which game promotions occurred
c. *Economic variables:*
   (10) PI = Consumer price index for Hawaii.

Special consideration was given to the advertising variables because advertising was expected to have both a cumulative and lagged effect on sales. The variable ADV1 represents a 50 percent weight on Speedy's current month's advertising expenditures, with weights of 100 percent, 80 percent, 70 percent, 60 percent, and 50 percent on those of the preceding five months, respectively. ADV2 has a 33 percent weight on the current month and 100 percent for the previous month. Because of the lagging, the data for the first 5 months were unusable, leaving 23 monthly observations on which to base the analysis.

Regression results are shown in Table 1. They reveal that for each class of store, an equation can be fitted with a high degree of explanatory power (as reflected in R^2).

Note that not all variables are relevant to each type of store. For example, the number of holidays is a significant explanatory variable only for tourist stores. Similarly, the promotions appear effective only at tourist stores. Some variables have different effects on different types of

Table 1

Estimated Coefficients and *t*-Statistics

Variable	Class of Store		
	Metropolitan	*Tourist*	*Rural*
HOLIDA	—	2,812(3.52)*	—
VISITO	—	231.6(1.06)	—
RAIN	−2,142(−1.25)	—	—
NOST	70,313(3.42)*	—	92,163(11.14)*
ADV1	.3862(1.07)	.4100(2.28)*	—
ADV2	—	—	.65027(3.49)*
CADV	.6519(1.97)*	.6320(2.39)*	−.4576(−2.57)*
NEWPRO	—	22,462(2.09)*	—
GAME	—	10,499(1.48)	—
CPI	1,827(4.68)*	1,164(4.06)*	−1,184(−1.95)*
Constant	−373,290	−148,990	221,780
Summary Statistics			
n	23	23	23
Standard error	17,478	11,730	12,702
R^2	.85	.91	.98
Durbin-Watson	2.05	1.94	2.21

* Significant at .05 level.

stores. Competitors' advertising (CADV) has a positive correlation with sales of metropolitan and tourist stores, but detracts from rural sales. In all cases, the advertising by Speedy Burger (when adjusted for lag) contributes to higher sales.

The estimated equations can be used to forecast aggregate sales by store types. Assumed values of the independent variables are substituted into the estimated relationship and a prediction is made. For example, suppose we expect the independent variable values next month for metropolitan stores to be:

RAIN = 1 inch (from Weather Service)
NOST = 5 (current level)
ADV1 = 98,716 (reflecting advertising expenses)
CADV = 127,233 (a "best guess")
CPI = 263.5 (from general economic forecast)

The forecast aggregate metropolitan sales are thus

$$\hat{Q} = −373,290 − 2,142(1) + 70,313(5) + .3862(98,716)$$
$$+ .6519(127,233) + 1,827(263.5)$$
$$= \$578,614.81$$

Questions:

a. Provide an interpretation for the estimated coefficient of the RAIN and CADV variables in metropolitan stores. Are the signs consistent with theory? Explain.

b. Interpret the coefficient of determination (R^2) for the TOURIST stores equation.

c. Based on the calculated Durbin-Watson statistics, should adjustments be made for autocorrelation in any model? Explain.

d. Given the set of independent variables, is there reason to suspect multicollinearity? If so, among what variables?

e. Given the definition of the HOLIDA variable, can you explain why it is significant to the TOURIST stores but not to the others?

References

Anderson, J. E., and M. Kraus. "Quality of Service and Demand for Air Travel." *Review of Economics and Statistics,* November 1981, pp. 533–40.

Barnes, R.; R. Gillingham; and R. Hagemann. "The Short-Run Residential Demand for Electricity." *Review of Economics and Statistics,* November 1981, pp. 541–52.

Bechdolt, B. "Cross-Sectional Travel Demand Functions: U.S. Visitors to Hawaii, 1961–1970." *Quarterly Review of Economics and Business,* Winter 1973, pp. 37–47.

Bryant, Keith W., and Jennifer L. Gerner. "The Demand for Service Contracts." *Journal of Business,* July 1982, pp. 345–66.

Carlson, Rodney L. "Seemingly Unrelated Regression and the Demand for Automobiles of Different Sizes, 1965–1975: A Disaggregate Approach." *Journal of Business,* April 1978, 243–62.

Farrar, D., and R. Glauber. "Multicollinearity in Regression Analysis: The Problem Revisited." *Review of Economics and Statistics,* February 1967, pp. 92–107.

Fujii, E. T., and J. Mak. "Forecasting Tourism Demand; Some Methodological Issues." *Annals of Regional Science,* July 1981, pp. 72–83.

Goldberger, A. "Best Linear Unbiased Prediction in the Linear Regression Model." *Journal of the American Statistical Association,* June 1962, pp. 369–75.

Gujarati, Damodar. *Basic Econometrics.* New York: McGraw-Hill, 1978.

Gylfasan, Thorvaldur. "Interest Rates, Inflation, and the Aggregate Consumption Function." *Review of Economics and Statistics,* May 1981, pp. 233–55.

Haitovsky, Y. "A Note on the Maximization of $\bar{R}^2$." *American Statistician,* February 1969, pp. 20–21.

Huang, Cliff, John J. Siegfried, and Farangis Zardoshty. "The Demand for Coffee in the United States, 1963–1977." *Quarterly Review of Economics and Business,* Summer 1980, pp. 36–50.

Houthhakker, H. S., and Lester D. Taylor. *Consumer Demand in the United States, 1929–1970—Analyses and Projections.* 2d ed. Cambridge, Mass.: Harvard University Press, 1970.

Johnston, J. *Econometric Methods.* 2d ed. New York: McGraw-Hill, 1972.

Leamer, Edward E. "Is It a Demand Curve, or Is It a Supply Curve? Partial Identification through Inequality Constraints." *Review of Economics and Statistics,* August 1981, pp. 319–25.

McLagan, D. L. "A Non-Econometrician's Guide to Econometrics." *Business Economics,* May 1973, pp. 38–45.

Nelson, G., and T. H. Robinson. "Retail and Wholesale Demand and Marketing Order Policy for Fresh Navel Oranges." *American Journal of Agricultural Economics,* August 1978, pp. 502–9.

Neter, J.; W. Wasserman; and M. Kutner. *Applied Linear Regression Models.* Homewood, Ill.: Richard D. Irwin, 1983.

Nevin, John R. "Laboratory Experiments for Establishing Consumer Demand: A Validation Study." *Journal of Marketing Research,* August 1974, pp. 261–68.

Savin, N. and K. White. "Estimation and Testing for Functional Form and Autocorrelation: A Simultaneous Approach." *Journal of Econometrics,* August 1978, pp. 1–12.

Schultz, Henry. *Theory and Measurement of Demand.* Chicago: University of Chicago Press, 1964.

8

Forecasting

Virtually every business and economic decision rests upon a forecast of future conditions. Successful forecasting aims at reducing the uncertainty that surrounds management decision making with respect to costs, profits, sales, production, pricing, capital investment, and so forth. If the future were known with certainty, forecasting would be unnecessary. Decisions could be made and plans formulated on a once-and-for-all basis, without the need for subsequent revision. But uncertainty does exist; future outcomes are rarely assured. Therefore an *organized* system of forecasting is often desirable.

Forecasting takes place at all levels of economic activity, with both long-range and short-range projections. There are many different ways to classify forecasting methods, but the four most commonly used methods are:

1. Mechanical extrapolations.
2. Barometric techniques.
3. Opinion polling and intention surveys.
4. Econometric models.

Although these methods are different, they should not necessarily be regarded as mutually exclusive. Some methods may be more suitable for preparing short-term forecasts such as monthly or quarterly predictions;

260

others may be better for long-term projections of a year or more. Some may be better for forecasting at the macro level, while others may be preferred for forecasting at the level of the firm. In many organizations, two, three, or even all four approaches may be used with various degrees of emphasis and sophistication.

Mechanical Extrapolations

Extrapolation procedures of one form or another are used extensively by business executives, economists, market researchers, and others engaged in forecasting activities. As a method of prediction, extrapolation may include procedures ranging from simple coin tossing to the projection of trends, autocorrelations, and other more complex mathematical techniques. Typically, extrapolation techniques are distinguished from other forecasting methods in that they are essentially mechanical and are not closely integrated with relevant economic theory and statistical data. Nevertheless, they are widely used by professional forecasters, probably because they are convenient and, for reasons to be given later, often seem to "work." A few of the more common forms used in business are worth noting.

Naive Models

Naive models are ordinarily thought of as "continuity" models, for they all state that the future value of the variable in question is in some way a function of its present or recent value. Thus, letting Y denote the realized value of the variable under investigation, $\hat{Y}$ (read: "Y-hat") its forecast value, and using subscripts to designate time periods, the following two naive models are typical examples:

1. *No-change model:* The predicted value of the variable for the next period will be the same as its actual value in the present period:

$$\hat{Y}_{t+1} = Y_t$$

2. *Proportional-change model:* The *change* in the value of the variable from the current period to the next period $Y_{t+1} - Y_t = \Delta Y_{t+1})$ will be proportional to the *change* in the value of the variable from the last period to the current period $(Y_t - Y_{t-1} = \Delta Y_t)$, thus

$$\hat{Y}_{t+1} = Y_t + k\Delta Y_t$$

The parameter k may be estimated by observation from historical data, by more refined methods such as averaging or statistical regression or by sheer hunch if there are inadequate data. If $k = 1$, the equation represents an equal-change model.

The great majority of all economic decisions (and probably political and social decisions as well) are made on the basis of naive models such as these. It is not difficult to see why this is so. Naive models are either straightforward or modified projections of the present or the recent past. Hence for most short-term decisions they provide the most feasible guides for forecasting, since they are simple to apply and require a minimum amount of data or computation.

Time-Series Analysis

A *time series* is a sequence of values corresponding to particular points, or periods, of time. Data such as sales, production, and prices, when arranged chronologically, are thereby ordered in time and hence are referred to as time series. The simple line chart is the most common graphic device for depicting a time series, with the dependent variable such as sales or production or prices scaled on the vertical axis, and the independent variable, time, expressed in years or months or any other temporal measure, scaled on the horizontal axis.

Why does a time series typically exhibit a pattern of fluctuations? The answer to this question has usually been that at least four sources of variation are at work in an economic time series:

1. Trend.
2. Seasonal variation.
3. Cyclical variation.
4. Irregular forces.

Trend represents the long-run growth or decline of the series. Seasonal variations due to weather and customs manifest themselves during the same approximate time periods each year (for example, Christmas, Easter, and other seasons when different types of purchases are made). Cyclical variations, covering several years at a time, reflect economic prosperities and recessions. And finally, irregular forces, such as strikes, wars, and boycotts, are erratic in their influence on a particular series but nevertheless must be recognized.

Of the four forces affecting economic time series, the seasonal factor is fairly easy to measure and predict. The irregular factor is unpredictable but can be adjusted by a smoothing-out process such as a moving average. Hence the trend, which represents persistent growth or decline, and cyclical variation, which is presumably recurrent, have occupied the chief attention of forecasters using time-series analysis.

Trend Projections.   As a forecasting procedure, the method of trend projection usually assumes that the recent rate of change of the variable will continue in the future. On this basis, expectations are established by projecting past trends into the future, using techniques such as regression analysis. (Trend estimates are more reliable if they are based on "deseasonalized" data; that is, seasonal influences should be removed from the data before trend is calculated.) Thus, companies often project sales, GNP, and so forth, several years into the future by this procedure. When predictions are based on trends of past relationships, the trend may be a simple unweighted line, or it may be weighted by attaching the greatest importance to the most recent period and successively lesser degrees of importance to periods in the more distant past.

A frequently used technique for determining the trend in a time series is to fit a regression line according to the least squares method that was discussed in Chapter 6. An example illustrating the least squares method is presented at the end of this section.

Trend models have been used both successfully and unsuccessfully in the past. Forecasts based on the years 1929, 1933, 1937, and 1973 were disastrous for companies that used this method. Yet the method continues in wide use because many economic time series do, for the most part, show a persistent tendency to move in the same direction for a period of time because of their inherent cumulative characteristics. Therefore, forecasts using the method of trend projection will be right as to the direction of change more times than they will be wrong. Unfortunately, trend projections fail to detect changes in direction until after they have occurred; but it is the prediction of turning points that is most important to management. If turning points can be detected in advance, management can alter its plans with respect to sales effort, production scheduling, credit requirements, and the like. Otherwise, the mere projection of trends implies a forecast of continuance and no essential change in policy.

Cyclic Models. When the trend and seasonal variation are removed from an annual series of economic data, the residual structure exhibits certain fluctuating characteristics that have been described by some economists as *business cycles*. World War II produced important changes in the structural variables of the economy, and apparently has thereby altered the business cycle. Consequently, cyclic models should not be used unless strong reasons exist for the timing and amplitude of the business cycle. Nevertheless, the use of cyclic models as a prediction method continues among forecasters in many business firms.

Relationships of the Variables. The most common practice in constructing forecasting models is to assume a multiplicative structure for the elements so that the relationship is expressed by the formula $O =$

$TSCI$, where O = total behavior, T = trend, S = seasonal variations, C = cyclical variations, and I = irregular variations. It is also possible to assume that the relationships are additive, $O = T + S + C + I$, or that they are both multiplicative and additive, such as $O = S + TCI$. Various theoretical possibilities exist, but in most practical problems the multiplicative structure is assumed. In any event, the problem is to isolate and measure each of these four factors by separating out of the total behavior O, the gradual long-term change T, the regular oscillations S occurring within a year, and the regular oscillations C occurring over several years, each measured independently of the others. This problem of assumed relationships between the series, however, is minor when compared with the following types of measurement problems that arise.

1.   In explaining the cyclical mechanism, whether for the total economy or for a particular firm, there is controversy over whether the methods of analysis are really valid. Analysts have shown that apparent cycles can result in a series not because a cycle actually exists but simply because of the way in which the data are processed. For example, the use of a moving average may induce an oscillation in a resulting series even if no real cycle exists. In general, summing or averaging successive values of a random series can result in cyclical behavior by the very act itself (known as the "Slutsky-Yule effect"). For these reasons, the conventional method of residual analysis used by most business firms in separating cyclical and random components of time series is by no means a universally accepted procedure. On the contrary, it has been strongly questioned by analysts for many years.

2.   The separation of trend and random forces in a time series has also been questioned. Various studies of economic series reveal that perhaps the trend in a series cannot be separated from the short-term movements, and that perhaps both may be generated by a common set of forces. If series of data are observed at fairly close intervals, the random changes from one term to the next may be large enough to outweigh substantially any systematic (causal) effect that may be present, so that the data appear to behave almost like a "wandering series." In such instances it is difficult to distinguish by statistical methods a genuine wandering series from one in which the systematic element is weak.

It is apparent that the mechanistic methods of processing time-series data—methods that are in extensive use by many business firms—have a number of shortcomings. Nevertheless, this does not mean that such methods need be discarded. They definitely have certain specific uses and are often well employed as a part of the forecaster's total kit of analytical tools. Their limitations as discussed here are based on their shortcomings when used as the only forecasting technique in complex forecasting problems. When properly utilized, there are a number of advantages that can be derived from the traditional methods of time-series analysis. These may be listed as follows:

1. The necessary data are usually minimal and often easily obtained either from within the company itself or from outside sources.
2. The analytical calculations, such as the moving average, are usually simple and repetitive, and therefore suitable for computer processing. Hence, these techniques may be particularly well suited for problems in which a large number of variables must be forecast.
3. Only moderate analytical skills are required of the forecasters themselves. The methods are fairly easy to understand and the data processing is straightforward.
4. The method is largely objective, although judgment is involved in choosing additive or multiplicative decomposition, fixed or changing seasonal factors, type of trend, and extrapolation of the cyclical component.
5. The resultant forecasts are usually reasonably accurate for the short run, say, a 12-month period.
6. Time-series analysis usually permits the calculation of the degree of error in the forecast. An interval of confidence for the predicted value strengthens the quality of the forecast itself. Forecast errors may be further reduced if identification of dependable trend and seasonal patterns can be made.
7. Once decomposition of the time series has been accomplished, the way is open for a causal analysis of the separate components.

Despite these advantages, time-series analysis, like every other tool, must be used with full awareness of its limitations:

1. Time-series analysis cannot be used when time-series data have not been accumulated; for example, projections are not possible for a new product or a new environment for which no historical records have been kept.
2. Forecasts based on extrapolation of trend, cyclical, and seasonal components of a series assume a strong persistence of time patterns from the past into the future. This may not always be a valid assumption.
3. Strict adherence to the time-series analysis technique fails to take advantage of the forecaster's knowledge of prospective developments. For example, the forecaster might know that advertising effort will be greater than in the past, and such knowledge should be used to modify the extrapolation.
4. Time-series analysis gives no information about the causal factors influencing the time-series components. It merely provides a basis for causal analysis.

Illustration of a Simple Forecasting Approach[1]

Let us suppose that we have been able to gather quarterly sales data for a particular product over the past five years and we want to forecast sales for the second quarter of next year. We begin by constructing the charts shown in Exhibit 8–1.

Exhibit 8–1 ——

Sales Forecast Using Unsophisticated Methods

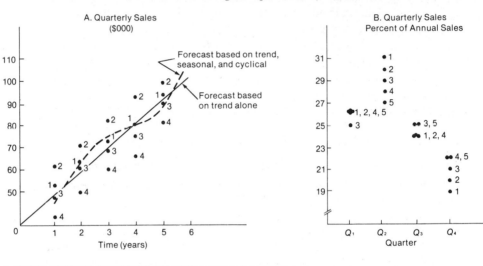

In part A of the exhibit, we begin by plotting the four quarterly sales for each year at the end of the year. This has the effect of removing the seasonal variation because we use the grouped observations to obtain an average. Then we rough in a solid linear regression line that represents the trend and a broken line in a smooth curve that more or less follows the average quarterly sales for each year. This broken line reveals the cyclical movement in the time series. We observe that at the end of year 6, sales are approximately 105 percent of the trend.

Looking at the solid trend line, we see that sales at the end of year 1 are $50,000 and they increase by $10,000 each year; that is,

$$\hat{Y}_{Qavg} = \$50,000 + \$10,000t$$

where t = number of years after year 1. For the sixth year, t = 5 and

$$\hat{Y}_{Qavg} = \$50,000 + \$10,000(5) = \$100,000$$

[1] Adapted from James L. Riggs, *Production Systems: Planning, Analysis, and control,* 3d ed. (New York: John Wiley & Sons, 1980), chap. 3.

But the broken, cyclical line indicates that this estimate is too low. Considering the probable cyclical movement, our forecast for sales becomes:

$$\hat{Y}_{Q_{avg}} = T \times C = \$100,000 \times 1.05 = \$105,000$$

Next, we must consider seasonal variation. To do this, we convert quarterly sales into percentages of annual sales for each of the five years. This removes the trend and cyclical effects from the data. We then plot—in part B of the exhibit—the five appropriate percentages for each of the four quarters. We are now in a position to obtain a weighted average of the data for any quarter.

Again using an "eyeball" approach and giving more weight to the more recent years, we estimate the weighted average percentage of annual sales to be about 28 percent in the second quarter. We multiply by four to obtain the seasonal effect; that is to say, if this rate of sales were to hold throughout the whole year, sales would be $4 \times 0.28 = 1.12$ times the annual average. Our forecast then becomes:

$$\hat{Y}_{Q_2} = T \times C \times S = \$100,000 \times 1.05 \times 1.12 = \$117,600$$

The only remaining consideration is the effect of irregular forces. We cannot predict what they will be, but we assume that they are normally distributed with a mean of zero and hence cancel themselves out. Thus our last equation becomes the final forecast.

Although this approach relies upon unsophisticated methods, this does not mean that the forecasts it produces are too crude to be valuable. On the contrary, one could spend considerably more time and not produce any substantial improvement. There are, of course, a number of factors to consider in choosing a forecasting method, and we discuss most of these later in this chapter.

Least Squares Method Applied to Trend Identification

Unquestionably the most widely used approach for finding the trend in a time series is the method of least squares that was explained in Chapter 6. As its name implies, this method involves fitting a regression line through a series of observed data points in such a way that the squared deviations from this line are minimized. The regression line is represented by the equation $\hat{Y} = a + bt$, where a and b are parameters to be determined and t is time. The parameters a and b are determined by solving the system of equations

$$\Sigma Y = na + b\Sigma t$$
$$\Sigma tY = a\Sigma t + b\Sigma t^2$$

where n is the number of observations.

Let us work with the example of a company that has been producing hand-operated nail-driving machines for five years. The plant has operated at near capacity for the last two years. Forecasts are needed to schedule production for the coming year and to provide estimates for future expansion of production facilities. Sales records for the five years have been tabulated by quarters as shown in Exhibit 8–2.

Exhibit 8–2_____

Data for Trend Analysis (quarterly sales in $000)

	1980	1981	1982	1983	1984
Quarter 1	$ 190	$ 280	$ 270	$ 300	$ 320
Quarter 2	370	420	360	430	440
Quarter 3	300	310	280	290	320
Quarter 4	220	180	190	200	220
Totals	1,080	1,190	1,100	1,220	1,300

To solve the equations, we need to find values for ΣY, Σt, ΣtY, and Σt^2. Accordingly, the annual sales data can be arranged as follows:

Year	Y	t	t^2	tY
1980	1,080	0	0	0
1981	1,190	1	1	1,190
1982	1,100	2	4	2,200
1983	1,220	3	9	3,660
1984	1,300	4	16	5,200
Sums	5,890	10	30	12,250

Then

$$5,890 = 5a + 10b$$
$$12,250 = 10a + 30b$$

Solving the equations simultaneously, we get

$$a = 1,084 \text{ or } \$1,084,000$$
$$b = 47 \text{ or } \$ 47,000$$

and

$$\hat{Y} = 1,084,000 + 47,000t$$

Our forecast for 1985 would be

$$\hat{Y} = \$1,084,000 + \$47,000(5) = \$1,319,000$$

The least squares method is a relatively quick way to calculate the trend line even when calculations must be done manually rather than with a computer. (The calculations can be made easier by letting the base year be the middle year in the series rather than the first year as we have shown.)

Moving-Average Techniques

Seasonal variation can be incorporated routinely into forecasts by means of a *seasonal index*, which can be calculated by a *moving-average* technique. A moving average is calculated by adding each period's value over some desired length of time and then dividing by the number of periods. Using data from the preceding example, we can illustrate a moving average and construct a seasonal index.

A table of four-period moving averages, centered moving averages, and seasonal indexes is given in Exhibit 8–3. The calculations used to construct the exhibit are made as follows. First, the four-period moving averages are calculated from four quarters of sales:

$$\frac{190 + 370 + 300 + 220}{4} = 270 \qquad \frac{370 + 300 + 220 + 280}{4} = 292$$

and so on (fractions are dropped). However, the four-period moving averages are centered *between* quarters. To get moving averages centered on the midpoints of the quarters, we calculate *centered moving averages*. For each quarter, the centered moving average is calculated as the average of the adjacent pair of four-period moving averages:

$$\frac{270 + 292}{2} = 281 \qquad \frac{292 + 305}{2} = 298$$

and so on. The seasonal indexes are calculated by dividing the centered moving average for the quarter into the actual sales for the quarter:

$$Q3: \frac{300}{281} = 1.07 \qquad Q4: \frac{220}{298} = 0.74$$

and so on.

Exhibit 8–4 shows the seasonal indexes arranged by quarter, together with their averages by quarter. Since these are rough estimates of seasonal index values, perhaps we can improve them by making some adjustments.

Exhibit 8–3_____

Moving Averages and Quarterly Seasonal Indexes

Year	Quarter	Sales in Units of $10,000	Four-Period Moving Average	Centered Moving Average	Seasonal Index
1980	1	190			
	2	370			
	3	300	270	281	1.07
	4	220	292	298	0.74
1981	1	280	305	306	0.91
	2	420	307	302	1.39
	3	310	297	296	1.04
	4	180	295	287	0.63
1982	1	270	280	276	0.98
	2	360	273	274	1.32
	3	280	275	279	1.00
	4	190	283	286	0.66
1983	1	300	300	301	1.00
	2	430	303	304	1.42
	3	290	305	307	0.94
	4	200	310	311	0.64
1984	1	320	312	316	1.01
	2	440	320	322	1.37
	3	320	325		
	4	220			

Exhibit 8–4_____

Data for Calculating and Adjusted Seasonal Index

Year	Q1	Q2	Q3	Q4
1	0.91	1.39	1.07	0.74
2	0.98	1.32	1.04	0.63
3	1.00	1.42	1.00	0.66
4	1.01	1.37	0.94	0.64
Totals	3.90	5.50	4.05	2.67
Average Seasonal Index	0.98	1.38	1.01	0.67

The first step is to normalize—that is, to make sure that the average of the four average seasonal indexes is 1. We find that:

$$\frac{0.98 + 1.38 + 1.01 + 0.67}{4} = 1.01$$

The small error could be eliminated by reducing each quarter's value by about 0.003.

Next, we examine the seasonal index values for trends or other patterns of behavior. The data in Exhibit 8–4 indicate that Q1 is increasing, Q2 is fairly stable, and Q3 and Q4 seem to be decreasing. These changes should be recognized and incorporated into an adjusted seasonal index. While there are more formal methods to make these adjustments, we shall be content to use an "eyeball" approach. This means that we exercise our best judgment to adjust the seasonal indexes upward or downward to recognize the trends, while insuring that the average of the four indexes is equal to 1. The results are as follows:

	Q1	Q2	Q3	Q4
Adjusted Seasonal Index	0.99	1.38	0.98	0.65

The last step is to make a forecast for each of the four quarters of the coming year; in this case, for 1985. We do this by multiplying the most recent centered moving average for the quarter by its respective adjusted seasonal index. The resulting quarterly forecasts for 1985 are:

Q1: 316(for 1984) × 0.99 = 312.84 or $313,000
Q2: 322(for 1984) × 1.38 = 444.36 or $444,000
Q3: 307(for 1983) × 0.98 = 300.86 or $301,000
Q4: 311(for 1983) × 0.65 = 202.15 or $202,000

Barometric Techniques

Whereas mechanical methods of forecasting, particularly time-series analyses, are used under the assumption that the future is an extension of the past, the use of barometric techniques is based on the idea that the future can be predicted from certain happenings in the present. Specifically, barometric methods usually involve the use of *statistical indicators*—selected time series that, when used in conjunction with one another or when combined in certain ways, provide an indication of the direction in which the economy, or a particular industry or product, is heading. The series chosen thus serve as barometers of economic change. Two particular applications of the barometric approach are commonly employed: leading series and pressure indexes. To some extent they may be overlapping, but we will discuss them separately for convenience.

Types of Indicators

The basic concept underlying the statistical indicator approach to business cycle analysis and forecasting is that various economic activities tend to move through the course of the business cycle in consistent but different time sequences. *Coincident indicators* are those that move approximately in phase with the aggregate economy and hence are measures of current economic activity. *Leading indicators* tend to reflect future changes in the trend of the aggregate economy. *Lagging indicators* are those that trail behind aggregate economic activities.[2] The relative position of these indicators in the business cycle is illustrated in Exhibit 8–5.

Exhibit 8–5

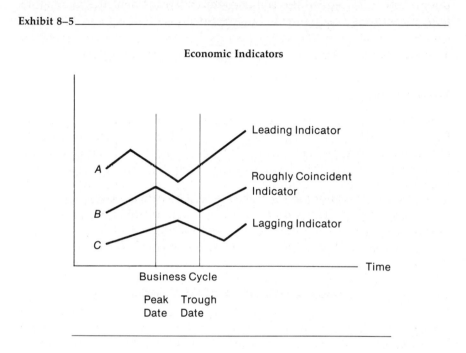

Economic Indicators

The relationships between leading, coincident, and lagging indicators usually have an economic basis. In many instances of leading indicators, for example, there are planning, contracting, or purchasing commitments that systematically lead to further economic activities or that are symptomatic of such activities. Coincident indicators reflect concurrent economic activities and are therefore the most direct of the three relationships. Current sales and production levels, for example, contribute toward establishing a more general level of economic activity. Finally, lagging indicators may sometimes be viewed as the residual in economic activities, as in the case of post-Christmas business inventories, or as a reflection of business or government commitments already under way.

---

[2] Although most economic indicators are related to the aggregate economy, some may be related to the sales volume of an industry or product.

But though experience is gained through historical evaluation, business executives are not nearly as interested in hindsight as they are in foresight. Consequently, of the three series discussed so far, lagging indicators are the least useful as an aid in formulating future business policy.

There are also two refinements of statistical indicators that are often used in forecasting. One is the diffusion index, which shows the direction and intensity of selected economic time series in a particular category, such as production or consumption. The other is the composite index, which highlights the timing and pattern of business cycle expansion and contraction. These indexes will be discussed in more detail after we take a closer look at the nature of leading indicators.

Leading Indicators

Forecasters have long sought leading indicators for predicting the future course of business. Andrew Carnegie used to count the number of factory chimneys belching smoke to tell whether business would increase or decline. The Brookmire Economic Service as early as 1911 utilized successive leads in stock, commodity, and money market series to forecast economic change. Today many business executives use their own leading indicators based on personal experiences and observations.

The most extensive periodic reports on business cycle indicators have appeared, since October 1961, in a monthly magazine entitled *Business Conditions Digest*, published by the U.S. Department of Commerce. This widely quoted source consists for the most part of tables and charts showing the movements of several hundred economic indicators over the business cycle. Accordingly, it is closely related to the work of the National Bureau of Economic Research, a private organization in New York that for decades has been the world's leader in business cycle research and analysis.

For forecasting purposes, chief interest centers on the several dozen economic series that in the opinion of the Bureau of Economic Analysis may be classified as leading indicators—economic measures that quite consistently precede the upturns and downturns of business activity. The movements of the series usually are shown against the background of the expansions and contractions of the general business cycle so that leads and lags can be readily detected and unusual cyclical developments spotted.

Exhibit 8–6 displays a page from the November 1982 issue of *Business Conditions Digest*. Each of the time series shown exhibits facets of business activity during the years 1948–1982. The vertical scale differs for each series as indicated in the title of the series. For example, the title of the first series indicates that the average workweek is measured in hours. Each issue of *Business Conditions Digest* also contains descriptions

Exhibit 8–6

Leading Indicators

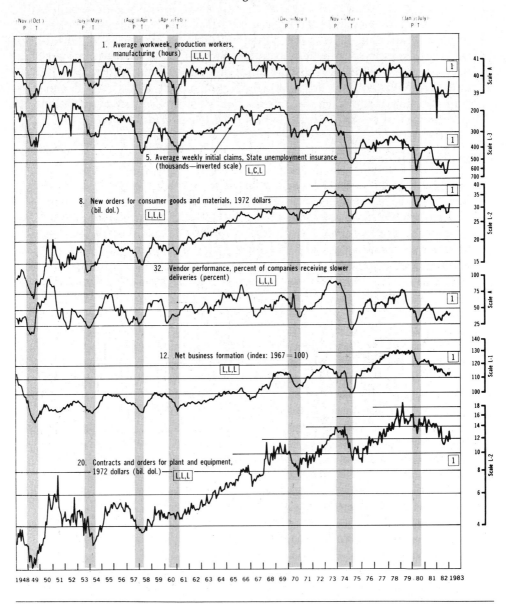

Source: Bureau of Economic Analysis, *Business Conditions Digest*, U.S. Department of Commerce, November 1982.

and sometimes technical discussions of various series and their usefulness in the story of business cycles.

Diffusion Indexes

The diffusion index was developed to answer the question of whether
a change in any particular indicator series is really forecasting a reversal
in the general trend or whether it is just an isolated development. The
large aggregate statistics developed by government agencies are extremely useful in macroeconomics as measures of the prevailing level of
economic activity. For example, the Commerce Department's measure
of gross national product (GNP) aggregates all production of final goods
and services into a single dollar-value figure; the physical output of all
manufacturing industries lumped together is measured by the Federal
Reserve's industrial production index; and the Bureau of Labor Statistics
publishes figures on the volume of employment in nonfarm industries.

As useful as these figures may be, they mask the important changes
that may be taking place in individual industries or markets, even
though these changes may in time have a major influence upon the
aggregate statistics. The overall economy may be expanding or contracting, but some business activities will be moving in the opposite direction. The diffusion techniques look at these variations of economic activity, rather than at the trend as a whole, and attempt to measure the
degree of dispersion.

To construct a diffusion index, the analyst first chooses a number of
indicator series (all of which are leading, coincident, or lagging) and
smooths each of the selected series, say, by means of moving averages.
Then for each time period, the analyst counts the number of series that
exhibit an increase in economic activity, converts that number to a percentage of the series examined, and plots it on the chart. Therefore,
whenever the plot point is above the 50 percent line on the chart, it
means that the majority of indicators predict expansion of the economy.
Below the 50 percent line means, of course, that the majority of indicators predict contraction. The intensity of the trend in either direction is
reflected in the distance of the plot point from the 50 percent line.

Diffusion indexes thus measure rates of change of the aggregate to
which the indexes apply, hence diffusion indexes tend to change direction before the aggregates do. This is a useful characteristic for forecasting purposes. Unfortunately, however, the lead of a diffusion index is
erratic. Many indexes tend to peak in the early stages of a business
expansion, then settle down at a moderate level until the onset of recession. At that point they may fall spectacularly but much too late to be of
any value in forecasting.

The prime difficulty with diffusion indexes is that efforts to increase their lead make them harder to interpret, while efforts to simplify their interpretation reduce their lead. Efforts to improve their lead usually require the inclusion of more and more leading series, but this results in increasing instability of the index. Despite the fact that diffusion indexes appear to derive reliability from the aggregation of more than one series, they must be used with caution. Leading indicators often give false signals, such as indicating a downturn in the business cycle that turns out to be merely a slowdown in the rate of expansion. Also, there is the danger of combining some indicators that may be potentially unreliable for a given situation with those of greater accuracy. In such cases, the probability of successful prediction is not increased by using additional series. Diffusion indexes become more reliable if three are constructed: one for leading indicators, one for coincident indicators, and one for lagging indicators. The student, however, is well advised to regard the diffusion indexes as *aids* to careful study and analysis of underlying economic phenomena rather than substitutes.

In spite of their shortcomings as reliable indicators of a coming trend, diffusion indexes provide a useful way of examining the breadth and vigor of movement in the business cycle. They cannot substitute completely for the judgment and experience of the forecaster, but they do provide a means of cross-checking judgment against the raw data of business statistics.

As an example, Exhibit 8–7 provides diffusion indexes for 12 leading indicators and 4 coincident indicators. The letter P refers to the peak of a business cycle and T designates its trough. (You might try to eyeball the series to see if the leading indicators forecast changes in the coincident indicators.)

Composite Indexes

A composite index is a weighted average of several individual indicators. The weight of each indicator is based upon its ability to perform well in six areas related to forecasting: (1) economic significance, (2) statistical adequacy, (3) consistency of timing at business cycle peaks and troughs, (4) conformity to business expansions and contractions, (5) smoothness, and (6) prompt availability. Composite indexes constructed for leading, coincident, and lagging indicators are illustrated in Exhibit 8–8. The dark stripes in this exhibit mark periods of economic contraction. The symbol P refers to the peak of a business cycle while T refers to its trough. As Exhibit 8–8 shows, there have been seven major economic contractions since 1948. The numbers in the chart indicate length of leads (−) and lags (+) in months from reference turning points; for

Exhibit 8–7

Diffusion Indexes and Rates of Change

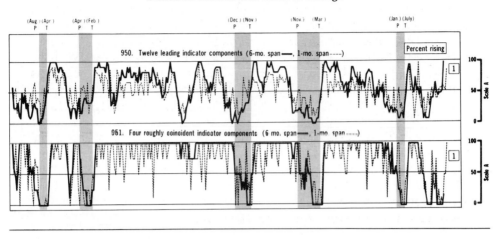

Source: Bureau of Economic Analysis, *Business Conditions Digest*, U.S. Department of Commerce, November 1982.

example, the leading indicators turned down nine months before the economy turned down in the 1973–75 recession.

In general it is these composites—particularly the composite of 12 leading indicators shown at the top of Exhibit 8–8—that are watched so closely by economists and the public. There is little doubt that over a span of time a composite index offers more reliable signals than does any single indicator, since much of the measurement error and "noise" associated with single indicators are eliminated. Because of these advantages, the composite indexes should be used if any leading indicator approach is used. Furthermore, criticism of this overall method should be made in reference to the composite indexes rather than any individual indicator.[3]

How Useful Are the Indicators?

How does the approach by the U.S. Department of Commerce—with its close resemblance to the indicator techniques long used by the National Bureau of Economic Research—avoid the difficulties that have

---

[3] A very good appraisal of the leading indicator approach can be found in Michael K. Evans, *Macroeconomic Activity: Theory, Forecasting and Control* (New York: Harper & Row, 1969), pp. 445–60.

Exhibit 8–8

Composite Indexes

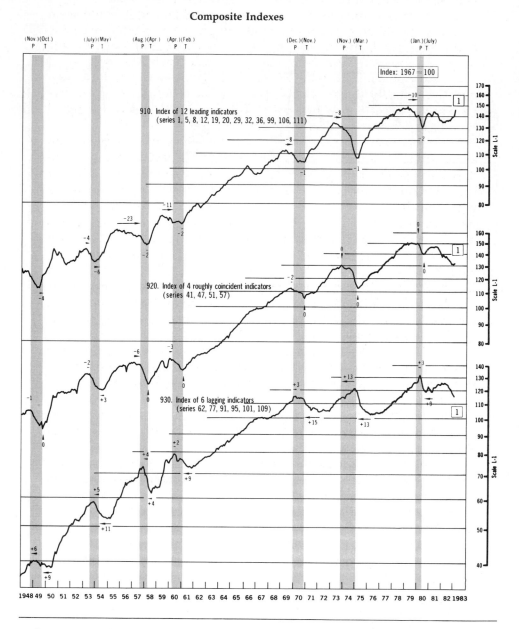

Source: Bureau of Economic Analysis, *Business Conditions Digest*, U.S. Department of Commerce, November 1982.

plagued indicator methods in the past? Does the indicator approach give false signals when a real recession or recovery is under way?

A number of leading series are available monthly, and it would seem that they should provide a useful guide for predicting the future course of the economy. Unfortunately, however, they are not as useful for this purpose as might at first seem because of the following limitations.

1. They are not always consistent in their tendency to lead. Frequently, some of the series will signal what turns out to be a true change, while the remaining series either fail to signal at all or else signal too late to be of much value for prediction.

2. It is not always possible to tell whether the series is signaling an actual future turning point of the economy or whether it is merely exhibiting a wiggle that is of no real significance. In order to be sure whether the variation is actually a true signal of impending change or merely a false start, it may be necessary to wait a few months for confirmation. But this, of course, destroys any forecasting advantage that the series may have in the first place, since the leading series can at best be used only for short-term forecasts up to about six months or so. Also, as Exhibit 8–8 shows, the leading indicators have exhibited very uneven lead times. In forecasting downturns the range is from only 4 months for the 1953–54 cycle to 23 months for the 1957–58 cycle. So even if it is known that a downturn (upturn) is coming, there is still uncertainty as to *when* it will come.

3. Even if the leading indicators could consistently signal the true turning points of the economy, they would still indicate only the direction of future change, while disclosing little or nothing about the magnitude of the change.

4. Indicator forecasting is not applicable to new-product situations. The development of indicators requires historical records that do not exist for new products.

5. Indicator forecasting cannot make use of the forecaster's knowledge of prospective market developments. It gives no information on the response of sales to company marketing strategy or external forces. These are probably the most cogent reasons that indicator forecasting should be used only in conjunction with other forecasting tools that are more specific to an industry or geographic area of interest.

6. There are certain technical difficulties inherent in indicator forecasting. Sometimes, indicators that lead company sales are hard to find. At other times, it requires an historical record extending over several cycles, a longer span than that required for short-run extrapolation procedures. This also may necessitate the accumulation of considerable data for several possible indicators until a good one is found. Other technical shortcomings include the fact that there is no way to obtain an estimate of error in the forecasts.

7.   Much skill and experience are necessary for the use of indicators as a forecasting tool. Forecasts of turning points require very fine judgment not only in the interpretation of historical records but also in the interpretation and evaluation of current evidence.

In the light of these criticisms, the use of leading series as a forecasting device would seem to be a very limited approach at best. However, indicators can be valuable forecasting tools when used in conjunction with other forecasting analyses, for several reasons:

1.   Indicators can be readily understood by those who make business decisions, which is a very important consideration for any tool.

2.   The indicator technique can be a great help in detecting turning points so that extrapolations of sales can be modified. Even an indication that a turning point may be at hand is useful information that can suggest that flexibility in plans is advisable.

3.   The quantity of data required for indicator forecasting is usually moderate once the right indicator has been found; periodic updating of an already available statistic may be all that is needed. Usually if the data need adjustment, they can be computerized.

Pressure Indexes

Acting on the idea that amplitude differences play a decisive role in the analysis of business cycles, economists have developed various ratio and difference measures called "pressure indexes" as guides to forecasting. Some examples of such indexes used in economic and business forecasting are the following:

1.   Durable goods production fluctuates much more widely than nondurable goods production over the course of a business cycle. Hence the ratio of durable to nondurable goods production is sometimes used as an indicator of cyclical change—the ratio tending to increase in prosperous periods and to decline before a business cycle downturn, although there is no clear-cut evidence of the latter.

2.   Purchasing agents, in predicting raw materials prices, frequently use a ratio of raw materials inventories to new orders for finished goods. Also, a somewhat rougher indication is obtained if production of finished goods rather than new orders is used in the denominator.

3.   The difference between the rate of family formation and the rate of housing inventory growth is a pressure indicator of the long-term demand for new housing. In the short run, on the other hand, factors such as disposable income and mortgage conditions are usually more influential in determining the actual rate of construction.

4.   Railroads approximate from six months to a year in advance the demand for new orders for railroad cars from the ratio of carloadings (seasonally adjusted) to cars in serviceable condition.

5.   The spread between common stock yields and corporate bond yields has sometimes been used as a predictor of stock prices. Classical market theory states that as the spread narrows, the advantage of owning stocks rather than bond declines, and money flows out of the stock market into the bond market.

These ratio and difference measures, as well as numerous others that can be devised, may not always be helpful in forecasting the magnitude of change. However, they do provide warning signals of impending developments and frequently an indication as to the future direction of change. When used in conjunction with other forecasting methods, pressure indexes can be useful guideposts for better prediction.

Opinion Polling and Intention Surveys

The opinion-polling or sample-survey technique of forecasting is a subjective method of prediction, amounting largely to a weighted or unweighted averaging of attitudes and expectations. The underlying assumption is that certain attitudes affecting economic decisions can be defined and measured far enough in advance so that changes in business trends can be predicted. The results are arrived at by asking people about their expectations or intentions as to future economic happenings. Various forms or types of surveys are used both in economic and in sales forecasting and are discussed below.

Surveys of Economic Intentions

Among the best-known studies made for forecasting economic activity or some particular phase of it are the following:

1.   Surveys of business executives' intentions on what to spend on plant and equipment, made independently by the McGraw-Hill Book Company, the Department of Commerce, the Securities and Exchange Commission, and the National Industrial Conference Board.
2.   Surveys of consumers' finances and buying plans, made primarily by the Survey Research Center of the University of Michigan under the sponsorship of both industry and government.
3.   Surveys of business executives' plans regarding inventory changes, made by the National Association of Purchasing Agents.

All of these surveys are made periodically. On the whole, the more successful ones have been the McGraw-Hill survey of expenditure plans for plant and equipment (capital-consuming plans) and the Survey Research Center's surveys of consumers' intentions. These account for most of the investment undertaken by the important capital-consuming industries. The record of these surveys has agreed rather well with actual expenditures, except for a few scattered years when the errors could be accounted for by unexpected international political events, such as war or the threat of war. Capital expenditure plans, since they are so dependent on changes in the structural environment of the economy, could not be expected to remain the same under such unusual circumstances. Other than these, however, the McGraw-Hill surveys have provided a basically sound analysis of capital expenditure plans. The surveys cover much the same ground as the government survey mentioned above but are available earlier (in *Business Week*) and are widely used for forecasting.

The Survey Research Center of the University of Michigan prepares surveys of consumer finances and buying plans. The surveys, based on samples of several thousand respondents, are designed to (1) evaluate recent developments among consumers; (2) provide data for testing hypotheses about economic behavior, that is, functional relationships among variables; and (3) determine intentions for consumer purchases of automobiles, houses, and major appliances. A single survey provides a cross section of data, while consecutive surveys yield time series of such data.

The results of these surveys have been both good and bad. On the one hand, the surveys seem to do well in foretelling some of the more important turning points of business. On the other hand, the surveys are less useful for predicting the magnitude of change. They have been best suited to predictions covering important decisions only a few months into the future because the average consumer's decisions are affected by a wide array of economic and emotional complexities.

Sales Forecasting

Opinion-polling methods are not confined to forecasting changes in economic conditions; many business firms use variations of the method in forecasting sales.

1. *Executive polling*, whereby the views of top management are combined and (subjectively) averaged, is frequently used. The assumption in the use of this approach is that there is safety in numbers since the combined judgment of the group is better than that of any single member. Hence the executives sit as a jury and pass judgment on the sales outlook for the coming year. Generally represented on the jury are people with a diversity of opinions—the sales, production, finance, purchasing, and administrative divisions. In those companies where forecasts of probable events are derived after a sifting and analysis of market reports, sales data, and formal economic forecasts, the executive-polling

approach may be quite successful. Without such careful evaluations, however, the method can easily degenerate into a guessing game yielding sloppy and unfounded predictions. Companies using the executive-polling approach may also combine it with statistical measures of trends and cycles or other analytical tools by raising or lowering the statistical forecast according to their subjective judgments.

2. *Sales force polling* is another variation whereby a composite outlook is constructed on the basis of information derived from those closest to the market. The sales forecast may be built up from the estimates of salespeople made in cooperation with branch or regional managers, or by going directly to jobbers, distributors, and major customers in order to discover their needs. One advantage is that this method utilizes the firsthand, specialized knowledge of those nearest to the market. It also gives salespeople greater confidence in their quotas developed from forecasts. Obviously, however, salespeople may be unaware of structural changes taking place in their markets and hence incapable of shaping their forecasts to account for those future changes. Also, sound forecasting requires more time and effort than most salespeople can ordinarily devote, and the result is more likely to be an off-the-cuff guess than a prediction. Furthermore, even their guesses may be biased by their quotas and the sales quota system. Accordingly, firms using this method may set up a system of checks and balances whereby the estimates of salespeople are compiled, checked, adjusted, and revised periodically in the light of past experience and future expectations.

3. *Consumer intentions surveys* are still another version of the opinion-polling method applied to sales forecasting. Some automobile companies, for instance, make sample surveys of automobile buying intentions, which they then project to a national level by weighting the estimate with the average purchase rate and an index of predicted incomes. Similar techniques are used by other firms in forecasting the sales of appliances, furniture, and other durable goods.

Econometric Models

Based on the idea that changes in economic activity can be explained by a set of relationships among economic variables, there has grown a branch of applied science known as *econometrics*. Breaking the word into its two parts, "econo" and "metrics," it is evident that its subject matter must deal with the science of *economic measurement*. And this is precisely what econometrics does: it explains past economic activity and predicts future activity by deriving mathematical equations that will express the most probable interrelationships among a set of economic variables. The economic variables may include disposable income, money flows, inventories, government revenues and expenditures, foreign trade, and so on. By combining the relevant variables, each a separate series covering a past period of time, into what seems to be the best mathematical arrangement, econometricians predict the future course of one or more of these variables on the basis of the established relationships. The "best mathematical arrangement" is thus a model that takes the form of an equation or system of equations that seems to describe best the past set of relationships according to economic theory. The model, in other words, is a simplified abstraction of a real situation expressed in equation form, and is used as a prediction system that will yield numerical results. To the extent that economic theorems and relationships can be verified by subjecting historical data to statistical analysis, then, at least in principle, econometrics stands as a compromise between pure "ivory tower" economic theory on the one hand and mere description of facts and occurrences on the other.

Single-Equation Models

Economic theory deals with the science of choices among alternatives, and its method is to construct simplified models of economic reality from which certain laws describing regularities in economic behavior are derived. When these models are quantitatively formulated, they may take the form of econometric models. Such models may be constructed for the total economy for predicting future levels of income, employment, and other aggregate economic variables, or they may be constructed for a particular firm or industry in order to predict sales, production, costs, and related economic variables. Both types of models can be useful, of course, in facilitating decision making and planning by government agencies, business executives, labor unions, political organizations, and similar groups with a direct interest in economic and business conditions. Hence, both types of models are often discussed and illustrated in the literature of econometrics.

One of the first steps in the construction of an econometric model is to specify the hypotheses that purport to explain the economic phenomena under investigation. Then these hypotheses are translated into a form suitable for testing, usually one or more mathematical equations.

For example, consider an elementary demand problem in which the industry sales S of a certain product during any given time period t is a function of the number of households H during the period and of consumers' disposable household income Y during the previous period. This model is expressed by the unspecified equation:

$$S_t = f(H_t, Y_{t-1})$$

If it is further hypothesized that the relationship among the variables is linear and not exact, the model becomes the specified equation

$$S_t = a + bH_t + cY_{t-1} + \mu_t$$

where a, b, and c are parameters to be estimated from the available data by certain statistical techniques, and μ is a "disturbance" term. Thus, if μ had been excluded from the equation, the relationship would mean that sales are completely determined by the household and income variables. However, by including μ, the equation recognizes that sales will be affected by additional factors besides households and incomes, and hence the forecasted estimates of sales that are derived from the equation will deviate from the actual or realized sales. These other factors represented by μ should be random in nature and, in a statistical sense, normally distributed so that μ will average out to zero. Then, once the parameters are estimated, certain statistical tests may be applied to evaluate the adequacy of the equation as a forecasting device. These were discussed with specific reference to demand forecasting in Chapter 7.

Simultaneous–Equations Models

There are many relatively uncomplicated problems in business and economics that can be solved by expressing the underlying structure in the form of a single mathematical equation. However, when a theoretical structure is complex, as is usually the case, there are simultaneous interrelations among the variables in the system. In that event, a system of equations can be developed to express the complex interactions among the variables. Such a system ordinarily requires a computer solution. The construction of such a model can be illustrated by the following simplified version of an actual model. Let:

$$C = \text{Consumption}$$
$$G = \text{Government expenditures on goods and services}$$
$$I = \text{Investment (net)}$$
$$K = \text{Net capital stock at end of period}$$
$$P = \text{Nonwage income}$$
$$W = \text{Wage income}$$
$$Y = \text{National income (or net product)}$$
$$t = \text{A given time period; } t - 1 \text{ denotes the previous time period}$$
$$a, b, c = \text{Parameters}$$
$$\mu_1, \mu_2, \mu_3 = \text{Disturbance terms or random influences that affect the dependent variable but are assumed to average out to zero}$$

In order to construct an econometric model, we must now specify various hypotheses that purport to explain the phenomena under investigation. These hypotheses are based on previous studies, empirical findings, or a priori reasoning. Then the hypotheses are translated into a form that is suitable for empirical verification and testing, usually into mathematical equations.

1.   Consumption in the current period depends on the current period's income and on consumption in the previous period:

$$C_t = a_0 + a_1 Y_t + a_2 C_{t-1} + \mu_{1t}$$

2.   Investment in the current period is determined by nonwage income earned in the current period and by the net capital stock available at the end of the previous period:

$$I_t = b_0 + b_1 P_t + b_2 K_{t-1} + \mu_{2t}$$

3.   Wages in the current period depend on income in the current period and on time. ("Time" is used as a substitute variable for all other variables that are unspecified but nevertheless exert an influence on wages.)

$$W_t = c_0 + c_1 Y_t + c_2 t + \mu_{3t}$$

4.   National income or net product in the current period is the sum of consumption, investment, and government expenditures in the current period. (In the real world there are some accounting differences between national income and net product, but these differences are assumed to be sufficiently unimportant to be neglected in this model.)

$$Y_t = C_t + I_t + G_t$$

5.   Nonwage income in the current period is the difference between national income in the current period and wage income in the current period:

$$P_t = Y_t - W_t$$

6.   Net capital stock at the end of the current period is equal to the last period's net capital stock plus current net investment:

$$K_t = K_{t-1} + I_t$$

This completes the set of hypotheses that we have expressed both in words and in equations for explaining the phenomena being investigated. Note that the last three statements are actually nothing more than definitions or mathematical identities that are needed to complete the model. For convenience, the six equations that comprise the model may now be grouped together as a system of equations.

$$C_t = a_0 + a_1 Y_t + a_2 C_{t-1} + \mu_{1t} \tag{1}$$
$$I_t = b_0 + b_1 P_t + b_2 K_{t-1} + \mu_{2t} \tag{2}$$
$$W_t = c_0 + c_1 Y_t + c_2 t + \mu_{3t} \tag{3}$$
$$Y_t = C_t + I_t + G_t \tag{4}$$
$$P_t = Y_t - W_t \tag{5}$$
$$K_t = K_{t-1} + I_t \tag{6}$$

It may be worth noting again that there is a reason for the use of the variables μ_{1t}, μ_{2t}, and μ_{3t} on the right side of the first three equations. These variables, called disturbance terms, allow for the fact that the other explicit independent variables in the equations do not account completely for the variations in the dependent variables.

For example, in Equation (1) consumption in the current period is determined by other factors in addition to income in the current period and consumption in the previous period. Some of these other factors may be both economic and psychological. Further, there may be errors in the data used to represent the relevant variables. All of these disturbances are represented in Equation (1) by the variable μ_{1t}. If we assume that no important independent variables have been omitted, then the disturbance terms reflect all of the unknown and unpredictable factors. Ideally, the variations in these "all other" factors will be small and random in nature, and will tend to cancel each other out so that their overall net effect on the dependent variable is zero. To the extent that this assumption is realized in practice, the remaining explicit variables in the equation will account for the systematic or causal movements in the dependent variable.

The reader should be aware that there is considerably more involved in econometric model building that the brief sketch presented here. Many theoretical and statistical problems exist that must be handled in actual model construction. These paragraphs have merely conveyed a bit of the flavor of the subject for those who are unfamiliar with it.[4]

Techniques of Macroeconomic Forecasters

A study of thirteen prominent macroeconomic forecasting organizations was conducted in 1981 by McNees.[5] As shown on Exhibit 8–9, five of the forecasters are commercial consulting firms (BMARK, CHASE, DRI, TG, and WEFA); four are university facilities (GSU, KEDI, RSQE,

[4] For a more detailed description, see Lawrence R. Klein and Richard M. Young, *An Introduction to Econometric Forecasting and Forecasting Models* (Lexington, Mass.: D.C. Heath, 1980).

[5] Stephen K. McNees, "The Recent Record of Thirteen Forecasters" (reprint), *New England Economic Review*, September–October, 1981, pp. 5–21. The reprint corrects several errors in the original article. See also McNees, "The Forecasting Record for the 1970s," *New England Economic Review*, September–October, 1979, pp. 33–53.

Exhibit 8–9

Summary Information on Thirteen Macroeconomic Forecasting Organizations

(1) Forecasting Organization	(2) Number of Macroeconomic Variables Forecasted	(3) Typical Forecast Horizon, Quarters	(4) Frequency of Release, Per Year	(5) Date Forecast First Issued Regularly	(6) Forecasting Technique(s) (Approximate Weights)
ASA (American Statistical Association and National Bureau of Economic Research Survey of regular forecasts, median)	8	45	4	1968	Most participants rely primarily on an "informal" GNP model; the majority also consider econometric model results.
BEA (Bureau of Economic Analysis, U.S. Commerce Department)	about 800	7	8	1967	Econometric model (65%), judgment (25%), current data analysis (5%), interaction with others (5%)
BMARK (Charles R. Nelson Associates, Inc., Benmark forecast)	3	4	4	1976	Time-series methods (100%)
CHASE (Chase Econometric Associates, Inc.)	about 700	10 to 12	12	1970	Econometric model (70%), judgment (20%), time-series methods (5%), current data analysis (5%)
DRI (Data Resources, Inc.)	about 1,000	8 to 12	12	1969	Econometric model (55%), judgment (30%), time-series methods (10%), current data analysis (5%)
GE (Economic Research and Forecasting Operation, General Electric Co.)	360	8	4	1962	Econometric model (50%), judgment (50%)
GSU (Economic Forecasting Project, Georgia State University)	215	8	12	1973	Econometric model (60%), judgment (30%), current data analysis (10%)
KEDI (Kent Economic and Development Institute)	1,699	10	12	1974	Econometric model (60%), judgment (20%), times-series methods (10%), interaction with others (10%)
MHT (Manufacturers Hanover Trust)	37	4 to 5	4	1970	Econometric model (50%), judgment (50%)
RSQE (Research Seminar on Quantitative Economics, University of Michigan)	about 100	8	3	1969	Econometric model (80%), judgment (20%)
TG (Townsend-Greenspan & Co., Inc.)	about 800	6 to 10	4	1965	Econometric model (45%), judgment (45%), current data analysis (10%)
UCLA (UCLA Business Forecasting Project, Graduate School of Management, University of California. Los Angeles)	about 1,000	8 to 12	4	1968	Econometric model (70%), judgment (20%), interaction with others (10%)
WEFA (Wharton Econometric Forecasting Associates, Inc.)	about 1,000	12	12	1963	Econometric model (60%), judgment (30%), current data analysis (10%)

Source: Stephen K. McNees, "The Recent Record of Thirteen Forecasters," *New England Review*, September–October 1981 (reprint), pp. 5–21.

and UCLA); two are corporate activities—one financial (MHT) and one nonfinancial (GE); and one is an activity of the federal government (BEA). The 13th "forecaster" (ASA) is simply the median forecaster of a survey.

The McNees study chose to compare forecast results on 15 of the most common macroeconomic variables, as follows:

1. Change in business inventories (billions of current dollars).
2. Civilian employment (millions)
3. Consumer price index (1967 = 100)
4. Federal government purchases of goods and services (billions of current dollars).
5. Gross national product (billions of current dollars).
6. Housing starts (millions of units).
7. Implicit GNP price deflator (1972 = 100).
8. Investment in residential structures (billions of current dollars).
9. Net exports of goods and services (billions of current dollars).
10. 90-day Treasury bill rate (percentage).
11. Nonresidential fixed investment (billions of current dollars).
12. Personal consumption expenditures, consumer durables (billions of current dollars).
13. Personal consumption expenditures, nondurable goods and services (billions of current dollars).
14. Real gross national product (billions of 1972 dollars).
15. Unemployment rate (percentage).

There are, of course, many other variables. As shown in column 2 of Exhibit 8–9, the number of variables forecasted ranged from as few as 3 to as many as 1,000.[6] Exhibit 8–9 also shows that 12 of the 13 forecasts are generated with the help of a large macroeconomic model of the U.S. economy. All of the models require input of the forecaster's assumptions about the future values of several exogenous variables, such as changes in economic policy of the federal government.

The models provide the basis for application of judgment, and according to column 6 of the exhibit, their outputs are weighted from 45 to 80 percent in development of the forecast. All forecasters in the Exhibit adjust the mechanical output of the econometric model in the light of newer data, revisions to data, past errors, feedback from users of their forecasts, and expected events of a nature not covered by the model. Sometimes judgmental adjustment includes the predictions of other forecasters. As shown in column 6 of Exhibit 8–9, judgmental adjustments carry weights of 20 to 50 percent.

---

[6] BMARK used the three variables (1) gross national product, (2) implicit GNP price deflator, and (3) real gross national product.

Several forecasters emphasized that the interaction between the model and the forecaster's judgment is a two-way street. The forecaster may elect to override the model's preliminary results, but those results may also modify the forecaster's judgment. Further, the relative weights given to the forecasting techniques employed will vary, not only from forecaster to forecaster, but also from prediction to prediction.

One forecasting organization, BMARK, uses an entirely different technique. Its forecasts are generated by autoregressive integrated moving average (ARIMA) time series equations. Thus its forecasts are based solely on the historical record of the predicted variable, and they are not judgmentally revised even if there is reason to suspect error. Consequently, they serve as benchmarks, or standards for comparison with the results of other techniques.

Evaluation of Forecasting

If forecasting is to be improved, there must be some way of measuring its performance. Having one's forecast checked against actual results and against the forecasts and opinions of others can be a disenchanting experience. For their own protection, as well as to encourage intelligent use of their products, economic forecasters should insist upon objective and systemic procedures for review and rigorous evaluation of their work.

These procedures must recognize that forecasting with complete accuracy is impossible and, fortunately, unnecessary, provided the forecasts are evaluated and used in the proper manner.

Auditing Past Performance

Checking a short-range forecast against the record, when all the data are at hand, is a fairly simple process. Evaluating long-range forecasts may be somewhat more complicated. Sometimes the statistical series has been altered; sometimes the forecast was hedged by unrealized assumptions or other restrictions. In either case, comparison with actual results may be difficult.

Forecast versus Actual

The simplest way to evaluate an unconditional forecast is to compare numbers with actual results and state the difference either in dollars or as a percentage of error. We can define forecasting error, ε, with respect to any one variable as the difference between a predicted value, P, and an actual value, A, over the forecast horizon, n, expressed in quarters.

When the forecast is generated, it is based upon the then current *estimate* of the predicted variable in the previous time period. When the *actual* value of the forecast base becomes known, the error in the base must be adjusted before the error in the forecast can be measured. The definition of forecast error thus becomes:

$$\varepsilon_{t+n} = P_{t+n} + (A_t - A_t^*) - A_{t+n} \tag{7}$$

where

n = The horizon of the forecast, in quarters
t = The base time
ε_{t+n} = Error in the forecast
P_{t+n} = Predicted value of the variable at the forecast horizon
A_t = Actual value of the variable in the base period
A_t^* = Estimated value of the variable in the base period
A_{t+n} = Actual value of the variable at the forecast horizon

Equation (7) actually measures forecasting error as the difference between the predicted cumulative change in the variable, $(P_{t+n} - A_t^*)$ and the actual cumulative change, $(A_{t+n} - A_t)$. This is quite desirable because we are usually more interested in the changes in a variable than we are in its future level.

Many economic variables, and especially those that exhibit trends, are commonly expressed as annual percentage changes. If we assume compound annual rates of growth, the percentage error can be defined as:

$$\varepsilon\% = \left[\left(\frac{P_{t+n}}{A_t^*} \right)^{4/n} - \left(\frac{A_{t+n}}{A_t} \right)^{4/n} \right] \cdot 100 \tag{8}$$

where n is the forecast horizon.

Summary Measures.   There are a number of summary measures that can be used to summarize individual errors, but most forecast users prefer the average absolute error, *AAE*, as an index of forecasting accuracy.[7]

$$AAE_n = \frac{1}{m} \sum_{t=1}^{m} |\varepsilon_{t+n}| \tag{9}$$

where

m = number of errors
n = horizon of the forecast
$|\varepsilon_{t+n}|$ = absolute value of the individual error

[7] Equations (7), (8), (9), and (10) have been provided by McNees, "The Recent Record of Thirteen Forecasters", p. 9.

Some forecast users prefer a summary measure that penalizes large errors, such as the square root of the mean squared error, RMSE:

$$RMSE_n = \sqrt{\frac{1}{m} \sum_{t=1}^{m} \varepsilon_{t+n}^2} \qquad (10)$$

As for academicians and practitioners, Carbone and Armstrong found the evaluation criteria shown on Exhibit 8-10:

Exhibit 8-10_____

Evaluative criteria and their relative importance as determined by forecasting practitioners and academicians

Criteria	Academicians*	Practitioners*
Accuracy		
R^2		2
Mean square error (MSE)	30	20
Geometric MSE	1	
Minimum variance	2	4
Theil's U test	3	1
Mean percentage error (MPE)	5	5
Mean absolute error (MAE)	12	14
Mean absolute percentage error (MAPE)	15	7
Minimax absolute error (MMAE)	2	
Random forecast errors	1	2
No specific measure	8	14
Ease of interpretation	26	29
Cost time	24	25
Ease of use implementation	26	18
Adaptive to new conditions	10	13
Universality	3	10
Capture turning points	5	6
Robustness	10	3
Incorporates judgemental input	4	2

* Out of the 206 persons surveyed, 70 Academicians and 75 Practitioners responded.
Source: Robert Carbone and J. Scott Armstrong, "Evaluation of Extrapolative Forecasting Methods: Results of a Survey of Academicians and Practitioners," *Journal of Forecasting*, April-June 1982, p. 216.

Evaluation. No matter how good the measurement of forecasting error might be, it is meaningless in isolation. Evaluation requires comparison with other forecasts made for the same period under similar conditions, but this is easier said than done. If all forecast users had exactly the same interests in terms of forecasted variables and horizons, it would be possible to rank the forecasters' past performances from best to worst, using the summary measures noted above. But this would be no guarantee that such performance will continue into the future.

Furthermore, forecast users do not have identical interests. Those who make economic policy are most concerned with macroeconomic aggregates like inflation and real growth. Most users, however, are mainly concerned about the products they buy and sell. The horizons of interest may vary from a few hours or days in financial markets to several years for those making capital budgeting decisions.

The solution to the problem is to treat each variable and horizon separately and let each forecast user consider what interests him. This means that no expert can say which forecaster is best. Each user must comb through an array of summary measures for each variable and horizon, as illustrated by Exhibit 8–11.

Exhibit 8–11 ——

Average Absolute Errors in Forecasted Gross National Product, 1976–1980 (in Billions of Current Dollars)

Forecaster	Forecast Horizon (Quarters)							
	1	2	3	4	5	6	7	8
Early-Quarter:								
ASA	17.2	24.7	30.9	35.4	36.6	—	—	—
BEA	20.5	24.3	29.3	32.6	33.3	39.2	—	—
BMARK	21.3	31.5	41.1	52.4	—	—	—	—
Chase	21.4	29.8	46.8	56.9	65.8	76.0	91.8	109.2
DRI	19.2	23.2	31.4	36.8	40.1	43.4	48.7	63.5
GSU	15.3	25.8	29.4	38.5	39.1	40.0	48.3	55.1
RSQE	15.6	25.0	35.6	30.3	39.1	53.3	—	—
WEFA	18.8	22.3	27.5	26.2	31.6	34.0	42.7	48.5
Mid-Quarter:								
KEDI	17.3	28.8	29.4	28.5	24.7	29.7	45.5	51.2
MHT	18.2	24.9	30.5	34.9	47.4	—	—	—
TG	14.6	24.1	24.0	34.9	36.4	34.6	37.4	—
UCLA	14.7	28.4	30.8	35.1	33.2	31.2	—	—
WEFA	13.0	23.7	25.3	27.5	32.8	32.8	37.6	44.4
Late-Quarter:								
Chase	12.7	29.4	44.3	56.8	67.4	78.8	94.9	111.0
DRI	8.4	25.4	25.4	33.9	40.0	41.6	47.0	56.6
GE	16.6	26.6	34.2	34.8	25.2	27.3	33.3	43.5

Source: Stephen K. McNees, "The Recent Record of Thirteen Forecasters" (reprint), *New England Economic Review*, September–October 1981, pp. 13–14.

Exhibit 8–11 shows the average absolute errors in billions of current dollars for quarterly forecasts of gross national product by the 13 forecasters of the previously referenced McNees study. The McNees study contains similar tables for the other 14 variables listed in the preceding section.

The errors are averaged from the second quarter of 1976 through the third quarter of 1980. The forecasters have been grouped according to the release dates of their forecasts. Early-quarter forecasts are based on the preliminary estimates of the preceding quarter's GNP. Mid-quarter forecasts are based on the first revision of last quarter's GNP. Late-quarter forecasts are made near the end of the quarter when many of the previous quarter's actual data are known. Note that two of the forecasters (Chase and DRI) made both early- and late-quarter forecasts, and one (WEFA) made both early- and mid-quarter forecasts.

Exhibit 8–11 demonstrates that even when relative magnitudes of error are tabulated for a single variable, it is difficult to rank the 13 forecasters. Partly this is because there are gaps in the forecast sets when some forecasters did not cover all quarters or all horizons in each forecast. A second difficulty is the disparity in timing of forecast release dates, as noted above.

As we have seen, evaluation of accuracy is not always fair or relevant and some additional considerations are appropriate. Whatever tests are made, they should be realistic and practical, keeping in mind that even the most elaborate statistical techniques leave wide margins for error. Bald comparisons with perfection prove nothing. Some of the questions that should be asked are these:

1. Did the forecast do what it was supposed to do?
2. Were the important changes forecast with respect to magnitude? Timing? Direction?
3. Should the errors have been anticipated by the forecaster?
4. *Above all, did the forecast enable better decisions to be made than would have been possible without it?*

Interim Review

The appropriate timing for interim review of forecasts depends upon so many factors that it is difficult to generalize. The best guide is to keep in mind what the interim review is for—to enable management to change an operating policy based on an erroneous forecast before it is too late. The interim review also enables the forecaster to update the forecast to reflect new developments and perform a running check on sources and methodology.

Sometimes the requirement for interim review is inherent in the forecasting schedule. This is common in short-range forecasting, where quarterly forecasts running four or five quarters ahead are made. These could be updated as new data are obtained, which could be monthly or quarterly, or whenever an exceptional event occurs. For longer-term forecasts, reviews might be instituted:

1. When the basic data from which the forecast was developed are changed, as when a published statistical series is revised.
2. When a key assumption undergoes an important change, such as a technological breakthrough.
3. When anticipated bounds on the forecast variable have been breached.

When there is a substantial deviation in the behavior of the forecast data, it is important to determine whether or not the validity of the forecast has actually been impaired. If the forecast represents an anticipated trend, then seasonal, cyclical, or random aberrations do not necessarily invalidate the trend. In the case of long-range forecasts, such as for 10 years, if the trend is off the forecast in the first 2 or 3 years, even by a wide margin, the interim review provides the opportunity to look again.

Forecasts should be accompanied by some measure of confidence. Any revisions brought about by the interim review should be announced promptly to all concerned. Reasons for the revisions should be explained concisely and frankly but without apology. Perfect forecasting does not exist and is not to be expected; therefore no apology is in order when perfection has not been achieved.

Selecting a Forecasting Method

There is no single forecasting method that is always more appropriate than other methods. In a sense forecasting is as much art as it is science. In many respects it is similar to the practice of general medicine, in which the practitioner must consider a wide variety of factors in diagnosing an illness and then prescribing for its cure. Among the factors a forecaster must consider are:

1. Availability and accuracy of historical data.
2. Time available to make the analysis.
3. Degree of accuracy expected.
4. Length of the forecast period.
5. Cost of making the analysis and preparing periodic forecasts.

The choice of a particular forecasting method should be decided by comparing the relative costs and benefits of each forecasting method. Of course, there is the inevitable trade-off: in order to improve accuracy and thereby lower the costs associated with an inaccurate forecast (excessive inventories, for example), we must use more resources—including time—in preparing the forecast. For example, at one extreme we have very elaborate and expensive econometric models that we hope will reduce forecast errors. At the other extreme we might use expert opinion.

Exhibit 8–12 illustrates these points and indicates an answer to the question of how much the firm should invest in forecasting. The answer

Exhibit 8–12_____

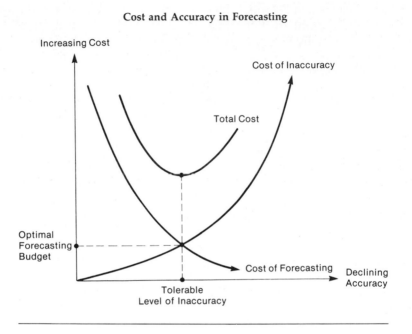

Cost and Accuracy in Forecasting

is: expand the forecasting function to the point at which the marginal cost of inaccuracy from a poor forecast is equal to the marginal cost of preparing a more accurate forecast. Unquestionably, there are difficulties in actually using the rule; nevertheless, it is a correct way of thinking about the problem.

Summary

In this chapter we have reviewed some of the tools and techniques available to the art and science of economic forecasting, and we have looked at some of the ways in which they are used. We have seen that mechanical extrapolations, barometric techniques, opinion polling, and econometric models all have uses in both long-term and short-term forecasting at all levels of economic activity.

The econometric method is the approach that is best suited for incorporating or utilizing the best features of all methods. Thus to an increasing extent, econometric models are making greater use of other forecasting methods such as leading indicators and up-to-date survey data. These statistics can be incorporated as variables in the model, and the latter can be revised as new information becomes available and new weights become necessary.

Sometimes econometric models have failed to provide better predictions for the following year than less costly models such as simple trend projections. Does this mean that econometric methods should be abandoned? Not at all; if our theoretical understanding and statistical data are good, econometrics can illuminate the darker areas and enhance our ability to predict. For econometrics, to a greater degree than other forecasting methods, is analytical in nature and process-oriented in approach. That is, econometric models almost always describe an ongoing process that yields a value for the dependent variable.

In any forecast, strong forces may come into play and modify existing relationships. The econometrician is aware of this and constantly watches for the emergence of new forces or changes in existing ones so that allowances can be made in the operating model. In this manner, a good econometric model automatically incorporates the necessary degree of built-in flexibility, thereby facilitating the model's use for forecasting purposes. Perhaps the most important use of naïve models, therefore, is that they provide a benchmark—a null hypothesis—against which the more sophisticated forecasting methods can be compared.

Whatever method is used, it seems likely that the forecaster's role in the decision-making activities of the firm is apt to grow rather than diminish. The forecaster's contribution to the welfare of the firm is to make management aware, on a timely and continuing basis, of the economic forces at work; and this requires that the forecaster must subject his or her own work to constant critical review. However, despite the improved techniques offered by use of computers, forecasting remains in large part an effort to predict human behavior. Forecasting, therefore, is at least as much art as science and seems likely to remain so in the foreseeable future.

Problems

1. Trend models or projections will usually yield correct forecasts, at least as to direction of change. If the distinction between a forecasting artist and a forecasting scientist is that the latter is correct more than half

the time, the use of trend models would seem warranted. Yet we have been critical of their use. Why? Discuss.

2.   "After all, in the final analysis, the best forecasting method is obviously the one that yields the highest percentage of correct predictions." Comment in the light of this chapter.

3.   Briefly discuss the nature and pros and cons of the following methods for forecasting business cycles:

a.   Trend projections.
b.   Leading indicators.
c.   Survey methods.
d.   Econometric model building.
e.   Any other method or technique.

4.   An economist at the Reading Company conjectured the model that sales in any given month are directly proportional to the square of buyers' incomes in the preceding month, plus a random disturbance.

a.   Write an equation for this month's sales and another equation for next month's sales, using the symbols y = sales, x = income, t = time, and μ = disturbance term.
b.   If sales this month are 36 and income last month was 3, what sales should be expected next month if income this month is 5?

5.   In the most current month the composite index of 12 leading indicators has just turned down; it has previously risen for six months in a row. How would you interpret this information?

6.   The diffusion index of 12 leading indicators shows a reading in the most current month of 0.75. How do you interpret this information?

7.   A naïve model of the demand for television sets asserts that annual sales of television sets varies *jointly* with the number of families during the year, income per family in the previous year, *plus* all other factors.

a.   Letting Z = sales, Y = income per family, X = number of families, t = time in years, and μ = all other factors, write the equation of the model.
b.   Assume that you are presented with the data in the accompanying table.

Year	Sales	Total Family Incomes	Number of Families
1	5	18.0	3
2	8	20.0	4
3	10	21.6	6
4	6	21.0	5

Assuming that the "all other factors" have always averaged out to zero, does the model seem to forecast accurately? If the number of families for year 5 is predicted to be 7, what will your sales forecast be?

8.   It has been observed that people's buying plans for the future are highly influenced by their most recent incomes. If true, what implication would this have with respect to the use of opinion-polling techniques in forecasting future consumption expenditure?

9.   Consider the forecasting model

$$Y_t = AK^t$$

where A and K are known constants. It is interesting to gain an apprecia-tion of the time path of the dependent variable Y_t for different values of A and K, and integer values of t representing *discrete time periods*.

a.   Let $K = 1$ and $A =$ any positive constant. Graph the time path of Y_t from $t = 0$ to $t = 5$, that is $0 \leq t \leq 5$.

b.   Let $K = 2$ and $A = \frac{1}{4}$. Graph the time path of Y_t for $0 \leq t \leq 5$. If your graph is correct, you will see why the time path of Y_t is said to *explode*. The direction of the explosion (i.e., positive or negative) depends on the algebraic sign of A. What happens if $A > 0$? $A < 0$? What does the magnitude of K determine?

10.   What are the four major sources of variation in a time series? Explain.

11.   The Bruxton Leather Goods Company introduced a new product in the first quarter of 1976. Its sales figures for the past eight years appear in the accompanying table.

			Quarter		
Year	1	2	3	4	Total
1976	150	120	100	200	570
1977	280	240	190	410	1,120
1978	240	220	180	280	920
1979	270	230	160	390	1,050
1980	290	250	180	440	1,160
1981	340	280	220	490	1,330
1982	300	220	190	420	1,130
1983	300	210	210	460	1,180

a.   Using the least squares method, determine the trend line and forecast sales for each quarter in 1984.

b.   Use a moving-average approach to forecast sales for the first two quarters of 1984. Compare these forecasts with your forecasts calculated in part (a).

Case Problem: General Steel Corporation

12.   For the past 10 years General Steel Corporation has been working actively with several foreign governments in planning heavy industrialization programs. As a result, General Steel now has subsidiary iron and steel manufacturing corporations in three foreign countries.

Two years ago the management of the company began exploring the possibility of opening a subsidiary corporation in Arcadia, a major industrial nation. Since the economic future of Arcadia is of obvious interest to the firm, General Steel's economists have been actively engaged in collecting data for the purpose of constructing an econometric model of that country.

According to recent studies by General Steel's economic research department, last year's corporate profits in Arcadia were about $42 billion. Although there is no way of being certain of how much Arcadia's federal, state, and local governments will spend next year, General Steel's economists estimate from present budget information that the amount should be around $75 billion. Also, an analysis of the most recent business cycle in Arcadia, covering several years, indicates that annual consumption expenditures have averaged $40 billion plus 70 percent of national income; investment expenditures have averaged about $20 billion plus 90 percent of preceding year's profits; and tax receipts have averaged about 20 percent of gross national product. GNP, of course, is composed of consumption, investment, and government expenditures, while national income represents the difference between gross national product and tax receipts.

Questions:

Let C = next year's consumption, Y = next year's national income, I = next year's investment, P = preceding year's profits, T = next year's tax receipts by government, G = next year's gross national product, and E = next year's government expenditures. Assume that all disturbance terms average out to zero.

a.   Construct an econometric model of Arcadia. (*Suggestion:* You should construct a five-equation model on the basis of the facts in the problem. Thus, your first equation should be for consumption, the second for investment, the third for tax receipts, the fourth for gross national product, and the fifth for national income. You may find it helpful to construct the model first by using lowercase letters such as a, b, c, d, e, to represent the constants, and then substituting the correct numbers for the constants.)

b.   Solve the system. [*Hints:* You want values of C, I, T, G, Y. The equations are not to be solved in chronological order. First solve Equation (2): Then, in solving (1) and the remaining equations, look for substitutions that can be made.] Here are the correct answers.

See if yours check. For next year: $C = \$259.9$ billion, $I = \$57.8$ billion, $T = \$78.5$ billion, $G = \$392.7$ billion, $Y = \$314.2$ billion.

c. Prepare a diagram of your model. Plot G on the x-axis and plot C, E, and I on the y-axis as functions of G; also, plot G as a function of G (a 45 degree line). Show that $C + I + E = G = 392.7$

d. Do some contingency forecasting. (1) Find the value for G if E happens to be $\$87$ billion rather than $\$75$ billion, with everything else held constant. (2) Find the value for G if Arcadia's average tax rate falls to 15.92 percent rather than the expected 20 percent, with everything else held constant (including E at $\$75$ billion).

e. Calculate the government deficit or surplus in the original forecast. Then calculate it for part (d) above. Finally, briefly discuss the relative effects of the two fiscal stabilizing tools—(1) changes in government spending and (2) changes in tax rates.

f. Discuss briefly some problems you might encounter in actually using this model to make economic forecasts.

g. In the above model, investment expenditures in one period depend upon the profits of the preceding period. Suppose, however, that the argument is made that investment expenditures in one period are actually more closely correlated to both *expected* profits P^* and the prevailing interest rate i in *that* period; that is, $I_t = f(P_t^*, i_t)$. Do you think this is a more realistic investment formulation? Explain. Discuss a major problem involved with actually using this formulation in a forecasting model.

References

Armstrong, J. Scott, "Forecasting with Econometric Methods: Folklore versus Fact." *Journal of Business,* October 1978, pp. 549–64.

Box, George E. P., and Gwilym Jenkins. *Time Series Analysis Forecasting and Control.* San Francisco: Holden-Day, 1976.

Burch, S. W., and H. O. Stekler. "The Forecasting Accuracy of Consumer Attitude Data." *Journal of the American Statistical Association,* December 1969, pp. 1225–33.

Butler, W. F., and R. A. Kauesh, eds. *How Business Economists Forecast.* Englewood Cliffs, N. J.: Prentice-Hall, 1966.

Carbone, Robert and J. Scott Armstrong, "Evaluation of Extrapolation Forecasting Methods: Results of a Survey of Academicians and Practitioners." *Journal of Forecasting,* April-June 1982, pp. 215–17.

Chambers, John C.; Satinder K. Mullick; and Donald D. Smith. "How to Choose the Right Forecasting Technique." *Harvard Business Review,* July–August 1971, pp. 45–74.

Chow, Gregory C. "Are Econometric Methods Useful for Forecasting?" *Journal of Business,* October 1978, pp. 565–71.

Cummings, J. M. "How Good Is Your Sales Forecasting? *Business Quarterly*, Spring 1971, pp. 54–63.

Dauten, Carl, and Lloyd Valentine. *Business Cycles and Forecasting.* 5th ed. Cincinnati: South-Western Publishing, 1977.

Gaudry, M., and M. Wills. "Estimating the Functional Form of Travel Demand Models." *Transportation Research* 12, 257–89 (1978).

Hanke, J. E., and A. G. Reitsch. *Business Forecasting.* Boston: Allyn & Bacon, 1981.

Makridakis, S., and S. C. Wheelwright. *Interactive Forecasting.* Palo Alto, Calif.: The Scientific Press, 1977.

————. *Forecasting Methods and Applications.* New York: John Wiley & Sons, 1978.

Montgomery, D. C., and L. A. Johnson. *Forecasting and Time Series Analysis.* New York, McGraw-Hill, 1976.

Moore, G. H., and J. Shiskin. *Indicators of Business Expansions and Contractions.* New York: National Bureau of Economic Research, 1967.

————. "Early Warning Signals for the Economy." *Statistics: A Guide to Business and Economics.* San Francisco: Holden-Day, 1976.

Okun, Arthur M. "On the Appraisal of Cyclical Turning-Point Predictors." *Journal of Business*, April 1960, pp. 101–20.

————. "The Predictive Value of Surveys of Business Intentions." *American Economic Review, Papers and Proceedings*, May 1962, pp. 218–25. See also the discussion by Daniel Brill, pp. 226–28.

Peterson, Ross S. *The Wharton Annual and Industry Forecasting Model.* Philadelphia: Wharton School, 1972.

Pindyck, R. S., and D. L. Rubinfeld. *Econometric Models and Economic Forecasts.* New York: McGraw-Hill, 1976.

Riggs, James L. *Production Systems: Planning, Analysis, and Control.* 3d ed. New York: John Wiley & Sons, 1981, chap. 3.

Silk, Leonard S., and M. L. Curley. *Business Forecasting.* New York: Random House, 1970, chaps. 3 and 4.

"Where the Big Econometric Models Go Wrong." *Business Week*, March 30, 1981, pp. 70–71.

Zarnowitz, Victor. "An Analysis of Annual and Multiperiod Quarterly Forecasts of Aggregate Income, Output, and the Price Level." *Journal of Business*, January 1979, pp. 1–33.

Zarnowitz, Victor, and Geoffrey H. Moore. "Sequential Signals of Recession and Recovery." *Journal of Business*, January 1982, pp. 57–85.

9

Production Analysis

Production analysis begins with the analysis of demand. Once demand for a given product or service has been determined, management decides the most profitable way to employ the firm's resources to produce that good or service. Such decisions involve an understanding of what economists call *production functions*.

A production function is simply an input-output relationship. It is analyzed and quantified during a production study. The goal of a production study is to determine the most economical input of resources to obtain a given level of output. Or conversely, it involves the determination of the maximum output obtainable from a given level and mix of inputs. A production study may pertain not only to the production of goods (such as automobiles, calculators, or pet foods), but also to the production of services (such as TV repair, hair styling, government assistance, or health care).

A study of production functions is also fundamental to cost analysis. Once a firm's production function has been identified, its cost function can be derived from it, provided the market prices of the input factors are known. Hence the study of production functions is even more basic than the study of cost functions.

This chapter is organized into two main sections:

1. *Theoretical production functions:* Here production is studied in terms of a relationship between output and input of single or multiple input

factors of production (resources). Emphasis is on the substitutability of inputs in the attempt to find the combination of inputs that will optimize production in the short run.

2. *Returns to scale:* Here production is studied in terms of the relative increase in output that takes place when all factors of production are increased simultaneously by the same proportion. Knowledge of possible returns to scale is crucial to long-range production planning and helps to determine whether or not the firm should expand.

Theoretical Production Functions

Production means the transformation of *input factors* of production into an *output* product over a span of time. Factors of production consist of many kinds of economic resources, such as labor, materials, machinery, and other capital assets that constitute the firm's production facilities. All of these inputs can be divided into two categories: fixed inputs and variable inputs. Fixed inputs, such as a firm's production facilities, are those whose quantity cannot be changed during the period of time under consideration. Fixed input, therefore, is a short-run concept. By contrast, a variable input is one whose quantity does change during a relevant time interval according to the level of production. Hours of labor, bags of fertilizer, kilowatt-hours of energy are all examples of variable inputs that can be increased or decreased as desired.

Like a demand function, a production function can be expressed as a schedule, a graph, or an equation such as $Q = f(X)$, where Q is the output quantity and X is the input quantity of some factor of production. In reality, however, output can never be ascribed to a single factor of production. Rather, it is the result of the combination of several input factors during the production process. The expression of the production function, therefore, is likely to be

$$Q = f(X_1, X_2, \ldots, X_n),$$

where Q, a specific output, is a function of the input factors, X_1, X_2, . . . , X_n, each of which represents a well-defined homogeneous class. For example, X_1 could be direct labor, X_2 could be indirect labor, X_3 could be raw materials, X_4 could be electrical power, X_5 could be floor space, and so forth. All of these factors of production are commonly aggregated into the two basic factors of capital, C, and labor, L, so that in general

$$Q = f(C,L)$$

It is important to remember that a production function relates to some given level of technology—it is a snapshot of a process frozen in time. If the technology changes through the upgrading of labor, materials, machinery, equipment, processes, or management, the production function changes accordingly.

Single Factor-Product Relationship

The most elementary form of production analysis and the one that provides the basis for more complex considerations in production management is the single factor-product relationship. It is concerned with the transformation of a single input into a single output while all other input factors are held constant. This relationship may be expressed conceptually by the equation $Q = f(X)$. However, since the quantity of the product, Q, will be the result of combining a variable quantity of some input factor, X, (e.g., skilled labor) with fixed quantities of other input factors (e.g., management, land, building, and equipment), the functional relationship can be more appropriately written as $Q = f(X_1 \mid X_2, X_3, \ldots, X_n)$. The vertical bar indicates that the input factors to the right are regarded as fixed in the production process under analysis, while the factor to the left is variable.

The fundamental problem in the study of the production function is to discover the probable nature of the input-output relationship. This is discussed in the literature of economic theory under several synonymous headings such as the "Law of Variable Proportions," or the "Law of Diminishing Returns." The nature and ramifications of this law are explained in the following example.

Suppose we are examining the effect of fertilizer on the production of watermelons. The output of watermelons depends upon a number of inputs besides fertilizer: soil (land), water (rain or irrigation), sunshine, temperature, and labor. By staking out and preparing test plots on a suitable piece of land, all of these inputs can be held constant, with fertilizer alone being allowed to vary.

Suppose we set up nine test plots, and in each plot we plant watermelon seeds from the same source. We use the first plot for control and therefore give it no fertilizer. On the other eight plots, we add increasing amounts of fertilizer. When the watermelons are harvested, the number of melons on each plot is tallied and each melon is weighed. The results are then tabulated by plot for comparative purposes. Hypothetical results are shown in Exhibit 9–1.

Besides the total product (output of watermelons) in Column (2), Exhibit 9–1 shows two other relationships that are of critical interest: average product (in Column [3]) and marginal product (in Column [4]). The average product is simply the total output divided by the total input, $AP_X = Q/X$. The marginal product is the change in output divided by the change in input, $MP_X = \Delta Q/\Delta X$. Although the MP_X is measured be-

Exhibit 9–1

Production of Watermelons on Nine Test Plots

(1) Amount of Fertilizer (sacks) X	(2) Total Product (pounds) Q	(3) Average Product (pounds/sack) $AP_X = Q/X$	(4) Marginal Product (pounds/sack) $MP_X = \Delta Q/\Delta X$
0	1,100	—	
10	2,200	220	110
20	4,800	240	260
30	7,600	253	280
40	9,800	245	220
50	11,600	232	180
60	12,200	203	60
70	11,800	169	−40
80	11,000	137	−80

tween discrete values of X, the units of input (sacks of fertilizer) are infinitely divisible; therefore the underlying function is continuous. The relationships tabulated in Exhibit 9–1, therefore, can be used as plot points to obtain the graphs shown on Exhibit 9–2.

The horizontal axis of Exhibit 9–2 represents the input quantity of fertilizer, X, in sacks. The vertical axis represents the output of water-melons, Q, in hundreds of pounds. The upper curve, TP_X, represents the production function, $Q = f(X)$. The graphs below represent the average product function, $AP_X = Q/X$, and the marginal product function, $MP_X = \Delta Q/\Delta X$.

What does the chart reveal? In other words, what are some of the fundamental properties of the production function?

The Law of Variable Proportions

First, Exhibit 9–2 as a whole reveals the operation of the *law of variable proportions*, also known as the *law of diminishing returns*. It shows that in a given state of technology and keeping other productive factors constant, additional units of a particular variable input will yield increasing re-turns per unit of the variable factor up to a point. Eventually, a point is reached beyond which further additions of the variable factor yield di-minishing returns per unit of input. That is to say, marginal product increases over a certain range of input up to a point, after which it decreases and eventually becomes negative.

In this illustration, the point of diminishing returns is reached at an input of about 25 sacks of fertilizer. This is indicated on the TP_X curve by

Exhibit 9–2

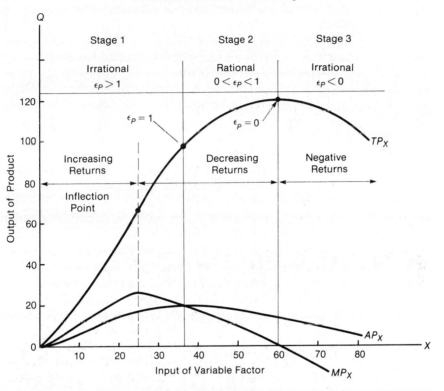

Production Function Relationships

the inflection point, that is the point at which the curve changes from concave upward to concave downward. This corresponds to the point at which the marginal product, MP_X, is at a maximum.

The law of diminishing returns applies to virtually all types of production functions, ranging from those that characterize agriculture and automobile production to those that emerge in retailing, textile operations, zinc mining, and the manufacturing of zippers. It is thus a phenomenon of great significance and generality.

The Total-Marginal Relationship

Second, Exhibit 9–2 reveals the change in the amount of total product that results from a unit change of input. Since the total product is plotted on the Q-axis, marginal productivity can be expressed as $MP_X = \Delta Q/\Delta X$, that is, as the rate of change in Q with respect to change in X. As long as this ratio, $\Delta Q/\Delta X$, is increasing, that is, as long as the MP_X curve is rising, the total product curve increases at an increasing rate and is convex to the X-axis.

The point on the X-axis at which the TP_X curve changes its curvature corresponds precisely to the point at which MP_X curve peaks, as shown by the broken line in the diagram. In the law of variable proportions stated above, it is the peak of the marginal product curve that is referred to as the point of diminishing (marginal) returns—the point prior to which there are increasing returns to the variable factor and beyond which there are decreasing returns. (Similarly, the peak of the average product curve represents the point of diminishing average returns.)

When the total product curve reaches its maximum (in this case when 60 sacks of fertilizer are used), the total product is neither rising nor falling. Hence, its slope is zero. Since the ratio $\Delta Q/\Delta X$ also defines the slope of the total product curve at a given point, it follows that when TP is maximum, MP_X is zero. Beyond its maximum, the total product declines; its graph must have a negative slope. The marginal product also must be negative, and it is—witness its drop below the X-axis. In summary, increasing returns to the variable factor exist when MP_X is positive and rising; decreasing returns occur when MP_X is positive and falling; negative returns are realized when MP_X is negative and falling.

The Average-Marginal Relationship

Third, Exhibit 9–2 reveals what may be called the average-marginal relationship. As long as the marginal product exceeds the average product, the average productivity of the variable factor increases as input increases. When the marginal product is less than the average product, the average product decreases as input increases. When the average product is at a maximum, the marginal product is equal to it.

A simple example will illustrate the average-marginal relationship. Suppose we have a group of students whose average age is 21. If a student over 21 joins the group, the average age will rise. If a student under 21 joins the group, the average age will fall. If a student who is just 21 joins the group, the average age is unchanged, since the marginal age and average age are equal.

It should be noted from the exhibit that even when the marginal productivity of the input turns down from its maximum point, the average productivity of the input factor is still rising. It will continue to rise as long as the marginal product is greater than the average product. It will reach its maximum when the marginal product and the average product are equal. *This* is the point of maximum production efficiency. However, it is not necessarily the point of maximum profit. In order to maximize profit, we must consider the cost of the input factors and the value of the output product. These matters will be discussed later in the chapter.

The Three Stages of Production

Fourth, Exhibit 9–2 illustrates the way in which economists customarily divide the typical production function into three stages. These are as follows:

Stage 1. This stage extends from zero input of the variable factor to the level of input where the average product is maximum. In this stage, the fixed factors are excessive relative to the variable input. Consequently, output can be increased by increasing the variable input relative to the fixed input. For example, if a large department store were understaffed with sales clerks, sales could be increased by hiring more clerks (the variable factor) relative to floor space and fixtures (the fixed factors). Throughout Stage 1, the marginal product is greater than the average product. The average product is a measure of efficiency, hence efficiency can be improved by increasing the variable input. Voluntary operation in Stage 1, therefore is considered to be irrational.

Stage 2. This stage extends from the end of Stage 1 (the point where the marginal product and the average product are equal) to the point where marginal product is zero and the total product is maximum. Management will seek to operate in Stage 2 because neither fixed nor variable inputs are being underused or counterproductively overused. Referring to the graph in Exhibit 9–2, as input increases from 38 to 60 units, both marginal product and average product decrease, but are positive. Total output, however, increases until it reaches a maximum when 60 units of X are input. At this point, $MP_X = 0$.

Stage 3. In this stage, which lies beyond Stage 2, the variable factor is excessive relative to the fixed factors, the marginal product is negative, and the total product is falling. It is completely irrational to produce in this stage. However, if the firm should inadvertently reach this stage, output can be increased by reducing the variable input relative to the fixed input (a short-run solution) or by increasing the fixed input relative to the variable input (a long-run solution).

The Elasticity of Production

Fifth, Exhibit 9–2 shows the elasticity of production, symbolized ε_P, which is defined as the rate of fractional change in total output, $\Delta Q/Q$, relative to a slight fractional change in variable input, $\Delta X/X$. Thus,

$$\varepsilon_P = \frac{\Delta Q/Q}{\Delta X/X} = \frac{\Delta Q}{\Delta X} \cdot \frac{X}{Q} = \frac{\Delta Q/\Delta X}{Q/X} \tag{1}$$

Since $MP = \Delta Q/\Delta X$ and $AP = Q/X$, we can rewrite production elasticity as

$$\varepsilon_P = \frac{\Delta Q/\Delta X}{Q/X} = \frac{MP}{AP} \tag{2}$$

That is, the elasticity of production is the marginal product divided by the average product. The range of elasticity of production (that is, whether it is greater than, equal to, or less than 1) will thus depend on the values of MP and AP and on whether the MP curve lies above, intersects, or lies below the AP curve. The elasticity of production varies at every point on the total product curve. This relationship accounts for the various values of ε_P shown in Exhibit 9–2 and helps to explain the three stages of production outlined earlier. In Stage 1, the elasticity coefficient is greater than unity (written $\varepsilon_P > 1$) because $MP > AP$. This means that a 1 percent change in the input causes more than a 1 percent change in the output. Therefore, it would pay to keep increasing the input at this stage.

At the beginning of Stage 2, $MP = AP$. Hence $\varepsilon_P = 1$, which means that a 1 percent change in input causes a 1 percent change in output. Throughout the rest of Stage 2 the marginal product is less than the average product, but it is not negative. Therefore, the percentage change in output is less than the percentage change in input, but it is greater than or equal to zero; that is, $1 \geq \varepsilon_P \geq 0$.

In Stage 3, the marginal product is negative, hence elasticity is also negative, that is, $\varepsilon_P < 0$. This means that the percentage change in output is negative with respect to any increase in input.

Optimal Relationships

In the previous discussion of the average-marginal relationship, it was noted that although peak efficiency occurs at the beginning of Stage 2, where $MP = AP$, this is not necessarily the point of maximum profit. To determine the optimum input-output relationship for maximum profit, we must shift the analysis from *physical* productivity to *economic* productivity. The precise amount of the input variable needed to produce maximum profit will depend upon the price of the input variable, the marginal product of the input variable, and the selling price of the output. To analyze the most profitable level of production in Stage 2, we need to understand the meaning and relationship of *marginal revenue, marginal cost, marginal revenue product,* and *marginal profit.*

Marginal revenue, MR_Q, is the additional revenue obtained when one more unit of output is sold. Therefore, at any given level of production, marginal revenue is equal to the selling price of the product.

Marginal cost, MC_Q, is the additional cost incurred when one more unit of output is produced. It measures the rate of change in total cost as output changes; i.e.,

$$MC_Q = \frac{\Delta TC}{\Delta Q} \qquad (3)$$

If the total cost changes as a result of a change in the quantity of the variable input, ΔX, while the price of the variable input, P_X, remains constant, then

$$MC_Q = \frac{P_X \cdot \Delta X}{\Delta Q} = P_X\left(\frac{\Delta X}{\Delta Q}\right) \qquad (4)$$

But $\frac{\Delta X}{\Delta Q}$ is the equivalent of $\frac{1}{\Delta Q/\Delta X}$. Since $\Delta Q/\Delta X = MP_X$, marginal cost may be calculated as the unit cost or price (P) of the variable input, divided by the marginal product; that is,

$$MC_Q = \frac{P_X}{MP_X} \qquad (5)$$

For example, suppose a worker earning \$10 per hour produces 50 units of output per hour. The marginal cost of labor is \$10/50 = \$0.20 per unit of output.

Marginal revenue product, MRP_X, is defined as the additional revenue that results from employing one more unit of input; that is,

$$MRP_X = MR_Q \cdot MP_X \qquad (6)$$

Marginal profit is the additional profit gained by the sale of one more unit of output. When marginal profit is zero, total profit (which is defined as total revenue minus total cost) is maximum. As we saw in Chapter 3, this will occur at the level of production at which marginal revenue, *MR*, equals marginal cost, *MC*. From Equation (5), it follows that maximum profit is earned when

$$MC_Q = \frac{P_X}{MP_X} = MR_Q \qquad (7)$$

From Equation (7) we see that $MR_Q \cdot MP_X = P_X$. Therefore, from Equation (6), profit is at a maximum when

$$MRP_X = P_X \qquad (8)$$

To sum up: If the price of the input factor is known, the price of the output is known, and the production function is known, the marginal product and marginal revenue product can be calculated; and the profit-maximizing firm will employ additional input up to the point at which marginal revenue product of that input is equal to its price. For example, suppose that each unit of output sells for $2 and that each unit of input costs $20. Optimal production occurs when

$$MRP_X = MR_Q \cdot MP_X = P_X$$
$$\$2 \cdot MP_X = \$20$$
$$MP_X = 10$$

That is, the firm will continue to increase production as long as the marginal product exceeds 10, and will stabilize production at the level where the marginal product equals 10.

The Production Function of Multiple Inputs

In the preceding section, we looked at production as a function of one variable input with all other input variables held constant. Our purpose was to gain a better understanding of factor productivity and its effect on the production function. In the real world, however, production always requires at least two input factors: *capital* and *labor*. Capital can be further identified in categories such as land, buildings, machinery, and equipment. Labor can also be identified by categories such as managerial, professional, skilled, semiskilled, and clerical.

To simplify study of multivariate production functions at this point we shall limit the number of independent variables to capital and labor, reflecting the basic production function:

$$Q = f(C, L) \tag{9}$$

If we are studying components of capital or labor, we can still aggregate any number of input factors into just two: the one we are most interested in, and all others combined. Alternatively, we can study two factors of interest with the understanding that all others are held constant. Either way, the multivariate function has one dependent and two independent variables. The problem then reduces to one of the following considerations:

1. Determining the minimum amount of variable factors needed to produce a given quantity of output.
2. Determining the maximum quantity of output that can be produced from given quantities of variable inputs.

To illustrate, we show the results of an agricultural experiment in which fertilizer with varying amounts of nitrogen and phosphates was applied to test plots. Exhibit 9–3 shows the outputs obtained from the 64 possible combinations of eight different inputs of phosphate and eight different inputs of nitrogen. Each combination has its own output, al-

Exhibit 9–3 _____

Crop Output (Bushels) as a Function of Varying Amounts of
Nitrogen and Phosphates in Fertilizer

Units of Nitrogen	Units of Phosphates							
	1	2	3	4	5	6	7	8
1	3	6	8	9	10	10	9	7
2	6	12	17	21	24	26	25½	24½
3	10	24	39	52	61	66	66	64
4	13	30	54	72	85	93	95	95
5	15	37	60	80	100	113	120	121
6	16	42	66	88	106	120	128	132
7	13	46	69	91	108	123	134	140
8	9	46	69	92	109	124	136	144

though some outputs are the same. They can be visually represented by a three-dimensional figure, as illustrated in Exhibit 9–4.

Since the input values are discrete, the production function is represented by a three-dimensional histogram. Each combination of input quantities forms the rectangular base of a block. The height of the discrete block represents output. Taken together, the tops of the blocks form a *production surface,* whose shape can be seen by following the rows of blocks, first in the X-direction and then in the Y-direction. The rough, stair-step nature of the production surface results from the *discrete* values of the input variables. To get a smooth surface, we must assume a *continuous* underlying production function for each of the input variables.[1]

Continuous Input-Output Curves and Relationships

The diagrams in Exhibit 9–5 have two horizontal axes in the base plane (XY-plane), along which units of input X and input Y are scaled in a positive direction only. Output is measured vertically. There is one output (Z) for each combination of inputs X and Y. Since an infinite number of combinations is possible, there is also an infinite number of outputs, each represented by a point in space. Taken together, these points form a smooth *production surface.*

_____

[1] In order for a production function to be truly continuous, the input variable units must be infinitely divisible. (This is true for the fertilizers in our example.) But even if input units are not divisible, it may be useful to pretend that they are. By assuming continuous underlying production functions, we are able to generalize the data, thus making the model more useful for purposes of prediction.

Exhibit 9–4

A Discrete Production Surface

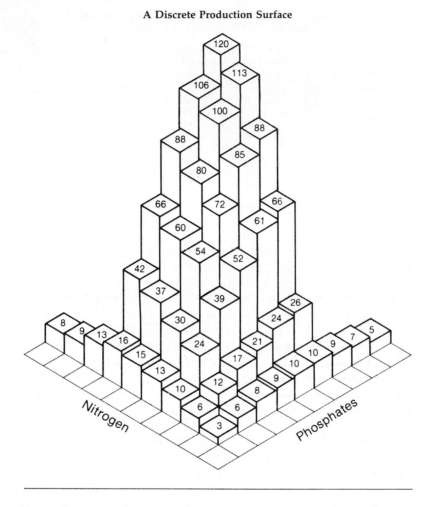

A production surface may be viewed as a hill, with greater outputs represented by greater height of the surface. Output is increased as we move up the hill. This is done by increasing one or the other of the inputs, or both at the same time. Thus on Panel A of the exhibit, if the quantity of input Y is held constant at Y_1, while input X is allowed to vary, a vertical slice at Y_1 and parallel to the X-axis produces the trace Y_1A on the production surface. Similarly, if the quantity of input X is held constant at X_1, a vertical slice at X_1 and parallel to the Y-axis will produce the trace X_1B.

These traces, or surface lines, are simply input-output curves. Each

Exhibit 9–5

Continuous Production Surfaces

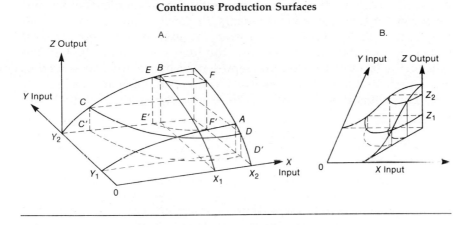

expresses a relationship between output and one variable input, while the other input is held constant at some specified level. Obviously, since infinitely many vertical slices can be made, there are infinitely many input-output curves that can be drawn. The *slopes* of the individual input-output curves indicate the *marginal products* of the variable inputs.

Panel A illustrates a production surface in which both individual input-output relationships are quadratic. Therefore, the slopes (marginal products) of the individual input-output curves are continuously diminishing. In contrast, Panel B illustrates a production surface in which the underlying production functions are cubic. As previously shown in Exhibit 9–2, in a cubic production function the slope (marginal product) of the individual input-output curves first increases, then decreases. Thus, with increasing inputs of both factors, the production surface is first convex and then concave to the *XY* base plane.

The figures in the exhibit illustrate production surfaces that result when the input-output curves for both factors are similar in shape. That is, both are quadratic in Panel A and both are cubic in Panel B. This need not be the case; the individual factor-output curves may be any shape. Consequently, any number of production surface shapes is possible, depending on the nature of the underlying univariate production functions.

Factor-Factor Relationships: Isoquants

A second type of relationship is revealed when the production surfaces in Exhibit 9–5 are sliced horizontally instead of vertically. The height of each horizontal slice represents a special output level, as indicated by Z_1 and Z_2 in Panel B. Associated with each horizontal slice is a contour line around the surface representing a constant level of output. Such contour lines are called isoquants. In Panel A, line CD is one such isoquant, while line EF is another isoquant representing a greater level of total output than CD. Obviously, the higher we go up the hill, the greater the level of total output represented by a particular isoquant. Since each isoquant is the result of various combinations of inputs, analyses of this type may be said to involve the study of factor-factor relations.

When the isoquants are projected downward onto the base, as shown by the dashed lines $C'D'$ and $E'F'$, we get a two-dimensional graph that is much easier to work with. It is customary in economic theory to work with the two-dimensional version of the isoquants rather than with their more cumbersome three-dimensional counterparts. Accordingly, it is in the two-dimensional framework that analyses of isoquants and other concepts of production are developed in the field of production economics. These concepts provide a powerful set of tools for management choice and decision making in business and economics.

Optimum Multiple Input Analysis

The multivariate production function provides a useful model for decisions involving input rates that lead to minimum cost or maximum profit. If inputs are measured in terms of dollars, and if it is assumed that the costs of all input combinations are known, the optimum input combination yields either minimum total costs for a given level of output or maximum output for a given level of total costs.

There are many different combinations of inputs that will yield a given level of output, but obviously the cheapest combination will maximize the producer's profit. Clearly the cheapest combination depends on the relative prices of the inputs. This leads to the following principle or decision rule, which is learned in elementary economics:

Principle: The least-cost combination of inputs is achieved when a dollar's worth of any input adds as much to total output as a dollar's worth of any other input.

Thus, letting MP_A denote the marginal product of A, and P_A the price of A, and similarly for other inputs $B, C, \ldots, N$, the equation of minimum cost is

$$\frac{MP_A}{P_A} = \frac{MP_B}{P_B} = \frac{MP_C}{P_C} = \cdots = \frac{MP_N}{P_N} \tag{10}$$

This *rule of minimum cost* states that if the price of an input rises, the producer should use less of it, thereby increasing its marginal product, and more of other inputs, thereby decreasing their marginal products. As an example, suppose a producer employs two inputs, A and B, which have the same unit price. Suppose further that at some given level of output, MP_A is 10 units per dollar and MP_B is 8 units per dollar. To minimize costs at the same output level, the producer should proceed as follows:

1. Reduce the input of B by 1 dollar's worth, thereby reducing output by 8 units.
2. Increase the input of A by 80 cents' worth, thereby increasing output by 8 units (that is, $\frac{4}{5}$ of the marginal product of 1 dollar's worth of B).

This trade-off between inputs reduces costs by 20 cents while maintaining output volume constant; it is the best result obtainable at the given volume.

The derivation of the rule of minimum cost, which is also often called the *least-cost hiring rule*, can be demonstrated by an *isoquant-isocost* approach that is analogous to the indifference-curve/budget-line approach to demand analysis that was discussed in Chapter 4. In our discussion of Exhibit 9–5, we defined isoquants as lines of equal output projected onto the base plane. Suppose we let the two inputs be labor, L (instead of X) and capital, C (instead of Y), as shown in Exhibit 9–6.

If we move along an isoquant from one point to another (as from point A to B to C on the isoquant Q_1), the loss in production from using less of C is exactly compensated by the gain from using more of L. In symbols,

$$-\Delta C \cdot MP_C = \Delta L \cdot MP_L$$

Dividing both sides of the equation by $\Delta L \cdot MP_C$, we get

$$\frac{\Delta C}{\Delta L} = -\frac{MP_L}{MP_C} \tag{11}$$

Thus the slope of the isoquant, $\Delta C/\Delta L$, indicates the rate at which one input may be substituted for the other at a given level of output. This rate is called the *marginal rate of technical substitution, capital for labor.* $(MRTS_{CL})$.[2]

The other half of the isoquant-isocost approach is the isocost line. "Isocost" means "equal cost," and an isocost line is a budget line that

---

[2] This may be compared to the marginal rate of substitution, X for Y (MRS_{XY}) that was presented in Chapter 4 as a part of demand analysis.

Exhibit 9–6

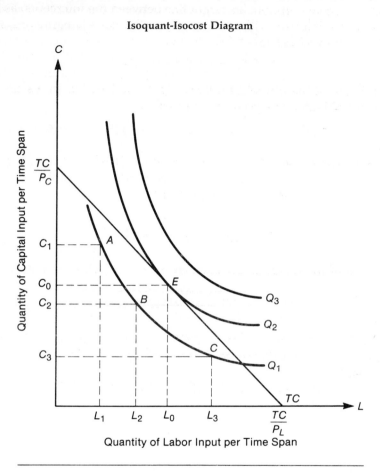

Isoquant-Isocost Diagram

defines the quantities of inputs that a given amount of money will buy in various combinations. In symbols,

$$TC = A \cdot P_A + B \cdot P_B + \cdots + N \cdot P_N \qquad (12)$$

which just says that if we use the input factors A, B, . . . , N, we multiply the quantity of each factor by its price and add up the results to get the total cost of our inputs.

In Exhibit 9–6, the isocost line TC represents the sum of money available for purchases of capital and labor, all of which must be spent. If we spend the entire budget on labor, we can buy TC/P_L units, and this is the L-intercept. If we spend the entire budget on capital, we can buy TC/P_C

units, and this is the C-intercept. If the prices of L and C are constant at all levels of consumption, a straight line between the intercepts, as illustrated on Exhibit 9–6, will trace out all possible combinations of L and C that can be purchased with TC dollars; that is

$$TC = L \cdot P_L + C \cdot P_C \tag{13}$$

To illustrate the optimum input-output relationship, let us take the original Cobb-Douglas production function

$$P' = 1.01L^{0.75}C^{0.25} \tag{14}$$

We take the partial derivatives to find the marginal products:

$$MP_L = \frac{\partial P'}{\partial L} = (0.75)(1.01)L^{-0.25}C^{0.25} \tag{15}$$

$$MP_C = \frac{\partial P'}{\partial C} = (0.25)(1.01)L^{0.75}C^{-0.75} \tag{16}$$

The ratio of the marginal products is:

$$\frac{MP_L}{MP_C} = \frac{(0.75)(1.01)L^{-0.25}C^{0.25}}{(0.25)(1.01)L^{0.75}C^{-0.75}} = \frac{3C}{L}$$

Suppose that the price of labor is \$12 per unit and the price of capital is \$2 per unit. How many units of labor and capital should an employer purchase?

Calling upon the least-cost hiring rule that $MP_L/P_L = MP_C/P_C$, we can write:

$$\frac{3C}{12} = \frac{L}{2}$$

Cross-multiplying,

$$6C = 12L$$
$$C = 2L$$

which means that regardless of the number of units to be produced, the employer should always use twice as many units of capital as of labor.

The foregoing procedure for finding the optimal ratio of inputs (using partial derivatives to find the marginal products) can be applied to any type of production function. However, the Cobb-Douglas type of production function has special properties (which are discussed in the next chapter) that make a much easier short-cut formula possible:

$$\frac{C}{L} = \frac{\text{Exponent of } C}{\text{Exponent of } L} \cdot \frac{\text{Price of } L}{\text{Price of } C} \tag{17}$$

Applying Equation (17) to the same problem, we get (as before):

$$\frac{C}{L} = \frac{.25}{.75} \cdot \frac{12}{2} = 2$$

$$C = 2L$$

Once the optimal ratio of inputs has been found, the maximum number of units that can be produced depends upon how much money is available to hire or purchase the input factors. In this example,

$$TC = LP_L + CP_C = 12L + 2C$$

Suppose that we have a maximum of $1,000 to spend on labor and capital. Then

$$12L + 2C = 1,000$$

But since $C = 2L$, we can substitute $2L$ for C, so

$$12L + 2(2L) = 1,000$$
$$12L + 4L = 1,000$$

$$L = \frac{1,000}{16} = 62.5$$

$$C = 2L = 125$$

When we put these values into the original equation, we get

$$P' = 1.01L^{0.75}C^{0.25} = (1.01)(62.5)^{0.75}(125)^{0.25} = 75.069$$

These approximately 75 units of output are the maximum that can be produced with a production budget of $1,000.

Theory of Returns to Scale

In our previous discussion of theoretical production functions, we allowed only one or two production factors to vary while holding all others constant, which is a short-run concept. Now we want to examine the input-output relationship when all production factors vary simultaneously in the same proportion. This is long-run analysis and it is concerned with scale relationships, a subject of enormous importance in production economics.

At first glance, it seems reasonable to expect that if we double all inputs at the same time, we will also double the output. In some industries this may be so. In other industries with different production functions, the yield from doubled inputs may be more or less than doubled. When all factors of production are increased simultaneously by some proportion, one of three results is possible:

1. *Increasing returns to scale:* Output increases by a greater proportion than the increase in inputs.

2. *Constant returns to scale:* Output increases in the same proportion as the increase in inputs.
3. *Decreasing returns to scale:* Output increases by a smaller proportion than the increase in inputs.

The concept of returns to scale can be illustrated with the aid of Exhibit 9–7.

Exhibit 9–7 ——————————————————————————————————

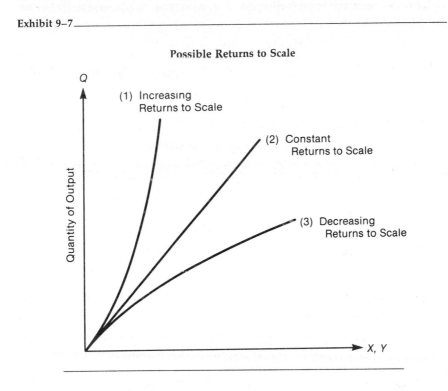

Possible Returns to Scale

The three curves in the exhibit represent three possible traces upon the production surface. The slopes of these curves indicate the proportional changes in output when inputs of X and Y are increased in the same proportion. That is, they indicate returns to scale. Curve (1) has an increasing slope, reflecting increasing returns to scale. Curve (2) has a constant slope, indicating constant returns to scale. Curve (3) has a decreasing slope, indicating decreasing returns to scale.

Testing Production Functions for Returns to Scale

When the production function is known, it can be analyzed algebraically for returns to scale. Suppose we have the production function

$$Q = f(X_1, X_2, X_3) \tag{18}$$

Now suppose we increase each input factor by the proportion k. Output will then increase by some proportion, h, resulting in

$$hQ = f(kX_1, kX_2, kX_3) \tag{19}$$

If $h > k$, the function has yielded increasing returns to scale. If $h = k$, the function has yielded constant returns to scale. If $h < k$, the function has yielded decreasing returns to scale. For example, suppose we have the production function

$$Q = 5X_1 + 3X_2 + 0.5X_3 \tag{20}$$

with initial inputs $X_1 = 3$, $X_2 = 1$, $X_3 = 2$. Total output, therefore, is

$$Q_1 = 5(3) + 3(1) + 0.5(2) = 19$$

Now we double the inputs to $X_1 = 6$, $X_2 = 2$, $X_3 = 4$. Output is then

$$Q_2 = 5(6) + 3(2) + 0.5(4) = 38 \tag{21}$$

Doubling the inputs ($k = 2$) has doubled the output ($h = 2$), therefore there are constant returns to scale, since $h = k$.

Homogeneous Functions.   If the constant term, k, can be factored out of Equation (19) above as k^n, the function is said to be homogeneous of degree n. For example, when the function

$$Q = 5X_1 + 6X_2 + X_3$$

is scaled up, we get

$$hQ = 5(kX_1) + 6(kX_2) + kX_3$$
$$hQ = k(5X_1 + 6X_2 + X_3)$$

The exponent of k is 1 ($k = k^1$), therefore $h = k$, and the function will yield constant returns to scale. But if we scale up the function

$$Q = 2.1X_1^{0.4}X_2^{0.3}X_3^{0.1}$$

we get

$$hQ = 2.1(kX_1)^{0.4}(kX_2)^{0.3}(kX_3)^{0.1}$$
$$= 2.1k^{0.8}X_1^{0.4}X_2^{0.3}X_3^{0.1}$$

Since 0.8, the exponent of k, is less than 1, $h < k$. Therefore, the function exhibits decreasing returns to scale. In general, the degree of homogeneity (indicated by the exponent of k) indicates returns to scale as follows:

1.   If $n > 1$, it means increasing returns to scale.
2.   If $n = 1$, it means constant returns to scale.
3.   If $n < 1$, it means decreasing returns to scale

Nonhomogeneous Functions.   When the production function is non-homogeneous because the scaling constant k cannot be factored out, the function can still be tested by employing the equation

$$hQ = f(kX_1, kX_2, kX_3)$$

and by assigning numerical values to the variables. For example, suppose we have the production function

$$Q = 10L + 0.6LCM + 2.1L^{0.4}C^{0.3}M^{0.2} \tag{22}$$

Examining this equation term by term, we see that each term has different returns to scale. The first term, $10L$, would yield constant returns to scale. The second term, $0.6LCM$, would yield increasing returns to scale. The third term, $2.1L^{0.4}C^{0.3}M^{0.2}$, would yield decreasing returns to scale. The overall return to scale would thus depend upon which term would exert the strongest influence when scaled up. To test this function for returns to scale, we need to select some set of reasonable values for the variables, then scale up and see what happens. Suppose we let $L = 10$, $C = 5$, and $M = 2$. Then substituting in Equation (22) above,

$$Q = 10(10) + 0.6(10)(5)(2) + 2.1(10)^{0.4}(5)^{0.3}(2)^{0.2} = 169.8$$

Now suppose we double the inputs, i.e., $k = 2$:

$$hQ = 10(20) + 0.6(20)(10)(4) + 2.1(20)^{0.4}(10)^{0.3}(4)^{0.2} = 698.3$$

Hence,

$$h = \frac{hQ}{Q} = \frac{698.3}{169.8} = 4.1$$

Since $h > k$, we conclude that the function exhibits increasing returns to scale.

Elasticity and Returns to Scale.   Since return to scale is defined as the ratio of percentage change in output to percentage change in input, it clearly is an elasticity of production. Thus for increasing returns to scale, $\varepsilon_p > 1$; for constant returns to scale, $\varepsilon_p = 1$; and for decreasing returns to scale, $\varepsilon_p < 1$.

Variable Returns to Scale

In the preceding discussion of returns to scale, we made the implicit assumption that the change in output proceeds along one of the smooth curves depicted in Exhibit 9–7 to yield increasing, decreasing, or constant returns to scale. In reality, however, the change in output may be more erratic, for the reasons outlined below:

1. *Indivisibility of some product services.* Rarely is it possible to increase all of the productive factors in the same proportion. As a consequence, some of the factors are always being underworked or overworked relative to others at most levels of output, and this results in alternations of increasing and decreasing returns. For example, doubling the rate of output of an assembly line may still require only one final inspector instead of two; one locomotive may have sufficient horsepower to pull 40 freight cars as adequately as 30; a salesperson may be able to take on a full line of goods instead of a single item at no significant increase in costs; and to a bank, the expense of investigating and managing a loan does not increase in proportion to the size of the loan. These examples from the fields of production, marketing, and finance illustrate that economies may result from stretching each input unit to its full capacity.

2. *Specialization.* Increased scale of operation provides the opportunity for specialization of both human and machine tasks, leading to gains in efficiency. Specialization of management is included in this category. Only large firms can afford resident accountants, lawyers, and economists. However, differences in the degree of specialization possible and the relative effects of labor and machine specialization can lead to varying effects on output.

3. *Machine capacity.* Equipment of larger capacity may be more efficient than smaller machinery. However, the scaling up of machine capacity is necessarily a step function, as compared to the scaling up of labor, which is more nearly a continuous process.

4. *Dimensional factors.* Doubling the diameter of a pipe quadruples its cross section and therefore its carrying capacity. Likewise, halving a pipe's diameter quarters its cross section and carrying capacity. Increase (or decrease) along one dimension of an input factor, accordingly, often yields disproportionate effects on output.

5. *Different rates of production in different machines.* Suppose Machine A fills 15,000 packages per day. Machine B wraps 20,000 packages per day. Both types of machines will be fully utilized only when the output is a multiple of 60,000 packages. Each increment of 60,000 would then fully utilize four of Machine A and three of Machine B. If output is *not* a multiple of 60,000 packages, however, one or both machines will be underutilized periodically, thereby causing fluctuations in output.

Management and Returns to Scale

If management does not fully understand the nature of the contribution that each input variable makes to the total production, attempts to improve profitability by increasing the scale of operations may yield some nasty surprises. This is beautifully illustrated in the following passage from a classic work:

There is a story of a man who thought of getting the economy of large scale production in plowing, and built a plow three times as long, three times as wide, and three times as deep as the ordinary plow and harnessed six horses to pull it, instead of two. To his surprise, the plow refused to budge, and to his greater surprise it finally took fifty horses to move the refractory machine. In this case, the resistance, which is the thing he did not want, increased faster than the surface area of the earth plowed, which was the thing he did want. Furthermore, when he increased his power to overcome this resistance, he multiplied the number of his power units instead of their size, which eliminated all chance of saving there, and since his units were horses, the fifty could not pull together as well as two.[3]

Given a particular technology, an expanding firm can expect to pass through a short phase of increasing returns to scale, then a long phase of constant returns to scale, and finally a phase of decreasing returns to scale. The last stage (decreasing returns) may be avoided through the implementation of an improved technology, which is often made possible by larger output. For example, as a firm grows, so do its data processing requirements. It may decide to install a computer rather than hire more clerks. This effectively alters the production function, of course, but it may or may not relieve the burden imposed on management by the growth of the firm.

In order to perform its function as coordinator, top management of a growing firm may be able to delegate authority, but ultimately decisions must emanate from a final authority if there is to be uniformity in performance and policy. As the firm grows, increasingly heavy burdens are placed on management so that eventually this factor of production is overworked relative to others and diminishing returns to management set in. Thus it is the growing difficulty of coordination that eventually stops the growth of any firm. To some extent, the development of new scientific methods and techniques of decision making may (1) reduce the time necessary to make a given number of correct decisions, or (2) increase the number of correct decisions that can be made in a given time period. However, this would only tend to postpone the realization of decreasing returns to scale rather than avoid them altogether.

For management, increasing, decreasing, or constant returns to scale reflect changes in production efficiency that result from scaling up productive inputs. But return to scale is strictly a production and cost concept. Management's decisions on what to produce and how much to produce must be based first of all upon demand for the product. After all, there is no profit in producing what cannot be sold, no matter how

---

[3] J. M. Clark, *Studies in the Economics of Overhead Costs* (Chicago: University of Chicago Press, 1923), p. 116.

efficiently it is produced. On the other hand, given a product for which there is a demand, there is no harm in reducing the profit margin on the product by increasing costs if the result will be greater total profit from a greater volume of sales.

In other words, return to scale is not the only consideration for management when making long-run decisions about production levels. Demand and other factors must also be included in the decision maker's deliberations.

Summary

Production analysis may be undertaken to determine (1) the most economical input of resources to obtain a given level of output, or (2) the maximum output that can be obtained from a given level and mix of inputs. Production of any good or service always requires input of two basic factors: capital and labor. In the short run, some elements of either capital or labor may be fixed and some may be variable. The study of production thus begins with the study of factor-product relationships, in which one factor is allowed to vary while all others are held constant.

Study of factor-product relationships has led to the law of variable proportions, also called the law of diminishing returns. This law says that as the input of a factor of production increases, the marginal output varies, and eventually declines and becomes negative. Total production will be maximum at the point where the marginal product is zero.

The analyst must remember that returns to scale and economies of scale are strictly production and cost concepts that have no links to demand. The ultimate decision regarding the size of the production facility must be based on the level of sales that is most profitable for the firm.

Problems

1. Explain underlying differences between the law of diminishing returns and decreasing returns to scale. How could these two concepts be utilized in decision making?

2. Draw an isoquant diagram, plotting the variables capital and labor. Then illustrate situations in which technological improvements result in:

a. Increased capital productivity.
b. Substitution of capital for labor.
c. Increased use of both capital and labor.

3. The condition of production equilibrium is indicated by the equation $MP_L/MP_C = P_L/P_C$. Prove this is true.

4. Determine whether the following production functions indicate constant, increasing, or decreasing returns to scale. Which of the functions is homogeneous?

a. $Q = 10C^{0.5}L^{0.5}$

b. $Q = 13C + 12L + 0.5M$

c. $Q = C + 2L + 0.7M^{0.3}$

d. $Q = 3C^2 + 8LM$

e. $Q = 1.09C^{0.3}L^{0.3}M^{0.3}$

f. $Q = \sqrt{3L^2 + 0.9C^2 + 4T^2}$

5. Simson's Inc., a clothing manufacturer located in Baltimore, doubled the size of its garment manufacturing factory, the number of machines in it, the number of employees, and the quantity of materials used. As a result the manufacturer's output increased from 200 to 420 garments per day.

a. Is this an example of increasing returns to scale (often called the economies of large-scale production)?

b. Simson's then doubled the quantity of managers and found the output fell to 370 garments per day. What do you suppose might have happened?

6. Division and specialization of labor are often cited as a partial explanation of the enormous increases in labor productivity that took place during the 19th century. In terms of isoquant curves, how would you fit division and specialization of labor into the concept of the production function? Explain.

7. An economics professor worked up the following production function for a privately operated business school:

$$Q = 15X^{0.7}Y^{0.2}Z^{0.3}$$

where

Q = Student enrollment
X = Number of professors
Y = Number of administrative personnel
Z = Number of support personnel

a. Determine the returns to scale. Is the function homogeneous?

b. Calculate the equations for the marginal product of professors and support personnel.

c. How many students could be enrolled if X = 42 professors, Y = 3.5 administrators, and Z = 53 support personnel?

d. With 3.5 administrators, 53 support personnel, and a tuition fee of $2,500, what is the optimum number of professors with average salaries of $35,000?

8.   Assume the tire industry has a production function of $P' = 0.2L^{0.61}C^{0.39}$. Tough Tread Tire Company has a weekly budget of $400,000 and estimates a unit of capital to cost $5.

a.   If the cost of labor is $9.50 per unit, what is the greatest output attainable?

b.   The union is presently demanding a wage increase that will raise the cost of labor to $11 per unit. If the budget and capital cost remain constant, how many workers will have to be laid off if Tough Tread continues to function at an optimal ratio of inputs? (Assume a 40-hour work week and that one unit of labor is equal to one hour of work.)

c.   Considering the above production function, how does aggressive union action result in unemployment?

9.   Weld-On Inc. produces three different types of glue. Each glue requires a separate manufacturing process, thus each has a unique production function, as indicated below:

$$\text{Watertight:} \quad Q = .65C^{.25}L^{.75}$$
$$\text{Woodbond:} \quad Q = C^2 + 3L$$
$$\text{Plastigrip:} \quad Q = 2C + 5L$$

where

Q = Units of glue produced
C = Units of capital used
L = Units of labor used

a.   What are the returns to scale for each product?
b.   Where should management concentrate its resources?
c.   What other factors and qualifications must be considered in following the strategy chosen in part (b)?

Case Problem: Westland Electronics Inc.

10.   Westland Electronics has been producing automated business telephone systems for the last 12 years. It just completed a two-year renovation of its production facilities, during which investments were made on robotic assembly systems. Westland believes the new system will be very cost-efficient, because it should lower labor costs and increase production capacity. If this proves to be true, Westland plans to intensify its move toward automation. The production research team at Westland estimates the company's capital production function to be

$$Q = 72X + 15X^2 - X^3$$

where

  Q = Number of business telephone systems produced
  X = Units of capital employed

Questions:
a. Does the capital production function exhibit increasing, decreasing, or constant returns to scale? Explain.
b. Westland is currently incorporating nine units of capital in production. What is the elasticity of production?
c. Westland sells all the business telephone systems it produces at $1,800 each; what is the current marginal revenue product for capital?
d. If additional capital can be purchased for $100,000 per unit, what recommendation would you make to Westland Electronics concerning further automation?
e. Why couldn't the decision on further automation have been made simply on the basis of elasticity?
f. Discuss some possible real-world effects of cost decreases in capital due to technological advancement, such as robotics and computers in production systems.

Case Problem: South Fort Electric

11. South Fort Electric operates a generating plant that converts natural gas to electrical power. After detailed analysis of the plant, management estimates the following production function:

$$Q = 5L^{0.7}C^{0.5}G^{0.8}$$

where

  Q = Hundreds of kilowatt-hours produced
  L = Thousands of labor hours
  C = Rate base (capital investment) in millions of dollars
  G = Natural gas in hundred thousands of cubic feet

South Fort Electric currently purchases natural gas for $22 per thousand cubic feet, employs 75,000 hours of union labor at $12 per hour, and maintains a $50 million rate base at the power plant. The public utilities commission has fixed electric power rates at $18 per hundred kilowatt-hours.

Questions:
a. What is the power plant's optimal level of natural gas consumption?
b. The public utilities commission permits a 10 percent return on rate base; at the optimal level of gas consumption, is it profitable for South Fort Electric to make additional capital investment?

References

Douglas, Paul H. "Are There Laws of Production?" *American Economic Review*, March 1948, pp. 1–41.

Gold, Bela. "Changing Perspectives on Size, Scale, and Returns: An Interpretive Survey." *Journal of Economic Literature*, March 1981, pp. 5–33.

Gould, J. P., and C. E. Ferguson. *Microeconomic Theory.* 5th ed. Homewood, Ill.: Richard D. Irwin, 1980, chaps. 5 and 6.

Johnston, J. "An Economic Study of the Production Decision." *Quarterly Journal of Economics*, May 1961, pp. 234–61.

Moroney, John R. "Cobb-Douglas Production Functions and Returns to Scale in U.S. Manufacturing Industry." *Western Economic Journal*, December 1967, pp. 39–51.

Mulligan, J. E. "Basic Optimization Techniques: A Brief Survey." *Journal of Industrial Engineering*, May–June 1965, pp. 192–97.

Nadiri, M. Ishaq, and M. A. Schankerman. "Technical Change, Returns to Scale, and the Productivity Slowdown." *American Economic Review*, May 1981, pp. 314–19.

Stokes, H. S., Jr. "An Examination of the Productivity Decline in the Construction Industry." *Review of Economics and Statistics*, August 1981, pp. 496–505.

10

Measurement of Production Functions

The measurement of production functions is a subject with a long and fascinating history. One of the early econometric studies of production functions was performed by C. W. Cobb and Paul H. Douglas at the University of Chicago. In a 1928 journal article[1] they postulated a function of the form

$$Q = aX_1^b X_2^c$$

as the production function for American manufacturing as a whole. Their work and later studies resulted in what has become known as the Cobb-Douglas production function. Since then, many studies of production in agriculture, manufacturing, and the utilities have used the Cobb-Douglas function to advantage, although in some industries production functions take other forms.

It was noted in the preceding chapter that a production process utilizes existing technology to transform input resources or factors of production into an output. The relationship between the input factors of production and the output is specified by the production function. In an empirical investigation of production, therefore, the goal is to develop a

---

[1] C. W. Cobb and P. H. Douglas, "A Theory of Production," *American Economic Review* March (suppl.), 1928, pp. 139–65.

mathematical model of the production function that can be used for one or both of the following purposes:

1. *Short-run analysis:* to determine the minimum amount of variable factors needed for producing a given output or for maximizing output through a combination of limited variable factors.
2. *Long-run analysis:* to determine returns to scale when all input factors are increased in the same proportion.

In this chapter, therefore, we will take a look at the methodology of production function measurement, the data that provide the raw material for production analysis, and the analytical tools that are used to discover meaningful facts about the production process. Accordingly, this chapter consists of three main sections:

1. *Production measurement:* In this section different methods of measurement will be described. Included will be a discussion of the kind(s) of data each type of measurement requires. The limitations of each method will also be examined.
2. *Selection of the production function:* Guidelines for selecting and fitting a production function to empirical data are suggested along with a discussion of the properties of the various equations that can be used to represent production functions.
3. *Some empirical studies of returns to scale:* This section presents representative empirical production studies of returns to scale in firms and industries.

Production Measurement

The production process being studied may be that of an individual economic entity such as a factory or service organization, or it may be that of an aggregation of economic units within specified economic, geographic, or political boundaries, such as an industry, a trading area, a state, or a nation. The methods used for estimating any production function, however, are the same regardless of whether the entity is an individual operating unit or an aggregate of units. What may differ between cases is the constitution of the data and/or the interpretation of the fitted function.

Methods of Measurement

Empirical estimates of a production function typically use one of the following statistical approaches:

1. Time-series analysis.
2. Cross-sectional analysis.
3. Engineering analysis.

Time-Series Analysis.   This approach uses historical observations as a data base. The data for a production study pertain to the amount and kind of input resources actually used, and the corresponding amount and kind of output actually produced in each time period. That is to say, a value of each variable is observed for each year, as illustrated by Exhibit 10–1.

Exhibit 10–1 _____

Format for the Collection of Time-Series Data

Year	Output	Capital Input	Labor Input	Materials Input
1970	xx	xx	xx	xx
1971	xx	xx	xx	xx
.	.	.	.	.
.	.	.	.	.
.	.	.	.	.
1985	xx	xx	xx	xx

For example, suppose we want to study production of rubber tires. We might gather data on how many tires were produced and how much capital, how much labor, and how much raw materials were used during each year from 1948 through 1978. We would then attempt to fit these data to one or more of the four most common production functions.

Analysis of time-series data is most appropriate for studies of production in a single firm that has not undergone significant changes in technology during the time span analyzed. To develop a production function for an industry is a different problem. Even if all firms in an industry have operated over the same time span, changes in capacity, inputs, and outputs may have proceeded at a different pace for each firm. Thus a cross-sectional analysis may be more appropriate.

Cross-Sectional Analysis.   Cross-sectional analysis deals with data collected at one particular time. The data thus might be likened to a snapshot, frozen in time. Instead of making observations of the variables for each year, the variables are observed for each firm in an industry. For example, we might gather data on how many tires were produced and how much capital, labor, and raw materials were used by each tire manufacturing firm in 1980. Then we would attempt to fit these data to one of the production curves. This data-gathering format is illustrated by Exhibit 10–2.

Exhibit 10–2

Format for the Collection of Cross-Sectional Data

Firm	Output	Capital Input	Labor Input	Materials Input
ABC	xx	xx	xx	xx
.	.	.	.	.
.	.	.	.	.
XYZ	xx	xx	xx	xx

Engineering Analysis.   When good historical data are difficult to obtain or not available, it may be possible for engineers or agricultural scientists to develop data from controlled experiments or from day-to-day working experience. These data are concerned with what the inputs and output ought to be with the most efficient combination of raw materials, capital equipment, and labor.

Limitations of the Methodology.   Each of the methods outlined above suffers from certain limitations.

1.   Time-series and cross-sectional studies are restricted to a relatively narrow range of observed values. For example, suppose that a factory consistently operates at 70 to 85 percent of capacity. Within that range, the estimated production function may yield a reasonably accurate prediction of inputs. But extrapolation of the production function to values outside that range may be seriously misleading. For example, marginal productivity might decrease rapidly above 85 percent capacity. The production function derived for values in the 70 to 85 percent range would not show this.

2.   Another weakness of time-series analysis is the assumption that all observed values of the variables pertain to one and the same production function. In other words, a constant technology is assumed. Some firms or industries may be stagnant enough to warrant such an assumption. Most firms and industries, however, find better, faster, or cheaper ways of producing their output. As their technology changes, they are actually creating new production functions. One way of coping with technological change is to make it one of the independent variables.

3.   Historical data for time-series analysis are gathered under the assumption that the combination of inputs chosen by the firm and the

resultant output are technically efficient. That is to say, the observed output is assumed to be the most that can be obtained from the observed inputs, and the observed inputs are assumed to be the minimum necessary (that is, the best mix) to provide the observed output. This may or may not be true. For example, if a plant is operating at less than normal or standard capacity, the input resources actually used may not be the minimum necessary to produce the recorded output. Theoretically, the production function includes only efficient combinations of input factors. If measurements are to conform to this concept, any years in which production was less than normal would have to be excluded from the data unless a way could be found to measure the capital input actually used rather than the stock of capital assets available. This is very difficult to do.

4.   The engineering method overcomes the weakness of a restricted range of observations that is characteristic of time-series data. Since engineering data are acquired by means of either experimentation or experience, the range of applicability is known and the full range, including zero input, can be used to develop the production function. However, the engineering data usually pertain to only part of the firm's production environment. Engineering data are generally confined to manufacturing activities, or in some cases, to only part of the firm's manufacturing activities. Engineering data do not tell us anything about the firm's marketing or financial activities, even though these activities may directly affect production.

Problems in the Measurement of Input and Output Variables

In its most elementary form, production consists of a flow of input resources into a production process from which there emerges an output flow of a single product. Ideally, the flow of output can be measured by the physical quantities used or consumed per period of time. Many situations arise, however, in which such simple measurement is not possible. For example, when the output consists of more than one product or service, when the inputs cannot be directly associated with the output, or when we desire a production function for an aggregation of economic entities, some other measurement must be developed. Since measurement of output poses problems somewhat different from those associated with the measurement of input, we shall discuss them separately.

Input Factors at the Plant or Firm Level.   Input factors for a firm's production process are customarily divided into three categories:

1.   *Direct inputs:* Resources, such as labor and materials, that go directly into the product are called variable inputs because the *total* of

these inputs varies with respect to *total* output. However, the *units* of input are constant with respect to each *unit* of output. For example, each unit of output might require a constant input of two component parts and 20 minutes of labor. The total number of component parts and hours of labor would depend upon the total number of units produced.

2.   *Indirect inputs:* Resources that are necessary for production but do not go directly into the product are often called *factory overhead*. This category includes indirect labor, manufacturing supplies, and utilities. These inputs vary with total output, but are not always constant with respect to each unit of output. For example, we cannot say that each unit of output requires x units of supervisory labor. However, we might say that each 1,000 units of output, or fraction thereof, requires one supervisor.

3.   *Capital inputs:* Land, buildings, machinery, equipment, tools, vehicles, and other capital assets utilized by the production process are called *fixed inputs* because they are fixed with respect to the total output. They are often lumped together as "overhead."

In most cases, flow measurements of direct inputs, such as hours of direct labor and units of direct material, are easily obtained from cost accounting records. Such reports may also include flow measurements of indirect inputs, such as hours of indirect labor, units of factory supplies, and units of utilities consumed. However, if the output consists of more than one product, it may be necessary to allocate portions of these inputs to each product.

A more serious problem arises when we attempt to measure the flow of fixed inputs such as land, buildings, equipment, machinery, vehicles, and other capital assets. Full-cost accounting procedures call for allocation of the cost of such assets to the firm's various products. Although it is not difficult to translate allocation of cost into allocation of physical quantities, such allocations are arbitrary and often highly subjective. Consequently, rather than attempting to measure the quantity of fixed assets that are actually used, many analysts prefer to measure the total quantity or *stock* of fixed assets that is in existence and *available* for use at a given point or over a given span of time. In essence, the analyst recognizes that production is a function of the firm's total assets as well as of direct inputs. Consequently, *flow* measurement may be used for variable and semivariable inputs, and *stock* measurement for fixed assets.

Output Measurement at Plant or Firm Level.   If the production model $Q = f(X_1, X_2, \ldots, X_n)$ provides for multiple inputs but only a single output, there is no problem. Output can be measured as the flow of physical units. If the output consists of joint products in fixed proportions, there is still no great problem, since measurement of one actually measures both. For example, when a steer is slaughtered for beef, the packing house gets one hide whether it is wanted or not. Measuring the number of carcasses automatically measures the number of hides. But if the output consists of joint products of variable proportions or multiple products, then there is a problem of measurement.

If the products are relatively homogeneous, output might be measured as the sum of common physical units. For example, output of gasoline, kerosene, diesel oil, fuel oil, and other products of an oil refinery might be lumped together and measured as barrels or gallons of refined petroleum products. But if the output consists of many dissimilar products, the sum of their physical units might be meaningless. For example, suppose that an electronics firm is producing integrated circuit chips that sell for a few dollars each, along with personal computers that sell for hundreds of dollars each. Output could be measured more meaningfully by the dollar value of the products made or shipped during the period of interest.

In some cases it may be necessary to use value data to measure input variables as well as output. In such cases, the value data of a time series must be adjusted for inflation by means of an appropriate price index, such as the consumer price index or the wholesale price index. For cross-sectional analysis, value data collected in different geographic areas should be adjusted to compensate for differences in prevailing wage rates and prices of raw materials.

Some production studies have been conducted using *value added* as the measurement of output. This greatly simplifies the production function, since value added is simply the gross value of the output minus the value of all goods and services used in its production.

Aggregate Production Analysis

As previously noted, a production function may be developed for certain aggregates of economic entities, such as for an industry, a geographical region, or an entire national economy. Such models depict the aggregate output, Q, as a function of aggregate labor (L) and aggregate capital (C):

$$Q = f(L, C)$$

However, the aggregate output, Q, is a composite of all the individual outputs, that is,

$$Q = (q_1, q_2, \ldots, q_n)$$

Similarly, the aggregate labor input, L, is a composite of all labor inputs, such as labor-hours:

$$L = (l_1, l_2, \ldots, l_n)$$

and the capital input, C, is the resultant of the amounts and types of capital inputs used at the firm's level:

$$C = (c_1, c_2, \ldots, c_n)$$

In the economy as a whole, or in a large segment of it, the elements of Q, L, and C could number in the hundreds. For example, if we are studying shoe manufacturing, the aggregate output of shoes would include hundreds of styles of shoes. In cases like this, some common unit of measurement must be used to express the value of the aggregate output. Usually this takes the form of an *index*, and the model is greatly simplified if an index can be used to represent each variable, both input and output.

There are a number of indexes that are readily available, such as the index of the gross national product (GNP) compiled by the U.S. Department of Commerce and the index of industrial production published by the Federal Reserve Board. Data on employment and hours worked are provided by the Bureau of Labor Statistics, and various other data are compiled by other federal and state agencies. However, reliable estimates of capital inputs are hard to obtain. It may be possible to construct a measure of the stock of capital available from gross investment and depreciation data published by the Department of Commerce. Other sources of data include corporations' annual reports, trade association publications, and the Commerce Department's periodic census of manufacturers and businesses. Whatever the source, the analyst must use extreme caution in dealing with the data.

Once appropriate indexes have been established, the development of an aggregate production function proceeds in the same way as the development of a firm's production function. However, the interpretation of the physical relationships is more difficult. For an individual firm, the production function relates to a specific technological process. For the economy, however, the production function relates to many technological processes employed by individual firms. The resulting model does not represent any particular firm, nor does it represent an average or typical firm, for there is no such thing.

For a particular industry, however, we might expect production processes, the mix of inputs, and proportional output to be similar for all firms. Even so, it would be risky to make inferences about the production function of a specific firm from the aggregate production function of the whole industry. One source of error could be the misinterpretation of certain inputs, such as specialized skilled labor, which might be *fixed* for the industry but *variable* for individual firms. Also, it is quite possible that individual firms might realize increasing returns to scale from expansion when returns to scale for the industry as a whole are limited.

Selection of the Production Function

Linear, quadratic, cubic, or power equations can be fitted to input-output data to derive production functions. Obviously, different processes may conform to different functions. In manufacturing, for example, the algebraic form of the function and the magnitudes of its coefficients will vary with such factors as floor area, arrangement of machines, work flows, quality of equipment, degree of mechanization, and magnitude of fixed inputs. In an agricultural study, factors such as climate, soil, variety of crop or livestock, and degree of mechanization will influence the final results. In view of so many diverse considerations, guidelines are needed for choosing a function that fits both the data and economic theory.

In addressing this problem, perhaps the most important thing to be said about the choice of algebraic production functions is that they are mathematical models that can at best only approximate the true input-output relationship. But this does not matter. What is important is that the hypothetical production function serve a vital analytic purpose as an abstraction of the real production process under the manager's supervision. However, to the extent that intangible factors, catalytic agents, and uncertainties attributable to breakage, spoilage, mistakes, poor communication, errors in judgment, and so forth are not accounted for in the algebraic formulation, the model must necessarily be accepted as only an incomplete approximation of the system rather than as a precise formula.

Our task is to choose an approximating function whose form reflects most accurately the production system being investigated. This is easier said than done, because the underlying scheme of a production function may be based on biological, psychological, physical, or other environmental factors as well as upon economic considerations. Fortunately, a considerable number of criteria, both economic and statistical, can be used to evaluate the individual properties of the various production functions. Included are such factors as the shape of each of the different curves, measures of marginal productivity and elasticity associated with each curve, and the relative ease or difficulty with which each production function lends itself to computational procedures.

A further constraint is imposed on the selection of the production function by the limitations of linear regression. If our interest lies in a single input variable while all others are held constant, the mathematical form of the function may be linear, quadratic, cubic, or exponential. If we want to model a multivariate production function, however, only a linear or power function may be used, since these are the only types that can be fitted by means of multiple regression.

Properties of Production Functions

When analyzing production functions in which total output, Q, is a function of a single input variable, X, we are most concerned with the measurement of the *average product, marginal product*, and *elasticity* of *production*.[2] These basic properties of the production function can be expressed in simple algebraic terms or graphically.

Average Product.   Given a production function $Q = f(X)$, in which output, Q, is expressed as a function of input, X, the average product is the ratio of output to input:

$$AP = \frac{Q}{X} = \frac{f(X)}{X} \tag{1}$$

Marginal Product.   The marginal product is the rate of change in output that results from a one-unit change in input. If inputs are in discrete units, the marginal product is

$$MP = \frac{\Delta Q}{\Delta X} \tag{2}$$

For a given production function, the marginal product is the first derivative of the function, which measures the slope of the curve:

$$MP = \lim_{\Delta X \to 0} \frac{\Delta Q}{\Delta X} = f'(X) \tag{3}$$

Elasticity of Production.   The elasticity of production, ε_P, is defined as

$$\varepsilon_P = \frac{\text{Percentage change in output}}{\text{Percentage change in input}} \tag{4}$$

As explained in the preceding chapter, at any given point (Q, X) on the production curve, the *point* elasticity of production is

$$\varepsilon_P = \frac{\Delta Q/Q}{\Delta X/X} = \frac{\Delta Q}{\Delta X} \cdot \frac{X}{Q} = \frac{\Delta Q/\Delta X}{Q/X} = \frac{MP}{AP} \tag{5}$$

The formula for *arc* elasticity, E_P, is

$$E_P = \frac{\dfrac{Q_2 - Q_1}{(Q_2 + Q_1)/2}}{\dfrac{X_2 - X_1}{(X_2 + X_1)/2}} = \frac{Q_2 - Q_1}{Q_2 + Q_1} \cdot \frac{X_2 + X_1}{X_2 - X_1} \tag{6}$$

---

[2] The basic relationships and concepts giving rise to these properties were explained in the preceding chapter. Brief summaries are given here for the sake of continuity in the context of measurement.

In applying this formula, it is assumed that the segment of the curve in question can be adequately approximated by a straight line. This is because the arc formula actually measures elasticity at a point halfway along a straight line between the endpoints of the arc.

In production economics, elasticity measures returns to scale. Consequently, as we shall see later, much empirical research has been directed toward determining the elasticities of production in various industries.

Linear Production Functions

The basic input-output relationship for empirical measurement is the simple linear equation,

$$Q = a + bX \tag{7}$$

where

Q = Total output
X = Input of a single variable
a, b = Parameters to be calculated by linear regression

This function exhibits the following properties:

1. The average product is:

$$AP = \frac{Q}{X} = \frac{a + bX}{X} = \frac{a}{X} + b \tag{8}$$

2. The marginal product at any point is

$$MP = \frac{dQ}{dX} = b \tag{9}$$

The marginal product of the linear production function is constant at all levels of production. Each additional unit of input yields b units of output, indicating constant productivity. Since this is not consistent with the law of diminishing returns, linear functions are rarely assumed in empirical research if output is expected to vary widely as a result of constant increases in input. For small variations in output, however, the linear assumption may be suitable.

3. From Equation (5) we can calculate the elasticity of production as

$$\varepsilon_P = \frac{b}{(a/X) + b} \tag{10}$$

From this equation we conclude that the elasticity is different for each value of X.

Quadratic Production Factors

Empirical studies of production frequently postulate the quadratic form

$$Q = a + bX + cX^2 \qquad (11)$$

Exhibit 10–3 shows four examples of this type of production function. The curves shown in this exhibit represent the results of studies of the relationship observed in four different years between inputs of fertilizer and outputs of vegetables in Alabama.

The curves of Exhibit 10–3 correspond to the equations

1st year: $Q = 0.1300 + 0.4920X - 0.0700X^2$
2nd year: $Q = 0.1128 + 0.5304X - 0.0786X^2$
3rd year: $Q = 0.1370 + 0.5854X - 0.0936X^2$
4th year: $Q = 0.1498 + 0.6324X - 0.1701X^2$

They are typical graphs of quadratic production functions, and they have the following properties:

1. A quadratic curve is a parabola, which has just one bend. The concavity of the curve $Q = a + bX + cX^2$ is determined by the sign of the parameter c. If c is positive the curve will open upward. If c is negative, as in Exhibit 10–3, the curve opens downward.
2. The constant parameter, a, which is calculated by regression analysis, is the Y-intercept that locates the curve upon the X,Y-plane. It has no economic significance with respect to production.
3. The average product is a downward-sloping curve if $c < 0$:

$$AP = \frac{Q}{X} = \frac{a}{X} + b + cX \qquad (12)$$

4. The marginal product is

$$MP = Q'(X) = b + 2cX \qquad (13)$$

The equation for the marginal product is linear with a constant downward slope if c is negative. This indicates that the marginal product continuously decreases and eventually becomes negative. The total product is at a maximum when the marginal product is zero.

5. The elasticity of production for a quadratic function is

$$\varepsilon_P = \frac{MP}{AP} = \frac{b + 2cX}{\dfrac{a}{X} + b + cX} \qquad (14)$$

As noted above, the MP function is a straight line, but the AP function is not linear, and the ratio MP/AP is not constant. Therefore,

Exhibit 10–3

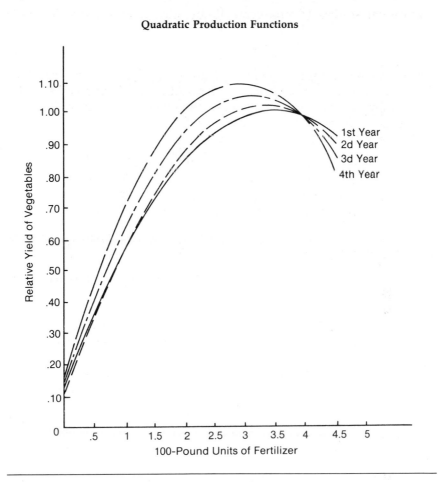

Quadratic Production Functions

1st Year
2d Year
3d Year
4th Year

Relative Yield of Vegetables

100-Pound Units of Fertilizer

elasticity is different at every point along the production curve. Furthermore, as X grows larger, elasticity declines until it becomes zero when $MP = 0$.

Cubic Production Functions

Exhibit 10–4 illustrates the traditional or classic production function that was discussed in the preceding chapter.

The data points in Exhibit 10–4 represent observed values of input and output. The vertical pattern of dots indicates that the inputs were available only in discrete units. Note that almost all of the dots are

Exhibit 10–4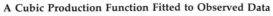

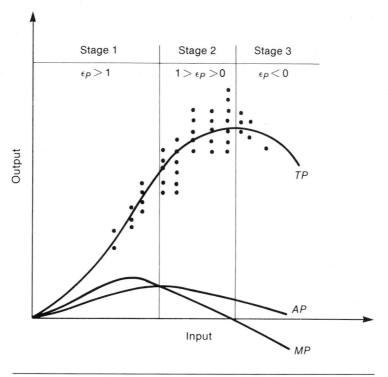

A Cubic Production Function Fitted to Observed Data

concentrated in Stage 2 of the production function. This indicates that management was usually able to keep production within the rational range.

The equation of the cubic production function is of the form

$$Q = a + bX + cX^2 + dX^3 \qquad (15)$$

in which the parameter d is negative. Some of the important properties of a cubic function are:

1. It allows for both increasing and decreasing marginal productivity, although this property is rarely needed for input of a single variable resource.
2. In the mathematically special, but economically sensible, case for which a is zero (that is, Q is zero when X is zero), the average product is

$$AP = \frac{Q}{X} = \frac{bX + cX^2 + dX^3}{X} = b + cX + dX^2 \tag{16}$$

That is, the average product is represented by a quadratic function; Stage 2 begins at the point where the average product is at a maximum and equal to the marginal product.

3. The marginal product is

$$MP = f'(X) = b + 2cX + 3dX^2 \tag{17}$$

Thus the marginal product is a quadratic function, which—since d is negative—first increases, then decreases. The input value at which MP is maximum marks the inflection point on the TP curve, at which the concavity changes from upward to downward.

4. The elasticity of production (for $a = 0$) is

$$\varepsilon_p = \frac{MP}{AP} = \frac{b + 2cX + 3dX^2}{b + cX + dX^2} \tag{18}$$

Since this ratio changes whenever X changes, elasticity is different at every point along the curve.

5. As shown on Exhibit 10–4, maximum production efficiency occurs when AP is maximum. This is the point at which $MP = AP$; that is (again for $a = 0$), when

$$b + 2cX + 3dX^2 = b + cX + dX^2$$

Collecting terms and solving for X, we obtain the equation

$$X = -0.5cd^{-1} \text{ or } -c/2d \tag{19}$$

This indicates the amount of factor X that is required when input resources are used most efficiently. For example, a cubic production expressing a relation between feed consumption and hog production is

$$Q = 65.2X + 7.0X^2 - 0.8X^3 \tag{20}$$

where

Q = Calculated output (dressed weight of hogs)
X = Daily feed input

From Equation (19) above, the maximum production efficiency input level (where $MP = AP$) is

$$X = -0.5cd^{-1} = -0.5 \left(\frac{7.0}{-0.8}\right) = 4.375 \text{ pounds}$$

At this level of input, output would be

$$Q = 65.2(4.375) + 7.0(4.375)^2 - 0.8(4.375)^3 = 352.24 \text{ pounds}$$

The average product (which is at a maximum) is

$$AP = \frac{Q}{X} = \frac{352.24}{4.375} = 80.5$$

or

$$AP = b + cX + dX^2 = 65.2 + 7(4.375) - 0.8(4.375)^2 = 80.5$$

The marginal product, calculated as

$$MP = b + 2cx + 3dX^2 = 65.2 + 14(4.375) - 2.4(4.375)^2 = 80.5$$

equals the average product at this level of input.

The level of input at which output would be at a maximum corresponds to the end of Stage 2, where $MP = 0$. In order to find this level of input, we must put Equation (17) into the standard form of a quadratic equation,

$$AX^2 + BX + C = 0 \tag{21}$$

which has the two solutions

$$X = \frac{-B \pm \sqrt{B^2 - 4AC}}{2A}$$

Rewriting Equation (17) in the standard form, we get

$$3dX^2 + 2cX + (b - MP) = 0$$

that is, $3d = A$, $2c = B$, $(b - MP) = C$. When $MP = 0$ (that is, at the input that maximizes output),

$$X = \frac{-2c \pm \sqrt{(-2c)^2 - 4(3d)(b)}}{2(3d)}$$

$$= \frac{-14 \pm \sqrt{(-14)^2 - 4(-2.4)(65.2)}}{2(-2.4)}$$

$$= \frac{14.0 \pm 28.67}{4.8} = -3.05,\ 8.89$$

Since a negative input is physically impossible, the input level for maximum output would be approximately 9 pounds. At this level of input, total output would be

$$Q = 65.2(9) + 7.0(9)^2 - 0.8(9)^3 = 570.6 \text{ pounds}$$

Linear, Quadratic, and Cubic Curve Fitting

Linear, quadratic, and cubic production functions of one input variable can all be fitted to empirical data by the least squares method of linear regression. Linear functions may be fitted without modification of the data, as explained in Chapter 6. To fit the quadratic or cubic function, we must first perform a transformation of the general equation by treating each power of X as an independent variable. Thus the general quadratic equation

$$Q = a + bX + cX^2$$

is transformed into the linear equation

$$Q = a + bX + cW$$

where $W = X^2$. In a similar manner, the general cubic equation

$$Q = a + bX + cX^2 + dX^3$$

is transformed into the linear equation

$$Q = a + bX + cW + dZ$$

where $W = X^2$ and $Z = X^3$. Multiple linear regression can then be used to determine the parameters a, b, c, and d, as explained in Chapter 7.

It should be noted that each general equation for linear, quadratic, and cubic functions contains a constant parameter, a, which is graphed as the Y-intercept of the curve. In theory, a should be zero for a production function, meaning that if there is no variable input there is no output that can be attributed to it. In practice, however, empirical investigations do not include zero input in the range of actual observations. Consequently, curve fitting by linear regression might generate a nonzero value for a. The only effect of such a value is to properly position the calculated curve upon the functional plane within the range of interest to the analyst. In other words, a nonzero constant in the production equation is a mathematical appendage that has no economic significance.

Power Production Functions with a Single Input

A power production function that expresses total product as a function of a single input has the form

$$Q = aX^b \tag{22}$$

Some of this function's properties are:
1. If we set the constant, a, equal to 1, Exhibit 10–5 shows that the curvature of the function depends on the exponent b, which in all practical problems is assumed to be positive. (A negative exponent would not make economic sense.) Thus if $b = 1$, the curve is a straight line. For $b > 1$ the curve is convex to the base, and for $b < 1$ it is concave to the base.

Exhibit 10–5

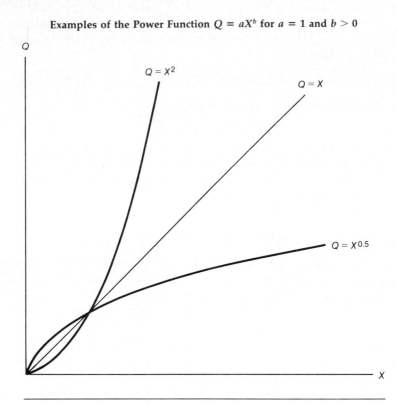

Examples of the Power Function $Q = aX^b$ for $a = 1$ and $b > 0$

Q

$Q = X^2$

$Q = X$

$Q = X^{0.5}$

X

2. The average product is

$$AP = \frac{Q}{X} = \frac{aX^b}{X} = aX^{b-1} \tag{23}$$

3. The marginal product MP is

$$MP = baX^{b-1} \tag{24}$$

The marginal product function allows for increasing, constant, or decreasing marginal activity, but not all three in any one function, as illustrated by the slopes of the curves in Exhibit 10–5. Thus if $b = 1$, both average and marginal product will be constant at the level a. This is the case for the linear function $Q = X$ in Exhibit 10–5. If $b > 1$, the marginal product will increase as X increases, but in a proportion dependent on the magnitude of b. For the curve $Q = X^2$ on Exhibit 10–5, $MP = 2X$. On the other hand, if $b < 1$, the marginal product will decrease as X increases, again in a proportion indicated by the magnitude of b. For the curve $Q = X^{1/2}$, $MP = (1/2)X^{-1/2} = 1/(2X^{1/2}) = 1/(2\sqrt{X})$.

$$\varepsilon_p = \frac{MP}{AP} = \frac{baX^{b-1}}{aX^{b-1}} = b \tag{25}$$

Thus we see that the elasticity of production is constant for all values of X and is equal to the exponent in the power function, which is an interesting and very convenient mathematical property.

5.   The function is linear when expressed logarithmically; that is, it can be written

$$\log Q = \log a + b \log X \tag{26}$$

Graphically, this means the equation plots as a straight line when expressed in its logarithmic form or in its original form on double logarithmic scales. Hence, for simplicity and convenience the equation is estimated statistically in logarithmic form.

Power Production Functions with Multiple Inputs

Production functions with multiple variable inputs are more realistic than those with only one. The general form for this type of power production function is

$$Q = aX_1^b X_2^c \dots X_n^m \tag{27}$$

where Q represents output from the variable inputs, X_i. The coefficient a and the exponents $b, c \dots , m$ are constants called parameters, because their values are established by the circumstances of their use. In production measurement, values of the parameters are estimated by linear regression.

The Cobb-Douglas functions mentioned at the beginning of this chapter are functions of this type, commonly with just two variable inputs, labor (L) and capital (C). The original Cobb-Douglas equation was of the form

$$P' = bL^k C^{1-k}$$

where

P' = Calculated or expected index of manufacturing output over a particular span of time

L = Index of employment in manufacturing industries

C = Index of fixed capital in manufacturing industries

k = Fractional exponent between 0 and 1

Thus, using annual data for the United States based on the period 1899 to 1922, the function that Cobb and Douglas derived for American manufacturing as a whole was

$$P' = 1.01L^{.75}C^{.25} \qquad (R^2 = .9409) \tag{28}$$

where the variables have the same meaning as described above, with all three indexes based on the year 1899 $= 100$. R^2 is the coefficient of multiple determination, and represents the proportion of variation in the dependent variable that was explained by the independent variables in the analysis. Thus, about 94 percent of the variation in P' was accounted for by L and C in this equation.

Let us examine some of the interesting implications of this analysis.

1. Note that this equation, a power function, is linear in the logarithmically but not in the original data. Thus, the equation expressed in its equivalent logarithmic form is

$$\log P' = \log 1.01 + .75 \log L + .25 \log C \tag{29}$$

2. The average products of labor and capital are:

$$AP_L = \frac{P'}{L} = \frac{1.01L^{.75}C^{.25}}{L} = 1.01L^{-.25}C^{.25} \tag{30}$$

$$AP_C = \frac{P'}{C} = \frac{1.01L^{.75}C^{.25}}{C} = 1.01L^{.75}C^{-.75} \tag{31}$$

3. The marginal products of labor and capital are the respective partial derivatives:

$$MP_L = .7575L^{-.25}C^{.25} \tag{32}$$
$$MP_C = .2525L^{.75}C^{-.75} \tag{33}$$

4. The elasticities of the individual inputs are

$$\varepsilon_{PL} = \frac{MP_L}{AP_L} = \frac{.7575L^{-.25}C^{.25}}{1.01L^{-.25}C^{.25}} = .75 \tag{34}$$

$$\varepsilon_{PC} = \frac{MP_C}{AP_C} = \frac{.2525L^{.75}C^{-.75}}{1.01L^{.75}C^{-.75}} = .25 \tag{35}$$

Because the function is linear in its logarithms, the elasticity of each individual input is simply its exponent. Thus, a 1 percent increase in labor results in a 0.75 percent increase in production, and a 1 percent increase in capital results in 0.25 percent increase in production. Since the exponents of these two independent variables are each less than 1, production is relatively inelastic with respect to any one input.

5. The Cobb-Douglas power function is also characterized by the convenient mathematical property of homogeneity that was discussed in the preceding chapter. This is readily illustrated if we multiply each of the input factors in Equation (28) above by some constant, k.

$$hP' = 1.01(kL)^{.75}(kC)^{.25} = 1.01k^{.75}L^{.75}k^{.25}C^{.25}$$
$$= 1.01k^{(.75+.25)}L^{.75}C^{.25} = k(1.01L^{.75}C^{.25})$$

Every Cobb-Douglas production function is always homogeneous of degree n equal to the sum of the exponents. This is true regardless of the number of productive input factors (independent variables) in the equation. In the original Cobb-Douglas model, input factors were restricted to capital and labor, and their exponents were chosen to add up to one, which restricted the model to production functions yielding constant returns to scale. Later models have relaxed these restrictions so that more than two input factors may be considered, and the sum of the exponents may be more or less than one. Returns to scale may be quickly determined by simply adding up the exponents of the independent variables to determine elasticity of the function as a whole. It should be emphasized, of course, that where the Cobb-Douglas type of production function has been used, especially at the intrafirm level, it has typically been in the later, rather than in its original form.

Some Empirical Studies of Returns to Scale

Returns to scale and attendant economies or diseconomies are among management's most important considerations in planning for growth. Consequently, many empirical studies of the production function have been performed to estimate elasticities of production, which measure returns to scale. Most of these studies have used a power function because of its convenient properties with respect to elasticity, which were noted in the preceding section.

Studies Using Time-Series Data

For their original study, Cobb and Douglas gathered time-series data on the U.S. manufacturing sector from 1899 to 1922, and converted the data into indexes (as explained in the preceding section).

One of the main problems that Cobb and Douglas sought to solve concerned the economic theory of *imputation:* How is the value of the final product to be allocated to the various factors of production (that is, capital, land, labor) that collaborated to produce it? In other words, How can we measure the contribution of each input factor to the value of the final product? To answer this question, they computed (by partial differential calculus) the marginal productivities of labor and capital, obtaining $.75PL^{-1}$ and $.25PC^{-1}$, respectively. On the basis of these quantities, they imputed the proportion of total product going to labor as $.75P$, and the proportion of total product going to capital as $.25P$, where P represents the actual index of production in any one year (as compared to P', which is the calculated index obtained from the derived production function).

At a later date, Cobb and Douglas revised the output and labor indexes to remove the secular trend from each index. They did this by calculating each annual index as a percentage of its overall trend value and by dropping the condition that the sum of the exponents equal 1. The result of these changes was the function

$$P' = .84L^{.63}C^{.30}$$

This equation indicates an elasticity of about ⅔ for labor and ⅓ for capital. Although the sum of the exponents is slightly less than 1, the difference is not statistically significant. Thus the Cobb-Douglas findings support their original hypothesis of constant returns to scale.

Since the seminal work of Cobb and Douglas, many other production studies using time-series data have been performed. Production functions have been estimated for major sectors of the economy, such as agriculture, mining, and manufacturing. Economists have also developed production functions for geographical regions, such as the Commonwealth of Massachusetts and the Australian states of Victoria and New South Wales. Production functions have even been determined for entire political economies, such as those of New Zealand, Norway, and Finland, as well as the United States.

A particularly interesting application of the Cobb-Douglas function was made in 1975 by a trio of investigators who applied it to time-series data to estimate and evaluate a police production function in the city of Los Angeles.[3]

One of the researchers' problems was to identify meaningful variables in the absence of a physical product. However, they could and did quantify output as the felony arrest rate, *FAR*, calculated as the number of arrests divided by the number of crimes committed. They also identified five independent variables that might be expected to influence the felony arrest rate:

MT = Number of motorcycle teams
FO = Number of field officers
NFO = Number of nonfield officers
CE = Number of civilian employees
XC = Number of newly released criminals in the community

In the first four of these variables, the number of employees in each class represents joint labor and capital input (for example, a motorcycle

---

[3] Jeffery I. Chapman, Werner Z. Hirsch, and Sydney Sonenblum, "Crime Prevention, the Police Production Function, and Budgeting," *Public Finance* Vol 30, no. 2 (1975), pp. 197–215.

officer and his motorcycle). The last variable, *XC*, is an indicator of police knowledge of a potential criminal population. All data were adjusted to eliminate the effect of population changes. The data were then converted to logarithms and multiple regression analysis was used to obtain the production function

$$FAR = 17.2MT^{.01}FO^{.718}NFO^{1.02}CE^{.74}XC^{.078}$$

The coefficient of determination was $R^2 = .9013$. The *t*-ratios for *FO*, *NFO*, and *CE* were 1.66, 2.29, and 2.16, respectively. The *t*-ratios for *MT* and *XC* indicated that these variables were statistically insignificant. The authors concluded that "the production function analysis indicated that increasing police resources significantly affects police output." The researchers also indicated that "there appears to be some indication of increasing returns (to scale) to the police agency as a whole."

This study suggests that analysis of production functions might be extended to many activities that produce professional services rather than just to those that produce a physical product. Merchandising activities would also seem amenable to a production function analysis.

Studies Using Cross-Sectional Data

Cobb-Douglas functions have been derived from cross-sectional data for various sectors of the economy in Australia, Canada, and the United States, and for a number of different industries in these as well as in other countries. In industry studies, cross-sectional data on firms within the industry are used. Industries studied so far include those that produce chemicals, clothing, coal, electricity, milk, railroad transportation, and rice.

One of the most noteworthy industry studies is Moroney's work on 18 manufacturing industries in the United States. The industries studied were broad groups, such as petroleum, coal, textiles, and primary metals. Moroney's objective was to determine returns to scale in each of these industries and he used cross sectional analysis rather than time-series data to avoid the problem of having to allocate changes of output observed in a time series between quantity of input and changes in technology.[4] The approach he chose was to estimate the parameters of the logarithmic form of a Cobb-Douglas production function by means of multiple regression analysis. Specifically, the model was

$$\log \gamma = \log \beta_0 + \beta_1 \log X_1 + \beta_2 \log X_2 + \beta_3 \log X_3 + e$$

---

[4] John R. Moroney, "Cobb-Douglas Production Functions and Returns to Scale in U.S. Manufacturing Industry," *Western Economic Journal*, December 1967, pp. 39–51.

where

γ = Value added
X_1 = Gross capital stock
X_2 = Production labor-hours
X_3 = Nonproduction labor-years
β_i = Elasticity of factor X_i
e = Error term

Exhibit 10–6

Output Elasticities in Several Manufacturing Industries, 1957

(1)	(2)	(3)	(4)	(5)	(6)	(7)
				Elasticity†		
			Production	Nonproduction		Coefficient of
	Number of	Capital	Labor	Labor	Total	Determination
Industry	Observations	β_1	β_2	β_3	$\beta_1 + \beta_2 + \beta_3$	R^2
Food and	41	.55529*	.43882*	.07610*	1.07021**	.9865
Beverages		(.12101)	(.12793)	(.03746)	(.02128)	
Textiles	21	.12065	.54881*	.33462*	1.00408	.9913
		(.17334)	(.21573)	(.08580)	(.02365)	
Apparel	24	.12762	.43705*	.47654*	1.04121	.9823
		(.08926)	(.08612)	(.09297)	(.03741)	
Lumber	23	.39170*	.50391*	.14533	1.04094	.9509
		(.09316)	(.12467)	(.10157)	(.06014)	
Furniture	22	.20458	.80154*	.10263	1.10875**	.9659
		(.15344)	(.18552)	(.07893)	(.05082)	
Paper and	30	.42054*	.36666*	.19723*	.98443	.9902
Pulp		(.04460)	(.09430)	(.07035)	(.01890)	
Printing,	17	.45900*	.04543	.57413*	1.07856**	.9888
etc.		(.05562)	(.17089)	(.19199)	(.03168)	
Chemicals	32	.20025*	.55345*	.33626*	1.08996**	.9701
		(.09879)	(.20996)	(.14650)	(.03693)	
Petroleum	17	.30783*	.54621*	.09309	.94713	.9826
and Coal		(.11162)	(.22207)	(.16847)	(.04489)	
Rubber and	16	.48071*	1.03317*	−.45754*	1.05634	.9912
Plastics		(.10535)	(.20567)	(.14574)	(.04139)	
Leather	11	.07597	.44124*	.52273	1.03994	.9897
		(.14921)	(.20105)	(.31491)	(.03916)	
Stone,	26	.63167*	.03165	.36592*	1.02924	.9614
Clay, etc.		(.10538)	(.22449)	(.20104)	(.04543)	
Primary	29	.37146*	.07734	.50881*	.95761	.9693
Metals		(.10260)	(.18842)	(.16433)	(.03454)	
Fabricated	33	.15110*	.51172*	.36457*	1.02739**	.9947
Metals		(.07426)	(.09379)	(.09204)	(.01589)	
Nonelectrical	30	.40382*	.22784	.38870*	1.02036	.9804
Machinery		(.12827)	(.18375)	(.20542)	(.03122)	
Electrical	25	.36796*	.42908*	.22905*	1.02609	.9832
Machinery		(.11869)	(.19225)	(.12937)	(.03640)	
Transportation	29	.23353*	.74885*	.04103	1.02341	.9719
Equipment		(.06969)	(.12572)	(.08809)	(.03915)	
Instruments	11	.20557	.81865*	.01978	1.04420	.9969
		(.15204)	(.20592)	(.16806)	(.02437)	

* Significantly different from zero at $P \leq 0.05$ (one-tail test).
** Significantly greater than one at $P \leq 0.05$ (one-tail test).
† Numbers in parentheses are standard errors of the regression coefficient.

Results of the regression analysis are shown in Exhibit 10–6. The following highlights are of particular interest:

1. The coefficients of multiple determination indicate that the power function was a very good fit in all cases.
2. In every industry except rubber and plastics, all of the input elasticities are positive, as expected. Furthermore, when standard statistical tests for significance are applied, 39 out of 54 elasticities are significantly different from zero at the .05 level of significance, indicating a good selection of variables.
3. The most important finding is the sum of elasticities in Column (6). These indicators of returns to scale rang from a minimum of .94713 for petroleum and coal to a maximum of 1.10875 for furniture. Elasticity of food and beverages, furniture, printing, chemicals and fabricated metals proved to be significantly different from 1 at the .05 level of statistical significance. Each of these five industries exhibits slightly increasing returns to scale.

Moroney concluded that the results of his studies supported the hypothesis that there is a broad range of "optimal" plant sizes in American

Exhibit 10–7_____

Estimates of Returns to Scale for Selected Industries

| (1) | (2) | (3) | (4) | (5) | (6) | (7) |
| | | | | | Elasticity | |
Industry	Country	Year	Labor β_1	Capital β_2	Raw Materials β_3	Total $\beta_1 + \beta_2 + \beta_3$
Food	United States	1967	.63†	.11		1.07*
Paper	United States	1967	.62†	.37	—	0.99*
Telephone	Canada	1972	.70	.41	—	1.11
Railroads	United States	1936	.89	.12	.28	1.29
Coal	United Kingdom	1950	.79	.29	—	1.08*
Food	United States	1909	.72	.35	—	1.07*
Metals and machinery	United States	1909	.71	.26	—	0.97*
Gas	France	1945	.83	.10	—	0.93*
Cotton	India	1951	.92	.12	—	1.04*
Jute	India	1951	.84	.14	—	0.98*
Sugar	India	1951	.59	.33	—	0.92*
Coal	India	1951	.71	.44	—	1.15
Paper	India	1951	.64	.45	—	1.09*
Chemicals	India	1951	.80	.37	—	1.17
Electricity	India	1951	.20	.67	—	0.87

* These sums are so close to 1 that the industries may be considered to show constant returns to scale.
† These values for β_1 are the sums of those originally found for production workers and nonproduction workers.
Source: Edwin Mansfield, *Microeconomics*, 3d ed. (New York: W. W. Norton, 1979), p. 164.

manufacturing, and that there are constant technological returns to scale in most industries. Similar studies by other investigators in the United States and other countries have yielded slightly different results. Some of these are shown in Exhibit 10–7.

In Exhibit 10–7, the sum of the elasticities in Column (7) is the measure of returns to scale. Of the 15 industries studied, 9 have elasticities greater than 1. However, 10 of the 15 (marked with an asterisk) have elasticities so close to 1 that we might consider them to exhibit constant returns to scale. This leaves four—railroads in the United States, coal in India, chemicals in India, and telephones in Canada—that showed increasing returns to scale in the years indicated.

Summary

The measurement of production functions is particularly important for long-range planning. In an empirical investigation of production, the goal is to develop a mathematical model that can be used to predict the output that can be obtained from any mix of inputs. Empirical studies can use any of three approaches to measurement: (1) time-series analysis, (2) cross-sectional analysis, or (3) engineering analysis. Input variables customarily are divided into three classes: (1) direct inputs of labor and materials, (2) indirect inputs that are necessary for production, and (3) capital inputs, often called "overhead." The first two classes are usually measured as a flow of physical resources into the production process. The capital inputs are more difficult to measure, however, because they must be arbitrarily allocated to particular products. Therefore, capital inputs are often measured in terms of the *stock* of capital resources available.

The measurement of output presents problems somewhat different from those encountered in the measurement of input. When more than one product is produced, output may have to be measured by dollar values rather than by quantities of product. Some studies have used *value added* as the output variable.

In the measurement of production in economic entities, both inputs and outputs are aggregates of the corresponding activities in component firms. These production models are greatly simplified by the use of an index to represent each of the variables.

A number of problems must be overcome in the measurement of production. Time-series and cross-sectional data are restricted to the relatively narrow range of observed values. This weakness may be overcome by the engineering method. Unfortunately, engineering data do not cover all of a firm's activities. Time-series and cross-sectional methods also assume that (1) the various observations represent the same

production function, and (2) the observed production process is technically efficient.

In analyzing production functions, we are most concerned with the
measurement of the average product, marginal product, and elasticity.
For univariate production functions,

$$\text{Average product} = AP = \frac{\text{Output}}{\text{Input}} = \frac{f(X)}{X}$$

$$\text{Marginal product} = MP = \frac{\text{Change in output}}{\text{Change in input}} = f'(X)$$

$$\text{Elasticity} = \frac{\text{Marginal product}}{\text{Average product}} = \frac{MP}{AP}$$

All types of production functions—linear, quadratic, cubic, and power
functions—can be estimated from observed data by means of linear
regression. However, the higher-order variables (X^2 and X^3) in quadratic or cubic functions must be transformed into independent variables. For example, $Q = a + bX + cX^2$ becomes $Q = a + bX + cW$, where
$W = X^2$. The cubic function $Q = a + bX + cX^2 + dX^3$ becomes $Q = a + bX$
$+ cW + dZ$, where $W = X^2$ and $Z = X^3$. The transformed equations then
can be fitted by multiple linear regression. The power functions must
also be changed into their logarithmic form: $\log Q = \log a + b \log X$ for a
univariate power function, and $\log Q = \log b_0 + b_1 \log X_1 + \cdots + b_n \log$
X_n for a multivariate power function.

Power production functions—including functions of the Cobb-
Douglas type—have the valuable property that the elasticity with respect to any input variable is equal to its exponent. Furthermore, the
sum of the exponents is the function's elasticity, which is a measure of
returns to scale. For this reason, the Cobb-Douglas form has been used
in many studies of returns to scale, especially in manufacturing industries. Many of these studies support the conclusion that there is a very
wide range of plant sizes that exhibit constant returns to scale.

Problems

1. Determine the equations for the average product, marginal product, and elasticity from the following production functions:
a. $Q = 3.5X + 400$
b. $Q = 15.7X + 20X^2 - 6.5X^3$
c. $Q = 15 + 7X - X^2$

2. A certain production function is given by the equation $Q = 20X -$
X^2, where X denotes input and Q is output.

a. Sketch the total, average, and marginal product curves from $X = 0$ to $X = 10$.

b. Write the equations for average and marginal output.

c. If each unit of X costs $5 while each unit of Q can be sold for $2, how many units of X should be utilized?

d. Regardless of the method you used to work part (c) prove the following proposition: A factor of production is employed up to a point where MRP (value of its marginal revenue product) is equal to its price.

e. Discuss the following comment: "Every factor of production is paid what it is worth."

3. Given the production function $Q = .84L^{.70}C^{.30}$, where $Q =$ units of output, $L =$ units of input labor, and $C =$ units of input capital:

a. What are the marginal and average products of labor and capital?

b. Show what the production elasticities of labor and capital are equal to their respective exponents.

c. Restate the production function as a linear function, and show that the production elasticities of labor and capital are the coefficients of their logarithms.

4. Burgundy Industries derived the following production function, where $Q =$ value of wine production, $R =$ total acreage planted in grapes, $L =$ units of labor, and $Z =$ units of pressing and bottling capacity:

$$Q = 0.25R^{0.3}L^{0.6}Z^{0.5}$$

a. Taken individually, if each of the above inputs increased by 10 percent, by how much would Q increase?

b. Taken together, if each of the above inputs increased by 10 percent, by how much would Q increase? What type of returns to scale are indicated by this production function?

5. King's cattle ranch has accumulated data on the weights of steers and on the amount of vitamin A added to the cattle-feed. They found the relationship between weight and vitamin A was best approximated by a quadratic form, $Q = a + bX + cX^2$. Explain how King's could use the least squares method to fit a production function.

6. For the benefit of its members, the American Corn Growers Association sponsored an analysis of the effects of phosphate fertilizer on corn production. They derived the following production function:

$$\hat{Q} = 43.2X + 7.5X^2 - 1.1X^3$$

where

$\hat{Q} =$ Estimated bushels of corn per acre
$X =$ Pounds of phosphates used per acre

a. If a farmer were to use 10 pounds of phosphates per acre, what would be his expected production?
b. What is the elasticity of production at 10 pounds of phosphates per acre?
c. Should the farmer increase or decrease the amount of phosphates used? Explain.
d. What is the maximum output possible and how many pounds of phosphates will be required?

Computer Problem: Caliber Manufacturing Inc.

7. In the past, Caliber Manufacturing has played it by ear when estimating production levels for its precision-honed rifle barrels. However, in the last few years the company has grown so quickly that rough estimates of needed output have resulted in both demand shortfalls and costly overproduction. In hope of increasing efficiency and better understanding of the relationship between inputs and outputs, the president of Caliber Manufacturing has hired a managerial economist. The economist tabulated the following data for the past 12 months of operations:

Month	Outputs (units)	Labor (hours)	Capital (units)
1	26,000	90,000	108,000
2	29,000	101,000	114,000
3	31,500	118,000	116,000
4	34,000	132,500	114,500
5	37,000	147,500	111,000
6	40,000	161,000	107,500
7	44,000	174,500	106,000
8	47,000	188,500	107,500
9	51,500	202,500	110,000
10	58,000	215,000	112,500
11	62,000	229,500	114,500
12	67,000	245,000	117,000

Questions:
a. What is the estimated linear production function in the form $Q = a + bX_1 + cX_2$?
b. Explain the significance of the linear production function parameters b and c.
c. Does the function exhibit increasing, decreasing, or constant returns to scale?
d. Transform the data to logarithms either by hand or through the computer. Using your adjusted data, what is the estimated production function in the Cobb-Douglas form, $P' = aX_1^b X_2^c$?
e. Does the Cobb-Douglas form exhibit increasing, decreasing, or constant returns to scale?

f. If labor costs $9 per hour and capital costs $11 per unit, what are the most efficient (least-cost) proportions of labor and capital under the Cobb-Douglas form?

g. Discuss possible benefits from a production analysis such as that performed on Caliber Manufacturing Inc.

References

Bernhardt, Irwin. "Sources of Productivity Differences among Canadian Manufacturing Industries." *Review of Economics and Statistics,* November 1981, pp. 504–12.

Caves, Douglas W.; Laurits R. Christensen; and Joseph A. Swanson. "Productivity Growth, Scale Economies, and Capacity Utilization in U.S. Railroads, 1955–75." *American Economic Review,* December 1981, pp. 994–1002.

Cobb, C. W., and P. H. Douglas. "A Theory of Production." *American Economic Review,* March (Suppl.) 1928, pp. 139–65.

Hildebrand, G. H., and T. C. Liu. *Manufacturing Production Functions in the United States, 1957.* Ithaca, N.Y.: Cornell University Press, 1965.

Huettner, D. A., and J. H. Landon. "Electric Utilities: Scale Economies and Diseconomies." *Southern Economic Journal,* April 1978, pp. 883–912.

Kopp, Raymond. "The Measurement of Productive Efficiency: A Reconsideration." *Quarterly Journal of Economics,* August 1981, pp. 477–504.

Mansfield, Edwin. *Microeconomics.* 3d ed. New York: W. W. Norton, 1979, chap. 6.

Schlutter, G., and P. Beeson. "Components of Labor Productivity Growth in the Food System, 1958–67." *Review of Economics and Statistics,* August 1981, pp. 378-87.

Walters, A. A. "Production and Cost Functions: An Econometric Survey." *Econometrica,* January–April 1963, pp. 1–66.

11

Cost Analysis

"A graduate class in economic theory would be a success if the students gained from it an understanding of the meaning of cost in all its many aspects."

These words—written in 1923 by the noted economist J. M. Clark in his classical work, *Studies in the Economics of Overhead Costs*—are still true today.

What prompted Clark to make this statement is the fact that the study of cost is extraordinarily complex, with all kinds of accounting, financial, economic, engineering, and even legal implications. As we might expect, there frequently is controversy over the nature of costs, how they should be defined, and what costs are relevant for decision making. Actually, most of the controversy evaporates once it is realized that there are different kinds of problems for which cost information is needed, and that the particular information required varies from one problem to another.

A thorough understanding of the concept of cost is necessary for a number of basic decisions that management must make for such things as pricing output, controlling costs, and planning future production. The first section of this chapter discusses the nature of cost and shows that costs may be classified in many ways. The discussion emphasizes the concept of *relevant costs*—those particular costs that should be considered when making a particular decision. The following section examines the cost-input-output relationship of economic theory, along with short-run and long-run costs. The last section focuses on economies and diseconomies of scale, as well as the advantages and disadvantages of growth. The measurement of cost and the development of cost functions are discussed in the next chapter.

The Nature of Costs

A glance at the multiplicity of cost concepts that are relevant to decision making should immediately dispel the notion that conventional accounting practices provide the firm with all necessary cost information for decision making. Conventional accounting practices recognize only those *explicit* historical costs (cash payments for wages, raw materials, taxes, and so forth) that can be recorded on the books under generally accepted accounting principles. Economists and managers recognize that there are other *implicit* costs that are never recorded in the books, but nevertheless must be considered in managerial decision making.

Whatever their nature, all costs involve a *sacrifice* of some kind. Costs may therefore be tangible or intangible, objectively or subjectively determined, monetary or nonmonetary. In an industrial society like ours, there are certain social costs associated with production, such as noise, congestion, and pollution. There are also psychic costs, that is, mental anguish or dissatisfaction that arise from the stresses and strains of a modern industrial society.

The point to be stressed here is that cost concepts differ depending on managerial uses and viewpoints. In practical work, the historical costs provided by accounting records are often sufficient to fulfill certain legal and financial requirements, such as tax returns, reports to the Securities and Exchange Commission, and annual reports to stockholders. But for decision making, where the concern is with predicting costs under alternative courses of action, conventional accounting usually leaves much to be desired. The most useful estimates of future costs frequently are derived by combining, adjusting, interpreting, modifying, or otherwise manipulating accounting data. In the well-managed firm, therefore, books of account are a source of basic information that must be weighed and analyzed in the decision-making process.

Accounting Cost versus Opportunity Cost

As indicated above, one of the most fundamental distinctions between two general concepts of cost is that between accounting (absolute) cost and opportunity (alternative) cost.

Accounting cost involves historical outlay of funds in payments for wages and salaries, materials purchased, and rent, utilities, interest, and so forth. Accounting costs also include estimated reductions in asset valuations, such as depreciation, amortization, or depletion expense.

Opportunity cost is concerned with the cost of forgoing certain opportunities or alternatives in favor of pursuing others. Opportunity cost stems from the fact that all resources are scarce. A resource that is used for one purpose cannot be used for something else at the same time. For example, if a firm chooses to invest $100,000 in a building instead of buying a $100,000 U.S. Treasury bond, the interest that could have been earned on the bond must be added to the building's explicit cost of $100,000. The basis of choice or decision where alternative costs are involved hinges on a comparison between what the firm is doing and what it could be doing, and it is the difference between those alternatives that constitutes the critical cost consideration.

A subdivision of opportunity or alternative cost is *implicit* or *imputed cost*. This never shows up in the accounting records, but it is nevertheless important for certain types of decisions. Rent never paid on idle land, depreciation on fully depreciated property still in use, interest on equity capital, and rent on company-owned facilities are examples of implicit costs.

Replacement Cost versus Original Cost

Economic analysis differs from accounting principles in the valuation of assets. Under generally accepted accounting principles, an asset is valued on the books at its original or historical cost. When substantial increases occur in general price levels, as in the years 1970–82, the true value of the asset is understated on the balance sheet, and the true income of the company is overstated on the income statement.

Many economists and cost accountants advocate valuation of assets at replacement cost, at least for management purposes. They point out that the firm has the alternatives of (1) using its assets to produce and sell a finished product or (2) disposing of its assets at current market prices. The sacrifice (cost) imposed by choosing to produce and sell is thus measured by the market value of the assets and not by their original cost.

The difference between the original cost and the current market value of goods made or purchased for sale is a profit or loss. But this profit or loss arises solely through holding goods through a period of rising or falling prices. It should not be attributed to the company's primary business operation, which is the making (or buying) and selling of goods. As for assets other than inventories, their original cost needs to be restated in current inflated dollars so that the true cost of their use can be charged against the company's operations. These problems are discussed in more detail in Chapter 13.

Fixed Cost versus Variable Cost

Economists generally divide costs into two major categories, fixed costs and variable costs. *Fixed costs* are those costs that do not vary with (i.e., are not a function of) output. They are costs that require a fixed outlay of funds each period, such as rent, property taxes, and similar "franchise" payments, interest on bonds, and depreciation when measured as a function of time (without any relation to output).[1]

It should be emphasized that the term "fixed" refers to those costs that are fixed *in total* with respect to volume of output. Total fixed costs are not fixed in the sense that they do not vary; they may vary and frequently do, but in response to causes that are independent of volume, such as plant size. It follows, of course, that since fixed costs are constant in total, they will vary *per unit* with the rate of output, continuously decreasing as output increases over the production range.

A term synonymous with fixed cost, at least to the economist, is *overhead cost.* To the cost accountant, this term is virtually the same as indirect cost. Overhead, in accounting literature, usually is composed of some fixed costs and some costs that are variable in nature. The distinction is unfortunate and can lead to misinterpretations in technical discussions if care is not taken in defining terms.

Variable costs are those costs that are a function of output in the production period. They vary directly, sometimes proportionately, with output. Over certain ranges of production they may vary more or less than proportionately with output depending on the utilization of fixed facilities and resources. Examples of variable costs include materials utilized, power, direct labor, factory supplies, and depreciation on a production (rather than time) basis.

In economic and accounting theory it is often assumed that variable costs are continuous functions of output when, in reality, some costs that remain fixed over considerable ranges of production increase by jumps, i.e., discontinuously, at various levels of output. Costs that exhibit this tendency have been classified as *semivariable (semifixed) costs.* They consist of a fixed and a variable portion, such as telephone expense, foremen's wages, and certain other expenses that remain constant for a wide range of production but then increase by definite jumps as output increases beyond certain levels.

---

[1] In the long run *all* costs vary. Therefore, fixed cost is a short-run concept. In fact, the definition of the short run is that period of time during which some inputs, and therefore some costs, are fixed.

Total Cost and Marginal Cost

At any given output level the sum of total fixed cost and total variable cost yields the total cost at that level of output:

$$TC = TFC + TVC \qquad (1)$$

When derived for successive levels of output, the resulting TC series thus represents a functional relationship between total cost and output.

Since in the short run, total variable costs comprise the only changing portion of total cost, any change in the aggregate will be a result of and equal to a change in total variable cost. This change, due to a change in output, is called *marginal cost*. That is, marginal cost is the change in total cost resulting from a unit change in output, and it equals the change in total variable cost. In economic theory, marginal cost is significant for decisions involving the company's allocation of resources and in product pricing, but it has other practical applications as well. At present it is sufficient to note that the concept of marginal cost should not be confused with the notion of differential or incremental cost discussed below.

The Concept of Relevant Incremental Costs

When a decision has to be made regarding a change in the volume of business, some costs will be altered as a result of the decision, but others will not. The only costs that are relevant to the decision are those that would be changed as a result of the decision, such as direct labor and direct materials. These are called *incremental costs*. Those costs that do *not* change as a result of the decision are called *sunk costs*. Since they are not affected by the decision, they are irrelevant. For example, a decision to add a second shift of workers would increase relevant variable costs, such as wages, materials, and supplies, but it would not change the cost of land, buildings, machinery, and other fixed assets.

A distinction may sometimes be made between *incremental cost* and *differential cost*. *Incremental cost* is the change in total cost (increase or decrease) that results from a decision, and that would not occur if the decision were not made. *Differential cost* is the difference in cost between two alternatives. However, for a go no-go type of decision where change in total cost represents the difference between implementing or not implementing a particular action, the terms incremental cost and differential cost are synonymous. The concept of relevant incremental cost may be illustrated by the following simple example.

Fred, a college student, wants to drive 500 miles round-trip to visit home at Christmas. He can't afford the trip unless he takes other students along to share the cost. In order to determine pro rata costs, he compiles the total cost data shown in Exhibit 11–1.

Exhibit 11–1_____

Estimated Annual Cost of Operating Automobile

Depreciation this year	$1,200
Interest on investment in car (at 15%)	900
License fees and taxes	50
Parking fees (at $10 per month)	120
Insurance	600
Gasoline (10,000 miles at 5¢ per mile)	500
Oil and grease	30
Tires (replaced every 30,000 miles for $240)	80
Repairs and maintenance	120
Total annual cost	$3,600

Therefore,

$$\text{Cost per mile} = \frac{\text{Total annual cost}}{\text{Annual mileage}} = \frac{\$3600}{10,000} = \$.36$$

and the total cost of a 500-mile round trip is $500 \times \$.36 = \$180$. On the basis of these calculations, Fred concludes that the pro rata cost for himself and four riders is $36 each for a total cost of $180. Assuming that the figures in the exhibit are reasonably accurate, is Fred's reasoning correct about the cost of the trip?

Ask yourself, what is Fred's objective? It appears that he merely wants to cover the cost of the trip on an equal-share basis. Therefore, he has two alternatives:

Alternative A: make the trip and charge each rider (including himself) enough to cover the cost.

Alternative B: Do not make the trip if the cost cannot be covered.

In comparing these alternatives, the only relevant costs are those that will be incurred if the trip is taken and avoided if it is not. These increased costs are the *incremental costs* which must be identified. The estimates of these are shown in Exhibit 11–2.

Exhibit 11–2_____

Incremental Costs of the 500-Mile Trip

Gasoline (5¢ per mile)	$25.00
Oil and grease (0.3¢ per mile)	1.50
Tires (0.8¢ per mile)	4.00
Repairs and maintenance (1.2¢ per mile)	6.00
Total incremental cost	$36.50

Thus 500 miles of driving will increase Fred's total cost by $36.50, not $180 as originally assumed. The incremental cost per mile is $36.50/500, or 7.3 cents, far less than his original estimated cost of 36 cents. The difference, of course, reflects the fact that his original estimate was based on all (fully allocated) costs, whereas the incremental estimate is based on only the additional costs of the trip. In any case, by charging a price per rider high enough to cover his original estimate of $180, he might not get any customers and thus end up not making the trip, all because of his failure to realize that in any decision-making problem *it is better to have a rough estimate of the right concept than an accurate estimate of the wrong one.*

It must be emphasized that incremental cost is a *short-run* decision-making concept, based on the existence of sunk costs that can be ignored as irrelevant. But in the long run, all costs must be recovered or the business will fail. If Fred intends to drive home on a regular basis, he will have to find a way to pay all of the costs listed in Exhibit 11–1.

Although the concept of incremental cost is simple enough—it involves only those costs that are affected by a decision—this does not mean that the concept is easy to apply. A single decision may have indirect as well as direct effects upon costs. For example:

1.   If the decision requires additional capital investment, the decision maker must consider not only incremental interest, but also any change in the firm's financial risk.

2.   Incremental costs need not vary only with output, product, or absolute cash outlays. In some situations, they may be placed in the same family with opportunity costs; that is, the incremental cost is the foregone opportunity of using limited resources in one activity instead of another.

For example, if floor space is used to make Product A instead of Product B, on which a profit of $50 per unit can be made, then the $50 forgone profit becomes a part of the cost of Product A. In contrast, the allocated rental cost of the floor space is irrelevant to this decision between Product A and Product B because the same rent will have to be paid in either case.

3.   The concept of incremental cost forces recognition of the fact that expenses vary differently in different dimensions of a business. For example, a trucking company, in considering taking on new business, may have the alternatives of (1) utilizing more trucks per day, or (2) getting more payload per truck. The choice of either alternative will result in separate incremental costs. The most economical policy would be to maintain a balance between the two, using each to the point beyond which the other would be cheaper, that is, where the incremental costs are equal.

For example, suppose that the trucking company is operating 10 tractor-trailer rigs, each with a 36-foot trailer. If each trailer is traded in for a 40-foot trailer, the result would be an 11 percent increase in cargo capacity without the purchase of additional tractors. On the other hand, the company could get an 11-percent increase in capacity simply by adding one 40-foot trailer to its fleet, but it would also have to buy a tractor to pull it.

4. In many agricultural processing operations (e.g., meat packing, sugar refining) the incremental cost of processing the main product does not equal the incremental cost of processing each of the various by-products, nor is it equal to their sum. For example, the incremental cost of turning a hog's carcass into pork roasts and chops does not equal the incremental costs, separately or collectively, of producing ham, bacon and sausage.

Incremental versus Marginal Cost.   The distinction between incremental cost and marginal cost is somewhat fuzzy, and the two terms are sometimes used as if they were synonymous. There is, however, a fundamental conceptual difference that should be recognized. The term *marginal cost* refers to the change in the total cost of output when one more unit is produced. One might also refer to the marginal cost of other business functions, such as sales, finance, and administration, as well as to the marginal cost of production in manufacturing, but the concept is restricted to *unitary change of output.*

Incremental cost is a broader concept that embraces *any* change in total cost of doing business. For example, a decision to introduce new machinery, develop a new product, or expand into different markets might involve marginal costs of production, but it would involve other costs as well. A decision to float a new security issue, install a data processing system, or launch a new advertising campaign is not directly reflected by a change in the cost of production. Nevertheless, there is a change in the total cost of doing business.

Incremental Analysis.   Incremental analysis considers incremental revenue as well as incremental cost in order to determine incremental profit. Incremental analysis is an analytical tool that can be applied to many practical decision-making problems. In all such problems, it is the difference between alternatives that provides the basis for making the correct decision. The decision maker must be sure, however, to consider *all* of the effects of each alternative, be they qualitative or quantitative. In Chapter 3, for example, we used the case of a tire manufacturer to illustrate the *quantitative* aspects of incremental analysis. However, we also pointed out that *qualitative* considerations might affect the decision.

The necessity for broad incremental analysis is particularly apparent in the case of a firm that is considering the introduction of a new product. At the very least, the person responsible for this decision must ask:

1. How would sales of the new product affect sales of existing products? Specifically, is the new product a substitute competing for sales? Is it a complement, enhancing sales? Would it round out the firm's product line? Or is it unrelated to existing products?
2. How would production of the new product affect production of existing products? Can the new product be manufactured with existing production facilities? Would the new product create a production bottleneck? How would production of the new product affect supplies of labor and materials? How would it affect maintenance and repair of machinery and equipment?
3. How would distribution of the new product affect the firm's distribution system? Would it require new channels?
4. What would be the long-run effects of the production and sale of the new product? What future investments might be required to replace worn-out facilities? Would future expansion or development of other products be affected?

Conclusions

The classification of cost concepts reveals various distinctions from both the economic and accounting standpoints. Because of this, we should not try to make one concept do the work of several. The corporation's obligations that must be met before dividends can be paid, the financial sacrifices or costs of production, and methods of valuing inventories are separate issues. In some companies, systems of cost analysis have been developed that coexist alongside but apart from formal books of account, although they are based on the same data. These systems are used to study differential costing, direct costing, and full costing for management purposes, unrestricted by the principles of financial accounting.

There is thus no single definition of cost of production that is applicable to all situations. Rather, the analyst must be sure to use the appropriate measure of cost in a given situation.

Theory of Cost: Cost-Output Functions

The fundamental starting point in cost theory is the principle that a unique functional relationship exists between cost and the rate of output for a firm. Admittedly, there may be independent variables other than output that will affect cost (e.g., production lot size and rate of plant utilization), but the costs of these are assumed to remain constant. Accordingly, they are held constant when cost curves are constructed.

The level of various cost curves—fixed, variable, total, average, and marginal—is affected by factor prices. When factor prices are constant, the exact nature (i.e., shape) of a given curve depends on the nature of the underlying production function. Curves thus derived are static in nature, meaning that they show only how costs differ under alternative output levels, all other things being equal.

Definition of Short Run and Long Run

In production economics, the *short run* is defined as that period of time during which some of the firm's input factors are fixed. For example, the costs of a firm's plant, machinery, and equipment are fixed for some time. Inherent in the notion of short run, therefore, is the idea of temporarily fixed resource commitments whose expense the firm incurs regardless of the level of output. Because of differences in the nature of their products (capital goods versus consumer goods), production processes (labor-intensive versus capital-intensive), plant size, and level of technology, different firms may have very different time frames constituting their short-run situations. This makes it virtually impossible to say, a priori, what is *the* short-run period for a given firm in a given industry.

The short run is an *operating* concept, since at any given time the firm is operating in the short run. The long run, which embraces many short runs, is a *planning* concept. Whereas decisions concerning day-to-day operations are based upon the firm's short-run cost functions, the firm's plans to expand are greatly affected by its long-run cost function. The *long run* refers to a period of time in which no input factors can be assumed to be fixed. All input factors can be changed in the long run, and therefore all long-run costs are variable.

The actual period of time that can be regarded as long-run depends upon the relationship of the firm's inputs to its production process. In general, the more capital-intensive a production process is, the longer will be the time period required to change *all* of the factors of production. For example, a new oil refinery might take three years or more to be built and placed in operation. A nuclear power plant or a dam might take even longer. In contrast, a service industry (e.g., a bank, an employment agency, or an insurance company) that employs relatively small amounts of capital may expand its entire operation in the few months required to hire and train more personnel.

Cost Behavior in the Short Run

Two factors determine the behavior of short-run costs: (1) the character of the underlying production function, and (2) the prices of the variable inputs to production. If technology remains constant as production increases, so that the production function does not change, the resulting cost curves are mirror images, or *inverses*, of the underlying production function. Hence, when one is convex, the other is concave. Thus the *shape* of the cost curve depends upon the shape of the production curve, but the *position* of the cost curve on the graphing plane depends upon the price of the input factor, X. If its price rises, the cost curve shifts upward, and vice versa.

Average and Marginal Cost Curves.   To understand a firm's cost structure and to have a theoretical basis for resolving various kinds of decision problems, it is important to examine several cost curves: (1) average total cost (*ATC*); (2) average variable cost (*AVC*); (3) average fixed cost (*AFC*); and (4) marginal cost (*MC*). All of these can be derived from total cost data. Thus, if Q represents output, then $ATC = TC/Q$, $AVC = TVC/Q$, and $AFC = TFC/Q$. For discrete functions, $MC = \Delta TC/\Delta Q$. For continuous functions, $MC = d(TC)/dQ$, that is, the first derivative of the function.

There are other methods as well that can be used to derive these curves from given output and total cost data, since $TC = TFC + TVC$ is the basic relationship and the quantities can be algebraically transposed as desired. For example, Exhibit 11–3 sets forth a cost schedule for the

Exhibit 11–3 _____

Cost Schedule for the Production of Tennis Rackets

Quantity of Production (000) Q	Total Fixed Cost ($000) TFC	Total Variable Cost ($000) TVC	Total Cost ($000) TC = TFC + TVC	Average Fixed Cost ($000) TFC/Q	Average Variable Cost ($000) TVC/Q	Average Total Cost ($000) TC/Q	Marginal Cost ($000) ΔTC/ΔQ
1	$50		$ 55.00				
2	50	$ 8.00	58.00	$25.00	$ 4.00	$29.00	$ 3.00
3	50		60.50				
4	50	13.00	63.00	12.50	3.25	15.75	2.50
5	50		65.00				
6	50	18.00	68.00	8.33	3.00	11.34	3.00
7	50		72.75				
8	50	28.00	78.00	6.25	3.50	9.75	5.25
9	50		86.00				
10	50	45.00	95.00	5.00	4.50	9.50	9.00
11	50	54.50	104.50	4.55	4.95	9.50	9.50
12	50	65.20	115.20	4.17	5.44	9.60	10.70
13	50		130.00				
14	50	99.10	149.10	3.57	7.08	10.65	19.10
15	50		174.75				
16	50	162.00	212.00	3.13	10.13	13.25	37.25
17	50		259.25				
18	50	269.50	319.50	2.78	14.97	17.75	60.25
19	50		399.00				
20	50	450.00	500.00	2.50	22.50	25.00	101.00

production of tennis rackets to illustrate the tabular method of cost analysis using discrete data.

Although the data in this exhibit are not complete, there is sufficient information to fill in the blanks. (The student may find it worth while to do so.) When the discrete data points are connected, the graphs of the average fixed cost, average variable cost, average total cost, and marginal cost are curvilinear, as illustrated in Exhibit 11–4.

Mathematically, average fixed cost (AFC) is a rectangular hyperbola that is asymptotic to the horizontal axis. This means that AFC is constantly decreasing, as shown in Exhibit 11–4. The exhibit also shows that marginal cost (MC) first decreases, than increases. Average variable cost (AVC) and average total cost (ATC) also first decrease, then increase, and ATC approaches AVC at higher levels of production.

Exhibit 11–4

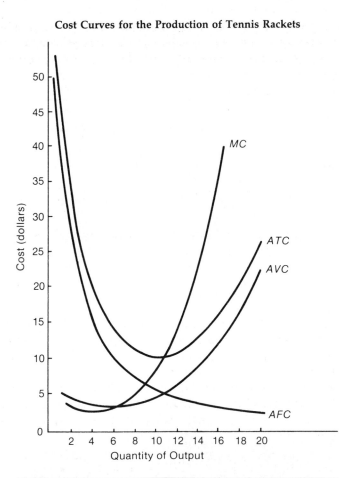

Cost Curves for the Production of Tennis Rackets

Note particularly that the marginal cost curve intersects both the average variable cost curve and the average total cost curve at their lowest points. That is to say, marginal cost is equal to average variable cost when average variable cost is at a minimum. Marginal cost is also equal to average total cost when average total cost is at a minimum.

This is easily verified by referring to the cost schedule in Exhibit 11–3. When the sixth unit is produced, the average variable cost of $3 is at a minimum and is equal to the marginal cost of $3. When the 11th unit is produced, average total cost of $9.50 is at a minimum, and is equal to the marginal cost of $9.50.

As with the total cost and total variable cost curves, the shape or curvature of the average and marginal curves is conditioned by the technical nature of the underlying production curves, and not by factor prices. A change in factor prices will shift the curves up or down on the graph, but will not change their shape because their slopes are not affected.

The natural consequence of a constant factor price for varying levels of output is an inverse relationship between (1) average variable cost and average product, and (2) marginal cost and marginal product. These relationships are derived as follows:

1. The average variable cost, AVC_Q, is defined as

$$AVC_Q = \frac{TVC_Q}{Q_X} = \frac{P_X \cdot X}{Q_X} = P_X\left(\frac{X}{Q_X}\right) \qquad (2)$$

where X = quantity of input factor X
P_X = unit price of input factor X
Q_X = quantity of output resulting from input of X.

The average product, AP_X, is defined as Q_X/X, which is the reciprocal of X/Q_X in Equation (2) above. Therefore,

$$AVC_Q = P_X\left(\frac{1}{Q_X/X}\right) = P_X\left(\frac{1}{AP_X}\right) = \frac{P_X}{AP_X} \qquad (3)$$

Given that the price, P_X, is constant, we see from Equation (3) that when AP_X increases, AVC_Q decreases, and vice versa. Logically, then, AVC_Q must be minimum when AP_X is maximum. This inverse relationship is illustrated by Exhibit 11–5.

2. Exhibit 11–5 also shows the inverse relationship between marginal product and marginal cost. Remember that marginal product and marginal cost are not affected by fixed input. Therefore, marginal cost, MC_Q, is defined as

$$MC_Q = \frac{\Delta TVC_Q}{\Delta Q_X} = \frac{\Delta X \cdot P_X}{\Delta Q_X} = P_X\left(\frac{\Delta X}{\Delta Q_X}\right) \qquad (4)$$

Exhibit 11–5

Relationship between Marginal Product and Marginal Cost, Average Product and
Average Variable Cost

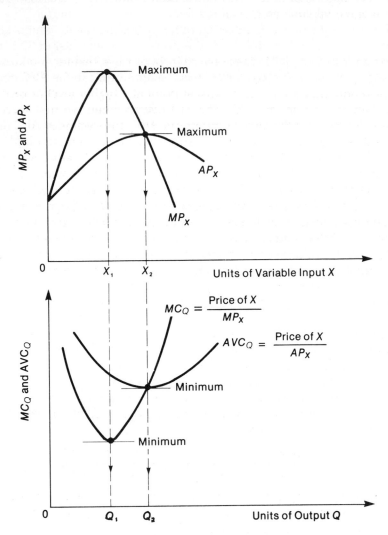

The marginal product, MP_X, is defined as $\Delta Q_X/\Delta X$, which is the reciprocal of $\Delta X/\Delta Q_X$ in Equation (4). Therefore,

$$MC_Q = P_X \left(\frac{1}{\Delta Q_X/\Delta X}\right) = P_X \left(\frac{1}{MP_X}\right) = \frac{P_X}{MP_X} \qquad (5)$$

Given that the price, P_X, is constant, we see from Equation (5) that when MP_X increases, MC_Q decreases, and vice-versa. Logically, then, MC_Q must be minimum when MP_X is maximum.

3. Average total cost, ATC, is the sum of average fixed cost, AFC, and average variable cost, AVC; i.e.,

$$ATC = AFC + AVC \tag{6}$$

Going back to Exhibit 11–4, we see that AFC grows smaller and smaller as output increases. Thus the ATC curve is asymptotic to the AVC curve. We also note that it reaches its lowest point at a higher level of production than for minimum AVC. This is because when we first increase production beyond the level of minimum AVC, the decline in AFC more than offsets the increase in AVC. As production continues to increase, however, we reach the point where increases in AVC begin to exceed decreases in AFC. This is where the ATC curve turns upward.

4. The most *production-efficient* level of production occurs where MP_X = AP_X and AP_X is maximum. This marks the end of Stage 1 and the beginning of Stage 2 of the classic production function that was illustrated by Exhibit 9–2 in Chapter 9, and coincides with the level where $MC_Q = AVC_Q$. This is *not* the most economical or *cost-efficient* level, however, because it does not consider AFC. The most economical, cost-efficient level of production occurs somewhere in Stage 2, at the point of minimum average total cost, ATC.

Elasticity of Total Cost.   Since the economic theory of cost deals with relationships between cost and output, can we measure responsiveness or sensitivity between these variables? The answer to this question, of course, involves the familiar concept of elasticity.

The elasticity of total cost measures the percentage change in total cost, TC, resulting from a 1 percent change in output, Q. Thus, at any point along the total cost curve,

$$\varepsilon_C = \frac{\Delta TC/TC}{\Delta Q/Q} = \frac{\Delta TC}{\Delta Q} \cdot \frac{Q}{TC} = \frac{\Delta TC/\Delta Q}{TC/Q} = \frac{MC}{ATC} \tag{7}$$

From this equation, it is apparent that the elasticity of total cost is the ratio of marginal cost to average total cost. The range of ε_C will thus depend on the values of MC and ATC.

If the total cost function is linear, or if it is nearly linear within the range desired, the elasticity of total cost, E_C, can be estimated with the arc formula,

$$E_C = \frac{\dfrac{TC_2 - TC_1}{(TC_2 + TC_1)/2}}{\dfrac{Q_2 - Q_1}{(Q_2 + Q_1)/2}} = \frac{TC_2 - TC_1}{TC_2 + TC_1} \cdot \frac{Q_2 + Q_1}{Q_2 - Q_1} \tag{8}$$

This formula gives a measure of the average elasticity for the range of output between Q_1 and Q_2.

Properties of Short-Run Cost Functions

The generalized or typical cost function of economics textbooks is the cubic function $TC = a + bQ - cQ^2 + dQ^3$. It is the inverse of the generalized (cubic) production function, which first exhibits increasing, then decreasing marginal product or returns to input. Consequently, as illustrated by Exhibit 11–6, the cost function exhibits first decreasing, then

Exhibit 11–6

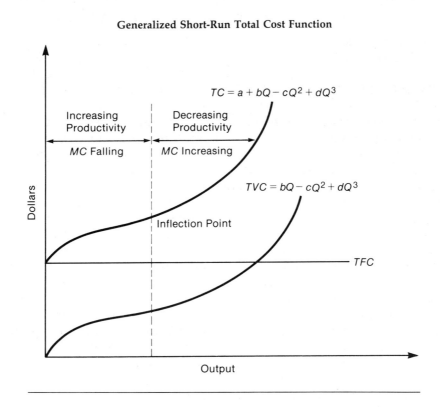

Generalized Short-Run Total Cost Function

increasing marginal cost. Marginal cost can be measured by the slope of either curve since the shapes of the TC and TVC curves are identical. The vertical distance between them is the constant total fixed cost, TFC.

The classic cost function, as illustrated by Exhibit 11–6, extends over the entire capacity of the production plant. Within that spread, there may be segments of the curve that exhibit linear or quadratic properties. If so, they will have the characteristics depicted on Exhibit 11–7, which shows the mathematical properties of linear, quadratic, and cubic cost functions.

In general, we note the following:

1. The constant parameter, a, represents total fixed costs. When it is removed from the total cost equation, the remainder represents total variable costs.[2]
2. Marginal costs are derivatives of the equations for total costs.
3. The quantity a/Q represents average fixed cost. When it is removed from the equation for average total cost, the remainder represents average variable cost.
4. Cost elasticity is the ratio of marginal cost to average total cost.

Economic interpretations of some of these mathematical properties are discussed below.

Linear Cost Functions.   Exhibit 11–8 illustrates the cost curves associated with a linear cost function.

As we shall explain in the next chapter, the results of empirical research suggest that firms in widely differing industries enjoy linear cost functions over a fairly broad range of what might be called normal production. One explanation for this phenomenon is that within this range of output, fixed input factors are readily divisible. This enables the fixed and variable inputs to be combined in minimum cost proportions at each level of output within the normal range of production. If the cost function were to be extended to include higher levels of output, however, the linear function would no longer be valid. This is because it does not recognize the law of diminishing returns. That is, the equation does not allow for total cost to turn upward, even as output levels approaching the physical capacity of the plant are reached.

Note that average variable cost (AVC) and marginal cost (MC) are constant and equal. The average total cost (ATC) curve is asymptotic to that of average variable cost. Within the normal range of production, the ATC curve flattens out and remains nearly constant.

Quadratic Cost Functions.   As shown in Exhibit 11–7, two types of quadratic functions are possible. The first type is described by the general equation $TC = a + bQ - cQ^2$. The associated cost curves are shown in Exhibit 11–9.

---

[2] When a cost function is obtained by regression analysis of production data, the data usually do not cover low levels of production. As a result, the constant term of the regression equation does not represent fixed cost. It merely indicates a Y-intercept that serves to properly locate the regression line in the production range of interest.

Exhibit 11–7

Cost Curves Associated with Various Cost Functions

Type of Equation	General Form	Total Fixed Costs TFC	Total Variable Costs TVC	Marginal Costs MC	Average Total Cost ATC	Average Variable Cost AVC	Cost Elasticity MC/ATC
Linear	$TC = a + bQ$	a	bQ	b	$\dfrac{a}{Q} + b$	b	$\dfrac{b}{\dfrac{a}{Q} + b}$
Quadratic I	$TC = a + bQ - cQ^2$	a	$bQ - cQ^2$	$b - 2cQ$	$\dfrac{a}{Q} + b - cQ$	$b - cQ$	$\dfrac{b - 2cQ}{\dfrac{a}{Q} + b - cQ}$
Quadratic II	$TC = a + bQ + cQ^2$	a	$bQ + cQ^2$	$b + 2cQ$	$\dfrac{a}{Q} + b + cQ$	$b + cQ$	$\dfrac{b + 2cQ}{\dfrac{a}{Q} + b + cQ}$
Cubic	$TC = a + bQ - cQ^2 + dQ^3$	a	$bQ - cQ^2 + dQ^3$	$b - 2cQ + 3dQ^2$	$\dfrac{a}{Q} + b - cQ + dQ^2$	$b - cQ + dQ^2$	$\dfrac{b - 2cQ + 3dQ^2}{\dfrac{a}{Q} + b - cQ + dQ^2}$

Exhibit 11–8

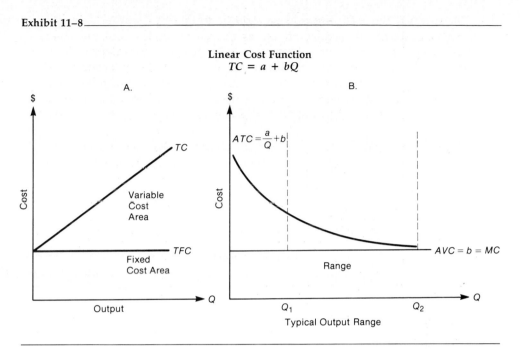

Linear Cost Function
$$TC = a + bQ$$

A.

B.

Typical Output Range

Exhibit 11–9

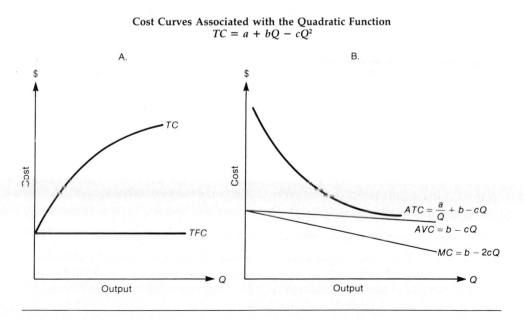

Cost Curves Associated with the Quadratic Function
$$TC = a + bQ - cQ^2$$

A.

B.

As always, the *ATC* curve is asymptotic to the *AVC* curve. Average variable costs fall at a constant rate as output increases, and marginal costs decrease even faster. Unfortunately for the firm, this happy situation is unlikely to occur in a normal range of output. It may occur at the start-up of production, where fixed factors are excessive in relation to variable inputs. Decreasing marginal costs thus are attributable to more efficient use of fixed factors, which also causes the average variable cost to decrease.

The second type of quadratic cost function is described by the equation $TC = a + bQ + cQ^2$. The associated cost curves are illustrated in Exhibit 11–10.

Exhibit 11–10

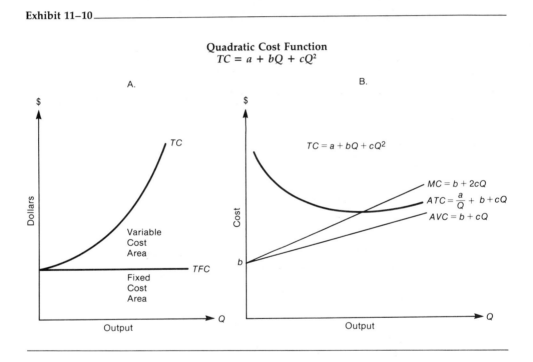

Quadratic Cost Function
$TC = a + bQ + cQ^2$

As shown in panel B, the *AVC* curve constantly increases, with *MC* rising even faster. Since the *ATC* curve is asymptotic to the *AVC* curve, it must cut through the *MC* curve. The intersection, where *MC* = *ATC* and cost elasticity is therefore 1, marks the most cost-effective level of production. To the left of this point, a 1 percent increase in output causes less than a 1 percent increase in cost, so an increase in output is in order. To the right of this point, however, a 1 percent increase in output causes greater than a 1 percent increase in cost.

Cubic Cost Functions. The typical total cost function of economics textbooks is not usually of a linear or quadratic form, but rather of the cubic type

$$TC = a + bX - cX^2 + dX^3$$

The shape of this curve is illustrated in Exhibit 11–11. Since the TC function is cubic, the ATC and MC curves are quadratic, first falling, then rising. The switch from decreasing to increasing marginal cost (when MC is minimum) corresponds to the inflection point of the curva-

Exhibit 11–11

Cubic Cost Curves and the Elasticity of Total Cost

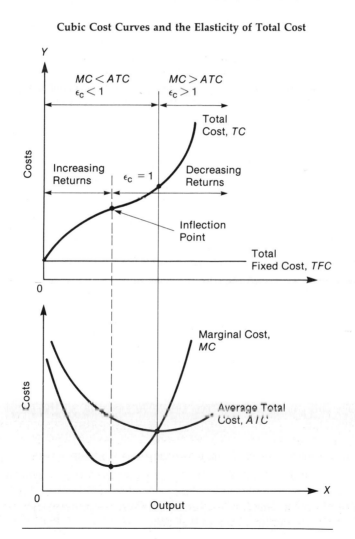

ture of the cubic function. The intersection of the MC and ATC curves, where $MC = ATC$ and $\varepsilon_C = 1$, marks the most cost-effective level of output. If the firm increases output to a higher level, it encounters increasing costs for such things as maintenance of machinery and overtime pay for labor. Total costs thus rise at an ever-increasing rate.

Cubic functions such as these represent, for the most part, strictly theoretical generalizations. Attempts that have been made to fit cubic curves to empirical data have met with varying and, at best, only moderate degrees of success (to be discussed in the next chapter). One reason that a cubic function does not readily fit empirical data is that the data usually are confined to the range of normal operations. As was shown earlier, the cost function in the normal operating range tends to be linear, and marginal costs are likely to be constant.

Cost Behavior in the Long Run

As we noted in the previous discussion, cost behavior in the short run is an *operating* concept. At any given time, now or in the future, the firm will operate an *existing* plant that incurs a set of fixed costs. Operational decision making thus is concerned with minimizing variable costs. In contrast, cost behavior in the long run is a *planning* concept. It is based on the premise that all input factors can be varied and that for each possible output level there is a least-cost combination of input factors. Therefore, it is possible to construct an optimal-sized plant for any desired level of production.

Because of the flexibility afforded in the long run, the firm must begin the planning process by first establishing the technology and production methods that are or will be available for the firm's expansion. The firm is then free to choose the plant and equipment size that is most suitable to its desired level of production. When the firm increases its plant size, however, some of the production factors will become fixed. The firm will again be operating in the short run, and a short-run average cost function will be established. This is illustrated by Exhibit 11–12.

The diagram shows the short-run average cost ($SRAC$) curves for four successively more efficient plant sizes. Each plant operates most efficiently at a level of output corresponding to the lowest point on its $SRAC$ curve. We call this level of output the *design capacity* of the plant.

If he or she is free to vary the plant size, the production manager will try to find the lowest average cost for each of several levels of production. Taking the smallest plant, it can be seen that the lowest short-run average cost occurs when M units are produced. The diagram shows, however, that M units can be produced at lower cost in the second plant. Pursuing this line of reasoning further, we conclude that it is most efficient to produce 0 to Q_1 units in Plant 1, Q_1 to Q_2 units in Plant 2, Q_2

Exhibit 11–12

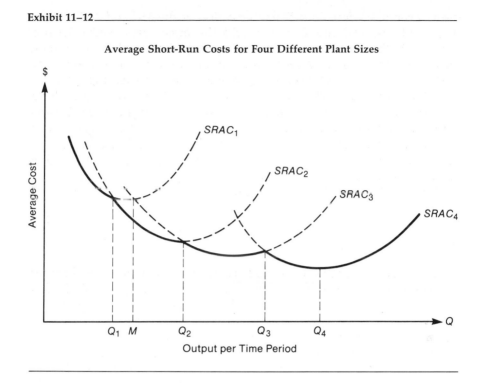

Average Short-Run Costs for Four Different Plant Sizes

to Q_3 units in Plant 3, and Q_3 to Q_4 units in Plant 4. This choice is indicated on the diagram by the solid line connecting these points. This solid line is the long-run average cost curve, *LRAC*.

Of course, a firm actually has many more than four plant sizes to choose from. Indeed, depending on the divisibility of productive units and their technical nature, there may be an infinite number of plant sizes available, each with its own short-run average cost curve and design capacity. When the points of intersection of all these *SRAC* curves are joined together, the result is the smooth *LRAC* curve illustrated by Exhibit 11–13.

In Exhibit 11–13, only five of the infinite number of possible *SRAC* curves have been drawn. Or, to put it another way, all but five of the intersecting *SRAC* curves have been erased. This leaves each of the remaining *SRAC* curves just tangent to the *LRAC* curve at the point of intersection with the (erased) *SRAC* curve for the next larger plant.

Exhibit 11–13 further illustrates the relationship between the long-run and short-run average cost functions. Suppose that the firm is producing Q_1 units of output in Plant 1, which has the short-run average cost curve $SRAC_1$. If the firm wants to expand output to Q_2 units, production

Exhibit 11–13

Short- and Long-Run Average Cost Functions

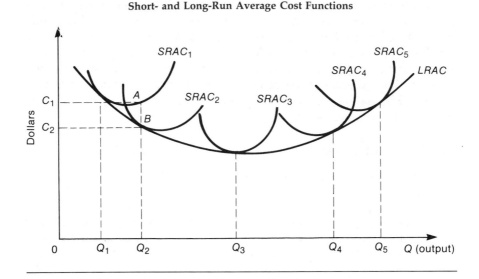

would take place at point A on $SRAC_1$, at a cost of C_1 dollars. But the cost would be substantially less in a larger plant with $SRAC_2$ at a cost of C_2 dollars. The reduction in cost would be $C_1 - C_2$.

The $LRAC$ curve envelops the entire family of $SRAC$ curves. The U shape of the $LRAC$ curve implies that expansion of plant size results in lower and lower unit costs until the optimum size is reached. This occurs at Q_3 units of output, where the $LRAC$ curve is at its lowest point. Thereafter, further increase in production will require successively larger plants and successively higher unit costs.

The $LRAC$ curve is tangent to only one point on each $SRAC$ curve. At the optimal plant size, the tangency occurs at the lowest point of both the short-run and long-run average cost curves, as shown by $SRAC_3$. For all other plant sizes, the tangency point occurs: (a) to the left of the minimum-cost point (design capacity) on all short-run curves that are to the left of the optimum curve $SRAC_3$, and (b) to the right of the minimum-cost point (design capacity) on all short-run curves that are to the right of the optimum curve. Therefore, for outputs less than Q_3, it is more economical to operate at less than design capacity, underutilizing a plant slightly larger than necessary. Thus, it would be cheaper to produce output Q_2 with a plant designated by $SRAC_2$ than with one represented by $SRAC_1$. Conversely, at outputs beyond the optimum level Q_3, it is more economical to operate at a somewhat higher level than design capacity, overutilizing a plant slightly beyond its design capacity. Thus, it is cheaper to produce Q_4 units with plant $SRAC_4$ than with $SRAC_5$.

The tendency for long-run average costs to fall as the firm expands its scale of operations is a reflection of cost economies that are frequently encountered with increasing size. The ultimate rise in the long-run curve is due largely to the eventual diseconomies of large-scale management. That is to say, as the firm becomes larger, decision making and coordination becomes more complex and difficult. Therefore, the burden of administration become disproportionately greater and diminishing returns to management set in.

The Effect of Demand Expectations on Average Cost

So far, we have considered the optimal-sized plant to be one with the lowest unit cost for a given level of output. This is something that can be estimated quite accurately. Unfortunately, however, the required level of output is not so easily determined. Rather, the given level of output is decided by *expected demand.*

To illustrate the importance of expected demand upon plant selection, consider the probability distributions of demand illustrated in Exhibit 11–14.

Exhibit 11–14

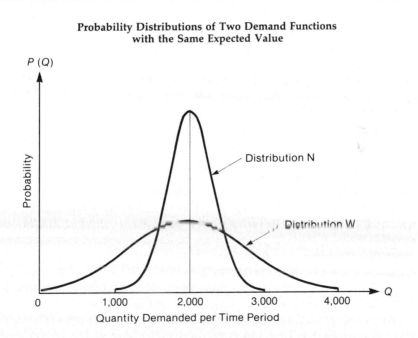

**Probability Distributions of Two Demand Functions
with the Same Expected Value**

P (Q)

Probability

Distribution N

Distribution W

0   1,000   2,000   3,000   4,000   Q

Quantity Demanded per Time Period

Exhibit 11–14 shows two possible probability distributions of demand for the same product. In both cases, the expected demand is the same—about 2,000 units. However, Distribution N shows a narrower range of deviation from the expected value than Distribution W.

Now suppose that we have a choice of two different plants to produce 2,000 units. The average total cost curves for them are as illustrated in Exhibit 11–15. Plant 1 is a highly mechanized (capital intensive) plant

Exhibit 11–15 _____

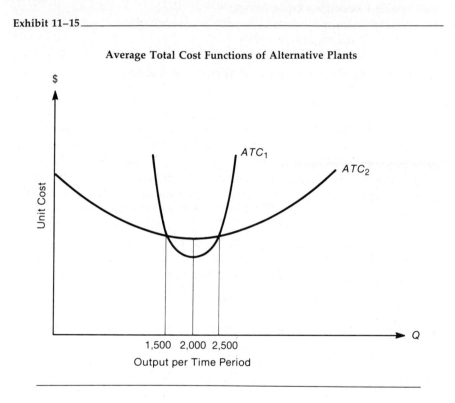

Average Total Cost Functions of Alternative Plants

designed to produce 2,000 units at its lowest unit cost. However, any deviation from this target output drives up costs very rapidly.

Plant 2 also achieves minimum average total cost at a production level of 2,000 units. However, it is a more general design, so that deviations from the target level of production escalate costs more slowly. From the diagram, it is clear that production between 1,500 and 2,500 units is less costly in Plant 1. Outside that narrow range, production is much less costly in Plant 2.

Which plant should we choose? The answer depends upon the probability distribution of demand combined with the cost at various levels. An appropriate yardstick might be the expected average total cost. It can be calculated for each plant by multiplying the unit cost (*ATC*) at each level of production (within the contemplated range of production) by the probability of demand for that quantity, then summing the products:

$$E(ATC_i) = \sum_{j=1}^{n} P_{ij}ATC_{ij}$$

where

$E(ATC_i)$ = Expected average total cost of *i*th plant design
P_{ij} = Probability of demand for the *j*th level of production in the *i*th plant
ATC_{ij} = Average total cost at the *j*th level of production in the *i*th plant
n = Number of output levels being considered

Economies and Diseconomies of Scale

In the preceding chapters on production, we discussed returns to scale (the proportionate increase or decrease that results from an increase in all input factors of production) as a long-run concept. If there are increasing returns to scale, then there are corresponding decreases in long-run unit cost, and we call this *economies of scale*. On the other hand, decreasing returns to scale result in increasing long-run unit cost, and we call this *diseconomies of scale*. Economies or diseconomies of scale may be obtained either within single plants, or for the firm as a whole.

Economies of Scale at Plant Level

There are at least eight different reasons that economies may be achieved when the plant size is enlarged more or less to scale:

1. *More efficient use of labor from the subdivision and specialization of labor.* For example, in a small manufacturing plant using, say, one machinist, the machinist might be required to sweep up around his machine. Thus he would be spending part of his time doing janitorial work at machinist's wages. As the plant expands, janitors could be hired for clean-up work at janitor's wages, leaving machinists free to spend all of their time doing what they do best.
2. *Machine execution of simplified work elements.* For example, computers are capable of performing repetitive tasks involving manipulation of data, and they can do it better, faster, and cheaper than human beings.
3. *In-house performance of specialized tasks.* For example, a small firm may use an outside duplicating service for occasional copying of documents. As the plant size grows, the increased need for copying may justify the purchase of a duplicating machine.

4. *Specialization and higher capacity of machines.* A machine that is designed to perform a specialized operation is usually more cost-efficient than a general-purpose machine. Higher capacity machines also offer savings. For example, a machine with twice as much capacity does not cost twice as much to buy or operate.

5. *Centralization and integration of manufacturing stages into a single continuous process.* An example is provided by steel mills in which raw steel goes into the rolling mills while it is still hot.

6. *Use or sale of by-products.* For example, when coke is made from anthracite coal, naphtha is obtained as a by-product. When gasoline is made from crude oil, other products such as kerosene, diesel oil, and fuel oil are also produced in the refining process. By-products are also common in the meat packing, chemical, and paper products industries.

7. *Quantity discounts on purchases.* A firm that buys in large quantities can demand and get volume discounts from suppliers.

8. *Savings on transportation costs by owning and operating the firm's own vehicles.* Many large companies own and operate more trucks than some of the smaller trucking companies.

Diseconomies of Scale at Plant Level

When a plant becomes too large, certain diseconomies may set in. Sheer size of a plant may cause bottlenecks in the production process and traffic jams in the employee parking lots. The movement of materials inside the plant may become more costly. Transportation costs outside the plant may also become excessive. If one huge plant is chosen rather than several geographically dispersed smaller plants, moving raw materials into the large plant and finished goods away from it become more costly. Finally, there is the matter of supervision and coordination, which becomes more complicated and more difficult as plant size increases.

Economies of Scale for Multiplant Firms

In multiplant firms, distinctive production and cost functions exist for the firm as a whole as well as for each of its component plants. Ideally, each plant would be of optimal size, meaning that no further economies are possible by changing plant size.[3] Even under such ideal circum-

---

[3] This does not mean that all plants are of the same size, even if they are producing the same output. It simply means that in each plant's geographic location, the cost environment is such that the minimum short-run average cost coincides with the minimum long-run average cost, as illustrated in Exhibit 11–13.

stances, there are three different shapes that could be assumed by the firm's long-run cost curve, as illustrated by Exhibit 11–16.[4]

In all three panels of Exhibit 11–16, Q^* indicates optimal plant size. We assume that the firm expands by adding more plants of optimal size.

Exhibit 11–16

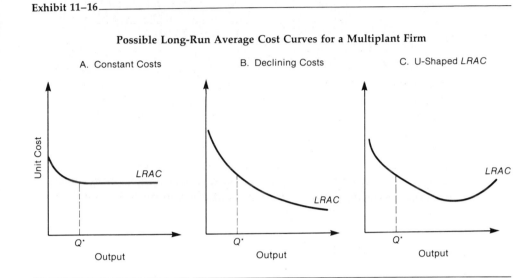

Possible Long-Run Average Cost Curves for a Multiplant Firm

A. Constant Costs   B. Declining Costs   C. U-Shaped *LRAC*

In Panel A, the *LRAC* curve for the firm levels off when optimal plant size is reached. No matter how many optimally sized plants are added to increase the size of the firm, no further economies of scale can be achieved.

In Panel B, long-run average cost for the firm continues to decline as additional (optimal-size) plants are added. Some of the reasons for economies of scale as the firm grows may be:

1. Putting several plants under one management economizes on top-echelon management. Also, a large firm can afford specialized staff, such as lawyers, tax accountants, and economists.
2. A larger firm may be able to serve the full range of its customers' needs, or use a common distribution system for many products, or use a common technology to manufacture a variety of products.
3. Large firms can realize the economies of mass marketing, with nationwide distribution and promotion.

---

[4] Empirical research has discovered all three types in the United States, with different shapes in different industries.

4. The large firm has a definite advantage in the financial markets. In general, large firms can negotiate lower interest rates on loans and lower costs of floating stock or bond issues to obtain capital.

In Panel C of Exhibit 11–16, economies of scale beyond Q^* are realized up to a certain size of the firm. After that, diseconomies of scale may set in, although there is some disagreement among economists about what happens to long-run average costs once economies of scale have been fully realized by the firm. Some economists think that long-run average costs then remain constant. Others think that they begin to rise because of problems of coordination and control by management.

Summary

A thorough understanding of the concept of cost is necessary for optimal allocation of resources to production, for pricing of the product, for control of costs, and for planning for future production. All costs involve sacrifice of some kind. Beyond that common ground, however, costs can be classified in many different ways, and cost concepts differ considerably, depending upon who uses them.

The theory of cost is concerned with both short-run and long-run costs. The short run is defined as that period of time during which some inputs, and therefore some costs, are fixed. Business firms always *operate* in the short run, and operational decision making is concerned with minimizing costs of variable inputs. *Planning*, however, is based on the concept that *all* inputs are variable in the long run.

Two factors determine the behavior of short-run costs: (1) the character of the underlying production function and (2) prices of the variable inputs. In analyzing the total cost function, we may develop and graph functions representing marginal cost, average fixed cost, average variable cost, and average total cost (which may also be called unit cost). The elasticity of cost measures the percentage change in total cost that results from a 1 percent change in the quantity produced. It is easily calculated as the ratio of marginal cost to average total cost, MC/ATC. The most cost-efficient level of production occurs when cost elasticity equals 1.

Economies of scale may be realized at either the plant level or firm level. Within the constraints of existing technology, it is possible to construct an optimally sized plant for whatever level of production is desired. In choosing a plant size, the probability distribution of expected demand must be considered. If the spread is narrow, a specialized plant designed to produce the expected demand at lowest cost might be appropriate. But if the spread is wide, it might be better to design a more generalized plant to give reasonable, but not necessarily the lowest, cost over a wider range of output.

In multiplant firms, economies of scale may arise over and above those realized from plants of optimal size. Such economies are most notable in the areas of management, marketing, and finance.

Problems

1.   Differentiate between incremental and sunk costs. Are all sunk costs fixed costs? Are all fixed costs sunk costs? Discuss.

2.   In estimating the annual cost of owning a fully paid-for $10,000 automobile, you might show the following cost entry: "Interest on investment at 15 percent: $1,500." What would this mean? Explain.

3.   Road-Ready Tire Company manufactures and sells about 1,000 tires a day at a unit cost of $16 and a wholesale price of $25. The company has an unexpected opportunity to sell additional tires under private labels to three different retail outlets. Thus, Able's Auto Accessories offers to buy 100 tires for $23 each; Baker's Auto Accessories offers to buy 100 tires at $20 each; and Charlie's Auto Accessories offers to buy 100 tires for $18 each. Road-Ready figures its unit costs on these additional tires to be $17 for the first 100 tires, $18 for the second 100 tires, and $19 for the third 100 tires.

a.   If there are no other considerations, which of these orders should Road-Ready agree to fill?

b.   What fundamental principles are involved here?

4.   Accuro Division of Metropolitan Instruments Company manufactures miniature calculators, which it sells to a limited number of exclusive dealers. Accuro's normal production rate is 260 units per week at a total cost of $3,200. At full capacity it can produce 340 units per week at a total cost of $3,800.

a.   What is the average cost per calculator under normal operating conditions?   3200/260

b.   What is the average variable cost per calculator? 3500/3200 · 600/80 = 6.5

c.   What is the total fixed cost? 3200 - 1950

d.   What is the average fixed cost per calculator under normal operating conditions?

e.   A foreign distributor offers to buy 50 calculators per week from Accuro over a one-month period, to be marketed under a different brand name. The distributor offers a price of $10 per calculator. Should Accuro accept the offer? What is the least price Accuro should accept for this kind of arrangement?

5.   The total cost function of a neckwear manufacturing company is $Q = 8 + 12X - 6X^2 + X^3$, where Q represents total cost (in hundreds of dollars per month) and X is output (in hundreds of ties produced per month).

a. What is the equation for average total cost?
b. What is the equation for average variable cost?
c. What is the equation for marginal cost?
d. Plot the total and fixed cost curves for $X = 0, 0.5, 1, \ldots, 5$. Plot the ATC, AVC, and MC curves for these values of X. Back up your graph with a complete cost schedule.

6. Dream Furniture Company has been experiencing operating losses in its plant for a number of months.
a. What cost factors should management consider in deciding whether to shut down its factory?
b. Is there a difference between abandonment and shutdown?
c. Is it possible for the company to recover part of its plant cost while operating at a loss? (Hint: What is the role of depreciation and its influence on cash flow?)

7. Motivated by rapidly increasing costs of diesel fuel, and by rather strong evidence that fuel economy depends upon vehicle speed, the Highway International Trucking Company has undertaken a study to determine fuel efficiency versus speed for its truck fleet. The "bottom line" of the study is an equation that relates miles per gallon MPG to miles per hour MPH:

$$MPG = 0.11 \; MPH - 0.001 \; MPH^2$$

a. Find the optimal speed to minimize fuel consumption.
b. The company estimates that diesel fuel will cost an average of $1 a gallon during the upcoming year. Calculate the fuel cost per mile if the fleet is driven at (1) the optimal speed, (2) 50 mph, and (3) 60 mph.
c. Suppose the company's drivers are currently paid by the route, rather than by mileage or hours (within limitations, of course). However, a suggestion has been made to utilize a new compensation scheme that would be based on hours; for example, drivers would be paid $15 an hour. Explain how each of these possible compensation arrangements (pay by the route, pay by the mile, and pay by the hour) is related to the optimal speed determined above. It is not necessary to find the precisely correct answer to the question, although a graph or an appropriately constructed table will help.

8. Speed-Marine builds motorboat engines. They recently estimated their annual total cost and total revenue functions to be:

$$TC = 80,000 - 600Q + 2Q^2$$
$$TR = 400Q - Q^2$$

where Q is the number of engines produced each year.
a. At what levels of production will Speed-Marine break even?
b. How many engines should be produced to maximize profit?

c. If the minimum satisfactory profit for Speed-Marine is $1,700, what is the amount of sacrificeable profits? (Hint: Review Chapter 1, Sales Maximization Theory.)

9.   Allied Wrench Inc. produces 9,000 multipurpose locking pliers that sell for $9.50 each. Its present cost function is estimated to be:

$$TC = 25,000 + 3.7Q$$

However, Allied is considering renovating its facilities. The new, technologically advanced plant would have an estimated cost function of:

$$TC = 34,000 + 2.5Q$$

The marketing department claims that the demand for the locking pliers fits a normal distribution with an expected mean value of 14,000 units per year.

a. What are the present TC, TFC, TVC, ATC, AVC, and MC?
b. Would you be in favor of renovating the plant?
c. What is the break-even point for both plant designs?
d. Which plant design is more specialized?
e. If leading economic indicators showed a recession is likely, would this alter your decision on whether to renovate?

Case Problem: Sealift Shipping Lines

10.   Sealift is a container shipping company based in Singapore. Business is expanding along with increasing trade in the Pacific, so management is investigating the purchase of new containers from a steel manufacturer in Japan. The present containers are cubic with a reinforced base and corrugated metal sides and top. They have 1,000 cubic feet of cargo space. The Japanese manufacturer reports that the reinforced base costs $7.00 per square foot and metal siding costs $3.20 per square foot. The containers can be built in any size.

Questions:
a. What is the present metal cost per cubic foot of cargo space?
b. Management is considering building larger containers in hopes of reducing costs. Sketch a graph of metal cost as it relates to cargo space (assume a cubic container). What is the optimal size container?
c. Discuss the problem of size. For example, how big do you build a warehouse, football stadium, or oil tanker?

Case Problem: Fertile Farm, Inc.

11.   The Fertile Farm corporation has fertilizer plants located all over the United States. Its phosphate division, located in Oakland, Califor-

nia, is presently under review by top management. Last year's prices for raw phosphates climbed by over 60 percent to $.75 per pound, and each bag of fertilizer contains four pounds of raw phosphates. The price rise is a result of environmental regulation levied on South Pacific island suppliers because of their strip mining practices. However, since new deposits of phosphates have been recently discovered in Florida, it is unknown whether prices will continue to rise.

Top management is attempting to find out how high phosphate prices can go before the Oakland fertilizer plant should shut down. To assist in this task, the accounting department has forecast the following costs for next year. Included is some important supplementary information.

Cost Forecast ($000)	Annual Production (000 bags)		
	70	100	120*
Raw materials, other than phosphates	$210	$300	$360
Variable manufacturing costs†	145	195	280
Fixed costs			
Insurance	20	20	20
Property taxes	12	12	12
Depreciation (building, equipment and other)‡	50	50	50
Maintenance§	70	70	70
Cost of capital‖	86	86	86
Totals:	$593	$733	$878

* Maximum production capacity is 120,000 bags.

† A charge of 30 cents per bag is included for depreciation on processing machinery. The machinery originally cost $360,000 and had an estimated life of 12 years if production averaged 100,000 bags per year. With four years of use remaining, the market value of the machines is only $25,000. However, to replace them would cost $600,000.

‡ This is a 10 percent annual write-off. The actual deterioration of these assets is not related to production; instead, it is based on time and obsolescence factors. Present market value is $150,000, with four years of useful life remaining. Replacement cost is expected to be $600,000.

§ One third of this amount is required whether or not the plant is operating.

‖ Fertile Farm requires a 10 percent return on investment.

Because of low farm prices and a very competitive fertilizer market, the price of Fertile Farm's phosphate fertilizer is expected to remain at $11.25 per bag for the foreseeable future. If management should decide to shut down, plant engineers estimate $10,000 in additional costs. Another factor in management's decision is a land-use hearing presently in the courts. If Fertile Farm wins the case, the plant's waterfront property can be rezoned from industrial to commercial, increasing its value from $500,000 to $2,400,000.

Questions:
a. Using the available cost figures, prepare a report for next year that analyzes the cost of shutting down for one year. Use this cost to show the break-even price that could be paid for phosphates at each level of production. Be explicit with regard to all costs.
b. What conclusions can be drawn from your cost analysis? Discuss other factors involved in the shutdown decision.
c. Because of the questionable returns of its phosphate division, management is considering termination of the Oakland facility. Assess the plant's profitability, assuming that phosphate prices remain stable. Should the facility be terminated?
d. What effect would the land-use ruling have on your decision?

Case Problem: Performance Motors Inc. (PMI)

12. PMI specializes in automobile modification. Recently it received a contract from a large Detroit auto manufacturer to modify 1,500 production cars with a high-performance package, which will increase the car's horsepower and handling capabilities. For meeting the terms of the contract PMI will receive $2,150 per car.

The chief accountant for PMI has spent a week going over the contract and estimates the following costs:

1. Direct labor, 33,000 hours at $18 per hour.
2. Parts needed from existing inventories originally cost $325,000. However, current replacement costs are $410,000.
3. Additional necessary parts will be purchased at a cost of $750,000.
4. A calibrated cylinder resurfacer will be required to increase engine compression. The machine rents for $65,000 for the life of the contract.
5. To finance the six-month project PMI will need a loan of $600,000, and its current credit standing results in an interest rate of 12.5 percent.
6. To consult on the project, a renowned Italian race car designer will be brought in at a cost of $39,000.
7. Variable overhead costs are allocated to projects by a $5 charge per direct labor hour.
8. To obtain the required return on capital, standard procedure at PMI is to charge a 75 percent profit margin on both direct labor costs and the purchase price of all materials used.

Slumping U.S. auto sales over the last few years have resulted in excessive capacity at PMI. Thus acceptance of this contract will not interrupt present or future production schedules.

Questions:

a. Which costs are relevant to PMI's decision? Is each cost explicit or implicit?
b. Should PMI accept or reject the auto modification contract?
c. Assume that the oil glut, through its effect in reducing gas prices, has spurred the demand for powerful, high-performance cars. PMI now has contracts to maintain production capacity for over two years. Under these conditions, have the relevant costs changed? Should PMI accept or reject the contract?

References

Anthony, Robert N. "What Should 'Cost' Mean?" *Harvard Business Review,* May–June 1970, pp. 121–31.

Bassett, Lowell. "Returns to Scale and Cost Curves." *Southern Economic Journal,* October 1969, pp. 189–90.

Berndt, Ernst R., and Catherine J. Morrison. "Capacity Utilization Measures: Underlying Economic Theory and an Alternative Approach." *American Economic Review,* May 1981, pp. 48–52.

Gould, J. P., and C. E. Ferguson. *Microeconomic Theory.* 5th ed. Homewood, Ill.: Richard D. Irwin, 1980, chap. 7.

Hirshleifer, Jack. "The Firm's Cost Function: A Successful Reconstruction." *Journal of Business,* July 1962, pp. 235–55.

Koot, Ronald S., and David A. Walker. "Short-Run Cost Functions of a Multiproduct Firm." *Journal of Industrial Economics* April 1970, pp. 118–28.

McElroy, F. W. "Return to Scale of Cost Curves: Comment." *Southern Economic Journal,* October 1970, pp. 227–28.

Miller, Edward, M. "The Extent of Economies of Scale: The Effect of Firm Size on Labor Productivity and Wage Rates." *Southern Economic Journal,* January 1978, pp. 470–87.

Shephard, A. Ross. "A Note on the Firm's Long-Run Average Cost Curve." *Quarterly Review of Economics and Business,* Spring 1971, pp. 77–79.

Stigler, G. J. "The Economies of Scale." *Journal of Law and Economics,* October 1958, pp. 54–71. (Reprinted in **G. J. Stigler.** *The Organization of Industry.* Homewood, Ill.: Richard D. Irwin, 1968, chap. 7.)

Walters, A. A. "Production and Cost Functions: An Econometric Survey." *Econometrica,* January–April 1963, pp. 1–66.

12

Empirical Estimation of Cost Functions

In the preceding chapter on cost analysis, we discussed both short-run and long-run cost functions. Knowledge of the firm's *short-run* cost function is essential for current operational decisions, such as finding the most efficient level of production, or pricing output. Knowledge of the firm's *long-run* cost function is essential for proper planning of the firm's future operations. It provides a guide to economies of scale and the optimum size for both plant and firm. In this chapter, we will discuss the techniques and problems of empirical measurement of costs and the consequent estimation of cost functions that reflect as closely as possible the actual cost-output relationship for a firm or group of firms, both in the short run and the long run.

Estimation of Short-Run Cost Functions

In this section we are concerned with the conceptual and empirical problems associated with the construction of short-run cost functions for a particular firm or group of firms. The analysis of short-run costs reveals how a firm's costs vary in response to changes in output within a time span short enough that the size of the plant may be regarded as fixed. Several methods exist by which an analysis of costs can be undertaken, but three of these, embracing accounting, engineering, and econometric approaches, are the most common.

Accounting method. Essentially, the method used by cost accountants is to classify the data into various cost categories (e.g., fixed, variable, semivariable) and then to take observations at the extreme and various intermediate output levels. In this manner linear or curvilinear cost functions are estimated and built up from the basic data, with little or no attention normally paid to formulating hypotheses or accounting for changes in factor prices or other conditions that may have affected costs.

Engineering method. In the engineering approach, emphasis is placed primarily on the nature of physical relationships such as pounds of supplies and materials used or rated capacity, and these relationships are then converted into dollars to arrive at an estimate of costs. This method uses knowledge of the firm's production facilities and technology to determine the most efficient combination of raw materials, capital equipment, and labor for the production of various levels of output. "Most efficient," of course, means "at the lowest average cost." In determining a firm's most efficient cost structure, the engineering method charges each unit of output with costs that *ought* to be incurred rather than with costs that have actually occurred in the past. This method may be particularly useful when good historical data are difficult or impossible to obtain.

Statistical or econometric method. The statistical approach combines regression analysis with economic theory to measure the net effect of output variations on cost. Its basic assumption is that the firm has been operating efficiently, or at least that inefficiencies can be isolated. Frequently the goal is to construct a cost function from time-series or cross-sectional data that will reflect as closely as possible the static cost curve of economic theory. However, since the empirical curve is at best only an average of past relationships, it is not an exact replica of the theoretical cost curves discussed in economics textbooks.

These three approaches to cost measurement should not be regarded as mutually exclusive or even competitive, but rather as supplementary and complementary to one another. As always, the emphasis placed on any method depends on the purpose of the investigation, that is, what it is that management really needs and wants, as well as the time and expense involved, considering the availability of data.

Objectives and Problems of Cost Measurement

Certain measurement problems concerning various adjustments in the data and other considerations must be taken into account when attempting to derive empirical functions from economic data. As in the measurement of demand and production, so too in the measurement of cost, there are problem areas of a methodological nature to be considered. Some of the more essential ones may be sketched briefly at this time.

Basically, the problem is to derive a cost function, expressed mathematically as an equation or geometrically as a curve, that will show the net relationship between the firm's costs and its rate of output. If the shape of the cost curve depended solely on the rate of output, solving the problem would be fairly simple. Unfortunately, costs depend on a number of factors in addition to output, so the problem resolves itself into eliminating these other cost determinants in order to arrive at a cost function that reasonably expresses the cost-output relation. Generally speaking, the following problem areas are among the important preliminary ones that must be handled in preparing the empirical analysis.[1]

1.   **Time Period of Measurement.**   The choice of an appropriate time period on which to base the analysis involves three important considerations: normality, variety, and length of observation.

Normality.   The time period should be a "normal" or typical one for the firm, so far as this is possible. This means that the period covered should be one that was reasonably static in that changes in technology, plant size, efficiency, and other dynamic occurrences that may have a significant bearing on costs were either nonexistent or at least at a minimum. Admittedly, a completely static period would probably be impossible to find. However, a period in which changes were relatively minor would be acceptable if the data could be adjusted to compensate for the differences; if not, the cost function will not reflect the typical type of cost behavior desired.

Variety.   The period should be one in which there were sufficiently wide variations in output so that enough observations for a regression analysis can be obtained. Further, if the results are to be used as a guide for future planning, the period should be recent enough to include data that will be basically relevant for the future. In many instances a minimum of 3 to 5 years is used as a source of data for a business cycle of, say, 7 to 10 years or thereabouts. On the other hand, if the normality conditions stated above are satisfied, a full business cycle may be preferable as an analysis period.

Length of Observation.   The period chosen should be one in which the observational unit (week, month, quarter, or year) is minimized to the extent that completeness of the data will permit. A small observation

---

[1] Of course, some of these problems pertain to the investigation of long-run as well as short-run costs.

unit such as a week, or perhaps a month, will allow measurement of slight output variations more readily, say, than will a year. Further, the cause-effect relationship between output and cost is more readily discernible with small rather than large observational units. Frequently, a month is the typical unit chosen in cost studies, although analyses have also been conducted on quarterly and annual bases because of technicalities involving inventory changes, cost reporting dates, and so forth.

2.   Technical Homogeneity.   Significant cost variations may be caused by differences in raw materials, equipment, frequency of production lags, and other changes in production conditions at different levels of output during the time span under study. In order to minimize such effects, the plant chosen for a statistical cost analysis should be characterized by an input and output structure that is as *technically homogeneous* as possible.

On the *input* side, this means that identical or very similar units within factor classes should be used. For example, use of identical or very similar units of equipment is necessary to prevent variations in cost due to different machines' being brought into production at different output levels. On the *output* side it means that the number of different products produced should, ideally, be small enough to facilitate measurement, and these products should not undergo significant cost changes (due, for example, to changes in composition or style) during the analysis period. If these conditions of output homogeneity are not met, the analysis may require that a weighted index of output be constructed for products or for classes of products, according to some logical criterion. Various approaches and techniques are possible.

Thus, in a study of production costs for steel, tons shipped rather than tons produced was found to be more useful because inventory fluctuations (the difference between production and shipments) were relatively small. In a cost study made for a clock manufacturer, the weights used for the output index were based on direct labor costs; in a cost analysis of a men's clothing factory, on the other hand, square feet of wool of a specific grade was chosen as the measure of output, from which conversion coefficients were derived for other types of materials used by the company.

In short, a number of preliminary measures must frequently be developed based on theoretical considerations. The particular one chosen is the one that accords best with economic analysis and statistical criteria.

3.   Cost Adjustment.   The third problem area in cost analysis involves decisions as to the proper choice of data and the types of adjustments needed to correct the data if they are to be recast into a meaningful cost function. The problem as a whole breaks down into three parts: cost inclusion, deflation, and cost-output timing.

Cost Inclusion.   Since the object is to arrive at a cost-output relation, the problem is to select only those elements of cost that vary with (are functionally related to) output. Thus, various kinds of overhead and allocated expenses that do not bear any relation to production rates should be excluded. Sometimes a series of preliminary correlations must be made to determine which costs should and should not be included in the final analysis. Also, it should be mentioned that total rather than unit (average) costs should be used in conducting most statistical cost analyses, for two main reasons: (1) the results are likely to be more reliable statistically because average cost is a ratio of two variables and therefore more susceptible to error, which in turn may cause magnified errors in the derived marginal cost function; (2) the marginal and average cost functions can be readily derived mathematically from the total cost function if desired, or the marginal and average cost figures can be derived by simple arithmetic if a cost table or schedule is constructed from the total cost equation.

Deflation.   In the construction of empirical cost functions, the data must often be "reduced" or deflated to a particular base period if the results are to be meaningful. Wages and equipment price indexes are readily available and are frequently used for such purposes, or the analyst may construct his own indexes if it seems desirable. In any event, the purpose of deflating the data is to adjust for significant inflationary changes in input prices during the analysis period.

Cost-Output Timing.   A third area of an adjustment often made addresses the problem of obtaining the correct correspondence of cost and output. Costs are not normally recorded in the books of account in such a manner that they are readily traceable to the output variations that created them. Usually, technical engineering estimates will be necessary if the correct timing associations are to be established between the two variables, cost and output.[2] Of particular importance in this respect are certain costs that are usually charged as a function of time, such as depreciation (normally on a straight line basis). These costs, or portions

---

[2] Some costs lead or lag the corresponding output. One example is the maintenance of machinery, buildings, and equipment. When production peaks at or near full capacity, routine maintenance may be deferred until a slack period occurs. When this maintenance finally is performed (during the first slack period), however, its cost properly belongs to the earlier period of high output. Charging maintenance costs elsewhere would result in a gross distortion of the cost function.

thereof, must first be adjusted or recalculated as a function of output rate before they can be incorporated in the overall cost function.

Identification of Relevant Costs

Some of the difficulties encountered during statistical cost analyses stem from an inaccurate identification of the costs that are relevant to the purposes of the study. Since managerial decision making is future-oriented, the only costs relevant to the decision are future costs. Historical costs available in a firm's records may point to the future, but they may have to be modified before they can be used for decision making.

It is also important to recognize that opportunity costs—not recorded on company accounts—have an important bearing on the future. Indeed, opportunity costs may be the largest and most important consideration in a short-run decision problem. That is to say, what the firm has not been doing but could be doing might be the key issue.

Procedure for Statistical Analysis

As we have just seen, the analyst must exercise great care in gathering data. The selection and adjustment of data, the choice of appropriate time periods, the problem of technical homogeneity, and the need for relevant data are very real and necessary concerns. Once these considerations have been addressed and adequate data gathered on output and associated costs, the analyst's next task is to develop cost schedules like the one illustrated in Exhibit 12–1.

Exhibit 12–1_____

Development of Cost Schedules

(1) Output (units) Q	(2) Total Cost TC	(3) Total Fixed Cost TFC	(4) Total Variable Cost TVC	(5) Average Total Cost $ATC = TC/Q$	(6) Average Variable Cost $AVC = TVC/Q$	(7) Marginal Cost $MC = \Delta TC/\Delta Q$
0	$100	$100	$ 0	—	—	$2.60
50	230	100	130	$4.60	$2.60	1.10
100	285	100	185	2.85	1.85	1.50
150	360	100	260	2.40	1.73	.
.	.	.	.	.	.	.
.	.	.	.	.	.	.
500	890	100	790	1.78	1.58	—

The first three columns in Exhibit 12–1 contain the empirical data gathered by the analyst. Column 1 contains the level of output arranged in ascending order. Column 2 contains the total cost associated with each level of output. Column 3 contains the fixed cost, which by definition does not change with the level of output. Column 4 contains the total variable cost, which equals $TC - TFC$. The remaining columns are easily calculated from the data by the formulas shown on the exhibit.

The complete table of Exhibit 12–1 is, of course, a presentation in tabular form of a set of *discrete* cost functions. What we want, however, is a set of *continuous* cost functions in the form of equations and graphs from which future costs at any level of production may be estimated. Once the preliminary considerations are out of the way, there remains the problem of choosing the type of equation or curve that seems to fit the data best, justified as much as possible by economic theory.

Least squares multiple regression is the method by which the data are best fitted to curves. This means that the analyst must choose among the three types of curves that can be fitted by the least squares technique: linear, quadratic, and cubic. The choice of one or the other depends upon how well the mathematical properties of the function represent the economics of the particular case. If there is no particular reason for choosing one, the data might be fitted with all three curves. In that case, the coefficient of determination, R^2, of the regression analysis would show which curve gives the best fit.

Examples of Short-Run Cost Studies

During the past five decades, economists have conducted many studies of short-run cost functions in widely differing industries. Most studies used time-series data, but some used engineering data. Regardless of the method used or the kind of industry that was investigated, they all reached the same conclusion: most short-run cost functions are linear over the normal range of output. That is to say, short-run marginal costs were constant while short-run average costs declined slightly, as previously depicted by Exhibit 11–8 in Chapter 11. While some U-shaped marginal and average cost curves were found to exist, they seem to be the exception rather than the rule. This is illustrated by Exhibit 12–2, which shows the results of some studies that were undertaken by statistical analysis of time-series data.

Eight of the 13 studies listed on Exhibit 12–2 found clear evidence of a linear cost function. Do studies such as these invalidate the theoretical curvilinear cost functions that we discussed in Chapter 11? Not at all. There are several reasons why the true underlying curvilinear cost function may not be apparent in an empirical investigation.

Exhibit 12–2

Some Empirical Investigations of Short-Run Costs

Investigator(s)	Date	Type of Industry	Findings
Broster	1938	Railways in United Kingdom	Operating cost per unit of output falls
Dean	1936	Furniture	Constant MC, SRAC "failed to rise"
Dean	1941	Leather belts	No significant increase in MC
Dean	1941	Hosiery	Constant MC, SRAC "failed to rise"
Dean	1942	Department Store	MC declining in one department, constant in two
Ehrke	1933	Cement	Ehrke interprets as constant MC, but Apel (1948) argues that MC is increasing
Eiteman and Guthrie	1952	Manufacturing	MC below AC at all outputs below capacity
Ezekiel and Wylie	1941	Steel	Declining MC, but large standard errors
Hall and Hitch	1939	Manufacturing	Majority have decreasing MC
Johnston	1960	Electricity in United Kingdom	ATC falls, then flattens, tending toward constant MC up to capacity
Johnston	1960	Multiple food products processing	Direct cost is linear; MC is constant
Lester	1946	Manufacturing	AVC decreases up to capacity levels of output
Mansfield and Wein*	1958	Railways in United Kingdom	Constant MC
Nordin	1947	Light plant	Increasing MC
Yntema	1940	Steel	Constant MC

* Used engineering method rather than time-series analysis.
Source: A. A. Walters, "Production and Cost Functions," *Econometrica*, January 1963, pp. 1–66.

1.   As econometrics textbooks point out, a curve fitted by the least squares regression method is the best we can get. Nevertheless, it is still only an approximation of the true function. If the true function is curvilinear but the curvature is slight, the fact that the line actually bends may not be detected because of random scatter or an insufficient number of observation points. This is no cause for concern. As Joel Dean reported in his study of a department store,

> "The unexplained scatter of observations is great enough to permit a cubic of the traditional form to be fitted in each case. However, the curvature would be so slight as to be insignificant from a managerial viewpoint, so that it could scarcely affect any economic conclusions which might be derived from the linear functions."[3]

2.   Aside from the mechanics of least squares curve fitting, the linearity of short-run cost functions may be explained by the way in which the fixed, or capital, inputs are actually used. Microeconomic theory holds that the employment or use of capital inputs is fixed in the short run. At low levels of output, capital inputs are underutilized. As production increases, a more favorable use of the capital (fixed) inputs causes marginal costs to fall, but at a decreasing rate of change, until the mix of fixed and variable input is optimal. At this level of production, marginal cost is at a minimum. After that, additional variable inputs put a strain on the capital inputs that is reflected as diminishing productivity and increasing marginal costs.

That is the theory. In actual production systems, however, the use of capital inputs may be matched with variable inputs in such a way that a fairly constant ratio is maintained. For example, a manufacturing firm can increase production by setting up an additional assembly line in which the ratio of capital (fixed factor) to labor (variable factor) remains constant. In other words, there is a variable employment of the fixed factor; hence the rate of usage of each unit of capital is almost constant regardless of the level of production. Under such circumstances, the law of diminishing returns does not hold. The marginal cost of output remains constant, and a linear cost function is the result.[4]

3.   Finally, we have to consider that these studies covered only those periods in which the firm was operating in its normal range of output. No observations were included at very low or very high levels. If the firm were operating at or near capacity, a very rapid increase in marginal costs could be expected. As the firm attempts to get more and more

---

[3] Joel Dean, *Managerial Economics* (Englewood Cliffs, N.J.: Prentice-Hall, 1951), p. 254.

[4] Researchers advancing this explanation distinguish between variable *employment* of the fixed factor (a short-run concept) and variable *magnitude* of the fixed factor (a long-run concept). For example, a large enough floor area can be used for either one or two assembly lines in the short run.

production out of its fixed facilities, it is likely that wage premiums will have to be paid either for overtime or for additional shifts. A third shift, especially, not only draws higher wages but also is less productive than a day shift. As the equipment is used more intensively, it breaks down more often, running up maintenance costs and creating hang-ups in production. Marginal or obsolete equipment may have to be used. Hiring standards may have to be lowered to get enough labor. In other words, everything the firm does to squeeze out the last ounce of capacity has to be done less efficiently, at greater cost.

This conclusion has been supported by surveys of manufacturing firms concerning the rates at which they would prefer to operate. Most firms respond that they prefer to operate in the neighborhood of 90 percent capacity. Apparently, these firms expect to achieve maximum efficiency and therefore minumum average total cost at about 90 percent of capacity. The clear implication is that getting the last 10 percent would cause marginal and average costs to rise.

Estimation of Long-Run Costs

As we pointed out earlier in this chapter, day-to-day operational decisions are short-run in nature. But planning for the future requires a study of long-run costs to determine whether or not management has achieved an optimal scale of plant for the technological level of manufacturing applicable to its industry. A long-run cost study is particularly important for three purposes:

1. *Expansion decision:* Appropriate expansion enables the firm to keep up with the industry. Consider, for example, the firm whose short-run situation develops the $SRAC_1$ curve in Exhibit 11–13 of the preceding chapter. If all firms were similarly poised, and assuming there were no barriers to entry or expansion, there would be a tendency for firms with larger plants (closer to $SRAC_3$) to enter the industry. There would also be a tendency for existing firms to expand their own facilities either through investment or mergers. In both cases, these movements would be made to obtain a more efficient base of operation, that is, lower unit costs and a decline in output price.

2. *Merger decision:* A long-run cost curve can help management to decide on the advisability of a merger. As already noted, a concern that expects economies of scale as a result of expanding its base of operations has a positive incentive to do so as long as the costs of such expansion do not exceed the benefits obtained. The long-run cost curve can at least serve as a guide in arriving at an answer.

3. *Evaluation of economic efficiency:* A final reason for studying the individual firm's long-run cost curve is that economies of scale are sometimes considered a public issue, especially in the case of antitrust allega-

tions. For example, if a potential merger has been shown to result in an unfair competitive advantage owing to anticipated cost savings among industry giants, the antitrust division of the Justice Department has sometimes stepped in to bar the arrangement. Alternatively, the federal government has also encouraged the merger or expansion of large companies when the public interest was thought to be served and/or the firms were controlled through further federal regulation. The economies of scale wrought by an integrated telephone system, the formation of the quasi-public Amtrak passenger rail system, and the "rescue" from bankruptcy of several aerospace and air carrier concerns through mergers provide examples. Similarly, the breaking up of General Motors into smaller units has been thwarted to date, perhaps in part because it has been successfully argued that the American consumer would ultimately suffer by paying higher prices for the passenger cars and other transport products of smaller, less efficient independent firms.

Methods of Estimation

Empirical investigation of long-run costs is similar to investigation of short-run costs, but considerably more complex. Since all costs are variable in the long run, the problem is to find the shape of the least-cost production curve for plants of different sizes. Some of the framework for the measurement of short-run cost functions applies to the measurement of long-run costs as well. However, there are additional problems in the measurement of size and cost in each of the methods discussed below.

Time-Series Analysis.   Regression analysis of time-series data is the most common method of short-run statistical analysis. In theory, it might be possible to extend the method to long-run cost analysis by examining the growth (increase in output level) of a single firm over a long span of time. More often than not, however, significant expansion of the firm is accompanied by significant changes in technology and other extraneous conditions. The resulting long-run cost curve would not be valid because the time-series data would actually pertain to a series of long-run cost curves rather than to the single curve that is desired.

Cross-Sectional Analysis.   Because of the difficulty described above, analysts rarely use time-series data for long-run cost studies. Rather, they use cross-sectional data to compare cost-output relationships of firms and plants whose sizes are different at some specific time. Therefore, the output level in each firm or plant becomes a primary independent variable.

While cross-sectional analysis eliminates many of the problems associated with time-series data, it creates some other problems of its own. For example, since all cross-sectional data pertain to the same time, there is no need to adjust for price inflation. But a number of other problems arise from differences among firms (or among plants in the same firm) in accounting methods, management practices, technology, and input factor prices. In particular:

1.   If a study involves a number of different-sized plants owned by a single firm, the very fact that plants are of different size indicates differences in technology.

2.   Regional differences may be expected in input factor prices, such as wage rates and the cost of transporting raw materials and finished goods into and away from the plant.

3.   Difficulties arise from differences in cost accounting practices among firms. For example, depreciation of assets and amortization of major expenses such as research and development are generally guided by tax laws rather than economic considerations. Even within the tax laws, different methods of depreciation and amortization are allowed, and these make a substantial difference in recorded costs. Many assets are valued at historical cost rather than at replacement or opportunity cost. Moreover, generally accepted accounting principles permit different methods of valuation of assets for costing purposes, such as FIFO (first-in, first-out) and LIFO (last-in, first-out).[5] On top of everything else, cost accountants must make arbitrary allocations of overhead costs and joint costs of production. The basis for such allocation may differ considerably from firm to firm and even from plant to plant within the same firm. All of these considerations add up to a very substantial distortion of the true cost/output relationship.

4.   Another statistically significant distortion may arise from different methods of payment for input factors. For example, total compensation for labor typically includes more than wage payments. Additional fringe benefits may include such things as vacation with pay, sick pay, health insurance, life insurance, retirement plans, profit sharing, and many other employee benefits. These "sweeteners" vary widely from firm to firm and their actual cost is extremely difficult to estimate.

5.   Even if these data problems are resolved satisfactorily, there is still the assumption that each firm is operating efficiently in the most efficient plant available for production at the level it has chosen. In other words, each firm is operating at the point on its long-run average cost *(LRAC)* curve at which its costs are minimal. If this assumption is not valid, then the derived cost curve will lie above the true *LRAC* curve, and costs will be overstated. Perhaps more important than cost overstatement would be the distortion of the true curvature, so that available economies (or diseconomies) of scale would be overstated.

---

[5] See Chapter 13 for more detailed explanation of FIFO and LIFO.

Engineering Method.   The engineering method of cost analysis rests upon a thorough understanding of the underlying physical production function and the analyst's ability to hold constant such factors as production technology and efficiency, product mix, and input factor prices. By developing standard costs based upon currently available production technology, the engineering method avoids many of the cost accounting problems of resource valuation and cost allocation. The cost analyst first determines the best (least-cost) combination of inputs to achieve a given level of output. Each input quantity is then multiplied by the input price. The output level and the sum of input costs then become coordinates of a point on the long-run cost curve. Since the sum of the input costs can be changed only by changing the mix of inputs, the effect is to isolate the effect of changes in input from all other factors.

Thus we see that the engineering method avoids the contamination of data by extraneous factors that is so troublesome in statistical methods. In particular, it avoids the mixture of old and new technology that is inherent in historical data. But the engineering method is not without its own problems—indeed, it suffers from at least three important limitations:

1.   Total costs associated with a product or line of products necessarily include costs of selling and distributing the product(s), plus some share of administrative costs, as well as the costs of production. But the engineering method deals only with the costs of production. The other costs are ignored except to the degree that they are arbitrarily allocated as overhead.

2.   The engineering method deals not with costs that have been actually incurred, but with costs as they ought to be under ideal conditions. This necessarily involves subjective opinion rather than facts, not only as to what the costs should be, but also as to what the ideal conditions are and the degree to which they can be achieved. Thus, given the same basic problem, no two analysts can be expected to reach the same conclusion.

3.   The engineering method deals with *currently* available technology and *current* factor prices. But the essence of long-run analysis is prediction of the *future*. The engineering method often gets into trouble when production functions are extended beyond the range of existing systems, or when they are extrapolated from pilot plant operations to full-scale facilities.

Survivor Method.   The survivor method was first developed in 1958 by George Stigler[6] of the University of Chicago, who was the winner of the Nobel prize in economics for 1982. The basic idea of the survivor method

---

[6] George J. Stigler, "The Economies of Scale," *Journal of Law and Economics*, October 1958, pp. 54–71.

is that the more efficient firms will survive over the long run, while less efficient firms will be driven out of the industry by competition. (More efficient firms are those with lower long-run average costs.)

The technique of the survivor method is to classify the firms in an industry by size, and then to determine the share of industry output or capacity that is provided by each class over a number of years. If the market share of a particular size-class grows larger over time, that size of firm or plant is deemed to be more efficient, with lower average costs. These empirical findings can then be interpreted to form a long-run cost curve. For example, suppose that both the smallest and largest classes suffered declining market shares, while the shares of middle-sized firms were increasing. This would indicate a U-shaped long-run cost curve, with economies of scale first increasing, then relatively constant, then decreasing.

The survivor method is more direct and easier to apply than other techniques for looking at economies of scale. It avoids problems of resource valuation and allocation of overhead cost required by the statistical method as well as the hypothetical aspects of the engineering method. However, it obviously cannot be used unless the industry has been established long enough for trends to become apparent. Furthermore, this method has the following limitations:

1. The basic premise of the survivor technique is that all firms operate in a highly competitive environment, in which survival depends upon the ability to minimize long-run average costs. Minimum costs imply maximum profits. However, many firms, and particularly large firms, manage to survive without attempting to maximize profits.
2. The survivor method will show that increasing or decreasing returns to scale may exist, thereby indicating an optimal size, but it does not show the relative inefficiency of operating at a scale larger or smaller than optimum. That is to say, it does not show whether operating at a different scale is *somewhat* inefficient, or *very* inefficient.
3. The survivor method is concerned with analysis over a long span of time. This makes it especially vulnerable to distortion caused by changing technology.

Some Results of Long-Run Cost Studies

Exhibit 12–3 summarizes the results of 16 empirical studies of long-run costs reported by Professor A. A. Walters and 1 reported by V. Gupta.

It is interesting to note that 13 of the 17 studies listed in Exhibit 12–3 used the statistical method of cross-sectional analysis. Seven of these 13

Exhibit 12–3

Results of Empirical Studies of Long-Run Costs

Investigator(s)	Date	Type of Industry	Method*	Findings
Bain	1956	Manufacturing (U.S.)	Q	Small economies of scale in multiplant firms
Gupta	1968	Manufacturing (India)	CS	*LRAC* L-shaped in 18 industries, U-shaped in 5, linear in 6
Moore	1961	Manufacturing (U.S.)	E	Economies of scale generally
Alpert	1959	Metals (U.S.)	E	Economies of scale to 80,000 lb/month then constant returns
Johnston	1960	Coal mining (U.K.)	CS	Wide dispersion of costs per ton
Dean and James	1942	Retail shoe store (U.S.)	CS	*LRAC* is U-shaped, but not because of diseconomies of scale
Holton	1956	Retailing (Puerto Rico)	E	*LRAC* is L-shaped, but Holton argues that inputs of management may be undervalued at high outputs.
Barts	1952	Railways (U.S.)	CS	*LRAC* either constant or falling
Barts	1960	Railways (U.S.)	CS	*LRAC* increasing in East, decreasing in South and West
Eads, Nerlove, and Raduchel	—	Airlines (U.S.)	CS,TS	No evidence of substantial economies of scale
Johnston	1960	Road passenger transport (U.K.)	CS	*LRAC* either falling or constant
Dhrymes and Kurz	—	Electricity (U.S.)	CS,TS	Substantial economies of scale
Gribbin	1953	Gas (U.K.)	CS	*LRAC* of production declines (no analysis of distribution)
Johnston	1960	Electricity (U.K.)	CS	*LRAC* of production declines (no analysis of distribution)
Lomax	1951	Gas (U.K.)	CS	*LRAC* of production declines (no analysis of distribution)
McNulty	1955	Electricity (U.S.)	CS	Average costs of administration are constant
Nerlove	1961	Electricity (U.S.)	CS	*LRAC*, excluding transmission costs, declines then shows signs of increase.

* CS = cross section, E = engineering, Q = questionnaire, TS = time-series, LRAC = long-run average cost.
Sources: A. A. Walter, "Production and Cost Functions," *Econometrica,* January 1963, pp. 1–66; V. Gupta, "Cost Functions, Concentration and Barriers to Entry in 29 Manufacturing Industries in India," *Journal of Industrial Economics,* November 1968, pp. 57–72.

found declining costs (increasing returns to scale) followed by constant costs. Three researchers chose the engineering method, and two of these three discovered essentially the same pattern. One researcher used a questionnaire to obtain data and discovered small economies of scale in multiplant manufacturing firms.

None of the studies reported by Walters used the survivor method. It has been used, however, first by Stigler and later by Allen. In 1930, 1938, and 1951, Stigler studied steel production by different-sized companies.[7] He found that returns to scale increased at low levels, decreased at high levels, and were nearly constant in the broad middle range. These results are depicted in Exhibit 12–4.

Exhibit 12–4

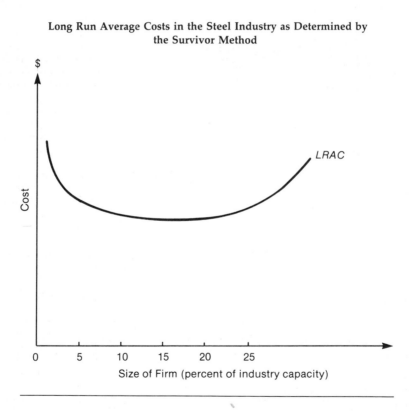

Long Run Average Costs in the Steel Industry as Determined by the Survivor Method

Stigler also examined the automobile industry, using the survivor method. This time he discovered an L-shaped curve. That is, economies of scale were achievable at low levels of production, followed by con-

---
[7] Ibid.

stant returns to scale, but there were never any diseconomies at high levels of output. In a later study of the Portland cement industry, using the survivor method, Allen also found an L-shaped long-run cost curve.[8] Many other researchers, using different methods, have obtained similar results. This has led researchers to advance the hypothesis that typical long-run average cost curves are L-shaped, as depicted in Exhibit 12–5, rather than U-shaped.

Exhibit 12–5

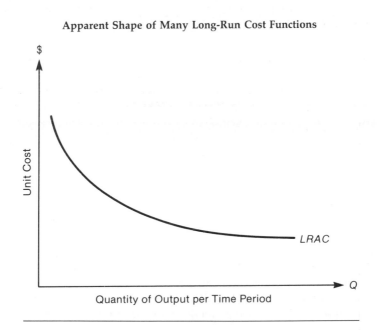

Apparent Shape of Many Long-Run Cost Functions

Conclusions

In the long-run, when a firm can change its use of any and all inputs, it will strive for just the right size to produce its output at the lowest possible cost. The right size depends upon the behavior of long-run costs as applied to a plant or to the firm as a whole. The long-run average cost ($LRAC$) curve for a plant will indicate its optimal size. When the firm has time to adjust all of its plants to optimal size, the $LRAC$ for the firm will indicate the optimal size of the firm. Thus the number and

---

[8] Bruce T. Allen, "Economies of Scale in the Portland Cement Industry, 1965–1971," working paper, Michigan State University; and "Vertical Integration and Market Foreclosure: The Case of Cement and Concrete," *Journal of Law and Economics*, April 1971, pp. 251–74.

size of the firms in a particular industry is largely determined by the behavior of long-run costs.

In theory, *LRAC* curves are U-shaped for both plant and firm. A number of empirical studies have found, however, that the LRAC curve did not turn up within the normal range of production. Consequently, the *LRAC* curve is L-shaped, indicating that there is room in those industries for firms or plants, as the case may be, to grow larger without increasing long-run average costs.

Problems of Empirical Estimation

The purpose of derived statistical cost functions is to isolate, from among the many factors that influence costs, the net effect of changes in output rates. In most of the studies that have been made, problems have been encountered that may be classified into two broad categories: *statistical* and *economic*. The statistical problems relate to difficulties in methodology and measurement; the economic problems concern the nature and validity of the results. Each may be treated separately for discussion purposes, even though there may be some overlapping in certain respects.

Statistical Problems

In the category of statistical problems, there are at least four broad classes: (1) measurement of output of diversified multiple products and the related problem of measuring the size of the firm; (2) dealing with technological change and the related problem of variation in the size of the firm; (3) measurement of costs of assets; and (4) choosing a measure of efficiency.

Measurement of Output of Multiple Products.   Most attempts to solve this problem have taken the form of weighting the quantity of each product by the proportion of total direct costs that is incurred by the product. In effect, this amounts to determining output as a function of costs, at least to some degree, when what is wanted is cost as a function of output. Despite this objection, however, it is difficult to see what other solution might be better, for the problem cannot easily be solved regardless of the sort of statistical procedures that may be employed.

Paralleling this problem is the difficulty of measuring the size of the firm in long-run studies. The more common practice has been to use assets or number of workers, the primary justification being that this provides a convenient way of measuring output by one input. A more accurate measure would appear to be sales, however, because in sales the various outputs are combined in proportion to their relative importance (prices).

Dealing with Technological Change.   Here the difficulties appear insurmountable. Whenever such change occurs, a new cost function, if not a new production function, comes into being and no amount of curve fitting will really compensate. At best, the results can only be roughly adjusted rather than accurately accounted for.

Closely related to this is the problem of variations in the size of the firm. What most analysts have done, rather than to solve these problems, is to avoid them, although carefully, by choosing firms and periods in which technological change and variations in size are absent. But when a problem is solved by avoiding its inherent difficulties, the solution is usually not very satisfactory.

Measuring Costs of Assets.   Statistical difficulties also exist in the measurement of the costs of assets. First, there is the problem of valuing raw materials inventory at cost or market. One argument is that they should not be valued in a cost study because they are not part of production. The other argument is that they should be valued, because an index of successful management is its ability to buy raw materials at low prices.

A further problem is the valuation of land. Accountants would value it at its definite and objective historical cost, but economists would hold that historical costs are irrelevant for decisions affecting the future. Nor would economists hold to current market value, because this is approximately equal to discounted future earnings, and the firm would always be earning the going rate of return on investment. (Problems of this type are discussed in the literature of capital budgeting.)

Choosing a Measure of Efficiency.   There are statistical considerations in choosing a measure of efficiency. For example, if rate of return on investment, a common measure, is used, companies paying high executive salaries instead of high dividends (as in smaller owner-officer corporations) will appear inefficient. One approach that has been suggested is to accept the corporation's decision as final; another is to adjust the salaries of officer-owned corporations to equality with nonofficer-owned corporations of equal size. Both methods are questionable, however, and the results of the two are quite different.

Still other problem areas could be mentioned, but enough has already been said to indicate the sort of difficulties frequently encountered in the empirical study of costs. It should be evident, therefore, that although studies of this kind can provide a useful guide for management planning, ambiguities exist in almost all such studies, and hence their practical value will depend upon how carefully they are interpreted.

Economic Problems

Many of the analysts who have investigated statistical cost functions have found a tendency for short-run total costs to be linear and hence marginal costs to be constant. Since this seems to contradict certain assumptions of economic theory, could it be that the theory is incorrect, unrealistic as to the facts, and hence in need of basic revisions? Various closely related explanations can be offered, all of which appear to contribute to the correct answer.

1.   Operating Range.   It is possible that the assumptions of economic theory are approximately correct, but total costs tend to be linear or nearly so within the practical operating range. If in empirical studies, wider ranges could be covered—closer to the output extremes of the total cost curve—the curve would bend in the end areas and thus yield decreasing and increasing marginal costs at these extremes.

2.   Constant Returns to Scale.   It is possible that the assumptions of economic theory are approximately correct, but constant marginal costs prevail over wide ranges of total cost. If this is true, it means that within the relevant range of the data, input or factor proportions are constant and therefore there are no significant economies or diseconomies of large-scale production. This leads to the inference that in the final analysis the only comprehensive test of efficiency is survival. If small firms tend to disappear and large ones survive, as in the automobile industry, we must conclude that small firms are relatively inefficient. If small firms survive and large ones tend to disappear, as in the textile industry, then large firms are relatively inefficient. In reality, however, we find that in most industries, firms of very different sizes tend to survive. Hence we conclude that in such industries there is no inherent advantage or disadvantage associated with size over a very wide range of outputs. In other words, it seems plausible to conclude that, in many different industries, constant returns to scale are a good approximation of reality.

3.   Dynamic Flexibility.   In a fluctuating, dynamic economy, firms have to be flexible so that they can adapt to changing business conditions. This means that they must be able to produce efficiently over a wide (normal) output range, and this in turn implies flat or nearly flat average and marginal costs, at least within that range.

It should be pointed out again that these three sets of explanations are not mutually exclusive. Each gives a valid partial account of why statistical total cost functions in industry have often been found to be linear, and marginal cost, therefore, to be constant.

Summary

Management requires knowledge of the firm's short-run cost function to make operational decisions and of the firm's long-run cost function to make planning decisions. Estimation of both short-run and long-run cost functions can be made from analysis of empirical data.

The goal of analysis is to construct a cost function that will reflect as closely as possible the static cost curve of economic theory. As discussed in the previous chapter, this is a cubic function, but it can have linear or quadratic segments.

Short-Run Estimation

For estimation of a short-run cost function, the most common method is statistical analysis of time-series data. When such data are not available, the engineering method may be used. In preparing for empirical analysis, the analyst must deal with at least four major problems:

1. Selection and adjustment of cost data to eliminate costs that should not be included, to account for inflation, and to obtain the proper correspondence between cost and output.
2. Selection of appropriate observation periods.
3. The need for technical homogeneity of both input and output.
4. Identification of relevant costs, including projection of historical costs into the future and inclusion of opportunity costs.

The procedure for statistical analysis is to gather the pertinent data, then fit a theoretical cost curve by means of least squares multiple linear regression. In a number of empirical studies, analysts have found clear evidence of a linear cost function. This does not invalidate the economic theory of diminishing returns. It merely indicates that the short-run cost function is approximately linear within the observed range of output.

Long-Run Estimation

Estimation of the firm's long-run cost curve is useful for guidance of the firm's expansion. The most common methods of estimation are statistical analysis of cross-sectional data, analysis of engineering data, and the survivor method. Each method has certain advantages and limitations.

Cross-sectional analysis eliminates many problems associated with time-series data. However, it must contend with difficulties that include:

1. Differences in technology among plants within a firm or firms within an industry.

2. Regional differences in input factor prices.
3. The nature of accounting data, which are usually the only cost data available.
4. Valuation of assets at historical cost rather than replacement or opportunity cost.
5. Arbitrary allocations of overhead costs and joint costs of production.
6. Different methods of payment for input factors, especially fringe benefits to labor.
7. The assumption that each plant and firm is operating efficiently, which may not be true.

The engineering method has certain distinct advantages, such as a constant, current technology as a basis for cost functions. By developing standard costs, the engineering method avoids many of the problems of resource valuation and cost allocation. However, the method suffers from certain limitations.

1. It is restricted to production costs and ignores selling, distribution, and administrative costs.
2. It deals with costs as they ought to be, rather than as they are.
3. It deals with current technology and current factor prices rather than the technology and costs of the future.

The survivor method is based on the premise that only the more efficient firms will survive competition over a long span of time. Its technique is to classify firms according to size, then to examine each size-class over the long run. If a certain size-class obtains a larger share of the market over time, that size is deemed to be more efficient, and vice versa.

A number of empirical studies have discovered long-run average cost curves that are either U-shaped with a very broad flat bottom, or else are L-shaped, with no cost upturn at the higher levels of output.

In general, empirical investigations have encountered two broad categories of problems: (1) statistical and (2) economic. Statistical problems fall into at least four broad classes:

1. Measurement of output of diversified multiple products and the related problem of measuring the size of the firm.
2. Dealing with technological change.
3. Measurement of costs of assets.
4. Choosing a measure of efficiency.

Economic problems arise when the results of the empirical investigation seem to contradict the law of diminishing returns with a linear cost function. This may be explained by the limited range of the input data. We conclude that studies of the cost function can provide a useful guide for management. Their practical value will depend upon how well they are interpreted.

Problems

   1.   In recent years large corporations have been actively pursuing merger possibilities.
a.   Why might mergers be beneficial?
b.   Do results of actual long-run cost studies support or reject the theory behind antitrust legislation against large corporate mergers?
   2.   Business, especially American business, is often accused of short-sightedness. Critics claim that many companies lack long-range planning and instead seem to focus on short-run profits.
a.   Given the availability of various methods of cost analysis, why don't more companies conduct long-run studies?
b.   We often read about "Japan Incorporated". How could this concept be more useful in long-range industrial planning?
   3.   The most efficient plant size in an engineering sense is one for which the *ATC* is as low as possible. Explain whether or not this is also the most efficient plant size in an economic sense, assuming your perspective is that of the individual firm.
   4.   An accountant in your company plotted a scatter diagram of production and cost data taken from the last six months of operations. Sketching in an approximate total cost curve *TC,* the accountant presents his work for your evaluation.

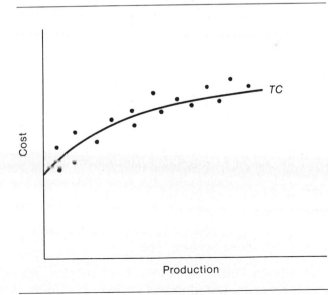

a. What type of cost analysis has the accountant made?
b. What form of cost equation best fits the given *TC* curve?
c. Is this *TC* curve a reasonable assumption for the company to follow?

    5. Flex-Rack Inc. has been experimenting with new tennis racket designs. Using a new fiber material, it plans to produce a small number of rackets for market testing. After analyzing available technology and production facilities, Flex-Rack estimated its total cost function for the new racket to be

$$TC = 975 + 18Q - .1Q^2$$

a. What type of cost analysis is Flex-Rack using?
b. Develop the cost schedule for output ranging from 0 to 100, using increments of 20 (but include the level of production at which *MC* = 0).
c. Using the cost schedule, graph the total cost function. Include curves for *TVC* and *TFC*.
d. On a second graph show the *ATC*, *AVC*, and *MC* curves.
e. What assumption is being made when Flex-Rack estimates cost according to the approximated cost function?

    6. Assume the following data on television manufacturers.

Plant Capacity (× 10,000)	Percentage of Industry Capacity	
	1972	*1980*
0.0– 1.5	9.8	6.6
1.5– 2.3	5.2	4.7
2.3– 3.4	4.3	4.8
3.4– 5.0	5.6	5.1
5.0– 7.3	6.2	5.9
7.3– 8.9	8.3	14.6
8.9–13.1	9.8	18.4
13.1–15.7	9.3	14.8
15.7–18.4	11.2	8.3
18.4–20.0	16.4	9.6
More than 20.0	13.9	7.2

a. What conclusions might be drawn about long-run costs for television manufacturers?
b. What type of cost analysis is being performed?
c. Which form of cost function best fits your conclusions?
d. What assumptions are necessary when using this technique of cost analysis?

Case Problem: Shadow Screen, Inc.

    7. Shadow Screen, Inc., located in Los Angeles, manufactures shadow screens for color television sets made in the United States and

West Germany. Output of its Los Angeles plant is exported to many Asian countries, such as Singapore, Hong Kong, and Korea, but not to Japan. Because of rising labor costs in the United States and increasing demand for its production in the Asian region, the management of Shadow Screen has decided to establish a manufacturing plant in Hong Kong, to be operational by the end of this year. Shadow Screen's industrial engineers estimate the cost function of the new plant to be

$$TC = \$800,000 + 40Q + .0025Q^2$$

where

TC = Total cost
Q = Units of production

Although Shadow Screen is a leader in the worldwide market, it is facing increasing competition in the Asian market from several French and German newcomers, and especially from several Japanese companies. Market demand in Asia is expected to be 500,000 units next year, and is expected to grow 20 percent annually for the next five years. Shadow Screen expects to sell 15,000 units next year, and to maintain its share of the market as it grows thereafter.

a. What is the expected total cost and average cost for sales of 15,000 units?
b. Calculate the output level that will yield the lowest average total cost.
c. In order to maintain a profit margin of 25 percent at a production level of 15,000 units, what price should be charged? What is the expected profit?
d. With a 20 percent annual increase in sales, when will the firm reach minimum average total cost?
e. Estimate Shadow Screen's market share and the most efficient market share for next year. Determine the potential for future competition in the industry.
f. Assume that the estimated cost function is subject to a standard error of ±$85,000. What is the probability of holding cost below $2 million next year?

Case Problem: Steel Producers of America

8. Because of the intense competition from both Europe and Japan, Steel Producers of America organized a group of experts to investigate cost structures in various ailing steel markets. Assume that the following cost-output data for the month of August represent steel producers manufacturing coil tension springs such as those used in automobile suspensions.

Company	Production	Cost/Unit
1	7,500	$53
2	11,000	54
3	14,500	52.5
4	15,000	51
5	18,500	49.5
6	19,500	50
7	28,000	47
8	67,000	43
9	118,000	43.5
10	150,000	43.5

Questions:

a.   Plot the data on an output-cost graph sketching a smooth curve of best fit.

b.   If all cost and output calculations were made at one point in time, what type of cost analysis does this represent? Is it a long-run or short-run analysis?

c.   Determine the relationship between output and cost. Does it exhibit increasing, decreasing, or constant returns to scale?

d.   Do the data perfectly fit your approximated cost curve? What might have caused deviations to occur?

e.   What advice for the future might the cost experts give to tension spring manufacturers?

f.   Discuss the pros and cons of applying this type of cost analysis to the U.S. computer industry.

References

Bain, Joe S. "Survival-Ability as a Test of Efficiency." *American Economic Review,* May 1969, pp. 99–104.

Benston, George J. "Multiple Regression Analysis of Cost Behavior." *Accounting Review,* October 1966, pp. 657–72.

─────────. "Economies of Scale in Financial Institutions." *Journal of Money, Credit and Banking,* May 1972, pp. 312–41.

Christensen, L. R., and W. H. Greene. "Economies of Scale in U.S. Power Generation." *Journal of Political Economy,* August 1976, pp. 655–76.

Dean, Joel. *Statistical Cost Functions of a Hosiery Mill.* Chicago: University of Chicago Press, 1941.

Douglas, Paul H. "The Cobb-Douglas Production Function Once Again: Its History, Its Testing, and Some New Empirical Values." *Journal of Political Economy,* October 1976, pp. 903–15.

Frech, Ted H. E., and Paul B. Ginsburg. "Optimal Scale in Medical Practice: A Survivor Analysis." *Journal of Business,* January 1974, pp. 23–36.

Hirshleifer, Jack A. "The Firm's Cost Function, A Successful Reconstruction." *Journal of Business,* July 1962, pp. 235–55.

Johnston, J. *Statistical Cost Analysis.* New York: McGraw-Hill, 1960, pp. 136–68. These pages summarize, in a few paragraphs each, the main features and conclusions of more than two dozen well-known statistical cost studies. Chapter 6, pp. 169–94, presents criticisms and evaluations of statistical cost analyses.

Longbrake, William A. "Statistical Cost Analysis." *Financial Management,* Spring 1973, pp. 48–55.

McGee, J. S. "Efficiency and Economies of Size." In *Industrial Concentration: The New Learning,* eds. H. Goldschmid, H. Mann, and J. Weston. Boston: Little, Brown, 1974.

Shepherd, William G. "What Does the Survivor Technique Show About Economies of Scale?" *Southern Economic Journal,* July 1967, pp. 113–22.

Walters, A. A. "Production and Cost Functions: An Econometric Survey." *Econometrica,* January–April 1963, pp. 1–66.

Weiss, Leonard W. "The Survival Technique and the Extent of Suboptimal Capacity." *Journal of Political Economy,* June 1964, pp. 246–61.

Williams, Martin. "Firm Size and Operating Costs in Urban Bus Transportation." *Journal of Industrial Economics,* December 1979, pp. 209–18.

13

Profit: Concepts and Measurement

Profitability is the ultimate test of management's ability to fulfill its coordinative functions of decision making and planning. In the final analysis, profits, not losses, provide the basis for a firm's well-being and growth in the marketplace. In this chapter we will examine the forces that contribute to or reduce profits. To start things off, we will survey some of the profit theories that have been proposed at one time or another. This will lead to a discussion of general aspects of profit measurement, followed by an analysis of problems inherent in the valuation of assets. Finally, the chapter will close with a discussion of the ways in which the economic analysis of profits may contribute to better decision making.

Profit Theories

The history of economic thought abounds in profit theories. Each of the many theories that have been offered, however, tends to focus upon just some small fraction of the various aspects of profit (e.g., its source, components, or function). Nevertheless, most profit theories can be classified as one of three major types:

1. Compensatory or functional theories.
2. Friction and monopoly theories.
3. Technology and innovation theories.

424

This classification is not all-inclusive. Furthermore, it should not be taken to mean that one type of theory may not contain elements of other types. It merely points out the main differences in orientation that have emerged historically in the course of thinking about profit. For this reason, this classification represents a fair arrangement of the major issues involved in profit analysis and a convenient starting point for approaching them in managerial decision making.

Compensatory or Functional Theories

This group of theories holds that economic profits (surplus) are the necessary payments to the entrepreneur in return for coordinating and controlling production. It is the entrepreneur who organizes the factors of production into a logical sequence, plans their efficient combination, and establishes policies to see that production is carried out. Profits, therefore, are the compensation for fulfilling these functions success-fully.

Functional theories were proposed in the early 19th century, before the advent of large corporations. At that time, the entrepreneur was regarded as a higher type of laborer, similar in certain ways to an individual proprietor. When attempts were made later, however, to apply functional theories to modern publicly owned corporations with their separation of ownership and control, the results appeared confusing and contradictory.

In the corporate form of business organization, the coordinative function is usually delegated by the owners (stockholders) to professional salaried executives. If executive remuneration is taken to be profits, despite its contractual form, the theory still leaves unexplained the residual income of the enterprise that goes to stockholders who exercise no active control. The only alternative, if functional theories are to be consistent with their original definition, is to allocate a share of the entrepreneurial function to stockholders. But attempts to do this are not in accord with the reality that the corporation is an organization of active leadership by managers and passive ownership by stockholders. With the growing importance of the large corporation as a dominant type of business organization in the American economy, functional profit theories lost much of their usefulness. In their place, a group of *friction* and *monopoly theories* emerged around the turn of the century.

Friction and Monopoly Theories

By 1900, the theory of a stationary economy had very nearly become a complete and unified system of thought. Against this background, the noted American economist, J. B. Clark, constructed an economic model that was intended to be a reconciliation of static theoretical laws and the dynamic world of fact. In modern times, this model has been called the *model of perfect competition*.

Fundamental assumptions of the model of perfect competition are the complete mobility of resources and the freedom of firms to enter and exit the market. Thus the economy is characterized by a smooth and friction-less flow of resources, with the system automatically clicking into equi-librium through the free play of market forces. Changes may occur that cause a departure from equilibrium, but so long as resources are mobile and opportunities are equally accessible to all economic entities (i.e., knowledge is perfect), the adjustment to a new equilibrium is accom-plished quickly and smoothly. In this type of economic equilibrium all factors of production receive their opportunity costs; and an enterprise's revenues exactly equal its costs (including the imputed wages and inter-est of the owner). Hence no economic surplus or profit residual can result.

In the real world, however, such surpluses do occur, and in accor-dance with the theory they can only be attributed to the frictions (or obstacles to resource mobility) and changes that actually characterize a dynamic economy. In the long run, according to the friction theory, the forces of competition eliminate surpluses, but surpluses continue to recur because new changes and new frictions continually arise. In con-trast to the functional theories previously outlined, profits are not attrib-utable to any particular function. Rather they are the result of institu-tional rigidities in the social fabric that prevent the working-out of competitive forces, thus giving a temporary advantage to the recipient of the surplus.

There is much empirical evidence to substantiate friction and monop-oly theories. The construction of the world's fair in Knoxville brought profit bonanzas to hotels, restaurants, and even homeowners with spare rooms to rent. The existence of patents and franchises enables many firms to establish legal monopolies and reap, therefore, larger profit than could otherwise be obtained. A favorable location for a business may cause the value of the site to exceed the rent paid for it. In general, the control of any resource whose supply is scarce relative to its demand provides a basis for pure or windfall profits. In such instances, greater than normal return would not arise if resources were sufficiently mobile to enter the market, or if the economy were frictionless (perfect) in its competitive structure. But social processes—such as customs, laws, and traditions—make these rapid adjustments impossible. Thus surplus profits do occur.

Technology and Innovation Theories

This group of theories holds that new technology gives rise to *inven-tions*, and inventions adapted to business use become *innovations*. Many inventions, of course, do not become innovations. But those that do, being dynamic phenomena, upset the equilibrium of an otherwise static system.

The original purpose of the innovation theory proposed by the late Professor Joseph Schumpeter was to show how business cycles result from these technological disturbances and from successive adaptations to them by business. His procedure was to assume a stationary system in equilibrium—in which all economic life is repetitive and goes on smoothly, without disturbance. Into this system a shock—an innovation—is introduced by an enterprising and forward-looking entrepreneur who foresees the possibility of extra profit. The quietude and intricate balance of the system are thus disrupted. The successful innovation prompts a large number of businessmen (followers rather than leaders) to plunge ahead and adopt the innovation. In turn, such mass rushes create and stir up secondary waves of business activity. When the disturbance finally subsides, the system settles into equilibrium once again, only to be disturbed later on by another innovation. Economic development thus takes place as a series of fits and starts (cycles) rather than as a smooth and continuous process.

From the business standpoint, an innovation may embrace any one of a wide variety of activities: the discovery of new markets, the differentiation of products (thereby yielding wider consumer acceptance), the development of a new product, and so on. In short, an innovation involves a new way of doing old things. We have seen many instances of highly profitable innovation, especially in the high-technology industries such as electronics. New products such as pocket calculators, home computers, and video games immediately come to mind as innovations marketed by the electronics industry, whose impact on business (and society) has been enormous. But there have been many other innovations, both in and out of the electronics industry. Especially noteworthy are new products that are spinoffs from space exploration. Successful development and marketing of such new products has resulted in a very high rate of return for those who were first in the field. However, because competition is severe in the high-technology industries, both domestically and internationally, the period of above-normal profits in such industries can be quite short.

When conceived in its broadest business sense as a new way of doing things (a definition that embraces more than just new product development), the innovation theory can go a long way toward explaining such great historical episodes as the rise of mercantilism and the Industrial Revolution. Certainly it can account for the underlying structural changes that have taken place in the history of American business.

The innovation theory focuses on the dynamic, uncertain, ever-changing nature of capitalism. It holds that the only limits to human progress are the inherent limits of human beings themsevles. (Even this may not be a serious restraint now with the advent of the robotic firm!)

From the standpoint of managerial economics, a theory's value is not so much determined by how well it explains the past or even the present, but how well it predicts the future. For this purpose, the innovation theory is somewhat inadequate because it cannot foresee whether or when an invention will become an innovation.

The Timing of Innovations.   Historically, there has generally been a substantial interval between invention and innovation. The time between invention and innovation (i.e., marketing) was 11 years for nylon, 14 years for the jet engine, 20 years for the xerographic copying process, and 22 years for television. The champion laggard was the fluorescent lamp, which was invented by Becquerel in 1859, but not marketed until 1938—a lapse of 79 years.

Since the scientific principles, technical know-how, materials, and skills—all the ingredients necessary to bring to the business world the reality of a new product, service, or method of production or of distribution—are in existence and available long before the innovation occurs, why does the innovation take place when it does, and neither sooner nor later?

On the surface, the answer is that an innovation takes place when the possibility for profit is recognized by someone willing and able to exploit the potential he or she believes to be inherent in the opportunity. The best time to introduce an innovation is when the expected present value of its profits is greatest. Unfortunately, the future stream of profits is so uncertain that this simple criterion cannot generally be applied.

Since the optimal timing of an innovation cannot be known, the decision whether and when to introduce an innovation depends upon an assessment of the structural environment, both institutional and otherwise, in which the innovating firm finds itself. The lag between invention and innovation is a function of many factors, such as the state of the technology, capital requirements, marketing know-how, anticipated demand, and expected profits. Above all, it is a function of the willingness (or unwillingness) of the entrepreneur to bear the risk of failure in the marketplace after extensive expenditure on research and development (R&D).

The Risks of Innovation.   If risk is defined as the probability of success, then the research side of research and development is somewhat more risky than the development side. For example, Mansfield has reported that less than 40 percent of privately funded R&D projects ever result in a commercial product.[1]

---

[1] Edwin A. Mansfield, *The Economics of Technological Change* (New York: W. W. Norton, 1968), p. 68.

In the area of pharmaceuticals and drugs, the market sees only one out of every 2,000 newly synthesized compounds.[2] In a study of one large firm, the firm initiated R&D projects with an estimated 80 percent chance of success, but actual successes occurred only half the time. Elements of risk that contributed to the 50 percent lack of success included the transfer of key personnel and changes in the firm's objectives.[3]

Some economists have suggested that large firms have an advantage over smaller firms because their size permits them to spread risk over more R&D projects. Empirical evidence contradicts this hypothesis.[4] Small independent investors and entrepreneurs have been more active and more successful in R&D because they have been more willing to take the associated risk.

The Rewards of Innovation. The rewards of innovation are the benefits that accrue not only to the innovating firm, but also to other firms and society as a whole. New processes that reduce costs or that can be used as production factors for other products may lead to a chain of innovations in other firms. For example, the introduction of nylon by Du Pont has led to a wide diversity of applications. Today, nylon fiber is used for everything from stockings to parachutes. Nylon is also used as a rustproof, lightweight substitute for metal fasteners, cabinet hardware, wheel bearings, and many other products. Some innovations, such as new medicines, produce far-reaching noncommercial effects, such as disease prevention and increased longevity.

In attempting to measure the rewards of innovation, researchers have used return on investment in the innovation as their yardstick. Mansfield found that return on investment in research and development ranged from 7 to 30 percent in chemicals, 40 to 60 percent in petroleum, and exceeded 15 percent in furniture, food, and apparel.[5]

In the investigation of social rates of return, researchers have defined the social benefits of innovation as roughly the sum of all private benefits that accrue because of the innovation and the social investment as the sum of all private investments in the innovation. Although research in this area has not been extensive, the findings to date indicate that the

---

[2] "Revisions in U.S. Patent Law, Still Pending," *Chronicle of Higher Education*, May 15, 1978, p. 6.

[3] Edwin A. Mansfield, *Industrial Research and Technological Innovation* (New York: W. W. Norton & Company, Inc., 1968), chap. 3.

[4] See John Jewkes, David Sawers, and Richard Stillerman, *The Sources of Invention* (New York: St. Martin's Press, 1959); D. Hamberg, "Invention in the Industrial Research Laboratory," *Journal of Political Economy*, April 1963, pp. 95–115; and Willard F. Mueller, "The Origins of the Basic Inventions Underlying Du Pont's Major Product and Process Innovations, 1920 to 1950," in *The Rate and Direction of Inventive Activity*, ed. Richard R. Nelson (Princeton, N.J.: Princeton University Press, 1962), pp. 323–46.

[5] Mansfield, *Industrial Research and Technological Innovation*, pp. 70–71.

social rate of return is considerably more than the private return to the originator of the innovation. For example, Mansfield found that the innovator of a certain machine tool enjoyed a return on R&D investment of 35 percent, while the social rate of return was 83 percent. In a detailed examination of 17 innovations, the median return to the innovator was 25 percent on the investment, while the median social return was 56 percent on all private investments in innovations.[6]

These findings indicate that it would pay society to encourage innovation, and this has been recognized by the federal government. One form of encouragement is the granting of patents which give the inventor exclusive rights to produce and market an invention for 17 years. Another form is a tax credit for qualified research expenses, which means that the government assumes part of the risk by paying part of the costs of innovation.

Profit Measurement

If economists, rather than accountants, were given the responsibility of recording financial data in the corporation's books, this section would perhaps not be necessary—and this comment is not intended as a criticism of accountants. On the contrary, one can only sympathize with accountants for the impossible position in which they are often placed as they try to provide a single set of financial statements that are supposed to be meaningful to every conceivable user—stockholders, creditors, labor unions, government agencies, management, and others (including managerial economists). Moreover, their task is made more difficult, if not impossible, by the requirement that they allocate to a given accounting period the "correct" revenues and costs; that is, from a continuing stream of revenues and costs, they must select those revenues and costs attributable solely to the period in question and not to previous and/or subsequent periods.

It should be realized that *the true profitability of any investment or business operation cannot be determined until the ownership of the investment or business has been fully terminated.* Hence, the requirement of measuring profits over a particular segment of the total life of the investment imposes a degree of arbitrariness that cannot be avoided. Although arbitrary allocation to a given accounting period is necessary with respect to both revenues and costs, the latter has received the greatest amount of attention, particularly in the areas of depreciation accounting and inventory valuation. Aside from the accounting aspects of cost (and profit)

---

[6] Edwin Mansfield et al., "Social and Private Rates of Return from Industrial Innovations," *Quarterly Journal of Economics*, May 1977, pp. 221–40.

measurement, however, there are certain important economic considerations that need to be addressed first.

Economic versus Accounting Measures of Profit

In the economic literature dealing with the determination of profit,
much attention is paid to discrepancies that might arise from the failure
to account for all costs. Chief among unrecognized costs are economic
costs that are overlooked while the more obvious costs, such as cash
outlays, development costs, and capital expenditures, are entered in the
books. There are, in fact, at least three possible sources of discrepancy:

1. The entrepreneur's wages (that is, those the entrepreneur could
   earn by working for someone else).
2. Rental income on land used in the business (which the owner could
   receive by leasing the property to another firm).
3. A minimum or "normal" profit (which would be just enough to
   compensate the owners for their capital investment and which presumably could be earned by putting the money to work in some-
   body else's business at equivalent risk).

These items are all deemed to be costs for the simple reason that an
entrepreneur who fails to secure a net revenue at least equal to their total
would, in the long run, withdraw from the business, hire out to another
firm, lease or sell the property, and invest his or her funds in some
alternative undertaking, thus improving his or her economic position.
This is the basis for the technical, *economic* meaning of *cost—the minimum
compensation necessary to keep a given resource or factor of production in its
stated employment in the long run.*

Frictions and various other market imperfections will cause resources
to remain in their existing employment at less than economic cost, and
there are many situations in which resource owners receive compensation in excess of economic costs. In the long run, however, there is
sufficient mobility of resources to tend to eliminate these discrepancies.
(Under dynamic, real-world conditions, changes always occur to redis-
tribute the discrepancies and introduce new ones.)

Cost, in the *economic* sense, is thus viewed as a *payment necessary to keep
resources out of* (the next most attractive) *alternative employment, since a*
payment that is below economic cost will result in an eventual shift of
the resource to the alternative opportunity—hence the term *opportunity
cost.*

Our specific concern with the problem of profit measurement raises
the question of how to deal with these potential discrepancies between
accounting and economic profit, for it follows from the discussion above
that economic profit or true surplus is equal to accounting profit less

certain unaccounted-for costs. Actually, the discrepancies are not too serious in the case of the corporation. Rather, they are most likely to exist in the small proprietorship.

In the corporation, management is hired and receives, presumably, and opportunity-cost wage. These wages are treated as expenses, along with the wage payments to all employees, and are deducted in determining final profit. Properties are ordinarily rented, and these rents are deductible in profit calculations. To the extent that real estate is owned rather than rented, it is frequently segregated into a special real estate or building corporation subsidiary from which the property is rented. If this is not done, the real estate is treated as part of the total investment that the firm seeks to use profitably (the rental value being readily determinable). This leaves, therefore, one possible source of discrepancy between accounting and economic profit—the earnings on the invested capital.

A corporation derives its long-term capital from one or a combination of three external sources: the sale of bonds, preferred stock, or common stock. The bondholder's contribution is obtained, however, at an opportunity-cost interest rate, and this cost is recognized in determining profit. As for the preferred stockholder, while legally an owner, his or her position is really that of a limited partner. Profit is computed before the preferred dividend is paid, and the board of directors can decide not to pay the preferred dividend if profits are insufficient. On the other hand, the amount of the preferred dividend is limited, no matter how large the company's profits may be. Thus, from the point of view of the common stockholder, the preferred dividend constitutes an opportunity-cost payment for the use of the preferred stockholder's capital, and nothing more. This is, of course, objectively determinable, and in fact is always deducted in determining net profits available for the common stock.

We are then left with only one significant element of discrepancy between accounting and economic profit: the cost of the use of the common stockholder's contribution (including reinvested earnings) to the corporation. This "normal profit" on the stockholder's capital is the amount by which accounting profit exceeds economic profit in the corporation. Furthermore, this element is measurable—it is the amount that would be earned elsewhere on investments of equivalent risk. Unless the existing investment process is capable of producing this opportunity rate of return, the capital will be gradually withdrawn.

Since the economist views profit as a surplus in excess of all opportunity costs, past outlays have only partial significance. Cost allocations arising from these past transactions must be modified by current facts. Thus, the profit earned in some period is equal to the growth in value of the enterprise from the beginning of the period to the end of the period (after adjusting for any distributions by, or contributions to, the firm during the period). This increase in value is a reflection, not only of what we ordinarily understand to be the results of operations during the period, but also of changes in asset values (plant, equipment, inventories) as well. Thus, *profit, in an economic sense, is the difference between the cash value of the enterprise at the beginning and end of the period*. This may be contrasted with the accounting concept of profit as the difference between total revenue and total expense during the accounting period.

Reasons for Measuring Profit

Various factors compel the periodic determination and reporting of profits. Periodic financial reports are required by:

1. Stockholders (owners), who want to know how their investments are faring.
2. Tax collectors, both state and federal, who want their shares of the profits, if any.
3. The Securities Exchange Commission, which requires certain financial reports from publicly held corporations.
4. Bankers and other financiers, who want to monitor the progress of firms in which they have investments.
5. Management, which needs financial data for decision making, control, and as a measure of success (or failure) of past decisions.

Given the discrepancy between the accountant's and the economist's conceptions of profit, certain problems emerge in the periodic calculation of profit for reporting purposes. In examining these issues in the sections that follow, we shall conduct our analysis from the economist's point of view.

Problems in Measuring Accounting Profit

Accountants, for legal and other reasons, are concerned only with historical facts. Further, generally accepted accounting principles decree that the books must carry only those entries that can be substantiated by reasonably objective evidence in the form of *source documents,* such as invoices, receiving reports, cancelled checks, and bank statements. Thus, accounting profit is an *ex post* concept based on past transactions as recorded on the company's books. Unfortunately, this leads to incomplete cost analyses. The failure to give consideration to certain economic costs has already been discussed. In addition to these oversights, even more serious errors arise from the generally accepted accounting techniques themselves.

The difficulties that exist in accounting methodology are not due to the failure of the accounting profession to produce the right techniques. Rather, they arise simply because the true profitability of an investment cannot be precisely determined until the process has been terminated. For any period other than the full life of the investment, profits can only be estimated. This in turn means that revenues and costs must, to some extent, be arbitrarily allocated to the period in question. The problem is that generally accepted and perfectly legal cost accounting methods can vary these allocated costs by as much as 40 percent. These wide variations are particularly apparent in the procedures for calculating depreciation expense and for the valuation of assets.

Depreciation of Assets

In carrying on a business activity, the firm's fixed assets other than land (e.g., buildings, machinery, and equipment) wear out or become obsolete from use and the passage of time. If the useful life of an asset is more than one year, it is considered to be a *depreciable asset*. The concept of depreciation is based on the premise that a depreciable asset produces revenues throughout its useful life. Therefore, in order for the company's annual income (profit) to be properly stated, a portion of the asset's cost is charged as an expense against the revenues in each fiscal year of the asset's life. This charge is called *depreciation*. The exact amount to be charged is established by company policy. However, for income tax reporting, depreciation must conform to federal and state laws.[7]

Since depreciation is an expense item, it serves as a direct reduction of the company's income. Thus the accounting measurement of profit depends in a very direct way upon the firm's methods of depreciation. The importance of this operating cost will vary widely from one company to another, depending on the composition of the firm's assets. Companies that are engaged in steelmaking, railroad and airline transportation, chemical processing, and the production of primary aluminum are characterized by extremely large depreciation charges. On the other hand, insurance companies, banks, investment funds, and advertising and merchandising establishments bear relatively small depreciation costs.

Methods of Depreciation

Depreciation methods can be grouped into two broad categories:

1. *Natural methods;* that is, methods that reflect the actual rate of wear and tear or obsolescence over the useful life of the asset. Natural methods include *straight-line* and *service-life* methods.

2. *Accelerated methods;* that is, methods that accelerate cost recovery. The sole purpose of accelerated methods is tax manipulation. This cate-

---

[7] Internal Revenue Service (IRS) rules and regulations with respect to all methods of depreciation are explained in IRS Publication 534, *Depreciation*. State laws usually follow the IRS rules.

gory includes the *declining-balance* method, the *sum-of-the-years'-digits* method, the *remaining-life* method, and the new *accelerated cost recovery system* (ACRS).

Under the rules laid down both in the generally accepted accounting principles and by the Internal Revenue Service (IRS), a company must decide what method of depreciation to use on each asset or class of assets. These methods need not be the same for all the firm's assets, and there are many methods to choose from. Moreover, the firm may legitimately keep two sets of depreciation records for the same assets. One set using natural methods may be used to prepare financial statements that more accurately reflect actual wear and tear or obsolence. The other set may use accelerated methods for preparation of income tax returns.

Straight-Line Method.   Under the straight-line method, the depreciable cost (original cost less the expected salvage value) is spread equally over the expected life of the depreciable asset. For instance, suppose a company car is purchased for $9,000. It has a useful life of three years, after which it can be sold for $3,000. The annual depreciation would be ($9,000 − $3,000) ÷ 3, or $2,000.

The straight-line method is not only simple and easy to apply, it is also theoretically correct for any asset that is used at a uniform rate. For that reason, the straight-line method is often used as a standard for comparison with other methods. It is also the basis for one method offered in the new accelerated cost recovery system (ACRS), created by the Economic Recovery Tax Act of 1981.

Service-Life Method.   For assets that are not used at a uniform rate, a service-life method may be more appropriate. When the rate of wear and tear is irregular, the useful life of the asset may be expressed either in terms of *working hours* or in terms of *units of production*. The depreciation that is charged then bears the same ratio to the asset's depreciable cost (cost less salvage) as the year's usage bears to the asset's useful life. For example, suppose that a bulldozer that cost $50,000 is expected to last for 20,000 hours of operation. If in one year, it is operated for 1,000 hours, depreciation would be (1,000/20,000) × $50,000 = $2,500. If in the next year, the machine is operated for 2,000 hours, the depreciation would be (2,000/20,000) × $50,000 = $5,000. Thus, in each year the depreciation charge reflects the actual portion of the assets's life that is used.

Depreciation and Tax Policy

For assets placed in service before January 1, 1981, the IRS permits the taxpayer to use "any method that is reasonable if you apply it consistently." This includes accelerated methods such as the declining-balance and the sum-of-the-year's-digits, as explained in IRS Publication 534, *Depreciation*. For assets placed in service after December 31, 1980, taxpayers are required to use the accelerated cost recovery system (ACRS) introduced by the Economic Recovery Tax Act of 1981. However, the ACRS provides an alternate system that is based upon the straight-line method.

Both the old and the new accelerated methods provide larger depreciation charges in the early years of an asset's life, and correspondingly smaller taxable income and taxes, than is the case with straight-line depreciation. If the asset in question is kept in the business for all or most of its useful life, depreciation charges fall off rapidly in later years to amounts substantially below those that would prevail under straight-line depreciation. Assuming no change in tax rates or in income before depreciation, taxable income and income taxes are substantially larger, thereby offsetting the lower taxes of earlier years. All other things being equal, however, the corporation still has the advantage, under accelerated methods, of having the productive use of cash that would otherwise be paid out in taxes were the straight-line method to be applied. Depending on the useful life of the asset, this cash can be used in the business for a number of years for any of a number of purposes, thereby reducing the need for outside financing.

Whether a company's choice of an accelerated method ultimately proves to have been wise depends on at least two factors, each of which is subject to change. Since accelerated methods result in only a postponement of taxes rather than a permanent avoidance of them, the wisdom or folly of adopting a given course of action depends on (1) the income tax rates prevailing at the time the deferred tax has to be paid, and (2) the level of taxable income at that time. Therefore, management must evaluate the future in terms of these uncertainties before adopting its depreciation policy.

But this is not all. Other considerations complicate the picture as well, so that decisions will vary from firm to firm even in the same industry. Among the more important complicating factors are: (1) current versus anticipated future working capital requirements, (2) the extent and timing of planned capital expansion programs, and (3) the fact that a present dollar is worth more than a future dollar (something that makes the company's cost of capital a very important consideration). The relative weight given to each of these considerations will depend, of course, upon current taxable income and the organizational form of the company.

Proprietorships and partnerships face a tax situation that differs considerably from that of corporations, since the entire profit or loss that a proprietorship or a partnership accrues is attributed to the owners as personal income. Because income tax rates are graduated, the actual tax that a partner or proprietor must pay depends not only on the size of the business income but also on whether or not he or she has other sources of income. Thus the selection of a method of depreciation is more difficult than in corporations, particularly if the partners have conflicting interests. Thus, accelerated depreciation has its greatest appeal for young, growing corporations with limited access to capital markets and relatively great need for funds to finance expansion.

Price Level Changes and Asset Valuation

Accountants, managers, and economists must evaluate three broad categories of assets:

1. Land, which is a fixed asset, but not depreciable.
2. Fixed assets other than land, almost all of which are depreciable.
3. Physical inventories of goods held for the purpose of manufacturing or trading.

Valuation of Land

The value of land may appreciate not only because of inflation, but also because of changes in its potential use. As a case in point, we take Castle and Cooke, Inc., parent of Dole Company, the packers of Dole pineapple. In the 19th century Castle and Cooke acquired extensive pineapple-growing land in Hawaii. In accordance with generally accepted accounting principles, this land is carried on the company balance sheet at its original cost of approximately $30 million, although its current market value is many times that amount.

The significance of this understatement of land value depends upon one's point of view. If profit is measured by the increase in value of the firm from one accounting period to the next, then we must conclude that the profitability of this concern has been grossly understated. On the other hand, if we assume that the firm will continue to use this land for growing pineapple, the appreciation of the land is irrelevant because it cannot be realized in terms of cash flow. However, much of this land represents potentially valuable building sites, and Castle and Cooke has already responded to growing population pressures by converting some of the land into housing developments. Therefore, the increased market value of the land can hardly be ignored when evaluating the profit potential of the company. The implication is that valuation of land assets must go beyond either cost or market value alone. Consideration of ways in which the land will be used is necessary to establish the economic value of land assets.

Valuation of Other Fixed Assets

In preparing balance sheets and income statements, accountants operate on the "going-concern" convention that the business will continue
indefinitely. Hence, on the assumption that the company will not sell its
fixed assets, it is customary to value these in terms of original cost rather
than current market value. Thus, generally accepted accounting practices prevent market fluctuations from entering into the fixed asset accounts.

If the asset is depreciable, the depreciation expense is recorded on the
income statement, and the net value of the asset is correspondingly
reduced on the balance sheet. If the asset is not depreciable, only the
balance sheet is affected. Accounting procedures do exist whereby the
increased (market) value of assets can be recorded on the books; however, the accounting profession has been very reluctant to use anything
other than historical cost as a basis for depreciation.

The subject of depreciation is complicated by controversy over three
of its aspects:

1. Its true function.
2. Its proper use as a tool for stimulating capital formation and for
    directing investment along lines deemed to be in the national in-
    terest.
3. The proper method for measuring it when reporting net income to
    stockholders and tax authorities.

As for its purpose, in theory, charging annual depreciation not only
matches costs with resulting revenues, it also provides for recovery, in
cash, of the original cost of the asset. This is supposed to provide for
replacement of the worn-out or obsolete asset. But in this era of substantial inflation, the mere recovery of nominal dollars spent years ago is not
sufficient to replace the asset today, even with an identical make and
model. The replacement problem is further complicated by the fact that
we are living in an era of rapid technological change; it may well be that
an identical replacement simply is not available. The improved replacement may provide greatly increased earnings in the future and thus be
well worth its greater cost. Such considerations require that a larger
portion of the reported income should be made available for the purchase of future assets rather than for distribution to owners.

As for the proper use of depreciation as a tool for stimulating capital
formation, this is primarily a political consideration that is built into the
tax laws. These laws are changed from time to time by the Congress.

Our primary concern is with the measurement of depreciation for
reporting income. Here the accounting profession, amid much controversy, has been unable to arrive at any satisfactory improvement on the
current method, which is to deduct a prorated recovery of historical cost

from current operating revenue. However, besides the replacement problem previously mentioned, a major objection to this procedure arises from inflation. The accounting procedure is to match increments of capitalized cost with resulting revenues, but the dollars that comprised the capitalized cost of years past are worth much more than the dollars of revenue that they presumably offset. From the economist's point of view, these accounting practices, by failing to recognize inflation, result in substantial distortion of the firm's financial position. The company's income is overstated on the income statement and the value of its assets is understated on the balance sheet.

Many accountants have also recognized this problem, and have offered three different solutions:

1. *Constant dollar accounting*, which is also called the general price-level model. This solution restates the historical cost from nominal dollars to constant dollars. The method of attack is to adjust the data by the application of appropriate indexes to obtain measurements in dollars of constant purchasing power. This approach is easy to compute, easy to understand, and completely objective.

2. *Current value accounting*, which abandons historical cost as a basis for valuation in favor of some measure of current value. Proponents of this approach argue that users of financial statements are more concerned with what the enterprise is worth now than what it cost in the past. The major drawback is that not all assets can be objectively evaluated.

3. *Current value/constant dollar accounting* is a method that would change both the unit of measurement and the historical cost model. Proponents of this approach argue that constant dollars should be used to measure current values of assets.

Constant-dollar accounting was approved by the American Institute of Certified Public Accountants (AICPA) in 1963, but only for supplemental information.[8] Its use in the provision of additional information was further encouraged in 1969 by the Accounting Practices Board (APB).[9]

Valuation of Inventories

If all goods purchased or manufactured within a given accounting period were sold during the same period, the only problem would be to determine the cost of the goods. But this is not the way a business normally operates. Goods are bought, stored, and sold throughout the accounting period. Under normal accounting procedures, the cost of

---

[8] Staff of the Accounting Research Division, "Reporting the Financial Effects of Price-Level Changes," *Accounting Research Study No. 6* (New York: AICPA, 1963).

[9] "Financial Statements Restated for General Price-Level Changes," *APB Statement No. 3* (New York: AICPA, 1969).

goods sold must be determined for the income statement so that their costs can be charged against the revenues from their sale. The cost of goods that remain in the inventory and that will produce revenues at a later date must be determined for the balance sheet, where they are listed as current assets.

Accountants insist that cost must be accepted as the primary basis for inventory valuation. If prices were constant and the quantity in stock always the same, accounting for inventory would present no particular problem. But when prices fluctuate, inventory replacement at varying costs raises the problem of measuring the costs to be applied both to goods sold and to goods remaining in the inventory. Accountants have devised various methods of measurement, but two methods, called first-in, first-out (FIFO) and last-in, first-out (LIFO), are most common.

In order to understand the difference between FIFO and LIFO a distinction must be made between the physical item and its cost. To help clarify this distinction, let us visualize a warehouse with two doors. Newly acquired goods enter by one door, sold goods exit by the other door. In between, the goods are stored in such a way that the order in which they are acquired is preserved. This means that the first item acquired is the first item sold. That is, the oldest merchandise is sold first. (This is normal practice regardless of the costing method used.)

Now suppose that each item entering through the acquistion door has a tag attached that states the item's cost. If the tag remains attached to the item, then the cost of the first item in is the cost of the first item out. That is FIFO—first-in, first-out. In contrast, suppose that as each item enters the warehouse, the cost tag is removed and placed upon a spike. Then as an item is sold and goes out the other door, an attendant removes one tag from the spike and attaches it to the sold item. The tag that the attendant removes from the spike is the last tag that was placed there by the attendant at the acquisition door. That is to say, the cost attached to the sold item is the most recent cost of acquisition. That is LIFO—last-in, first-out.

Effects of Inventory Valuation by FIFO.   When prices are rising, the value of goods sold or used up is recorded at the earlier, lower price levels. The item entitled "cost of goods sold" on the income statement therefore is below the replacement cost of the goods sold. This means that gross profit is overstated. On the other hand, if prices are falling, cost of goods sold will be reported on the income statement at a value greater than replacement cost. This means that gross profit is understated. In other words, unless prices are completely stable, FIFO will cause gross profit to be either overstated or understated. On the balance sheet, however, the valuation of goods remaining in the inventory is at or near current replacement cost. Therefore, whether prices are rising or falling, the valuation of inventory on the balance sheet is fairly accurate.

Effects of Inventory Valuation by LIFO.   The effects of LIFO on the income statement and balance sheet are directly opposite to those of FIFO. Under LIFO, whether prices are rising or falling, goods sold or used up are evaluated at the latest prices of acquisition. Hence the cost of goods sold, as reported on the income statement, is at or near replacement cost. This means that gross profit is fairly stated whether prices are rising or falling. This is the chief virtue of LIFO.

On the balance sheet, however, goods remaining in the inventory are valued at the earlier costs of acquisition. In a time of falling prices, this would cause the value of the inventory to be overstated. In a time of rising prices, the value of the inventory will be understated. In companies that maintain a safety stock—that is, a minimum level of inventory on hand—the inventory can retain items valued at costs that date back many years. Under this circumstance, the value of the inventory may be grossly understated on the balance sheet. Furthermore, if the company ever has to dip into the safety stocks, some very strange things can happen to the income statement.

For example, suppose that a company has been on LIFO for a 10-year period during which prices were moving up steadily and operations were proceeding at a pace that permitted stocks to be maintained at desired physical levels. Labor difficulties set in, and a strike is called that forces the company to operate out of inventory for a prolonged period. Soon the inventory that has been carried at prices that prevailed 10 years earlier is brought into sales, and huge inventory profits are realized. It is even conceivable, in fact, that these very large profits result in reported earnings far in excess of those realized for the equivalent period before the strike began. For these reasons there has developed in some quarters a disenchantment with LIFO valuation and a desire to return to what is felt to be the more logical and realistic FIFO approach.

The Economic Concept of Replacement Cost Accounting

While there are very cogent reasons why accountants insist upon using historical costs to value assets and also refuse to recognize any profits held in the inventory, there are equally persuasive arguments in favor of relaxing such practices for the purposes of decision making. From an internal, managerial perspective, the economist's concept of replacement cost accounting can be quite useful. Accounting procedures approach replacement cost accounting with the LIFO method of inventory valuation. However, because of the undesirable aspects of LIFO, a more generalized replacement cost approach would be preferred, to be uniformly applied to both inventories and fixed assets. The essential idea is to report a profit figure that reflects the revenues and costs of the present period, not the revenues of the present year and the costs of the previous years. The difference between the accounting concept and the economic concept can be illustrated by the following example:

Suppose that a hypothetical company deals in a completely homogeneous product and makes all transactions in cash; suppose further that it has the following balance sheet as of December 31, 1983:

Cash	$30,000
Inventory: 3,000 units @ $10.............	30,000
Total assets	$60,000
Owner's equity........................	$60,000

Now suppose the following activities take place in 1984:

Sales:	20,000 units @ $15	$300,000
Purchases:	3,000 units @ $10	30,000
	15,000 units @ $11	165,000
	5,000 units @ $12	60,000
Operating expenses:		20,000

The firm's income statement as of December 31, 1984, would depend upon whether it used FIFO or LIFO:

	FIFO	LIFO
Sales: 20,000 units @ $15................	$300,000	$300,000
Cost of goods sold:		
Beginning inventory:		
3,000 units @ $10...................	30,000	30,000
Purchases:		
3,000 units @ $10..................	30,000	30,000
15,000 units @ $11..................	165,000	165,000
5,000 units @ $12..................	60,000	60,000
Cost of goods available		
for sale	285,000	285,000
Less ending inventory:		
FIFO: 5,000 units @ $12.............	60,000	—
1,000 units @ $11.............	11,000	—
LIFO: 6,000 units @ $10.............	—	60,000
	71,000	60,000
Net cost of goods sold	214,000	225,000
Gross profit on sales....................	86,000	75,000
Operating expenses.....................	20,000	20,000
Operating income	$ 66,000	$ 55,000

The difference of $11,000 in operating income is due solely to the difference in the method of inventory valuation, and these results reveal ample grounds for the continuing controversy in the accounting profession. But by invoking the economist's definition of profit—the difference between the cash value of an enterprise at the beginning and end of the period—perhaps we can clarify the issue. In our hypothetical example, the change in cash on hand is:

Cash on hand, January 1		$ 30,000
Plus sales		300,000
		$330,000
Subtract:		
Purchases	$255,000	
Operating expenses	20,000	$275,000
Cash on hand, December 31		$ 55,000

There are also on hand 6,000 units of merchandise that are valued at their replacement cost of $12 per unit for a total of $72,000. That is to say, if the 6,000 units could be returned to the supplier at the last price paid ($12), the cash value of the enterprise clearly would be

Cash	$ 55,000
Inventory: 6,000 @ $12	72,000
Cash value of the firm, Dec. 31.	$127,000

The increase in cash value of the firm (profit) is

Cash value of the firm, Dec. 31	$127,000
Less: Cash value of the firm, Jan. 1	60,000
Economic profit	$ 67,000

The $67,000 profit can be further divided into its two components: *trading profit* and *holding profit*. Traders are well aware that goods that are sold must be replaced if business is to continue. Trading profit, then, may be defined as net sales minus operating expenses and the current replacement cost of the goods that were sold. For our hypothetical company, trading profit is:

Sales		$300,000
Operating expenses	$ 20,000	
Replacement cost:		
20,000 units @ $12	240,000	260,000
Trading profit		$ 40,000

Holding profit or loss is defined as the increase or decrease in replacement cost of an item held in inventory. This profit has nothing to do with the trading skills of the persons managing the enterprise. It is more a capital gain or loss that results from a general increase or decrease in prices. For our hypothetical company, holding profit is:

$$
\begin{array}{l}
6{,}000\ (\$12.00 - \$10.00) = \$12{,}000 \\
15{,}000\ (\$12.00 - \$11.00) = 15{,}000 \\
5{,}000\ (\$12.00 - \$12.00) = -0- \\
\hline
\phantom{5{,}000\ (\$12.00 - \$12.00) = }\ \$27{,}000
\end{array}
$$

The trading profit of $40,000 plus the holding profit of $27,000 adds up to the economic profit of $67,000.

The purpose of the foregoing illustration has been twofold: (1) it sheds some light on the FIFO-LIFO controversy as it relates to economic decision making, and (2) it provides an opportunity to show how the economist's definition of profit can lead to better profit analysis. A decision maker should be in a better position to understand and evaluate profit performance when profit is viewed in the comprehensive manner shown above, rather than as a single figure without any breakdown and separation of its basic sources. Further, the economist's concept of net income avoids the necessity of stating the inventory value at a historical cost that is substantially different from its current replacement cost, as is the case with LIFO.

Summary

The history of economic thought abounds in profit theories, but most of them fall into three major categories:

1. *Compensatory or functional theories,* which hold that profit is the entrepreneur's reward for coordinating and controlling the enterprise.
2. *Friction and monopoly theories,* which explain profit as the result of frictions that prevent the smooth operation of the model of perfect competition.
3. *Technology and innovation theories,* which hold that profits are the rewards for innovation, that is, the adaptation of an *invention* to business use.

In the measurement of profit, there is a difference between generally accepted accounting methods and economic concepts. The accountant calculates profit as the difference between total revenue and total costs. The economist would divide the accountant's profit into two parts. One part, called *normal profit,* represents recovery of opportunity costs, which are not recognized by accountants. The remainder represents *economic profit* (which is sometimes called *surplus profit* or *excess profit*).

Accounting methods have great difficulty with charges for depreciation of assets and with the valuation of assets, especially goods carried in inventories. Depreciation methods can be grouped into two broad categories: (1) *natural methods,* which reflect the actual rate of wear and tear or obsolescence, and (2) *accelerated methods,* which are used to manipulate taxes by accelerating cost recovery.

From the economist's point of view, accounting practices that use historical cost for asset valuation result in substantial distortion of the values of three broad categories of assets:

1. *Land,* which may increase in nominal value due to inflation, or in real value due to changes in potential use.
2. *Fixed assets other than land,* almost all of which are depreciable.
3. *Physical inventories of goods* which are held for the purpose of manufacturing or trading.

The standard accounting practice of basing depreciation on historical cost in nominal dollars results in substantial distortions on both the balance sheet and the income statement. On the balance sheet, assets are undervalued in terms of current dollars. On the income statement, the charge for depreciation is understated, thus causing taxable income to be overstated.

This problem has been recognized by many accountants as well as by economists, and three different solutions have been proposed:

1. *Constant dollar accounting,* which states depreciation charge and asset valuation in dollars of constant purchasing power.
2. *Current value accounting,* which abandons historical cost in favor of some objective valuation of the asset in current dollars.
3. *Current value/constant dollar accounting,* which combines the other two methods.

Valuation of inventories is necessary to determine cost of goods sold and to determine the value of goods remaining in the inventory for the firm's balance sheet. The two most common methods of inventory valuation are FIFO (first-in, first-out) and LIFO (last-in, first-out). The FIFO method assigns the earliest costs to the income statement as cost of goods sold and retains the latest costs for the balance sheet. The LIFO method does just the opposite. But neither FIFO nor LIFO can result in an accurate valuation on both the income statement and the balance sheet unless prices are completely static.

The economist's solution is to value both goods sold and goods retained in inventory at replacement cost. Profit can then be calculated as the difference in the firm's cash value at the beginning and end of the period. This economic profit can be divided into two parts:

1. *Trading profit (loss)* is the direct result of trading activities of the firm. It is defined as net sales minus operating expenses and the *replacement cost* of goods sold.
2. *Holding profit (loss)* is a capital gain or loss that results from a general increase or decrease in prices while goods are being held for sale.

Neither the accounting profession nor the Internal Revenue Service will accept replacement cost accounting for preparation of financial statements. However, it can and should be used for managerial purposes, as it provides a more accurate indication of the success or failure of the firm's activities.

Problems

1. It has been argued that the major difference between accounting profit and economic profit is that accountants recognize depreciation while economists do not. Do you agree with this position? If economists do recognize depreciation, is it measured in the same way that accountants measure it? Discuss these issues.

2. In reporting financial leases, large business firms are now required to "capitalize" future lease payments and record the capitalized value as a liability and also as an asset. Both of these values are then reduced as lease payments are made. Previously, these lease payments were treated as ordinary expenses in the year in which they were made. From the economist's point of view, explain which method you believe more accurately measures the value of the firm at any given time.

3. In the following situations, explain why you would suggest using a straight-line or accelerated depreciation method.
a. A new corporation with a low credit rating.
b. A corporation currently operating at or below the break-even point but expecting future long-run profits.
c. A corporation that estimates that its taxable income will remain steady for the next 10 years.
d. A corporation in an industry targeted by government for incentive tax breaks over the next five years.

4. Describe carefully three currently acceptable methods of depreciation accounting for assets acquired before January 1, 1981, and explain the profit-reporting consequences of each.

5. Westphall Products, Inc., is a new firm with a promising long-run future. However, the company expects to show income tax losses

during the first five years of operation. Moreover, during this period it must acquire about $2 million of assets that qualify for the full 10 percent investment tax credit and for accelerated depreciation as well. Westphall's president is attempting to arrange financing for these assets. The local bank is willing to extend a 10-year loan at an interest rate of the prime plus 3 percent. However, the bank's loan officer indicated that she knew of a wealthy private investor who would most likely buy the assets and then in turn lease them to Westphall at an effective interest cost of the prime rate only. The president is suspicious of this latest arrangement since he cannot understand how an individual could possibly charge a lower interest rate than a bank. Explain how the above situation might be possible.

6.   Accelerated depreciation and shorter service lives are both merely substitute methods of adjusting depreciation for changes in the price level. True or false? Explain.

7.   Suppose you bought a house 20 years ago for $45,000 and sold it this year for $145,000. During this period the accumulated depreciation on the house was $25,000, leaving a book value of $20,000.

a.   Did you make an accounting profit? If so, how much?

b.   Is your accounting profit your "real" profit? Explain.

8.   Vincent quit his $18,000 a year job to work full-time on his growing wholesale vodka distributorship. He began the year with $10,000 in cash and 700 bottles of premium vodka. The following is a record of purchases made during the year.

Date	Number of Bottles	Price/Bottle
January 1	100	$7.50
March 7	500	8.25
May 14	1,000	8.50
July 2	800	8.50
October 3	500	9.00
December 6	600	9.50

At the end of the year, Vincent calculated total sales of $50,000 and operating expenses of $2,700. The ending inventory is 650 bottles, and the current purchase price of a bottle of vodka is $9.50.

a.   What is the ending cash value of Vincent's distributorship?

b.   What is the total economic profit for operations during the year?

c.   Divide the total economic profit into trading and holding profit.

d.   Should Vincent stay in business?

9.   The Midwest Electric Power Company purchased plant and equipment in the following years:

Year	Asset	Estimated Life (years)	Price Index
1964	$ 20,000	25	50
1967	40,000	20	100
1973	100,000	40	150
1984	125,000	25	200
1985	60,000	10	300

a.   Assuming that these assets were purchased on January 1 of the year in which they were acquired, compute the total depreciation charge for 1985 based on original cost. Assume straight-line depreciation.

b.   Compute the total depreciation charge for 1985 in terms of 1985 dollars.

c.   The company's revenues for 1985 are $100,000. Fuel expenses are $18,000; labor expense, $9,000; taxes, $25,000. Prepare two profit and loss statements, one without the adjusted depreciation and one with depreciation adjusted according to the price index.

d.   On the basis of your calculations, what is the effect of the adjustment in depreciation on the company's operating income? Are stockholders better or worse off? Discuss.

10.   Jack's Radio Wholesalers, Inc., has accumulated the following information on its KX-15 speakers during 1983:

Date	Units	Price/Unit
January 1 (inventory)	600	$18.00
March 11 (purchase)	650	18.50
July 9 (purchase)	700	19.75
November 20 (purchase)	400	20.50
December 1 (purchase)	200	21.00
December 31 (inventory)	650	

a.   Calculate the value of inventory on January 1, 1984, using both FIFO and LIFO.

b.   What effect would each method of inventory valuation have on Jack's income statement?

c.   What effect would each method have on Jack's balance sheet?

Case Problem: Wilco Machine Tools

11.   Accountants at Wilco Machine Tools are working on the following financial statements:

WILCO MACHINE TOOLS
Comparative Balance Sheets
($000)

	Dec. 31, 1982	Dec. 31, 1983	
		(LIFO)	(FIFO)
Assets			
Cash............................	$245	$502	$502
Inventory	90	___	___
Total assets..................	$335	$____	$____
Equities			
Owner's equity	$335	$____	$____

Inventories and Purchases, 1983

Date	Units	Price/Unit
Jan. 1 (inventory)	1,200	$
Mar. 15 (purchase)	1,700	85
June 15 (purchase)	2,000	90
Sept. 25 (purchase)	2,500	95
Dec. 25 (purchase)	1,200	105
Dec. 31 (inventory)	1,400	

Note: Average selling price during the year was $150.

WILCO MACHINE TOOLS
Income Statement
For the Year Ended December 31, 1983

Sales	$
Cost of goods sold..............	_____
Gross profit....................	
Operating expenses..............	135,000
Net profit before tax..........	$_____

Questions:

a. Complete Wilco Machine Tools' balance sheet and income statement using both FIFO and LIFO methods of inventory valuation.

b. Which inventory valuation method would be preferable for:
   (1) Tax purposes?
   (2) Showing potential investors?

c. From an economist's view, thoroughly analyze 1983's operations.
d. Discuss why an economist's view might be better for decision making.

References

Anthony, Robert N. "The Trouble with Profit Maximization." *Harvard Business Review,* November–December 1969, pp. 126–34.

Anthony, Robert N., and G. A. Welsch. *Fundamentals of Management Accounting.* 3d ed. Homewood, Ill.: Richard D. Irwin, 1981.

Curran, Ward S. "Depreciation in Economic Theory and Capital Budgeting." *Quarterly Review of Economics and Business,* Spring 1968, pp. 61–68.

Horngren, Charles T. *Cost Accounting: A Managerial Emphasis.* 5th ed. Englewood Cliffs, N.J.: Prentice-Hall, 1982.

Pyle, William W., and Kermit D. Larson. *Fundamental Accounting Principles.* 9th ed. Homewood, Ill.: Richard D. Irwin, 1978, chap. 20. This text provides a basic, but thorough, discussion of general price-level-adjusted accounting (GPLA) methods.

Solomons, David. "Economic and Accounting Concepts of Incomes." *Accounting Review,* July 1961, pp. 374–83.

14

Profit: Planning and Control

Profit planning refers to operating decisions in the areas of product line, volume of production, and pricing. Whatever the firm's profit goals may be, profit planning must take into account the expected demand for the firm's products, its capacity to meet the demand, and all of its costs. A good profit plan will establish objectives and prescribe the means for achieving the objectives. It will also establish a timetable for actions necessary to carry out the plan. Profit management not only is a vital function for directing short-run operations but also is essential for optimizing investment and financing decisions in the long run.

There are a number of approaches to profit planning that are commonly used by accountants and economists. In this chapter we shall discuss three of these:

1. The profit budget.
2. Break-even analysis.
3. Regression analysis.

Each of these may be used separately or in combination with others, depending on the information available and the purpose of the analysis.

451

The Profit Budget

Profit planning generally begins with a profit budget derived from a projected or pro forma income statement. It is based upon the most recent income statement of the firm, with appropriate adjustments for expected changes in costs, prices, and anticipated demand over the period covered by the profit budget. From these figures, of course, either a profit or a loss can be forecast. The profit budget is used for *coordination* and *control* of the firm's activities as well as for *planning*. Therefore, good practice requires that it be flexible, with periodic review and revision.

The *planning* aspect of profit budgeting enables managers at all levels to anticipate their needs for work force, materials, equipment, and financial resources, and to plan accordingly.

The *coordinating* aspect of profit budgeting is a side effect of the preparation and periodic revision of the budget. The executive who is responsible for drawing up the budget cannot perform the necessary duties without extensive consultation with, and input from, department heads. The very process of drawing up a budget forces a coordination of the firm's activities that otherwise might not take place.

The *control* aspect of the profit budget, unlike coordination, is not automatic. Nevertheless, when the budget is used properly, it enables management to maintain a systematic check on the results of current operations and their relation to previous forecasts. When wide variations between predictions and results are observed, the causes can be analyzed to discover ways to improve profitability.

Break-Even Analysis

Break-even analysis is a technique of profit planning that has been used for many years by accountants, business executives, and some economists. It is essentially a device for integrating costs, revenues, and output of the firm in order to illustrate the probable effects of alternative courses of action upon net profits. The technique contains many variations and applications, and only a few of its essential characteristics are highlighted here in order to provide a basic understanding of its nature and relation to managerial decision making.

The economic basis of break-even analysis stems from the cost-output and revenue-output functions of the firm, as illustrated in Exhibit 14–1.

The diagram in the exhibit shows the total revenue curve, TR, the total cost curve, TC, and the corresponding net profit curve, NP, as functions of output. It represents the short-run cost and revenue data for a single firm under static conditions, that is, given a fixed plant and no changes

Exhibit 14–1

Cost-Volume-Profit Relationships

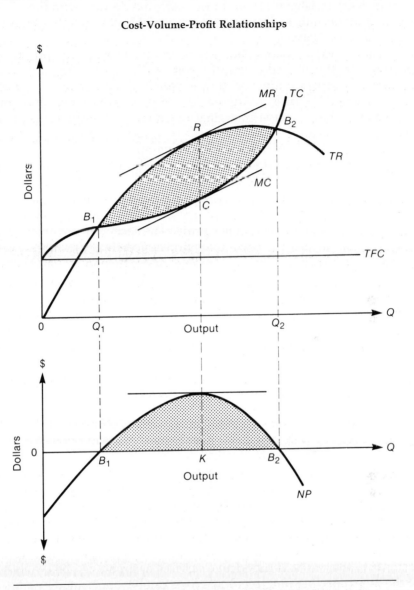

in technology. The total revenue curve, determined by price per unit times the number of units sold, is concave downward, indicating that the firm can sell additional units only by charging a lower price per unit.

The total cost curve represents the sum of total fixed costs and total variable costs *(TFC + TVC)*. As outlined in a previous chapter, total fixed costs are those costs that do not vary with (i.e., are not a function of) output. Total variable costs are those costs that do vary with (i.e., are a function of) output. In Exhibit 14–1 the variable cost area lies between the *TC* and *TFC* curves.

The difference between total revenue and total costs is net profit, *NP*, as shown by the shaded area in Exhibit 14–1 (upper panel); it may be plotted as a separate function (lower panel). Total net profit is maximized where $TR - TC$ is maximum, at output *K*. At this level of output, the slope of the *TR* curve (marginal revenue, *MR*) is the same as the slope of the *TC* curve (marginal cost, *MC*), indicating that $MR = MC$; and the slope of the *NP* curve is zero. The graph reveals two break-even points at the output level Q_1 and Q_2, at which the firm's revenues just cover its costs so that net profit is zero.

The curvilinear functions depicted in Exhibit 14–1 may pertain to a very wide range of outputs. At the first break-even point, the firm first recovers its costs, and beyond lies profit. The second break-even point, however, may actually lie beyond the firm's capacity to produce. Consequently, within a relatively narrow range of production around the first break-even point, linear representations of *TC* and *TR* functions provide adequate approximations of the underlying curves and are much easier to develop and interpret.

The Linear Break-Even Chart

With a few modifications, the upper panel of Exhibit 14–1 forms a basis for the construction of the break-even chart shown in the upper panel of Exhibit 14–2.

The modifications that change the curves of Exhibit 14–1 to the straight lines of Exhibit 14–2 rest mainly on two assumptions:

1.   If further units of the product can be sold at the same price, the firm's revenues can be represented by a linear total revenue (sales) curve, *TR*, emanating from the origin. This would apply to a firm in a purely competitive industry. But the case may also be applicable to many business firms in other competitive situations (e.g., oligopoly) if the product can be sold without a break in the price over wide ranges of output.

2.   If further units of productive services or inputs can be purchased at the same price per unit, the firm's costs can be represented by a linear total cost curve, *TC*, emanating from the intersection of the total fixed cost line, *TFC*, with the vertical axis. (The underlying production function must also be linear.) The assumption of a linear total cost curve may also be quite reasonable over a wide range of output, as evidenced by various empirical studies of costs that have been made by economists and engineers (see Chapter 12).

Exhibit 14–2

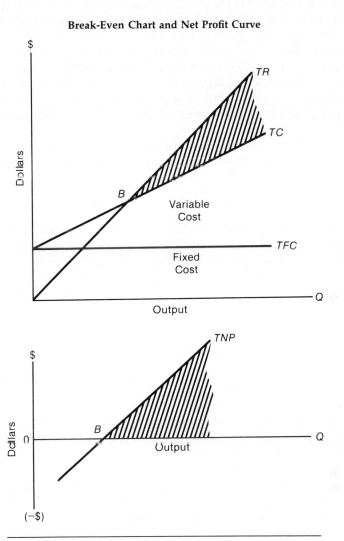

Break-Even Chart and Net Profit Curve

The upper panel of Exhibit 14–2 has been constructed from its theoretical counterpart on the assumption of a linear relationship between output and expense or sales. Thus it reveals the profitability of operations at each output level within the firm's normal production range. Since the sales and cost curves are straight lines, there is only one break-even point, which occurs at B. The shaded area represents net profit, which is also shown by the TNP curve in the lower panel of the chart.

Contribution Margin

Business executives do not usually think of profit in the economic sense as total revenues less total costs. Instead, for short-run decisions where a portion of the firm's capital is already a sunk investment and hence immobile, they use a more appropriate profit concept known as *contribution margin* or *contribution profit*—the difference between receipts and variable expenses. Thus, if a product sells at $1 per unit and the variable expenses total 30 cents, each unit sold recovers its variable expenses plus 70 cents. The 70 cents is the contribution margin, since it contributes to the recovery of fixed expenses and the earning of profit.

Exhibit 14–3 illustrates the concept of contribution margin and its

Exhibit 14–3

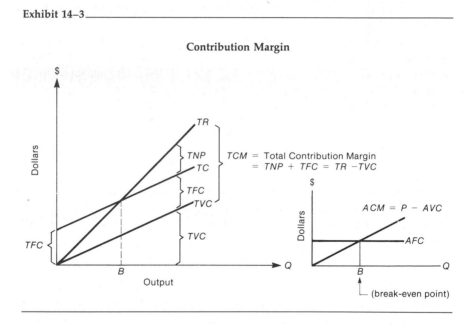

Contribution Margin

relationship to total revenue and elements of cost. On the left panel, TR = total revenue, TC = total cost, TFC = total fixed cost, TVC = total variable cost, TNP = total net profit, and TCM = total contribution margin. On the right panel, ACM = average contribution margin, P = price, AVC = average variable cost, and AFC = average fixed cost. On both panels, B = breakeven level of production.

The left panel of Exhibit 14–3 reveals the following relationships:

$$TCM = TR - TVC = TNP + TFC$$

Therefore, if $TNP = 0$, then $TCM = TFC$. This occurs at the break-even point. We also see that

$$TR = TCM + TVC = TNP + TFC + TVC$$

The right panel illustrates the definition of the average contribution margin *(ACM)* as the difference between unit price and average (unit) variable cost. The break-even point occurs where the average contribution margin is equal to the average (unit) fixed cost.

As Exhibit 14–3 stands, it conveys all of the information commonly used by break-even analysts in profit planning and control. The original data for the construction of the chart are frequently obtained directly from the published profit and loss statement of the firm. Sometimes a single statement is used and the lines are extrapolated backwards on the assumption that linear relationships prevail and that the observations selected are typical. Sometimes several statements are used, representing different output levels; the points are plotted as a scatter diagram and the revenue and cost curves may then be sketched in freehand as regression lines.

On the horizontal axis, any measure of output, such as physical units, percentage of capacity, or dollar sales, may be used. When the company's income statement is the source of the data, sales are usually the measure of output since the other indicators are not ordinarily given. In any event, when used for profit planning, the chart shows:

1. The output required to net a given revenue.
2. The revenue to be expected from a given output.
3. The output or sales volume required to break even.

For levels of output beyond those shown in the diagram, the revenue and cost curves are generally projected on the assumption that the underlying relationships remain unchanged up until the level of full capacity.

Algebraic Techniques

The assumption of linear revenue and cost functions permits the development of simple algebraic procedures for handling break-even problems. First, let us define the following symbols:

Q = Quantity of output in units

P = AR, the price per unit of output, or average revenue, assumed to be a constant (on a graph the slope of the TR function is determined by P)

TR = $P \cdot Q$, the total revenue received from the sale of Q units of product

TFC = Total fixed cost

AVC = Average variable cost

ACM = $P - AVC$ = average (unit) contribution margin

TC = Total cost, equal to $TFC + Q(AVC)$.

TCP = $TR - TVC$ = $Q(ACM)$ = total contribution profit

$\pi = TNP = TR - TC$, the net profit from sale of Q units of product.

$B =$ Break-even point.

To derive a formula for the break-even point in terms of quantity sold, we first observe that, by definition, break-even means the point at which $TR = TC$. Substituting, we get

$$P \cdot Q_B = TFC + TVC$$
$$= TFC + AVC \cdot Q_B$$
$$Q_B(P - AVC) = TFC$$

Hence the break-even quantity is

$$Q_B = \frac{TFC}{P - AVC} = \frac{TFC}{ACM} \tag{1}$$

That is to say, the break-even quantity is calculated as the total fixed cost divided by the unit contribution margin.

From this basic equation, there are three ways of expressing the break-even point: (1) as a number of units sold, (2) as a dollar volume of sales, or (3) as a percentage of plant capacity. Each of these calculations requires a different expression of the contribution margin as the denominator in Equation (1) above. To illustrate, suppose an airline can carry a maximum of 10,000 passengers per month on one of its routes at a fare of $85. Variable costs are $10 per passenger, and fixed costs are $300,000 per month.

1.   Break-Even Quantity.   If we want to find the number of passengers necessary to break even, we calculate by Equation (1) that it is

$$Q_B = \frac{\$300,000}{\$85 - \$10} = \frac{\$300,000}{\$75} = 4,000 \text{ passengers}$$

Note that Equation (1) establishes TFC/ACM as the break-even quantity. Hence, at the break-even point,

$$TR = P \cdot Q = P\left(\frac{TFC}{ACM}\right) = \$85\left(\frac{\$300,000}{\$75}\right) = \$340,000$$

and

$$TC = TFC + TVC = TFC + Q(AVC) = TFC + AVC\left(\frac{TFC}{ACM}\right)$$

$$= \$300,000 + \$10\left(\frac{\$300,000}{\$75}\right) = \$340,000$$

thus $TR = TC$.

2. Break-Even Sales. If the break-even point is desired in terms of sales dollars, the contribution margin is expressed as the fraction of price or revenue that contributes to payments of fixed costs and profit:

$$S_B = \frac{TFC}{1 - (AVC/P)} \tag{2}$$

or

$$S_B = \frac{TFC}{1 - (TVC/TR)} \tag{3}$$

In Equation (2) the contribution per unit is calculated from the ratio of average variable cost to unit price (AVC/P). In Equation (3) the contribution margin is calculated on a total-sales basis from the ratio of total variable cost to total revenue (TVC/TR). The resulting ratio is the same in either case, and in both cases the calculated ratio is subtracted from 1 to yield the fraction of revenue that contributes to payment of fixed costs.

For the airline example, if we want to find the ticket sales necessary to break even, we can use Equation (2):

$$S_B = \frac{\$300,000}{1 - (\$10/\$85)} = \frac{\$300,000}{.8824} \approx \$340,000$$

This answer agrees with our earlier calculation that the break-even quantity is 4,000 passengers, since $4,000 \times \$85 = \$340,000$.

3. Break-Even Percentage of Capacity. If the break-even point is desired in terms of a percentage of plant capacity, the unit contribution margin is multiplied by the plant capacity to obtain the maximum dollar value that the plant can contribute to fixed cost and profit. Total fixed cost can then be expressed as a percentage of this value by the formula

$$\%_B = \frac{TFC}{(P - AVC)Q_{max}} \cdot 100 \tag{4}$$

where Q_{max} is the plant capacity in units of production. Or, to put it another way, the breakeven percentage of plant capacity is the breakeven quantity, Equation (1), divided by plant capacity, then multiplied by 100 to get a percentage.

Again taking the airline example, if we want to find what load factor (i.e., average percentage of seating capacity filled) must be achieved to break even, we calculate:

$$\%_B = \frac{\$300,000}{\$75(10,000)} \cdot 100 = 40 \text{ percent}$$

Planning for Profit

In order to project the production and sales necessary to meet a planned profit goal, the planned profit is treated as an additional increment of fixed cost. The basic equations then become:

$$Q_B = \frac{TFC + \pi}{P - AVC} = \frac{TFC + \pi}{ACM} \tag{5}$$

where π = planned profit and ACM is expressed in dollars, or

$$S_B = \frac{TFC + \pi}{1 - \dfrac{AVC}{P}} = \frac{TFC + \pi}{1 - \dfrac{TVC}{TR}} = \frac{TFC + \pi}{ACM} \tag{6}$$

where ACM is expressed as a percentage of unit price or total revenue, or

$$\%_B = \frac{TFC + \pi}{(P - AVC)Q_{max}} (100) = \frac{TFC + \pi}{(ACM)Q_{max}} \tag{7}$$

where Q_{max} is the plant capacity, in units.

Taking our preceding example of the airline, suppose that management sets a profit target of $200,000. Then the break-even points would be

$$Q_B = \frac{\$300,000 + \$200,000}{\$75} = 6,667 \text{ passengers}$$

$$S_B = \frac{\$300,000 + \$200,000}{1 - (\$10/\$85)} = \frac{500,000}{.8824} \approx \$566,667$$

$$\%_B = \frac{\$300,000 + \$200,000}{75(10,000)} (100) = 66.67 \text{ percent of capacity}$$

In this example, no provision was made for payment of income taxes. In general, if r denotes the tax rate expressed in decimal form, then profit after taxes, PAT, is related to profit before taxes, PBT, in the following way:

$$PAT = PBT - (r)(PBT)$$

that is,

$$PAT = (1 - r)PBT$$

hence

$$PBT = \frac{PAT}{1 - r}$$

Thus, in the example above, at the corporate tax rate of 46 percent, a profit after taxes of $200,000 would require a profit before taxes of

$$PBT = \frac{\$200,000}{1 - .46} = \frac{\$200,000}{.54} = \$370,370$$

That is, a 46 percent tax on $370,370 is $170,370, leaving $200,000 profit after taxes.

This calculation can be incorporated directly into the break-even sales planning formula if desired:

$$S_B = \frac{\$300,000 + (\$200,000/0.54)}{.8824} \approx \$759,753$$

Similarly, if management is contemplating an action that will involve additional fixed commitments (e.g., floating a new bond issue that will require the firm to make periodic interest payments in the future), these increments in fixed cost can be added to the numerator of the above formula, and the additional sales revenue needed to cover these extra costs can thus be calculated.

Break-Even Point Alternatives

As shown on Exhibit 14–4, profit is represented on a break-even chart by the area between the total-revenue and total-cost curves beyond the first break-even point. Obviously, this area can be enlarged by increasing the volume of sales. However, the increase in units sold is eventually limited by plant capacity. The profit area can also be enlarged by shifting the break-even point to a lower level of production and sales. This can be achieved by manipulating three variables: (1) fixed cost, (2) variable cost, and (3) price.

To illustrate these concepts, we have depicted on Panel A of Exhibit 14–4 linear cost relationships based on the following data:

$$\text{Plant capacity} = 100 \text{ units per day}$$
$$AVC = \$7 \text{ per unit}$$
$$P = \$12 \text{ per unit}$$
$$TFC = \$400 \text{ per day}$$
$$Q_B = 80 \text{ units per day}$$
$$TR \text{ (at capacity)} = \$1,200 \text{ per day}$$
$$TC \text{ (at capacity)} = \$1,100 \text{ per day}$$

The shaded area in Panel A represents profit at levels of production beyond the break-even point.

Exhibit 14-4

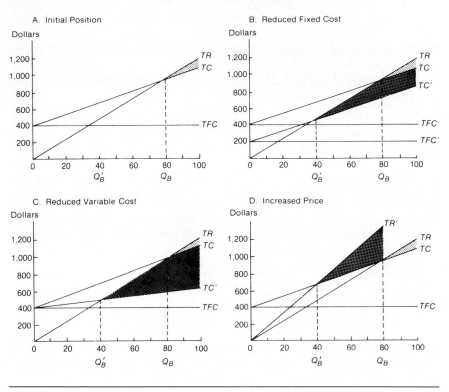

Break-Even Point Alternatives

If we want to reduce the break-even point to 40 units (Q'_B), we might do it in one of three ways:

1. Reduce Fixed Cost. From Equation (1) we note that the break-even point could be reduced in direct proportion to a decrease in total fixed cost. Therefore, we can reduce the break-even point to 40 units if we can cut fixed costs (TFC') to $200, because

$$Q'_B = \frac{TFC'}{(P - AVC)} = \frac{\$200}{\$12 - \$7} = 40 \text{ units}$$

the darker shaded area on Panel B represents the gain in profit.

2. Reduce Average Variable Cost. Reduction of the break-even point to 40 units (Q'_B) might be achieved by a reduction in average variable costs (AVC'). This alternative reduction in variable cost may be computed from Equation (1) as

$$Q'_B = \frac{TFC}{P - AVC'}$$

or

$$AVC' = P - \frac{TFC}{Q'_B} = \$12 - \frac{\$400}{40} = \$12 - \$10 = \$2 \text{ per unit}$$

The darker shaded area on Panel C indicates the increase in profit. However, it should be noted that a 50 percent reduction in the break-even point requires more than a 70 percent reduction in variable cost.

3. Increase Price. The increase in price necessary to achieve a break-even sales volume of 40 units (Q'_B) may be computed from Equation (1) as

$$Q'_B = \frac{TFC}{P' - AVC}$$

or

$$P' = \frac{TFC}{Q'_B} + AVC = \frac{\$400}{40} + \$7 = \$17$$

With an increase in price, a decrease in the quantity sold might be expected. Panel D shows that even with sales reduced to 80 percent of capacity, a sizable increase in profits could result.

Margin of Safety

In the preceding illustrations, only one of the variables (price, total variable cost, or total fixed cost) was changed at a time, but in reality they may all be changed simultaneously. One way of measuring the overall effect of multiple changes is to look at the ratio of profit to total fixed cost. This margin of profit stands between the profit the firm is making and the loss it would take if sales drop below the break-even point. Hence it is called the *margin of safety*, and the larger it is, the better.

The margin of safety (MS) may be calculated in two ways; first,

$$MS = \frac{\pi}{TFC} \tag{8}$$

with profit, π, and total fixed cost, TFC, expressed in dollars. But profit is made on units sold in excess of the break-even quantity, and the break-even quantity is determined by total fixed cost. So the same margin of safety may be expressed as a ratio of quantities:

$$MS = \frac{Q_S - Q_B}{Q_B} \tag{9}$$

where

Q_S = Total number of units sold
Q_B = Break-even quantity

To illustrate this concept, let us suppose a firm produces solid-waste disposal units that are sold to stores, factories, and other commercial users for \$35,000 each. The plant is currently producing 48 units per year, which represents 60 percent of its 80-unit capacity. Total fixed cost is \$600,000 and the average variable cost per unit is \$20,000.

The firm is contemplating a change in design that will increase the average variable cost by \$1,000 per unit. Also an advertising campaign will be launched, at a cost of \$120,000, to announce that the new improved model will sell for \$2,000 less than the old one. The marketing manager estimates that these measures will increase sales to 90 percent of plant capacity. Assuming that the marketing manager is right, what will be the effects on the break-even sales volume and on annual profits?

To answer these questions, we note first of all that four alternatives are available, as follows:

Alternative A. Maintain current conditions for which the break-even quantity is

$$Q_B = \frac{TFC}{P - AVC} = \frac{\$600,000}{\$35,000 - \$20,000} = 40 \text{ units}$$

The annual profit is

$$\pi = Q_S(P - AVC) - TFC$$
$$= 48 (\$35,000 - \$20,000) - \$600,000 = \$120,000$$

The margin of safety is

$$MS = \frac{\pi}{TFC} = \frac{\$120,000}{\$600,000} = 0.20$$

or

$$MS = \frac{Q_S - Q_B}{Q_B} = \frac{48 - 40}{40} = 0.20$$

Alternative B. All of the contemplated changes are carried out; that is, production is increased to 90 percent of capacity, variable costs increase by $1,000 per unit, price is cut by $2,000 per unit, and $120,000 is spent on advertising. The new break-even quantity is

$$Q_B = \frac{\$600,000 + \$120,000}{\$33,000 - \$21,000} = \frac{\$720,000}{\$12,000} = 60 \text{ units}$$

At 90 percent capacity, $0.90(80) = 72$ units will be manufactured and sold. The net profit will be

$$\pi = 72(\$33,000 - \$21,000) - \$600,000 - \$120,000 = \$144,000$$

which is an increase of $24,000. The margin of safety, however, has not changed, since it is

$$MS = \frac{Q_S - Q_B}{Q_B} = \frac{72 - 60}{60} = 0.20$$

Alternative C.   Obtain the same net profit as Alternative B, but without the advertising. The break-even quantity is

$$Q_B = \frac{\$600,000}{\$12,000} = 50 \text{ units}$$

and the quantity sold would be

$$Q_S = \frac{\pi + TFC}{P - AVC} = \frac{\$144,000 + \$600,000}{\$12,000} = 62 \text{ units}$$

The margin of safety would increase to

$$MS = \frac{62 - 50}{50} = 0.24$$

Alternative D.   Get the same profit with the advertising but without the price cut. The break-even quantity is

$$Q_B = \frac{\$720,000}{\$14,000} = 52 \text{ units}$$

and the quantity sold is

$$Q_S = \frac{\$144,000 + \$720,000}{\$14,000} = 62 \text{ units}$$

The margin of safety decreases to

$$MS = \frac{62 - 52}{52} = 0.19$$

To summarize the alternatives:

Alternative	Sales Quantity	Break-Even Quantity	Profit	Margin of Safety
A	48	40	$120,000	.20
B	72	60	144,000	.20
C	62	50	144,000	.24
D	62	52	144,000	.19

Thus the break-even quantity and margin of safety both point to Alternative C as the best choice.

Comparing Different Kinds of Plants

The break-even approach can be used to make cost comparisons among plants that have different fixed and variable cost structures. For example, a capital-intensive plant generally involves larger fixed costs but smaller variable costs than a plant that is labor intensive. The cost advantage of this type of plant depends, then, upon the output rate: at small output rates it is more costly, but as output increases so does its cost advantage. To illustrate this point, let us return to the manufacturer of solid-waste disposal units and imagine that business has improved substantially and plans are now under way to build another manufacturing plant. Two designs have been submitted by the firm's engineering department and management must choose one of them.

Design A consists of merely duplicating the existing facility, in which case the total cost equation is expected to remain

$$TC_A = \$600,000 + \$21,000Q$$

Design B is a new design that utilizes more capital equipment. Its estimated total cost curve is

$$TC_B = \$780,000 + \$18,000Q$$

To find the production level at which neither design has an advantage, we simply set their cost equations equal to each other and solve for Q:

$$TC_A = TC_B$$
$$\$600,000 + \$21,000Q = \$780,000 + \$18,000Q$$
$$\$3,000Q = \$180,000$$
$$Q = 60$$

We interpret the answer to mean that for output of less than 60 units, Plant A is more efficient. For output of more than 60 units, Plant B is more efficient. For output of 60 units, they are equally efficient.

Another dimension to this kind of problem, as well as for the others previously discussed, can be introduced into the example by imagining that management is not sure of the output rate. Let us assume, however, that a sales forecast has produced the following results:

1. Most likely sales (that is, the mean), $\mu = 70$.
2. Standard deviation of the distribution, $\sigma = 25$.
3. The probability distribution is normal.

This information is contained in Exhibit 14–5. The straight line shows the cost advantage of Plant B, which is $3,000 per unit above the 60-unit output rate (i.e., $3,000Q - 60(3,000) = 3,000Q - 180,000$, as shown on the graph). Along with this function, the probability distribution for sales is shown. Now we can ask the question: What is the probability that sales will equal or exceed 60 units?

Exhibit 14–5

Cost Advantage of Plant B and Sales Probability Distribution

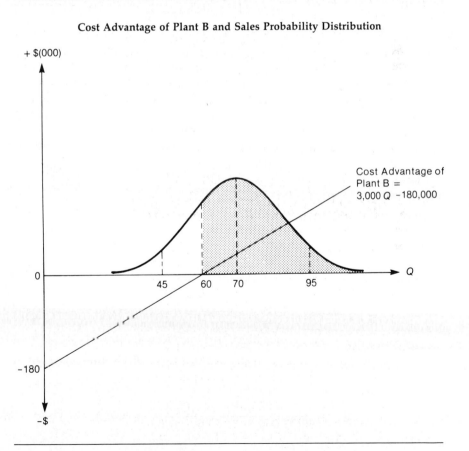

The shaded area under the probability distribution measured as a percentage of the total area under the distribution answers this question. The answer is easily found by referring to Table E in the Appendix at the end of the text and carrying out the following steps:

1. Find the appropriate Z value:

$$Z = \frac{X - \mu}{\sigma} = \frac{60 - 70}{25} = \frac{-10}{25} = -0.40$$

2. Find the percentage value in the table relating to this Z value; it is 0.1554.
3. Determine the shaded area; it is $0.500 + 0.1554 = 0.6554$.

Thus, the probability is a little more than 65 percent that Plant B will be more profitable than Plant A. Of course, management might also use the same technique to determine the probabilities for other output rates.

Operating Leverage

Even among plants with the same output capacity, the cost structure may vary from a labor-intensive plant with relatively lower fixed costs and higher variable costs to a capital-intensive plant with relatively higher fixed costs and lower variable costs. If both types charge the same price for their outputs, the capital-intensive firm will have a higher contribution margin. This means that the capital-intensive firm will experience greater variation in profit as sales increase or decrease. That is to say, the capital-intensive firm will have more operating leverage.

Operating leverage is a measure of the extent to which fixed production facilities, as distinguished from variable inputs, enter the firm's operations. The degree of operating leverage can be obtained from a formula that utilizes the contribution margin concept. For break-even analysis assuming linear relationships, the degree of operating leverage (OL) at any level of production, Q, can be calculated as the ratio of the total contribution profit to net profit:

$$OL_Q = \frac{TCP_Q}{\pi_Q} = \frac{Q(P - AVC)}{TCP_Q - TFC} = \frac{Q(P - AVC)}{Q(P - AVC) - TFC} \tag{10}$$

In the preceding example, at a production level of 60 units, Design A (which is more labor intensive) has an operating leverage of

$$OL_A = \frac{60(33,000 - 21,000)}{60(33,000 - 21,000) - 600,000} = 6.0$$

At the same level of 60 units, Design B (which is more capital intensive) has an operating leverage of

$$OL_B = \frac{60(33{,}000 - 18{,}000)}{60(33{,}000 - 18{,}000) - 780{,}000} = 7.5$$

Since operating leverage measures the sensitivity of profit to changes in the level of production and sales, it is actually the *sales elasticity of profit*:

$$\varepsilon_\pi = \frac{\Delta\pi/\pi}{\Delta Q/Q} = \frac{\Delta\pi}{\Delta Q} \cdot \frac{Q}{\pi} \tag{11}$$

To illustrate, let Plant B's production rise from 60 to 61 units. Then,

$$\pi_{60} = 60(\$33{,}000 - \$18{,}000) - \$780{,}000 = \$120{,}000$$
$$\pi_{61} = 61(\$33{,}000 - \$18{,}000) - \$780{,}000 = \$135{,}000$$

At a level of 60 units of production and sales,

$$\varepsilon_\pi = \frac{15}{1} \cdot \frac{60}{120} = 7.5$$

This is identical to the value for the operating leverage computed earlier. It means that at a level of activity where 60 units are produced and sold, a 1 percent increase in production and sales will result in a 7.5 percent increase in profit. At the same level of production in Plant A, which has a lower operating leverage of 6.0, a 1 percent increase in production and sales results in only 6.0 percent increase in profits.

For any given level of sales, operating leverage is greater for the more capital-intensive firm. However, the more capital-intensive firm will have a higher break-even point than the labor-intensive firm. Therefore, whether or not the capital-intensive firm enjoys a cost advantage depends upon its output. At lower levels of production, the labor-intensive plant has an advantage. At higher levels, the capital-intensive firm has an advantage. There is an output at which they are equally efficient, as we saw above.

Evaluation of Break-Even Analysis

Break-even analysis is a general method of profit planning and control, based on the assumption that there is a unique functional relationship between the profits of a firm and its level of output. Output, as stated earlier, may be measured in terms of physical units, dollar value of sales, percentage of plant capacity, or any other relevant index. Profit, on the other hand, is more explicit and usually represents the difference between receipts and expenses for the period under study. As an analytical device, break-even methods have as their chief advantages simplicity, ease of comprehension by management, and relative inexpensiveness compared with other more sophisticated techniques. Most, if not all, of the required data can be taken directly from the firm's cost accounting records and financial statements.

The static profit-output relationship that underlies the notion of break-even analysis assumes a continuation of the same relative sales and expense patterns. It takes no account of uncertainty, that is, the possible changes in revenues and costs that result from changing business conditions. Thus, the assumption in break-even analysis that there is a *simple relationship* between profit and output is an oversimplification of the facts. Profit depends on output, to be sure, but it also is affected by production processes, selling effort, the composition of demand, and a multiplicity of other factors internal and external to the firm.

A characterization of profit more in keeping with the facts would thus take into account its *multiple relationships*. To the extent that firms experience rapid changes in their main cost components, in their sales mixture, in their advertising and promotional policies, and/or in their technology and product design, the oversimplified traditional break-even techniques must be applied with great caution and due consideration of their weaknesses. However, when properly used, cost-volume-profit analysis provides the necessary background for decisions about such things as pricing strategies, promotion and advertising expenditures, channels of distribution, and output contracting.

Regression Analysis

Another method commonly used in profit planning is regression analysis. How does this procedure relate to profit prediction?

Essentially, the goal is to discover a functional relationship between the company's profits and one or more indicators of national economic change such as the Federal Reserve Board's Index of Industrial Production, disposable income, bank debits, and so forth. The underlying assumption of this method of profit prediction is that the well-being of the firm, as measured by its profits, is directly determined by business conditions in the economy; the company, in other words, is a product of its environment. Profits are thus treated as a dependent variable, and the relevant measures of national economic change are independent variables.

In practice, this approach to profit forecasting is greatly enhanced when some logical lead-lag relationship can be found between the company's profits and one or more external variables. For example, the American Radiator & Standard Sanitary Corporation (now known as

American Standard, Inc.) utilized the fact that there was approximately a four-month lag between its own sales and the regularly published Dodge index of residential contracts awarded, thereby facilitating its profit forecast on plumbing and heating supplies.

Where logical lead-lag relationships cannot be found, the independent variables must themselves be forecast before a prediction of profits can be made. In that event, the accuracy of the profit forecast will depend directly upon (1) the accuracy of the forecast made for the independent variables, and (2) the extent to which these external variables are truly related to the company's profits. The first condition can be partially hedged by selecting indicators that are frequently forecast by various government and private agencies—variables such as gross national product, disposable personal income, the Federal Reserve Board's Index of industrial production, and so forth—so that the various predictions can be cross-checked, weighted, and evaluated. The second condition requires more of a subjective judgment supported by economic reasoning as to which variables will most closely affect the company's present and future earnings. Discovering the relevant data and choosing the appropriate period for the analysis (such as the most recent business cycle with the data expressed quarterly) are probably the most difficult aspects of this type of regression analysis.

Decentralized Profit Centers

At the beginning of this chapter, we noted that profit budgeting is intimately connected with control of the company's operations. There are two primary means of control: (1) clear statements of policies and procedures that control behavior before it occurs, and (2) reaction to feedback that corrects behavior while it is occurring or immediately thereafter. It is in this second area that the profit budget serves as a yardstick by which managerial or organizational performance can be measured and corrected if necessary.

As an organization grows larger and more complex, the task of top management becomes more and more difficult. Many companies have resolved this problem through decentralization. A truly decentralized firm is organized as a combination of semiautonomous units, each of which is a profit center. Largely as a result of the fabulous success achieved by General Motors with decentralized organization, this technique has won increasing favor among many of the larger manufacturing companies. It has been adopted by such well-known industrial giants as General Electric, Ford, Chrysler, and Westinghouse Electric. Divisional managers are given authority to plan their selling campaigns, establish selling prices, determine their material and personnel requirements, select their sources of supply from either inside or outside the company, and determine their marketing and distribution channels. In other words, the division manager's responsibility and authority tends to be complete with respect to all *short-run* decision making.

The top executive group of the parent firm retains responsibility for all matters of long-run policy, particularly with respect to capital expenditures; the establishment, disestablishment, and merger of decentralized divisions; and the selection and evaluation of divisional managers. In fulfilling this last responsibility, there is a tendency for top management to use profit as a yardstick by which to measure a division manager's performance. After all, profit is the ultimate measure of the firm's well-being. However, top management soon learns that determining and using profit measures for purposes of internal control are more difficult and controversial matters than establishing profit measures for the company as a whole.

Divisional Profit

In a decentralized firm, management responsibility has been delegated to the heads of divisional units, and there is a need for appropriate profit measures for evaluating performance of subordinate executives and guiding decisions of the divisional managements. A profit measure that will function properly must exclude all factors over which the divisional managers have no control. This means that it must be independent not only of the decisions handed down from the top but also from the superior or inferior performance of other divisions with which the one in question does business.

One can begin to appreciate now why the problem of internal profit measurement is so difficult:

1. *Allocation of cost.* Many facilities and services may be used jointly by two or more divisions of the company (e.g., general administrative services, research, maintenance personnel, and equipment). Furthermore, one division is likely to use more of these common facilities and services than another, and the amount of such use is not necessarily related to the volume of a division's business, thereby complicating the problem of allocating such costs among the various operating units.

2. *Interdivisional transactions.* It is also very likely that one division will have a business relationship with another involving a transfer of goods, by-products, and/or services. If established market prices exist for such transfers, the problem is relatively simple, but if no market prices exist, a system of (arbitrary) transfer prices must be established. Since the purchasing division has no control over the efficiency with which such products and services have been produced (and for which there are no established market prices to permit objective testing of their

supply prices), it should not be placed in a position of having its own performance hindered or helped by the supplying division's performance.

The preceding discussion leads to the conclusion that divisional net profit, determined in a simplistic manner, is a highly unsatisfactory measure for internal day-to-day decision making and executive evaluation. In order to make divisional profit a meaningful figure, therefore, it is necessary to add back two major costs:

1. Nondivisional expenses that have been charged to the division as part of its burden for supporting the company overhead.
2. Nonvariable or overhead costs of the division itself, incurred as a result of decisions made either by an earlier divisional manager or by the top executive group (with which rests responsibility for long-term capital commitments).

We then come up with a figure that may be called *controllable divisional profit*, which is essentially the earnings available after deducting from divisional revenues all variable divisional costs such as cost of goods sold and administrative and selling expenses, as well as any overhead costs directly subject to the control of division managers.

Evaluating Managerial Performance

Even after controllable divisional profit has been determined, there remains the problem of evaluating the divisional management. By what yardstick should it be measured? Comparisons of absolute dollar figures are meaningless when divisions differ in such things as size, products, marketing conditions, and operating equipment.

Perhaps we should use return on investment (*ROI*), but the problems in applying this yardstick are also quite formidable. We have already mentioned the transfer pricing problem, but there are at least three other major difficulties in using *ROI* as a yardstick.

1. *Differences in depreciation base and methods.* Obviously, accelerated depreciation decreases return on investment. On the other hand, fully depreciated assets no longer create depreciation expense and hence increase *ROI*. Leasing of assets in effect hides them from view and also increases *ROI* on the diminished investment base.
2. *Relative riskiness of investments.* Return on investment takes no account of the fact that one investment may be riskier than another. Given that two investments are equally successful in achieving their expected return, the one with the higher risk can be expected to yield the higher return—but this does not reflect superior management performance.

3. *Effect of evaluation period.* Evaluation usually takes place once a year, but large investments frequently take considerably more than a year to pay off. In the meantime, of course, *ROI* might be quite low or nonexistent.

Conclusion

In many respects, the task of evaluating departmental performance within a division is just as formidable as the task of evaluating divisions of the firm. One of the stickiest and most persistent problems at both levels is the fair and equitable allocation of fixed overhead costs. What one manager may consider to be fair and equitable might be bitterly resented and protested by another.

Whatever procedure is adopted, there does seem to be one universal rule: If the evaluation or cost allocation scheme does not lead managers to make decisions that benefit the organization as a whole, then it must be changed or discarded.

If discussion of decentralized control seems to raise more questions than answers, it is because that is the nature of the problem. It is unlikely that anyone has developed a completely satisfactory, universally applicable method for evaluating managerial performance, and possibly no one ever will. In many situations, it might make more sense to forget profits altogether and evaluate efficiency instead, as measured by minimization of costs.

A better way would be simply to compare actual division performance with its budgeted performance. After all, the budget is a negotiated document with performance goals and objectives that have been agreed to by the manager and his superiors. The manager who meets or beats his budgeted performance should be congratulated and rewarded accordingly. The manager who fails to meet his budgeted performance had better have a good explanation or else suffer the consequences.

Summary

A profit budget serves the functions of planning, coordination, and control of the firm's activities. The budgeting process enables managers to anticipate their needs, and forces coordination of the firm's activities that otherwise might not take place. The control function is not automatic, but by means of suitable reports, it enables management to maintain a systematic check on the company's operations in terms of planned versus actual results.

Break-even analysis is an adjunct to profit planning that graphically or algebraically portrays the probable effects of alternative courses of action. It can be used to determine the output required to net a given revenue, or the revenue to be expected from a given output, or the sales volume required to break even. It can also be used to compare the profitability of different types of plants (capital-intensive versus labor-intensive).

Break-even analysis is simple, easy to understand by management, and relatively inexpensive to perform. Its weakness is the assumption that profit is a simple function of output. In reality, profit is also affected by production processes, selling effort, the composition of demand, and a multiplicity of other factors both internal and external to the firm.

Regression analysis is also commonly used for profit forecasting. Its goal is to discover a functional relationship between the company's profits and one or more indicators of national economic change.

On the control side, a formidable task is the evaluation of divisions and divisional managers of a decentralized firm, and departmental performance within divisions. One of the toughest problems at both levels is the fair and equitable allocation of fixed overhead costs. Whatever procedure is adopted, it must lead managers to make decisions that benefit the whole organization. The best method of evaluation may be simply to compare actual performance with budgeted performance.

Problems

1. What is meant by contribution margin? Can it be positive when total profit is negative? Can it be negative when total profit is positive?

2. Return on investment (*ROI*) is frequently used to evaluate the profit performance of semiautonomous divisions within a corporation. Discuss some limitations of using this method. Can you suggest an alternative approach? Explain.

3. In break-even analysis, if a linear revenue function is used, one is assuming that all units of output are sold at a constant price. What assumption is made when a nonlinear revenue curve is used? Is either of these assumptions very realistic from a practical point of view? Discuss.

4. Kona Coast Inn manages 7 two-bedroom apartment units that rent for $95 a day and 20 one-bedroom cabin units that rent for $60 a day. The inn also manages 30 single room units and 15 double-room units, which rent for $40 and $50 a day, respectively. After the occupants leave, the cost of cleaning and preparation for new occupants is $18 each for the apartment and cabin units, and $9 each for all other types of accommodations. Annual lease for the property is $200,000, and other fixed costs for managing and maintaining the property are $50,000 on a 300-day annual basis. The average stay at the facility is 2½ days, and the occupancy closely follows the proportion of available facilities.

a. What percentage of facilities must be rented each day to break even?

b. How many of each type of accommodations must be rented each day (on the average) to make an annual profit of $50,000?

5. This & That Boutique offers all of its merchandise for sale at $20 per unit. The total cost of producing Q units is given by $C = 40 + 4Q + 0.02Q^2$. Using algebraic methods, show:

a. The number of units that must be produced and sold to maximize profit.

b. That marginal revenue equals marginal cost at the profit-maximizing value of Q.

c. The break-even output.

6. Data for last month's activity at a division of the Albritton Company appear below:

| | Product | | | |
	A	B	C	Total
Sales.....................	$100,000	$60,000	$90,000	$250,000
Variable costs..........................	50,000	50,000	60,000	160,000
Allocated fixed costs	24,000	14,400	21,600	60,000
Profit (loss) before taxes	$ 26,000	$ (4,400)	$ 8,400	$ 30,000
Federal income taxes	13,000	2,200*	4,200	15,000
Net profit	$ 13,000	$ (2,200)	$ 4,200	$ 15,000

* Indicates a credit.

a. Using the data, construct a break-even diagram for the division as a whole. Calculate the break-even sales volume.

b. Sales in the upcoming month are expected to change as follows: (1) Product A, up 10 percent; (2) Product B, down 20 percent; and (3) Product C, up 5 percent. Based on this new product mix information, construct another break-even diagram and, again, calculate the break-even sales volume. Also, determine the divisional profit or loss for the upcoming period.

c. Albritton's president feels the division should eliminate Product B because of its previous profit performance and the pessimistic forecast for the upcoming month. Indicate whether or not you agree with this decision.

7. Suave Hats, Inc., manufactures men's hats and sells them at $25 each. Its total fixed cost is $6,000 per week, and its average variable cost is $13 per unit.

a. What is the company's break-even sales volume?

b. What would the company's profit be at its normal production capacity of 2,000 hats per week?

c.   The company has been operating at its normal production capacity. The union threatens to strike, so the management of Suave decides to produce an additional 500 hats for inventory at an estimated average variable cost of $15 per hat. What will be the incremental profit (or loss) on the sale of the 500 additional hats?

d.   After some negotiation, the company and the union agree on a new labor contract. Meanwhile, the company has been able to dispose of only 300 of the 500 additional hats at its regular price of $25. However, a department store has offered to take the remaining 200 hats under a private label at $14 each. If the management of Suave accepts the offer, what will be the incremental effect of these 500 units?

8.   National Outerwear manufactures and sells men's raincoats at a price of $40 each, for which the average contribution profit is $15 per coat. Last year total fixed costs were $5.4 million; this year, through a major cost reduction effort, they are expected to be $3.9 million.

a.   How many raincoats did National Outerwear need to sell last year in order to break even?

b.   How many must it sell this year in order to break even?

c.   How many raincoats must the company sell this year in order to earn a profit before taxes equal to 20 percent of sales?

9.   Calvin Levine is planning to go into the designer jeans business. He projects the following costs for the first year of operation

Rental payments	$1,500 per month
Direct Labor	$ 9.50 per hour
Raw materials	$ 6 per pair of jeans
Overhead	$ 975 per week
Interest on capital	$1,350 per month

It takes 20 minutes of direct labor to assemble a pair of pants, and Calvin sells his designer jeans for $39.50 a pair.

a.   How many pairs of jeans must be sold to break even the first year? (Assume a 50-week year.)

b.   If profits total $38,500 for the first year, what is Calvin's safety margin?

c.   After a successful first year, Calvin foresees a decline in designer jeans demand as a result of a weakening economy. If Calvin wants a break-even point of 2,300 units, how much of a reduction in fixed costs would be necessary?

d.   What three alternative methods are available for reducing the break-even point? Using each of these methods, what adjustments must be made to meet Calvin's break-even point of 2,300 units?

e.   Considering the uncertain demand conditions faced by Calvin, which of the three methods for reducing break-even points is most appropriate? Why?

10.   IBN Water Purification Inc. is evaluating two possible designs for a new production facility to replace their present obsolete facility. The total cost functions for the two facilities are

$$TC_1 = 550,000 + 600Q$$
$$TC_2 = 300,000 + 825Q$$

Both plants would produce an identical desalination device that sells for $2,600 per unit. IBN foresees no change in demand and intends to estimate sales from an average of the last seven years:

Year	Sales ($000)
1	$1,100
2	1,075
3	1,200
4	1,250
5	1,150
6	1,100
7	1,125

a.   Calculate the operating leverage for both plant designs.
b.   Find the level of production at which neither plant design has an advantage.
c.   Which plant design is labor intensive and which is capital intensive? Explain.
d.   Considering the sales information given, which plant design has a greater probability of cost savings?
e.   Graph the cost function for the plant design with greater expected savings, over a normal distribution of the past sales data.

11.   Dutch Line Furniture Company produces natural oak wood chairs. Presently, production is running at 3,500 per year, which is plant capacity. Currently, the chairs sell for $135 each, variable costs are $50 each, and fixed costs total $120,000 per year. Because of excess demand, Dutch Line is planning to expand plant capacity by 1,500 chairs. The plant expansion will incorporate some new high-speed equipment resulting in a reduction of variable costs by 15 percent, but an increase in fixed costs by 40 percent. Because of their reputation for quality, Dutch Line can sell every chair it produces.

a.   What is the break-even output before and after the plant expansion?
b.   What is the degree of operating leverage at current capacity?
c.   What would be the degree of operating leverage at capacity after plant expansion?
d.   Will the plant expansion increase or decrease the margin of safety at capacity?
e.   Would you advise Dutch Line to expand? Explain.

Case Problem: U.S. Automobile Industry

12.   Since the Japanese auto influx of the late 1970s, the big three U.S. auto manufacturers have tried reducing prices, giving rebates, and offering discount financing in order to increase sales. Common sense tells us that sales are elastic to price. In other words, by lowering the price we can increase sales. However, with further analysis it becomes apparent that there are actually two forms of elasticity to be considered when adjusting prices:

Price elasticity of demand, which measures the effect that price reductions will have on demand and thus on revenues.

Cost elasticity, which measures the effect that increased sales volume will have on production and thus on costs.

Of course, both elasticities should be considered by U.S. auto manufacturers when they attempt to compete through price reductions. However, corporations using such price reductions have focused on price elasticity of demand while often neglecting the effects on costs.

Actual demand studies conducted on new automobiles have estimated price elasticities of demand ranging from 0.5 to 1.5. The higher the coefficient of elasticity, the greater the percentage increase in quantity demanded that will result from a price decrease. For our analysis assume a liberal elasticity measurement of 1.5, which should maximize any benefits from a price reduction. We will explore the effects of an auto manufacturer's reducing car prices by $400.

The auto industry is considered an oligopoly market structure. Thus competition can be expected to meet any price reduction, as indicated by the rebate war of the late 1970s and the interest rate competition during 1982–83. As a result, price reductions are not a relative advantage but instead a general price change by all producers. Assume the following conditions before price reductions:

Average car price	$9,000 per car
Expected sales volume ($9,000 per car)	1,000,000 cars
Average total cost	$8,200 per car
Total variable cost	$6,400,000,000

Questions:
a.   Calculate the present total fixed cost, average fixed cost and average variable cost.
b.   What is the present break-even point?
c.   What is the change in total revenue resulting from the $400 price reduction?
d.   Calculate the profit before and after the price reduction.

e. Because of the price reduction, revenues have been reduced by $400 per car. Was there any effect on the cost per car? What is the average total cost after reducing the price?

f. Discuss possible conclusions from your calculations.

g. Would higher or lower variable cost, relative to total cost, help justify price reductions? Explain.

h. The following formula is used to determine the price elasticity of demand necessary for a given price reduction while keeping profits constant:

$$Q = \frac{P}{\overline{N} - P + [1 - (V/C)]\overline{C}}$$

where

Q = Percentage increase of output quantity required
P = Price decrease in dollars
$\overline{N}$ = Net profit per unit at the old price
$\overline{C}$ = Cost per unit (i.e., average total cost) at the old price
V/C = Ratio of total variable cost to total cost

The elasticity coefficient is then

$$\text{Elasticity} = \frac{Q(\overline{N} + \overline{C})}{P}$$

At what elasticity would the $400 price reduction be justified?

i. What advice would you give to the auto manufacturers? Why do U.S. manufacturers continue to give price reductions?

j. Discuss possible recessionary effects on auto sales.

Case Problem: Monkeypod Ltd.

13. Monkeypod Ltd. is a newly formed company in the Hawaiian wood products industry. It will specialize in monkeypod bowls for sale to both tourists and island residents. Before constructing any production facilities, management conducted a market research study with the following results:

Island	Demand/month (1983)
Oahu	8,000
Maui	3,000
Kauai	2,300

The facilities development team suggested two possible alternatives for plant construction:

1. Build one large plant on Oahu with a capacity of 16,000 units per month, fixed cost of $32,000 per month, and variable cost of $4 per unit.
2. Build three plants, one on each island, with production capacities of 10,000 units on Oahu, 4,000 units on Maui, and 3,000 units on Kauai. The total fixed cost for the three facilities would be $40,000 per month with variable costs of $3.50 per unit.

Questions:
a. What are the total cost equations for each alternative?
b. Given the market survey results, which of the given production alternatives should be chosen?
c. If the monkeypod bowls sell for $9.50 each, how much profit will be realized from your chosen alternative?
d. If the demand for bowls is expected to rise significantly next year, would this alter your decision? Explain.
e. Discuss possible reasons for the differing cost structures between the two production alternatives.
f. Discuss the economies of scale being exhibited.

References

Horngren, Charles T. *Cost Accounting, A Managerial Emphasis.* 5th ed. Englewood Cliffs, N.J.: Prentice-Hall, 1982.

Meimaroglou, M. C. "Break-Even Analysis with Stepwise Varying Marginal Costs and Revenue." *Budgeting,* November 1964, pp. 1–7.

Percival, John. "Operating Leverage and Risk." *Journal of Business Research,* April 1974, pp. 223–31.

Reinhardt, U. E. "Breakeven Analysis for Lockheed's Tri-Star: An Application of Financial Theory." *Journal of Finance,* September 1973, pp. 821–38.

Riggs, James L. *Engineering Economics.* 2d ed. New York: McGraw-Hill, 1982. The discussion on multiple products and nonlinear break-even analysis in chapter 3 is particularly recommended.

15

Pricing, Output, and Nonprice Competition in Different Market Structures

In previous chapters we discussed possible objectives of the firm and the profit-maximization model, determinants and measurement of demand, the production function and the concept of optimal employment of resources, and the nature and behavior of costs, including economies of scale and profit planning and control.

Having studied these elements, we are now in a position to examine how demand, production, cost, and profit objectives interact to determine the market structure within which the firm operates. We can also see how market structure determines price/output decisions that every firm must make.

In the first section of this chapter, we examine four important determinants of market structure: (1) sellers' characteristics, (2) buyers' characteristics, (3) product characteristics, and (4) conditions of market entry and exit. In following sections, we describe and analyze the market structures known as (1) perfection competition, (2) pure monopoly, (3) monopolistic competition, and (4) oligopoly. In the last section, we discuss nonprice competition provided by product differentiation and advertising. Finally, in Appendix 15A, a more rigorous discussion of profit-maximizing equilibrium is presented.

Special topics on pricing and pricing practices are discussed in the next chapter. Key points covered in the next chapter include pricing objectives and methods, price discrimination, pricing of multiple products, pricing of joint products, and transfer pricing.

Market Structures

A *market* is a collection of buyers and sellers of products that have some degree of substitutability.[1] *Market structure* refers to the nature and degree of competition in the market for a particular good or service.

The general theory of pricing postulates a spectrum of market structures that range from *perfect competition* at one extreme to *pure monopoly* at the other. In between, a number of intermediate market structures are possible, but for convenience they are divided into two classes of imperfect competition: *monopolistic competition* and *oligopoly*.

There are a number of determinants that might be used to indicate the market structure for any particular product or group of products. As might be expected, many of these determinants are interdependent.

In general, determinants of market structure may be grouped into five major categories: (1) the number and nature of the sellers, (2) the number and nature of the buyers, (3) the nature of the product, (4) the conditions of entry into and exit from the market and (5) possible economies of scale. Each of these categories is discussed in more detail in the following subsections.

The Effect of Sellers' Characteristics on Market Structure

The nature and degree of competition is influenced by the *number* and *size* of the firms operating in the market in relation to the size of the market. Thus the continuum of market structures ranges from many sellers in perfect competition, no one of which can produce a significant portion of the total market supply, to only one seller in a pure monopoly. Agricultural commodities provide particularly good examples of markets with many relatively small sellers, while utilities offer examples of markets close to pure monopolies.

The Effect of Buyer Characteristics on Market Structure

The nature and degree of competition is also influenced by the number and size of the buyers in the market. If there is only one large buyer (the condition is called monopsony) or only a few buyers (this condition is called oligopsony) there cannnot be much competition among suppliers.

---

[1] There is a tendency to regard *market* and *industry* as synonyms. They are not synonymous unless all goods produced by the industry are substitutes. For example, the standard classification Motor Vehicles and Parts embraces such diverse products as large semitrailer trucks and small Volkswagen sedans. These products are hardly substitutes, nor are they sold to the same set of buyers. Therefore, this particular industry has more than one market. In this chapter, we shall use the word *industry* to mean that part of the standard industrial classification that constitutes a market as defined above.

Monopsony or oligopsony characterizes government purchases of complex systems, the market for automotive components purchased by the large automobile manufacturers, local labor markets where there is only one large employer, and local agricultural markets where the entire crop is purchased by a few large processors.

The Effect of Product Characteristics on Market Structure

The most important characteristic of a firm's product is the degree to which the product is differentiated from all others in the same market. Product differentiation thus is closely related to elasticities of demand. Products that are close substitutes, as indicated by high positive cross-elasticity coefficients, will be marketed in a different structure from products with greater or lesser differentiation. At one extreme, a perfectly elastic standard product (no differentiation) is a necessary condition for perfect competition. At the other extreme, a product with no close substitutes (extreme differentiation) is a necessary condition for pure monopoly.

Conditions of Entry and Exit

Economic theory holds that profitability within a particular market will attract the entry of new firms, and lack of profitability (losses) will drive weaker firms out.[2] In the model of perfect competition, both entry and exit are assumed to be free from any obstruction. At the other extreme, a pure monopoly can exist only if barriers to entry are so high that no other firm can enter the market.

There are many potential barriers to the entry of new firms into a particular market, and the height of these barriers plays a crucial role in determining the structure of the market. Factors that may bar market entry include the following:

1. Costs of developing a differentiated product plus promotional costs necessary to penetrate the market.
2. Demand conditions, especially price elasticity.
3. Control by existing firms over the supply of the factors of production.
4. Control by existing firms over channels of distribution.
5. Legal and institutional factors, such as patents and franchises.
6. Potential economies of scale.
7. Capital requirements.
8. Technological factors.

---

[2] *Profitability* refers to profit in excess of normal profit (which is equal to opportunity cost).

All of these apply to firms already in the market as well as to those that may wish to enter it. This has led to some disagreement over what constitutes a barrier to entry, an issue that is complicated by further disagreement over the definition of "market entry." On the one hand, a school of thought typified by Bain holds that entry occurs whenever there is production of new output, regardless of whether it is produced by a new or existing firm. With this definition of entry, the Bain school holds that a barrier to entry is any advantage held by existing producers over potential producers.[3]

A different viewpoint is presented by Stigler, who defines entry as the emergence of new firms not previously in the market. A barrier to entry is any cost that must be borne by the firm seeking to enter but not borne by those who are already established in the market.[4]

In either case, the height of a barrier to entry is a major determinant of market structure. Many of the highest and longest-lasting barriers to entry are those thrown up by government decrees and actions. Governments limit the number of potential competitors in many markets with licensing requirements and zoning restrictions. A notorious example is the taxi business in New York City, where only a limited number of licenses are granted by the city government. Taxicab medallions (needed for legal operation) sell for nearly $60,000, which is a rough estimate of the surplus profit cabs are each expected to earn because of their limited numbers.

Government agencies routinely grant exclusive franchises to favored firms for such things as parking concessions, garbage collection, radio and television broadcasting, air transportation, trucking, and postal service. In some cases, the government sells such a franchise to the highest bidder so that some of the economic profits go into the public treasury, but this is not always the case.

Economy of Scale

Possible economies of scale in production provide the best explanation of why there are large firms in some industries, but not in others. When large economies of scale are possible, firms that can grow large enough to achieve such economies have a competitive edge. Consequently, the market comes to be served by a small number of firms, each of which is large enough to attain the available economies of scale. When the economy of scale is such that it can be fully achieved only if one firm provides all that is demanded, then a natural monopoly exists.

---

[3] Joe S. Bain, *Barriers to New Competition* (Cambridge, Mass.: Harvard University Press, 1965).

[4] George J. Stigler, *The Organization of Industry* (Homewood, Ill.: Richard D. Irwin, 1968), pp. 67–70.

Having examined the determinants of market structure, we are now ready to discuss the firm's output and pricing decisions in terms of four classic models: (1) perfect competition, (2) pure monopoly, (3) monopolistic competition, and (4) oligopoly.

Perfect Competition

The model of perfect competition envisions a market structure with the following characteristics:

1. *Many small sellers of a homogeneous or standard product.* Market supply is the aggregate production of all sellers, but no one seller produces enough to significantly affect market supply. However, if all sellers move in the same direction at the same time, market supply will be affected. For example, a low market price for wheat in one year may cause all wheat farmers to reduce their plantings for the next year.

2. *Many small buyers.* Since the product is homogeneous, buyers are indifferent to the source of the product. Market demand thus is the aggregate demand of all buyers, no one of which is large enough to significantly affect demand. However, if all buyers move in the same direction at the same time, they will shift the demand curve. For example, there is an upsurge in the demand for eggs at Easter time, or in the demand for lettuce in hot weather.

3. *Free entry.* In the long run, there is free entry into and exit from the market. Barriers to entry or exit are either very low or nonexistent.

4. *Free mobility of economic resources.* There are no artificial restraints upon supply, demand, or price of either input factors of production or output of the product, and all resources are freely mobile.

5. *Perfect information.* Each buyer and seller operates under conditions of certainty, being endowed with complete knowledge of prices, quantities, costs, and demand.[5]

6. *The firm is a price taker and quantity adjuster.* Market price is determined by the equilibrium between market supply and market demand. Consequently, individual firms have nothing to say about prices, but can sell all they can produce at the market price. (The firm's demand curve is a horizontal line.) Therefore, the firm's only decision is how much to produce in order to maximize profit (or minimize loss).

Although some of the assumptions of the perfectly competitive model may seem unrealistic, use of the model in economic theory has been

---

[5] The model of *pure* competition, as opposed to *perfect* competition, does not require perfect information on the part of buyers and sellers. In pure competition, buyers and sellers are to various degrees unaware of pertinent market facts.

increasing in recent decades for two quite different reasons. One reason is that the model can be used as an ideal, or yardstick, against which all other models can be compared and evaluated. The other reason is that the model has been quite accurate in *explaining* and *predicting* behavior of the market and the firm in certain circumstances.

Short-Run Equilibrium

We begin our analysis with market equilibrium between the market supply curve, S, and the market demand curve, D, as shown in Panel A of Exhibit 15–1. The market-clearing price is thus established as P dol-

Exhibit 15–1

Profit-Maximizing Price and Output for a Firm in Perfect Competition

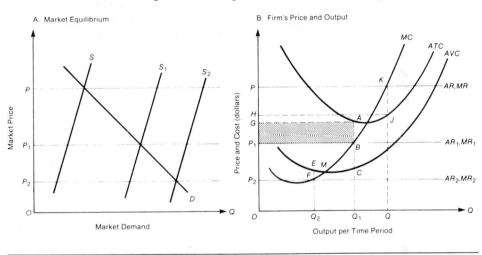

lars. A firm can sell all it wishes at the market price. Its demand curve, therefore, is a horizontal line that represents both average revenue, AR, and marginal revenue, MR, each of which is equal to the market price, P. This situation is depicted in Panel B, along with the curves representing the firm's marginal cost, MC, average total cost, ATC, and average variable cost, AVC. These cost curves include a "normal" profit equal to the firm's opportunity cost.

As we have noted in previous chapters, the firm's profit will be maximized when marginal cost equals marginal revenue. This occurs at point K in Panel B, indicating an optimal production of Q units and a price of P dollars. The unit price, P, is greater than unit cost, ATC, by JK dollars.

This represents unit profit. Hence there is a total economic profit represented by the rectangle *JKPH*.

As an algebraic example, suppose we let the price $P = \$10$. The firm's total revenue thus is

$$TR = P \cdot Q = 10Q \tag{1}$$

from which we derive the marginal revenue

$$MR = \frac{dTR}{dQ} = 10 \tag{2}$$

Now let us assume the cost function

$$TC = 4 + 4Q + Q^2$$

from which we derive the marginal cost

$$MC = \frac{dTC}{dQ} = 4 + 2Q. \tag{3}$$

The firm's total profit is

$$\pi = TR - TC = 10Q - 4 - 4Q - Q^2 = -4 + 6Q - Q^2$$

In order to maximize profit, we take the first derivative and set it equal to zero:

$$\frac{d\pi}{dQ} = 6 - 2Q = 0$$

Hence,

$$Q^* = 3$$

where the asterisk indicates optimum value.

To complete the exercise, we take the second derivative and check its sign to see whether Q^* represents a maximum (negative sign) or a minimum (positive sign):

$$\frac{d^2\pi}{dQ^2} = -2$$

Hence π is maximum at Q^*. That is, profit is at a maximum when $Q = 3$. When $Q = 3$, $MC = 4 + 2Q = 10$, which is equal to marginal revenue. At any greater level of production, $MC > MR$, and at any lower level of production, $MC < MR$.

The maximum profit is obtained by inserting the optimal level $Q = 3$ into the profit function:

$$\pi = -4 + 6Q - Q^2 = 4 + 6(3) - (3)^2 = \$13$$

The same result can be obtained by letting marginal revenue equal marginal cost to find the optimal output:

$$MR = 10 = 4 + 2Q = MC$$
$$2Q = 6$$
$$Q^* = 3$$

Now let us suppose that the market equilibrium is upset by events that cause a shift in either the demand or the supply curve. A good example is the bumper grain crop of 1982, which shifted the supply curve to the right and drove the price down below cost for many farmers. The change in price calls, of course, for a different optimal quantity of production.

To illustrate, suppose the supply curve shifts to S_1 on Panel A of Exhibit 15–1, creating a new market price of P_1. Now the firm's $MR = MC$ at B on Panel B, and $Q^* = Q_1$. The price is now greater than unit variable cost, AVC, but less than total unit cost, ATC. Consequently, the firm will lose some, but not all of its fixed costs, represented by the rectangle ABP_1G. The firm will continue to produce in the short run, since there is still a positive contribution margin, BC, for each unit (i.e., $ATC = AVC + AFC = Q_1C + CA$).

If, however, the market price drops to P_2, which is below the firm's minimum average variable cost, the firm cannot recover all of its variable costs, to say nothing of its fixed costs. Hence, it would be forced to shut down.

The Firm's Short-Run Supply Curve.   We see in Exhibit 15–1 that at each different price, the firm will produce at the level where $MR = MC$. The points of intersection between the MR curve and MC curve follow the MC curve as the price changes. Hence the firm's short-run supply curve is simply its marginal cost curve, except that the lower end of the supply curve terminates at point M, where $MC = AVC$. Below this point, the firm is not able to recover variable costs and therefore will not produce anything.

Long-Run Equilibrium

Since both entry and exit are free, the existence of economic profit will attract new firms into the market, while losses will squeeze some firms out. In the long run the firm can also adjust the size of its plant for maximum efficiency and can choose the market in which it will operate, in each case with an eye for profit.

Adjustments to the number of firms in the market will continue until long-run equilibrium is reached. At equilibrium all economic profit is squeezed out, and each firm earns a normal profit, no more and no less.

Thus the product is priced at the lowest possible average cost in the long run. The process is illustrated in Exhibit 15–2.

Exhibit 15–2 shows how the market and the firms within it arrive at long-run equilibrium with demand held constant. Given the demand

Exhibit 15–2 _____

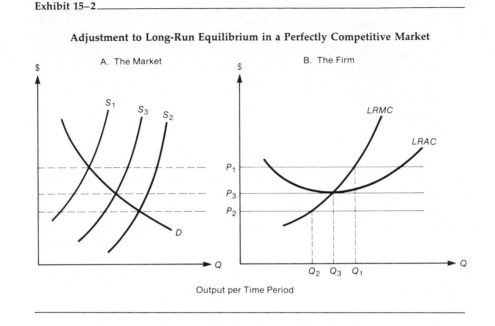

Adjustment to Long-Run Equilibrium in a Perfectly Competitive Market

A. The Market

B. The Firm

Output per Time Period

_____

curve D and the supply curve S_1 in Panel A, a market-clearing price of P_1 becomes established. Panel B shows the long-run average cost, LRAC, and long-run marginal cost, LRMC, of a typical plant in this market. At a price of P_1, Q_1 units can be produced at a substantial economic profit.

The economic profit being earned by firms in the industry attract new firms. Their added production shifts the supply curve to S_2, which lowers the price to P_2. Each firm reduces its output to the optimal quantity Q_2, but all firms lose money at that price. The weaker firms will then drop out, shifting the supply curve back to the left. Equilibrium is re-established with a market supply of S_3 and a price of P_3. At this price, where $P = LRAC$ and $LRAC = LRMC$, the typical firm earns no economic profit while producing and selling the product at the lowest possible long-run average cost.

The Market's Long-Run Supply Curve.   If the market demand curve shifts, the market supply curve and the market equilibrium point also shift, as depicted in Exhibit 15–3. When the initial and final equilibrium

Exhibit 15–3

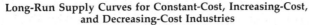

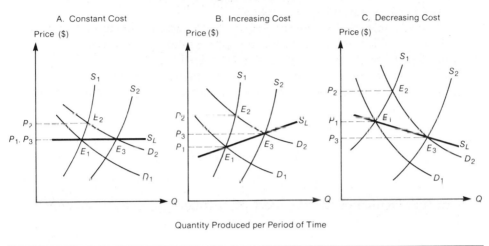

Long-Run Supply Curves for Constant-Cost, Increasing-Cost,
and Decreasing-Cost Industries

Quantity Produced per Period of Time

points are connected, we get the long-run market supply curve, which
may be horizontal, rising, or falling, depending upon whether production costs remain constant, rise, or fall as production increases.

Each of the panels in Exhibit 15–3 depicts what happens to market
supply and market price when demand is increased. We begin with
initial equilibrium at point E_1 in Panel A, which is the intersection of the
market demand curve D_1 with the market supply curve S_1. The market-
clearing price is P_1.

Then, for any one of a number of reasons, the demand curve shifts to
D_2. Market equilibrium is now at E_2, with a market price of P_2. At this
price, economic profits attract new firms into the market. Those firms
increase the market supply, causing the supply curve to shift to the
right. New market equilibrium is gained at E_3, with a market price of P_3.
However, P_3 is the same price as P_1. When the initial equilibrium point,
E_1, is connected with the final equilibrium point, E_3, the resulting long-
run supply curve is horizontal because prices of the input factors of
production were not driven up as new firms entered the market. This
has happened because this particular industry does not require a significant share of the total supply of the resources that it uses.

Panel B depicts the same sort of transition from initial equilibrium at
E_1, with price P_1, through interim equilibrium at E_2, with price P_2. This
time, however, the long-run supply curve connecting E_1 and E_3 has an
upward slope, and the final price, P_3, is higher than the initial price, P_1.

This is because the industry depicted in Panel B requires a significant share of the total resources available. Therefore, when new firms enter the industry, they must bid up the prices of input factors in order to obtain a sufficient supply. Therefore, their minimum long-run average costs (which equal price) are greater.

Panel C again depicts the transition from E_1 and P_1 through E_2 and P_2 to E_3 and P_3. This time, the long-run supply curve slopes downward and the ultimate price, P_3, is lower than the initial price, P_1. This occurs because new firms expanding production encounter economies of scale that cause the costs of input factors to decrease when they are used in larger quantities.

Pure Monopoly

The model of pure monopoly lies at the opposite end of the market structure continuum from perfect competition. In general, monopoly power exists anywhere along the continuum where the seller exercises some degree of control over a product's price and quantity in the market. This broad definition covers any seller outside of perfect or pure competition, and takes in most firms in the American economy.

Characteristics of pure monopoly are:

1. *One seller.* There is only one seller, who supplies the entire market.
2. *No close substitute.* The seller's product is so differentiated from others that no close substitute exists.
3. *No entry allowed.* Barriers to entry are so high that no other firm can enter the market.

The assumption of insuperable barriers to entry is crucial to the maintenance of the monopoly in the long-run. This means that even when the monopolist is earning economic profits, additional suppliers are unable to enter the market. The most common barriers to entry are:

1. Legal or institutional factors, such as patents or franchises.
2. Economies of scale that require very large capital outlays.
3. The monopolist's control of input supplies.
4. Demand conditions, such as the market's inability to absorb additional production.
5. Technology controlled by the monopolist.

Real-world examples that completely fulfill all of the conditions for pure monopoly are rare, if they exist at all. However, the position of pure monopoly is approached by firms providing electricity, natural gas, telephone communications, cable TV service, and some transportation services. These monopolies arise because the economies of scale are such that it is most efficient to let one firm produce and sell all that is demanded at a market-clearing price. These are called *natural monopolies*. Usually, such firms are granted a government franchise to monopolize a defined area in exchange for submitting to government regulation.

Monopolies may also arise in other ways:

1. Patents may be granted, which give the inventor exclusive rights to a product or technological process for 17 years.
2. Franchises may be granted to an authorized exclusive producer/seller in a given area. These may be granted by the government (e.g., airport parking lots) or by another firm (e.g., automobile deal erships granted by manufacturers).
3. A firm may own or control the sole source of a key raw material.

Since the monopoly has complete control of output and price, it can set the output and price to maximize profit. It does so by setting $MR = MC$ to find the optimal output.

Monopolist's Short-Run Output and Pricing Decision

Since the monopolist supplies the entire market, the monopolist's demand curve is the downward-sloping market demand curve, as illustrated by Exhibit 15–4.

Exhibit 15–4 depicts a monopolist's demand curve, D, marginal revenue curve, MR, unit cost, ATC, and marginal cost, MC. Maximum profit (or minimum loss) is obtained when marginal revenue equals marginal cost. If the depicted cost structure prevails, output will be Q units, which will clear the market at a price of P. The unit cost will be C, enabling the monopolist to enjoy an economic profit represented by the shaded rectangle, $ABCP$.

To illustrate the monopolist's output and pricing decision, suppose a monopolist is faced with demand and cost functions as follows:

$$Q = 2{,}000 - 5P,$$

or

$$P = 400 - 0.2Q$$

and

$$TC = 100 + 4Q + 0.4Q^2$$

so that

$$MC = 4 + 0.8Q$$

Exhibit 15–4

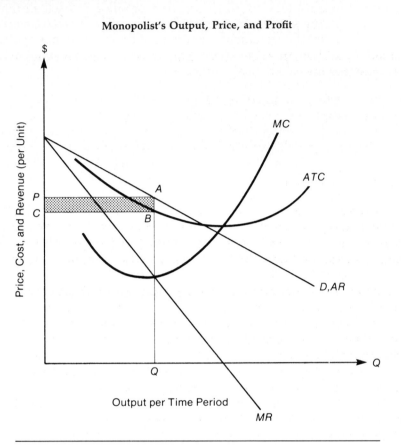

Therefore,

$$TR = P \cdot Q = (400 - 0.2Q)Q = 400Q - 0.2Q^2$$
$$MR = 400 - 0.4Q$$

Maximum profit occurs at the level of output and price where $MR = MC$:

$$400 - 0.4Q = 4 + 0.8Q$$
$$-1.2Q = -396$$
$$Q^* = 330$$

and

$$P^* = 400 - (0.2)(330) = \$334$$

Alternatively, total profit, π, is

$$\pi = TR - TC = 400Q - 0.2Q^2 - 100 - 4Q - 0.4Q^2$$
$$= -0.6Q^2 + 396Q - 100$$

Maximum profit occurs at the value of Q for which the first derivative of this function is zero:

$$\frac{d\pi}{dQ} = -1.2Q + 396 = 0$$
$$Q = 396/1.2 = 330$$
$$\pi = -0.6(330)^2 + 396(330) - 100 = \$65,240.$$

Long-Run Equilibrium

Since the monopolist has no competition—entry of new firms is effectively barred—pure economic profit is not eliminated in the long run as it is in the case of perfect competition. Hence the monopolist's long-run problem is to adjust plant size as demand conditions warrant to achieve maximum profit in the long run.

If the monopolist has been incurring a short-run loss and cannot find a plant size that will at least eliminate the loss, the monopolist goes out of business. But if the monopolist is earning a profit in the short run (or, at worst, suffering a temporary loss), he must determine whether a plant of different size and cost, with a different price and output, will yield a greater profit. In making this determination, the relevant consideration is long-run marginal cost, as illustrated by Exhibit 15–5.

In Exhibit 15–5, the monopolist begins with the short-run output, Q_1, and price, P_1, which is established by the intersection of the MR curve and the short-run marginal cost curve, $SRMC_1$. At this level of production and sales, using plant 1, the monopolist is earning the pure profit, ABP_1C_1. However, long-run cost equilibrium is achieved at the level where marginal revenue is equal to long-run marginal cost, $LRMC$. This calls for Q_2 units, at a price of P_2, from a plant whose $SRAC$ is just tangent to $LRAC$ at Q_2 units of production. Under these conditions profit is enlarged to the area EGP_2C_2. This is the best the monopolist can do, but he *can* do it because in the long run, his plant can be any size he pleases and he has no competition.

Monopolistic Competition

The extremes of perfect competition and pure monopoly are theoretical models that are remote from many actual market situations. Thus in the late 1920s and early 1930s, many economists attempted to develop

Exhibit 15–5

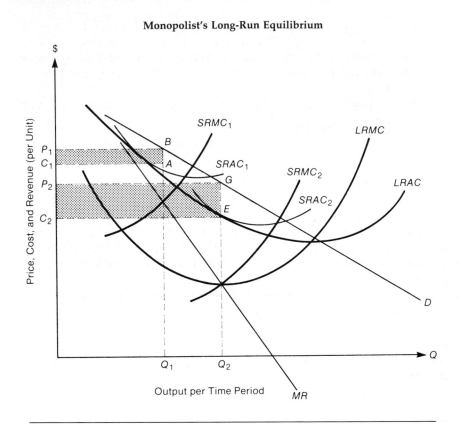

Monopolist's Long-Run Equilibrium

models of imperfect competition that could characterize market structures between those two extremes. One of the most notable achievements of one of those economists, Edward Chamberlin, was his model of monopolistic competition.[6]

Chamberlin's model pictures an industry with four distinguishing characteristics:

1. There are a very large number of small firms offering slightly differentiated products in a market in which barriers to entry are very low.
2. The market consists of firms that produce similar products that are close substitutes for one another. The substitutability of these prod-

---

[6] E. H. Chamberlin, *The Theory of Monopolistic Competition* (Cambridge, Mass.: Harvard University Press, 1933).

ucts provides the element of competition in monopolistic competition.

3. Because of product differentiation, each firm possesses a monopoly over its own version of the general product. Therefore, each firm may set its own price, but within limits imposed by competition. Product differentiation thus provides the element of monopoly in monopolistic competition.

4. Some barriers to entry do exist so that entry is not completely free. Nevertheless, entry is relatively easy.

Short-Run Equilibrium

Because of the large number of close substitutes, the demand curve for any one product is expected to be downward sloping and highly elastic. Because its product is differentiated, the firm in monopolistic competition is free to choose its output level and set its price with maximum profit as its objective. However, there are limits to this freedom. If the firm can persuade its customers that its product is superior to close substitutes and worth a higher price, it may be able to charge a higher price than its competitors—but not much higher, because the competing products are still close substitutes.

The firm's demand curve will depend upon the total demand for the whole product group and the firm's share of that market. The firm may use advertising and other forms of nonprice competition to increase demand for its product, but these efforts may be offset by similar efforts by the firm's competitors.

Under these circumstances, it is not possible to draw a stable, unambiguous demand curve for the firm. However, to the extent that each firm is able to know or estimate its demand curve, it will behave in the same way as a monopolist. That is, the firm will seek to maximize profit by producing at the level where $MR = MC$, as was shown in Exhibit 15–4. Like the monopolist, the firm in monopolistic competition may earn an economic profit, or only a normal profit, or it may suffer a loss. In the short run, then, there is little or no difference between the analysis of monopoly and the analysis of monopolistic competition.

Long-Run Equilibrium

If firms in monopolistic competition are observed to be making economic profits, other firms will be tempted to enter the market. However, there is a cost barrier to be overcome, because the new firm must spend enough on research and development to come up with a differentiated product, then spend enough on advertising and promotion to penetrate the market. Thus entry is not completely free, but it is relatively easy.

Exhibit 15–6

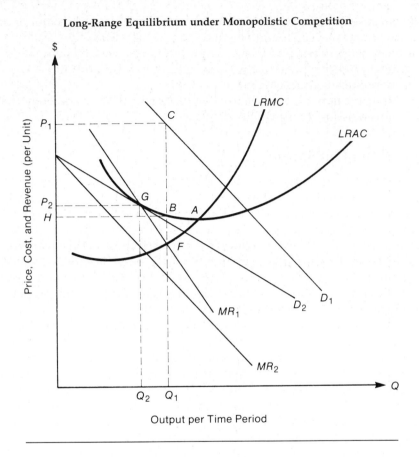

Long-Range Equilibrium under Monopolistic Competition

Output per Time Period

Exhibit 15–6 illustrates the equilibrium process. The exhibit depicts a firm with the lowest long-run average cost, *LRAC*, equal to long-run marginal cost, *LRMC*, at point *A*. When the firm faces the downward sloping demand curve, D_1, and its associated marginal revenue curve, then $MR_1 = LRMC$ at point *F*. The optimal output quantity is Q_1, which clears the market at a price of P_1 and a unit cost of *H*. The firm earns an economic profit represented by the rectangle $HBCP_1$.

The economic profit available in this market attracts new firms. When they enter the market, every firm's share becomes somewhat smaller. Each firm's demand curve shifts to the left and grows somewhat more elastic. If the typical firm's new demand curve settles below the *LRAC*, it means that all firms in that position are losing money, and the weaker firms will be forced out of the market. When they leave, the demand curves of the remaining curves shift back to the right and grow somewhat less elastic.

The market finally settles down into long-run equilibrium where each firm's demand curve (D_2) is just tangent to its $LRAC$. In Exhibit 15–6, the firm is at long-run equilibrium when producing Q_2 units at a price P_2, which is just equal to the long-run average cost at point G. In other words, the competition in monopolistic competition tends to squeeze out economic profits in the long run. Unlike perfect competition, however, equilibrium does *not* occur at the point of the lowest long-run average cost, i.e., at point A. Does this mean that monopolistic competition is less efficient than perfect competition? Technically, yes, but only if you place no value on having a variety of products to choose from. A price slightly higher than the minimum possible $LRAC$ and a slightly excessive unused capacity in each firm is what consumers gladly pay for the privilege of choice.

Illustrative Problem.   April Showers Company is a medium-sized manufacturer of sprinkler heads. Recently, the firm has developed a square-spraying sprinkler head that greatly improves lawn watering and reduces water requirements in comparison with conventional circular-spraying sprinkler heads. The firm's engineers estimate the total cost function to be

$$TC = 500,000 + 400Q$$

where Q = output in units of 1,000 sprinkler heads. The cost function includes a return on investment of 15 percent. The firm's marketing department estimates demand will be

$$Q = 2,500 - .5P$$

where P is the price per 1,000 sprinkler heads.
a.   Determine the profit-maximizing output and price.
b.   What is the profit at the optimum output?
c.   Determine sales-maximizing price and profit.
d.   Determine output, price, and profit at long-run equilibrium. (Assume a parallel shift in the demand curve.)
e.   What is April Showers' demand function at long-run equilibrium?

Solution:
a. $Q = 2,500 - 0.5P$, hence the inverse demand equation is $P = 5,000 - 2Q$.
Therefore,

$$TR = (5,000 - 2Q)Q = 5,000Q - 2Q^2$$

Let π = profit. Then

$$\pi = TR - TC = 5{,}000Q - 2Q^2 - 500{,}000 - 400Q$$
$$= -2Q^2 + 4{,}600Q - 500{,}000$$

Taking the derivative and setting it equal to zero,

$$\frac{d\pi}{dQ} = -4Q + 4{,}600 = 0$$
$$Q^* = 4{,}600/4 = 1{,}150 \text{ units at optimum profit}$$
$$P^* = 5{,}000 - 2Q^* = 5{,}000 - 2(1{,}150)$$
$$= \$2{,}700 \text{ per } 1{,}000 \text{ sprinkler heads}$$

b.

$$\pi = -2Q^2 + 4{,}600Q - 500{,}000$$
$$= -2(1{,}150)^2 + 4{,}600(1{,}150) - 500{,}000 = \$2{,}145{,}000$$

c.

$$TR = PQ = P(2{,}500 - .5P) = 2{,}500P - .5P^2$$
$$MR = 2{,}500 - P = 0$$
$$P = \$2{,}500 \text{ for maximum sales revenue}$$

At $P = \$2{,}500$,

$$Q = 2{,}500 - .5(2{,}500) = 1{,}250 \text{ units}$$
$$\pi = -2(1{,}250)^2 + 4{,}600(1{,}250) - 500{,}000 = \$2{,}125{,}000$$

d.   Since the demand curve shifts in parallel fashion until it is tangent to the *ATC* curve, its slope remains the same, i.e., -2.0. Therefore, the new demand function at the point of tangency is $P = a - 2Q$, where a is a constant that will be evaluated in Part (*e*) below. To find the slope of the *ATC* curve, we calculate the *ATC* function and take its derivative:

$$ATC = \frac{TC}{Q} = \frac{500{,}000 + 400Q}{Q} = (500{,}000 + 400Q)Q^{-1}$$
$$= 500{,}000Q^{-1} + 400$$
$$\frac{dATC}{dQ} = -500{,}000Q^{-2} = -\frac{500{,}000}{Q^2}$$

To find the output level and price at equilibrium, recall that at equilibrium, the new demand curve is tangent to the *ATC* curve at the point where their slopes are equal. Hence,

$$-2.0 = -\frac{500{,}000}{Q^2}$$
$$2.0Q^2 = 500{,}000$$
$$Q^2 = 250{,}000$$
$$Q = 500$$
$$P = ATC = \frac{500{,}000 + 400(500)}{500} = \$1{,}400$$

e.   Substituting $P = 1,400$ and $Q = 500$ into the demand equation $P = a - 2.0Q$ from Part (*d*), we get

$$1,400 = a - 2.0(500)$$
$$a = 1,400 + 1,000 = 2,400$$

Hence the new demand function is

$$P = 2,400 - 2.0Q$$

or its inverse

$$Q = 1,200 - 0.5P$$

Evaluation of Monopolistic Competition

The model of monopolistic competition has been criticized chiefly on the ground that it cannot be empirically verified or demonstrated.[7] If products are only slightly differentiated and there are a large number of small sellers, the firm's demand curve is so nearly horizontal that the model of pure competition provides an adequate explanation. In markets where there are strong brand preferences, it usually turns out that there are a small number of sellers dominating a limited market; thus the market is actually an oligopoly. And, of course, if a small business sells a product for which there are no close substitutes, the firm enjoys a monopoly.

One of the key assumptions of the model of monopolistic competition is that firms are relatively small and so numerous that an action by one firm has little or no influence upon other firms. This assumption is clearly unrealistic.[8] An action such as a price change by one firm may have no effect at all on firms in distant markets, but it may strongly influence other firms nearby. Again the oligopoly model is more realistic. For example, the Yellow Pages of the telephone book for Honolulu list 30 retail hardware stores. But when the city is divided into the neighborhood markets where people actually buy hardware, each market has only two or three stores.

Oligopoly

As noted above, many economists argue that the vast majority of business firms, whether large or small, operates under the market structure

---

[7] Harold Demsetz, "The Welfare and Empirical Implications of Monopolistic Competition," *Economic Journal*, September 1964, pp. 623–41 and "Do Competition and Monopolistic Competition Differ?" *Journal of Political Economy*, January–February 1968, pp. 146–68.

[8] Lester G. Telser, "Monopolistic Competition: Any Impact Yet?" *Journal of Political Economy*, March–April 1968, pp. 312–15.

of oligopoly. The term *oligopoly* is used to describe a market in which the dominant share of the market is supplied by a small number of firms. Oligopolies display the following characteristics:

1. *A small number of firms.* The firms may be large or small in absolute terms, depending upon the size of the market. (All oligopolistic firms are large relative to the market because they are so few.)
2. *Products may be homogeneous or differentiated.* Their products may be homogeneous, such as steel, cement, or newsprint; or differentiated, such as automobiles, cereals, beer, and soap.
3. *Interdependence.* The key feature of an oligopoly is the interdependence and competitive interaction among its members. Whatever one firm does affects all others. The greatest uncertainty facing management is not *whether* competitors will react to a decision—it is certain that they will—but *how* they will react.

All models of oligopoly recognize the interdependence of firms therein, but there is no generally accepted equilibrium theory that explains the output and pricing decision of all oligopolies. Many models of oligopoly have been proposed, but discussion in this chapter will be limited to three of the most prominent:

1. Price leadership models.
2. Kinked demand curve model.
3. Cartelization and formal collusion.

In the next chapter, on pricing practices, we shall discuss other models such as cost-plus pricing models and market share models.

Price Leadership Models

In many oligopolies, a pattern has been observed in which one firm sets a price and all the others follow. Three distinct patterns of price leadership that have been observed most often are (1) barometric, (2) collusive, and (3) dominant firm.

Barometric Price Leadership.   Barometric price leadership gets its name from the fact that one firm acts as a "barometer," reflecting changing market conditions or costs of production that require a change in price. First one firm, then another, may fulfill this role by announcing price changes that they hope will be followed by others in the market. If other firms do not agree with the barometer firm's assessment of the market or cost situation, a series of higher or lower price changes may be announced by competing firms until a general consensus is reached, either by trial and error or by explicit collusion.

The barometric price leader need not have any great amount of market power, nor does there need to be a dominant firm. The barometric price leader will lead only if the changes it makes are agreeable to the rest of the industry. There is no glory and no particular gain from being the leader. Indeed, sometimes the first firm to announce a price increase must endure a great deal of harsh criticism. Consequently, there is no struggle for power, and the role of the barometric price leader easily passes from one firm to another. For example, Bethlehem Steel is just as apt to announce a price change as U.S. Steel.

Collusive Price Leadership. In the United States, outright collusion is generally illegal. One of the major difficulties in enforcing the antitrust laws is that most leader-follower arrangements do not spring from formal collusion. Instead, they stem from the fact that firms that are producing similar products under similar cost conditions, for sale in the same market, are very likely to arrive at the same pricing decisions at the same time without consulting one another. Firms engaged in such behavior are aware of what they are doing, of course, so it may be termed "tacit collusion."

In the late 1940s, the courts responded to tacit collusion with the doctrine of "conscious parallelism," under which a number of firms were prosecuted.[9] In later years, however, the courts have tended to treat evidence of conscious parallelism as merely one of a set of circumstances that may indicate noncompetitive behavior. Parallel pricing is such common behavior that the doctrine of conscious parallelism is unenforceable in the courts unless it can be shown that parallel pricing is against the best interest of the individual firms concerned. Examples of such behavior would include keeping price rigid when demand is falling, raising prices when large amounts of excess capacity are present, or identical bids and prices from firms with large amounts of excess capacity.

Dominant Firm Price Leadership. The model of dominant firm price leadership envisions a market in which one firm has become the leader because it is bigger or because it has a lower cost structure than other competing firms. Because of its market power, the dominant firm can behave as if it were a monopoly, setting its output and price to yield maximum profit. The competing firms may sell all they wish at the dominant firm's price. Thus they behave as if they were price takers in a purely competitive market. This model is illustrated by Exhibit 15-7.

---

[9] See *United States* v. *Socony Vacuum Oil Co.*, 310 U.S. 150 (1940); *American Tobacco Co.* v. *United States*, 328 U.S. 781 (1946); *Triangle Conduit and Cable Company et al.* v. *Federal Trade Commission*, 162 F. 2d, 175 (1948). Also see Donald F. Turner, "The Definition of Agreement Under the Sherman Act: Conscious Parallelism and Refusals to Deal," *Harvard Law Review*, February 1962, pp. 655–706.

Exhibit 15–7

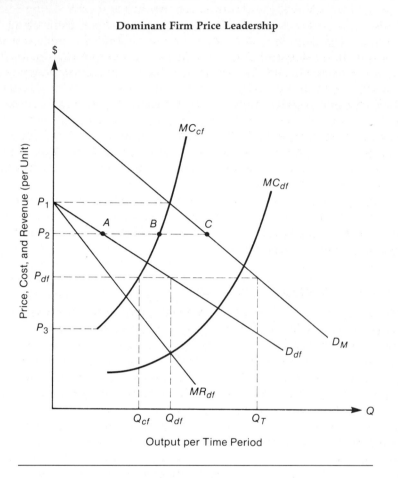

Dominant Firm Price Leadership

Output per Time Period

The model begins with the market demand curve, D_M, and a marginal cost curve for the dominant firm, MC_{df}, which is lower than the collective marginal cost of the competing firms, MC_{cf}. The curve MC_{cf} is also the supply curve for the competing firms. At a price of P_1, the competing firms would be willing to supply the entire market. Hence, the dominant firm's demand would be zero at that price and the P-intercept of curve D_{df} is at P_1. At a price of P_2, the competing firms would be willing to supply P_2B units, since the competing firms' MR is just the price that is equal to MC_{cf} at point B. This leaves BC units for the dominant firm to supply. From this fact, we can plot point A on D_{df} such that

$P_2A = BC$. If additional points are needed, they can be obtained by following a similar procedure for successively lower prices.

When the dominant firm's demand curve has been established, its marginal revenue curve, MR_{df}, can be derived. The dominant firm establishes the output quantity, Q_{df}, and price, P_{df}, at which $MC_{df} = MR_{df}$. The competing firms can sell Q_{cf} units at that price, and the total supplied to the market is $Q_T = Q_{df} + Q_{cf}$.

What keeps the competitors in line? Presumably it is the realization that the dominant firm is the most efficient firm with the lowest cost structure. Therefore, it could drive the competition out if it chose to do so. Probably, however, it does not resort to price-cutting techniques that would destroy the competition because of the ever-present threat of antitrust action by the federal government.

Although dominance has been identified in a number of industries in the past, dominance typically does not last very long. The position of the dominant firm is eroded by the growth of markets, the entry of new firms, and technological change.

The Kinked Demand Curve Model

The kinked demand curve as an explanation of price rigidity in oligopolies was postulated in 1939 by Sweezy[10] and by Hall and Hitch.[11] As illustrated in Exhibit 15–8, the model assumes that the firm is operating in an oligopoly where there is strong interaction among competing firms. The firm's demand function is graphed as two connected line segments that have different slopes. The resulting kink at their intersection is associated with the firm's current price for its product. If the firm cuts its price in an effort to enlarge its share of the market, its interacting competitors do the same. Consequently, the firm's demand moves down the lower, less elastic portion of the demand curve, producing a relatively smaller increase in sales with respect to the proportion of price reduction. But if the firm raises its price, the interacting competitors refuse to go along. Consequently, the firm's demand moves along the upper, more elastic portion of the kinked demand curve, producing a relatively larger loss of sales with respect to the proportion of price increase.

Since the kinked demand curve has two different slopes, the model derives two different MR curves with a gap between them at the output level of the kink. The kink in the demand curve will be more pro-

---

[10] Paul M. Sweezy, "Demand Under Conditions of Oligopoly," *Journal of Political Economy*, August 1939, pp. 568–73.

[11] R. L. Hall and C. J. Hitch, "Price Theory and Business Behavior," *Oxford Economic Papers*, May 1939, pp. 12–45.

Exhibit 15–8

Kinked Demand Curve Model of Oligopoly

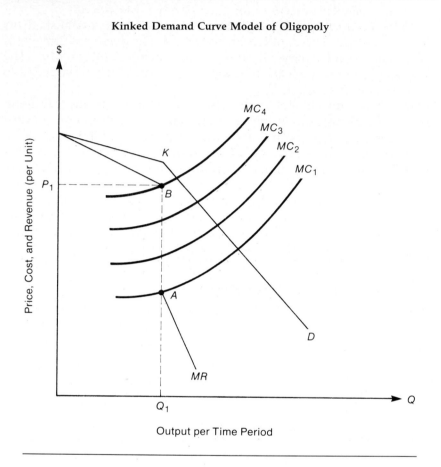

Output per Time Period

nounced and the width of the gap therefore greater when the following conditions exist:

1. There are only a small number of firms in the market.
2. The size of most firms in the market is about the same.
3. The products are standard, or nearly so.
4. There is no collusion.

As shown in Exhibit 15–8, the discontinuity in the MR curve allows many different marginal cost curves to pass through the gap between points A and B, and all of them would equal MR at Q_1 units of output. This means that the firm could experience increases in marginal costs all the way from MC_1 to MC_4 without any incentive to change its price. If the kinked demand curve shifts to the right in response to increased

Exhibit 15–9

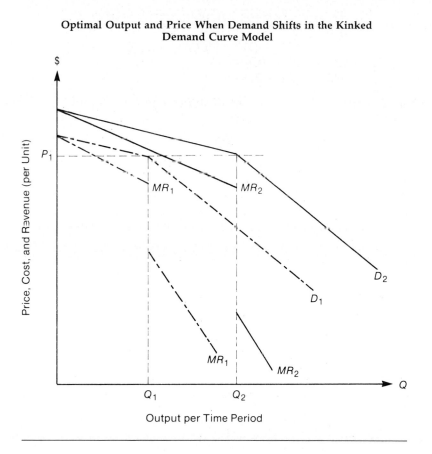

Optimal Output and Price When Demand Shifts in the Kinked
Demand Curve Model

demand, the firm will respond by increasing output. But, as shown in
Exhibit 15–9, the kink may remain at the same price level.

Illustrative Problem. Safe Ride Products faces the following seg-
mented demand curve for its new road emergency kit:

$$D_1: \quad Q_1 = 85 - P_1 \qquad \text{or} \quad P_1 = 85 - Q_1 \tag{4}$$
$$D_2: \quad Q_2 = 32.5 - 0.25P_2 \quad \text{or} \quad P_2 = 130 - 4Q_2 \tag{5}$$

where

Q = Output in thousands of units
P = Price in dollars

The firm's total cost, TC, is

$$TC = 375 + 25Q + .6Q^2 \tag{6}$$

Step 1. Calculate MR_1, MR_2, and MC from Equations (1), (2), and (3).

$$TR_1 = P_1Q_1 = (85 - Q_1)Q_1 = 85Q_1 - Q_1^2$$
$$MR_1 = 85 - 2Q_1$$
$$TR_2 = P_2Q_2 = (130 - 4Q_2)Q_2 = 130Q_2 - 4Q_2^2$$
$$MR_2 = 130 - 8Q_2$$
$$MC = 25 + 1.2Q_2$$

Step 2. Find the kink, or point of intersection of D_1 and D_2. At the intersection, $Q_1 = Q_2 = Q$; hence

$$85 - Q = 130 - 4Q$$
$$3Q = 45$$
$$Q = 15$$
$$P = 85 - 15 = 130 - 4(15) = \$70$$

Step 3. Graph the kinked demand curve model and note that the MC curve passes through the discontinuity or gap between MR_1 and MR_2.

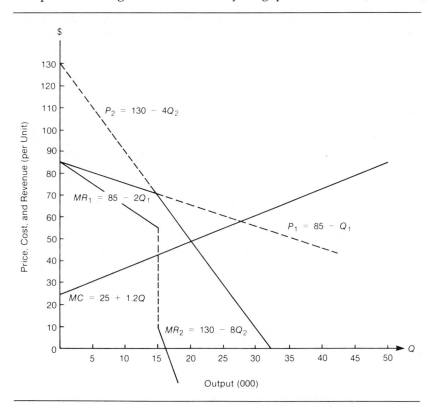

Step 4. Note the upper and lower limits of the gap:

$$MR_1 = 85 - 2Q = 85 - 2(15) = \$55$$
$$MR_2 = 130 - 8Q = 130 - 8(15) = \$10$$

Hence *MC* can range from a low of \$10 at $Q = 15$ to a high of \$55 at $Q = 15$ without changing the optimal output (15 units) and price (\$70).

Step 5. Calculate total profit at the forecast total cost.

$$\pi = TR - TC = 70(15) - 375 - 25(15) - .6(15)^2 = \$165(000)$$

Evaluation of the Kinked Demand Curve Model.   The kinked demand curve model has been criticized on several counts:[12]

1. There are other valid explanations for price rigidity, such as nationally advertised prices, catalogued prices, reluctance to disrupt customer relations, and fears that recurrent price cuts may trigger a price war.
2. The model does not explain how the firm arrived at the kink in the first place.
3. The assumption that price cuts will be matched by the competition, but that price increases will be ignored, may not be true.

Empirical evidence has given little support to the model as a theory of long-run pricing strategy in oligopolies. It may have some validity as an explanation of short-run pricing behavior in a new industry in the early stages of development.

Cartels and Formal Collusion

In an oligopoly, where there is a small number of producers, all firms could benefit if they could get together and behave as if they were a monopoly. If they could agree upon prices, output, market areas, use and construction of productive capacity, advertising expenditures, and the purchase and use of inputs, then they could squeeze the last drop of economic profit out of the market. When such an agreement is reached openly and formally, the group is called a *cartel*. If a covert, informal agreement is reached, it is *collusion* or *conspiracy*.

Cartels are legal in Europe and many other parts of the world, and multinational American firms may become involved in them in foreign markets. For example, U.S. airlines can legally be members of the International Air Transport Association (IATA) cartel. But within the United States, all forms of cartelization are illegal under most circumstances. Collusive agreements about prices are always illegal. Most other agreements about other important market variables have almost always been

---

[12] George J. Stigler, "The Kinky Oligopoly Demand Curve and Rigid Prices," *Journal of Political Economy*, October 1947, pp. 432–49. See also Walter J. Primeaux and Mark R. Bomball, "A Reexamination of the Kinky Oligopoly Demand Curve," *Journal of Political Economy*, July–August 1974, pp. 851–62; and Walter J. Primeaux and Mickey S. Smith, "Pricing Patterns and the Kinky Oligopoly Demand Curve," *Journal of Law and Economics*, April 1976, pp. 189–99.

invalidated by the courts, but there are important exceptions. Most notably, certain farm products, such as milk, are marketed under cartel-like arrangements.

Cartelization arises because firms want to eliminate uncertainty and improve profits by stabilizing market shares, stabilizing prices, reducing competition, putting excess capacity to work, or outlining spheres of interest and eliminating unnecessary promotional costs. Cartelization or collusion is most successful when most, if not all, of the following specific structural conditions are present in a market.

1. *Small number of sellers.* This makes it easier to reach and enforce an agreement.
2. *Similar cost conditions for all sellers.* This makes for equitable profits.
3. *Minimal or nonexistent product differentiation.* This makes it easier to agree upon a set of rules and eliminates the need for exceptions to the rules.
4. *Inelastic demand.* This enables the cartel to increase the price of the product without incurring a commensurate decrease in sales.
5. *High barriers to entry.* To avoid competition, new firms are kept from entering the market.
6. *Stability of the industry.* This enables the cartel to make and enforce rules.
7. *Depressed economic conditions.* In hard times, firms seek ways to avoid cut-throat competition, thus making cartelization more attractive.
8. *Little or no excess capacity.* This makes it easier for the cartel to allocate production quotas without creating a temptation to cheat.

The establishment of a price and the subsequent allocation of market shares to members of a cartel are similar to the allocation of production to multiple plants of a single firm; that is, the optimal allocation occurs when $MC_A = MC_B = \ldots = MC_N = MR$ of the cartel, as shown in Exhibit 15–10.

Exhibit 15–10 shows a simple two-firm cartel. Firm A has the marginal cost curve MC_A and Firm B has the marginal cost curve MC_B. The cartel's total production is the total produced by both firms. Hence the cartel's marginal cost curve, MC_T, is just the horizontal summation of $MC_A + MC_B$. In the total market, which has the demand curve D_M and the marginal revenue curve MR_M, the intersection of MC_T and MR_M determines the cartel's profit-maximizing output of Q_T units at a price of P_C. Each firm may receive an allocated share of the profits by producing at the level at which the firm's marginal cost is equal to marginal cost for the cartel at the cartel's profit-maximizing level. This results in the production of Q_A units by Firm A and Q_B units by Firm B. Since the cartel's price is always higher than the average total cost of the least efficient member, all firms in the cartel will make a profit; but the lower-cost

Exhibit 15–10

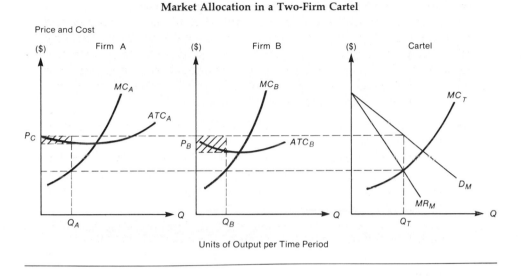

Market Allocation in a Two-Firm Cartel

Units of Output per Time Period

(more efficient) firms will make more profit than the higher-cost (less efficient) firms.

The foregoing paragraph illustrates the allocation of output according to the firm's individual outputs, but there are other bases as well. Among these are historical market shares, plant capacity (which may be determined in a number of different ways), and a bargained solution based on economic power. The problem is that while firms may all agree that maximizing the cartel's profits is beneficial, they seldom agree that the division of the spoils is equitable. This leads to cheating—subversion of the agreement—by individual members.

Since the cartel's price is always higher than the free-market price without the cartel, most or all of the firms in the cartel will develop some excess capacity. The most efficient firms will develop the most excess capacity. The temptation to cheat is always very strong among all firms, but for the most efficient firms with excess capacity and relatively constant or decreasing unit cost, the temptation may prove to be irresistible. As shown in Exhibit 15–11, the cheating firm (in this case, Firm B) can greatly increase its profits by slightly undercutting the cartel price to the point where $MR_B = MC_B$, and their excess capacity is put to work.

Cheating on the agreement is one of the major reasons why cartels eventually break up. Other reasons are:

1. The presence of maverick firms in the market that won't go along with the cartel. For example, in the Organization of Petroleum Ex-

Exhibit 15-11 _____

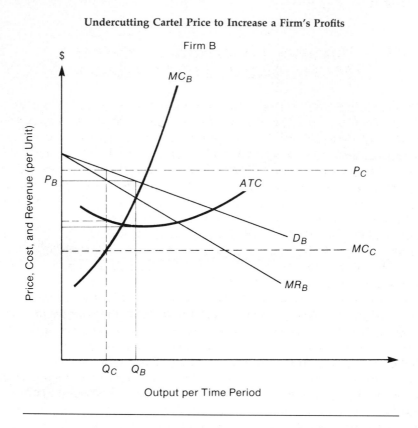

Undercutting Cartel Price to Increase a Firm's Profits

Firm B

porting Countries (OPEC), Iran decided in 1983 not to go along with OPEC market share allotments and price fixing because the country desperately needed oil revenues to support development projects and its war with Iraq.

2. Periodic adoption of new corporate strategies to meet changing business conditions, which may cause members to drop out of the cartel.

3. The entry or potential entry of strong competitors into the market. Mexico, Norway, and the United Kingdom have all refused to join OPEC after discovering large amounts of oil in their respective territories.

4. Frequently changing supply and demand conditions that make the cartel price structure obsolete. OPEC's struggle to maintain the cartel price in the face of a worldwide increase in the supply of oil and a

decrease in demand (because of conservation) provides a good example.

Nonprice Competition: Product Differentiation and Advertising

The preceding discussions of market structures revealed price as a means of competition. However, price competition at best merely moves the seller along the firm's demand curve. Moreover, a price cut designed to increase sales provokes quick retaliation by competitors. Product differentiation can provide effective competition in a much more subtle way. Product competition is perceived by competitors as much less aggressive than price competition, and their reaction is much slower. Furthermore, the advertising that is necessary to establish product differentiation in the mind of the consumer can have the salutary effect of shifting the firm's demand curve to a higher level.

Product differentiation may be broadly defined as anything that causes a buyer to prefer one product to another. Therefore, product differentiation, if it exists at all, exists in the mind of the consumer. It isn't necessary for the difference to *be* real—it is only necessary for the consumer to *think* it is real. This persuasion may be the result of incessant advertising and other forms of promotion that instill brand name recognition. For example, a store may offer Clorox bleach, Purex bleach, and a store brand in identical bottles and identical quantities at three different prices. The contents label on each bottle may reveal identical chemical composition of the contents. Yet customers will pay more for the highly advertised brands. Apparently they perceive a difference in the products by virtue of brand name recognition. This, of course, reveals the intimate connection between product differentiation and promotion.

Of course, there can be and are some real differences among similar products. These may arise from many sources, such as:

Patents, trademarks, copyrights.

Differences in quality and durability.

Differences in design, style, fit, color, and packaging.

Conditions surrounding the sale, such as the courtesy of sales personnel, a convenient shopping location, a comfortable air-conditioned store, and convenient shopping hours.

Guarantees and warranties, including policies on return of merchandise.

Method, time, and cost of delivery.

Availability of repair services.

The Role of Advertising

Advertising, which is the principal cost of product differentiation, can provide consumer information by describing the goods and services available and by identifying their sellers. The theory of information developed by Stigler holds that advertising can reduce search costs for both buyers and sellers.[13] From a welfare standpoint, informative advertising is quite desirable. Nevertheless, a considerable amount of product differentiation can result from advertising that is uninformative, or even deceptive and untruthful. Advertising thus has the potential of making the marketplace more perfect or of disrupting its functioning, and therein lies the problem in any discussion of the welfare role of advertising. Despite all the claims of proponents and opponents, advertising is neither all good nor all evil. Without *informative* advertising, however, there can be little effective product differentiation in the consumer's mind, which is the only place it matters.

Measurement of Product Differentiation

It is much easier to talk about the degree of product differentiation in qualitative terms than to settle upon a meaningful quantitative measurement. There are four quantitative measurements of product differentiation that have been proposed at one time or another:[14]

1.   *Advertising-to-sales ratio.* This is the measurement most often used, and advertising as a percentage of sales ranges from less than 1 percent for automobiles and petroleum products to more than 20 percent for drugs and cosmetics. (The higher the ratio, the less real differentiation exists in the products.) The difficulties with this measurement are twofold:

a.   Products may be visibly differentiated by nonadvertising selling costs, such as distinctive packaging
b.   Advertising and sales data are rarely available to a researcher at the level of the firm.

2.   *The coefficient of cross elasticity of demand.* As explained in Chapter 5, cross elasticity measures the change in the demand for one product in

---

[13] George J. Stigler, *The Economics of Advertising* (Homewood, Ill: Richard D. Irwin, 1944).

[14] Lester Telser, "How Much Does It Pay Whom to Advertise?" *American Economic Review*, May 1961, pp. 194–205.

response to a change in the price of another product, which is either a substitute or complement. Measurement of differentiation, however, applies only to substitutes. The general idea is that the higher the cross elasticity, the less product differentiation exists between substitutes. This measure also suffers from a pair of difficulties. First, the second product must be a carefully selected, close substitute. For example, a low cross elasticity between two makes of refrigerators might indicate a high degree of product differentiation. But if the cross elasticity between corn and pig-iron is near zero, it merely indicates that the products are not substitutes. The second difficulty is that the cross product must undergo significant price changes before cross elasticity can be observed and measured.

3.   *Entropic measurement.* Entropy is a term drawn from thermodynamics by way of communication theory. It refers to the degree of randomness. An entropic measurement of product differentiation looks at the extent of customer loyalty to a brand or a merchant. On a scale of 0 to 1, a homogeneous product would rate a 0, because customers would buy completely at random from any seller in the market. At the other extreme, if the product is so different that customers always buy a particular brand or from a particular merchant, the entropy measurement would be 1. Entropic measurement is highly subjective in nature. Further, it is unable to distinguish between the effects of product differentiation and the effects of price upon consumer behavior.

4.   *Product-differentiation barriers.* This approach measures the degree of product differentiation as high, medium, or low by the extent to which it acts as a barrier to market entry by new firms. Such classification is based not only on advertising-to-sales ratios, but also on any other facet of product differentiation that the observer is aware of. This approach requires a knowledgeable observer, and the results can be no better than the quality of information possessed by the classifier.

Summary

A *market* is a collection of buyers and sellers of products that have some degree of substitutability. *Market structure* refers to the nature and degree of competition within a market. The five major indicators of market structure are (1) the number and nature of sellers, (2) the number and nature of buyers, (3) the nature of the product, (4) the conditions of entry and exit, and (5) possible economies of scale.

The general theory of pricing postulates a continuum of market structures that ranges from perfect competition at one end to pure monopoly at the other. Perfect competition envisions a market with many small sellers and buyers of a homogeneous product. Market price is set at the

equilibrium between market supply and market demand, and both buyers and sellers must either take it or leave it. All resources are completely
mobile, and market entry and exit are free from all barriers. Thus when
an economic profit is being made, enough new firms will enter the
market to drive the price down and squeeze out all economic profit.
Long-range equilibrium is thus obtained when the price is set equal to
the lowest possible long-run average cost.

In pure monopoly, there is only one seller of a product that has no
close substitute. A natural monopoly exists when economies of scale are
so great that it is most efficient for one firm to supply the entire market.
Other monopolies may arise from patents or franchises or from control
of raw materials. The monopolist faces a downward-sloping demand
curve. However, since the barriers to entry are so high that no competitor can enter the market, the monopolist is free to optimize profit at the
level of production and sales for which marginal revenue equals marginal cost. This may or may not create an economic profit, depending
upon the monopolist's cost relative to demand.

Between the extremes of perfect competition and pure monopoly lies
the realm of imperfect competition, in which two market structures have
been postulated: (1) monopolistic competition and (2) oligopoly. Monopolistic competition envisions a market in which there are many small
sellers of weakly differentiated products that are close substitutes. Because of product differentiation, each firm has a limited monopoly over
its own version of the product. Therefore, the firm faces a downward-
sloping, highly elastic demand curve and sets its output and price where
$MR = MC$, the same as in a pure monopoly.

The situation differs from pure monopoly, however, in that the firm
faces competition. Firms seeking to enter the market must undergo the
cost of developing a differentiated product and the promotional cost of
penetrating the market. Thus a cost barrier to entry exists, but entry still
is relatively easy. As new firms enter, the demand curves for all firms
shift to the left and become more elastic. At long-run equilibrium, the
firm's demand curve is just tangent to its long-run average cost ($LRAC$)
curve. Since the demand curve slopes downward, the point of equilibrium is somewhat to the left of the lowest possible $LRAC$. Thus a slightly
higher price than would be obtained in perfect competition is the premium consumers pay for a wide selection of available goods.

The term oligopoly denotes a condition of imperfect competition in
which a few sellers supply most of the market with products that may be
either homogeneous or differentiated. The most outstanding feature of
oligopoly is the interdependence of its members, such that any decision
by one firm affects all other members. Three models of oligopoly have
been discussed:

1. Price leadership models, in which one firm takes the lead in establishing a price and the others follow.
2. The kinked demand curve model, which assumes that the competition will follow a firm's price decreases but not its price increases.
3. Cartelization and formal collusion, in which sellers act in concert as if they were a monopoly, to maximize profits.

All of the foregoing models focus on price competition. At best, however, price competition merely moves the firm along its established demand curve. Nonprice competition in the form of product differentiation and advertising can do even better—it can shift the entire demand curve to a higher level.

Product differentiation may be broadly defined as anything that causes the consumer to prefer one product to another. Product differentiation exists in the mind of the consumer. It need not be real as long as the consumer thinks it is real. Thus, anywhere from one fourth to three fourths of all advertising is "fluff" designed to persuade the consumer that the advertiser's product is different though it really is not. Good, informative advertising is necessary to bring real differences to the consumer's attention.

Four approaches have been tried to measure product differentiation: (1) advertising-to-sales ratio, (2) coefficient of cross elasticity, (3) entropic measurement, and (4) product-differentiation barriers. None of these approaches has proved to be very accurate or meaningful.

Problems

1. Name a few industries that might provide examples of perfect competition, monopolistic competition, oligopoly, and pure monopoly. Do the characteristics of these industries fit the theoretical market stuctures exactly? What problems are encountered when applying theoretical models to real-world markets?

2. Agriculture is often characterized as operating in a perfectly competitive market. Does one farmer actually compete with another farmer? If so, in what way?

3. The OPEC cartel effectively increased oil prices during the 1970s, resulting in tremendous profits for member countries. What economic factors led to disunity among OPEC ranks in 1983? What are the effects?

4. In 1982, traces of heptachlor were discovered in the State of Hawaii's milk supply. Although the problem was corrected, demand for milk fell by 20 percent. In 1983, both the State Dairy-owners' Association and individual producers were advertising to increase the fallen demand

for dairy products. Is there a difference in the motives of these two advertisers?

5.   Explain how monopolistically competitive firms are similar to perfectly competitive firms, and how they differ.

6.   List the reasons why research, development, and innovation are more likely to occur under oligopoly than under any other market structure.

7.   Many firms contribute money and executives' time to so-called "social responsibilities" such as charities and civic projects. Is such behavior consistent with maximizing profit in the long run? Under what market structures would firms be most likely and least likely to engage in such behavior? Explain.

8.   Security Lock, Inc. is a major American producer of magnetic door locks. In recent years, Security Lock has suffered substantial short-run losses in the international market because of cut-throat price competition from companies in England, France, and West Germany. However, these companies have also suffered substantial losses, and so have proposed that Security Lock join them in an international cartel that would give the four firms a high degree of monopoly power. Since their biggest market would be the United States, the cartel has asked Security Lock to propose production and pricing policies for their approval. Assuming that Security Lock's participation is legal, how could Security Lock proceed?

9.   Fisco Farms is a relatively small producer of wool in New Zealand. Fisco's total cost function is

$$TC = 6,500 - 600Q + 20Q^2$$

where

Q = hundreds of pounds (cwt.) of wool
TC = Total cost in dollars

If the market price for wool is $10 per pound,
a.   Determine Fisco's profit-maximizing output and price.
b.   Determine the maximum total profit.
c.   Determine ATC at the maximum profit output.
d.   Suppose wool prices decline to $5 per pound, with no change in cost. Should Fisco continue to operate?
e.   Describe the condition of long-run equilibrium in a competitive market. How is such an equilibrium obtained?
f.   What are Fisco's ATC and output at long-run equilibrium?

10.   The Sharpit Manufacturing Company dominates the manufacture of pencil sharpeners because of its highly cost-efficient operation.

Its market research department estimates demand for the Sharpit brand pencil sharpener as

$$Q = 600 - 0.5P$$

where

Q = Output in units
P = Price per unit in dollars

The production department reports that

$$TC = 50,000 + Q^2$$

where

$$TC = \text{Total cost}$$

a. Calculate the profit-maximizing output and price.
b. Calculate profit at profit-maximizing output.
c. Calculate revenue-maximizing output and profit at that level.
d. What is the level of output and profit at minimum average total cost?
e. What is the price elasticity of demand at the most profitable price?

11.   When Ace Mini Computer Company developed a compact computer that could be fitted in an ordinary briefcase, at first there was no competition in the marketplace. The estimated demand and total production cost were

$$Q = 3,000 - 2P$$
$$TC = 250,000 + 650Q$$

where

P = Price of computer in dollars
Q = Demand for computer in units

a. Determine profit-maximizing output and price. Also find total profit.
b. Determine the revenue maximizing output, price, and profit.
c. A few years later, there are many similar products on the market, although some product differentiation is evident. Because of the competition, Ace's sales have declined and its demand curve has shifted in a parallel fashion so that all economic profit has been eliminated. Assuming that Ace's cost function remains the same, determine its output and price at equilibrium.
d. Determine the new demand equation for Ace Mini Computer.

12.   Carbine Inc. is one of four major manufacturers of high-quality specialty steel. Attempting to establish pricing and production policies has been difficult for Carbine because its demand curve has reacted

inconsistently. An economist hired by Carbine to analyze the situation found the following demand and cost functions:

$$P_1 = 550 - Q$$
$$P_2 = 750 - 3Q$$
$$TC = 15,000 + 200Q + .3Q^2$$

where

P = Price of steel per ton
Q = Output in thousands of tons
TC = Total cost in thousands of dollars

a. Describe the market structure and model that seems to fit the data given above.
b. Graph the curves for demand, MR, and MC.
c. Determine Carbine's profit-maximizing price and output.
d. Determine the maximum profit.
e. Purchasing newly developed furnaces changes Carbine's total cost function to $TC = 17,500 + 125Q + .3Q^2$. Determine the new profit-maximizing price and output. What is the maximum profit?

13. Suppose the railway freight car manufacturing industry consists of seven firms, which produce four basic types of freight cars:

Flat cars, used for such goods as lumber, pipe, automobiles, and heavy machinery.

Hopper cars, used for such goods as sand, gravel, coal, and other bulk materials.

Box cars, used for such goods as grains, fertilizers, dry chemicals, and general merchandise.

Tank cars, used for transportation of liquids of any type.

In addition to price, industry demand is sensitive to factors such as:

Forecast demand for rail transportation.

Prime rate of interest.

Railroad earnings per ton-mile.

Among the seven firms, Bethlehem Car Company is considered to be dominant because of its lower cost of production. Consequently, when Bethlehem sets the price, the other firms are forced to follow that price in order to compete at all. However, Bethlehem will allow the competing firms to sell all they wish to sell at that price. Bethlehem's market research indicates that industry demand for box cars in the coming year will be

$$Q_M = 40,000 - 0.5P$$

where

Q_M = Market quantity demanded in units

P = Price in dollars

Bethlehem's expected cost function for the manufacture of boxcars is

$$TC_B = 100{,}000 - 15{,}000Q_B + 2.5Q_B^2$$

Further, it has learned that the marginal cost of boxcar production by the smaller competing firms (which is derived by summing the MC of the six smaller firms) is

$$MC_C = 50{,}000 + 2Q_C$$

a. Determine Bethlehem's demand curve and marginal revenue curve.
b. Determine the profit-maximizing output and price for Bethlehem Car Company.
c. Determine the output for the combined competing firms.
d. What conditions are necessary for Bethlehem Car Company to continue in its dominant role?

Discussion Topics

14.   *Fortune's* 500, May 3, 1983, ranks General Motors as the second largest corporation in the United States, boasting 657,000 employees and over $60 billion in total sales. It has been said that giant oligopolies—such as General Motors, General Electric, and Alcoa—are primarily responsible for producing higher quality consumer goods, and that breaking them up to obtain more active price competition could be counterproductive. Do you agree or disagree? Critically analyze your position both pro and con.

15.   Where economies of scale have led to formation of large oligopolies, barriers to entry of new firms are extremely high in terms of both required technical know-how and required capital investment. For example, the five leading U.S. steel manufacturers average over $7 billion in assets. Can you suggest desirable methods to overcome these barriers in steel as well as other oligopolistic industries?

16.   George Stigler, a Nobel prize winning economist, has argued that government is primarily responsible for the existence of monopoly. He cites public utilities, federal and state labor laws, agricultural support programs, local building codes, and licensing restrictions as examples of government-sponsored monopoly that increase inefficiencies. Do you agree or disagree? Explain. What is the significance of the government's 1983 breakup of AT&T?

17.   Your local power company and the U.S. Postal Service, with its more than 659,000 employees in 1981, are close to pure monopolies.

How can their performance be evaluated to decide whether they are doing an efficient job?

References

Bain, Joe S. *Barriers to New Competition.* Cambridge, Mass.: Harvard University Press, 1965.

Baumol, William J. *Economic Theory and Operations Analysis.* 4th ed. Englewood Cliffs, N.J.: Prentice Hall, 1977.

Chamberlin, E. H. *The Theory of Monopolistic Competition.* Cambridge, Mass.: Harvard University Press, 1933.

Demsetz, Harold. "The Welfare and Empirical Implications of Monopolistic Competition." *Economic Journal,* September 1964, pp. 623–41.

————. "Do Competition and Monopolistic Competition Differ?" *Journal of Political Economy,* January–February 1968, pp. 146–68.

————. "Barriers to Entry." *American Economic Review,* March 1982, pp. 47–57.

Dorfman, Robert, and Peter O. Steiner. "Optimal Advertising and Optimal Quality." *American Economic Review,* December 1954, pp. 826–36.

Hall, R. L., and C. J. Hitch. "Price Theory and Business Behavior." *Oxford Economic Papers,* May 1939, pp. 12–45.

Koch, James. *Industrial Organization and Price Level.* 2d ed. Englewood Cliffs, N.J.: Prentice-Hall, 1980.

Nelson, Phillip. "The Economic Consequences of Advertising." *Journal of Business,* April 1975, pp. 213–41.

Palda, Kristian S. "The Measurement of Cumulative Advertising Effects." *Journal of Business,* April 1965, pp. 162–79.

Pyatt, F. G. "Profit Maximization and the Threat of New Entry." *Economic Journal,* June 1971, pp. 242–55.

Silberston, Aubrey. "Survey of Applied Economics: Price Behavior of Firms." *Economic Journal,* September 1970, pp. 511–82.

Stigler, George J. *The Economics of Advertising.* Homewood, Ill.: Richard D. Irwin, 1944.

————. "The Economics of Information." *Journal of Political Economy,* June 1961, pp. 213–25.

————. "Price and Non-Price Competition." *Journal of Political Economy,* February 1968, pp. 149–54.

————. *The Organization of Industry.* Homewood, Ill.: Richard D. Irwin, 1968, pp. 67–70.

Sweezy, Paul M. "Demand Under Conditions of Oligopoly." *Journal of Political Economy,* 1939, pp. 568–73.

Telser, Lester. "How Much Does It Pay Whom to Advertise?" *American Economic Review,* May 1961, pp. 194–205.

————. "Monopolistic Competition: Any Impact Yet?" *Journal of Political Economy,* March–April 1968, pp. 312–15.

Turner, Donald F. "The Definition of Agreement Under the Sherman Act: Conscious Parallelism and Refusals to Deal." *Harvard Law Review,* February 1962, pp. 655–706.

Appendix 15A | Market Power and Profit-Maximizing Advertising

Market power may be defined as the ability to influence noticeably the price or quantity of some commodity in the market. In the models of market structure that were discussed in this chapter, market power ranged from zero for firms in perfect competition to complete control for a pure monopoly.

We have also seen that the element of monopoly in imperfect markets requires product differentiation, and the greater the differentiation, the greater the monopoly power. Further, we have seen that differentiation is promoted by informative or persuasive advertising. Finally, we have seen that in all market structures, profit-maximizing equilibrium exists at the level of production and sales at which marginal revenue equals marginal cost, with a price established by the demand function for that level of sales. Thus the three great action variables are *price, product,* and *promotion.*

Most firms have some control over the principal action variables of price, product, and promotion. In equilibrium, maximum profit will be realized when the last dollar spent on each action variable results in the same incremental profit. In mathematical notation,

$$\frac{M\pi_P}{C_P} = \frac{M\pi_A}{C_A} = \frac{M\pi_Q}{C_Q} = \cdots = \frac{M\pi_N}{C_N} \tag{1}$$

where

$M\pi_i$ = Marginal profit from ith action
C_i = Cost of ith action
P = Subscript indicating price
A = Subscript indicating advertising and other forms of promotion
Q = Subscript indicating changes in product composition, quality, packaging, etc.
N = Subscript of the Nth of N actions

523

Measurement of Market Power

The best known measurement of market power is the Lerner index:

$$I = \frac{P - MC}{P} \qquad (2)$$

where

P = Price
MC = Marginal cost
I = Index of market power

The numerator of the Lerner index represents economic profit. Under conditions of perfect competition, where all economic profit is squeezed out, $MR = P = MC$ and the Lerner index = 0, indicating that the firm has no market power at all. The maximum magnitude of the Lerner Index is 1, which could occur only if $MC = 0$. As long as $P > MC$, the Lerner index is positive; but if $MC > P$, it would be negative.

When the firm is maximizing profits at equilibrium, where $MR = MC$, the Lerner index is the reciprocal of the price elasticity of demand. This can be shown with the aid of the formula for marginal revenue that was developed in Footnote 2 of Chapter 5:

$$MR = P \left(1 - \frac{1}{|\varepsilon_D|} \right) \qquad (3)$$

At equilibrium, $MR = MC$; therefore,

$$MC = P \left(1 - \frac{1}{|\varepsilon_D|} \right) \qquad (4)$$

Expanding the right side,

$$MC = P - \frac{P}{|\varepsilon_D|} \qquad (5)$$

Subtracting P from both sides,

$$MC - P = - \frac{P}{|\varepsilon_D|} \qquad (6)$$

Reversing the signs,

$$P - MC = \frac{P}{|\varepsilon_D|} \qquad (7)$$

Dividing both sides by P,

$$\frac{P - MC}{P} = \frac{1}{|\varepsilon_D|} = I \qquad (8)$$

From the explanation of price elasticity in Chapter 5, the student should recognize that Equation (8) is equivalent to saying that the Lerner index measures market power in terms of the deviation of the slope of the demand function from zero.

Profit-Maximizing Advertising

It has been demonstrated by Dorfman and Steiner[1] that when the product (and other) variables are held constant, the profit-maximizing advertising-to-sales ratio is

$$\frac{A}{S} - \frac{P - MC}{P} \cdot \varepsilon_{Q \cdot A} \tag{9}$$

where

A/S = Advertising/sales ratio

$\dfrac{P - MC}{P}$ = Lerner index of market power

$\varepsilon_{Q \cdot A}$ = Elasticity of output with respect to advertising expenditures

Equation (9) may be interpreted as saying that the more market power a firm has, the more of its sales dollar it will spend on advertising. This is because there is a strong correlation between market power and product differentiation; and the fundamental purpose of advertising is to establish product differentiation in the mind of the consumer.

With some algebraic manipulation, Equation (9) also shows how the effects of advertising expenditure upon product price are related to the firm's advertising/sales ratio, as follows:

Step 1. Begin with Equation (9)

$$\frac{A}{S} = \frac{P - MC}{P} \cdot \varepsilon_{Q \cdot A} \tag{9}$$

Step 2. Rewrite the Lerner index as the reciprocal of the price elasticity of demand:

$$\frac{A}{S} = \frac{1}{\varepsilon_{Q \cdot P}} \cdot \varepsilon_{Q \cdot A} \tag{10}$$

Step 3. Replace the elasticity symbols with their definitions.

$$\frac{A}{S} = \frac{1}{\dfrac{\Delta Q/Q}{\Delta P/P}} \cdot \dfrac{\dfrac{\Delta Q/Q}{\Delta A/A}}{1} = \dfrac{\dfrac{\Delta Q/Q}{\Delta A/A}}{\dfrac{\Delta Q/Q}{\Delta P/P}} \tag{11}$$

---

[1] Robert Dorfman and Peter O. Steiner, "Optimal Advertising and Optimal Quality," *American Economic Review,* December 1954, pp. 826–36.

Step 4. Carry out the indicated division by inverting the denominator.

$$\frac{A}{S} = \frac{\Delta P/P}{\Delta Q/Q} \cdot \frac{\Delta Q/Q}{\Delta A/A} \tag{12}$$

The right-hand term is the elasticity of quantity sold with respect to advertising.

Step 5. Simplify the fraction

$$\frac{A}{S} = \frac{\Delta P/P}{\Delta A/A} = \frac{\text{Percentage change in price}}{\text{Percentage change in advertising expenditures}} = \varepsilon_{P \cdot A} \tag{13}$$

Equation (13) says that the more sensitive price is to expenditure on advertising, the more of the sales dollar will be spent on advertising, which is just a formal acknowledgment of a common-sense notion.

The problem with the theoretical work above is that it ignores the passage of time. However, there is ample empirical evidence to support the concept that advertising expenditures more nearly have the properties of an investment than an expense. That is, the returns do not necessarily come in the same time period as the expenditure. On the contrary, returns from good advertising campaigns will continue to be received for many years to come.[2] The appropriate measurement of advertising returns, therefore, is the present value of a future stream of profits, as follows:

$$PVA = \sum_{t=1}^{n} \frac{S_t - C_t}{(1 + r)^t} = \sum_{t=1}^{n} \frac{\pi_t}{(1 + r)^t} \tag{14}$$

where

PVA = Present value of advertising in base year, $t = 0$
S_t = Sales in year t
C_t = Cost of sales in year t
π_t = Profit in year t
r = Firm's discount rate

The advertising should be undertaken if $PVA \geq 0$. In spite of the empirical evidence that advertising is an investment, the accounting profession continues to treat it as a periodic expense. No allowance is made for the image, goodwill, and future profits prospects that are

---

[2] One study found that it took seven years for the company to reap 95 percent of the sales generated by its advertising dollars. (See Kristian S. Palda, "The Measurement of Cumulative Advertising Effects," *Journal of Business,* April 1965, pp. 162–79; also Palda, *The Measurement of Cumulative Advertising Effects* (Englewood Cliffs, N.J.: Prentice-Hall, 1964).

being generated. Consequently, the real value of the firm's assets is considerably more than its book value. If expenditures for advertising and other product-differentiating activities were spread over the life of such investments, then much of the higher profit rates that have been attributed to firms that spend large amounts for product differentiation might disappear.

16

Pricing Practices
and Decisions

In the theoretical frame of reference established in the preceding chapter, simple models of various market structures were constructed to explain the firm's output and pricing decisions under *static* conditions of cost and demand. In each model, the firm's objective was assumed to be maximization of profit, and the objective was achieved by adjusting output so that marginal revenue was equal to marginal cost.

In the *dynamic* environment of the real world, managements have fairly well-defined pricing objectives that are based upon *planned* profits and *long-range* profit horizons as well as short-run profits. They understand that pricing decisions made today may affect the firm's profitability in the future. Consequently:

1. Specific pricing policies may differ among firms, reflecting different orders of priorities among competing objectives rather than any simple concept of profit maximization.
2. Management must deal with multiple objectives, a changing environment, and the output and pricing of multiple products for which demand may not be known.
3. There is a realization among managements that the typical situation of multiproduct and multimarket operations requires a simultaneous decision with respect to price, cost, and product characteristics. Pricing and marketing strategies pertaining to individual prod-

528

ucts and markets thus tend to be viewed not in isolation but in the global context of the entire firm as a decision-making enterprise.

4. In large multiproduct and multimarket firms, there are particularly complex problems of joint production and joint distribution costs, as well as considerable lack of knowledge with respect to basic cost-output and cost-sales relationships. Pricing, therefore, is frequently done for broad product groups within the framework of the company's overall profit position and objectives. Hence it is possible that the costing of products ends up as a result rather than a cause of price policy.

These are some of the reasons why empirical research about pricing practices finds that many firms set their prices without formally analyzing marginal relationships. A thorough understanding of pricing practices may reveal, however, that although there is constant adjustment to the uncertain environment, in the long run the firm's pricing decisions do not deviate very far from the $MR = MC$ profit-maximizing approach.

In this chapter, we are concerned with the pragmatic side of pricing decisions. Our discussion will focus on five major topics:

1. Pricing objectives.
2. Pricing methods and approaches.
3. Price discrimination. $\Longrightarrow$ *policy of non discrimination*
4. Optimal pricing of multiple products.
5. Transfer pricing (which is discussed in Appendix 16A at the end of the chapter).

Pricing Objectives

Some years ago, the Brookings Institution, a prominent research organization in Washington, D.C., sponsored a well-known study of the pricing objectives of 20 major American corporations.[1] The typical and collateral pricing goals of these 20 companies tended to fall into four categories, namely:

1. Pricing to achieve a target return on investment.
2. Pricing to stabilize prices or outputs.
3. Pricing to realize a target market share.
4. Pricing to meet or match competition.

Although today, in light of inflationary experience and higher capitalization costs, the rates of returns on investment uncovered by the study would probably be considered outdated, the pricing goals by which they

---

[1] See Robert V. Lanzillotti, "Pricing Objectives in Large Companies," *American Economic Review*, December 1958, pp. 921–40.

were obtained are still worth considering. We therefore examine each of the above pricing objectives, using the Brookings study as a framework for our discussion.

Pricing to Achieve a Target Return on Investment

A *target-return price* is a price that is designed to yield a predetermined average return on capital used for specific products, product groups, and divisions. Most firms tend to use stockholders' equity (net worth) plus long-term debt in measuring return on capital. In allocating fixed costs among products or divisions, firms usually use a standard cost system based on an assumed rate of production—typically 70 to 80 percent of capacity—and an assumed product mix as "normal."

Some of the essential features of target-return pricing may be conveniently listed as follows.

1. Company accountants and industrial engineers establish estimates of standard costs based on standard volume—the latter usually measured by the long-run rate of plant utilization. The margins added to these standard costs are designed to yield the target rate of return on investment over the long run. The margins are thus based on the averaging of fluctuations in cost and demand over the business cycle; hence, short-run changes in volume or product mix do not unduly affect price.

2. Companies are aware that a rigid adherence to target-return pricing may not always be possible, depending on the degree of market protection afforded the particular product. This is especially true of new products, where an orderly "stepping down" of prices may be necessary over the long run as competing products become available.

3. Since target returns are established on the basis of "normal" or average periods, year-to-year profits may at times be higher or lower than the predetermined targets. This is a bit of evidence that tends to support the belief that firms probably do not as a general rule set prices so as to maximize profits, at least in the short run.

4. New products have been particularly singled out for target-return pricing by most companies. At firms such as Du Pont, Union Carbide, Alcoa, and General Foods, either of two types of pricing strategies are often used: (a) a relatively high price policy may be adopted with planned step-down rates for "skimming" the market by exploiting the inelasticity of demand in different markets (as long as current or potential competition permits); (b) a relatively low or "penetration" price policy may be adopted to develop mass markets quickly, in anticipation of a rapid expansion of the market and higher returns later. It should be emphasized, however, that the target approach to pricing is not limited to new products; it has also been applied extensively to high-volume, low-unit-profit items including steel, aluminum, and chemicals.

A concomitant issue with regard to the target-return criterion is the selection of the profit target itself. Executives who have been asked this question have responded by saying that their company's margins are based on one or more of the following considerations:

What is believed to be a "fair" or reasonable return.
Industry custom.
A desire to equal or better the company's recent average return.
What the company felt it could get.
Use of a specific profit target as a means of stabilizing industry prices.

Independent of the specific criteria of choice, however, is the fact that the target rate in most cases is regarded by the various firms as a long-run objective. It tends to average about 15 percent after taxes, with a range of 10–20 percent.

There is a close relationship between target return on investment as a pricing *objective* and cost-plus as a pricing *method*. In most companies cost-plus pricing, in one form or another, is the chief means of obtaining the objective. The "cost" may be based on an estimate of standard cost and standard volume for a specific group of products; the amount of the "plus" may vary with the pricing executive's goal—whether it be a target return on investment, price stabilization, or some other objective.

Pricing to Stabilize Prices or Outputs

Several companies emphasized the drive for *stabilized prices* as an important objective. Their justification for specifying this goal was presumably based on a philosophy that holds that if a firm's general level of prices is sufficient to yield adequate returns during periods of recession, the level should not be raised as high as the traffic will bear in periods of prosperity. This also implies, of course, that in pricing individual products, an effort will be made—conditioned in each case by the pricing executive's conscience—not to exploit the situation by raising prices beyond reasonable limits of "cost-plus."

The objective of stabilizing prices may be quite impossible to achieve in times of high inflation when increases in costs are frequent and substantial. In such times, management is more apt to pursue a target return on investment.

Pricing to Realize a Target Market Share

Pricing to achieve a minimum or maximum *market share* was an objective cited frequently by the various companies. For example, General Electric stated that its products rarely have more than 25 percent of any given market, and that it is the company's policy not to exceed 50 percent because it would then become too vulnerable to competition.

There is undoubtedly some incompatibility between a target-return approach and a market-share policy: a company desiring to increase its share of the market will probably find that it must place decreasing emphasis on a strict adherence to a predetermined target.

Pricing to Meet or Match Competition

Pricing to meet or to match competition was sometimes cited as the objective of a pricing policy. To some extent this type of policy, if it can be called such, may be due largely to executive fears—fear of losing competitive status in the marketplace and fear of violating the antitrust laws concerning price discrimination.

Pricing Methods and Approaches

A firm may pursue its pricing objectives through a variety of methods and approaches; however, we shall limit our discussion to the two most important methods: (1) cost-plus pricing; and (2) incremental cost pricing.

Cost-Plus Pricing

The most widely used method of pricing is known as cost-plus pricing. It is a procedure whereby the price is determined by adding a fixed markup of some kind to the cost of acquiring or producing the product. Thus development of a cost-plus price requires two basic steps: (1) determination of the relevant cost; and (2) determination of what the "plus" should be.[2]

Determination of the relevant cost differs somewhat among the three basic types of business: manufacturing, merchandising, and service. In turn, determination of the "plus" will depend, in part, on how the cost was determined.

---

[2] The "plus" of cost-plus may be expressed as a markup on the cost or as a profit margin on the price. For example, if a product costing $8 is priced at $10, there would be a 25 percent markup on cost or a 20 percent profit margin on the price. Conversion from one expression to the other is quite easy by means of the formulas:

$$\text{Markup on cost} = \frac{\text{Margin on price}}{1 - \text{Margin on price}} \tag{1}$$

$$\text{Margin on price} = \frac{\text{Markup on cost}}{1 + \text{Markup on cost}} \tag{2}$$

Cost-Plus Pricing in Manufacturing.   Cost-accounting methods have been developed that enable manufacturers to establish a *standard unit cost* for each product that they make. Standard unit costs normally are developed as a part of the firm's budgeting process, and are based upon forecasted demand for the product and expected prices of the input factors of production. Thus the standard unit costs are carefully predetermined target costs that should be attained at the forecast level of production.

Cost-accounting procedures that provide for allocation of all overhead costs (selling, administrative, and financial costs) to the product are available. However, cost accounting procedures are not standardized and different companies may deal with the allocation of overhead costs in different ways. If all costs have been fully allocated to the product, the markup is all profit. If some overhead costs have not been allocated, then the markup must be high enough to cover the unallocated costs as well as profit.

Cost-Plus Pricing in Merchandising.   The cost of goods sold in merchandising is simply the wholesale price, to which an allocated share of the shipping costs paid by the merchant may or may not be added. The markup must be sufficient to cover all other costs in addition to profit. That is to say, a merchant will allocate overhead costs to the "plus" side of cost-plus rather than to the cost side.

Cost-Plus Pricing in Service Industries.   Customers of auto repair shops, TV repair shops, plumbers, electricians, and other tradesmen expect to be billed on a *time and materials* basis. That is, there will be one charge for the hours worked and another charge for the parts used. The price of labor and the price of the materials may both be calculated on a cost-plus basis. In each case, the wholesale cost of the materials and the wages actually paid to the workman must be marked up enough to cover all overhead costs as well as profit.

"Time and materials" does not always mean the actual time required to complete the job. In some cases, the charge for time may be based upon a standard, such as the flat-rate manual used by auto repair shops. The flat-rate charge for time has permeated the professions as well, and particularly the medical profession. In part, this is due to the way in which medical insurance companies set allowable fees for specific treatments.

The "Plus" in Cost-Plus

The markup added to cost may be the same for all of the firm's products, or different for each one. It may be expressed as a set number of dollars or, more likely, as a percentage of cost. The specific formula used by a particular firm may be geared to long-standing industry practice, or to competitive conditions, or to break-even analysis, or to capital investment requirements. If the firm's pricing objective is a target return, then the plus in cost-plus must include the contribution that each unit must make to achieve the stated objective at the forecast level of sales.

In any case, the plus in cost-plus must include a satisfactory profit. This does not necessarily lead to the same price as marginal analysis, whereby the level of sales is set such that $MR = MC$. The profit-maximization model using marginal analysis is a short-run concept, whereas cost-plus pricing is a long-run concept. For example, if management believes that a larger share of the market will improve long-run profitability, the quickest way to enlarge market share is to reduce price.

The behavior of automobile manufacturers after World War II provides a case in point. No automobiles were manufactured during the war years, 1942–45; consequently, there was an enormous pent-up demand. The manufacturers could have reaped a huge short-term profit by jacking up the price. However, they felt that their long-term interests were better served by lower prices that would expand not only the ownership of automobiles, but also the dealer network to serve the expanded market.

Evaluation of Cost-Plus Pricing

Some of the main reasons for using cost-plus pricing are the following:

1. It offers a relatively simple and expedient method of setting price by the mechanical application of a formula.
2. It provides a method for obtaining adequate ("fair") profits, when demand cannot be precisely estimated.
3. It is desirable for public relations purposes even at the expense of short-run profits because it provides a rationale for a price increase that customers will accept.

Some of the main criticisms of cost-plus pricing are as follows:

1. Cost-plus pricing fails to take into account demand as measured in terms of buyers' desires and purchasing power. This criticism does not stand up under empirical investigation. As previously noted, standard costs of manufacturing are based on forecasted demand. Second, firms that market different product lines often have a different markup policy for each line, according to demand elasticities and competitive pressures. Third, clear evidence that firms using cost-plus pricing do pay attention to demand was provided by the airline industry when deregulation took place. Widespread introduction of discounts and special fares indicated that the airlines were paying close attention to de-

mand conditions and to their competition. None of the foregoing means that cost-plus pricing leads to the same profit as operating at the level where $MR = MC$, and there is no empirical evidence to support such a notion.

2. Cost-plus pricing fails to recognize the roles of such important cost concepts as avoidable cost and opportunity cost as guides for pricing decisions.[3] This, of course, is a generality that may be true in some cases, but is certainly not true in all. There is nothing in the cost-plus method to prevent inclusion of opportunity costs. They may be included in the cost, just as is done in marginal analysis; or they may be considered as normal profits to be included in the markup.

3. Cost-plus pricing fails to reflect competition in terms of rivals' reactions and the possible entry of new firms. For example, in an industry that prices by the cost-plus method, if company margins are above the level necessary to cover operating costs and yield "normal profits" per unit at capacity, new firms will tend to enter the industry as long as no considerable excess capacity is already present. The results will be a smaller market share for each firm, and therefore higher unit overhead costs and lower profits per firm. The same thing, of course, can be said about the profit-maximizing model. Indeed, as was shown in the previous chapter, this is how an industry moves from short-run profit maximization to long-run equilibrium.

Cost-Plus versus Marginal Analysis

As we noted in the preceding subsection, cost-plus pricing is basically a long-run concept, while marginal analysis to maximize profits deals with pricing in the short-run. But even in the short run, cost-plus may be preferred to marginal analysis simply because marginal analysis requires information about demand and cost with a degree of precision that is always difficult and sometimes impossible to obtain.

Besides the statistical problems of demand estimation that were discussed in Chapter 7, there are the added problems of product interdependence both inside and outside the firm and the uncertainty of competitors' actions in the future. Cost estimation encounters the same statistical problems as demand estimation, with the additional complications of joint costs and the allocation of overhead. Add to all these problems the uncertainties inherent to the future, such as weather, economic conditions, and labor union demands, and it is easy to see why managements may turn to something a little less complicated than marginal analysis.

---

[3] *Avoidable costs* are the firm's expenses of doing a job as compared with its expenses if it does nothing. The difference represents the sacrifices or potential savings that the firm can avoid by doing nothing.

This does not mean that marginal analysis should be abandoned by the firm that uses cost-plus pricing. On the contrary, marginal analysis provides a useful basis for evaluating the firm's pricing policies, provided enough information can be obtained. Acquiring information, of course, is expensive. The cost of acquiring information must be added to the other costs before analysis takes place.

Incremental Cost Pricing

"The economist who understands marginal analysis has a full-time job in undoing the work of the accountant!"

This quotation is indicative of a viewpoint that has long been held by many economists. It simply refers to the fact that accounting practices and most business executives' thinking are permeated with cost allocation directed at average rather than incremental cost. Thus, in any business, there is likely to be a substantial difference between the costs of each company activity as it is carried on the accounting books and the "extra" costs—the so-called incremental costs—that determine whether or not the activity should be undertaken. For many kinds of pricing decisions, the incremental costs are the only "true" and relevant costs to be considered.

Incremental cost provides business executives with an essential guide for short-run production and pricing decisions. For if a business executive is considering, say, a reduction in price in order to increase sales, the executive must know whether the resulting gain in revenue from the additional volume, that is, the incremental revenue, will more than cover the increase in costs. If the incremental revenue exceeds the incremental cost, profits will be expanded accordingly.

Thus, while incremental costs should not *determine* a product's price, they should set a "floor"—and demand conditions a "ceiling"—within which the range of many profitable pricing decisions should be made. "Fully distributed" cost, on the other hand, is an economically invalid criterion for certain types of short-run pricing decisions, since it is based on arbitrary apportionments of unallocable costs among various products, departments, and divisions. It is manifestly absurd and illogical to hold a certain product or group of products economically responsible for any given share of unallocable costs. Whether the particular price of a product is above or below its fully distributed cost is of no economic significance as far as its minimum price is concerned in a particular short-run pricing decision. In the long run, however, all costs must be recovered.

The appropriate use of incremental analysis requires a thorough examination of the *total* effect of the decision in question, both in the short run and the long run. For example, the decision to introduce a new product should be based on *all* changes in costs and revenues that will result from the decision. This includes the effects on production, cost, and sales of all other products as well as the newcomer. Will production of the new product cause any bottlenecks? Will it increase the requirement for maintenance or shorten the useful life of existing machinery and equipment? If the new product is a substitute or complement for one or more of the firm's other products, how will the other products' sales be affected? Thus we see that the relatively simple concept—consider only those factors that are changed by the decision—is not easy to apply.

Price Discrimination

Price discrimination, or differential pricing, has been a subject of heated controversy for many years. It involves both economic implications and regulatory problems. The economic aspects are our concern in this section. The regulatory aspects are discussed in the next chapter.

What is meant by the term *differential pricing?* Generally, it is a method that can be used by some sellers to tailor their prices to the specific purchasing situations or circumstances of the buyer. Specifically, it may be defined as the practice by a seller of charging different prices to the same buyer or to different buyers for the same good, without corresponding differences in cost.[4]

Degrees of Price Discrimination

For analytical purposes, it is convenient to distinguish between three classes of differential pricing:

First Degree.   In differential pricing of the first degree, the seller charges the same buyer a different price for each unit bought, thereby extracting the maximum total receipts. This is a purely theoretical situation, usually studied in elementary economics. By shading the price down to the buyer for each additional unit purchased, the seller obtains a larger total revenue than if the same price per unit were charged for all units bought. In real life, of course, in order to sell a given quantity of goods, all units are sold at the same price. As illustrated by Exhibit 16–1, Q_4 units would be sold at a price of P_4 dollars. The triangle $P_0M_4P_4$ represents the additional revenue that could be realized under first de-

---

[4] From a theoretical standpoint, a better statement would define differential pricing or price discrimination as the sale of technically similar products at prices that are not proportional to marginal costs. However, the law that deals with price discrimination does not distinguish as to the type of cost, thus leaving wide margins for interpretation.

Exhibit 16–1

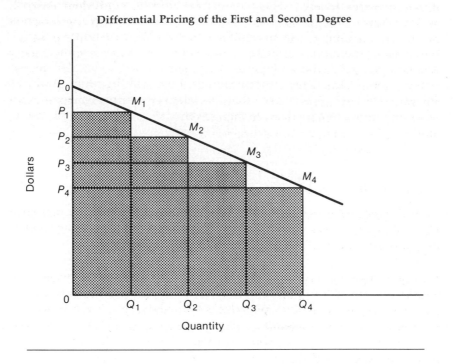

Differential Pricing of the First and Second Degree

gree differential pricing, but never is. This triangle is called *consumer's surplus,* as explained in Chapter 4.

Second Degree. Differential pricing of the second degree, more commonly known as volume discounting, involves the same underlying principle as first-degree differential pricing, except that the seller charges different prices for blocks of units instead of for individual units. The result is a "stair-step" pricing effect illustrated graphically by Exhibit 16–1. The illustration shows that for 0 through Q_1 units, the price is P_1 dollars; from Q_1 to Q_2 units the price is P_2 dollars; from Q_2 to Q_3 units the price is P_3 dollars; and for Q_3 to Q_4 units, the price is P_4 dollars. By charging a higher price for smaller quantities, the buyer receives a higher total revenue than if a single price were charged. The additional revenue is represented by the shaded areas above the line P_4M_4. However, some of the consumers' surplus remains, as indicated by the unshaded triangles above the line P_4M_4.

Third Degree. Differential pricing of the third degree occurs when the seller segregates buyers according to income, geographic location, individual tastes, kinds of uses for the product, or other criteria, and charges different prices to each group or market despite equivalent costs in serving them. Thus, as long as the demand elasticities among different buyers are unequal, it will be profitable to the seller to group the buyers into separate classes according to elasticity, and charge each class a separate price. This is what is referred to more generally as market segmentation, that is, the carving up of a total market into homogeneous subgroups according to some economic criterion. From the standpoint of pricing, the criterion usually employed is that of demand elasticity, and it is often applied in a practical manner via certain indirect means, as will be seen shortly.

The Conditions for Differential Pricing

Three practical conditions are necessary if a seller is to practice price discrimination effectively: (1) multiple demand elasticities, (2) market segmentation, and (3) market sealing.

Multiple Demand Elasticities.   There must be differences in demand elasticity among buyers due to differences in income, location, available alternatives, tastes, or other factors. If the underlying conditions that normally determine demand elasticity are the same for all purchasers, the separate demand elasticities for each buyer or group of buyers will be approximately equal and a single rather than multiple price structure may be warranted.

Market Segmentation.   The seller must be able to partition (segment) the total market by segregating buyers into groups or submarkets according to elasticity. Profits can then be enhanced by charging a different price in each submarket.

Market Sealing.   The seller must be able to prevent—or natural circumstances must exist which will prevent—any significant resale of goods from the lower- to the higher-priced submarket. Any leakage in the form of resale by buyers between submarkets will, beyond minimum critical levels, tend to neutralize the effect of different prices and narrow the effective price structure toward a single price to all buyers.

In view of these conditions, what practical techniques can sellers use to establish a structure of price differentials? In the following paragraphs the techniques employed will be differential structures based on: (1) quantity, (2) time, and (3) product use. This classification, it will be seen, cuts across the three degrees (forms) of price discrimination but places major emphasis on the most interesting and important one—price discrimination of the third degree.

Quantity Differentials

Three types of quantity differentials are particularly worth noting because of their significance in business practice. They are: (1) cumulative discounts, (2) quantity discounts, and (3) functional discounts. Each of these deserves some separate comment.

Cumulative Discounts.   Cumulative discounts are based upon total quantity bought over a period of time (such as a year). They are granted by sellers primarily as a concession to large buyers, or for the purpose of encouraging greater buyer loyalty, or because they may reduce costs by facilitating forward planning in production, stabilize seasonal output variations, and reduce investment in inventories.

Quantity Discounts.   Based upon the amount of the purchase at one time and its delivery to one location, quantity discounts are granted in order to encourage larger orders so as to reduce the costs of selling, accounting, packing, delivery, and other handling and shipping costs.

Functional Discounts.   Based upon the trade classification of the buyer (e.g., wholesaler, jobber, retailer, etc.), functional discounts are also commonly referred to as "distributor discounts." Since these discounts are granted to distributors according to the latter's position in the product's channel of distribution, the various differentials have the purpose of inducing distributors to perform their particular marketing functions.

Time Differentials

A second class of differential pricing achieves market segmentation through the medium of *time*. As in other kinds of price differentials, the object from the seller's standpoint is to capitalize on the fact that buyers' demand elasticities vary, but in this case as a function of time. Thus two classes of time differentials may be distinguished, extending from the narrowest to the broadest "slice of time."

Clock-Time Differentials.   When demand elasticities of buyers vary within a 24-hour period, the seller has the opportunity of exploiting these differences through price differentials. The most common examples of this are the differences between day and night rates on long-distance telephone calls, and the differences between matinee and evening admission charges in movies and theaters.

When price differentials are based on clock time, the object of the seller is to charge a higher price for the product in the more inelastic period and a lower price during the more elastic interval. Telephone rates and theater prices are thus an interesting contrast.

Calendar-Time Differentials. Price differentials may be based not only on elasticity differences within a day, but on differences between days, weeks, months, or seasons as well. In addition to telephone rates and theater prices, which exhibit weekend variations in addition to intra-day (i.e., clock-time) price differences, other examples of calendar-time price differentials are found in the sale of services by recreational facilities such as golf courses, tennis courts, and swimming pools; the sale of food by some restaurants; and seasonal variations in the sale of clothing, resort accommodations, and vacation trips. Calendar-time differentials thus refer to any variable price structure based on time that extends beyond the 24-hour period of clock time.

Seasonal variations, since they occur within a year and are due strictly to weather and custom, are more broadly a function of time in that variations in weather and in custom (e.g., Christmas and Easter buying) are recurrent and fairly periodic. Hence, seasonal variations may justifiably be placed in the category of calendar-time differentials from the standpoint of the seller who is considering this type of pricing structure. Perhaps cyclical variations could also be included if they were fairly regular and periodic in the calendar sense, which they are not for the economy as a whole but may be for certain (relatively few) business firms.

Product Use Differentials

A third classification of price discrimination is the segregation of buyers according to their use of the product. For example, electric and gas companies establish separate rate structures for residential and commercial users; telephone companies distinguish between residential and business phones; movie theaters, barber shops, and public carriers set separate charges for adults and children despite equal time and space costs of serving both groups; and railroads sell freight transportation service at different prices to different groups according to the goods shipped.

What conditions must exist for a seller to establish an effective structure of price differentials according to product use? At least two conditions are essential:

1. There must be a difference in demand elasticity among buyers as to product use.
2. The seller must be able to segment these buyers into fairly homogeneous groups.

Profit Maximization with Price Discrimination

To illustrate profit maximization with price discrimination, suppose that a firm is making a single product and selling it in two different

Exhibit 16–2

Price Discrimination in Two Markets

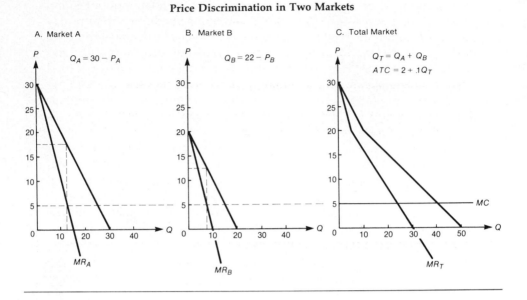

A. Market A

$Q_A = 30 - P_A$

MR_A

B. Market B

$Q_B = 22 - P_B$

MR_B

C. Total Market

$Q_T = Q_A + Q_B$

$ATC = 2 + .1Q_T$

MC

MR_T

markets that have different demand functions and price elasticities as shown on Exhibit 16–2. What should be the price and quantity sold in each market in order to maximize the firm's profit? Let's take a step-by-step approach to analysis of the problem:

Step 1. Identify the demand function in each market in terms of Q:

$$\text{Market A:} \quad Q_A = 30 - P_A \quad \text{or} \quad P_A = 30 - Q_A \tag{3}$$

$$\text{Market B:} \quad Q_B = 22 - P_B \quad \text{or} \quad P_B = 22 - Q_B \tag{4}$$

Step 2. Find the total quantity demanded, Q_T, in both markets:

$$Q_T = Q_A + Q_B \tag{5}$$

Step 3. Identify the total cost function, TC:

$$TC = (2 + .1Q_T)Q_T = 2Q_T + .1Q_T^2$$

$$= 2Q_A + 2Q_B + .1Q_A^2 + .2Q_AQ_B + .1Q_B^2 \tag{6}$$

Step 4: Develop the profit function as total revenue minus total cost:

$$\pi = TR - TC = (30 - Q_A)Q_A + (22 - Q_B)Q_B - TC$$
$$= 30Q_A - Q_A^2 + 22Q_B - Q_B^2 - 2Q_A - 2Q_B - .1Q_A^2 - .2Q_AQ_B - .1Q_B^2$$
$$= 28Q_A - 1.1Q_A^2 + 20Q_B - 1.1Q_B^2 - .2Q_AQ_B \tag{7}$$

Step 5. Take the partial derivatives of Equation (7) and set them equal to zero:

$$\frac{\partial \pi}{\partial Q_A} = 28 - 2.2Q_A - .2Q_B = 0 \tag{8}$$

$$\frac{\partial \pi}{\partial Q_B} = 20 - 2.2Q_B - .2Q_A = 0 \tag{9}$$

Step 6. Solve the system of equations developed by Step 5:

$$(28 - 2.2Q_A - 0.2Q_B = 0)1 = 28 - 2.2Q_A - 0.2Q_B = 0$$
$$(20 - 0.2Q_A - 2.2Q_B = 0)11 = 220 - 2.2Q_A - 24.2Q_B = 0$$
$$\overline{\phantom{(20 - 0.2Q_A - 2.2Q_B = 0)11 = {}} -192 \qquad\qquad + 24.0Q_B - 0}$$
$$Q_B = 8 \tag{10}$$

$$28 - 2.2Q_A - 0.2Q_B = 28 - 2.2Q_A - 0.2(8) = 0$$
$$- 2.2Q_A = -26.4$$
$$Q_A = 12 \tag{11}$$

Step 7. Find the profit-maximizing price:

$$P_A = 30 - Q_A = 30 - 12 = \$18 \tag{12}$$
$$P_B = 22 - Q_B = 22 - 8 = \$14 \tag{13}$$

Step 8. Verify your solution by proving that $MR_A = MR_B = MR_T = MC$:

$$TR_T = TR_A + TR_B = (30 - Q_A)Q_A + (22 - Q_B)Q_B$$
$$= 30Q_A - Q_A^2 + 22Q_B - Q_B^2 \tag{14}$$

$$MR_A = \frac{\partial TR_T}{\partial Q_A} = 30 - 2Q_A = 30 - 2(12) = 6 \tag{15}$$

$$MR_B = \frac{\partial TR_T}{\partial Q_B} = 22 - 2Q_B = 22 - 2(8) = 6 \tag{16}$$

$$MC_T = \frac{dTC}{dQ_T} = \frac{d(2Q_T + 0.1Q_T^2)}{dQ_T} = 2 + 0.2Q_T$$
$$= 2 + 0.2(12 + 8) = 6 \tag{17}$$

Step 9. Determine maximum total profit achieved by price discrimination. From Step 4:

$$\pi = 28Q_A - 1.1Q_A^2 + 20Q_B - 1.1Q_B^2 - 0.2Q_AQ_B$$
$$= 28(12) - 1.1(144) + 20(8) - 1.1(64) - 0.2(12)(8)$$
$$= \$248$$

Step 10. Determine maximum total profit that can be achieved without price discrimination. From Step 2:

$$Q = Q_A + Q_B = 30 - P_A + 22 - P_B = 52 - P_A - P_B \tag{18}$$

Without price discrimination, $P_A = P_B = P$, hence from (18)

$$Q = 52 - 2P \quad \text{and} \quad P = 26 - 0.5Q \tag{19}$$

$$\pi = P \cdot Q - TC = 26Q - 0.5Q^2 - 2Q - 0.1Q^2$$
$$= 24Q - 0.6Q^2 \tag{20}$$

$$\frac{d\pi}{dQ} = 24 - 1.2Q = 0$$
$$Q = 20$$
$$P = 26 - 0.5(20) = \$16$$

Substituting $Q = 20$ into our profit function, we get

$$24(20) - 0.6(20)^2 = \$240$$

Since profit is maximized when $MR = MC$, the profit maximizing total quantity is the same whether or not there is price discrimination; but profit is greater when we discriminate.

Alternate Calculation. The preceding routine, using partial derivatives, can be extended to more than two markets. If we are looking at only two markets, there is an alternate method that avoids partial derivatives and the need to solve a system of equations. At Step 4, instead of developing the profit function, we set $MR_A = MR_B$ to obtain their optimal relationship. (They must be equal to each other at optimum, since each is equal to MC.)

$$MR_A = 30 - 2Q_A = 22 - 2Q_B = MR_B$$
$$Q_A = Q_B + 4 \tag{21}$$

Marginal cost in terms of Q_B is:

$$2 + 0.2Q_T = 2 + 0.2(Q_A + Q_B) = 2 + 0.2Q_A + 0.2Q_B$$

$$= 2 + 0.2(Q_B + 4) + 0.2Q_B = 2 + 0.2Q_B + 0.8 + 0.2Q_B$$

$$= 2.8 + 0.4Q_B \tag{22}$$

At maximum profit, $MR_B = MC_T$:

$$22 - 2Q_B = 2.8 + 0.4Q_B$$
$$2.4Q_B = 19.2$$
$$Q_B = 8$$
$$Q_A = Q_B + 4 = 8 + 4 = 12.$$

Optimal Pricing of Multiple Products

Our discussion so far has been based on the assumption that the firm produces only one product. In modern industry, however, the typical firm produces several products, and this multiplicity creates four different kinds of relationships:

1. *Demand relationships* arise when the products are either substitutes or complements for each other. In either case, a price change for one product will affect demand for the other according to their cross elasticities.
2. *Cost relationships* arise when multiple products are produced in the same facility. Some costs remain directly chargeable to each product, but other costs, such as rent, utilities, and taxes, are shared by all.
3. *Production relationships* arise when more than one product results from a single production process. Usually there is a primary product and one or more by-products which may be produced in either fixed or variable proportions. Disposing of the by-products may be profitable or costly, depending upon their nature.
4. *Capacity relationships* arise when the firm is able to use excess or idle capacity to produce one or more additional products. As new products are added, the sharing of fixed costs alters the optimal output and price structure for all products.

Product Line Pricing ~Chpt. 5~

Many firms produce *product lines;* that is, groups of products that are related either as substitutes or complements. The key economic feature with respect to pricing a company's product line is the cross elasticity of demand as discussed in Chapter 5.

Pricing of Substitute Goods.   The production of substitute goods by a firm is an effort to segregate market sectors that have different demand elasticities. For example, Procter & Gamble produces Ivory, Zest, Safeguard, Camay, and Lava handsoaps for people with different tastes and preferences. General Motors produces Chevrolet, Pontiac, Buick, Oldsmobile, and Cadillac automobiles for buyers of different income levels as well as different tastes.

Although each of these product lines competes with similar products of other companies, they also compete "in house" with each other. There are numerous examples of firms that produce substitute products for internal as well as external competition. These include meat packers, automobile manufacturers, tire makers, clothing producers, cigarette firms, soap companies, and pharmaceutical houses, to name only a few. Pricing policies that push the sales of one product may consequently hurt the sales of another of the firm's products as well as other firms' competing products. How then should these products be priced? In practice, two common methods of product-line pricing for substitute goods can be distinguished.

The procedure followed by many producers is to set prices on their entire line of products by the same method. Essentially, a markup method of pricing is used on the entire line of products, with the same margin used for all similar products in the line. The specific technique is to price the products in proportion to costs, with the choice of costs being either full costs or "transformation" costs, the latter representing the labor and overhead expenditures required to transform (convert) raw materials into finished products.

A second approach commonly used in product-line pricing is to price the product by varying the size of the margin with the level of costs. Thus, the more costly the product, the higher the margin, and hence the higher the price. Pricing of automobiles is a good example of this approach.

Both of these methods, despite their widespread use in industry, suffer because they take no account of differences in demand, differences in competitive conditions, and differences in the degree of market maturity of each product in the line. Further, the accounting methods used to divide joint costs among products of the same firm are not at all justified economically, being wholly arbitrary and thus resulting in prices that reflect the arbitrary allocation of common costs.

What, then, should be the appropriate method for setting price? Ideally, the optimum price in a market sector is the one that yields the largest total contribution margin. Approached in this way, the product-line price structure would aim at the correct objective: that of *exploiting the differences in demand elasticities between market sectors*, as explained in the previous section.

Pricing Complementary Goods

The second type of demand interrelation is complementarity. The degree of complementarity among users can take one near-extreme form of fixed proportions (e.g., watch cases and watch mechanisms, automobiles and engine blocks, houses and furnaces); it may take different degrees of variable proportions (e.g., turpentine and paint, cameras and film, stereo phonographs and records); or it may take the most remote form when the various products in the line are not jointly related in use but merely augment the firm's general reputation (e.g., dentifrices and soap by a firm such as Procter & Gamble, where the ultimate product being sold is personal hygiene). In the last case, all products of a firm can be viewed as complementary if they enhance one another's acceptability, but in any event the fundamental pricing principles are not materially altered.

The ultimate objective, as with substitute goods, is to arrive at a price structure that produces the largest total contribution margin according to the separate demand elasticities of market segments. An essential difference, however, is this: where complementary goods are concerned, a decrease in the price of one leads to an increased demand for the others, so that the cross elasticity is substantially negative.

The practical consequence of this is that sellers will frequently find it more profitable to price an item low or even at a loss, in the hope of selling the complementary item at an above-average margin.

Loss Leaders.   Loss leaders illustrate one type of product-line pricing of complementary goods. Most commonly encountered in retailing, this practice refers to selling a commodity at less than invoice cost or at a price sharply below customary price, and publicizing the fact through advertising. The intention is (1) to draw in customers who will buy other products and/or (2) to arouse consumer interest that will eventually shift the demand curve to the right.

In the first case, the complementarity is between different products at the same time, and the direct losses on the loss leader are unimportant if they are more than offset by the indirect gains on the complementary items. In the second case, the complementarity reveals a time dimension between present and future demand, with the hope that present losses will encourage future sales and profits. Magazine trial subscriptions and student rates on theater tickets are two examples.

For a loss leader to be effective, the negative cross-elasticity coefficient between the loss item and the other products must be large (ideally, infinite); the direct or price elasticity should be low (ideally, zero); and the supply elasticity should be high so that the direct losses do not merely outweigh the indirect complementary gains. Frequently, purchases of loss leaders will be rationed (e.g., one to a customer) at the depressed price. Implicitly, this reduces the demand elasticity and limits the direct losses suffered by the seller while still evoking sales on the complementary commodities. Further, the good should be well known, widely and frequently purchased, unsuitable for storage by consumers, and standardized so that its customary price is widely known and its bargain price quickly recognized.

Thus, the phrase *loss leader* is actually a misnomer, for intelligent management can in reality increase its profits by careful selection and pricing of loss leaders. Given the prices of other products, a change in the price of the loss leader can produce larger sales of all products so that the increment in revenues exceeds the increment in costs. Hence the fact that the leader's marginal cost is greater than its marginal revenue is irrelevant; the true marginal revenue of the leader is the change in the firm's *total* revenue with other outputs (or prices) remaining the same. Therefore, a good loss leader is always a profit leader.

Tie-In Sales.   *Tie-in sales or contracts* afford a second concrete illustration of complementarity commonly discussed in marketing literature.

The practice consists of requiring buyers to combine other purchases with the featured goods so that in effect the seller is offering the purchaser a joint product. Normally, the featured or "lever" commodity must be difficult to substitute, not easily dispensed with, and relatively more inelastic in demand than the subsidiary item. An ideal opportunity for tie-in sales exists when the seller possesses an exclusive and essential patent, as in the classic example of the American Shoe Machinery Company, which compelled shoemakers to purchase other materials and intermediate products as a condition of purchasing shoe machinery. (The practice was ruled to be illegal.) Packaged sales, offering the chance to "buy one and get one free," may be considered a type of tie-in practice and are often encountered as a method of introducing a new product.

Two-Part Tariff.   Still another illustration of complementarity in pricing and somewhat similar to tie-in sales is the *two-part tariff*. Here the buyer pays two prices for a joint product consisting of a fixed and a variable component. For the fixed portion, the buyer pays a set price independent of utilization; and for the variable flow of services, the buyer makes separate payments. Examples include the basic installation charge for electric wiring or gas transmission lines and the variable payments dependent upon use; the minimum charge for public utility services and the variable payments for units purchased; or the entry fee to an amusement park (or the cover charge in a nightclub) and the variable payments for each individual entertainment.

Utilizing Plant Capacity

One reason for pursuing a multiple-product strategy is to make full use of plant capacity. Whenever existing production fails to utilize the firm's productive resources at an optimum level (which is not necessarily 100 percent of capacity), a certain portion of its fixed inputs are being wasted. If another product can be produced and sold at a price greater than its incremental cost, it would pay the firm to do so.

Looking at the situation from another angle, if the fixed costs can be spread over more products, the firm's profitability will be enhanced. This leads to a persuasive argument that business firms are more in the business of selling their unique productive capacities than they are of selling this or that product.[5] For example, a firm with technical expertise in computer technology may search for a family of products and services to embody its competence. The terminal point of this line of reasoning is

---

[5] This approach was originally developed by Eli Clemens, "Price Discrimination and the Multiple Product Firm," *Review of Economic Studies* 29 (1950–51), pp. 1–11.

to view the firm's capacity solely in terms of the existing skills of its employees and to see its product mix as the most convenient—and most profitable—expression of those skills.

The process of selling plant capacity in the form of a variety of products can be illustrated with the aid of Exhibit 16–3, which depicts a plant

Exhibit 16–3

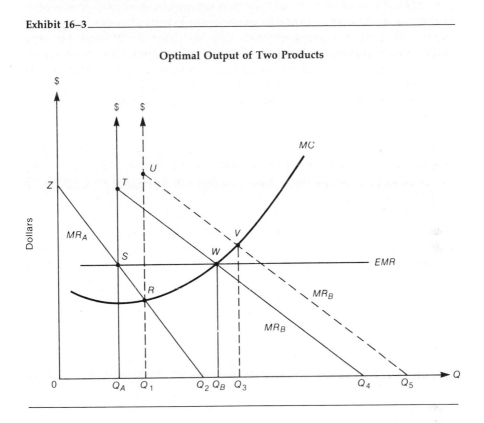

Optimal Output of Two Products

that is capable of producing two products, A and B, with no significant difference in cost factors. What is the optimal level of output for each product?

1. There is only one marginal cost curve, MC, regardless of which product is being produced.

2. The marginal revenue curve for Product A extends from the Y-intercept at Z to the X-intercept at Q_2. If only Product A is produced, the profit-maximizing output is Q_1 units, which is the level at which $MR = MC$ (at point R).

3. The productive capacity beyond Q_1 units is free to produce Product B. Therefore, suppose that we cut off production of Product A at Q_1 and begin production of Product B. The quantity Q_1 then becomes the

origin for our diagram of the marginal revenue of Product B. The marginal revenue line MR_B extends between U and Q_5, crossing the marginal cost curve at V, which corresponds to an aggregate output of Q_3 units of Products A and B. That is, we would produce Q_1 units of Product A and $(Q_3 - Q_1)$ units of Product B.

4. If we look above Q_1, we see that the production of Q_3 units of A and B is not optimal, for the marginal revenue of B at point U is clearly greater than the marginal revenue of A at point R. We can increase profits by producing fewer units of A and putting the resources saved into production of B.

5. On our diagram, we change the product mix by sliding the triangle UQ_1Q_5 to the left. As we do so, the intersection between MR_C and MC (at V) moves down the MC curve. At the same time, the intersection between MR_A and MC (at R) moves up the MR_A curve. This movement continues until $MR_A = MR_B = MC$. This equilibrium occurs at points S and W on the horizontal line of equal marginal revenue, EMR. The optimal production quantities then are Q_A units of Product A and $(Q_B - Q_A)$ units of Product B.

This process can be extended to any number of products as long as the marginal cost curve does not change. Exhibit 16–4 depicts the way in which prices may be determined for three products being produced in optimal quantities; that is, when $MR_A = MR_B = MR_C = MC$. The prices P_A, P_B, and P_C are picked off the respective demand curves D_A, D_B, and D_C for the quantities Q_A, Q_B, and Q_C.

The model depicted by Exhibit 16–4 assumes that the firm is able to invade new markets with each additional product, and that in each market the price is greater than marginal cost. The new markets are entered in the order of their profitability. Thus we see that for each successive product on Exhibit 16–4, the price is somewhat lower and the marginal cost somewhat higher. Equilibrium is reached when no more markets can be found in which new products may be sold for a price greater than marginal cost, or when the firm's productive capacity has been reached.

Limitations of the Model. This model has several weaknesses: first, it ignores demand interdependence, and second, it assumes the firm's capacity can be easily altered to produce a variety of products. Actually, the model can be reshaped to handle either of these cases, although the arithmetic can become somewhat complex. With respect to plant capacity, the issue may not be so much a matter of whether adjustments can be made in a physical sense as it is a matter of the costs involved in making them. For example, when an airliner is divided into two sections, the physical aspect of creating the new product—seats in a first-class section—is accomplished quite easily by putting a partition in the

Exhibit 16–4

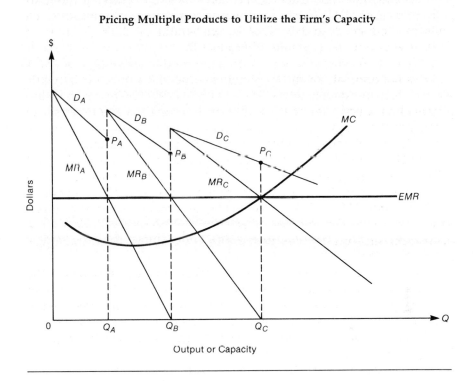

Pricing Multiple Products to Utilize the Firm's Capacity

Output or Capacity

aircraft and providing first-class passengers with a "free" cocktail and other amenities. But the important economic question is whether or not the greater incremental revenues from the new product can offset the added costs.

With respect to demand interdependence, the market conditions for a single product may range from near monopoly to pure competition. In many cases, the firm may arrive at equilibrium in the perfectly elastic market of pure competition in which $P = MR = MC$. This is a common condition that almost all multiproduct firms encounter sooner or later; that is, they produce some products on which they make no profit. Such products may eventually be discontinued, but in many cases products that make no profit, or even suffer slight losses, are continued for strategic reasons other than profit. For example, products may be retained to round out the firm's product line, to retain customer goodwill, or to keep open channels of distribution that might otherwise be closed.

Loss leaders, as previously discussed in this chapter, are examples of products priced at a loss for strategic reasons. Closely akin is the grocery supermarket practice of keeping markups very low on staple items such as flour, salt, coffee, and soap. Price elasticity is high on staple items because of competition and the consumer's knowledge of what the prices "ought to be." Thus advertising of low prices on staple items has an effect similar to advertising of loss leaders.

In some cases, no-profit or loser products are necessary to keep the organization intact. Construction companies and consulting firms of all types often will "buy a contract" (offer their services below cost) in order to keep their labor force intact between more profitable projects. In such cases, the incremental short-run loss of buying the contract has to be weighed against the costs of replacing professional staff or skilled labor when a more lucrative contract is obtained.

Optimum Pricing of Joint Products

Joint products result from production processes that naturally yield multiple products. A decision to run the production process automatically produces the entire product group. For example, the processing of sugar cane results in a by-product called *bagasse*, which is the residue of the cane stalk after the juice has been squeezed out. By-products may be used, or sold, or otherwise disposed of. Bagasse, for example, is burned to make steam to generate electricity. By-products that cannot be used or sold create a problem (and a cost) of disposal.

The ratio or proportion of joint products may be either fixed or variable. For example, the slaughter of one steer produces one carcass and one hide, a proportion that never changes. In contrast, a petroleum refinery always produces a spectrum of products ranging from gasoline to fuel oil, but it does control and can vary the proportions of the various outputs.

Joint Products in Fixed Proportions of One to One.   Since there is only one production process, there is no economically sound way to allocate costs to the individual products. The demand curves, however, can be and usually are quite different for the main product and the by-products. Determination of the optimal output and prices involves optimization of the total marginal revenue from all products in relation to marginal cost. We shall explain the procedure with the help of Exhibit 16–5.

Exhibit 16–5 depicts two cases of the joint products A and B produced in the fixed proportion $1:1$. In order to maximize profit we must find the level of production at which $MR_T = MC$; however, there is a complication: neither product may be sold beyond the quantity where its individual $MR < 0$. This is because a negative marginal revenue means we would be losing money on each unit sold. In both panels, $MR_B = 0$ at Q_M units of joint production.

Exhibit 16–5

Output and Price Determination of Joint Products A and B Produced in Fixed Proportion

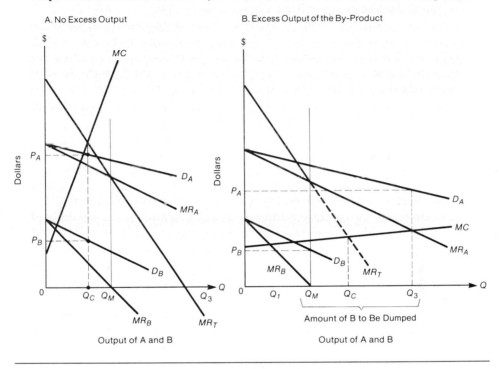

A. No Excess Output

B. Excess Output of the By-Product

Output of A and B

Output of A and B

Amount of B to Be Dumped

The step-by-step procedure for determining optimal output and price goes as follows:

Step 1. Develop or obtain the demand function for Product A (D_A on the graphs) and its related marginal revenue (MR_A).

Step 2. Develop or obtain the demand function for By-product B (D_B on the graphs) and its related marginal revenue (MR_B).

Step 3. Add MR_A and MR_B (vertically) to obtain MR_T.

Step 4. Obtain the total cost function and take its derivative to get marginal cost, MC.

Step 5. Observe the value of Q at which $MR_B = 0$ (Q_M on the graphs).

Step 6. Observe the level of Q at which $MR_T = MC$ (Q_C on the graphs).

Step 7. Compare Q_C to Q_M. If $Q_C \leq Q_M$, then the optimal output and sales level for both products is Q_C. This condition is illustrated on Panel A. Go to Step 9.

Step 8. If $Q_C > Q_M$, as illustrated on Panel B, then the maximum quantity of By-product B that can be sold is Q_M. To find the optimal quantity of the main Product A, find the level at which $MR_A = MC$. This is at Q_3 on Panel B. Of course, Q_3 units of By-product B will also be produced, but the quantity $Q_3 - Q_M$ will be dumped, destroyed, or otherwise disposed of, because selling it means losing money on every unit sold. In the past, the cheapest method of disposal has too often been indiscriminate dumping. Legal and environmentally sound disposal methods may incur additional costs. These additional costs can be quite substantial, and thus provide a powerful incentive to find new uses and new markets for the unwanted product.

Step 9. Use the demand functions of A and B to find the prices at which the optimal quantities may be sold. Thus, in both panels, Product A would sell for P_A dollars, and By-product B would sell for P_B dollars.

Step 10. Calculate the profit function at optimum output and sales.

Now let us use a numerical example to illustrate the procedure just explained. Suppose a firm produces the main Product, A, and its By-product, B, in a 1:1 ratio. Demand functions for the two products are $Q_A = 800 - 2P_A$ and $Q_B = 150 - P_B$. The joint cost function is $TC = 600 + 4Q + 3Q^2$. Find the optimal prices and quantities to be sold.

1. Find the marginal revenue of A:

$$Q_A = 800 - 2P_A \quad \text{or} \quad P_A = 400 - 0.5Q_A \tag{23}$$
$$TR_A = (400 - 0.5Q_A)Q_A = 400Q_A - 0.5Q_A^2 \tag{24}$$
$$MR_A = 400 - Q_A \tag{25}$$

2. Find the marginal revenue of B:

$$Q_B = 150 - P_B \quad \text{or} \quad P_B = 150 - Q_B \tag{26}$$
$$TR_B = (150 - Q_B)Q_B = 150Q_B - Q_B^2 \tag{27}$$
$$MR_B = 150 - 2Q_B \tag{28}$$

3. Find the total marginal revenue:

$$MR_{A+B} = 400 - Q_A + 150 - 2Q_B = 550 - Q_A - 2Q_B \tag{29}$$

But, since the output ratio is $Q_A = Q_B = Q$,

$$MR_{A+B} = 550 - Q_A - 2Q_B = 550 - 3Q \tag{30}$$

4. Find the joint marginal cost:

$$TC = 600 + 4Q + 3Q^2 \tag{31}$$
$$MC = 4 + 6Q \tag{32}$$

5. Equate joint marginal cost with joint marginal revenue:

$$4 + 6Q = 550 - 3Q$$
$$9Q = 546$$
$$Q = 60.67 \tag{33}$$

6.   Find the maximum sales of By-product B. From equation (6):

$$MR_B = 150 - 2Q_B = 0$$
$$2Q_B = 150$$
$$Q_B^* = 75 \tag{34}$$

7.   Since $Q < Q_B^*$, the quantity to be produced and sold is the same for both products, namely 60.67 units. We find the price from equations (1) and (4):

$$P_A = 400 - 0.5(60.67) = \$369.67 \tag{35}$$
$$P_B = 150 - 60.67 = \$89.33 \tag{36}$$

8.   Total profit is:

$$
\begin{aligned}
\pi &= TR_A + TR_B - TC \\
&= 60.67(369.67) + 60.67(89.33) - 600 - 4(60.67) - 3(60.67)^2 \\
&= \$15,962.30
\end{aligned}
$$

Joint Products in Fixed Proportions Other Than a One-to-One Ratio.
If the joint products are produced in fixed proportions other than 1:1, we must first remember that the cost function pertains to output of the main product. Therefore, we want to establish a ratio of $1:x$, where x is the number of units of by-product per unit of the main product. For example, suppose that the demand and cost functions remain the same for Product A and By-product B of the previous example, but the production technology changes so that the production ratio becomes $Q_A:Q_B = 2:3$.

We note that the ratio 2:3 is the same as the ratio 1.0:1.5. Hence $Q_A = Q$ and $Q_B = 1.5Q_A$. By making appropriate substitutions of $1.5Q_A$ for Q_B and vice versa, the procedure described above for a 1:1 ratio can be followed.

Joint Products in Variable Proportions and Fixed Product Prices.
When proportions of joint products are variable, it becomes necessary to determine what proportions and what level of output will maximize profit. When the firm is able to vary the proportions of the joint products, optimal pricing soon becomes quite complex because a large number of combinations must be considered. Conceptually, what is needed is a set of isocost curves that will depict the locus of all combinations of output that can be produced for a given total cost. One such set is depicted on Exhibit 16–6.

1.   The curvilinear isocost curves on Exhibit 16–6 are called product transformation curves, or production possibility curves. Each curve represents all possible variations in the proportional output of Products A

Exhibit 16–6

Output Determination of Joint Products with Variable Proportions and Fixed Product Prices

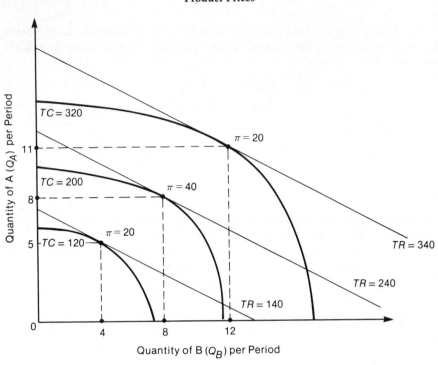

and B for a given constant cost. The curves are concave to the origin to reflect the reasonable assumption that it becomes increasingly difficult to produce more of one product and less of the other as we approach the ends of the curve. As we move outward from the origin, each curve reflects a higher level of total cost. The levels shown are for $TC = 120$, $TC = 200$, and $TC = 320$.

2. Exhibit 16–6 also shows a set of isorevenue lines. They represent all combinations of output of Products A and B that will produce the same revenue. The lines are straight because they are drawn under the assumption of constant product prices—in this illustration $P_A = \$20$ and $P_B = \$10$.

3. An optimal combination of A and B can be found for any given isocost by finding its tangency with an isorevenue line. For $TC = 120$,

$Q_A = 5$ and $Q_B = 4$; for $TC = 200$, $Q_A = 8$ and $Q_B = 8$; and for $TC = 320$, $Q_A = 11$ and $Q_B = 12$. Finally, the diagram suggests that there is also an optimal total budget for producing the two joint products. As in most other situations, this optimal output occurs at the point of profit maximization. In our illustration this occurs with a budget of 200. However, there are an infinite number of budgets that would have to be examined to determine whether any of these offers a profit greater than 40. Again, the use of the calculus or linear programming can be helpful in searching for the point of maximum profits.

Joint Products in Variable Proportions and Variable Product Prices.   If we relax the assumption of fixed product prices, a graphic solution is a bit more tedious but not difficult to understand; and since variable prices are a much more realistic assumption—at least for wide variations in output—it is worth the effort. Again, we work with two products (A and B) and assume linear demand curves for each.

1.   The diagram in Exhibit 16–7 uses all four quadrants of the traditional Cartesian graph—however, there are no negative values for any variable in any of the four quadrants. Think of it this way: increasing distance from the origin in any direction corresponds to greater positive values for the two variables plotted in that quadrant.

2.   In quadrant IV, we show an isocost curve for quantities of A and B. The trick now is to find a point on this isocost curve that gives us values for Q_A and Q_B such that the marginal revenues of the two products are equal. (The marginal revenue of A is shown in quadrant II and that of B in quadrant I.) This is accomplished by fitting a rectangle in the diagram in the manner shown. Once we find the quantities (Q_A and Q_B) that yield equal marginal revenues, it is a simple matter to find optimal prices by going up to the demand curves to find P_A and P_B. (For practice in understanding the diagram, you should satisfy yourself that only one rectangle can be drawn for the isocost curve that is given.) Also, as in the previous example, we would have to search all possible isocost curves to determine an optimal total output of the two products.

3.   The two previous examples illustrate a more general principle for finding an optimal combination for any number of joint products. It is:

$$\frac{MR_A}{MC_A} = \frac{MR_B}{MC_B} = \cdots = \frac{MR_N}{MC_N}$$

This general formula should be familiar to you from Chapter 4, in which consumer behavior theory was discussed, and from the discussion in Chapter 9, related to finding an optimal combination of factors of production.

Exhibit 16–7

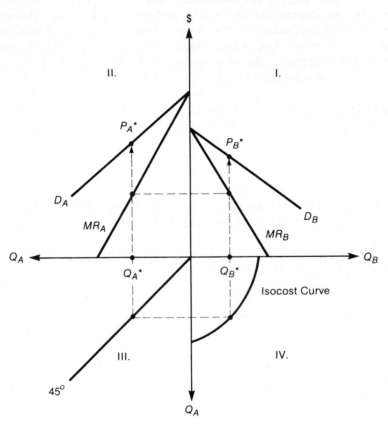

Price and Output Determination for Joint Products with Variable Proportions and Variable Product Prices

Summary

In the static world of economic theory, simplified models of market structure show how the firm may maximize profit by producing at a level where marginal revenue equals marginal cost. In the dynamic real world, however, managements must deal with multiple objectives, multiple products, multiple markets, and a considerable degree of uncertainty.

Empirical research has discovered several objectives that may be pursued in establishing prices: (1) to achieve a target return on investment;

(2) to stabilize prices or outputs; (3) to realize a target market share; or (4) to meet or match competition. The firm may pursue its pricing objectives through a variety of methods, but the two most important methods are *cost-plus pricing* and *incremental cost pricing*.

The *cost-plus method* of pricing consists of two parts: (1) establishing the cost and (2) establishing the plus, or markup. The determination of relevant cost differs somewhat among manufacturing, merchandising, and service industries, and the way in which the markup is determined will depend upon what is included in cost. In all cases, however, the cost-plus must include a satisfactory profit. This may be less than maximum in the short run in order to improve profits in the long run. Thus cost-plus is a long-run pricing concept closely related to target return objectives.

Incremental cost pricing provides business executives with an essential guide for short-run production and pricing decisions. The appropriate use of incremental analysis requires a thorough examination of the total effect of the decision in question, both in the short run and the long run. Then a price can be set that will cause incremental revenue to exceed incremental cost.

Price discrimination, also known as *differential pricing*, is defined as the practice of charging different prices to different buyers of the same product without corresponding differences in cost. It exists in three degrees:

In first degree price discrimination, the seller charges a different (lower) price for each successive unit bought, thereby extracting the maximum total receipts. It is purely theoretical and does not exist in real life.

Differential pricing of the second degree is more commonly known as volume or quantity discounting. Quantity discounts may be based upon either one-time or cumulative purchases, or may be offered according to the function of the buyer (such as wholesaler, jobber, retailer) in the chain of distribution.

Differential pricing of the third degree occurs when the seller is able to segregate and seal off markets according to the price elasticities of the buyers. Different markets can then be charged different prices, with higher prices in the more inelastic groups. Differentials may be based on time (either clock time or calendar time) or product use. Whatever the basis for discrimination, profit is maximized when the marginal revenue in each market is equal to the marginal cost of the product; i.e., $MR_A = MR_B = \ldots = MR_N = MC$.

When the firm produces multiple products, relationships arise in the areas of demand, cost, production, and capacity. In pricing substitute goods, the firm competes with itself as well as with other firms, and two approaches to pricing have been detected. One is to price the entire line by the same method, such as a percentage markup on cost. The other method is to vary the profit margin with the level of costs; that is, to place a higher markup on more costly goods. A better way would be to exploit any differences in price elasticities of the various products.

In pricing complementary goods, lowering the price of one good increases demand for both. Hence for many products sold in retail stores, loss leaders (goods sold at or below cost) have proved to be very profitable. Tie-in sales and two-part tariffs are also commonly used in pricing complementary goods.

Joint products present a different problem, since the by-product arises automatically in production of the main product. Optimal pricing requires that the joint marginal revenue equal marginal cost; however, the by-product may not be sold beyond the quantity at which its marginal revenue falls to zero. Joint products may be produced in fixed proportions or in variable proportions, with either fixed or variable prices for both inputs and output. Thus the problem of pricing joint products can become very complicated. The general principle to be followed is that the ratio of marginal revenue to marginal cost should be the same for all products.

Problems

1. ′ If most firms tend to set prices on the basis of costs, for example, cost-plus, why should companies ever show losses on their profit and loss statements?

2. Would you expect the markup on staple items (potatoes, flour, and sugar as examples) in a supermarket to be higher or lower than the markup on nonstaples? From the perspective of the *individual* supermarket, which of the two product groups has the more elastic demand? Does the relationship between markup and elasticity, generally recognized as being inverse, seem to hold for staples and nonstaples? Finally, which of the two groups would include the more attractive candidates for a loss leader? Explain.

3. In the book publishing business, it is inherent in the royalty arrangement that the publisher's pricing policy results in an economic conflict between the author and the publisher. In the great majority of cases, the author's royalty is a percentage of the total revenue that the publisher receives on the sale of the book. The publisher, however, determines the price of the book (and also incurs all costs of manufacturing, promotion, and distribution). It follows that *the price that maximizes profit for the publisher is higher, and the output lower, than the price and output that maximize royalty payments for the author.* Why? Demonstrate this proposition graphically, using marginal analysis.

4. The A-2-Z Company manufactures small electrical appliances that are sold in markets built up by substantial promotion of the A-2-Z brand. Among its better known products is a food blender. At a standard production level of 100,000 units, the standard fully allocated cost is $10 per unit, of which $6 is average variable cost. The normal markup on cost is 50 percent. The firm receives an offer from a Canadian firm to buy 50,000 units, with the Canadian firm's brand imprinted, at a price of $12. Manufacture of the additional 50,000 units will require a second shift, and will increase standard variable costs to $8 per unit. Should A-2-Z Company accept the Canadian firm's offer?

5. Identify the pricing principle(s) involved in each of the following pricing practices:

a. The price of liquid detergent per ounce is found to decrease with larger-sized containers.

b. A movie theater charges one price for adults, a second for children, and a third for students.

c. A bakery charges only half as much for day-old bread as it does for fresh bread.

d. There is a several hundred dollar difference between comparably equipped Chevrolets, Pontiacs, and Cadillacs.

e. A photo-processing concern charges 35 cents each for between 1 and 5 prints from a negative, 30 cents for between 6 and 10 prints from the same negative, and 25 cents each for more than 10 prints from the negative.

f. On a certain round-trip flight, an airline charges $30 less for passengers flying weekdays than for those taking the same flight on weekends.

g. Subscriptions to many periodicals are cheaper if more than a year's subscription is purchased. Also, often the publisher offers a substantial discount to students and educational institutions.

h. Many utilities charge different prices to private versus industrial users.

6. Saturn Publishing Company publishes two monthly magazines called *Action* and *Brisk*. The company charges the same price for both magazines, but the sales of *Brisk* are about twice those of *Action*. Both magazines are among the leaders in their field, with combined sales of 5 to 6 million copies a month. In this sales range, therefore, the marginal cost of producing the two magazines is practically constant. Further, it has been established on the basis of previous pricing experiments in various markets that the elasticity of demand is equal for the two magazines at the present price.

Recently, the president of the company asked whether it is consistent with profit maximization for the two magazines to have the same price.

The sales manager replied that in order for Saturn to maximize its profits, it ought to charge a higher price for *Brisk* than for *Action*, since demand is greater for the former.

The president has called you in as a consulting economist to settle the question. Both the president and sales manager studied economics while in college and are fairly familiar with such concepts as average revenue, marginal revenue, marginal cost, and so forth. Can you provide them with an analytical solution to the problem?

7. The World Cup Company manufacturers two types of professional quality tennis rackets. The *Champion* is of regular dimension and the *Winner* has a larger hitting area, but the two rackets may be considered as substitutes in the marketplace. The demand functions are

$$Q_C = 800 - 4P_C + 8P_W$$
$$Q_W = 300 + 2P_C - 6P_W$$

where

Q = Quantity demanded
P = Price
C = Subscript denoting the Champion
W = Subscript denoting the Winner

Their cost functions are

$$ATC_C = 10 + 0.5Q_C$$
$$ATC_W = 15 + 0.125Q_W$$

where ATC = average total cost (fully allocated unit cost).
a. Determine optimum output and price for each racket.
b. Determine profit for each type of racket at optimum output.

8. The Kentucky Pride Distillers make and distribute a premium grade whiskey in two distinct markets in the Midwest. Estimated demand functions in the two markets are

$$Q_1 = 180 - 2P_1$$
$$Q_2 = 70 - 0.5P_2$$

while unit cost is

$$ATC = 10 + 0.1Q$$

where

P_1 and P_2 = Prices in markets 1 and 2 per case of six bottles
Q_1 and Q_2 = Quantity demanded in markets 1 and 2 (in cases)
ATC = Average total cost (fully allocated unit cost per case)

a. Assume that price discrimination is possible, then calculate:
    (1) Profit-maximizing sales level and price for each market.

(2) Maximum profit for the firm.

(3) Price elasticity of demand for each market at optimum sales level.

b. Calculate profit-maximizing sales level and price if price discrimination is not practiced.

c. Compare the firm's profits with and without price discrimination.

9. The Green Pastures Dairy produces butter and cottage cheese from each ton of milk in fixed proportions of one unit of butter to one unit of cottage cheese. The dairy's economic advisor has estimated demand for the two products as

$$P_B = 75 - Q_B$$
$$P_C = 60 - 3Q_C$$

where P = price, Q = quantity demanded, and the subscripts B and C represent butter and cottage cheese, respectively. The cost of the joint production of butter and cheese is

$$TC = 300 + 15Q + Q^2$$

where TC = total cost in dollars.

a. Determine the optimal quantity of each product to be produced and sold in order to maximize profit.

b. Determine the optimal price of each product.

c. Calculate maximum total profit on both products.

10. Excelsior Wood Products produces millwork from raw lumber. The production process is such that for every two units of their primary product (Product A) they get three units of salable scrap (By-product B). Their cost function is

$$TC = 600 + 4Q + 3Q^2$$

and their demand functions are

$$Q_A = 800 - 2P_A$$
$$Q_B = 150 - P_B$$

a. Find the sales level and price for each product that will maximize profit.

b. Calculate the maximum profit from both products.

Case Problem: The Pricing of a Special Program

11. The dean of the school of business administration at a large university believed that a number of professional businesspeople in the city would have an interest in preparing for the CMA (Certified Managerial Accountant) examination given each year. A report was pre-

pared suggesting that a review course be offered by the business faculty of the school, with classes held during evening hours when classroom space is available.

A preliminary market study indicated that a tuition fee of $500 would attract 20 students for total revenues of $10,000. The participating faculty would be paid a bonus—expected to be $8,000—for their services, and all other direct costs would be small enough to ignore.

The dean recommended approval of the program on the basis of its $2,000 contribution. The university's controller, however, opposed it. He indicated that indirect costs at the university usually match direct costs dollar for dollar. This means that all activities must be able to show a contribution equal to their direct costs in order to be acceptable.

Dean's Response: The important question is whether or not the program uses university facilities that could be used in some other activity. If the answer is yes, what contribution (monetary or other) do these activities offer? If they are worth more than $2,000, run them; if they are worth less than $2,000, run the CMA program. In any case, *never* look at the fixed overhead or some artificial means of allocating it.

Controller's Response to the Dean: Decisions such as these always look good when they are made in isolation from all other decisions, but we must look at the total picture. If we allow one program to run without meeting its full costs, we will soon be asked by others to run their programs at less than full cost. Pretty soon half the university is on an "incremental cost only" basis. Who then covers the fixed overhead? Incremental analysis is all right as long as you stick to one decision, but it breaks down when a policy issue must be considered and our primary concern is policy.

Who is right—the dean or the controller?

References

Cowling, Keith, and A. J. Rayner. "Price, Quality, and Market Share." *Journal of Political Economy,* November–December 1970, pp. 1292–1309.

Darden, B. R. "An Operational Approach to Product Pricing," *Journal of Marketing,* April 1968, pp. 29–33.

Eckstein, Otto, and Garry Fromm. "The Price Equation." *American Economic Review,* December 1968, pp. 1159–83.

Hall, R. L., and C. J. Hitch. "Price Theory and Business Behavior." *Oxford Economic Papers,* May 1939, pp. 12–45.

Koch, J. V. *Industrial Organization and Prices.* 2d ed. Englewood Cliffs, N.J.: Prentice-Hall, 1980.

Lanzillotti, Robert F. "Pricing Objectives in Large Companies." *American Economic Review,* December 1958, pp. 921–40.

McGuigan, James R., and R. Charles Moyer. *Managerial Economics.* 2d ed. St. Paul, Minn.: West Publishing, 1979.

Pappas, James L., and Eugene F. Brigham. *Managerial Economics.* 4th ed. Hinsdale, Ill.: Dryden Press, 1983.

Maurice, S. C., and Charles W. Smithson. *Managerial Economics.* Homewood, Ill.: Richard D. Irwin, 1981.

Okuguchi, Koji. "On the Stability of Price Adjusting Oligopoly Equilibrium under Product Differentiation." *Southern Economic Journal,* January 1969, pp. 244–46.

Scherer, F. M. *Industrial Market Structure and Economic Performance.* 2d ed. Skokie, Ill.: Rand McNally, 1980.

Schneidau, R. E., and Ronald D. Knutson. "Price Discrimination in the Food Industry: A Competitive Stimulant or Tranquilizer?" *American Journal of Agricultural Economics,* December 1969, pp. 1143–48.

Silberston, Aubrey. "Surveys of Applied Economics: Price Behavior of Firms." *Economic Journal,* September 1970, pp. 511–82.

Sizer, John. "The Accountant's Contribution to the Pricing Decision." *Journal of Management Studies,* May 1966, pp. 129–49.

Yandle, Bruce, Jr. "Monopoly-Induced Third-Degree Price Discrimination." *Quarterly Review of Economics and Business,* Spring 1971, pp. 71–75.

Appendix 16A | Decentralization and Transfer Pricing

As business firms grow, top management must resolve three central problems: (1) how to allocate resources, activities, and responsibilities to subordinate units, (2) how to create incentives for high performance, and (3) how to coordinate and evaluate the performance of the subordinate units. As we noted in Chapter 14, solution of these problems often involves decentralization of the organization into autonomous divisions.

The autonomous divisions of a decentralized firm are expected to be profit or investment centers, but they are really more than that. In a truly successful decentralization, each division contributes to the success of the company by contributing to the others' success as well as its own. One of the ways in which divisions cooperate is the production of goods or services by one division for use by another division. Since the transfer of such products involves a transaction between autonomous divisions, it becomes necessary to establish a transfer price at which the product may be sold by one division and purchased by the other.

Transfer is not confined to exchanges between divisions, but applies to any exchange of goods or services between organizational units. Thus the allocation of service-department costs to production departments by cost accountants is actually a form of transfer pricing. However, since we are concerned with economic rather than accounting aspects of transfer pricing, and for the sake of simplicity, we shall confine our discussion to exchanges between divisions.

The Nature and Objectives of Transfer Pricing[1]

Information about transfer prices affects many crucial decisions about the acquisition and allocation of the firm's resources. Ideally, transfer prices should provide each manager with the information necessary to coordinate his or her inputs and outputs with other units so that profits are maximized for the firm as a whole.

When goods and services are exchanged between divisions, the monetary values to be assigned to these exchanges is often the most trouble-

---

[1] For a more complete discussion, see Charles T. Horngren, *Cost Accounting: A Managerial Emphasis*, 5th ed. (Englewood Cliffs, N.J.: Prentice-Hall, 1982), chapter 19, from which much of the material in this Appendix has been extracted.

some aspect of the firm's control system. In establishing transfer prices, three inherent and sometimes conflicting problems must be solved:

1. *Goal congruence.* This is the problem of insuring that the division management's goals coincide with those of the firm.
2. *Incentive.* This is the problem of providing division managers with the incentive to pursue the firm's goals rather than their own.
3. *Autonomy.* This is the problem of providing guidance without undermining the division managers' authority and freedom to make independent decisions.

There is no all-inclusive rule that will invariably lead to the optimal economic decision because the three problems of congruence, incentive, and autonomy must all be dealt with at the same time. In any particular situation, however, the following general rule may provide a useful first step in analysis: *The lowest transfer price should be the sum of (1) incremental cash outlay (which sometimes may be approximated by variable costs) and (2) opportunity costs for the firm as a whole.*

Incremental cash outlay means the cash outflows that are directly associated with the production and transfer of the goods or services in question. *Opportunity costs* means the maximum contribution to profits that is foregone by the firm if the goods are transferred internally. If an external market exists, the opportunity cost is market price less outlay cost. If no outside market exists, the opportunity cost might be zero; but it also might be the foregone proceeds from sale of the productive facilities, or foregone profits from their use to produce something else.

We see then that there are two basic circumstances under which transfers and transfer pricing take place: (1) when there is an external or *intermediate* market for the goods or services and (2) when there is not. Since the latter circumstance is perhaps the most common and most troublesome, we shall discuss it first.

Transfer Pricing When There Is No External Market

We shall begin this section by showing that in the absence of an external market, the correct transfer price is the marginal cost of the seller. Then we shall show some of the many variations in determining what the marginal cost is.

Transfer Pricing at Marginal Cost

Suppose a firm has two divisions. Division A manufactures a critical component (for which there is no external market) of the final product.

Division B completes assembly and packaging of the final product and markets it to the public. Since there is no external market for Division A's product, Division B must buy its entire supply from Division A; hence, the production by Division A is precisely equal to the demand by Division B. The situation is illustrated by Exhibit 16A–1.

Exhibit 16A–1

Transfer Pricing with No External Market

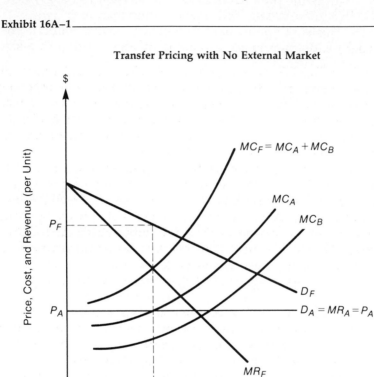

Quantity per Time Period

Exhibit 16A–1 shows Division A's marginal cost curve, MC_A, Division B's marginal cost curve, MC_B, and the firm's marginal cost curve, MC_F, which is the vertical summation of $MC_A + MC_B$. The diagram also shows the firm's demand curve for the finished product, D_F, and its derived marginal revenue curve, MR_F. To optimize the *firm's* profits, the production and sales level is set so that $MR_F = MC_F$. This calls for Q_F units to be sold at a price of P_F dollars.

Division A's marginal revenue will be the transfer price. Since this price, once established, remains a constant, Division A's demand curve is a horizontal line on which $MR_A = P_A$. Since Division A seeks to maximize profit, the transfer price (which equals marginal revenue) must be equal to marginal cost at Q_F units of production.

Having established that the transfer price should equal marginal cost at the desired level of sales, we still have to determine what the marginal cost is, and this is not always easy.

Variations in Calculating the Transfer Price

If the transfer price is based upon *actual* fully allocated costs, the buyers *might* reap the benefit of efficiencies in the seller's operation, but they are more apt to bear the burden of inefficiencies over which they have no control. This is because full recovery of actual costs provides the selling division with no incentives to control costs. Consequently, many firms allow only *standard* costs as transfer prices.

Standard costs may solve the inefficiency problem but still lead to dysfunctional decisions in the short-run. For example, suppose that a firm desires to market a product at a price of $16. The firm has two divisions: Division A produces a component at a variable cost of $6 per unit, to which they add a standard overhead allocation of $4. Their transfer price to Division B thus is $10. Division B's costs amount to $8; hence, their total cost is $18. Since the market price is $16, they will not market the product, for to do so would entail a loss of $2 on each unit sold.

But, keeping in mind that the allocated overhead costs are going to be incurred by the firm whether or not the product is marketed, the firm could benefit in the short run by setting the transfer price equal to variable cost. The incremental costs are $6 in Division A plus $8 in Division B, for a total of $14. The price of $16 would yield an incremental profit of $2 to be applied to the firm's fixed costs.

Despite its limitations, full cost is in common use as the base for cost-plus transfer pricing that approximates an external market price, whether or not one exists. One variation in this procedure is to transfer the goods at standard variable cost, then add a periodic lump-sum charge for overhead and profit. In this way, the buyer's decisions are not influenced by the seller's fixed costs or profits.

Another variation of the cost-plus approach is for top management to impose a transfer price equal to variable cost, then prorate the firm's profits between the contributing divisions. Proration can be negotiated in a number of ways, including the basis of standard variable costs in each division.

Another variation is a system of dual pricing in which one price is used for economic decision making, but a different price is used for evaluation of performance. Taking our previous example, Division A would charge Division B its variable cost of $6, but would get credit for a $10 sale. In effect Division A would get a corporate subsidy of $4 per unit. Both division managers would be happy, but the company might not be. The difficulty is that both managers have lost their incentives to hold down costs.

Transfer Pricing When an External Market Exists

When there is an external market for the selling division's product, the selling division may produce more or less than the buying division needs. If the selling division produces more than the buying division needs, the surplus can be sold in the external market. If the selling division produces less than the buying division needs, the buying division can obtain the rest of its needs in the external market. Either way, the selling division is free to pursue maximization of its own profit. The transfer price, however, will depend upon whether or not the external market is perfectly competitive.

Transfer Pricing with a Perfectly Competitive External Market

For the case of a perfectly competitive external market, we shall illustrate the derivation of a transfer price with the aid of Exhibit 16A–2.

On Exhibit 16A–2, the external demand for the selling division's product, D_S, is shown as a horizontal line, which also represents the marginal revenue, MR_S, which is equal to the price, P_S, in the external market.[2] Since the selling division can sell all it wishes at that price, its profit is maximized by production of Q_S units, at which level its marginal revenue, MR_S, equals marginal cost, MC_S. Demand for the buying division's product is represented by the line D_B, from which the buying division's marginal revenue, MR_B, is derived. The buying division's marginal cost, MC_B, is equal to the price of the transferred product, P_S, plus MC_M, which is the buying division's marginal cost of completing and marketing the final product.[3]

Optimal sales for the buying division are Q_B units, as determined by the intersection of the MC_B and MR_B curves. Hence, the selling division

---

[2] James R. McGuigan and R. C. Moyer, *Managerial Economics* 2d ed. (St. Paul, Minn.: West Publishing, 1979), pp. 378–81.

[3] In some firms, the two divisions might be a production division and a marketing division. In that case, the transferred product is the ultimate product, and MC_M represents promotional, selling, and perhaps administrative costs.

Exhibit 16A–2

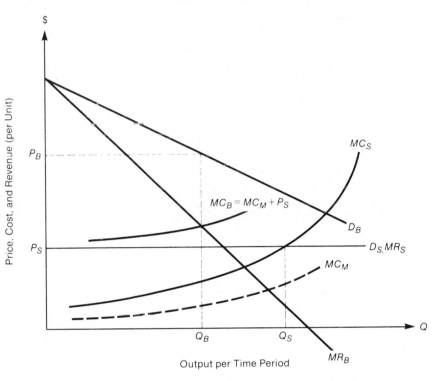

Determination of Transfer Price When a Perfectly Competitive External Market Exists for the Product

will supply the buying division with Q_B units, and sell the remaining output, $Q_S - Q_B$, in the external market.

To illustrate, suppose that a company is organized into a production division and a marketing division that sells the product domestically in the firm's own retail stores. However, the manufacturing division can also export as much of its output as it wishes to foreign distributors at a price of $25 per unit.

The marketing division's demand is

$$Q_M = 50,000 - 1,000P_M$$

which is the same as

$$P_M = 50 - .001Q_M$$

and its total cost in addition to the transfer price paid to the production division is

$$TC_M = 225{,}000 + 10Q_M$$

The production division's total cost is

$$TC_P = 375{,}000 + 12Q_P + .0005Q_P^2$$

Since the production department can sell as much as it wants to, either to the marketing division or abroad, its marginal revenue is the market price of $25 per unit. Its marginal cost is

$$MC_P + \frac{dTC_P}{dQ_P} = 12 + .001Q_P$$

At optimum production, $MR = MC$, or

$$12 + .001Q = 25$$
$$Q = 13{,}000 \text{ units.}$$

For the marketing division, total cost including purchase of the product, is

$$TC_M = 225{,}000 + 10Q_M + 25Q_M$$
$$= 225{,}000 + 35Q_M$$

so that

$$MC_M = 35$$

Marginal revenue for the marketing division is computed as follows:

$$TR_M = P_M Q_M = (50 - .001Q_M)Q_M$$
$$MR_M = 50 - .002Q_M$$

At optimum, $MR_M = MC_M$:

$$50 - .002Q_M = 35$$
$$.002Q_M = 15$$
$$Q_M = 7{,}500$$

Hence the production division would produce 7,500 units for sale to the marketing division at $25 per unit and 5,500 units for export at the same price. The marketing division would sell the product at a price of

$$P_M = 50 - .001Q_M$$
$$= 50 - .001(7{,}500) = \$42.50$$

Transfer Pricing with Imperfectly Competitive External Market

When an external market exists for the selling division's product but is not perfectly competitive, the problem becomes one of price discrimination in two markets, as discussed in Chapter 16. The profit-maximizing rule for the seller is that the marginal revenue in each market shall be equal to marginal revenue for the total market, which shall be equal to marginal cost. Hence, the transfer price to the buying division is just the selling division's marginal cost. This can be illustrated with the aid of Exhibit 16A–3.

Exhibit 16A–3 _____

Transfer Pricing with an Imperfectly Competitive External Market

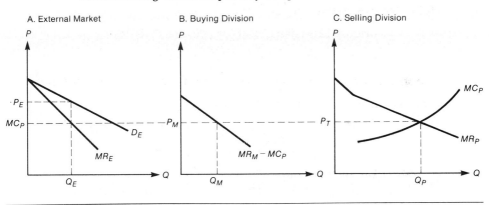

A. External Market   B. Buying Division   C. Selling Division

Panel A of Exhibit 16A–3 presents the downward-sloping demand curve of the imperfect external market and its associated marginal revenue curve, MR_E.

Panel B presents the net marginal revenue of the buying division, which is equal to marginal revenue on division sales, MR_M, minus the transfer price, P_T, which is equal to the marginal cost, MC_P, of the selling division.

Panel C presents the marginal revenue of the selling division, which is the horizontal summation of the division's marginal revenue in both markets, i.e., $MR_E + MR_M$. The selling division's optimal output level is Q_P units, at which level $MR_P = MC_P$.

At the transfer price of P_T dollars, the buying division will purchase Q_M units of the selling division's product. In the external market, the optimum sales level is Q_E units, which will clear the market at a price of P_E dollars.

To further illustrate, suppose that we have the following cost and demand functions:

$$P_E = 120 - .002Q_E$$
$$P_M = 125 - .0025Q_M$$
$$TC = 250,000 + 12Q + .005Q^2$$

where

P = Price
Q = Quantity produced or sold
E = Subscript denoting external market
M = Subscript denoting marketing division
$Q = Q_E + Q_M$

Marginal cost of production is

$$MC = 12 + .001Q = 12 + .001Q_E + .001Q_M$$

Marginal revenue of external market is

$$MR_E = 120 - .004Q_E$$

Net marginal revenue of marketing division is

$$MR_M - MC = 125 - .005Q_M - 12 - .001Q_E - .001Q_M$$

Setting combined marginal revenue equal to marginal cost:

$$MR_{E+M} = MR_E + MR_M = MC$$
$$120 - .004Q_E + 125 - .005Q_M - 12 - .001Q_E - .001Q_M$$
$$= 12 + .001Q_E + .001Q_M$$

Gathering terms:

$$233 - .005Q_E - .006Q_M = 12 + .001Q_E + .001Q_M$$
$$- .006Q_E = - 221 + .007Q_M$$
$$Q_E = 36,833 - 1.167Q_M$$

Set marginal revenue of the external market equal to marginal cost:

$$MR_E = MC$$
$$120 - .004Q_E = 12 + .001Q_E + .001Q_M$$
$$- .005Q_E = -108 + .001Q_M$$
$$Q_E = 21,600 - .2Q_M$$

Now we have two equations in two unknowns. Solving simultaneously:

$$Q_E = 36,833 - 1.167Q_M$$
$$\underline{Q_E = 21,600 - .2Q_M}$$
$$0 = 15,233 - .967Q_M$$

$$Q_M = 15,753$$

$$Q_E = 21,600 - .2(15,753) = 18,449$$
$$P_E = 120 - .002(18,449) = \$83.10$$

$$Q = Q_M + Q_E = 15,753 + 18,449 = 34,202$$
$$P_T = MC = 12 + .001(34,202) = \$46.20$$

Comments on Market Prices as Transfer Prices

One of the difficulties with market prices is that few markets are perfectly competitive; and even when they exist, price comparisons are meaningless unless grade, quality, delivery terms, credit terms, and service terms are precisely the same as those of the selling division. Another difficulty is that distress prices may prevail in the marketplace. This will require a difficult choice between short-run and long-run benefits to the supplying division, buying division, and the company as a whole.

The market price approach to transfer pricing is most useful when it simulates an arm's-length, bargained, open-market transaction. If the selling division has the option of not selling internally and the buying division has the option of not buying internally, and if an arbitration procedure is available for settling disputes, then market pricing of transferred goods on services satisfies the three problems of congruence, incentive, and autonomy. Further, the buying division often gains the advantages of better quality and more dependable supply and delivery than it could obtain at the same price on the open market.

The usefulness of market pricing depends, however, upon the firm's ability to obtain reliable price quotations from other manufacturers. In many cases, a lower internal price might be justified when internal transactions reduce costs. This leads to the idea of negotiated market prices that split cost savings between the buying and selling divisions.

International Transfer Pricing[4]

When transactions between divisions or subsidiaries of a multinational company take place across national boundaries, the buying and selling units must meet the differing requirements of their respective jurisdictions with respect to customs duties, tax rates, rules of competition, and customary business practices. The differences create problems with respect to transfer pricing, but they also create opportunities to

---

[4] Material in this subsection has been extracted from Stefan H. Robock and Kenneth Simmonds, *International Business and Multinational Enterprises* 3d ed. (Homewood, Ill.: Richard D. Irwin, 1983), pp. 532–36.

increase profits to the firm by manipulation of transfer prices. These opportunities include the following:

1. *Tax savings.* By producing the transfer product in a low-tax country, then charging high transfer prices to units in high-tax countries, taxable earnings are shifted to the low-tax environment.
2. *Reduced duties.* Low transfer prices on goods shipped into high-tariff countries keep the dutiable base and duty low.
3. *Repatriation of dividends.* In countries where direct repatriation of dividends is restricted, income can be shifted out of the country by charging higher transfer prices for goods brought in.
4. *Lower deposits on import licenses.* In countries where a deposit is required to obtain permission to import goods, a low transfer price will hold down the size of the required deposit.
5. *Financing of new subsidiaries.* Unusually low transfer prices to a new subsidiary can help it to show a healthy profit and thereby obtain local credit.
6. *Control of public and labor relations.* In situations where high profits might cause customers or local governments to demand lower prices or might encourage labor unions to demand higher wages, the payment of higher transfer prices can lower the visible profits.

Despite all these opportunities for profitable manipulation of transfer prices, most American firms claim that they deal with foreign subsidiaries "at arm's length." In both buying and selling, the foreign subsidiaries are treated as if they were independent companies. The only exceptions were subsidiaries in developing countries such as India and Pakistan, where tax rates on distributed profits are 70 percent or more.

Several constraints have acted to bring about arm's-length transactions. Among these are the profit-center concept and the expanding role of tax and customs authorities.

1. *The profit-center concept.* Manipulation of transfer prices may destroy the value of profits as a measure of performance. There are two methods of manipulating transfer prices within the profit-center concept. One is to share the total realized profits between the parent company and subsidiary. The other is to keep two sets of books. One set would be for tax and other local purposes, and the other set would be for management control purposes. In either case, it is debatable whether the gain from manipulating transfer prices is greater than the resulting cost and increased complexity of measuring performance.

2. *Expanding role of tax and customs authorities.* Governments are aware of the possibilities of transfer price manipulation to reduce taxes and customs duties. Most nations have stepped up their surveillance of multinational business operations within their borders so as to maximize

their tax revenues or assure fair treatment of their subsidiaries. The United States is foremost in the world in this regard. The U.S. Treasury's transfer-price review program covers not only the sale of tangible goods, but also the transfer of intangible property such as patents and trademarks, the use of tangible property, and the pricing of money and services.

The general rule developed by the Treasury is called the *arm's-length formula*. Several methods have been presented by the Treasury for conformance to the arm's-length formula, but the general principle is that the two parties must bargain as if they were independent entities. However, even the U.S. regulations appear to leave room for a company to reduce its transfer price in order to meet competition or to penetrate a new market. Consequently, most companies still have the opportunity to increase systemwide profits and to support marketing goals by judicious use of alternative transfer-pricing strategies.

Problems

1. Suppose that a vertically integrated firm consists of two divisions: (1) a manufacturing division, which completes the product, and (2) a marketing division, which sells the product. What should the transfer price be in order to maximize the firm's profit?

2. Suppose that a vertically integrated firm consists of two divisions: Division A manufactures an essential component for the firm's product. The product is completed, packaged, and marketed by Division B. What should Division A's transfer price be:
a. If there is no external market for Division A's product?
b. If there is a perfectly competitive external market for Division A's product?
c. If there is an imperfectly competitive external market for Division A's product?

3. The Flamingo Corporation is organized into two autonomous divisions for the manufacture and sale of power lawn mowers. The Small Engine Division produces gasoline engines of a type that can be bought or sold in outside competitive markets at a price of $30 each. At that price, the Small Engine Division has a 20 percent margin of profit. Their marginal cost, MC_E, is $.08Q_E$, where Q_E is the number of engines produced and sold in any market. The Lawn Products Division buys the engine and manufactures the remaining components. Marginal cost, MC_M, of the finished lawn mower is $0.1Q_M$ plus the cost of the engine. Demand for the finished product is

$$Q_M = 750 - 5P_M$$

where

Q_M = Quantity demanded
P_M = Price of each lawn mower.

a. When the Lawn Products Division buys engines from the Small Engine Division, what should the transfer price be?
b. What is the profit-maximizing output level and price for the Lawn Products Division?
c. What is the profit-maximizing output level and price for the Small Engines Division?
d. How many engines should be exchanged between the divisions and how many should be bought or sold on the open market?

References

Dean, Joel. "Decentralization and Intracompany Pricing." *Harvard Business Review*, July–August 1955, pp. 65–74.

Hirshleifer, Jack. "On the Economics of Transfer Pricing." *Journal of Business*, July 1956, pp. 172–84.

———. "Economics of the Divisionized Firm." *Journal of Business*, April 1957, pp. 96–108.

Horngren, Charles T. *Cost Accounting: A Managerial Emphasis*. 5th ed. Englewood Cliffs, N.J.: Prentice-Hall, 1982, Chapter 19.

Keegan, Warren J. *Multinational Marketing Management*. Englewood Cliffs N.J.: Prentice-Hall, 1974, pp. 268–69.

McGuigan, James R., and R. Charles Moyer. *Managerial Economics*. 2d ed. St. Paul, Minn.: West Publishing, 1979.

Robock, Stefan H.; Kenneth Simmonds; and Jack Zwick. *International Business and Multinational Enterprises*. 3d ed. Homewood, Ill.: Richard D. Irwin, 1983, pp. 532–36.

Thomas, A. *A Behavioral Analysis of Joint-Cost Allocation and Transfer Pricing*. Urbana, Ill.: Stipes Publishing, 1980.

17

The Economic Role
of Government

Although the American economic system is often described as "free enterprise," it is not and never has been a *laissez faire* system. In Article I, Section 8 of the U.S. Constitution, the first 8 of the 18 clauses that spell out the powers of Congress pertain to economic matters. Thus the traditional government functions of maintaining law and order and providing for the national defense were expanded to include overseeing the economic system to make sure that it does not break down and that it operates in the public interest.

If all business could be conducted in the market structure of perfect competition, far less government intervention in the marketplace would be necessary. In the real world, however, most market structures are imperfect. They have certain flaws and limitations that require government intervention to promote the general welfare, as mandated by the Constitution. These limitations include the following:[1]

1. Although the benefits of competition are recognized, the private enterprise system does not guarantee that competition will exist. Disproportionate market power can be wielded by organized labor as well as by big business.
2. Inequality of opportunity persists for blacks, Hispanics, women, and other minorities.

---

[1] As identified by the Committee for Economic Development (CED) in a Review and Discussion Guide entitled "Redefining Government's Role in the Market," p. 2.

3. The private enterprise system necessarily disregards the public interest in products and services that are consumed collectively for the benefit of all. Examples are parks, highways, traffic signals, weather forecasts, police and fire protection, and national defense.
4. The market economy does not provide for desirable social conditions such as clean air and water, clean streets, and safe living and working conditions.

In particular, Congress has been granted the power to provide for the general welfare and to regulate commerce. Under these clauses, federal government intervention in the marketplace has taken four major forms:[2]

1. *Antitrust policy* seeks to control concentration of economic and political power in the marketplace and keep it within acceptable limits by maintaining a market structure that is efficient in performance and fair to all. This is done by prohibiting unnatural monopolies and unfair competition.
2. *Regulation* seeks to preserve freedom of choice and consumer sovereignty in the marketplace and desirable social conditions such as clean air and water, clean streets, and safe living and working conditions. Regulation controls the activities of business firms, including natural monopolies such as public utilities, for the benefit of the consumer or society as a whole.
3. *Incentives,* in the form of tax policy or subsidies, encourage business firms to conduct research and development, to undertake new ventures, and to modify production schedules to increase external social benefits or decrease external social costs (such as pollution).
4. *Public ownership* provides for production by the federal government of public goods and services such as airports, seaports, inland waterways, interstate highways, bridges, dams, and national forests, national parks, wilderness areas, and other recreational facilities.

Although the four forms of government intervention listed above are clearly economic in nature, the necessary legislation and subsequent regulatory enforcement soon become *political* actions because of the maneuvering of special interest groups. The most prominent of these groups are representatives of agriculture, labor, various industries, small business, the professions (medicine, law, education), environmentalists, and consumers. Within each of these broad categories, there are hundreds of smaller, more specialized groups, all clamoring for leg-

---

[2] In the following discussions of government intervention, the primary reference is to intervention by the federal government. However, it should be recognized that some forms of intervention, such as regulation of utilities, is more apt to be performed at the state or local level. The word *government* will be used here to encompass whatever level of government is appropriate to the subject being discussed.

islative or executive attention. Competing or cooperating with others, whichever is expedient, each special interest group seeks legislation or executive orders to advance its particular cause. Consequently, the laws and executive directives that are intended to provide economic support and regulation of private enterprise are actually the result of a political bargaining process.

The CED suggests four ways in which government can strengthen market forces and overcome market limitations:

1. "Establish fair rules and protect against predatory action and restricted competition."
2. "Recognize rights and enforce contracts."
3. "Establish standards of performance where society in general is concerned."
4. "See to it that buyers have information so that they are neither ignorant nor misled when making buying decisions."[3]

A full-scale study of government intervention in the U.S. economy is far beyond the scope of this book. Rather, in this chapter we shall provide an overview of government activities designed to support and regulate business. We shall attempt to explain the economic underpinnings of regulation and to outline the more important types of regulation that business decision makers may have to deal with. In particular, we shall discuss:

1. Economic externalities and government intervention to deal with externalities.
2. Regulation of natural monopolies.
3. Restraint of market power and unfair competition by means of antitrust policy.
4. Enforcement of the antitrust laws.
5. Behavior of the regulatory agencies.
6. Intervention for the protection of society.
7. The trend toward deregulation.

Economic Externalities

An externality is a market imperfection that arises when persons not directly involved in an economic transaction nevertheless receive benefits or bear costs as a result of that transaction. Since externalities are not reflected in the market price of goods or services, the result is a misallocation of resources. Without some sort of intervention in the marketplace, too little will be produced of goods with beneficial (positive) exter-

---

[3] CED Guide, "Redefining Government's Role in the Market," p. 3.

nalities, and too much of goods with harmful (negative) externalities. Externalities may arise from either production or consumption, as discussed in the following sections.

Production Externalities

In Chapters 9 and 11, we discussed the *internal* economies or diseconomies of returns to scale as the firm expands its operations. But there can be *external* economies or diseconomies of production as well. An external economy of production arises when an increase in the firm's production results in some benefit to society (persons outside the firm) for which the firm is not compensated in the prices of its products. Social benefits from expanded production may arise in at least two different ways:

1. *By direct service to others.* For example, if a firm expands production by building a new plant in a small town, merchants in the town will profit when the new plant's employees spend their wages.
2. *By indirect cost reduction to other firms.* For example, when Henry Ford introduced the automobile assembly line, the increased production of automobiles greatly increased the demand for steel. Since large economies of scale were possible in the steel industry, all users of steel benefited from Ford's innovation.

An external diseconomy of production arises when expansion of the firm's production results in adverse effects (social costs) that are not paid for by the firm and are therefore not reflected in the prices of its products. For example, increased output of a manufacturing plant may put strains on the local transportation system that increase costs for all users.

But there can also be negative externalities associated with a production process whether or not it expands. The example that is most often cited, perhaps because it is the most serious, is the industrial pollution of air or water. If a firm dumps noxious or toxic wastes into a river, municipalities downstream must spend large sums on purification. If a firm spews wastes into the air, both health and property of downwind residents may be adversely affected.

Consumption Externalities

An external economy of consumption arises when the purchase and consumption of a good or service results in utility for people who do not pay for the good or service. For example, suppose that the owner of an old house in run-down condition pays a contractor for a thorough remodeling and renovation. The house increases in value, and that is what the owner paid for. But if (as often happens) the improvement in that house causes the whole neighborhood to look better, then values of all homes will rise. The neighbors get a "free ride," or positive externality.

An external diseconomy of consumption arises when the purchase and consumption of a good or service results in disutility for people not involved in the transaction. Again taking house remodeling as an example, suppose that all the neighbors except one renovate and remodel their homes. By comparison with the others, the lone exception will look even worse than before and will suffer a loss in value.

The Economic Impact of Externalities

Some externalities, such as the pleasure gained from viewing a well-tended garden or the discomfort of standing on a crowded bus, may seem to have no great social significance, and certainly cannot be given a dollar value. Yet when they are taken all together, externalities have a profound economic impact.[4]

It is no accident that industries tend to cluster in particular locations. We associate steel with Pittsburgh, automobiles with Detroit, rubber with Akron, and financial institutions with New York. This clustering has taken place because new firms were attracted to locations where established firms provided positive externalities such as pools of skilled labor, specialized financial institutions, suppliers of raw materials, and transportation systems—all developed at the expense of firms already in place. Locations that lack these necessities, such as the inner-city ghettos and underdeveloped countries, are much less attractive to industry.

Consumption patterns are also conditioned by consumption externalities. The fortunes of the garment industry, for example, turn upon their ability to induce the purchase of new styles before old garments are worn out. Those who are unable or unwilling to buy the new styles may suffer a diseconomy—they may feel dowdy or behind the times even when well dressed in yesterday's styles.

Managers of both private and public enterprises need to be aware of the economic and social effects of externalities that stem from their operations. The private firm's management should analyze the firm's operations to determine what positive or negative externalities may be generated in the normal course of business. If positive benefits are identified, they should be emphasized in the firm's public relations activities. If negative externalities are recognized, the firm should seek to remedy them by internal action, if possible. If not, the firm should prepare for

---

[4] Externalities must not be confused with secondary price effects. Secondary price effects take place *within* the market system. For example, sale of wheat to the Soviet Union in 1972–73 caused a rise in the price of wheat products in the United States. Externalities are conveyed *outside* of the price system directly to the persons affected.

and attempt to influence the remedies that may be imposed by government.

The management of a public enterprise also must identify the positive and negative externalities that its activities may generate. The negative externalities call for a remedy, of course; but it is the positive externalities that must be most clearly understood, because they may be the only justification for continuing or expanding the public enterprise.

Misallocation of Resources

The most serious consequence of either positive or negative externalities, regardless of whether the enterprise is private or public, is the misallocation of resources. In the case of positive externalities, the result is underutilization; that is, society is not using enough resources in the production of a particular good or service. This case is illustrated by Exhibit 17–1.

Let's say that Exhibit 17–1 depicts the marginal revenue, *MR*, and marginal cost, *MC*, of a firm that is manufacturing solar energy systems.

Exhibit 17–1

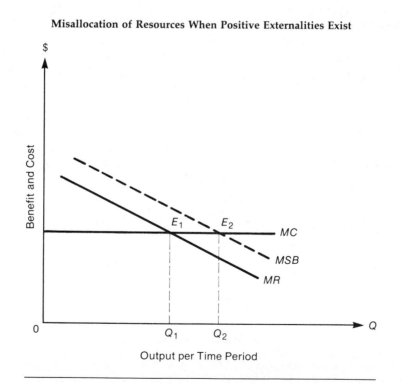

Misallocation of Resources When Positive Externalities Exist

For simplicity's sake, we have given the firm a constant marginal cost. At equilibrium, E_1, where $MR = MC$, the firm maximizes profits by producing Q_1 units.

Now let's say that the firm's solar energy systems reduce the demand for imported oil with the result that oil prices go down. This means that the production costs of all products that use oil (especially transportation) go down. Clearly there is an external social benefit from the production of solar energy systems. If we add the value of the positive externality to the price of the product, the result is the marginal social benefit curve, MSB. Thus if the firm could be paid for the social benefit it generates, equilibrium would be at E_2. Optimal output would be Q_2, which would require a greater allocation of resources to production of solar energy systems. The difference between Q_2 and Q_1 represents underproduction and therefore underutilization of resources.

Similarly, misallocation of resources when negative externalities exist can be illustrated by Exhibit 17–2.

Again for simplicity's sake, Exhibit 17–2 depicts a firm with constant

Exhibit 17–2_____

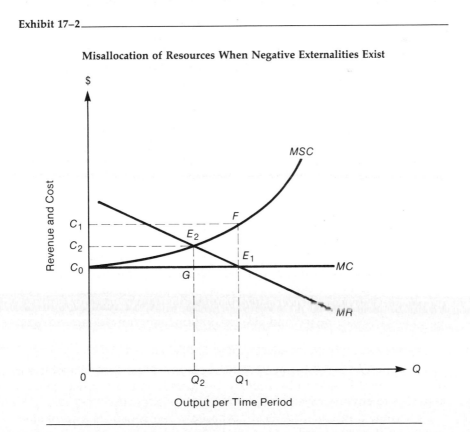

Misallocation of Resources When Negative Externalities Exist

Output per Time Period

marginal cost. However, there is a negative externality, say pollution, that grows more costly as production increases. This is represented by the marginal social cost curve, MSC. As long as the firm does not pay for the pollution it causes, equilibrium occurs at E_1, where $MR = MC$. The cost of pollution is represented by the rectangle $C_0C_1FE_1$, all of which is borne by society at large. But if the firm must pay for pollution, its equilibrium would be at E_2, and production would be cut back to Q_2 units. The cost of pollution would be reduced to the rectangle $C_0C_2E_2G$, all of which would be borne by the firm and its customers. The difference between Q_1 and Q_2 represents overutilization of resources.

Whether externalities are positive or negative, the problem is that the private firm, which controls the level of production, has no incentive to produce either more or less than the profit-maximizing output, at which the firm's marginal revenue equals the firm's marginal cost. Consequently, there is substantial government intervention in the marketplace either to supply the missing incentives to produce more when the externality is beneficial or to produce less when the externality is harmful.

Incentives for Beneficial Externalities

When beneficial externalities exist, some people pay while others get a "free ride." There are two basic ways of solving the free ride problem: (1) prevent those who do not pay from receiving any benefits, or (2) insure that everyone who receives benefits pays.

The first technique is often employed by private enterprise. For example, suppose that a developer plans to renovate all of the houses in a blighted city neighborhood. If he buys and remodels them one at a time, the surrounding property owners get a free ride as the value of their properties increases, too. The solution is for the builder to buy all of the old houses at the same time. Then the increase in value of surrounding properties will be *internalized* as each one is renovated.

The second technique is more suitable to government action, and may result in the provision of public goods paid for by taxation.

Public Goods. If the beneficial externality is nonexclusive, meaning that people cannot be excluded from its benefits no matter who pays for it, the good is classed as a *public good*. Examples of public goods are national defense, police and fire protection, immunization, and education.

If the good is not only nonexclusive, but also of a nature such that its consumption by one person does not reduce the amount available for others, then it is said to be a *pure public good*. If a pure public good is available to anyone, it is available to all at no extra cost.

Government intervention is appropriate when beneficial externalities exist and it is not feasible to exclude free riders from those benefits.

Thus there is general agreement that the government should provide pure public goods, such as flood-control dams, police and fire protection, and national defense. Unfortunately, there is no way to measure the economic benefits of public goods. Consequently, there is no agreement on how much of these goods should be provided. The decisions on what to provide and how much to provide thus become political rather than economic decisions.

Many different goods are partly private and partly public. In such cases, the government may provide incentives for the expansion of private production with a subsidy rather than (or in addition to) the direct provision of the public good. For example, the installation of solar heating devices clearly provides benefits for which a householder is willing to pay. But society at large also benefits by a reduction in the demand for energy that requires importation of foreign oil. Therefore, both federal and state governments have encouraged solar installations by giving tax credits.

Grants of Operating Rights

Production of goods or services with positive externalities may also be promoted by grants of operating rights in areas of the public domain or where substantial public goods are involved. A classic example is control of the airwaves by the Federal Communications Commission (FCC). The spectrum of radio frequencies is a natural resource that exists in a limited quantity but is not depleted by use. It belongs to nobody in particular, but to everybody in general. Therefore, if it were not regulated, the price for its private use would be zero. At that price, it might well be overused or used inefficiently. Consequently, the government regulates use of radio frequencies and limits usage to selected licensees.

The number of licenses that can be granted is necessarily limited by the physical restrictions of the radio frequency spectrum. Each license gives its holder the right to use only a particular frequency or set of frequencies. Once granted, the license is almost always renewed routinely unless it is shown that renewal of the license would be harmful. In effect, an FCC license is a semipermanent monopoly grant. Consequently, economists have suggested that FCC licenses be periodically auctioned off to the highest bidders, thus capturing some of the monopolists' economic profits for the public treasury.

Federal, state, and sometimes municipal regulatory agencies also grant public franchises in the form of charters or licenses to many other industries. These include banks and other savings institutions, insurance companies, securities dealers, and others.

Public franchises are granted only to those firms that can demonstrate financial soundness, fiscal responsibility, and the ability to serve the needs of the public in their area. Any time that a firm fails to meet these criteria, its right to operate may be withdrawn. Since the mere threat of withdrawing operating rights is usually sufficient to ensure compliance, grants of operating rights can be an effective form of regulation. Many critics point out, however, that it can be rendered ineffective if there are no clear, consistent, and workable standards of performance. Television programming is most often cited as a case in point.

There are two schools of thought with respect to this type of regulation. One is that it is designed for the conservation and efficient use of scarce resources. The conservation motive may be detected in much of the licensing in the field of communications, and to a lesser degree in regulation of natural gas, oil, water, and electric power. However, an increasing number of economists have subscribed to the second view: that such regulation is promoted by power blocs that want to seal off part of the market to protect themselves from competition.

Grants of Patents.   A U.S. patent is an exclusive right conferred by the federal government on an inventor for a limited period. It authorizes the inventor to make, use, transfer, or withhold an invention, which the inventor might do even without a patent; but it also gives the inventor the right to exclude others or to admit them on particular terms, a power which the inventor enjoys only with a patent.

Patents thus are means of promoting invention by granting temporary monopolies to inventors (currently 17 years). But the patent system, it is held, has also been used as a means of controlling output, dividing markets, and fixing prices of entire industries. Since these are perversions of the patent law that have a direct effect on competition, they have been subject to criticism by the antitrusters, and the courts have increasingly come to limit the scope and abuses of patent monopoly. Among the chief issues have been the standard of patentability, the right of nonuse by the patentee, the use of tying contracts, the employment of restrictive licenses, and the practices of cross licensing and patent pooling.

Subsidies.   Subsidies are the direct or indirect payment of money or other benefits to private institutions to encourage the production of goods or services with positive externalities.

One of the most successful subsidies in American history was provided by the Pacific Railroad Act of 1862, which made possible the construction of the nation's first transcontinental railroad. In addition to free rights of way, the act gave the Central Pacific and Union Pacific railroad companies 10 square miles of land and a minimum of $16,000 for each mile of track laid. This subsidy not only facilitated construction of the railroad, but also provided land for sale to settlers who could be expected to do business with the railroad. Thus it expedited settlement of the West.

Subsidies may be direct or indirect. Direct subsidies generally take one of two forms:

1. *Low-cost financing.* For example, FHA and VA financing has broadened home ownership by subsidizing the construction industry.
2. *Special tax treatment.* Examples include:
   a. *The investment tax credit* for certain types of business investments that result in social benefits such as job creation or energy independence.
   b. *Depletion allowances,* which encourage the development and exploitation of natural resources.

At the municipal level, some communities have lured industry with a combination of low-cost financing and tax moratoriums.

Indirect subsidies by the federal and state governments include the entire transportation infrastructure—a network of highways, waterways, seaports, and airports that makes interstate commerce possible. Government construction of dams has also indirectly subsidized a number of industries. Besides the benefits of flood control, water may be provided for irrigation of farmlands. The creation of artificial lakes has also created a demand for marinas, campgrounds, motels, recreational vehicles, boats, camping equipment, and all of the other paraphernalia associated with water sports and recreation.

Subsidies may be granted for reasons other than dealing with externalities. A case in point is the U.S. maritime industry, which has received approximately $10 billion in direct subsidies since 1936. In addition, U.S. shipyards and shipowners receive indirect subsidies in the form of laws that require shipment of certain cargos on U.S. vessels and laws that make the financing of new ships less costly. How does the federal government justify this expense? The Maritime Administration most often cites three reasons:

1. To maintain *employment* in both the operation and the construction of ships.
2. To aid in the *balance of payments* between imports and exports by requiring certain imports to be carried by ships operating under the U.S. flag.
3. To provide a merchant marine that is adequate for *national security* in time of war.

Taxation to Reduce Negative Externalities

One way of reducing the production of a negative externality is to direct its cost back upon the firm. This can be done on a regular basis by taxation and on an irregular or ad hoc basis by fines and penalties for prohibited behavior. For example, a truck's license tag will cost many times more than an automobile tag, on the grounds that its heavier weight will do more damage to the roads. However, a limitation is imposed on how much the loaded truck can weigh, even when properly licensed. If the truck exceeds this weight, additional taxes in the form of fines and penalties will be imposed on its operator.

Undesirable behavior can also be controlled by subsidies. For example, the Internal Revenue Code offers special tax breaks to firms that install pollution control devices. Alternatively, it would be possible to tax or fine the firm for emitting pollution. The choice of control method—subsidy or taxation—raises an important political issue. A subsidy implies that the firm has the right to pollute, and that society is willing to pay it to forgo that right. Taxation implies that society owns the environment and has a right to clean air and water. Therefore, the polluter must pay damages for the harm being caused. When the potential for harm is great, taxation can be raised to a prohibitive level, causing the undesirable activity to cease altogether.

Example.   A firm engaged in the manufacture of lead-acid batteries for heavy-duty equipment begins the manufacturing process with the smelting of ore to extract lead. In this process, there is a discharge of particulate matter, some of which is later used in the manufacture of the batteries. The unused portion is dumped into the air, creating a substantial amount of air pollution.

A local citizen's group, concerned about the health of the community, persuades the city to impose a pollution tax upon the particulates discharged by the plant.

Each unit of output, Q, is composed of one unit of lead, Q_L, and one unit of particulate matter, Q_P. The firm's demand for lead is

$$P_L = 9{,}044 - 8Q_L \qquad (1)$$

and its demand for particulates is

$$P_P = 800 - 2Q_P \qquad (2)$$

The firm's total cost is

$$TC = 50{,}000 + 16Q + 8Q^2 \qquad (3)$$

1.   What is the firm's optimal output, price, and profit before the pollution tax is imposed?

First, Q_L and Q_P are joint products; hence $Q = Q_L = Q_P$. The marginal revenue of lead is

$$TR_L = (9{,}044 - 8Q_L)Q_L = 9{,}044Q_L - 8Q_L^2$$
$$MR_L = 9{,}044 - 16Q_L$$

The marginal revenue of particulates is

$$TR_P = (800 - 2Q_P)Q_P = 800Q_P - 2Q_P^2$$
$$MR_P = 800 - 4Q_P = 0$$

$Q_P^* = 200$ units when $MR_P = 0$, meaning that the firm will use a maximum of 200 units of particulates and dump the rest. The marginal cost of joint production is:

$$TC = 50,000 + 16Q + 8Q^2$$
$$MC = 16 + 16Q$$

At optimum, joint $MR = MC$:

$$MR_L + MR_P = MC$$
$$9,044 - 16Q_L + 800 - 4Q_P = 16 + 16Q$$

Since $Q = Q_L = Q_P$, we drop the subscripts:

$$36Q = 9,828$$

and $Q = 273$ units of lead and 273 units of particulates, which is more particulates than can be used profitably. Therefore, optimal production occurs where $MR_L = MC$:

$$9,044 - 16Q = 16 + 16Q$$
$$32Q = 9,028$$
$$Q = 282$$

Hence the firm should produce 282 units of lead and 282 units of particulates; of which 200 units of particulates would be used and 82 units dumped into the air.

Prices would be

$$P_L = 9,044 - 8(282) = \$6,788/\text{unit}$$
$$P_P = 800 - 2(200) = \$400/\text{unit}$$

The firm's profit would be

$$\pi = TR_L + TR_P - TC$$
$$= 9,044Q_L - 8Q_L^2 + 800Q_P - 2Q_P^2 - 50,000 - 16Q - 8Q^2$$
$$= 9,044(282) - 8(282)^2 + 800(200) - 2(200)^2 - 50,000$$
$$- 16(282) - 8(282)^2$$
$$= 2,550,408 - 636,192 + 160,000 - 80,000 - 50,000 - 4,512$$
$$- 636,192$$
$$= \$1,303,512$$

2. What is the minimum tax that must be charged in order to completely eliminate pollution by the firm?

The actual production of particulates without the tax is 282 units, of which 82 are being dumped in the air.

$$MR_P = 800 - 4Q_P = 800 - 4(282) = -328$$

The tax will have to be greater than \$328 to cause the firm to seek an alternative to dumping the unwanted particulates in the air. Another way of arriving at the same answer is to consider that MR_P (the marginal revenue of Q_P) becomes negative after 200 units. Each of the 82 units dumped avoids a loss of revenue of \$4, since $MR_P = 800 - 4Q_P$; hence, $82 \times \$4 = \$328$ tax makes dumping the 82 units as costly as using them. In that case, the firm would cut production back to 273 units, the level at which $MR_L + MR_P = MC$, as calculated above.

Government Control of Operations

Like subsidies and tax policies, operating controls are also intended to reduce undesirable externalities by mandating some actions and prohibiting others. Unlike subsidies and tax policies, operating controls rely upon nonmonetary incentives, although fines and even imprisonment can be used to punish violators.

While control of pollution immediately comes to mind, the fact is that almost every facet of business activity is subject to some government regulation that falls within the general category of intervention for the protection of society, as will be discussed later in this chapter.

Regulation of Public Utilities

A natural monopoly occurs when economies of scale are such that the long-run average cost declines throughout the entire range of production that can be absorbed by a particular market. This means that maximum efficiency (lowest cost production) can be achieved only when one firm produces all that the market demands.

The situation of continuously falling long-run average costs is characteristic of capital-intensive industries with relatively large fixed costs. As the fixed costs are spread over more and more units, the average or unit cost declines. As long as average cost is declining, marginal cost is less than average cost. Thus almost all utilities—gas, electric, water, sewers—and many transportation facilities are natural monopolies.

The existence of a natural monopoly poses a dilemma because, as we saw in Chapter 15, a monopoly seeks to maximize profits by restricting output, as illustrated by Exhibit 17–3.

Exhibit 17–3 shows the market demand curve, D, its associated marginal revenue curve, MR, the monopolist's long-run marginal cost

Exhibit 17–3

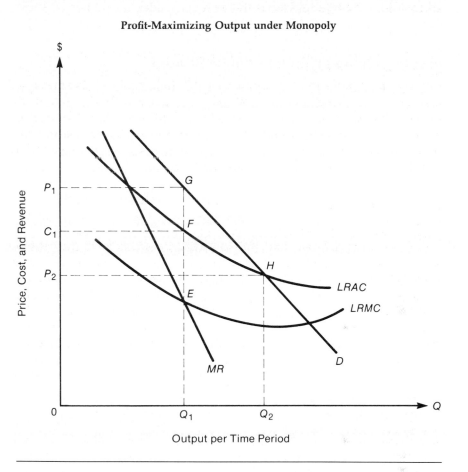

Profit-Maximizing Output under Monopoly

curve, *LRMC*, and long-run average cost curve, *LRAC*. The *LRAC* curve includes normal profit. Left to its own devices, the monopoly will reach equilibrium at *E*, where $MR = LRMC$. By producing Q_1 units at a price of P_1 dollars and a cost of C_1 dollars, the monopoly will earn an excess (economic) profit of $(P_1 - C_1)$ dollars per unit for a total profit represented by the rectangle P_1C_1FG. Clearly, however, the monopoly could increase production all the way to Q_2 units by giving up its economic profit. At a price of P_2 dollars, the monopoly would recover all of its long-run average cost (which includes normal profit or required return on investment).

Obviously, the general public would be better off with the monopoly producing more output at a lower price. The question is: How can it be induced to do so? The most common answer is: By regulation of prices and profits. That simple answer, however, hides a number of sticky problems.

Problems in Regulation of Public Utilities

Although Exhibit 17–3 presented the theoretical foundation for regulation of natural monopolies, in reality it is not possible to determine precisely the amount of fixed assets necessary to support a given level of production nor the precise *LRAC* schedule. Further, in the case of utilities, the *LRAC* schedule represents the joint costs of serving several classes of customers (such as residential, commercial, and industrial), each of which has its own demand schedule and price elasticity. Therefore, there are many different combinations of rate schedules that could be used to produce the required level of profit, but there is no rational way in which costs can be used as a basis for the user class rates.

From these difficulties come the problems of pricing the output, determining the appropriate level of investment, and the encouragement of inefficient production. In addition there are problems with regulatory delays and costs. These problems are all related, but they are separated for the sake of discussion in the paragraphs that follow.

Pricing the Output.   Theoretically, the regulated price is such that the monopoly recovers its fixed and variable costs plus an allowed return on investment (*ROI*). The actual output, however, will be determined by the actual demand at the price set by the regulatory commission.

If the regulating agency has guessed wrong about demand, and has set the price too high (such as at P_1 on Exhibit 17–3), the regulated monopoly will enjoy some degree of economic profit. However, since the *ROI* is limited, the excess profits will be allocated to system expansion, thus becoming part of the investment base on which allowed *ROI* is calculated. The firm will grow at a faster-than-optimal rate. If the price is set too low, the required *ROI* will not be attainable, and the firm will not expand.

Appropriate Level of Investment.   The utility's allowable return on investment (*ROI*) is calculated as a percentage of the *rate base*, which is roughly equal to fixed assets. If the allowed *ROI* is more than the cost of capital, it will pay the utility to shift to more capital-intensive methods of production by expanding fixed assets. On the other hand, if the allowed *ROI* is too low, the utility may not expand its capacity rapidly enough to satisfy future demand, and might be forced to continue less capital-intensive but relatively inefficient methods of production. Either way, regulation can lead to something less than an optimal combination of the input factors of production.

Encouragement of Inefficiency.   Since a regulated monopoly is guaranteed a certain return on investment, there is little incentive to be careful about costs. Inefficiency thus tends to be protected, as illustrated by Exhibit 17–4.

Exhibit 17–4_____

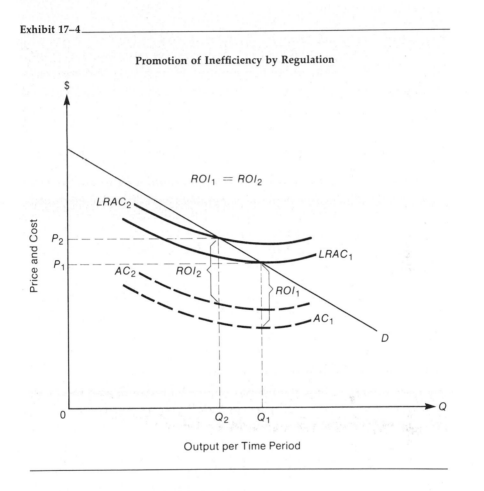

Promotion of Inefficiency by Regulation

Output per Time Period

On Exhibit 17–4, the subscripts 1 and 2 designate two regulated utilities operating under similar circumstances at different locations. That is, the two firms face identical cost functions and are allowed the same ROI by their regulatory agencies, i.e., $ROI_1 = ROI_2$. The curves labeled AC_1 and AC_2 represent their respective cost functions, not including normal profit. The curves labeled $LRAC_1$ and $LRAC_2$ represent their respective long-run average costs, including normal profit, or ROI.

At the regulated price of P_1 dollars, both firms produce Q_1 units of output. Firm 1, being more efficient, also earns the full allowed return on investment (ROI_1). Firm 2, however, being less efficient, cannot earn the full allowed *ROI*. Firm 2 therefore asks for and receives a rate increase from its regulatory agency. The price increase to P_2 allows Firm 2 to earn the full allowed return on investment (ROI_2), while continuing its inefficient operation.

Regulatory Costs and Delays.   Regulatory costs stem from two major sources. First, there are the routine administrative costs of maintaining a regulatory commission and of maintaining necessary records within the regulated monopoly. Second, there are the careful and expensive economic analyses that are made by both proponents and opponents of a proposed rate increase. Ultimately, all of these costs are borne by consumers.

In addition to cost, the regulatory process imposes a substantial delay between the time a necessary rate increase is proposed and the time it is approved. This is because regulation of natural monopolies is a political process. The regulatory commission members are either elected directly, or else are appointed by elected officials who must answer to the electorate, who are the monopoly's customers. When a rate increase is proposed, it cannot be approved until public hearings have been held, at which time all who wish to be heard may testify. The monopoly's customers are naturally opposed to any rate increase, and they are able to put a great deal of political pressure upon the regulatory commission. Often they succeed in denying or at least delaying reasonable and necessary rate increases.

The Effects of Inflation

Regulatory lag can work either for or against the regulated monopoly. For example, during the 1950s and 1960s, economies of scale and technological improvements resulted in lowered costs, while reduction in rates lagged behind. In the 1970s and early 1980s, however, the tide turned. Inflation and high interest rates drove up costs while rate increases lagged behind. Utilities, starved for funds, began to delay repairs and postpone investments in new equipment. Consequently, the quality of service suffered.

Inflation also magnifies the distortion caused by the use of average cost in setting rates. As we saw on Exhibit 17–3, it is assumed that economies of scale keep the marginal cost below average cost. However, regulatory commissions are prone to calculate average costs from historical (book) costs, rather than current replacement costs. Consequently, marginal cost is actually greater than the average cost on which the regulated price is based. Setting prices below the marginal cost of production encourages wasteful use by the consumer.

Restraint of Market Power and Unfair Competition

Throughout our history, there has been a libertarian distrust of power, whether it be political or economic. The elaborate system of checks and balances established by the Constitution serves to prevent concentration of political power. On the economic side, incorporation laws passed in the 1850s enabled stockholders to pool their economic resources without having to pool their political resources also. The effect has been to permit the coexistence of big business with democracy.

The growth of big business in this country has been watched by the people with mixed feelings of pride and suspicion, with clear recognition that economic power and political power go hand-in-hand. Consequently, antitrust policy has been used whenever necessary to prevent undue concentration of corporate power.

Antitrust Laws

Conventional wisdom says that in order to preserve a market economy, natural monopolies must be strictly regulated and unnatural monopolies must be prohibited altogether.[5] The federal government's chief weapons in preventing monopolies and maintaining fair competition have been acts passed by Congress since 1890, commonly called the antitrust laws. The most important antitrust laws are the Sherman Antitrust Act, the Clayton Antitrust Act, the Federal Trade Commission Act, the Robinson-Patman Act, the Wheeler-Lea Act, and the Celler-Kefauver Antimerger Act. The substantive provisions of the antitrust laws may be outlined as follows.

The Sherman Act (1890). This was the first attempt by the federal government to regulate the growth of monopoly in the United States. The provisions of the law were concise (probably too concise). It declared as illegal:

1. Every contract, combination, or conspiracy in restraint of trade which occurs in interstate or foreign commerce.
2. Any monopolization or attempt to monopolize, or conspiracy with others in an attempt to monopolize, any portion of trade in interstate or foreign commerce.

Violations of the act were made punishable by fines and/or imprisonment, and persons injured by violators could sue for triple damages.

---

[5] Exceptions to the rule are monopolies created by franchises, patents, and copyrights. However, the government does place certain limits upon the rights bestowed by such grants.

The act was surrounded by uncertainty by failing to state precisely which kinds of actions were prohibited. Also, no special agency existed to enforce the law until 1903, when the Antitrust Division of the U.S. Department of Justice was established under an assistant attorney general. In order to put some teeth into the Sherman Act, therefore, Congress passed the Clayton Act and the Federal Trade Commission Act.

The Clayton Act (1914).   Aimed at practices of unfair competition, the Clayton Act was concerned with four specific areas: price discrimination, exclusive and tying contracts, intercorporate stockholdings, and interlocking directorates. About each of these it said:

1.   For sellers to discriminate in prices between purchasers of commodities is *illegal,* where the effect is substantially to lessen competition or tends to create a monopoly. However, such discrimination is permissible where there are differences in the grade, quality, or quantity of the commodity sold; where the lower prices make due allowances for cost differences in selling or transportation; and where the lower prices are offered in good faith to meet competition.
2.   For sellers to lease, sell, or contract for the sale of commodities on condition that the lessee or purchaser not use or deal in the commodity of a competitor is *illegal* if such exclusive or tying contracts substantially lessen competition or tend to create a monopoly.
3.   For corporations engaged in commerce to acquire the shares of a competing corporation, or the stocks of two or more corporations competing with each other, is *illegal* if such intercorporate stockholdings substantially lessen competition or tend to create a monopoly.
4.   For corporations engaged in commerce to have the same individual on two or more boards of directors is an interlocking directorate, and such directorships are *illegal* if the corporations are competitive and if any one has capital, surplus, and undivided profits in excess of $1 million.

Thus, price discrimination, exclusive and tying contracts, and intercorporate stockholdings were not declared by the Clayton Act to be absolutely illegal but rather, in the words of the law, only when their effects *"may be substantially to lessen competition or tend to create a monopoly."* On interlocking directorates, however, the law made no such qualification; the fact of the interlock itself is illegal, and the government need not find that the arrangement results in a reduction in competition.

The Federal Trade Commission Act (1914).   The Federal Trade Commission Act served primarily as a general supplement to the Clayton Act by stating broadly and simply that "unfair methods of competition in commerce are hereby declared unlawful." Essentially, both the Clayton Act and the Federal Trade Commission Act were directed toward the prevention of abuses, whereas the Sherman Act emphasized the punishment of abusers. Moreover, under the Federal Trade Commission Act, the Federal Trade Commission (FTC) was established as a government antitrust agency with federal funds appropriated to it for the purpose of attacking unfair competitive practices and safeguarding the public by preventing the dissemination of false and misleading advertisements. It was no longer necessary to await private suits brought by private parties on their own initiative and at their own expense in order to curb unfair practices in commerce.

The Robinson-Patman Act (1936). Frequently referred to as the "Chain Store Act," the Robinson-Patman Act was passed to provide economic protection to independent retailers and wholesalers, such as grocers and druggists, from "unfair discriminations" by large sellers attained "because of their tremendous purchasing power." The act, which amended Section 2 of the Clayton Act dealing with price discrimination, made the following practices illegal:

1. Charging different prices to different buyers on sales that are otherwise identical.
2. Selling at different prices in different parts of the country "for the purpose of destroying competition or eliminating a competitor."
3. Selling "at unreasonably low prices" where the purpose is to destroy competition or a competitor.
4. Discriminating in price.
5. Paying brokerage commissions to buyers or to intermediaries under their control.
6. Granting allowances, services, or facilities by sellers to buyers, whether for services rendered by the buyer or not, that are "not accorded to all purchasers on proportionally equal terms."

The Wheeler-Lea Act (1938). An amendment to part of the Federal Trade Commission Act, the Wheeler-Lea Act was passed to provide consumers, rather than just business competitors, with protection against unfair practices. The act makes illegal "unfair or deceptive acts or practices" in interstate commerce. Thus, a consumer who may be injured by an unfair trade practice is, before the law, of equal concern with the merchant who may be injured by an unfair competitive practice. The act also defines "false advertising" as "an advertisement other than labeling which is misleading in a material respect," and makes the definition applicable to advertisements of foods, drugs, curative devices, and cosmetics.

The Celler-Kefauver Antimerger Act (1950). The Celler-Kefauver Antimerger Act is an extension of Section 7 of the Clayton Act, which made it illegal for corporations to acquire the stock of competing corporations. But that law, the FTC argued, left a loophole through which monopolistic mergers could be effected by a corporation acquiring the *assets* of a competing corporation. The Antimerger Act plugged the loophole in the Clayton Act by making it illegal for a corporation to acquire the stock *or assets* of a competing corporation if the effect may be "substantially to lessen competition, or to tend to create a monopoly." The act thus bans all types of mergers—*horizontal* (similar plants under one ownership, such as steel mills), *vertical* (dissimilar plants in various stages of production, integrated under one ownership), and *conglomerate* or *circular* (dissimilar plants and unrelated product lines)—provided the commission can show that the effects *may* substantially lessen competition or tend toward monopoly.

The intent of Congress in passing the act was that there be a maintenance of competition. Accordingly, the act was intended to apply to mergers of large firms or of large with small firms, but not to mergers among small firms that may be undertaken to strengthen their competitive position.

Measurement of Economic Concentration

Since the early 1930s, an impressive number of economic studies have been made to discover the degree to which an index such as value of shipments, assets, employment, income, and sales are concentrated in a few large firms. Study bases have included nonbanking corporations, total manufacturing, particular manufacturing industries, and the output of manufactured products. A typical finding of such a study is shown on Exhibit 17–5.

Exhibit 17–5 illustrates the *concentration ratio* approach, which measures the percentage of an industry's output provided by its four largest firms. Commonly used indexes are sales, value added, assets, number of employees, and, as on Exhibit 17–5, value of shipments. The same indexes may also be used in the *market share* approach, which indicates the percentage of an industry's output provided by a single firm. Concentration ratios, however, are the measures that are most frequently used to gauge monopoly power.

How good are the concentration ratios as a measure of monopoly power? The harsh answer is, *worthless*. Given a set of data, the degree of concentration will vary according to the choice of the *base* (all businesses, all manufacturing, all nonfinancial corporations, all industries, and so forth); choice of the *unit* (plant or firm, single-product or multiproduct

Exhibit 17–5

Concentration Ratios: Percentages of Industry Output Produced by the Four Largest Firms in Selected Industries in 1972

Industry	Percentage of Industry Output (value of shipments)
Primary aluminum	100
Motor vehicles	93
Cigarettes	84
Aircraft engines and parts	77
Photographic equipment	74
Tires and inner tubes	73
Aircraft	66
Soap and detergents	62
Electronic computing equipment	51
Radio and television sets	49
Shipbuilding and repair	47
Construction machinery	43
Toilet preparations	38
Petroleum refining	31
Pharmaceutical preparations	26
Book publishing	19
Fluid milk	18
Bottled and canned soft drinks	14
Women's and misses' dresses	9

Source: U.S. Bureau of the Census.

firm); and choice of the *index* (assets, employment, output, income, or sales). By selecting only two options for each of these three qualifiers, it is possible to get six different concentration ratios from the same data. Hence, within limits, it is possible to manipulate the data to show whatever the researcher wants to show.

A more serious obstacle is the usual lack of homogeneity of the input data. For example, if all nonbanking corporations are chosen as the base, this includes regulated monopolies such as railroads and utilities (whose assets amount to half the assets of the 200 largest corporations) along with firms operating in highly competitive industries (such as Sears Roebuck, Macy's, and A&P) and other firms that have little or no control over either their input or output markets.

Concentration ratios by industry usually follow the *Census of Manufactures'* classification, which defines industries, in part, by the materials and processes they use. The result is that one industry grouping may contain firms that produce noncompeting products; while firms that produce competing products may be grouped in different industries. In the same manner, concentration ratios by product follow a classification that defines products, in part, by the materials, production processes, and degree of manufacturing integration required in their production, with the result that a single product may have multiple listings.

If output data are national when markets are actually regional, or if heterogeneous goods are lumped together in a single category, the concentration ratio may be seriously understated. On the other hand, if the data are limited to domestic production, ignoring competition from imports or from close substitutes that may be listed in another category, the concentration ratio may be seriously overstated.

We see, then, that concentration ratios tell us very little either about the structure of markets for particular products or about the index of concentrated power. We conclude, therefore, that *measures of economic concentration are not measures of monopoly power,* as the critics of big business would have us believe. Such measures *might* reveal the results of monopolistic restriction or collusion—but they are just as apt to reveal the results of innovation, market development, lower costs and prices, and superior management. They are also apt to hide from view the influences of competition and countervailing power.

Thus in response to the charge that a few giant corporations have gained monopoly power we see that the evidence available does not substantiate the charge. As for charges that concentration has grown over the years and that competition has declined as a result, we can say only that there is no evidence to support such a view. When the various studies of concentration are put together, we find that:

1. The growth of big business both in numbers and size is proportional to the growth of the economy as a whole.
2. Some industries, such as transportation, communications, and finance, have a relatively high degree of concentration, while there is a relatively low degree in trade and service industries.
3. The roster of the nation's 500 largest firms changes every year, with some old firms dropping off and some new ones added, although the larger firms in the more concentrated industries tend to remain.
4. From 1900 to 1946, concentration ratios declined slightly. Since 1947, there has been stability or possibly a slight increase: the evidence is too murky to tell which.

We conclude that it is impossible to say whether concentration in the economy as a whole has been increasing, stable, or decreasing. Over any long period of time, some concentration ratios for individual industries, product groups, or product classes rise while others fall, and the overall picture is not clear.

Mergers

A merger is an integration of two or more firms under a single ownership. Mergers play an important role in a free enterprise economy, in that less efficient firms are swallowed by the more efficient. Thus mergers often result in redeployment of productive assets and facilitate the efficient flow of investment capital. But it is also possible for mergers to have an adverse effect on competition by:

1. Reducing the number of firms capable of entering concentrated markets.
2. Reducing the number of firms with the capability and incentive for competitive innovation.
3. Increasing the barriers to entry in concentrated markets.
4. Diminishing the vigor of competition by increasing actual and potential customer-supplier relationships among leading firms in concentrated markets.

Mergers may be classified as horizontal, vertical, or conglomerate.

Horizontal Mergers.   A horizontal merger is one in which different plants producing similar products are brought under a single ownership. Three reasons are often advanced for such expansion:

1. To meet the demands of a growing market.
2. To take advantage of economies of scale in production and distribution.
3. To increase market share and market power.

With respect to economies of scale, few mergers result in actual savings in production costs. The merger is more likely to result in the closing of redundant, inefficient plants and the elimination of excess capacity in the industry (a desirable result). Substantial savings can be realized in the costs of selling and distributing the product, but the most compelling reason is the desire for increased market power.

Vertical Mergers.   A vertical merger is one in which firms engaged in different stages of the chain of production and distribution are united under one ownership. For example, a manufacturing firm might integrate backward to obtain control of a source of raw material or forward to obtain control of sales outlets for its products. Two major reasons for vertical mergers exist:

1. *To reduce costs.* For example, substantial cost reductions were obtained in the steel industry when the furnaces were integrated with the rolling mills, thus eliminating costly reheating steps in the production process.

2. *To gain control over the economic environment.* For example, Firestone has complete vertical integration from rubber plantations to manufacturing facilities to retail outlets. Their supply of raw materials is secure, as is their access to the ultimate consumer of their tires and other rubber products.

Vertical mergers may also enhance the firm's market power. However, they are not controlled unless they result in a monopoly, or have undesirable horizontal effects at one level or another of the chain of production and distribution.

Conglomerate Mergers. A conglomerate merger is one in which different companies producing different products are brought under a single ownership. Such diversification enables the acquiring company to spread risk, find good use for idle capital, add a line of products to its marketing capacity, or simply gain in economic power.

Reduction in risk comes about when the merging firms are able to reduce the variability of their earnings. To illustrate, suppose two firms are operating in different markets (i.e., making and selling different products). Suppose also that each firm has expected (mean) earnings of $20 million with a standard deviation of $4 million.

Operating separately, each firm bears the risk that actual profits may deviate from the expected value by as much as 20 percent. But if the firms combine in a conglomerate merger, the standard deviation for the firm will depend upon the correlation of variation in profits between the two markets, according to the formula

$$\sigma_T = \sqrt{\sigma_1^2 + \sigma_2^2 + 2\rho\sigma_1\sigma_2} \qquad (4)$$

where

σ_T = Standard deviation of expected profits for the conglomerate
σ_1, σ_2 = Standard deviation of expected profits in Markets 1 and 2, respectively
$\rho(\text{rho})$ = Correlation coefficient between σ_1 and σ_2

At one extreme, variability of expected profits in the two markets might have a perfect negative correlation, so that $\rho = -1$.
In that case,

$$\sigma_T = \sqrt{4^2 + 4^2 + 2(-1)(4)(4)} = 0$$

meaning that the merger has removed all risk of variability in expected profits, since negative variations in one division are precisely offset by positive variations in the other.

At the other extreme, variability of expected profits in the two markets might have perfect positive correlation, so that $\rho = +1$. In that case,

$$\sigma_T = \sqrt{4^2 + 4^2 + 2(1)(4)(4)} = 8$$

which means that the two firms have gained no improvement in risk, since variability of expected profits continues to equal 20 percent of the $40 million combined earnings of the conglomerate.

If there is no correlation between variability of expected earnings in the two markets, then $\rho = 0$, and

$$\sigma_T = \sqrt{4^2 + 4^2 + 2(0)(4)(4)} = \sqrt{32} = 5.66$$

which is about 14 percent of the expected profits of $40 million. In other words, *the merger of two companies making and selling totally unrelated products may reduce risk for both firms.* This is perhaps the strongest motivation for corporate diversification by the merger route, but there are others:

1. The firm may lack the necessary management skills for internal diversification. These skills may be acquired in a merger.
2. Internal diversification pits the firm against established competition. A merger may absorb one competitor.
3. A firm with stagnant technology may acquire research and development facilities and personnel by merging with a firm in a technologically advancing industry.
4. Merger avoids the start-up costs and time delay associated with a totally new operation.
5. Merger may enable the firm to utilize excess capacity in raw materials, plant facilities, managerial talent, capital resources, or distribution systems.
6. Merger may justify the cost of full-time staff specialists at top management level, such as legal staff, internal auditors, and economists.
7. A large conglomerate may be able to effect savings in total capital requirements. This is because the timing of the cash flows required by the divisions makes the total requirement less than the sum of the division requirements.
8. A large conglomerate can also effect savings in the cost of capital. For example, there is at least 3 points difference in the interest rate charged a small borrower and the prime rate charged a large borrower.
9. A large conglomerate can realize savings in promotional costs for one or more of the following reasons:
   a. A high level of advertising expenditures commands quantity discounts from all forms of advertising media.

     b.   Large expenditures on advertising result in relatively more efficient promotional techniques.

     c.   When one of the parties to a merger possesses a well-known trademark, it may be transferred to other product lines.

10.   A large conglomerate can provide the nationwide dealer and service network that is essential to the sale of durable goods.

The Controversy over Mergers

The role of big business and the degree of government intervention needed to guard against the real or imagined evils of big business are long-standing bones of contention. In addition, since the late 1960s, the economy has had to contend with inflation, recession, monetary devaluation, trade imbalances, and a continuing energy crisis, which have intensified the controversy.

On one side we have a group of economic and political reformers who charge that (1) economic power is concentrated in a few corporate giants to the extent that it amounts to unregulated monopoly; (2) this concentration has grown over the years; and (3) competition has declined as a result. We might call these advocates the anti-big-business group. Arrayed against them is a pro-big-business group of economists and politicians who argue that bigness in some cases is not only desirable but also necessary; and that competition has not been impaired in industries dominated by the giants, although the degree and type of competition may often go unrecognized. Both sides advocate changes in the antitrust laws, but the changes they want and the reasons for them are quite different.

Anti-Big Business Proposals for Reform of Antitrust Laws.   The anti-big-business reformers insist that the "engine of monopoly" controls much of the American economy. As a result, they say, American industry is dominated by large firms with strong monopoly powers, with the consequence of serious misallocation of economic resources, causing inflation and unemployment.

The more radical of these reformers desire public ownership of the largest corporations. Others advocate the dissolution of large firms into smaller competing firms (such as separating Chevrolet Division from General Motors), especially if it can be shown that dissolution would not impair the efficiency or technological progress of the smaller firms thus created. This reform could take place through court decrees under existing law, or, if necessary, the law should be changed to expedite the dissolution.

These reformers also advocate the elimination of all exceptions to the antitrust laws, thus removing the exemptions now enjoyed by labor unions, transport industries, and some others. They also believe that protective legislation that aids special-interest groups and tends to strengthen their monopolistic position, such as tariffs, import quotas, and patent laws, should be revised.

The anti-big-business group's case rests, of course, upon its contention that the concentration of industry in the hands of a few large companies creates monopoly power, and the group supports its contention with studies of economic concentration. But, as we have shown, the measures of concentration that they use are so badly flawed that they are worthless.

Pro-Business Proposals for Reform of Antitrust Laws. The pro-big-business group points out that the anti-big-business reformers confuse bigness with monopoly. Even in an industry dominated by giants there is more than one giant, so that the situation is one of oligopoly, not monopoly. Furthermore, both in economic theory and in actual practice, oligopolies are fiercely competitive although they avoid *price* competition. Competition takes place in service, convenience, quality, style, or some other attribute that serves to distinguish one company's product from another's.

The traditional 19th-century assumptions about competition that are embedded in the antitrust laws are hopelessly outdated, they say. In the late-20th-century economy characterized by vast technological advancement, market growth, and rapid product development, nonprice competition is workable competition that should be preserved and enhanced by the antitrust laws. Fundamental revision of these laws is necessary to recognize that nonprice competition is more relevant than price competition in today's oligopolistic economy, even though price competition is easier to observe and measure.

The pro-big-business group argues that antitrust laws must recognize that merely being big is not evil. Economic efficiency and bigness are often closely related. Proponents of big business cite the need for U.S. firms to expand in order to compete efficiently with giant foreign multinational corporations in both the U.S. and world markets. They contend that antitrust enforcement should be aimed at anticompetitive behavior, not at mere size or growth.

The pro-big-business group argues that big businesses are more competitive than their numbers alone would indicate, for two reasons: first, there is competition with products from other industries (for example, a producer of aluminum must compete with producers of copper, steel, and plastics as well as with other producers of aluminum); and, second, sellers in the output market are buyers in another input market, where the large firms from whom they buy may exercise countervailing power. They also point out that big businesses can achieve economies of scale that are not possible with large numbers of small firms, and that big businesses have the financial resources to support large-scale research and development.

There are varying degrees of truth and falsity in the arguments advanced by both sides, and there is no clear indication of what antitrust policy the government should follow. It seems evident that many instances of business practice have acted to reduce competition and are to be condemned. On the other hand, it is equally evident that a merger that creates a larger firm able to challenge the industry's giants would lead to greater economic efficiency and increased competition. Furthermore, as trade barriers are lowered, it is important to evaluate competition on an international basis.

Recent Developments

Waves of merger acquisitions tend to rise and fall as conditions change in the economy. When return on investment is low and inflation keeps pushing up the costs of production, corporations may seek higher returns by investing in other companies. In 1981, a number of large mergers were proposed and opposed and not always consummated. By the end of the year, however, 2,395 mergers and acquisitions had been recorded, which was the largest number since 1974. In dollar value 1981 broke all records for the third year in a row, with acquiring companies paying $82.9 billion for their acquisitions. In some cases, takeover offers to common stockholders were 50 percent or more above market value. The year also saw 12 transactions that exceeded $1 billion in value.

Technically, every merger is subject to scrutiny by the Antitrust Division of the Justice Department. On June 14, 1982, the Antitrust Division issued new guidelines that would enable companies seeking mergers to determine whether or not their proposal might be challenged. The guidelines included the following policy statement:

"While challenging competitively harmful mergers the Department seeks to avoid unnecessary interference with that larger universe of mergers that are either competitively beneficial or neutral. In attempting to mediate between these dual concerns, however, the Guidelines reflect the congressional intent that merger enforcement should interdict competitive problems in their incipiency".[6]

This phraseology is taken to mean that the Department of Justice recognizes that once a merger takes place, it can't be unscrambled. Therefore, policy is to prevent harmful mergers from taking place. In order to determine whether or not a proposed horizontal merger is

---

[6] U.S. Department of Justice, Antitrust Division, *Merger Guidelines* (Washington, D.C.: U.S. Government Printing Office, 1982), p. 3.

harmful, the Justice Department will examine: (1) concentration and market shares, (2) ease of entry of new firms into the industry, and (3) other factors that "affect the likelihood that a merger will create, enhance or facilitate the exercise of market power."[7] In particular, the Department will consider factors that relate to the ease and profitability of collusion.

In evaluating a vertical merger or conglomerate merger, the Department examines its horizontal effect in three major areas of concern: (1) elimination of specific potential entrants into the market, (2) barriers to entry in primary or secondary markets, or both and (3) facilitating collusion. In the third category the Department is particularly concerned about vertical integration to the retail level, about the elimination of a disruptive buyer in a downstream market, and the possible evasion of rate regulation by a public utility.

Enforcement of the Antitrust Laws

Although Congress succeeded in passing the antitrust laws, it failed to define, and left up to the courts to interpret in their own way, the meaning of such terms as "monopoly," "restraint of trade," "substantial lessening of competition," and "unfair competition." For business executives, therefore, these are areas of uncertainty that need to be understood if decisions are to be made and plans formulated to guide a firm's future course of action.

Enforcement of antitrust laws is very similar to enforcement of traffic laws. The law against speeding is self-enforcing to the extent that every driver knows about it and takes precautions against violating the law, or at least against getting caught. Everybody supports the law against speeding, but hardly anyone gets upset when someone does it. At the same time, the amount of speeding that takes place depends to a large extent upon how vigorously the law is enforced.

In the same fashion, business executives are aware of the antitrust laws and desire to avoid actions that will attract the attention of the Antitrust Division of the Department of Justice or the Federal Trade Commission. Consequently, antitrust compliance plays a large role in business planning for expansion. The more vigorous the antitrust enforcement, the more wary become the business planners.

When enforcement of antitrust laws becomes necessary, it is effected on a case-by-case basis. That is, an order or decision resulting from an action is applicable not to all industry but to only the defendants in the particular case. Cases tried under the Sherman Act may originate in the

---

[7] Ibid., p. 22.

complaints of injured business executives, suggestions made by other government agencies, or the research of the Antitrust Division of the Department of Justice. About 90 percent of the cases, it has been estimated, arise from complaints issued by injured parties. The Federal Trade Commission Act, on the other hand, is enforced by the FTC and, when its orders become final, through suits brought by the Department of Justice. Finally, with respect to the Clayton Act, the FTC and the Justice Department have concurrent jurisdiction in its enforcement, and in practice it is usually a matter of which agency gets there first.

Initiation of antitrust prosecution is, of course, a political as well as a legal action. That is, the kind of cases that will be prosecuted depends upon the political philosophy of the executive branch of government. Members of the FTC and the key personnel of the Justice Department and the Antitrust Division are political appointees. We can expect them to be attuned to the views of the president. Therefore, the tenor of antitrust prosecution may change with a change of presidents.

Sherman and Clayton Acts

Section 14 of the Clayton Act fixes the responsibility for the behavior of a corporation on its officers and directors and makes them subject to the penalties of fine or imprisonment for violation of the antitrust laws. In 1974, violations of the Sherman Act were upgraded from misdemeanors to felonies. Maximum imprisonment was increased from 1 year to 3 years, and the maximum fines (per officer) were increased from $50,000 to $100,000 for individuals and from $50,000 to $1,000,000 for corporations. Fines can be pyramided by exacting the maximum penalty for each count of an indictment (e.g., monopolizing, attempting to monopolize, conspiring, restraining trade) and by imposing the maximum fine upon each of the defendants in a suit (e.g., a trade association, each member of the association, and each of the directors and officers of the member firms). Other penalties are also possible as provided in other acts.

Business executives who want to avoid risking violation of the law may consult with the Justice Department by presenting their proposed plans for combination or other particular practices. If the plans appear to be legal, the department may commit itself not to institute future criminal proceedings, but it will reserve the right to institute civil action if competition is later restrained. The purpose of a civil suit is not to punish but to restore competition by providing remedies. Typically three classes of remedies are used.

1. *Dissolution, divestiture,* and *divorcement* provisions may be used. Examples include an order to dissolve a trade association or combination, to sell intercorporate stockholdings, or to dispose of ownership

in other assets. The purpose of these actions is to break up a monopolistic organization into smaller but numerous competitors.

2. An *injunction* may be issued. This is a court order requiring that the defendant refrain from certain business practices, or perhaps take a particular action that will increase rather than reduce competition.

3. A *consent decree* may be employed. This is usually worked out between the defendant and the Justice Department without a court trial. The defendant in this instance does not admit guilt, but agrees nevertheless to abide by the rules of business behavior set down in the decree.

Finally, the laws are also enforced through private suits. Under the Sherman Act, injured parties (individuals, corporations, or states) may sue for treble damages including court costs; under the Clayton Act, a private plaintiff may also sue for an injunction—a restraining order—whenever threatened by loss or damage resulting from some firm's violation of the antitrust laws.

Restrictive Agreements

The state of the law as to restrictive agreements of virtually any type among competitors is reasonably clear, and the courts have almost always, with few minor exceptions, upheld the government in such cases. In general, a restrictive agreement is regarded by the government as one that results in a restraint of trade among separate companies. It is usually understood to involve a direct or indirect, overt or implied, form of price fixing, output control, market sharing, or exclusion of competitors by boycotts or other coercive practices. It makes no difference whether the agreement was accomplished through a formal organization such as a trade association, informally, or even habitually identical behavior frequently referred to as "conscious parallel action" (e.g., identical price behavior among competitors). It is the effect, more than the means, that is judged.

Monopoly

Concerning monopoly, the state of the law is less certain and the position of the courts less consistent than in cases involving restrictive agreements. Moreover, there has been a fundamental change in the attitude of the courts since 1945. Prior to that time, it was the position of the court that the mere size of a corporation, no matter how impressive, is no offense, and that it requires the actual exertion of monopoly power, as shown by unfair practices, in order to be held in violation of the law. This has been called the "good trust versus bad trust" criterion.

But decisions handed down in various antitrust cases since 1945 reversed this outlook. In the case against the Aluminum Company of America (ALCOA) in 1945, in which Judge Learned Hand turned the trend in judicial thinking on monopoly [148 F 2d 416], it was the court's opinion that:

1. To gain monopolistic power even by growing with the market, i.e., by reinvesting earnings rather than by combining with others, is nevertheless illegal.
2. The mere size of a firm *is* an offense, for the power to abuse and the abuse of power are inextricably intertwined [pp. 427–28].
3. The company's market share was 90 percent and that "is enough to constitute a monopoly; it is doubtful whether 60 or 64 percent would be enough; and certainly 33 percent is not" [p. 424].
4. The good behavior of the company which, prior to 1945, would have been an acceptable defense to the court, is no longer valid, for "Congress did not condone 'good' trusts and condemn 'bad' ones; it forbade all" [p. 427].

With this decision, Judge Hand put an end to the "good trust versus bad trust" criterion that had been used by the courts for almost a quarter of a century, beginning with the U.S. Steel case in 1920 and supplemented by the International Harvester case in 1927. And despite the doubtfulness of the measure of monopoly power and hence whether the charge of monopoly was really proven in this case, subsequent court decisions have never repudiated the doctrines enunciated by Judge Hand, although they have tempered them somewhat. Thus, at the present time, the judgment of monopoly is based on such factors as the number and strength of the firms in the market; their effective size with respect to the technology, competition with substitutes, and competition with foreign trade; national security interests in maintaining strong productive facilities and maximum scientific research; and the public's interest in lower costs and uninterrupted production (as later stated in 1950 by Judge Knox in his decree for a remedy in the aluminum case).

The trend, on the basis of subsequent cases, indicated that monopoly may be held illegal without requiring proof of intent and even if the power were lawfully acquired; and the power may be condemned even if never abused, especially if it tends to limit or bar market access to other firms. However, the recent settlements of the AT&T and IBM cases indicate that the Antitrust Division has returned to the criterion that bigness per se is no offense. By coincidence both the AT&T case and the IBM case were settled on the same day—January 8, 1982.

The AT&T Case.   The government's suit against American Telephone and Telegraph Company is the biggest antitrust action since the Rockefellers' Standard Oil Trust was broken up in 1911. The Antitrust Division of the Justice Department filed suit in November 1974, charging that AT&T had abused its telephone monopoly by freezing out competitors in equipment and long-distance service. While the case dragged on, telephone equipment manufacturers, data-processing companies, and cable-television systems had to try to plan in a state of uncertainty, while the Commerce Department worried about the possibility that the Japanese would gain an advantage in telecommunications.

Finally, after the government had spent about $25 million to prosecute the case, and AT&T had spent about $360 million defending itself, the adversaries reached an out-of-court settlement that William Baxter, assistant attorney general, said "completely fulfills the objectives of the Antitrust Division and is also very much in the interests of AT&T and its shareholders."

The nature of the settlement was a sort of "good news, bad news" announcement for AT&T and the other interested parties. From AT&T's point of view, the bad news was that it had to spin off the 22 Bell-system telephone companies in which it had controlling interest. These companies' $80 billion assets represented about two thirds of AT&T's total assets. This was bad news for local Bell-system customers, too, because the newly independent companies will no longer have local telephone service subsidized by AT&T's long-distance earnings.

More bad news for AT&T was the loss of the monopoly on long-distance telephone service. But that is good news for long-distance callers, who can now enjoy the benefits of price competition in long-distance service. The good news for AT&T was that it can keep its minority interest in two Bell-system local telephone companies and continue to operate Bell Laboratories and its manufacturing arm, Western Electric. Best news of all, it is now free to enter into competition on cable TV, video-text communications, and digital data transmission, where the greatest growth in communications promises to be.

Even after spinning off two thirds of its assets, AT&T will remain a very large company, with annual profits between $2 billion and $3 billion. Access to the rapidly growing data communications industry will let the company grow even larger. It does seem, therefore, that the mere size of a firm is no longer an offense, and the Antitrust Division concentrated on finding a practical and workable solution. The ultimate effect on consumers remains to be seen.

The IBM Case. The government filed suit against IBM in 1969, charging that at one time IBM monopolized the computer market by selling its products only in packages and by pricing its new equipment below cost. Again the remedy sought was divestiture, requiring that IBM be broken up into several smaller companies.

The government's suit inspired the filing of 16 private suits as well, all of which IBM won in federal courts. IBM management promised the government a stiff fight and gave it to them, spending $300 million in the process, and causing government expenditures of $26 million in what Yale law professor Robert H. Bork characterized as "the Antitrust Division's Vietnam". In the meantime, rapid technological change in the computer industry, including changes in marketing methods pursued by all competitors, so weakened the government's case that the Antitrust Division decided to drop it.

IBM, of course, claimed complete vindication. William Baxter, as spokesman for the Antitrust Division, stated that it would be very difficult to argue convincingly that episodes of bad conduct by IBM that occurred many years ago had anything to do with IBM's maintenance of its market share. He said it would not be inaccurate to describe IBM's share of the computer market as a monopoly position, but this did not mean that the Sherman Act had been violated. To be a violation, the market share would have to be obtained unlawfully or maintained by illegal acts. The government was not able to prove this.[8]

We do not know whether the courts are ready to overturn the precedent set by Judge Hand; but it seems clear that the Antitrust Division of the Reagan Administration is quite willing to ignore it and go back to the old criterion that market power must cause damage to merit prosecution.

Federal Trade Commission

Since its establishment by Congress in 1914, the FTC has served as a watchdog over business, charged with attacking "unfair or deceptive acts in commerce." Under the Federal Trade Commission Act, the FTC is authorized to prevent unfair business practices as well as to exercise, concurrently with the Justice Department, enforcement of relevant provisions of the Clayton Act as amended by the Robinson-Patman Act. Accordingly, the FTC has taken action against agreements that have tended to curtail output, fix prices, and divide markets among firms, thereby striving to maintain competition as well as to prevent unfair methods.

In enforcing the laws relating to monopoly, unfair trade, and deception (including such laws as the Export Trade Act, the Wool Products Labeling Act, the Fur Products Labeling Act, and the Flammable Fabrics Act), the FTC utilizes three procedures:

1. The *cooperative* method, which involves conferences on an individual and industrywide basis in order to secure voluntary compliance by business executives with respect to the rules of fair competition.

---

[8] News dispatch datelined Washington, D.C., *Los Angeles Times*, January 9, 1982.

2. The *consent* method, whereby the commission may issue a stipulation to the violator stating that the company agrees to discontinue the illegal practices.
3. The *compulsory* method, which involves legal action based upon the issuance of formal complaints.

In general, the commission obtains its evidence for making complaints from its own investigations, from injured competitors, from consumers, and from other government agencies. About 10 percent of the cases actually selected arise from the commission's own investigations; the remaining 90 percent are derived from the other sources, particularly from the complaints of injured parties.

Problems of Enforcement

The pace of antitrust enforcement necessarily rises and falls with the Congressional appropriations for the Antitrust Division of the Department of Justice and the Federal Trade Commission. But even when a large budget is available, the Antitrust Division is not able to keep an eye on every possible violator. Furthermore, the average case that is taken to court requires more than five years of litigation, during which hundreds of thousands of pages of exhibits and testimony must be examined. The first problem, then, is to select which cases to prosecute.

From an economic viewpoint, the optimal allocation of antitrust resources would satisfy the equation:

$$\frac{MG_1}{P_1} = \frac{MG_2}{P_2} = \cdots = \frac{MG_n}{P_n} \tag{5}$$

where

MG_i = Marginal gain in consumer surplus caused by the ith antitrust action

P_i = Cost (price) of the ith antitrust action[9]

This equation suggests that the "trust busters" should choose their cases to provide the greatest increase in consumer surplus per dollar spent in prosecuting the case. This may be efficient, but is it just? The small complainant against a large corporation could hardly obtain satisfaction under such a criterion. How, then, do the Department of Justice and the FTC select cases for prosecution? Several studies have at-

---

[9] James V. Koch, *Industrial Organization and Price*, (Englewood Cliffs, N.J.: Prentice-Hall, 1980), p. 483. The analogy to the least-cost hiring rule discussed in Chapter 9 should be obvious.

tempted to answer this question, with no definitive results. Both the Justice Department and the FTC exhibit interest in industries that are large oligopolies. But antitrust actions are brought against firms, not against industries.

The second problem in antitrust law enforcement is one for the courts. When a firm and its officers are convicted, how shall they be punished? Following Becker's marginal analysis of the economics of crime,[10] Posner suggests that the penalty should equal the damage done to society.[11]

The Becker-Posner analysis implies first of all that penalties should be flexible upwards, so that individuals and firms have no incentives to violate antitrust laws. As it stands now, the maximum fine for collusion is $1 million. If the firm stands to gain $10 million from collusion, there is a strong incentive to break the law, especially if the probability of being caught and convicted is less than 100 percent.

The Becker-Posner analysis also implies that behavior that does not result in a net loss to society should not be prosecuted even if it is technically illegal. This would be especially true of certain violations of the Robinson-Patman Act, since that act seems to be designed to protect individual competitors rather than competition. If rigorous nonpredatory pricing by a more efficient firm drives a less efficient firm out of business, how should society react? After all, the less efficient firm's resources are now free to be used more efficiently. It would seem that society gains, so why punish efficiency in a competitor?

Four kinds of penalties are actually imposed upon antitrust violators:

1. Fines for both individuals and corporations.
2. Prison terms for individuals.
3. Treble damages to be paid to specific injured parties.
4. Structural remedies such as dissolution, divestiture, and the separation of firms.

The first three may be effective if the fines and damages are great enough and the prison terms long enough. But the efficacy of the structural remedies is very much in doubt. For example, Elzinga examined the court-ordered remedy in 39 merger cases and concluded that 75 percent of them did not accomplish their purpose.[12]

---

[10] Gary S. Becker, "Crime and Punishment: An Economic Approach," *Journal of Political Economy*, March–April 1968, pp. 169–217.

[11] Richard A. Posner, *Antitrust Law: An Economic Perspective* (Chicago: University of Chicago Press, 1976), p. 221.

[12] Kenneth G. Elzinga, "The Antimerger Law: Pyrrhic Victories?" *Journal of Law and Economics*, April 1969, pp. 43–78.

Intervention for Protection of Consumers and Workers

One of the basic assumptions of the perfectly competitive market structure is that the consumer possesses complete information about products, prices, and every other facet of market activity. Thus there is market failure to the extent that reality falls short of this ideal, and the Congress has considered it necessary for the federal government to intervene with laws to insure truthful advertising about products and truthful information about the cost of credit. The Congress has also been concerned about the risks of injury associated with consumer products and in the workplace, and about protection of the environment in general.

Misrepresentation of Products

The first law forbidding sellers to misrepresent their product was the Federal Trade Commission Act of 1914. This act forbade misrepresentation because it is an unfair form of competition, but the effect is to protect consumers as well as competitors. Misrepresentations prohibited by this act include:

1. Raising prices before announcing a sale at reduced prices so that prices are not actually reduced for the sale.
2. Claiming that a product is being sold below cost when it is not.
3. Claiming that the product will do things that it will not do, such as restoring lost youth or curing the common cold.
4. Misrepresenting the origin of the product, such as putting a "Made in USA" label on goods actually made in Taiwan.
5. Misrepresenting the quality, character, or composition of a product, such as touting gold-plated jewelry as solid gold or cheap glass as crystal.

The foregoing list is just a small sample of the many deceptive acts and practices that are forbidden by the FTC Act. In addition, it was amended by the Wheeler-Lea Act of 1938 to prohibit false or deceptive advertising of foods, drugs, medicines, corrective devices, and cosmetics. In recent years, the FTC has been requiring advertisers to provide data to back up their claims, and this has taken a lot of the "fluff" out of advertising copywriting. Advertisers who are unable to back up their claims with hard data may be required to run an equal amount of corrective advertising in the same media.

The Food and Drug Act of 1906 also forbids adulteration and mislabeling of food or drugs sold in interstate commerce. This act was strengthened to include cosmetics in 1938, and recent amendments have pertained to pesticides, herbicides, and food additives. Pesticides and herbicides must be tested for human toxicity and approved by the FDA before sale. Food additives must be proven safe.

Truth-in-Lending Law

The Consumer Credit Protection Act of 1968 requires the lender to make a complete and accurate disclosure of the terms of credit, in plain language. In particular, the cost of credit must be expressed in two ways:

1. As the absolute amount, in dollars and cents, of interest and related credit charges.
2. As an annual rate of interest on the unpaid balance.

The borrower's right to pay off the loan ahead of schedule, without penalty, must also be spelled out.

Consumer Product Safety Commission

The Consumer Product Safety Commission was established in 1972 and charged with the mission of reducing product-related injuries to consumers. Other objectives include informing consumers so that they can compare and evaluate the safety aspects of various products, and developing uniform safety standards for many goods.

In its first five years of operation, the commission grew to 890 employees in 13 field offices, and its budget to $39 million. The commission also became notorious for concentrating on trivia as it recalled more than 20 million unsafe items. On the average, 83 percent of the owners of these items ignored the recall, even when a refund, repairs, or replacement was offered.

The commission has been criticized from both sides. Consumer advocates charged that resources have been wasted on relatively unimportant products, while development of safety standards for more commonly used products was neglected. Business executives complained about the excessive cost of complying with unreasonable standards. In the late 1970s the commission was reorganized to stress more rational priorities, and its 1984 budget was cut to $32 million.

Environmental Protection Agency (EPA)

Cars rolling off Detroit's assembly lines now have antipollution devices as standard equipment. The dense black smokestack emissions that used to symbolize industrial prosperity are rare and illegal sights. Plants that once discharged water into a river must now apply for permits that are almost impossible to get unless the plants install expensive water treatment equipment.

Since its creation in 1970, the EPA has become one of the most powerful governmental agencies in the United States. It monitors air, water, pesticides, toxic chemicals, and waste materials, and it is responsible for overseeing a program of grants for sewage treatment plants, the largest public works program in U.S. history. In performing its duties, the EPA has substantially reduced the deterioration of the environment.

All of this has not been done without monumental problems. Businesspeople point out that the EPA regulations are forcing their costs up. According to the Commerce Department, capital expenditures for the control of air and water pollution totaled $7.7 billion in 1975 alone, and it is predicted that between 1975 and 1984 industry will have to spend $258 billion just to meet the provisions of existing legislation. There are other complaints too, such as increased paperwork, delays caused by the EPA's own foot-dragging, and the nonexistence of technology advanced enough to meet all of the requirements. In addition, the EPA has been accused of contributing to the inflation rate and causing unemployment.

The effects of additional costs to business are most important in those industries that exhibit high elasticity for their goods. If prices increase dramatically for these goods, demand will fall. If elasticity is low, prices can increase with little effect on demand. The steam boiler industry provides a good example of this. Foreign boilers are good substitutes for U.S. boilers, so an increase in costs for domestically produced boilers will result in greater demand for those produced overseas.

However, we are not totally unsympathetic to the EPA. In many cases the agency has bent over backward to minimize the impact of its regulations on industry. When seven steel plants in Ohio employing 24,000 people threatened to close rather than install water treatment equipment, the EPA excused them from meeting 1977 water standards. In the steam boiler example, action aimed at producing an immediate reduction in noise pollution was seen to be unacceptable because of the impact such action would have on the economic well-being of the individuals the action was supposed to benefit. Thus, even though there were compelling health reasons to establish immediately noise abating standards in the industry, it was not politically feasible for the government to force such a change.

The future of EPA activity boils down to a choice between the carrot and the stick. The current administration favors a policy of economic incentive rather than coercion as a means to accomplish certain goals. Proposed incentives include a pollution tax that would replace the old method of simply forcing industry to comply with EPA regulations.

Government officials and business executives are becoming more and more aware that it is possible for a healthy environment and a healthy economy to coexist.

Other Regulations

1. Improvements in the fuel efficiency of automobiles and control of exhaust emissions—mandated by the Environmental Protection Agency (EPA)—and safety standards imposed by the National Highway Traffic Safety Administration (NHTSA) have added hundreds of dollars to the cost of each car.
2. Firms that handle food products and drugs are subject to regulation under the Pure Food and Drug Act.
3. Industrial working conditions are governed by labor laws and health and safety regulations developed by the Occupational Safety and Health Administration (OSHA). OSHA regulations outline safety standards for noxious gases and chemicals, harmful substances such as asbestos, noise levels, and other occupational hazards.
4. All but the very smallest businesses are subject to regulation of hiring and firing practices, and mandates for equal treatment of men and women have been developed and are enforced by the Equal Employment Opportunity Commission (EEOC).
5. Minimum wage laws put a floor under wages, and wage and price controls have imposed ceilings from time to time.
6. The Food, Drug and Cosmetic Act (1962) requires that drugs be proved effective before they can be marketed and that relevant information about each product be stated on its label.
7. Truth in packaging policy requires clear and accurate labeling of products sold in drug and grocery stores, showing contents, net quantity, name of manufacturer, and number of servings.
8. The Fair Credit Reporting Act (1971) grants consumers the right to examine their credit files, requires a rejected credit applicant to be informed of the reasons for rejection, establishes procedures for settling disputes, and prohibits credit discrimination based on race, religion, color, sex, marital status, or age.
9. The Magnuson-Moss Warranty Act (1975) requires warranties written in plain English, clearly indicating what parts are and are not covered, and clearly stating how the consumer may exercise the rights granted by the warranty.
10. Mail order firms must fill orders within 30 days or refund the customer's money.
11. The Real Estate Settlement and Procedures Act (1974) requires mortgage lenders to explain settlement costs for both buyer and seller in advance of the sale.

The economic consequences of regulation are not always apparent and are often impossible to measure. When the potential social costs are catastrophic, as they would be in the case of nuclear accidents, offshore oil well blowouts, and the like, there are really no alternatives to regulations designed to prevent such occurrences. Nor are there any easy alternatives to regulation when the externalities are difficult or impossible to measure, such as threats to public health or the chance of death or injury to workers. But when regulations seem to do no more than add to the firm's cost, the firm may be more interested in avoiding the regulation than in reducing the negative externalities. It is by no means clear that direct operating regulation is any more effective than tax or subsidy policies.

Behavior of the Regulating Agencies

We have seen that the chief instrument of government intervention is the regulatory agency, which is supposed to be working for the public good. But there are many different opinions as to what the public good may be, and regulatory agencies often are accused of engaging in strange economic behavior.

A regulatory agency is established by the act of a legislative body, which also outlines the composition, functions, and operating criteria of the agency. But the legislative mandate is usually broad enough and vague enough to allow the agency a great deal of latitude in working out the details of its operations. The attitude of the agency may sometimes be established by its director. The longer the agency operates, the more deeply entrenched become the collective practices of its bureaucracy. These questions arise: What determines the philosophy of the regulatory agency? What governs the behavior of the regulators?

The Capture Theory

Regulatory agencies are supposed to operate in the public interest by molding firms' behavior toward socially desirable ends. But the capture hypothesis advanced by George Stigler in 1971 holds that no matter why regulating agencies are established, they end up by promoting the interests of the firms they are supposed to be regulating.[13]

The capture theory notes that the state's power to prohibit or compel and to give or take money in the form of subsidies or taxes is the power to help or hurt any particular industry. Since regulatory agencies have

---

[13] George J. Stigler, "The Theory of Economic Regulation," *Bell Journal of Economics and Management Science* (Spring 1971), pp. 3–20; see also George J. Stigler, *The Citizen and the State: Essays on Regulation* (Chicago: University of Chicago Press, 1975).

the power to control prices and the entry of new firms (as, for example, the ICC has in the trucking industry), they are the ideal means of running a de facto cartel, if only they can be captured by the industry. Consequently, regulation may be actively sought by an industry despite some of the petty annoyances of the regulations.

Capture of a regulatory agency by the industry it regulates is not too difficult for two reasons:

1. A regulatory agency must have a good working knowledge of the industry it regulates. Consequently, its key personnel are apt to be hired from the industry. Further, there is a natural tendency for friendly personal relationships to develop from frequent contact between regulators and industry executives.
2. The industry's product is just one of many that are bought by consumers, who are also apt to be completely unorganized. For the firms, however, regulation is a vital interest. Consequently, at any regulatory hearing, firms will be well prepared and well represented at whatever cost is necessary, while consumers or the general public will not be.

Stigler asserts that firms in regulated industries will most often seek the following favors from the government:

1. *Direct money subsidies.* A good example is the maritime industry, which has received approximately $10 billion in direct subsidies since 1936.
2. *Control over entry of new competitors.* Examples are (1) Federal Deposit Insurance Corporation (FDIC) regulations restricting the rate of entry into commercial banking; the American Medical Association control of medical training and licensing; and until recent deregulation, Interstate Commerce Commission (ICC) restrictions on the licensing of new trucking firms.
3. *Control over marketing of substitutes and complements.* A classic example is the suppression of margarine sales by butter producers.
4. *Price fixing.* Examples are the freight rates established by regulatory agencies overseeing all forms of transportation by land, sea, or air.

Stigler contends that pro-industry policies of regulatory agencies are to be expected under the current system of selecting and rewarding regulators, and that they will continue unless the system is changed.

The Share-the-Gains, Share-the-Pains Theory

Sam Peltzman's approach focuses on the motivation of regulators to retain their positions.[14] A prudent regulator, whether elected or ap-

---

[14] Sam Peltzman, "Toward a More General Theory of Regulation," *Journal of Law and Economics* (August 1976), pp. 211–40.

pointed, can retain the job by maximizing the approval of his constituency. The regulator's constituency consists of three disparate groups:

1. The legislative body that established the agency and monitors its behavior.
2. The industry that is being regulated.
3. Customers of the industry that is being regulated.

Each of these groups will have something to say about the agency's performance, and the opinion of each group must be given some weight. The Peltzman model suggests that the regulators perform a balancing act, leaning first one way, then the other, but always ending up in a neutral position.

In Peltzman's view, the agencies do not allow themselves to be captured by one side or another—that would be far too risky for the regulators. They can be moved by pressure if there is no counterpressure, but they will seek the middle ground. For example, if a product proves to be unsafe, an agency may tighten its standards, but not until the manufacturer has had an opportunity to redesign the product. When it comes to safety, an agency will usually err on the side of excessive prudence. The regulator's motto is "Better safe than sorry." Thus children's toys are barred from the market on the basis of what a child *might* do, rather than on what children ordinarily do.

While there is no doubt that government regulations impose substantial costs on producers, there is no single answer to the question of who pays the bill. If we assume that regulation is imposed even-handedly upon all firms within a particular industry, the answer will depend upon two circumstances: (1) the market structure in which the firm sells its products, and (2) whether or not close substitutes exist.

If demand is inelastic or if no close substitutes exist, increases in marginal costs can be passed on to customers. But in markets where demand is highly elastic and close substitutes do exist, some and perhaps most of regulatory cost increases must be absorbed by the firm's owners, employees, and suppliers.

The Trend toward Deregulation

Although government regulation of the American economy began more than 100 years ago, it has greatly expanded and has become increasingly burdensome during the past two decades. Consequently, there has been generated in the business community a widespread opinion that regulation has gone too far and needs to be reevaluated. This opinion was shared by the Ford and Carter administrations and was one of the planks in President Reagan's campaign platform. It was also shared by enough members of Congress to win passage of the Airline Deregulation Act of 1978.

Since then, Congress has substantially deregulated common carrier trucking, interstate movers of household goods, railroads, the petroleum industry, and banks and other depository institutions. The drive for deregulation is gaining momentum in the early 1980s and we will no doubt see a substantially different business environment before this decade is over.

Reasons for Deregulation

Economists and business executives who press for deregulation do not quarrel with the reasons for government intervention that have been set forth in this chapter. Rather, they criticize the inefficient and wasteful administration of regulation and the excessive costs of regulatory methods that have failed to produce desirable outcomes. Three reasons for deregulation are cited most often:

1. *Excessive and inefficient regulation.* According to a study by the U.S. Department of Commerce, the percentage of GNP under regulation increased from 8.2 percent in 1965 to 23.7 percent by 1975. Fully 77 percent of the increase was caused by growth in health and safety regulations.[15] These are the regulations most often complained about. In too many cases, government regulators have not only specified the standards that must be met, but also have specified the means of compliance, whether or not the specified means are cost-effective. It would be more efficient to simply specify the desired results, and then leave it up to the firms to find the best way to comply.

Another complaint is the sheer mass of regulations. By 1980, the *Code of Federal Regulations* totaled 800,000 pages and occupied 52 large bookshelves. Furthermore, regulations emanating from different agencies are frequently contradictory to the point where compliance is impossible. For example, USDA rules that a sausage maker's kitchen floor must be washed frequently for sanitary reasons, but OSHA demands that it be kept dry for safety reasons.

2. *Excessive cost.* In a study of the annual cost of federal regulation in 1976, Murray Weidenbaum, later to become chairman of President Reagan's Council of Economic Advisors, estimated the administrative costs at $3.2 billion and the compliance costs at $62.9 billion, for a total of $66.1 billion.[16] In a study made for the Joint Economic Committee,

---

[15] Paul W. MacAvoy, "Overview of Regulatory Effects and Reform Prospects," in *Reforming Regulation*, eds. T. B. Clark, M. H. Kosters, and J. C. Miller, III (Washington, D.C.: American Enterprise Institute, 1980).

[16] Murray Weidenbaum, *Business, Government and the Public,* 2d ed. (Englewood Cliffs, N.J.: Prentice-Hall, 1981).

Weidenbaum estimated the 1979 costs of regulation to be more than $100 billion.

As Milton Friedman has observed, "There is no such thing as a free lunch," and these costs would not be excessive if commensurate benefits could be shown on the other side of the ledger. Unfortunately, this cannot be done. Measuring benefits is even more difficult than measuring costs, especially where the benefit is an improvement in safety. Nevertheless, the discipline of attempting a cost-benefit analysis of proposed regulations might bring out many facts that are now overlooked.

Another problem is that costs tend to rise exponentially as we approach perfection. For example, the cost of reducing air pollution by, say, 85 percent, might be within reason. But the cost of getting rid of that last 15 percent might be astronomical and far more than it is worth. At some point there is an equilibrium between costs and benefits. The regulators and the regulated need to work together to find that point. But it is unlikely that an industrial society can ever be totally safe and totally unpolluted.

3. *Market distortions and inefficiencies.* Market distortions and inefficiencies caused by regulation are manifested in three different ways. First, when goods not produced in a natural monopoly are price-controlled, the inevitable result is poor distribution, shortages, and inefficient consumption. This was the case when the price of oil was regulated, and is the case with natural gas (the next candidate for deregulation). Second, regulation that controls or denies entry into the market stifles the vigorous competition that leads to better products and better service at lower cost to the consumer. Third, regulation of natural monopolies too often protects inefficient production at excessive cost.

Is Antitrust Policy Necessary?

Although most efforts at deregulation are directed toward government intervention for the protection of society, antitrust policy has also come under fire. Actually, five different evaluations of antitrust policy can be detected in the literature:

1. *First opinion.* The very existence of free enterprise depends upon antitrust legislation, which is both actually and potentially beneficial. There is no proof to back up this opinion, so it is largely an expression of faith.

2. *Second opinion.* Antitrust laws would be good if enforced, but the enforcement agencies have been deliberately starved for funds and personnel, and the government actually favors development of monopoly and oligopoly.

3. *Third opinion.* Substantial changes in the antitrust laws are needed to increase their effectiveness. Antitrust laws should be enforceable and

thus inspire sufficient respect that they will be obeyed in fear of swift and certain punishment if violated. Thus extensive enforcement would not be necessary. Most commentators belong to this group.

4. *Fourth opinion.* Antitrust laws are applicable only to the United States. They have monopolistic, perhaps imperialist, results overseas. For example, it really doesn't matter to Central American banana growers whether the price of bananas is set in a free market in the United States or by a cartel.

5. *Fifth opinion.* It is questionable whether there is any connection between antitrust policy and economic growth, employment, and wage and price levels. The holders of this opinion recognize the difficulty of measuring results of antitrust policy. They suggest it would be useful to compare the performance of an economy before and after antitrust, and note that the U.S. growth rate in the last quarter of the 19th century was greater than after World War II. They also suggest comparison of the economies of countries where monopoly has been high, such as Japan, and where it has been low, such as Brazil.

The Effects of Deregulation

There is no doubt that deregulation will remain one of the main economic issues of the 1980s, so it will be quite some time before all the evidence is available. But we can see some of the effects of deregulation that has already taken place.

Deregulation of the Airline Industry.   Before deregulation took place, many airline executives predicted that it would introduce an era of cut-throat competition on the more profitable long-haul routes while eliminating service on the profitable short-haul routes. These fears have proved to be unfounded, in part because the airlines have always been very competitive on everything except price. Now price competition has reduced fares while increasing load factors as the less popular flights were dropped. New short-haul feeder lines have sprung up to continue service to the smaller cities. From the consumer's point of view, deregulation is a success.

Deregulation of Depository Institutions.   The Depository Institutions Deregulation and Monetary Control Act of 1980 is the widest reform of the banking system since the 1930s. Depository institutions include commercial banks, thrift institutions, savings and loan associations, mutual savings banks, and credit unions. The main purpose of the act is to remove or diminish differences among the depository institutions with regard to the types of deposits they can offer, the rates of interest they can pay, the reserves they must hold, and their access to Federal Reserve services. Two of the most noticeable results for consumers are the availability of higher interest rates on various types of deposits and the ability to write checks on accounts in the thrift institutions. All "Regulation Q" restrictions on interest rates payable on savings will be phased out by 1986.[17]

Settlement of the AT&T Case.   Although the AT&T case was an antitrust suit, its settlement effectively deregulated long-distance telephone service and opened it to competition. The result has been a proliferation of firms offering cut-rate long-distance service. For example, in the spring of 1983, four such firms were competing with the local telephone company in Honolulu. However, local customers of the Bell system companies that were spun off from AT&T may find their telephone bills increasing, since AT&T was subsidizing local service with its profits from its long-distance monopoly.

Summary

Government intervention in the American economy was provided for in the Constitution and is necessary to compensate for market failure. Market failure arises from two main sources:

1. *Externalities.* These arise when persons not involved in a market transaction nevertheless receive benefits or bear costs as a result of the transaction. The most serious externality is pollution of water and air.
2. *Structural failure.* This occurs as the market structure departs from perfect competition and goes into oligopoly or monopoly. A special class of structural failure is the natural monopoly, which is regulated.

   Government intervention to deal with externalities is designed to provide incentives to increase the output of beneficial externalities or decrease the output of harmful externalities. Incentives to increase output may include grants of operating rights, patents, subsidies, and tax relief. The government may also provide public goods, such as roads and dams, and public services, such as police and fire protection and national defense, that would not be provided by private industry. Incentives to decrease harmful output include tax penalties and government control of operations.

   A natural monopoly occurs when economies of scale are such that

---

[17] Regulation Q of the Federal Reserve System puts a ceiling on the rate of interest that can be paid by commercial banks on demand deposits and savings account.

the long-run average cost declines throughout the range of production that can be absorbed by a market. Natural monopolies are regulated by public utility commissions, which set the price high enough to provide an adequate return on investment.

Market power and concentration are controlled by antitrust laws. The chief prohibitions contained in the antitrust laws may be summarized as follows:

1. It is flatly *illegal*, without any qualification, to:
   a. Enter a contract, combination, or conspiracy in restraint of trade (Sherman Act, Section 1).
   b. Monopolize, attempt to monopolize, or combine or conspire to monopolize trade (Sherman Act, Section 3).
2. When and if the effect may be substantially to lessen competition or tend to create a monopoly, it is *illegal* to:
   a. Acquire the stock of competing corporations (Clayton Act, Section 7).
   b. Acquire the assets of competing corporations (Clayton Act, Section 7, as amended by the Antimerger Act in 1950).
   c. Enter exclusive and tying contracts (Clayton Act, Section 3).
   d. Discriminate unjustifiably among purchasers (Clayton Act, Section 2, as amended by Robinson-Patman Act, Section 1).
3. In general, it is also *illegal* to:
   a. Engage in particular forms of price discrimination (Robinson-Patman Act, Sections 1 and 3).
   b. Serve as a director of competing corporations of a certain minimum size (Clayton Act, Section 8).
   c. Use unfair methods of competition (Federal Trade Commission Act, Section 5).
   d. Use unfair or deceptive acts or practices (Federal Trade Commission Act, Section 5, as amended by Wheeler-Lea Act, Section 3).

Thus the laws taken as a whole are designed not only to prevent the growth of monopoly but to maintain competition as well.

Federal and state governments also intervene to protect the health, safety, and welfare of society. It is in this area that the government has been most active in the 1970s. Because the effects of regulation were often much different from what was intended, and because of excessive zeal on the part of some regulatory agencies, a reaction has resulted in strong demands for deregulation. Deregulation has already taken place in the airline industry, the trucking industry, the petroleum industry, the railroad industry, and for depository institutions, and it seems to be only a matter of time before it will take place in the natural gas industry. Whether the results will be good or bad remains to be seen.

Problems

1. Critically evaluate the following government policies:
a. Tax credits for installation of solar energy devices in private homes.
b. The investment tax credit for businesses.
c. Medicare.
d. Import taxes (tariffs).
e. Excise taxes.
f. Sales taxes.
2. Discuss three different ways of dealing with pollution. Who bears the cost? In your opinion, which way is preferable?
3. Critically evaluate the economic impact of government policy toward:
a. Transportation subsidies (maritime, highway, rail, and air).
b. Agricultural subsidies (dairy products, grains, tobacco).
4. Suppose that two unregulated firms were allowed to compete in the production and sale of electrical power in the same city.
a. What would the economic impact be?
b. How could the economic results be improved?
5. The Friendly Electric Company has petitioned the public utility commission in its state for permission to practice "time of day" pricing. This means that electricity consumed during certain hours of the day—late at night, for example—would be priced lower than electricity consumed during periods of peak demand. The company argues that this pricing scheme will enable it to lower overall rates. Evaluate this proposal.
6. Paradise Valley Electric Power Company is regulated by a public utilities commission (PUC) of which you are a member. The PUC has established an allowable rate of return for the utility of 16 percent before taxes. The utility's costs have risen substantially due to inflation, and they have requested a rate increase to yield 20 percent before taxes. The following pertinent information has been verified:
1. The rate base (assets) is $3 billion.
2. The average operation of machinery and equipment is 50 percent of capacity, and generates 12 billion kilowatt-hours (kwh) of electricity per annum.
3. Operating costs average 6.5 cents per kwh, not including return on investment (ROI).
a. Calculate the price per kwh if the before-tax rate of return is held to 16 percent.
b. Calculate the price per kwh if the before-tax rate of return is increased to 20 percent.

7. Suppose that tomorrow morning, all grocers in Chicago, without previous public notice, raised their prices for milk by 3 cents per quart. Does this action prove the existence of an agreement or constitute an offense on the part of the grocers? What would your answer be if the automobile manufacturers without notice announced a 5 percent price increase next year on all new model cars? Explain.

8. In an industry characterized by price leadership without prior arrangement, is there likely to be a charge of combination or conspiracy leveled against that industry if (*a*) prevailing prices are announced by the industry's trade association rather than by a leading firm; (*b*) all firms in the industry report their prices to their industry trade association; (*c*) all firms in the industry quote prices on a basing point system, that is, the delivered price is the leader's price plus rail freight from the leader's plant; and (*d*) all firms follow the leader not only in price but in product and sales policies as well? (These four questions should be answered as a group rather than individually.)

9. "To say that the degree of competition depends on the number of sellers in the marketplace is like saying that football is more competitive than tennis." Do you agree? Explain. (*Hint:* Can you describe different forms of competition, in addition to price competition, that exist in American industry?)

10. It is generally stated that growth, stability, and flexibility are three primary objectives of mergers. (*a*) With respect to growth, it has been said that "a firm, like a tree, must either grow or die." Evaluate this statement. (*b*) Why may instability be a motive for merger? Instability of what? (*c*) What is meant by flexibility as a motive for merger? (*Hint:* Compare flexibility with vulnerability.)

11. (Library research) Examine the IBM case in detail. What antitrust provisions were alleged to have been violated? How extensive were the alleged damages? Was corporate morality ever an issue? Did government prosecution have any effect on IBM's corporate policies or on the general public?

12. The Hygrade Cement Company is located in a small midwestern city with a population of 80,000. The company's manufacture of Portland cement employs about 10 percent of the town's work force and provides 100 percent of its air pollution. Because of complaints about the plant's discharge of particulate matter into the air, the city council is considering actions to induce or force the firm to reduce its air pollution. Three alternatives are being considered:

1. Require the firm to reduce its discharge of particulates by 85 percent.
2. Impose a tax of $7 per ton of particulates discharged.
3. Leave the situation unchanged.

Each alternative has consequences for the town's employment as well as for the firm's profits, as follows:

Action	Impact on Profits	Impact on Employment
Reduce discharge 85%	−40%	−18%
Tax discharge	−20	−8
Forget it	0	0

a. What do you think the council should do? Why?
b. Are there other factors that should be considered?
c. Why does the 85 percent reduction in particulates have such a drastic effect on employment?

  13.   In considering regulation to improve automobile safety, there is considerable controversy over the requirement to install air bags that will automatically inflate to cushion the impact of a head-on crash. Opponents of the air bags advocate seat belts instead. They argue that the seat belts are not only much cheaper than air bags, but also are effective in rollovers and other crashes where air bags are useless. Proponents of the air bags counter with the argument that seat belts don't work when people don't use them, but air bags require no action on the part of occupants of the car. What are the economic arguments for and against the following proposals?
a. Compulsory installation of air bags.
b. Compulsory installation of seat belts and stiff fines for people who do not use them. (Some countries already have this law.)
c. Car buyer should have the right to choose whether he wants seat belts or air bags or both or neither.

  14.   The Intellectual Club is a group of economists, environmentalists, and ex-officials of the government of a certain developing country in Southeast Asia. In 1973, a local firm entered a joint venture with one of Japan's largest steel companies to produce locally a fine specialty steel. However, the production process was such that sulfur products were discharged into the air. The Intellectual Club complained bitterly about the air pollution, but the government refused to shut down a plant that was providing employment, paying taxes, and otherwise providing the economic benefits that flow from a primary industry. However, the government indicated it would entertain the idea of a pollution tax if the Intellectual Club could justify such a tax and determine how much it should be. The Club learned that the steel plant had installed certain equipment that partially recovered sulfur from the plant's smokestacks. The recovered sulfur was used in the production process

or sold. When steel and sulfur are jointly produced in a constant ratio of 1 unit of steel, Q_A, to one unit of sulfur, Q_B, their respective demand functions are estimated as:

$$P_A = 5,000 - 2Q_A$$
$$P_B = 400 - Q_B$$

Total cost of joint production of steel and sulfur is:

$$TC = 20,000 + 5.6Q + 2.8Q^2$$

a. Determine optimal output, prices, and profit without a pollution tax.
b. Estimate the minimum tax that must be charged to induce the firm to eliminate the sulfur pollution.
c. Critically evaluate the economics of externalities as it pertains to the emigration of a polluting industry to other nations.

   15.   Provide the economic rationale for deregulation of the following industries:
a. Trucking.
b. Airlines.
c. Oil.
d. Gas.
e. Communications.

Case Problem: HPOWER

   16.   In 1981, the LMC Corporation proposed construction of a plant to convert Honolulu's garbage into electrical power. The proposed plant, which became known as HPOWER, would take trash and garbage that presently goes into landfills and, in cooperation with Hawaiian Electric Company, burn it to make steam for the generation of five megawatts of electrical power. The proposed site for HPOWER was next to an old sugar mill in the suburban community of Waipahu (population 30,000), 14 miles from downtown Honolulu.

   The selection of Waipahu as the site for HPOWER was for economic reasons. After careful study of other possible sites, the Waipahu site was chosen because its central location would minimize the cost of hauling garbage as well as the cost of transmitting the power generated. However, after two years of planning, the proposal ran into a storm of opposition from Waipahu residents who feared the increased traffic of garbage trucks and who did not like the idea of having a garbage disposal plant in their backyards. HPOWER became a hot political issue in the 1982 elections, when it was voted down. However, the available landfill sites will all be full in two or three years, and the city is entertaining new proposals for generation of electrical power from garbage.

Questions:

a. Assume you are a resident of Waipahu in opposition to HPOWER. Justify your position.
b. Take a position as a nonresident of Waipahu.
c. Take a position as president of LMC Corporation.
d. Take a position as mayor of the City and County of Honolulu.
e. If you were a member of the City Council, which has the power to accept or reject similar proposals, what criteria would you follow to reach a decision?
f. Explain how an economic issue such as HPOWER can become a political issue.

Case Problem: The Nader Recommendations

17. Several years ago a Nader task force investigating antitrust activity came up with the following recommendations:
1. To limit size of any one firm to $2 billion in assets.
2. Break up any industry with a 50 percent concentration ratio for the four largest firms in the industry, or with an eight-firm concentration ratio of 70 percent or more.
3. Require the top 500 corporations to divest an amount of assets equal to the assets of any firm that they acquire.
4. Levy a 100 percent tax on all advertising expenditures of any firm that possesses incipient market power in excess of a certain percentage of sales revenue.
5. Convert any defense contractor whose business with the government exceeds 75 percent of sales revenue over a five-year period into a public corporation to preserve the public interest.

Questions:

a. Critically evaluate each of the five recommendations.
b. Do you agree that highly concentrated industries have greater economic power and tend to have larger profits? Why? Justify your answer with some concrete evidence.
c. The crucial issue involved here is whether or not monopoly power can benefit the American public. In your outside readings have you noted situations where this type of power does work to the benefit of the American people?

Case Problem: Price Discrimination

18. A new management has recently assumed control of the fifth largest company in one of the nation's major industries. The industry is strongly oligopolistic and has had a long history of price leadership.

The new management is headed by an aggressive president who has announced interest in expanding the company's market share through planned price reductions. The president, however, is aware of the likelihood that any general price reductions would be promptly matched by competitors, and hence little if anything would be gained. Moreover, the four larger firms in the industry control about 90 percent of the output, and are therefore in a relatively strong position to withstand the damaging effects of a price war.

The president has decided, therefore, to adhere to the outward historical pattern of price leadership as far as the industry is concerned, but to engage in secret price concessions with potential customers whenever necessary to attract their business. For example, he will continue to publish his previous prices and he will follow the price leader as long as total demand is high and there is no major price resistance by buyers. However, if it ever becomes apparent that an important sale may be lost because of the price, a lower price will be negotiated in order to retain the customer.

Questions:

The president of the company has hired you as an antitrust economist to advise him on the following questions.

a. How will the president's strategy stand up in view of the Robinson-Patman Act?

b. The president proposes to cut prices in New England where the demand for the product is more elastic, and to maintain prices elsewhere. What do you advise with respect to the Robinson-Patman Act?

c. The president has several personal friends in Congress. What would you advise him to do about the Robinson-Patman Act? Be specific.

Case Problem: The AT&T Case

19. Refer to the AT&T antitrust case in the text of this chapter.

Questions:

a. Leonard Hyman, analyst at Merrill Lynch, Pierce, Fenner & Smith described the AT&T divestiture as a wrenching experience for AT&T. "It's going to split apart the family," he said, "But the business that will remain is still an enormous entity, with annual profits of $2 billion to $3 billion." In the light of this statement, critically evaluate the statement by William Baxter, the assistant attorney general, that the agreement "completely fulfills the objectives of the

Antitrust Division and is also very much in the interests of AT&T and its shareholders."

b. In your opinion, what are the political issues or politics involved in settlement of the case? Can you provide any evidence to support your opinion?

c. This case took six years and the expenditure of at least $385 million, all of which will eventually be paid by taxpayers and users of telephone services. Can you think of ways the system might be reformed to avoid such enormous costs of litigation?

d. In your opinion, has the AT&T settlement served the public interest? Establish and categorize criteria upon which to base your opinion.

e. Testimony by former Defense Secretary Harold Brown established a security link between national defense and the communications industry. Should there be a national policy of protecting certain monopolies in the interest of national security? How could such a criterion be applied to antitrust cases?

Case Problem: Value Hardware

20. Value Hardware operates 23 stores in southern California. Total sales climbed to a record $9 million in 1982 with an average contribution margin of 30 percent. Value Hardware's management attributes much of its current success to an exclusive six-year contract with LS Corporation for dealership in Olympia paints. The contract began in January 1980. Olympia paints accounts for about 20 percent of total sales, but an additional 20 percent of sales are attributable to purchases of complementary goods such as paint brushes, step ladders, and so forth.

In 1983, the LS Corporation, makers of Olympia paints, merged with a national chain of hardware stores. As a result of the merger, LS Corporation pulled Olympia paints out of the Value Hardware stores. Although Value Hardware replaced Olympia with another brand, sales of paint dropped 25 percent and total sales were down 10 percent in 1983.

Previous projections by Value Hardware's management forecast that Olympia paint sales could be expected to increase 5 percent per year for the duration of the six-year contract. However, future sales of the replacement line of paints were not expected to increase above the 1983 level. On January 1, 1984, Value Hardware filed an antitrust suit for triple damages against LS Corporation.

Questions:

a. What antitrust laws might Value Hardware allege were violated?

b. Analyze the total economic losses sustained by Value Hardware as a result of cancellation of the Olympia paint dealership.

References

"Antitrust: New Life in an Old Issue." *Time,* June 28, 1971, pp. 70–72.

Bailey, Elizabeth E. "Contestability and the Design of Regulatory and Antitrust Policy." *American Economic Review,* May 1981, pp. 178–83.

Baumol, William J. "Contestable Markets: An Uprising in the Theory of Industry Structure." *American Economic Review,* March 1982, pp. 1–55.

Becker, Gary S. "Crime and Punishment: An Economic Approach." *Journal of Political Economy,* March–April 1968, pp. 169–217.

Caves, Richard. *American Industry: Structure, Conduct, Performance.* 4th ed. Englewood Cliffs, N.J.: Prentice-Hall, 1977.

Christiansen, Gregory B., and Robert H. Haveman. "Public Regulations and the Slowdown in Productivity Growth." *American Economic Review,* May 1981, pp. 320–25.

Dorfman, Robert. "Incidence of the Benefits and Costs of Environmental Programs." *American Economic Review,* February 1977, pp. 333–40.

Elzinga, Kenneth G. "The Antimerger Law: Pyrrhic Victories?" *Journal of Law and Economics,* April 1969, pp. 43–78.

"FTC vs. Business." *Business Week,* December 13, 1976, pp. 52–60.

Gatti, James F. *The Limits of Government Regulation.* New York: Academic Press, 1981.

"Government Intervention." *Business Week,* April 4, 1977, pp. 42–93.

"Is John Sherman's Antitrust Obsolete?" *Business Week,* March 23, 1974, pp. 47–56.

Kahn, Alfred E. *The Economic Regulation.* New York: John Wiley & Sons, 1971.

Koch, James V. *Industrial Organization and Prices.* 2d ed. Englewood Cliffs, N.J.: Prentice-Hall, 1980.

McGuigan, J. R., and R. C. Moyer. *Managerial Economics,* 3d ed. St. Paul, Minn.: West Publishing, 1983, from which Problem 12 was adapted.

Meadows, Edward. "Bold Departures in Antitrust." *Fortune,* October 5, 1981, pp. 180–88.

Miller, E. M. "Do Economies of Scale Attract Entry?" *Antitrust Bulletin,* Fall 1980, pp. 583–87.

Misham Ezra J. "The Postwar Literature on Externalities: An Interpretative Essay." *Journal of Economic Literature,* March 1971, pp. 1–28.

Oster, Sharon. "Product Regulations: A Measure of the Benefits." *Journal of Industrial Economics,* June 1981, pp. 395–409.

Peltzman, Sam. "The Gains and Losses from Industrial Concentration." *Journal of Law and Economics,* October 1977, pp. 229–63.

————. "Toward a More General Theory of Regulation." *Journal of Law and Economics,* August 1976, pp. 211–40.

Posner, Richard A. *Antitrust Law: An Economic Perspective.* Chicago: University of Chicago Press, 1976.

Redefining Government's Role in the Market. Committee for Economic Development, 1979.

Scherer, Frederic M. *Industrial Market Structure and Economic Performance.* 2d ed. Skokie, Ill.: Rand McNally, 1980.

Stelzer, Irwin M. *Selected Antitrust Cases,* 6th ed. Homewood, Ill.: Richard D. Irwin, 1981.

Stigler, George J. "The Theory of Economic Regulation." *Bell Journal of Economics and Management Science*, Spring 1971, pp. 3–21.

"The Odds in a Bell-IBM Bout." *Business Week*, January 25, 1982, pp. 22–26.

The Wall Street Journal, January 9, 1982.

U.S. Department of Justice, Merger Guidelines (June 14, 1982).

Uttal, Bro. "How to Deregulate AT&T." *Fortune*, November 1981, pp. 70–75.

Waters, L. L. "Deregulation—For Better, or For Worse?" *Business Horizons*, January/February 1981, pp. 88–91.

Weidenbaum, Murray L. *Business, Government and the Public.* Englewood Cliffs, N.J.: Prentice-Hall, 1979.

18

Capital Budgeting: Investment Selection

Capital budgeting involves planning expenditures for assets, the returns from which will be realized in future time periods. Thus, there are two fundamental types of decisions that must be made.

Investment Selection

These decisions will determine both the total amount of capital expenditures to be undertaken in the planning period and the specific projects selected. Typical decisions in this area include the following:

1. *Expansion decisions*, such as building or acquiring additional plant facilities.
2. *Replacement decisions*, such as the replacement of existing equipment.
3. *"Seed" investment decisions*, such as research and development, advertising, market research, training, and professional consulting services.
4. *Operating investment decisions*, such as increasing inventories or accounts receivable, or development of a new product line.

Financing Investment

Ideally, these decisions are made in conjunction with investment decisions, and they involve:

638

1. The amount and kind (debt or equity) of financial capital to be raised.
2. The amount of dividends to be paid to the owners and the amount of earnings to be retained in the corporation and invested on their behalf.

Each of these types of decisions requires a comparison of rates of return and costs of capital on alternative investments. Hence an explanation of the theory and measurement of these concepts is necessary. To visualize how the capital budgeting parts fit together, let us look at an overview of the capital budgeting process as illustrated in Exhibit 18 1.

Exhibit 18–1

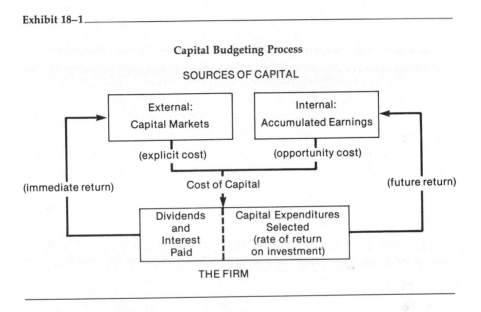

Capital Budgeting Process

SOURCES OF CAPITAL

Sources of capital to the firm are presumed to be: (1) the capital markets, which include many different types of financial intermediaries, and (2) earnings of the firm accumulated from previous time periods. Each specific source of capital has its own cost, which becomes a component part of the overall cost of capital to the firm. From the total capital available, interest obligations are first to be paid, then management must decide how much capital to retain in the firm and invest for the shareholders' future return and how much to pay in current dividends.

Finally, the diagram indicates that the criterion for investment selection within the firm is the rate of return on investment. This chapter deals with this rate-of-return concept and investment selection in general. The cost of capital is discussed in the following chapter. Taken together, they form the core of capital budgeting.

Rate of Return

Among laypeople, the common conception is that the rate of return on an investment is simply the ratio of annual receipts to original cost. This meaning is only approximately correct; it is precisely true for a special type of investment, namely, a permanent, nondepreciating, nonappreciating asset producing a periodical, uniform income stream. To the extent that the liquidating or resale value of the asset is, at the time the investment is terminated, greater or less than the original outlay, the true rate of return will be greater or less than the rate as defined above.

In reality, it is rarely possible to predict the precise liquidating or resale value of an investment; hence, in the typical case, the *true* rate of return on an investment to a given owner cannot be known until the ownership has terminated and the actual liquidation value is known. This liquidation value and the income stream produced by the investment are combined to obtain a measure of the true rate of return. However, for many practical situations we want to estimate the rate of return before, rather than after, the investment is made, in order to have some preliminary idea of the investment's profitability. The method of accomplishing this is described below.

Time Value of Money

A fundamental concept that must be understood when talking about rate of return is the notion of the *time value of money*.[1] By this is meant that dollars at different times cannot be directly comparable unless they are first expressed in terms of a common denominator. The common denominator that is commonly used is the interest rate.

Thus, if money can be invested at 12 percent interest, then a dollar today is not the same as a dollar next year, because a dollar today can be invested so that it is worth $1.12 next year. Similarly, $1.12 next year is not equivalent to $1.12 in the following year, because $1.12 next year can be invested at 12 percent so as to be worth $1.12 plus 12 percent of that amount, or a total of $1.254 in the following year.

It is clear that this process, which is known as *compounding*, can be extended as far into the future as we like. Further, by this process, we can equate a given sum of money at the present time with another sum of money at any future time. Thus, in line with the above example, the

---

[1] The concept of the time value of money was introduced in Chapter 1. It is restated here for the convenience of the student.

sum of $1 today is, at 12 percent interest, equivalent to $1.12 next year, or to $1.254 in the following year, or to still greater amounts in later years.

The reverse of compounding is *discounting*. Whereas in compounding we move from the present to the future, in discounting we move from the future back to the present. Thus, at 12 percent interest, how much is $1.254 two years from now worth today? We know from the previous example that $1 now is worth $1.254 two years from today at 12 percent. Therefore, we may say that $1.254 two years hence discounted at 12 percent has a *present value* of $1.

By showing how dollars at different times can be made equivalent through the common denominator of an interest rate, we may define and illustrate the meaning of "rate of return."

Definition: The *rate of return* on an investment is the interest rate that equates the present value of the cash returns on the investment with the present value of the cash expenditures relating to the investment. That is, the rate of return on an investment is the interest rate at which an investment is just repaid by its discounted receipts.

As already stated, many people think of the rate of return on an investment as the annual net receipts or cash flow from the investment divided by the total amount of the investment. Thus, if an investment of $1,000 in a parcel of land were to yield forever a rent of $200 per year, then the rate of return would be $200 ÷ $1,000 = 20 percent. In this case the entire $200 is return on capital, since no part of this amount is used to pay back the original investment of $1,000. To obtain the present value of this investment, we must "capitalize" it. This is done by dividing the income ($200) by the rate of interest (20 percent) that will make the present value of the investment equal to the present cost of the investment. Thus, $200 ÷ 0.20 = $1,000. Hence, according to the above definition of rate of return on investment, the reason 20 percent is the rate of return on this investment is because it is the only interest rate that equates the present value of the income stream to the present value of the cost of the investment. That is, it is the only interest rate that when applied to the cash flow or net receipts will precisely recover the investment.

If the $1,000 had been invested in an asset with a finite life, then part of the cash flow of $200 would represent return on capital, and part would represent the amount needed to recover the initial investment. In cases where the annual receipts include both interest and principal, the rate of return is more difficult to compute. For this purpose, interest tables have been devised to facilitate the computations.

There are many types of problems that arise in calculating rate of return. They involve the nature of the variations in cash flow, the length of life of the investment, and, of course, the amount of the investment. Most of the problems, however, can usually be grouped into three classes, as illustrated by Case I, Case II, and Case III, which follows.

Case I: Present Value of a Uniform Series: PVUS

The first case involves the present value of a uniform series, abbreviated PVUS. This case relates to an investment that will yield a constant income stream over its life.

Example.   A new machine costs $10,000, requires no increased investment in working capital, and is expected to yield a $3,000 (before tax) profit per year for 10 years, at which time its scrap or resale value will be negligible. Assume straight-line depreciation and a 50 percent tax rate. (*a*) What is the rate of return on this investment? (*b*) If management requires at least a 10 percent return on any new investment, would this investment qualify? (*c*) At a 10 percent rate of return, what is the present value per dollar of investment? Of what use is this type of measure?

Solution.   (*a*)   One way of conveniently solving for rate of return is to begin by setting up a table such as Exhibit 18–2.

Note that depreciation is calculated only for the purpose of arriving at income after taxes. As far as cash flow, column (7), is concerned, it may be estimated by subtracting taxes from operating profit, or by adding in the amount of depreciation when income after taxes, column (6), has

Exhibit 18–2

Calculation of Cash Flow (cost of asset: $10,000; life of asset: 10 years)

(1)	(2)	(3)	(4)	(5)	(6)	(7)
	Operating Profit and Capital Recovery	*Depreciation (Straight Line)*	*Taxable Income (2) − (3)*	*Taxes 50% of (4)*	*Income after Taxes (4) − (5)*	*Cash Flow (2) − (5) or (6) + (3)*
Year						
1	$3,000	$1,000	$2,000	$1,000	$1,000	$2,000
2	3,000	1,000	2,000	1,000	1,000	2,000
3	3,000	1,000	2,000	1,000	1,000	2,000
.	.	.	.	.	.	.
.	.	.	.	.	.	.
9	3,000	1,000	2,000	1,000	1,000	2,000
10	3,000	1,000	2,000	1,000	1,000	2,000
CR*	0	—	—	—	—	0

* CR denotes capital recovery. It includes the forecasted resale or scrap value of the asset, plus the return of additional working capital that may have been required by the investment.

been determined. Thus, depreciation is conceived as a *source of cash* in the sense that profits are reduced because expenses are increased each year by the amount of depreciation, leaving that much less profit for distribution to stockholders and that much more for the replacement of fixed assets. Thus, by investing $10,000 now, management expects an after-tax cash flow of $2,000 a year for 10 years.

What interest rate will equate these sums? To answer this question, we have to utilize Table A of the Appendix at the end of this text, which gives the present value of an annuity of $1 at specified interest rates for a given number of years. That is, figures in the body of the table tell us the amount that must be invested now, at the rate of compound interest shown across the top, to produce an income of $1 a year for the years shown on the left side of the table. The chart, of course, shows similar information.

First, we set up our equation, using k to denote the discount rate and n the number of years.

$$\$10,000 = \$2,000 \begin{bmatrix} \text{PVUS} \\ k = ? \\ n = 10 \end{bmatrix}$$

Therefore,

$$\begin{bmatrix} \text{PVUS} \\ k = ? \\ n = 10 \end{bmatrix} = \frac{\$10,000}{\$2,000} = 5.000$$

Thus, an investment of $10,000 that yields $2,000 per year is proportional to an investment of $5 that yields $1 per year. Looking at Table A of the Appendix, we note that at $n = 10$, the closest number to the present value or discount factor of 5.000 is represented by an interest rate of 15 percent. Hence, 15 percent is very nearly the rate of return on this investment. (A closer estimate can be obtained by linear interpolation, resulting in 15.1 percent, but the slight gain in accuracy thus obtained is probably not worth the extra effort.)

(b) If management requires at least a 10 percent return on capital, then this investment would surely qualify since its rate of return is about 5 percent greater than the minimum acceptable rate.

Note: The concept of a minimum acceptable rate of return on an investment has been given the technical name of *cost of capital*. In this case, therefore, the cost of capital is said to be 10 percent. (A fuller discussion of cost of capital is presented in the next chapter.)

(c) At a rate of return (or cost of capital) of 10 percent, the present value factor in Appendix Table A for $n = 10$ is 6.145. Hence 6.145 × $2,000 = $12,290, which is the present value of the discounted cash inflow. The net present value of the investment, then, is $12,290 − $10,000 = $2,290; and the present value per dollar of investment, called the profitability index or benefit/cost ratio, is $12,290 ÷ $10,000 = 122.9 percent. The profitability index provides a convenient method for screening proposals and for ranking investments that require identical cash outlays. For investments of differing magnitude, however, ranking by a profitability index should be used with caution, as illustrated by Exhibit 18–3.

Exhibit 18–3

Profitability Index versus Net Present Value

Project	Funds Required	Profitability Index or Benefit/Cost Ratio	Net Present Value
A. Buy new machine	$ 100,000	127% or 1.27	$ 27,000
B. Expand advertising	100,000	122% or 1.22	22,000
C. Expand plant	1,500,000	119% or 1.19	285,000
D. Renovate existing plant	800,000	115% or 1.15	120,000
E. Replace truck fleet	900,000	102% or 1.02	18,000

Clearly, these projects are ranked correctly if the only criterion is the amount returned per dollar invested. However, if the firm is able to raise the capital to execute Project C, or even Project D, the overall benefit to the firm will be much greater even though the profitability index is less. Project C, for example, will yield more than 10 times as much as Project A, even though its profitability is 8 percent less.

Case II: Present Value of a Nonuniform Series, or Present Value of Single Payments: PVSP

When the income stream or cash flow varies substantially from year to year, it is necessary to obtain a separate discount factor for each year's cash flow. This requires the use of the table or chart in Table B of the Appendix. Here the figures in the body of the table reveal the amount that must be invested now, at compound interest, to yield a single payment of $1 in a specified future year. The table thus gives the present value of $1, and hence can be used to find the present value of any single payment. The corresponding chart, of course, conveys similar information. There are also "canned" computer programs available to calculate the discounted value of any payment.

Example.   The cash flow (i.e., after taxes and before depreciation) on an investment of $1,000 with an expected life of five years is, for each year, estimated to be: $400, $350, $300, $250, and $200. Capital recovery at the end of the five years is expected to be zero. (*a*) What is the rate of return on this investment? (*b*) If the firm's cost of capital is 12 percent, what percent would it lose (or gain) by undertaking this investment? What about a cost of capital of 25 percent? Discuss.

Solution.   (*a*)   In this case the cash flow is already given, in contrast to the previous example where it had to be calculated before the rate of return could be determined.

A convenient trial-and-error procedure for handling this type of problem (i.e., in which the cash flows are nonuniform) is shown in Exhibit 18–4. Thus the actual cash flow is also the present value at 0 percent

Exhibit 18–4

Effect of Discount Rate (*k*) on Present Value of Nonuniform Future Cash Inflows

Year	Cash Inflow	Trial No. 1 k = 0% Discount Factor	Trial No. 1 k = 0% Present Value	Trial No. 2 k = 10% Discount Factor*	Trial No. 2 k = 10% Present Value	Trial No. 3 k = 20% Discount Factor*	Trial No. 3 k = 20% Present Value
1	$400	1	$ 400	0.91	$ 364	0.83	$332
2	350	1	350	0.83	291	0.69	242
3	300	1	300	0.75	225	0.58	174
4	250	1	250	0.68	170	0.48	120
5	200	1	200	0.62	124	0.40	80
Total			$1,500		$1,174		$948
Ratio B/A†			1.5		1.17		0.948

* Discount factors rounded to the nearest hundredth.
† Where *A* = Present cost of the investment.
  B = Present value of returns from the investment.

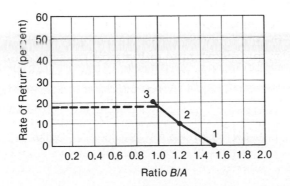

interest or, equivalently, at 0 percent interest the actual cash flow has the same present value no matter when it is received. In this case, the present value at 0 percent is $1,500, and the B/A ratio (the ratio of the present value of the investment to the present cost of the investment) therefore is 1.5. For convenience, we plot this point on the chart of Exhibit 18–4 and label the point with the number 1 to represent trial number 1.

Note that this point lies to the right of the heavy vertical line that represents the true rate of return at which B/A equals 1. This means that we have discounted the cash flow at too low a rate of interest and that a higher discount rate is necessary.

As a second trial, we try 10 percent, and we enter the appropriate discount factors from Appendix Table B, which give the present value of $1. These discount factors are then multiplied by the corresponding cash flow figures and the resulting products are totaled. The B/A ratio is now 1.17, and this point is plotted as the point 2 on the chart. Since point 2 is still to the right of the heavy vertical line, a third trial is necessary.

On trial 3, we try a 20 percent discount rate. The present value now results in a B/A ratio of 0.948, which we plot as point 3 on the chart. Connecting the points, we perform a graphic linear interpolation between points 2 and 3, resulting in a rate of return of about 18 percent as shown by the dashed line. Of course, the closer the two points are on each side of the heavy vertical line, the closer will be the estimate of the true rate of return as determined by the line that connects the two points. This is because we are performing a *linear* interpolation of a *curvilinear* function, since the discount factors in Appendix Table B are derived from the power function

$$PVSP = (1 + k)^{-n}$$

where k is the rate of interest per period and n is the number of periods. Note that a straight line between points 1 and 3 does *not* pass through point 2; rather, the straight-line segments 1–2 and 2–3 suggest the underlying curve.

In most instances, a close estimate can be obtained by the third trial. Sometimes, however, further trials may be necessary, and any number of additional columns may be used for this purpose.

Of course, the interpolation can be done directly, without the use of a graph. Thus, at the interest rates of 10 percent and 20 percent, we have:

	Interest Rate	*Present Value*	
$0.10 \begin{cases} x \begin{cases} 0.10 \\ 0.10 + x \\ \end{cases} \\ \quad\ 0.20 \end{cases}$		$\left. \begin{matrix} \$1,174 \\ \$1,000 \end{matrix} \right\}\$174 \\ \ \\ \$\ \ 948 \end{matrix} \right\}\$226$	

Setting up the proportion:

$$\frac{x}{0.10} = \frac{174}{226}$$

Cross-multiplying:

$$226x = 17.4$$

and hence

$$x = 0.077$$

Therefore, the interpolated rate of return is

$$0.10 + 0.077 = 17.7\%$$

We can get a closer approximation of the rate of return if we choose interest rates that are closer together, such as 15 percent and 20 percent. At an interest rate of 15 percent, the discounted cash flow amounts to $1,055. (The student should verify this figure, using the discount factors in Appendix Table B, rounded to two decimal places.) Then following the same procedure for interpolation, we have:

	Interest Rate	*Present Value*		
	0.15	$1,055		
0.05 { x { 0.15 + x	$1,000 } $55	} $107
	0.20	$ 948		

Setting up the proportion:

$$\frac{x}{0.05} = \frac{55}{107}$$

Cross-multiplying:

$$107x = 2.75$$

and hence

$$x = 0.026$$

Therefore, the rate of return is

$$0.15 + 0.026 = 17.6\%$$

The student should verify that if 16 percent and 18 percent are chosen and the discount factors are rounded to two decimal places, interpolation again gives an estimated rate of 17.6 percent.

(b) If the firm's cost of capital is 12 percent, it would earn nearly 6 percent over that amount by undertaking this investment. At a cost of capital of 25 percent, it would lose more than 7 percent by undertaking this investment. Note that the *B/A* ratio computed in the table becomes the profitability index by converting the ratio into a percentage (i.e., by moving the decimal point two places to the right).

Case III: Present Value of a Uniform Series and Present Value of a Single Payment: PVUS and PVSP

This case combines some of the features of the two previous cases and hence may be treated briefly.

Example. The cost of a new machine is $44,000, and an additional $6,000 in working capital will be required to finance the added inventory and accounts receivable that will result from the estimated increase in sales. The economic life of the machine is expected to be seven years, at which time the scrap or resale value is predicted to be about $9,000.

Assuming straight-line depreciation and a forecasted cash flow of $12,000 a year, calculate the rate of return on this investment, using both graphic and formula methods.

Solution. Note that the predicted cash flow is given, and hence need not be derived as was done in the first problem. We may begin, however, by listing the essential factors to be considered.

(1)	Cost of asset	$44,000
(2)	Working capital needed	6,000
(3)	Total investment	$50,000
(4)	Scrap or resale value	9,000
(5)	Economic life (years)	7
(6)	Allowed depreciation, (1) − (4)	35,000
(7)	Depreciation per year, (6) ÷ (5)	5,000
(8)	Capital recovery, (2) + (4)	15,000

Graphic Method. The solution is shown in Exhibit 18–5. On the first trial (at a discount rate of 0%), the *B/A* ratio of 1.98 is relatively high or far to the right of the heavy vertical line. As a second trial, let us try 15 percent. At this discount rate, which gives a discount factor of 4.16 (from Appendix Table A) for the uniform portion of the cash flow and 0.38 (from Table B) for the single-payment portion, the *B/A* ratio comes to 1.11. This is much closer to the true rate, as can be seen on the chart. Hence, only one more trial should be necessary for a graphic interpolation. Thus, after the third trial of 20 percent, we can estimate graphically a true rate of return of about 19 percent, as shown by the dashed line on the chart.

Exhibit 18–5

Calculation of Rate of Return (uniform and nonuniform payments)

Year	Cash Inflow	Trial No. 1 k = 0%		Trial No. 2 k = 10%		Trial No. 3 k = 20%	
		Discount Factor	*Present Value*	*Discount Factor*	*Present Value*	*Discount Factor*	*Present Value*
1	$12,000						
2	12,000						
3	12,000						
4	12,000	7	$84,000	4.87*	$58,440	3.61*	$43,220
5	12,000						
6	12,000						
7	12,000						
7	15,000‡	1	15,000	0.51†	7,650	0.28†	4,200
Total			$99,000		$66,090		$47,420
Ratio B/A§			1.98		1.32		0.95

* Discount factors from Appendix Table A rounded to the nearest hundredth.
† Discount factors from Appendix Table B rounded to the nearest hundredth.
‡ Capital recovery, including the forecasted resale or scrap value of the asset and the return of additional working capital needed to finance it.
§ Where A = Present cost of the investment.
    B = Present value of returns from the investment.

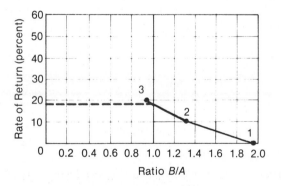

Formula Method. When the formula approach is used, we calculate the present value at two different rates of interest, just as in the graphic method above, and then interpolate algebraically. Thus suppose we decide to start at a trial interest rate of 15 percent.

$$\$12,000 \begin{bmatrix} PVUS \\ k = 15\% \\ n = 7 \end{bmatrix} + \$15,000 \begin{bmatrix} PVSP \\ k = 15\% \\ n = 7 \end{bmatrix} = ?$$

$$\$12,000(4.16) + \$15,000(0.38) = \$55,620$$

This means that in order to receive the given cash flow, the required investment at 15 percent interest would have to be $55,620 instead of $50,000. This interest rate, therefore, is too low. Hence we try a higher interest rate, say 20 percent.

$$\$12,000 \begin{bmatrix} \text{PVUS} \\ k = 20\% \\ n = 7 \end{bmatrix} + \$15,000 \begin{bmatrix} \text{PVSP} \\ k = 20\% \\ n = 7 \end{bmatrix} = ?$$

$$\$12,000(3.61) + \$15,000(0.28) = \$47,520$$

This means that in order to receive the given cash flow, the required investment at 20 percent interest would have to be $47,420 instead of $50,000. This discount rate, therefore, is too high. To find the correct discount rate, which is somewhere between 15 percent and 20 percent, we interpolate as follows.

$$
\begin{array}{ccc}
 & \textit{Interest} & \textit{Present} \\
 & \textit{Rate} & \textit{Value} \\
0.05\left\{ x\!\!\left\{ \begin{array}{c} 0.15 \\ 0.15 + x \\ 0.20 \end{array} \right. \right. & & \left. \begin{array}{c} \$55,620 \\ \$50,000 \\ \$47,520 \end{array} \right\}\!\!\$5,620 \right\}\!\!\$8,100
\end{array}
$$

Setting up the proportion:

$$\frac{x}{0.05} = \frac{\$5,620}{\$8,100}$$

Cross-multiplying:

$$\$8,100x = \$281$$

and hence

$$x = 0.035$$

Therefore, the rate of return is

$$0.15 + 0.035 = 18.5\%$$

Note, therefore, that the so-called formula method involves the same calculations as the graphic method, until the interpolation stage is reached. At that point, the graphic technique provides results that are quite adequate for decision purposes, while the algebraic interpolation provides only a slightly more accurate estimate. Either method may be used for most practical problems. The only advantage of the graphic technique is that it provides a good visual indication of the closeness of each approximation to the desired $B/A = 1$ ratio.

Some Analytical Aspects of Rate of Return

The approach used in previous sections to calculate the yield on an investment in assets is called the discounted cash flow (DCF) method. Despite various short-cut devices that have been developed to give rough approximations of the rate of return, the discounted cash flow method is the only one that produces the correct measure. In order to see why this is so, it is first necessary to review and clarify some technical points stated at the beginning of this chapter.

The Common Concept of Rate of Return

Let us recall that most people think of the rate of return on investment as simply the ratio of annual receipts to original cost. Actually, however, this definition is correct for only a special kind of investment, namely a permanent, nondepreciating, nonappreciating asset producing a periodically uniform income stream. To the extent that the liquidating value or resale value of the asset is, at the time of liquidation or sale, greater or less than the original outlay, the true rate of return will be greater or less than the rate as defined above. Since at the time the investment is made one rarely is able to predict its precise liquidating or resale value, it follows that in the typical case the *true rate of return on an investment to a particular owner cannot be known until the ownership has terminated*. Hence, prior to actual termination of ownership, it is necessary to accept the best estimated rate of return as a reasonable measure of the investment's profitability.

The Technically Correct Concept

What, then, is the technically correct meaning of rate of return? As we have seen, a precise definition is:

Definition: The *rate of return* on an investment is the interest rate that equates the present value of cash receipts expected to flow from the investment over its lifetime with the present value of all expenditures relating to the investment.

To minimize unnecessarily complicating aspects without doing violence to either the concept or the conclusions, it is usual to assume that the investment involves only an initial outlay of funds. Where additional outlays are expected to be required in the future, however, these are simply discounted down to the present and added to the original outlay to determine the total present value of outlays. Thus, the total cost of the investment may be expressed as:

$$I_C = C_0 + \frac{C_1}{1 + k} + \frac{C_2}{(1 + k)^2} + \cdots + \frac{C_n}{(1 + k)^n} \qquad (1)$$

where C_0 is the initial cost outlay, $C_1, C_2, \ldots, C_n$ are a series of future outlays, I_C is the sum of all outlays properly discounted to represent the present value of the investment, and k is the interest or discount rate.

The project will also produce a flow of cash earnings over its life that must be similarly discounted down to the present. Thus:

$$I_R = \frac{R_1}{1 + k} + \frac{R_2}{(1 + k)^2} + \cdots + \frac{R_n}{(1 + k)^n} + \frac{S}{(1 + k)^n} \qquad (2)$$

where $R_1, R_2, \ldots, R_n$ are a series of cash revenues received at the end of each of the respective periods over the life of the investment, S is the liquidating or salvage value at the end of n periods, and I_R is the present value of this stream of future receipts.

Equation (1) expresses the present value of the investment in terms of the outlays connected with it; Equation (2) expresses the investment's value in terms of the cash revenues that will flow from it. If we select that rate of discount k in such a way that I_C and I_R are equal, then k is defined as the rate of return on the investment. Also, by setting Equation (1) equal to Equation (2), we arrive at Equation (3), which is the most common expression of the internal rate of return (IRR) approach to capital budgeting:

$$C_0 = \frac{R_1 - C_1}{1 + k} + \frac{R_2 - C_2}{(1 + k)^2} + \cdots + \frac{R_n - C_n}{(1 + k)^n} + \frac{S}{(1 + k)^n} \qquad (3)$$

Finally, if we let k_0 equal the firm's cost of capital and use it to discount the cash flows, we then have

$$NPV = -C_0 + \left[\frac{R_1 - C_1}{1 + k_0} + \frac{R_2 - C_2}{(1 + k_0)^2} + \cdots + \frac{R_n - C_n}{(1 + k_0)^n} + \frac{S}{(1 + k_0)^n} \right] \qquad (4)$$

where NPV is the net present value of an investment and is used in the NPV capital budgeting approach. Since these two approaches have fundamental differences, they will be discussed shortly in more detail.

Rate of Return, Economic Theory, and Decision Making

The rate of return on investment, technically defined by Equations (1) and (2), is a well-conceived theoretical concept that goes by various aliases in the economic literature. Among the more important of these are *marginal efficiency of capital,* a phrase made famous by John Maynard Keynes, and the closely related concept of *internal rate of return* used by Kenneth E. Boulding and others. But while it is a concept well founded in theory, it presents many practical problems to anyone desiring to apply it to actual cases, for we must realize that the solution for k depends on both the amounts and the timing of the cash flows, both of which are estimates. Hence, the rate of return can itself be only an estimate, so that insistence on a precise solution for k would be unrealistic. It is worth repeating at this point that the *rate of return on an investment can never be stated with precision until the ownership of the investment has been terminated.*

What guides are needed for making correct capital budgeting decisions? Actually, two measures are required: one is the internal rate of return and the other is the firm's cost of capital on the project. Given these two choice indicators, economic theory states that profit maximization requires adherence to the following fundamental principle of marginal analysis:

> *Fundamental Principle:* All projects whose estimated rates of return exceed the cost of capital are undertaken to the point where the rate of return of the marginal product just equals the cost of capital.

As an alternative and more practical approach to choosing projects, k may be set equal to the firm's cost of capital, and the sum of the cash flows from alternative projects can be discounted by the value of k. Projects may then be ranked according to their present value per dollar of investment. As a further step, greater realism can be incorporated in the ranking process by "weighting" each project with an appropriate risk factor that reflects the probability of realizing the estimated return.

Ranking of Capital Investments

Capital budgeting theory holds that the firm should raise the necessary capital for all nonconflicting proposals that promise to increase the value of the stockholders' shares. In the real world, however, there are many reasons why the firm cannot or should not raise enough capital for all of the investment opportunities that it faces. Hence the decision maker may be confronted not only with conflicting or mutually exclusive proposals (e.g., buy new machines or renovate machine shop) but also with the necessity for capital rationing. In either case, the decision maker's problem is to rank investment proposals in such a way that the available capital may be fully invested in the most profitable combination.

The critical factor in ranking investments is the measurement of the expected return. In the preceding sections of this chapter, we defined two methods of measuring the return: the net present value (NPV) method and the internal rate of return (IRR) method. The relationship between the two methods is illustrated in Exhibit 18–6.

Exhibit 18–6 depicts evaluation of an investment proposal that will cost $23,000 and provide net cash inflows of $6,000 per year for 10 years.

Exhibit 18–6

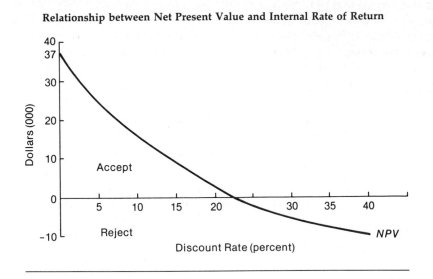

Relationship between Net Present Value and Internal Rate of Return

The *NPV* line traces the net present value of the investment at various discount rates. If we ignore the time value of money, the project will return $60,000 − $23,000 = $37,000. Ignoring the time value of money is equivalent to a discount rate of zero, so we can establish the *Y*-intercept at $37,000. The *NPV* line curves downward and to the right, indicating that *NPV* decreases as the discount rate increases. The internal rate of return (IRR) is measured at the *X*-intercept where the *NPV* is zero. In Exhibit 18–6 the internal rate of return is 22.7 percent. The zone of acceptance is the area under the *NPV* line and above the *X*-axis, where the cost of capital (discount rate) is less than or equal to the internal rate of return and the corresponding *NPV* is equal to or greater than zero. The zone of rejection is the area under the *NPV* line and below the *X*-axis, where the cost of capital (discount rate) is greater than the internal rate of return and the corresponding *NPV* is therefore negative.

Conflict between NPV and IRR Methods

Despite the harmony between net present value and internal rate of return illustrated in Exhibit 18–6, there can be a conflict between conclusions reached via the net present value method and those reached via the internal rate of return method, because the implicit assumptions differ with respect to reinvestment of cash flows. The net present value method assumes that cash inflows are reinvested at a rate equal to the cost of capital (or whatever discount rate is chosen as the cutoff criterion), and all projects are evaluated against the same assumed rate of reinvestment. In contrast, the internal rate of return method assumes that cash inflows are reinvested at the internal rate of return for the project, which means that different projects have different assumed rates of reinvestment. This can lead to conflicting conclusions with respect to the ranking of investments, as illustrated by Exhibit 18–7.

Exhibit 18–7

Cash Flows for Two Mutually Exclusive Proposals

Year	Cash Flow	
	Project A	Project B
0	$(22,856)	$(22,856)
1	8,500	0
2	8,500	5,000
3	8,500	10,000
4	8,500	15,000
5	8,500	19,516
Total cash inflow	$ 42,500	$ 49,516
Less initial investment	22,856	22,856
Net cash inflow	$ 19,644	$ 26,660
Net present value*	$ 5,636	$ 5,783
Internal rate of return	25.0%	22.0%

* At a discount rate of 15 percent.

In Exhibit 18–7 we have two mutually exclusive proposals to be ranked in order of desirability. Both proposals have the same initial cost, but the magnitude and timing of the cash flows are quite different. Since they are mutually exclusive, only one can be selected.

If we evaluate by the net present value method, all cash flows in both projects are discounted by the same 15 percent cost of capital, and the implicit assumption is that all cash flows can be reinvested to yield 15 percent. This seems to be an even-handed basis for judgment, and Project B clearly is superior since it has a larger net present value.

If we evaluate by the internal rate of return method, we see that Project A has an internal rate of return of 25 percent, compared with only 22 percent for Project B. But this is because we have made the implicit assumption that the cash flows from Project A will be reinvested at 25 percent, while the cash flows from Project B can be reinvested at only 22 percent. There seems to be no logical reason why the $8,500 received from Project A in year 2 would bring 25 percent in another investment while the $5,000 received from Project B in the same year would yield only 22 percent. We must conclude, then, that ranking by rate of return is erroneous in this case.

Which method should be used? The answer depends upon the appropriate rate of reinvestment for the cash flows. The net present value method is generally regarded as superior because all projects under consideration are rated against the same assumed rate of reinvestment, which should be the cost of capital.

Reinvestment and the Rate of Return

The above discussion clearly shows the importance of the assumption one makes about the reinvestment of cash flows as they become available over future time periods. Using another example, let us look more closely at this assumption.

A bridge is to be constructed across a river, and the choice of materials (to simplify the illustration) is between steel and wood. A steel bridge would last, say, 40 years; a wooden bridge would have to be replaced in, let us say, 8 years. The advantage of the steel bridge is its lower annual maintenance costs. Its major disadvantage is the much larger investment required. Assuming that there is no preference for either type of bridge in terms of the quality of service, the investment decision will hinge on a comparison of annual costs (comprising maintenance costs and the investment's capital recovery cost), and the alternative involving the least annual cost would be the proper economic choice. The fact that the steel bridge would be much more durable does not alter the decision, for implicit in the analysis is the assumption that the wooden bridge can be replaced after each eight-year period at *exactly the same* cost, maintenance disbursements, durability, and salvage value (if any), and that the same will be true for the steel bridge when the time comes to replace it. Thus, the annual costs computed for the original bridge are implicitly assumed to repeat indefinitely into the future.

This is, in short, an "other things being equal" approach. When it is not possible to plan otherwise, or to predict whether the "other things" will change in one direction rather than another, it is the only meaningful approach to use. In terms of the above example, the choice between the less durable wooden bridge and the longer-lived steel bridge is determined by what we consider today to be the correct economic decision. Our hope is that it will prove to be the right decision in the long run; and whether or not we are right will depend on economic and technological conditions eight years from now. Any factors that would make the replacement economics more favorable eight years from today (lower prices and wage costs, more efficient construction methods, more durable materials that cost no more than the wood does today) would be added reasons for selecting the wooden bridge today. Inflationary factors would make the choice of the steel bridge more attractive.

Thus, the reinvestment problem, as stated earlier, is not a new one, and is only one aspect of all investment decisions that must be made in a continuing and perpetuating society or firm. The sophisticated decision maker takes all factors into consideration, whenever possible, and acts accordingly. The more dynamic the industry and the more uncertain the external forces that act upon the firm, the greater are the number and importance of the factors likely to cause discrepancies between anticipated and actual results. In such cases, investment decisions are likely to be biased in favor of very short payouts. In more stable and predictable industries (such as public utilities), long payout investments are much more common.

Investment Selection and Risk

Up to this point, we have assumed decision making under certainty in the investment selection decision. Of course, this is quite unrealistic, and we need to broaden our analytical framework to include the concepts of risk and uncertainty. With most investments, the annual cash flow estimate for a project represents (or at least should represent) the expected value of a distribution of actual cash flows, each weighted by an appropriate probability estimate. In fact, some cash flow estimates may be the product of joint probability distributions for both cash inflows and outflows, and little imagination is required to appreciate the complex process of arriving at a single best estimate of an annual cash flow. Moreover, the project's life may also be uncertain; yet, even when all these factors are taken into consideration and adjusted for their relative risks, there still remains the task of integrating the entire process into the discounting formula.

The Certainty-Equivalent Method

There are a number of techniques available to express IRR or NPV on a risk-adjusted basis. However, one method—the certainty-equivalent approach—is an extension of utility theory that we first discussed in Chapter 2, and hence it is a logical choice for elaboration here.[2]

---

[2] It is also considered a theoretically sound approach; see A. A. Robicheck and S. C. Myers, "Conceptual Problems in the Use of Risk-Adjusted Discount Rates," *Journal of Finance*, December 1966, pp. 727–30.

The certainty-equivalent approach begins by assessing the risk characteristics of each project's annual cash flows, as explained above; then it
is necessary to reduce the cash flows to certainty-equivalent amounts.
These reductions are derived from the decision maker's willingness to
trade off risk and return as the diagram in Exhibit 18–8 illustrates. On

Exhibit 18–8

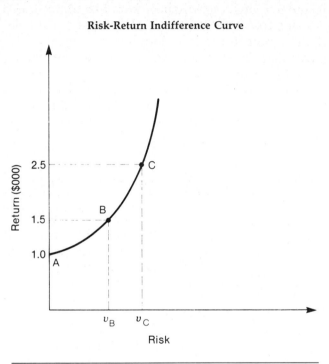

Exhibit 18–8, the decision maker is assumed to have three investment
choices: A, B, and C. A has zero risk and offers a return of $1,000; B and
C are risky but offer returns of $1,500 and $2,500, respectively, while
their degree of risk is measured by their coefficients of variation v_B and
v_C, respectively.[3] The function connecting the three points is presumed
to be the decision maker's risk-return indifference curve. Hence, project
A is viewed as no better (or worse) than projects B and C; in short, they
are risk-adjusted, equivalent-yield investments, with the added returns
attached to B and C being exactly offset by their greater riskiness.

---

[3] The coefficient of variation is defined and explained in Chapter 3; a more detailed
discussion of risk and return is also presented there.

From the exhibit, certainty-equivalent weighting factors (α-values) are determined for B and C in the following manner:

$$\alpha_B = \frac{\$1,000}{\$1,500} = 0.667$$

$$\alpha_C = \frac{\$1,000}{\$2,500} = 0.400$$

These α-values are then used in the discounting formula that yields r^*, the certainty-equivalent internal rate of return for the ith investment:

$$C_0 = \sum_{t=1}^{n} \frac{\alpha_i(R_t - C_t)}{(1 + r^*)^t}$$

Or α-values can be used to determine the certainty-equivalent net present value (NPV'):

$$NPV' = \sum_{t=1}^{n} \frac{\alpha_i(R_t - C_t)}{(1 + r')^t} - C_0$$

where r' is the rate of return on a risk-free investment (e.g., the rate on U.S. Treasury securities). This last expression is more often used in the literature, but in either case the decision rule for accepting or rejecting investments remains: (1) accept all projects for which $r^* > r'$; or (2) accept all projects with positive NPV'.

The dollar amounts used in the above example were selected arbitrarily and they should not be viewed as having unique importance. However, the derived α-values are unique in the sense that they are applicable to all projects having risk characteristics of v_A or v_B. In other words, the decision maker should be consistent in treating investment risk by matching α-values with v-values or whatever statistic is used to measure risk. However, as a practical matter, rather than having a wide range of α-values, it might be more convenient and more easily understood if these values are expressed for broad categories of risk such as high risk (α_1), medium-high risk (α_2), and so forth. This procedure would do no theoretical injustice and would make the process more manageable.

Other Methods for Handling Risk

In addition to the certainty-equivalent approach, two other methods are frequently used to incorporate risk analysis into the investment selection decision: (1) the risk-adjusted discount rate approach, and (2) a probability distribution approach. With the risk-adjusted discount rate approach, a decision maker must first specify the degree of risk in a particular investment decision. If the risk is greater than the risk of an "average" investment, a risk premium is added onto the "average" discount rate used to calculate net present values. (The average discount rate is generally viewed as the firm's weighted average cost of capital, a term that will be developed in the next chapter.) Investments with less than the average risk are then discounted at lower rates.

This method, however, has at least two major limitations. First, the determination of the risk-adjustment factor has no greater objectivity than the determination of α-values in the certainty-equivalent approach. Second, by making a single adjustment to the discount rate, which is then applied to each annual cash flow, no allowance is made for period-to-period risk adjustments as is the case with the certainty-equivalent approach.

The probability distribution approach calculates a net present value amount for each possible outcome related to an investment. For example, suppose a project that costs $2,000 will produce a certain cash flow of $1,000 per year; however, the number of years this flow will continue is not known with certainty but can be expressed in probabilistic terms. So let us assume that three periods are possible with the following probabilities: (1) two years, $p = .2$; (2) three years, $p = .5$; and (3) four years, $p = .3$. Assuming a discount rate of 10 percent, we have the following expected net present value:

$$
\begin{aligned}
(1,000 \times 1.736 - 2,000) \times .2 &= -52.8 \\
(1,000 \times 2.487 - 2,000) \times .5 &= +243.5 \\
(1,000 \times 3.170 - 2,000) \times .3 &= +351.0 \\
\hline
E(NPV) &= 541.7
\end{aligned}
$$

In addition to the $E(NPV)$, a standard deviation can be calculated to determine the degree of variation in net present value, which then is used to assess the project's risk. Of course, the decision maker must still determine a risk-return trade-off function before a decision can be reached, and to this extent the probability distribution approach is no different from the certainty-equivalent and risk-adjusted-discount rate approaches.

After examining these other two methods of handling risk, it is clear that each has its advantages and disadvantages. In the final analysis, the choice of a particular method should be made on the basis of operational simplicity and ease of understanding, rather than on the basis of strong theoretical arguments.

Short-Cut Methods and Business Practices

Both the internal rate of return formulation and the cost of capital method are used in business to solve the problem of selecting economically worthwhile investments. However, there are also short-cut devices and rule-of-thumb techniques that have been developed to facilitate capital-budgeting decision making. None of these, it should be emphasized, yields the correct answer that is obtained by the discounted cash flow procedure; at best they provide only rough approximations. One of the more commonly used of these techniques is described briefly below.

Payout, Payoff, or Payback Period

Business executives have frequently used a short-cut method of allocating capital funds by estimating the length of time required for the cash earnings on a given investment to return the original cost to the owner. This measure is referred to in various parts of the literature as the payout, payoff, or payback period. It is used as both a before- and after-tax measure (the latter being the more important), and its expression in terms of cash earnings is a recognition of the fact that depreciation charges should be included in the earnings figures, that is, earnings are measured before depreciation.

By way of simplifying the use of this tool, it is typical to estimate a uniform flow of annual earnings over the life of the project. Hence, if the original investment is represented by I and the uniform (average) annual cash flow is represented by E, the payout period P is expressed as

$$P = \frac{I}{E}$$

Under the conditions stated above, it is clear that, given the life of the project, profitability will vary inversely with the payout period and that, given the payout period, profitability will vary directly with the life of the project. It is, therefore, easy enough to understand the insistence of management on short-payout investments. However, the tool is often too blunt to be used in selecting among alternative projects that differ as to cost, payout, and productive life. In such cases, a more precise instrument is needed. It is worth pointing out, at the risk of being obvious, that a short payout is not necessarily coincident with high profitability. Thus, if the productive life of the project is even shorter than the payout period, the return on the investment will be negative; and if the project life and payout period are equal, the investment return is zero. In either case, an economic loss is incurred.

The relationship between the before-tax and after-tax payout depends on both the tax rate and the productive life of the project.[4] Representing

---

[4] Discussion of an after-tax payout seems meaningful only for projects that are actually profitable, that is, their productive life is greater than the before-tax payout period.

depreciation by D and assuming a 50 percent tax rate, the after-tax payout becomes

$$P' = \frac{2I}{E + D}$$

As a limiting value, for projects of perpetual life (or, for practical purposes, extremely long-lived projects such as hydroelectric plants and dams), the depreciation charge approaches zero and the after-tax payout approaches twice the value of the before-tax payout. Hence, with a 50 percent tax rate, the after-tax payout will, for all depreciable investments, lie somewhere between the before-tax payout at the lower limit and twice that value at the upper limit.

An argument is sometimes offered that the payback method deals with project risk, albeit in an indirect manner. This argument is based on the notion that for most projects risk is perceived as increasing over time, which means that cash flows received in more distant years are thought to be riskier than those received in current years. Thus, ranking projects on the basis of their payback periods also ranks them according to their relative riskiness. However, this is not a direct measurement of risk since it fails to consider the dispersion or variation of cash flows for any given year. In other words, a project may pay for itself in a few years *if* the estimated cash flows for those years are actually received; but if there is a high probability that the cash flows will not be received, then the project must still be considered risky despite its short payout period.

Summary

Capital budgeting is concerned with the evaluation of investment proposals to determine whether or not they should be undertaken. In order to make these decisions, we must have information about: (1) the cash flows over time of an investment, (2) the cost of capital to the firm, and (3) the degree of risk in an investment. Two methods, both involving discounted cash flows, are frequently used in practice: (1) the internal rate of return approach, and (2) the net present value approach. Both were discussed in this chapter, but the internal rate of return as an analytical tool was highlighted. Both techniques require that future economic cost, revenue, and taxes be forecasted, and that these data be arranged in a year-by-year timetable of new cash flows extending into the future for the life of the project. The timetable thus reveals for each year the net after-tax effect on the company's cash receipts and payments. No distinction is made between capitalized outlays and current operating transactions except to the extent that these affect corporate income taxes. Finally, the net cash flows are discounted, yielding a measure of rate of return or of present value, which then becomes the choice indicator or criterion for comparing—and accepting or rejecting—particular investment proposals.

In addition to the mechanics of discounted cash flow analysis, we considered the problems of ranking investments by each method. In this respect, the primary consideration is the assumption one makes about the reinvestment of cash flows as they become available over time. We concluded that net present value is the more theoretically sound approach.

Risk in capital budgeting arises from the fact that all calculations are based on estimates of future events. Variability of cash flows, both income and outgo, is to be expected, and the actual results may be quite different from the planning estimate. Risk may be analyzed by means of a number of approaches, and we highlighted the certainty-equivalent method of expressing cash flows. This approach has a firm theoretical foundation in utility theory and is relatively easy to incorporate into the discounting formula.

Finally, we discussed a common business practice in investment analysis, the payback method.

Problems

    1. *a.* Carefully explain the concept of cash flow, contrasting it with net income.

       b. Determine the annual cash flows for the following investment that is expected to have a four-year life:

         (1) Investment cost = $4,000, fully depreciable for tax purposes (straight-line method, no salvage value, and a tax rate of 40 percent).

         (2) Annual net income after depreciation but before taxes = $1,500.

       c. If the required rate of return on an investment of this type is 20 percent, should the investment be made? Support your answer.

    2. Which of the following, if any, should be added to, or deducted from, the cost of a new machine in deciding whether to purchase it? (Disregard all tax considerations.)

    a. A fee paid to a consultant for advice on whether the machine should be acquired or not.

    b. The cash salvage value of the old machine.

    c. The original cost of the old machine and its present book value.

    d. Cost of removing the old machine.

    e. Installation costs on the new machine.

f. The cost of training operators for the new machine.

g. An additional investment in accounts receivable and inventory that will be needed.

3. Under what conditions might a firm be better off to select a project with a rapid payback than one with the highest rate of return?

4. Explain the fundamental difference between the net present value (NPV) and internal rate of return (IRR) methods of investment analysis.

5. Three investments—A, B, and C—are compared in the accompanying diagram. Answer the following questions related to the diagram.

a. Is one investment preferable to the other two at all discount rates? Explain.

b. Provide a brief interpretation of points (1), (2), (3), and (4).

c. Describe the cash flow pattern for investment C.

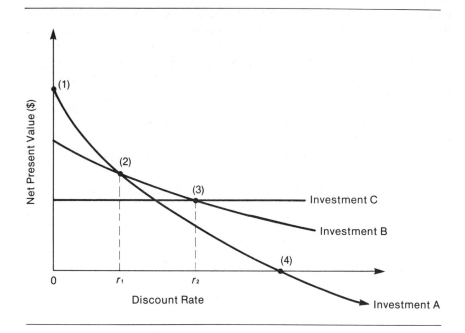

6. The formula for finding the present value *P* of an amount *F* to be received in the future, assuming an interest rate of *i* percent, is:

$$P = F\left[\frac{1}{(1 + i)^n}\right]$$

a. How, then, would you determine the future value *F* of an amount *P* invested at *i* percent for *n* years?

b. A wealthy uncle intends to give you a gift upon graduation. You have a choice of a new car for $10,000, or an investment trust of the same amount invested in securities that will earn 8 percent interest compounded annually for the next 40 years. Since you are now 22 years old and plan to retire at age 62, the trust would fit rather nicely into your plans. Now, how much will you have in the trust in 40 years? Finally, if you expect inflation to average 6 percent a year over the next 40 years, what will be the purchasing power equivalent of the fund's terminal value?

7. Concrete Products Company, a large manufacturer of concrete building materials, needed $240,000 worth of aggregates (at then current prices) over a period of two years. It learned that the Acme Sand and Gravel Company owned deposits that were more than enough for its needs. However, Acme was a small company without enough equipment to produce at the required rate and without enough capital to expand. In order to secure the necessary supply of raw materials, Concrete Products agreed to supply Acme with the necessary capital by paying for one year's supply in advance, discounted at 12 percent. Acme in return agreed to provide a constant daily flow of sand and gravel into the Concrete Products plant, with monthly billings against the prepaid amount. The contract was signed and Concrete Products paid Acme $107,160.

At the end of the first year Concrete Products, wanting to insure itself against a price increase, again proposed to make advance payment of $107,160 for the second year's supply, but Acme's new controller objected. "The 12 percent discount rate is reasonable," he told Acme's president, "but you were cheated on the payment for the first year and you shouldn't let yourself be cheated again. The correct amount is $112,550."

Explain the controller's objection.

8. The XYZ Company is considering two mutually exclusive projects, each requiring an initial investment of $15,000 and each lasting for five years. The estimated cash inflows are given in the accompanying table.

			Period		
Project	1	2	3	4	5
A	3,000	3,000	3,000	5,000	5,000
B	—	5,000	12,000	8,000	5,000

The firm's cost of capital is 20 percent. Find
a. The net present value.
b. The rate of return.
c. The profitability index for each proposal.

9.   The Jason Company is considering replacing one of its old machines with a new and more efficient one. The old machine is still in good working condition and will last physically for at least 20 more years.

The new machine, delivered and installed, costs $10,000 and is expected to save $1,900 annually in direct costs as compared with the old machine. The new machine has a 10-year economic life, with zero salvage value.

The Jason Company can borrow money at 10 percent, but it does not expect to negotiate a loan for this particular purpose. The management of the company requires a return of at least 20 percent before taxes on this type of investment. Disregard all taxes for the time being.

a.   Assuming that the old machine has a zero book value and a zero salvage value, should the company buy the new machine?

b.   Suppose the present machine, now four years old, originally cost $8,000 and has been depreciating at a straight-line rate of 10 percent. Its present book value, therefore, is equal to original cost less accumulated depreciation, or $8,000 − $3,200 = $4,800. Its salvage value, however, is zero. Should the Jason Company buy the new machine?

c.   Suppose, in part (b), that the salvage value is currently $3,000 but will decline to zero if the machine is held for another 10 years. Should the company purchase the new machine?

d.   What if the annual savings were cut in half and the economic life were doubled? In other words, if the annual savings were $950 for 20 years, should the company purchase the new machine? (Assume everything else is the same as in part (a) above.)

e.   Assume now that the Jason Company must pay a 50 percent tax, that it uses straight-line depreciation, and that the company's cost of capital is 10 percent after taxes. If the facts are the same as for part (a), should the company buy the new machine?

10.   The London Shipping Company is considering investing $28,000 in new conveying equipment. It is estimated that the new equipment will result in direct labor savings of $11,000 annually over the 10-year life of the equipment, and that an additional $10,000 in working capital will be required, which will be entirely recovered at the end of the 10-year period. If the company requires a 20 percent minimum return on investment, should it go ahead with this project? (Disregard tax and depreciation considerations and assume a zero salvage value.)

11.   The certainty-equivalent approach of dealing with risk in the investment selection process is sometimes criticized as being too subjective. Do you believe this criticism is justified? Can you think of some objective way of dealing with risk in investment situations?

12.   Two mutually exclusive investments, A and B, are available to decision maker Jones. However, because A has a three-year life while B's is five years, Jones feels she cannot make a decision. Discuss, bringing the topic of reinvestment into your answer.

Case Problem: Hamakua Plantation

13.   Hamakua Plantation is an agricultural corporation formed to pursue diversified agriculture on former sugar cane lands on the Big Island of Hawaii. One of its holdings is a ten-acre lot planted in papayas. Because of numerous problems with plant disease, the high cost of labor required for harvesting and packing the fruit, and difficulties with transportation of the fruit to market, the firm has been clearing no more than $100 per acre per year on papayas. This has caused management to seek an alternate use for the land. One suggestion has been made to plant the ten acres in macadamia nuts, for which there is a growing market, with supply unable to keep up with demand. However, it takes six years from planting to the first crop, and 11 years to reach full production.

Working with experts from the College of Tropical Agriculture at the University of Hawaii, Hamakua's controller has assembled the following estimate of costs and revenues over the first 11 years after planting:[5]

Initial investment:

Equipment and buildings	$7,000
Establishing the planting (10 acres)	1,250
	$8,250

Annual costs may be classified as:
1.   Orchard maintenance, which includes weed control, fertilizing, pruning, inarching, rat control, and raking and burning leaves.
2.   Harvesting, which includes gathering, husking, drying, and sorting the nuts.
3.   Depreciation of buildings and equipment
4.   Overhead, which includes land rent, taxes, indirect labor, and interest on investment.

---

[5] Based on J. T. Keeler and E. T. Fukunaga, *The Economic and Horticultural Aspects of Growing Macadamia Nuts Commercially in Hawaii.* (Agricultural Bulletin No. 27, Hawaii Agricultural Experiment Station, University of Hawaii, June, 1968).

Annual costs per acre are projected as follows:

Year	Maint-enance	Harvest-ing	Deprec-iation	Over-head	Total Cost/Acre	Sales	Profit/(Loss)/Acre
1	$269	$ –0–	$ 80	$146	$ 495	$ –0–	$ (495)
2	195	–0–	80	146	421	–0–	(421)
3	266	–0–	80	146	492	–0–	(492)
4	244	–0–	80	146	470	–0–	(470)
5	412	–0–	80	146	638	–0–	(638)
6	338	419	110	159	1,026	669	(357)
7	368	673	110	159	1,310	1,560	250
8	389	900	110	159	1,558	2,234	676
9	409	1,019	110	159	1,697	2,674	977
10	429	1,127	110	159	1,825	3,120	1,295
11	429	1,151	110	159	1,849	3,343	1,494

The company's cost of capital is 15 percent, and because of other income, it is in the 46 percent tax bracket.

Question:

Prepare a suitable analysis to determine whether the company should continue growing papayas on the ten acres in question, or whether the firm would be better off in the long run to switch to macadamia nuts.

References

Bierman, Harold, Jr., and Seymour Smidt. *The Capital Budgeting Decision.* 4th ed. New York: Macmillan, 1975.

Clark, John J.; T. J. Hindelang; and R. D. Pritchard. *Capital Budgeting: Planning and Control of Capital Expenditures.* Englewood Cliffs, N.J.: Prentice-Hall, 1979.

Durand, David. "Comprehensiveness in Capital Budgeting." *Financial Management,* Winter 1981, pp. 7–13.

Hertz, David B. "Investment Policies That Pay Off." *Harvard Business Review,* January–February 1968, pp. 96–108.

————. "Risk Analysis in Capital Investment." *Harvard Business Review,* January–February 1964, pp. 95–106.

Jean, William H. *Capital Budgeting: The Economic Evaluation of Investment Projects.* Scranton, Pa.: International Textbook, 1969.

Lewellen, Wilbur G.; Howard P. Lanser; and John J. McConnell. "Payback Substitutes for Discounted Cash Flow." *Financial Management,* Summer 1963, pp. 17–23.

Lewellen, Wilbur G., and Michael S. Long. "Simulation Versus Single-Value Estimates in Capital Expenditure Analysis." *Decision Sciences,* October 1972, pp. 19–33.

Man, James C. T. "Survey of Capital Budgeting Theory and Practice." *Journal of Finance,* May 1970, pp. 349–60.

_____. "The Internal Rate of Return as a Ranking Criterion." *Engineering Economist,* Winter 1966, pp. 1–3.

Rappaport, Alfred, and Robert A. Taggart, Jr. "Evaluation of Capital Expenditure Proposals Under Inflation." *Financial Management,* Spring 1982, pp. 5–13.

Schall, Lawrence D.; Gary L. Sundem; and William R. Geijsbeek, Jr. "Survey and Analysis of Capital Budgeting Methods." *Journal of Finance,* March 1978, pp. 281–87.

Solomon, Ezra. "Alternative Rate of Return Concepts and Their Implications for Utility Regulation." *Bell Journal of Economics and Management Science,* Spring 1970, pp. 65–81.

Weston, J. Fred, and Eugene F. Brigham. *Essentials of Managerial Finance.* 6th ed. Hinsdale, Ill.: Dryden Press, 1982.

19

Capital Budgeting: Financial Policy

Measuring a project's rate of return, or establishing its superiority or inferiority relative to other projects by whatever measure one might choose, is only one important step in constructing the final capital budget. Thus, having determined that the rate of return on a project is, say, 15 percent, do we accept it or not? It would be manifestly imprudent to rely on some intuitive figure that "sounds good" or "seems attractive," and so it becomes necessary to establish a standard that will divide projects into two broad groups: those that are acceptable and those that are not. As we shall see, this standard is the firm's cost of capital. Moreover, the cost of capital, along with rates of return on available projects, determines the optimal amount of total investment that should be undertaken during the planning period. Let us use demand and supply concepts to illustrate this investment selection process.

If the various proposed projects were arrayed in descending order according to their estimated rates of return, together with the dollar amounts of capital required by the respective projects, we would have constructed what constitutes the firm's *demand* schedule for capital. Overlaying this with a capital *supply* schedule, the intersection point would indicate, theoretically at the least, the desired volume of investment to be undertaken. All projects promising a return in excess of the intersection rate would be accepted; those with estimated rates less than the critical rate would be rejected.

Exhibit 19–1

Demand and Supply Approach to the Capital Budgeting Process

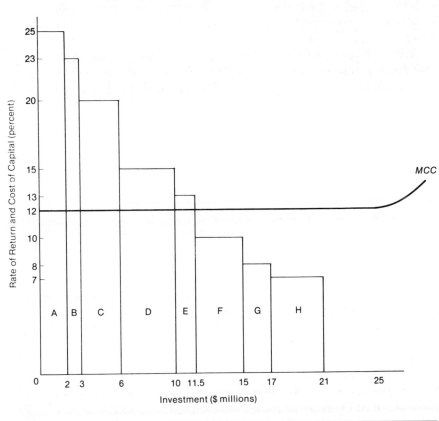

Investment ($ millions)

The diagram in Exhibit 19–1 illustrates a demand-supply equilibrium. The firm is presumed to have eight different investments—designated A through H—available for selection during the current planning period. Project A has the highest rate of return, 25 percent, and requires an outlay of $2 million; project H has the lowest return, 7 percent, and involves an outlay of $4 million; rates of return on the other projects are between these two extremes. The MCC line in Exhibit 19–1 is the firm's capital supply schedule. It shows the marginal cost of capital the firm must pay with respect to the amount of capital it plans to raise either internally or externally. The curve in the diagram shows that MCC is level up to $25 million. After that, however, the MCC line begins to increase, perhaps reflecting market concerns over the amount of capital the firm can invest profitably during a given period of time without substantially altering the risk exposure of owners or creditors. Or a rising *MCC* line might also indicate that as the firm seeks larger amounts of capital, it eventually must rely upon investors who are less familiar with the financial opportunities of the firm than its regular creditors and shareholders and therefore require higher rates of return as a condition for investing in the firm.

Finally, the diagram shows that projects A, B, C, D, and E should be undertaken, since their rates of return exceed the marginal cost of capital. By similar reasoning, projects F, G, and H should be rejected. Following this plan, the total investment for the upcoming period would be $11.5 million.

Cost of Capital

As we have seen, a firm's cost of capital is an essential criterion for investment decision making. Accordingly, the theory and measurement of cost of capital are of fundamental importance in business finance.

At the outset, we shall define cost of capital or, more specifically, marginal cost of capital as the cost of acquiring the next increment of capital to be utilized by the firm. How do we measure a firm's cost of capital? The most widely recommended method is to calculate the weighted average of the current cost of funds to the firm from all sources. This amounts to calculating the cost of debt and the cost of equity, as explained below.

First, let us note a fallacy in reasoning that often arises when calculating cost of capital. Suppose that the cost of debt funds is 10 percent before taxes (or 5 percent after taxes) and the cost of equity money is 15 percent. If an investment project under consideration is to be financed by debt, it is tempting to think that the cost of capital for the project is the cost of debt, because the new project is giving rise to additional debt financing. This thinking is fallacious, however, for the following reasons.

In order for a firm to be able to borrow money, that is, engage in debt financing, it must have an adequate equity base. This is necessary because when a firm incurs debt, it also incurs the legal obligation to make periodic interest payments before its earnings can be distributed to owners or stockholders. Hence the existence of an equity base provides a safety cushion for creditors.

Obviously, the greater the proportion of total assets that are financed by debt instead of equity, the greater the potential economic loss to the owners in case of a decline in earnings. On the other hand, if the firm can earn more on its total assets than the interest rate it pays on its debt, the owners will benefit by receiving higher earnings. This is known in business finance as "trading on the equity," or by the preferred term *leverage*.

Calculating Cost of Capital

This leads to the notion that an "optimum" or "best" financial structure exists for each firm, or at least a range within which the proportions of debt and equity, or the debt/equity ratio, is approximately ideal. Accordingly, when a firm incurs additional debt financing, it is thereby using up some of its existing equity base. If it continues, the financial structure (i.e., the entire right-hand side of the balance sheet as in terms of the ratio of debt to equity) will become unbalanced in favor of debt.

Logically, therefore, it is often recommended that the calculation of cost of capital should be based on a weighted average of *all forms of financing* that the firm currently uses, including all forms of debt as well as equity. Further, the estimates should be based on current market costs of debt and equity rather than on historical costs or book values, because decisions for investment are to be made in the present on the basis of current rather than past information. Exhibit 19–2 illustrates the weighting procedure used to calculate the cost of capital this way.

Exhibit 19–2

Calculating Cost of Capital

Method of Financing	(1) Current Market Value	(2) Proportion of Total	(3) Current Market Cost Before Taxes	(4) Current Market Cost After Taxes (50%)	(5) Weighted Cost (2) × (4)
Long-term debt	$ 35,000	35%	8%	4%	1.4%
Preferred stock	10,000	10	8	8	0.8
Common stock	30,000	30	20	20	6.0
Retained earnings	25,000	25	18	18	4.5
Totals	$100,000	100%			12.7%

Note from this example that the cost of debt is an expense or deductible item for income tax purposes, whereas the cost of equity is not.[1] The

---

[1] Of course, if the firm does not earn a profit, there are no income taxes and the cost of debt is the full interest rate. Likewise, if the firm earns $100,000 or less, the tax rate is lower and the cost of debt is higher.

cost of capital, in this case 12.7 percent, is the minimum that must be earned on the total assets of any project. Of course, management may also wish to add a safety margin to this estimate, but the current cost of capital at least indicates the minimum prospective profitability necessary to undertake a particular investment.

Each method of financing brings some net amount of funds into the firm (after paying costs such as underwriting) and requires some future cash outflows, such as interest payments, repayment of principal, or payment of dividends. The discount rate that equates the present value of the net inflows with the present value of the expected outflows is the explicit cost of the particular source of financing. The general equation, then, for the explicit cost of any method of financing is

$$I_0 = \frac{C_1}{1 + k} + \frac{C_2}{(1 + k)^2} + \cdots + \frac{C_n}{(1 + k)^n} \tag{1}$$

where I_0 is the net income, or yield, of the method of financing; C_t is the cash outflow in the period t where, $t = 1, 2, \ldots, $ n; and k is the discount rate that expresses the before-tax cost of the method of financing. This approach is used in making the cost estimates for each specific source of capital.

Cost of Debt

The explicit cost of debt is determined not only by the rate of interest specified in the debt instruments but also by the method of repayment, the yield of the debt issue (i.e., the net cash inflow after paying all expenses of the debt issue), and the assumptions that are made about the tax rates expected over the life of the debt.[2]

The first step in calculating the cost of debt is to determine the periodic cash outflows, which are the C_t in Equation (1). The interpolation technique used in Cases II and III in the preceding chapter can then be used to find the before-tax cost of debt, which is k in Equation (1).

For example, let us suppose that a firm that normally pays a 46 percent income tax issues one hundred 8 percent bonds, each with a face value of $1,000, all maturing in five years. The payout will be a uniform series of $8,000 per year for five years, plus a single payment of $100,000 to retire the bonds at end of five years. From the present-value equations (on Tables A and B of the Appendix) for a discount factor of 8 percent, we calculate the present value of the cash outflow as ($8,000 × 3.99271) + ($100,000 × 0.68058) = $100,000, which, of course, is the total face value of all the bonds. Thus we see that if the yield is equal to the face

---

[2] There are also implicit costs of debt such as working capital requirements, issuing of additional debt, and others. Obviously, these must also be considered in the decision to raise capital through debt or by other means.

value, the cost is equal to the stated interest rate. The after-tax cost in this case would be $0.08 \times (1.0 - 0.46) = 4.32$ percent.

If the yield is less than the face value of the securities, the before-tax cost will be greater than the stated interest rate. For example, if the yield were $95,000, we would interpolate from present value tables to find the before-tax cost of debt is 9.32 percent, and the after-tax cost is $9.32 \times 0.54 = 5.03$ percent.

If the yield is greater than the face value, the before-tax cost of debt will be less than the stated interest rate. For example, if the yield were $105,000, the before-tax cost of debt would be 6.81 percent and the after-tax cost would be 3.68 percent.

In the case of mortgages and serial bonds, periodic payments are made on the principal as well as on the interest. For example, suppose that one hundred 8-percent serial bonds yield $95,000 and are scheduled to be retired at the rate of 20 bonds per year. The cash outflow would be:

			Year		
Cash Outflow	1	2	3	4	5
Principal	$20,000	$20,000	$20,000	$20,000	$20,000
Interest	8,000	6,400	4,800	3,200	1,600
Total outflow	$28,000	$26,400	$24,800	$23,200	$21,600

The present value of the cash outflow at 8 percent discount is: ($28,000 $\times$ 0.92593) + ($26,400 $\times$ 0.85734) + ($24,800 $\times$ 0.79383) + $23,200 $\times$ 0.73503) + ($21,600 $\times$ 0.68058) = $100,000. At a discount rate of 11 percent, the present value is $92,887. Then, by interpolation, the before-tax cost of debt is 10.11 percent and the after-tax cost is 5.46 percent.

Cost of Preferred Stock

Preferred stock has features of both debt and equity. Like bonds or mortgage loans, preferred stock specifies a rate of return to the investor that is fixed as a percentage of the face (par) value of the instrument. Unlike debt, however, the payment of these dividends is not a legal requirement. If the company falls upon hard times, the directors can omit the preferred dividend without danger of being forced into bankruptcy.

For tax purposes payment of dividends on preferred stock is a distribution of earnings rather than a tax-deductible expense. Thus while preferred stock provides financial leverage, its cost is much higher than for debt as long as the firm is profitable. On the other hand, the financial risk of debt is largely avoided when preferred stock is used instead.

In determining the cost of preferred stock financing, we assume that the directors intend to pay the preferred dividends on time, and we therefore treat preferred stock as a perpetual debt. The cost, then, is simply the annual dividend divided by the yield. For example, if a firm obtains a yield of $98 per share on an issue of par $100, 7 percent preferred stock, the cost is $7/$98 = 7.14 percent. If the preferred stock has a call option and the company intends to call it in after some specific time, Equation (1) may be used to calculate the cost.

Cost of Equity Capital

Equity capital consists of funds obtained from the sale of common stock plus the retained earnings of the firm. The market price of a common stock is based upon investors' expectations and attitude toward risk. Each investor has in mind some minimum rate of return (from dividends and capital gains) that constitutes a threshold of investment. He or she will invest when the expected rate of return is at or above this threshold, and will disinvest when it falls below the threshold. Thus the cost of equity capital may be defined as the minimum rate of return that will leave the market price of the common stock unchanged.

The investor makes a decision to invest, hold, or disinvest on the basis of the market price of the common stock. In return for the price of a share, the investor expects to receive a future stream of income composed of periodic dividends and, finally, the market price of the stock when it is sold. Since these increments of income are to be received in the future, they must be discounted to reflect the time value of money. The market price of common stock, then, is simply the present value of the expected value of a future stream of income, which can be expressed by the equation:

$$I = \frac{D_1}{1 + k} + \frac{D_2}{(1 + k)^2} + \cdots + \frac{D_n}{(1 + k)^n} + \frac{S}{(1 + k)^n} \qquad (2)$$

where $D_1, D_2, \ldots, D_n$ are a series of cash dividends received at the end of each of the respective periods over the life of the investment; S is the market value at the end of n periods; k is the investor's discount rate (required rate of return); and I is the present value of the investment.

To show why this is so, suppose that an investor buys a share of common stock at a price of $100, expecting to receive a dividend of $5 at the end of one year and then be able to sell the stock for $110. The return will be the gain over the original investment, $15, divided by the investment; which gives a return of 15 percent. If we substitute these data into Equation (2) and solve for k, we get the same answer, 15 percent.

Now let us suppose that the investor decides to keep the stock for two years before selling, basing this decision on information or belief that the second-year dividend will be $6.26, and that the price of the stock at the end of two years will be $120. When we substitute into Equation (2) and solve for k, we again get $k = 15$ percent. This illustrates that the price of the stock is the present value of a discounted stream of dividends plus a discounted terminal value. But the terminal value is just the price that another investor is willing to pay, which is a discounted stream of dividends plus a discounted terminal value, and so on. Thus we see that the price of a stock is based on a stream of earnings in perpetuity.

If the company's dividends are expected to grow at some constant rate, then the dividend in any period is equal to the most recent dividend multiplied by the compound growth factor. By manipulation of Equation (2) it can be shown that the cost of equity capital, k_e, is the ratio of the next expected dividend, D_1, to the current price, P_0, plus the rate of growth, g:

$$k_e = \frac{D_1}{P_0} + g \qquad (3)$$

This assumes, however, that dividends will grow at a constant rate forever. There may be firms for which this is a reasonable expectation, but in other cases the rate of growth can be expected to taper off from time to time. If both the timing and the magnitude of changes in the growth pattern can be estimated, then Equation (2) can be used to derive the cost of equity capital.

But what about companies that pay no dividends? Not only do their stocks often sell well, but they sometimes sell for very high prices. How does this happen? The answer, of course, is that investors expect a terminal value high enough that they are willing to forego dividends. In the meantime the company is reinvesting its earnings, which it hopes will mean greater earnings in the future. How can the cost of capital be estimated for a company that pays no dividends? One way is by examining the growth in the market price of the stock. For example, if the stock price has increased over several years at a compound rate of 10 percent and this growth is expected to continue, one might accept 10 percent as the cost of equity capital.

Earnings-Price Ratio. The earnings-price ratio is just one of many pieces of information that investment analysts use to evaluate a stock. In two special situations, the earnings-price ratio may reflect the firm's cost of equity capital. The first case is that of the firm whose earnings per share are expected to remain constant and that pays out all earnings as dividends. The other case is a firm that does not have investment opportunities yielding more than the cost of equity capital but can invest a constant proportion of its earnings in projects that provide a perpetual return just equal to the cost of equity capital. In situations where the investors expect growth in the corporation's earnings, the earnings-price ratio is a very uncertain measure of the firm's cost of equity capital, since earnings-price ratios of less than the yield on government bonds are quite common.

Cost of New Stock Issues.   When a new issue of stock is sold, the net yield to the firm will be somewhat less than the market price of the stock because of flotation costs. Consequently, the cost of equity capital on new financing will be somewhat higher than the market would indicate. Flotation costs include the difference between the sale price and the proceeds received by the company (called the *underwriting spread*), registration expenses, and other out-of-pocket costs such as printing and postage.

Cost of Retained Earnings

Although today it is recognized that the use of retained earnings is not cost-free, as some writers have contended in the past, there still is much controversy over the measurement of the cost. Some authorities feel that the cost of equity capital should be adjusted downward to reflect the tax effect, but a strong case can be made for simply using the cost of equity capital as the cost of retained earnings.

There is general agreement that the cost of retained earnings is an opportunity cost equal to the value of the dividend foregone by the stockholders. This cost may be defined as the rate of return that permits the shareholder to be indifferent between (1) a cash dividend payment and (2) the investment project financed by retained earnings.

In a world free of taxes, we might reason that if the firm paid out all of its earnings as dividends, then the only way the firm could attract these earnings back into its capital structure would be to sell stock. The price of the stock would be determined by the cost of equity capital as previously defined: hence, the cost of retained earnings is just the cost of equity capital. On the other hand, there are those who point out that even in a world without taxes, there still are brokerage fees. Therefore the stockholder could not be indifferent unless the cost of equity capital were somewhat higher than the cost of retained earnings. More precisely, the cost of retained earnings would be the cost of equity capital multiplied by 1 minus the brokerage rate. For example, if the brokerage rate is 1 percent, the cost of retained earnings would be 99 percent of the cost of equity capital.

In the real world, of course, there are taxes as well as brokerage fees and they are levied at different rates. The personal income tax rate on ordinary income may be 2.5 times as much as the rate on long-term capital gains; dividends, with the exception of a small exemption, are taxed as ordinary income. It can be shown that the cost of retained earnings is the cost of equity capital multiplied by the ratio $(1 - t_p)/(1 - t_g)$, where t_p is the personal income tax rate on ordinary income and t_g is the personal income tax rate on capital gains. For example, if the investor were paying the maximum 50 percent personal income tax and 1 percent brokerage fees, the cost of retained earnings would be $(1 - 0.50)/(1 - 0.20) \times (1 - 0.01) = 61.875$ percent of the cost of equity capital.

This is a very neat solution except for the problem of determining the composite personal tax rate for all stockholders. Rough estimates suggest that for the average investor the personal tax rates are 40 percent on personal income and 16 percent on capital gains, but there can be very large institutional stockholders which are tax exempt. In very small firms or closely held corporations, it might be possible to ascertain the tax rate by questioning all stockholders. In large publicly held firms, this would be impossible and estimates would have to be used.

Another approach to evaluating the cost of retained earnings is the external-yield criterion. In this approach, the cost of retained earnings is defined as the forgone opportunity to invest in other firms of similar risk. This criterion is not affected by, and need not be concerned with, personal tax rates, as it simply measures what the firm could get by direct investment. The external-yield criterion is economically justifiable and can be applied consistently. As a general rule, however, since we assume equilibrium in the marketplace between risk and return, we would expect the external yield to be the same as the cost of equity capital to the firm.

Leverage and the Cost of Capital

Going back to Exhibit 19–2, it is reasonable to ask: How were the amounts in column (2) arrived at in the first place? Since long-term debt has the lowest cost, would it not be logical to raise as much capital as possible from this source and thereby lower the weighted average cost? For example, if additional bonds were sold for $15 million and the proceeds used to buy back and retire common stock, the weighted average cost of capital (k_0) would decline to 10.3 percent. But why stop here; why not continue until there is nothing but debt in the capital structure? What factors usually impede such an excessive use of debt? Finally, is there an optimal debt/equity ratio?

Optimal Debt/Equity Ratio

It is generally quite well understood that when a firm engages in debt financing it exposes itself to risks that, once the debt begins to approach a rather sizable amount relative to the total capital structure, increase in rapid geometric fashion compared with the increase in the debt itself. This is reflected, of course, in the leveraged effect on corporate earnings, but it also results in a reduction of the earnings yield (earnings-price ratio) of the stock.

Let us look in more detail at the relationship between the cost of capital and the debt/equity (D/E) ratio by examining Exhibit 19–3, which illustrates this relationship for one set of hypothetical conditions.

Exhibit 19–3

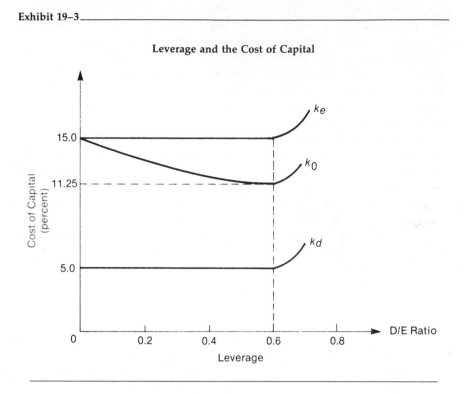

Leverage and the Cost of Capital

To keep things simple, preferred stock and retained earnings are ignored, leaving only the cost of debt k_d and the cost of equity k_e to consider. When the debt/equity ratio equals zero, k_0 (the weighted average cost of capital) $= k_e$; then, as debt is brought into the capital structure, and assuming its cost is less than the cost of equity, k_0 declines. Specifically, we know

$$k_0 = ak_d + (1 - a)k_e$$

where a is the proportion of total capital in the form of debt.

The diagram in Exhibit 19–3 shows k_e = 15 percent and k_d = 5 percent and k_0 declining until the debt/equity ratio of 0.6 (a = 0.375) is reached. At this point it begins to rise since both k_d and k_e increase in response to a growing apprehension on the part of both owners and creditors about the future solvency of the firm. In short, each group now demands a higher return because of the added risk exposure placed upon them.

Of course, optimal debt/equity ratios can be expected to vary among industries and even among firms within a given industry, depending upon the unique circumstances in each. For example, firms with rather stable sales and earnings, such as public utilities, tend to have high debt/equity ratios; yet there are wide variations among individual firms within the public utility industry, which are usually a reflection of the sales and earnings stability of each firm's principal customers. Also, it is not necessary that k_d and k_e turn up at the same point, as indicated in the diagram. This is done for ease of the presentation and does not reflect a theoretical or pragmatic argument.

There is considerable controversy, of both a theoretical and practical nature, as to the real-world existence of optimal debt/equity ratios. While we cannot explore the vast literature in this area—indeed, during the early 1960s it dominated the field of finance—the consensus now seems to favor the approach we have presented. Those interested in pursuing the topic further should consult the references at the end of this chapter, starting with the Franco Modigliani and M. H. Miller article in the June 1958 issue of the *American Economic Review*, since that was the genesis of the controversy.

The Cost of Capital Reformulated

To close our discussion of leverage and prepare us for the next section, let us reformulate the costs of equity and debt capital. As we have seen, these reflect investors' valuations of a company's stock and debt instruments, respectively. Investors, of course, in determining these values, consider a variety of factors, and certainly one that is most important is the rate of return available on a risk-free investment such as a Treasury security.[3] In a sense, this risk-free rate establishes a rate "base"

---

[3] Risk-free means the investor expects to receive both the promised interest and face value of the security at its maturity date. In fact, many government securities are purchased at a discount from their face value, and the investor actually achieves the expected yield by receiving the face value at maturity. Notice that risk-free does not mean the investor can *always* recover the amount initially invested in the government security before its maturity date. If interest rates happen to increase after the purchase of the security, its market value declines, and sale at this time results in a loss. To this extent the security is not risk-free.

upon which all other rates depend; and when viewed in this manner a firm's cost of capital can be formulated as:

$$k_0 = R_F + \rho_1 + \rho_2$$

where

R_F = Rate of return on the risk-free investment

ρ_1 = A risk premium on the firm's securities, reflecting its business risk

ρ_2 = A risk premium for the degree of leverage in the firm's capital structure

An exposition of this formulation appears in Exhibit 19–4.

Exhibit 19–4

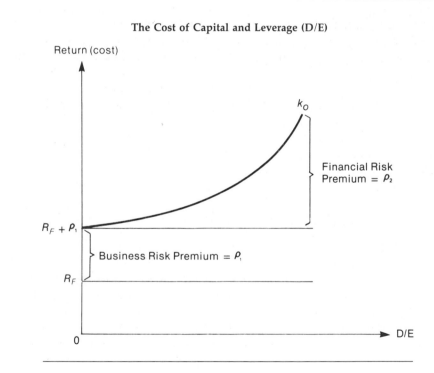

The Cost of Capital and Leverage (D/E)

As discussed, values for ρ_1 will depend upon the business activity of the firm; for example, banks typically have very low risk premiums because of the relative stability of their earnings over time, while automobile manufacturers have much higher premiums that reflect the inherent instability of their activities.

External Factors and the Cost of Capital

Up to this point, our discussion of the cost of capital has been limited to those factors that management can control: (1) the amount of capital to raise, and (2) the manner—debt or equity—in which it is raised. As we have just seen, however, the cost of capital is a market-determined figure that reflects all the perculiarities and disturbances of the market. Let us look at these market forces and how they affect the firm's cost of capital and the capital budgeting process overall.

The Federal Authorities

The two most important determinants of the risk-free interest rate R_F (and therefore of the cost of capital) are: (1) the federal government, making itself felt through the operations of the Treasury Department, and (2) the policies of the Federal Reserve authorities. While matters pertaining to money and credit are officially the province of the "Fed," the Treasury's operations are too important for their effects on the capital markets to be ignored.

The Treasury enters the money market each Monday with an offer of 91-day bills. Generally, this offering is simply a refunding of a similar volume of maturing bills, but even when this is the case the Treasury must set a rate that will (1) be taken by the market without shaking it unduly, and (2) be generally in line with the objectives of the Federal Reserve authorities. In addition to these weekly bill offerings, the Treasury enters the market less regularly with longer maturing securities for sale. These not only must be fitted into the existing structure and be reasonably consistent with monetary objectives but also must suit the Treasury's own purposes, namely: (1) to provide the desired volume of funds, and (2) to lengthen or shorten the average debt as desired by the Treasury's policy-making officials.

The Fed, in which is vested the responsibility for pursuing monetary and credit policies designed to promote economic growth and stability, actually sets the pattern of rates that prevail in the market. Through the exercise of controls over the rediscount rate, member bank reserve requirements, and selective credit controls (such as margin requirements for stock purchases), and, most important, by controlling the actual volume of commercial bank reserves, the Fed produces a marked effect on the general level of the rate structure. Moreover, some feel its open-market operations are capable of shaping the rate structure itself. This is possible by concentrating market operations on the shorter or longer end of the maturity scale, as the case might be.

While other forces, discussed below, have important effects on the general structure of rates, the government bond market is almost entirely subject to the operations of what amounts to the monolithic force of the federal authorities.

Of course, changes in the yield of one type of debt instrument very quickly spill over and produce similar changes in all other debt obligations—public and private—which in turn lead to changes in equity yields, and ultimately the entire yield structure on all assets is influenced to some degree. This portfolio-balancing approach to investment selection explains partially the mechanism whereby changes in policy by central authorities have an effect on investment spending within the firm by increasing or decreasing its cost of capital. So, for example, when credit standards and member bank reserves are altered by the Fed, or when the Treasury engages in massive new credit offerings, we expect R_F to change and certain reactions to take place within the firm. The passage below, describing events surrounding the federal income tax rebate that was proposed and then aborted in 1977, illustrates this process.

> The argument for such a policy was that it would stimulate consumer spending, and thus stimulate aggregate output and employment. However, there was considerable concern that the policy would cause an upward revision of short-term interest rate expectations if . . . the Treasury would have to increase its borrowing substantially during the second half of 1977 to finance the increased deficit. Under such circumstances, much, if not all, of the alleged stimulus that would be provided by the tax rebate could be offset by the negative impact of higher interest rate expectations on firms' decisions to invest in real capital. Such a negative effect arises because the higher the expected level of future interest rates, the less profitable the income stream associated with each particular investment project.[4]

Public Psychology

We will here interpret *public psychology* very broadly and treat it rather briefly. However, this brevity should not be construed as implying a lack of importance. On the contrary, the firm's cost of capital is embedded in the market place and to this extent the psychology of the market is crucially important. Public psychology includes such elements as "consumer optimism," "investor confidence," and "business outlook." These frequently point in the same direction at the same time, and their effects are most importantly felt on the yields that prevail on security issues other than Treasury debt obligations. Thus, while it is true that

---

[4] Albert E. Burgher, Richard W. Lang, and Robert H. Rasche, "The Treasury Bill Futures Market and Market Expectations of Interest Rates," *Review*, Federal Reserve Bank of St. Louis, June 1977, p. 2.

the federal authorities have an enormous effect on all yields by setting the pattern through their government bond operations, that is, by setting R_F, the question of how, and to what degree, other yields will respond depends on public psychology. In other words, the values of ρ_1 and ρ_2 can be expected to change as a reflection of investors' enthusiasm or pessimism regarding an individual firm or the market as a whole. Thus, whether the spread between bond and stock yields will be narrow or wide, or whether it will favor one type of investment over another, depends more on the factors subsumed under "public psychology" than directly on the Fed's credit policies.

Individual Factors

Thus far we have considered market forces that affect the general level and pattern of rates. Within this pattern must be fitted each individual security (investment); and the forces that have been discussed apply also to the individual issue. But, in addition to these general forces, the individual investment is subject to specific forces.

The decision to raise the tariff on lead imports or to subsidize investment in energy-saving devices can be expected to affect specific industries or companies more than others, although it is conceivable that their effects might be traceable to many other segments of the economy. Similarly, if the outlook for automobile or housing demand is not promising, the yields on the securities of the companies involved will reflect this fact. In short, many of the factors discussed above as part of public psychology can be found to apply, at times, with particularly telling force to specific companies rather than to industry in general. All of these factors, those of both general and specific import, can in fact be classed under the heading of that all-embracing term "uncertainty." We are then able to say simply that yields on Treasury securities are lowest because there is no question of default involved, that high-quality bonds offer somewhat higher yields, and so on down the scale to low-grade equities on which expected dividend and earnings yields are large because of their large risk. For any given equity, of course, current dividends and earnings might be zero. But the possibility exists, reasonable or not, that future earnings will permit payments that will make the current price attractive, that is, at least in line with prices of other securities.

Summary

The cost of capital must be known before investment selection can be undertaken, since otherwise it would be impossible to determine a cutoff point with respect to all the investment alternatives available to the firm. The cost of capital tells us which investments should be undertaken and which should be rejected.

Calculation of the cost of capital is made for each increment of capital raised either internally or externally; hence, the expression *marginal cost of capital* (MCC) is frequently used. The MCC is a weighted average of all capital increments available to the firm and is used in a mix that the firm considers optimal. In general, this financing mix refers to the amount of debt in a firm's capital structure relative to the amount of owners' equity: the debt/equity (D/E) ratio. In an optimal D/E ratio, the weighted average cost of capital would increase if the D/E ratio either increased or decreased. D/E ratios vary considerably among firms in different kinds of industries and even within a given industry.

A convenient formulation of a firm's cost of capital is $k_0 = R_F + \rho_1 + \rho_2$, which means that the weighted average cost of capital k_0 depends upon a risk-free rate of return R_F available to investors plus a business risk premium ρ_1 plus a financial risk premium ρ_2 placed upon the firm's stocks and bonds. This formulation shows clearly the influence of federal authorities (the U.S. Treasury and the Federal Reserve System) on the firm's cost of capital, since increases or decreases in the value of R_F cause the firm's cost of capital to change in the same direction. This formulation can also be used to illustrate the influence market psychology has on k_0 since values for ρ_1 and ρ_2 may not be stable but rather reflect continuous market appraisals and reappraisals of the firm's earning prospects and risks.

Problems

1.   What is a firm's potential internal supply of capital?

2.   The L Company follows of policy of paying 35 percent of cash earnings in dividends and reinvesting 65 percent in replacement of existing facilities and for expansion. Assuming that this is their guiding principle in determining capital expenditure planning, what do you think of this method? Can you see why, if used in a more sophisticated manner along with other guides, it might be a practical approach to the problem of capital budgeting?

3.   Is financing by retained earnings less costly than financing by the sale of new stock? What difficulty is encountered in determining the cost of retained earnings?

4.   When may a firm be considered to have an optimal capital structure?

5.   "A truly democratic policy which all businesses should pursue is 100 percent distribution of cash earnings, the corporate capital being

replenished by offering of stock subscriptions. Only in this way would the stockholders truly control the corporation's capital, and the free market forces would truly allocate resources among competing firms in the most optimum manner." Discuss.

6. Leviathan Industries estimates the cost of its equity capital with the following formula:

$$k_e = R_F + \rho_1 + \rho_2$$

where R_F is the current yield on Treasury bills (0.08); ρ_1 reflects Leviathan's business risk and is believed to have a value of 0.04; and ρ_2 is a function of the debt/equity ratio currently estimated as $0.1 \ (D/E)^2$. If Leviathan's after-tax cost of debt capital is equal to 0.05 for all values of D/E, determine graphically (or by any other means) Leviathan's optimal D/E ratio. Is it realistic to expect k_d to be uninfluenced by changes in the D/E ratio? Explain.

7. The argument is sometimes made that Federal Reserve policy (or U.S. Treasury action) is not effective if firms raise most of their capital internally. Discuss whether or not you agree with this point, clearly detailing how actions of the central authorities affect (at least theoretically) investment decisions within the firm.

8. The Honolulu Pump Company is trying to reach a decision on whether or not a $10 million expansion of its manufacturing facilities should be undertaken. The company is planning a $40 million bond issue later in the year, and if the project is selected it would be financed primarily by the proceeds from this issue. The after-tax rate of interest on the bonds is estimated to be 5 percent, and the company's weighted average cost of capital is expected to be 12 percent after the bond issue. The expansion project has an internal rate of return of 10 percent, and the company's controller feels the investment should be undertaken since its return covers the cost of the debt that will be used to finance it. The president is not sure this is the correct choice since the internal rate of return is less than the overall cost of capital. Discuss what you believe to be the correct approach.

References

Alberts, W. W., and S. H. Archer. "Some Evidence on the Effect of Company Size on the Cost of Equity Capital." *Journal of Financial and Quantitative Analysis*, March 1973, pp. 229–45.

Arditti, Fred D., and Milford S. Tysseland. "Three Ways to Present the Marginal Cost of Capital." *Financial Management*, Summer 1973, pp. 63–67.

Bierman, Harold, Jr. *Strategic Financial Planning.* New York: Free Press, 1980.

Brigham, Eugene F. *Financial Management Theory and Practice.* 3d ed. Hinsdale, Ill.: Dryden Press, 1982.

Modigliani, Franco, and M. H. Miller. "The Cost of Capital, Corporation Finance and the Theory of Investment." *American Economic Review,* June 1958, pp. 261–97. "The Cost of Capital, Corporation Finance and the Theory of Investment: Reply." Ibid., September 1958, pp. 655–69. "Taxes and the Cost of Capital: A Correction." Ibid., June 1963, pp. 433–43. "Reply." Ibid., June 1965, pp. 524–27.

Moyer, R. Charles; James R. McGuigan; and William J. Kretlow. *Contemporary Financial Management.* St. Paul, Minn.: West Publishing, 1981.

Quirin, G. D., and J. C. Wiginton. *Analyzing Capital Expenditures: Private and Public Perspectives.* Homewood, Ill.: Richard D. Irwin, 1981.

Sundem, Garry L. "Evaluating Capital Budgeting Models in Simulated Environments." *Journal of Finance,* September 1975, pp. 977–92.

Valentine, J. L., and E. A. Mennis. *Quantitative Techniques for Financial Analysis.* Rev. ed. Homewood, Ill.: Richard D. Irwin, 1980.

Appendix 19A | Application of the Valuation Model

While the valuation procedures detailed in Chapter 19 are straightforward and perhaps simple enough, our understanding of them would be enhanced by seeing an actual application of their use. To this end, the Securities Research Division of Merrill Lynch, Pierce, Fenner & Smith, Inc., published a most interesting example in their July/August 1978 issue of *Investment Strategy*.

Parts of this publication are presented here to illustrate the use of the valuation model described in Chapter 19, and we hope students will see the similarities between this example and many topics presented in the chapter. In fairness to Merrill Lynch, let us hasten to point out that we are presenting only one of four parts of their valuation approach, and for completeness interested readers should see the entire report.

One final comment: The nine-step process described below can also be used for valuation of an individual firm; that is, its use is not limited to the market as a whole. Apart from the issue of whether or not the model results in an accurate valuation of the market or of an individual security, at the very least it draws management's attention to those factors that are usually important in the valuation process. Certainly, if it does this it has made a sufficient contribution.

Valuation

Our valuation work has four principal aspects:

1. A valuation model that incorporates such fundamental influences as interest rates, earnings, dividends, and risk expectations.
2. Secular analysis of implications for return and risk on the basis of postwar trends in factors such as the bond-stock yield spread, the spread between yields on high and low grade bonds, profitability, and the flow of investment funds.
3. Valuation analysis for key market sectors on the basis of relative price-earnings multiples, relative prices, earnings performance, and long-term financial trends as measured by such variables as return on capital and the sources and uses of cash flow.
4. Analysis of technical influences including key elements of the supply of and demand for common stocks.

689

Summary for Market Outlook

Our dividend valuation model (Exhibit 19A–1) shows that, given our scenario of a continued increase of both short- and long-term rates, with a peaking of Moody's Aaa corporate bonds at 9¼ percent in the fourth quarter, plus a likelihood of a recession or at least a growth recession in

Exhibit 19A–1 _____

Earnings and Dividends Outlook

	EPS 1977	Change 1978/1977	Est. EPS 1978	Change 1979/1978	Est. EPS 1979
S&P 500	$10.89	7.9%	$ 11.75	5.5%	$ 12.40
S&P 400	11.57	7.6	12.45	6.0	13.20
DJIA	89.10	15.3	102.70	3.2	106.00
S&P 500 Dividends	4.67	8.1	5.05	6.9	5.40
S&P 400 Dividends	4.96	15.6	5.40	6.5	5.75
DJIA Dividends	45.84	3.2	47.30	3.3	48.85

early 1979, then the downside risk for the S&P 400 is about 20 percent from its current level of 106. This risk level is implied by a trough P/E ratio of 6.5 and $12.83 earnings per share based on the average of our analyst's estimates for 1978 and 1979. Our downside risk is a moving target subject to a rolling readjustment as events unfold. Note that this model is not meant to do cyclical pinpointing, a common type of misuse, but is instead a way of evaluating stock prices within a long-term perspective. For example, the 1970 bull market occurred with a risk premium close to zero. This excess was not corrected until several years had passed.

Valuation Model

A valuation model is intended to serve two purposes: first, it serves as a quantitative benchmark for evaluating a current or expected level of stock prices on the basis of expectations and assumptions about such fundamental influences as economic growth, interest rates, dividends, earnings, and risk; second, it serves as a framework for understanding the interrelationships among those fundamental influences and the impact changes in those influences have on the valuation of stocks. The fundamental model that we use is essentially the Gordon-Shapiro dividend-valuation model, which contends that stock prices represent the investor's present valuation of an expected stream of dividends.

The mathematical formula used to derive price on the basis of the dividend is

$$P = \frac{D_0(1 + G)}{1 + K} + \frac{D_0(1 + G)^2}{(1 + K)^2} + \frac{D_0(1 + G)^3}{(1 + K)^3} + \cdots + \frac{D_0(1 + G)^\infty}{(1 + K)^\infty}$$

in which dividends grow at rate G and are discounted at the investor's required rate of return K to derive a present value of the expected stream of dividends. While the expected stream of dividends theoretically can be infinite under this formula, the low value of a dollar discounted two decades into the future means that for practical purposes it is the expectations of the first 20 years or so that determine the investment decision. The equation above can be restated by mathematical means as[1]

$$P = \frac{D}{K - G}$$

That equation can be translated into a price-earnings multiple by dividing each side by E, or earnings, as follows:

$$P/E = \frac{D/E}{K - G}$$

$(K - G)$ means required rate of return K minus growth rate G. Because the required rate of return K is equal to yield plus appreciation, $K - G$ is equivalent to yield, which is D/P, the dividend divided by the price:

$$P/E = \frac{D/E}{D/P} = \frac{\not{D}}{E} \times \frac{P}{\not{D}} = P/E$$

A theoretical forecast of P/E, or the theoretical price-earnings multiple, can now be stated as:

$$P/E \text{ (theoretical forecast)} = \frac{D/E \text{ or payout ratio (forecast)}}{\text{Required yield (forecast)}}$$

Our goal is to project a theoretical market price by means of an intermediate-term outlook for earnings and the price-earnings multiple as developed from the model. Our earnings outlook is generated from the projections of our analysts. Our theoretical P/E can be derived by forecasting the payout ratio and required yield in a nine-step process:
1. Forecast intermediate-term earnings.
2. Forecast intermediate-term dividends.

---

[1] Students should see that this formula can be rearranged to

$$K = \frac{D}{P} + G$$

3. Derive a forecast of the payout ratio on the basis of steps 1 and 2.
4. Forecast on an intermediate-term basis the long-term interest rate for a relatively risk-free instrument.
5. Evaluate the risk premium entailed in owning common stocks instead of bonds as a function of secular and cyclical risk influences; the risk premium is measured as a percentage of the interest rate.
6. Derive total return required by investors for owning common stock by adding steps 4 and 5.
7. Derive the nominal growth rate of dividends as a function of return on equity using the reinvestment rate as a proxy for growth (ROE × reinvestment ratio).
8. Subtract growth as determined in step 7 from required total return in order to derive required yield.
9. Determine the forecast of P/E by dividing step 3 by step 8.

Our forecasts of earnings and dividends are those indicated previously. The historical test of the model is shown below. The examples show how the model is used. The fit of the actual P/E to the theoretical P/E is not surprising because the two sides of the equation are mathematically identical.

Basic Formula: $P/E = \dfrac{D/E}{K - G}$

$$= \frac{\text{Payout ratio}}{\underset{\substack{\text{Aaa corporate} \\ \text{bonds rate}}}{} \times \underset{\substack{(1 + \text{Risk} \\ \text{premium ratio})}}{} - \underset{\substack{(\text{ROE} \times \\ \text{Reinvestment ratio})}}{}}$$

Example 1:

Theoretical P/E (1961–70) $= \dfrac{54.6}{5.4(1.56) - 5.2} = 16.9$

Actual $P/E = 17.2$

Example 2:

Theoretical P/E (1971–74) $= \dfrac{44.4}{7.7(1.34) - 7.1} = 13.8$

Actual $P/E = 14.7$ (decline of 15% from 1961–70)

Note that:

The payout ratio decreased by 19 percent.

The interest rate rose by 43 percent.

Risk-premium ratio declined by 39 percent.

The absolute risk premium declined by 13 percent.

The growth factor increased by 37 percent (ROE × reinvestment ratio).

The yield remained constant; rising interest rates counterbalanced declining risk and rising nominal growth.

The implied total return rose by 23 percent.

This example shows the complex interaction of influences that subsequently caused the decline in the P/E.

Valuation Forecast

While the Gordon-Shapiro model appears straightforward enough on the surface, it is usually in a static form. Application in the real world requires analysis and judgment within a dynamic framework. A purely mechanical approach to valuation will not work and should not be given an unjustified air of precision. For example, in the early post–World War II period the yields on stocks exceeded the yields on bonds, implying a very high risk premium and very low growth despite such favorable growth characteristics as a high implied internal growth rate, a high return on investment, strong growth of dividends, and rising cash flow as shown in Exhibit 19A–2 (columns 2, 3, 4, 5). As market perceptions caught up with reality, total return was pushed up (21–23 percent; column 8) beyond the expectations that were based originally on the negative spread between bond and stock yields or the implied total return (9½ to 12 percent) as calculated from the stock yield (4–6 percent) and implied (retrospectively) growth (5½ to 6 percent) of the 1950–58 period. The risk/premium ratio, which ranged from 317 percent to 185 percent (column 12), offered investors an excess return in light of growing prosperity and increasing confidence. Consequently, price-earnings multiples rose (column 13).

Because both the real and perceived conditions that affect total return can vary greatly, we have adopted a two-phase approach to valuation.

Phase 1 consists of the utilization of the Gordon-Shapiro model, which focuses on the intermediate-term outlook and recent history of interest rates, earnings, dividends, and risk. Assumptions about those influences typically are made in a cyclical context.

Phase 2 consists of adjusting the current risk and growth influences on the basis of the long perspective of different stages of the postwar period. The adjustment is subjective but is based on quantitative observations. Thus, the model's cyclical assumptions are adjusted to reflect assumptions about changes in the structure of the economy and the financial markets. Those assumptions on secular trends are made by

Exhibit 19A–2

Secular Market Trends (S&P 400) Segmented by Business Cycle

	(1)	(2)	(3)	(4)	(5)	(6)	(7)	(8)	(9)	(10)	(11) Implied Common Stock Risk Premium	(12)	(13)
Business Cycle (trough to trough)	Payout Ratio	Return on Book Equity	Implied Internal Growth Rate (1.0 − Col. 1) × Col. 2	Actual Average Dividend Growth Rate	Cash Flow Margin (through 3Q77) All Corp.	Yield	Implied Total Return (Col. 3 + 6)	Actual Total Return NYSE Sample	Moody's Aaa Corporate Bond Rate	Ratio of Yield to Bond Rate	Absolute (Col. 7 − 9)	As Percentage of Aaa Rate (Col. 11 ÷ 9)	P/E Multiple
1950–54	52.8%	13.3%	6.3%	4.3%	11.7%	5.8%	12.1%	22.4%	2.9%	200%	9.2%	317%	9.1
1954–58	54.6	12.3	5.6	7.1	12.5	4.1	9.7	21.6	3.4	121	6.3	185	13.3
1958–60	59.4	10.2	4.1	1.1	12.6	3.4	7.5	17.8	4.2	81	3.3	79	17.5
1961–70	54.6	11.5	5.2	4.9	13.1	3.4	8.4	8.3	5.4	59	3.0	56	17.0
1971–74	44.4	12.7	7.1	5.1	12.1	3.2	10.3	−3.9	7.7	42	2.6	34	13.8
1975–79 E	42.0	13.5	7.8	8.3	13.0	4.9	12.7	15.3	8.5	58	4.2	49	8.6

comparing key influences that affect future growth in the current cycle in relation to past cycles.

$$\text{Theoretical } P/E = \frac{0.43}{9.25(1.56) - 7.8}$$

$$= 6.5 \times \text{Theoretical price} = 6.5 \times \$12.83 = 83(\text{S\&P } 400)$$

The 43 percent payout ratio is based on expectations for 1978 and 1979. The 9.25 percent interest rate is based on peak expectations for Moody's Aaa corporate bonds for late 1978 to early 1979. The 7.8 percent growth is implied by the reinvestment ratio and book return on investment and is nominal. The 56 percent risk/premium ratio is based on the expectation of some further secular increase as well as some cyclical correction. The EPS base is derived from an averaging of 1978 and 1979 earnings. The current multiple of the S&P 400 on this basis is 8.2 (late June), which implies a 41 percent risk premium based on the other assumptions in the model. In trying to measure the changes in the risk premium in past bear markets by identifying separately the effects of changing interest rates, earnings and payout influences from the change in the price-earnings multiple, we found that the maximum cyclical variation in the risk premium is relatively small, ±10 percent (i.e., ±5.0 percent on a 50 percent risk premium ratio).

Appendix

Discount Tables and Charts; Common Logarithms; Statistical Tables; Derivative Formulas

Table A

Present Value of a Uniform Series: PVUS

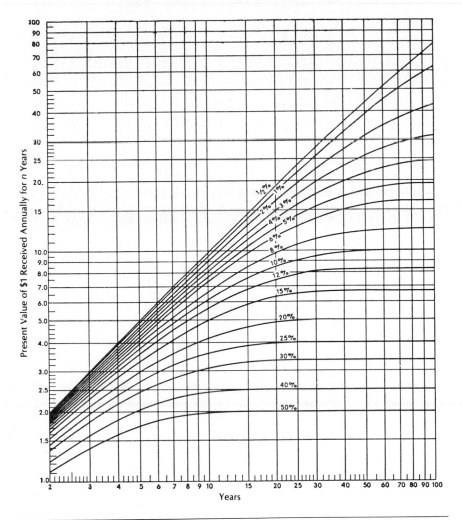

Source: Adapted from Sherman Hanish *Economic Analysis for Engineering and Management Decision Making* (New York: McGraw-Hill, 1962).

Table A (concluded)

Present Value of $1 Received Annually for N Years

$$PV = \left[\frac{1 - (1 + k)^{-N}}{k} \right]$$

Years (N)	1%	2%	4%	6%	8%	10%	12%	14%	15%	16%	18%	20%	22%	24%	25%	26%	28%	30%	35%	40%	45%	50%
1	0.990	0.980	0.962	0.943	0.926	0.909	0.893	0.877	0.870	0.862	0.847	0.833	0.820	0.806	0.800	0.794	0.781	0.769	0.741	0.714	0.690	0.667
2	1.970	1.942	1.886	1.833	1.783	1.736	1.690	1.647	1.626	1.605	1.566	1.528	1.492	1.457	1.440	1.424	1.392	1.361	1.289	1.224	1.165	1.111
3	2.941	2.884	2.775	2.673	2.577	2.487	2.402	2.322	2.283	2.246	2.174	2.106	2.042	1.981	1.952	1.923	1.868	1.816	1.696	1.589	1.493	1.407
4	3.902	3.808	3.630	3.465	3.312	3.170	3.037	2.914	2.855	2.798	2.690	2.589	2.494	2.404	2.362	2.320	2.241	2.166	1.997	1.849	1.720	1.605
5	4.853	4.713	4.452	4.212	3.993	3.791	3.605	3.433	3.352	3.274	3.127	2.991	2.864	2.745	2.689	2.635	2.532	2.436	2.220	2.035	1.876	1.737
6	5.795	5.601	5.242	4.917	4.623	4.355	4.111	3.889	3.784	3.685	3.498	3.326	3.167	3.020	2.951	2.885	2.759	2.643	2.385	2.168	1.983	1.824
7	6.728	6.472	6.002	5.582	5.206	4.868	4.564	4.288	4.160	4.039	3.812	3.605	3.416	3.242	3.161	3.083	2.937	2.802	2.508	2.263	2.057	1.883
8	7.652	7.325	6.733	6.210	5.747	5.335	4.968	4.639	4.487	4.344	4.078	3.837	3.619	3.421	3.329	3.241	3.076	2.925	2.598	2.331	2.108	1.922
9	8.566	8.162	7.435	6.802	6.247	5.759	5.328	4.946	4.772	4.607	4.303	4.031	3.786	3.566	3.463	3.366	3.184	3.019	2.665	2.379	2.144	1.948
10	9.471	8.983	8.111	7.360	6.710	6.145	5.650	5.216	5.019	4.833	4.494	4.192	3.923	3.682	3.571	3.465	3.269	3.092	2.715	2.414	2.168	1.965
11	10.368	9.787	8.760	7.887	7.139	6.495	5.988	5.453	5.234	5.029	4.656	4.327	4.035	3.776	3.656	3.544	3.335	3.147	2.752	2.438	2.185	1.977
12	11.255	10.575	9.385	8.384	7.536	6.814	6.194	5.660	5.421	5.197	4.793	4.439	4.127	3.851	3.725	3.606	3.387	3.190	2.779	2.456	2.196	1.985
13	12.134	11.343	9.986	8.853	7.904	7.103	6.424	5.842	5.583	5.342	4.910	4.533	4.203	3.912	3.780	3.656	3.427	3.223	2.799	2.468	2.204	1.990
14	13.004	12.106	10.563	9.295	8.244	7.367	6.628	6.002	5.724	5.468	5.008	4.611	4.265	3.962	3.824	3.695	3.459	3.249	2.814	2.477	2.210	1.993
15	13.865	12.849	11.118	9.712	8.559	7.606	6.811	6.142	5.847	5.575	5.092	4.675	4.315	4.001	3.859	3.726	3.483	3.268	2.825	2.484	2.214	1.995
16	14.718	13.578	11.652	10.106	8.851	7.824	6.974	6.265	5.954	5.669	5.162	4.730	4.357	4.033	3.887	3.751	3.503	3.283	2.834	2.489	2.216	1.997
17	15.562	14.292	12.166	10.477	9.122	8.022	7.120	6.373	6.047	5.749	5.222	4.775	4.391	4.059	3.910	3.771	3.518	3.295	2.840	2.492	2.218	1.998
18	16.398	14.992	12.659	10.828	9.372	8.201	7.250	6.467	6.128	5.818	5.273	4.812	4.419	4.080	3.928	3.786	3.529	3.304	2.844	2.494	2.219	1.999
19	17.226	15.678	13.134	11.158	9.604	8.365	7.366	6.550	6.198	5.877	5.316	4.844	4.442	4.097	3.942	3.799	3.539	3.311	2.848	2.496	2.220	1.999
20	18.046	16.351	13.590	11.470	9.818	8.514	7.469	6.623	6.259	5.929	5.353	4.870	4.460	4.110	3.954	3.808	3.546	3.316	2.850	2.497	2.221	1.999
21	18.857	17.011	14.029	11.764	10.017	8.649	7.562	6.687	6.312	5.973	5.384	4.891	4.476	4.121	3.963	3.816	3.551	3.320	2.852	2.498	2.221	2.000
22	19.660	17.658	14.451	12.042	10.201	8.772	7.645	6.743	6.359	6.011	5.410	4.909	4.488	4.130	3.970	3.822	3.556	3.323	2.853	2.498	2.222	2.000
23	20.456	18.292	14.857	12.303	10.371	8.883	7.718	6.792	6.399	6.044	5.432	4.925	4.499	4.137	3.976	3.827	3.559	3.325	2.854	2.499	2.222	2.000
24	21.243	18.914	15.247	12.550	10.529	8.985	7.784	6.835	6.434	6.073	5.451	4.937	4.507	4.143	3.981	3.831	3.562	3.327	2.855	2.499	2.222	2.000
25	22.023	19.523	15.622	12.783	10.675	9.077	7.843	6.873	6.464	6.097	5.467	4.948	4.514	4.147	3.985	3.834	3.564	3.329	2.856	2.499	2.222	2.000
26	22.795	20.121	15.983	13.003	10.810	9.161	7.896	6.906	6.491	6.118	5.480	4.956	4.520	4.151	3.988	3.837	3.566	3.330	2.856	2.500	2.222	2.000
27	23.560	20.707	16.330	13.211	10.935	9.237	7.943	6.935	6.514	6.136	5.492	4.964	4.524	4.154	3.990	3.839	3.567	3.331	2.856	2.500	2.222	2.000
28	24.316	21.281	16.663	13.406	11.051	9.307	7.984	6.961	6.534	6.152	5.502	4.970	4.528	4.157	3.992	3.840	3.568	3.331	2.857	2.500	2.222	2.000
29	25.066	21.844	16.984	13.591	11.158	9.370	8.022	6.983	6.551	6.166	5.510	4.975	4.531	4.159	3.994	3.841	3.569	3.332	2.857	2.500	2.222	2.000
30	25.808	22.396	17.292	13.765	11.258	9.427	8.055	7.003	6.566	6.177	5.517	4.979	4.534	4.160	3.995	3.842	3.569	3.332	2.857	2.500	2.222	2.000
40	32.835	27.355	19.793	15.046	11.925	9.779	8.244	7.105	6.642	6.234	5.548	4.997	4.544	4.166	3.999	3.846	3.571	3.333	2.857	2.500	2.222	2.000
50	39.196	31.424	21.482	15.762	12.234	9.915	8.304	7.133	6.661	6.246	5.554	4.999	4.545	4.167	4.000	3.846	3.571	3.333	2.857	2.500	2.222	2.000

Source: Adapted from Norman Barish, *Economic Analysis for Engineering and Management Decision Making* (New York: McGraw-Hill, 1962).

Present Value of a Single Payment: PVSP

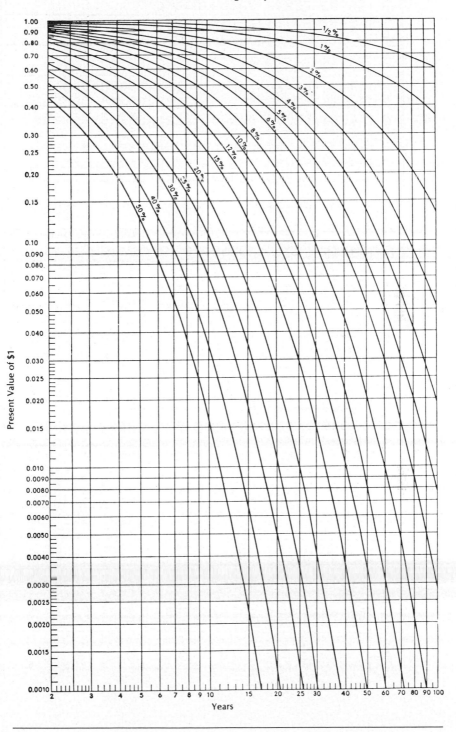

Present Value of $1

Years

Table B (*concluded*)

Present Value of $1

$$PV = (1 + k)^{-x}$$

Years Hence	1%	2%	4%	6%	8%	10%	12%	14%	15%	16%	18%	20%	22%	24%	25%	26%	28%	30%	35%	40%	45%	50%
1	0.990	0.980	0.962	0.943	0.926	0.909	0.893	0.877	0.870	0.862	0.847	0.833	0.820	0.806	0.800	0.794	0.781	0.769	0.741	0.714	0.690	0.667
2	0.980	0.961	0.925	0.890	0.857	0.826	0.797	0.769	0.756	0.743	0.718	0.694	0.672	0.650	0.640	0.630	0.610	0.592	0.549	0.510	0.476	0.444
3	0.971	0.942	0.889	0.840	0.794	0.751	0.712	0.675	0.658	0.641	0.609	0.579	0.551	0.524	0.512	0.500	0.477	0.455	0.406	0.364	0.328	0.296
4	0.961	0.924	0.855	0.792	0.735	0.683	0.636	0.592	0.572	0.552	0.516	0.482	0.451	0.423	0.410	0.397	0.373	0.350	0.301	0.260	0.226	0.198
5	0.951	0.906	0.822	0.747	0.681	0.621	0.567	0.519	0.497	0.476	0.437	0.402	0.370	0.341	0.328	0.315	0.291	0.269	0.223	0.186	0.156	0.132
6	0.942	0.888	0.790	0.705	0.630	0.564	0.507	0.456	0.432	0.410	0.370	0.335	0.303	0.275	0.262	0.250	0.227	0.207	0.165	0.133	0.108	0.088
7	0.933	0.871	0.760	0.665	0.583	0.513	0.452	0.400	0.376	0.354	0.314	0.279	0.249	0.222	0.210	0.198	0.178	0.159	0.122	0.095	0.074	0.059
8	0.923	0.853	0.731	0.627	0.540	0.467	0.404	0.351	0.327	0.305	0.266	0.233	0.204	0.179	0.168	0.157	0.139	0.123	0.091	0.068	0.051	0.039
9	0.914	0.837	0.703	0.592	0.500	0.424	0.361	0.308	0.284	0.263	0.225	0.194	0.167	0.144	0.134	0.125	0.108	0.094	0.067	0.048	0.035	0.026
10	0.905	0.820	0.676	0.558	0.463	0.386	0.322	0.270	0.247	0.227	0.191	0.162	0.137	0.116	0.107	0.099	0.085	0.073	0.050	0.035	0.024	0.017
11	0.896	0.804	0.650	0.527	0.429	0.350	0.287	0.237	0.215	0.195	0.162	0.135	0.112	0.094	0.086	0.079	0.066	0.056	0.037	0.025	0.017	0.012
12	0.887	0.788	0.625	0.497	0.397	0.319	0.257	0.208	0.187	0.168	0.137	0.112	0.092	0.076	0.069	0.062	0.052	0.043	0.027	0.018	0.012	0.008
13	0.879	0.773	0.601	0.469	0.368	0.290	0.229	0.182	0.163	0.145	0.116	0.093	0.075	0.061	0.055	0.050	0.040	0.033	0.020	0.013	0.008	0.005
14	0.870	0.758	0.577	0.442	0.340	0.263	0.205	0.160	0.141	0.125	0.099	0.078	0.062	0.049	0.044	0.039	0.032	0.025	0.015	0.009	0.006	0.003
15	0.861	0.743	0.555	0.417	0.315	0.239	0.183	0.140	0.123	0.108	0.084	0.065	0.051	0.040	0.035	0.031	0.025	0.020	0.011	0.006	0.004	0.002
16	0.853	0.728	0.534	0.394	0.292	0.218	0.163	0.123	0.107	0.093	0.071	0.054	0.042	0.032	0.028	0.025	0.019	0.015	0.008	0.005	0.003	0.002
17	0.844	0.714	0.513	0.371	0.270	0.198	0.146	0.108	0.093	0.080	0.060	0.045	0.034	0.026	0.023	0.020	0.015	0.012	0.006	0.003	0.002	0.001
18	0.836	0.700	0.494	0.350	0.250	0.180	0.130	0.095	0.081	0.069	0.051	0.038	0.028	0.021	0.018	0.016	0.012	0.009	0.005	0.002	0.001	0.001
19	0.828	0.686	0.475	0.331	0.232	0.164	0.116	0.083	0.070	0.060	0.043	0.031	0.023	0.017	0.014	0.012	0.009	0.007	0.003	0.002	0.001	
20	0.820	0.673	0.456	0.312	0.215	0.149	0.104	0.073	0.061	0.051	0.037	0.026	0.019	0.014	0.012	0.010	0.007	0.005	0.002	0.001	0.001	
21	0.811	0.660	0.439	0.294	0.199	0.135	0.093	0.064	0.053	0.044	0.031	0.022	0.015	0.011	0.009	0.008	0.006	0.004	0.002	0.001		
22	0.803	0.647	0.422	0.278	0.184	0.123	0.083	0.056	0.046	0.038	0.026	0.018	0.013	0.009	0.007	0.006	0.004	0.003	0.001	0.001		
23	0.795	0.634	0.406	0.262	0.170	0.112	0.074	0.049	0.040	0.033	0.022	0.015	0.010	0.007	0.006	0.005	0.003	0.002	0.001	0.001		
24	0.788	0.622	0.390	0.247	0.158	0.102	0.066	0.043	0.035	0.028	0.019	0.013	0.008	0.006	0.005	0.004	0.003	0.002	0.001	0.001		
25	0.780	0.610	0.375	0.233	0.146	0.092	0.059	0.038	0.030	0.024	0.016	0.010	0.007	0.005	0.004	0.003	0.002	0.001	0.001	0.001		
26	0.772	0.598	0.361	0.220	0.135	0.084	0.053	0.033	0.026	0.021	0.014	0.009	0.006	0.004	0.003	0.002	0.002	0.001				
27	0.764	0.586	0.347	0.207	0.125	0.076	0.047	0.029	0.023	0.018	0.011	0.007	0.005	0.003	0.002	0.002	0.001	0.001				
28	0.757	0.574	0.333	0.196	0.116	0.069	0.042	0.026	0.020	0.016	0.010	0.006	0.004	0.002	0.002	0.002	0.001	0.001				
29	0.749	0.563	0.321	0.185	0.107	0.063	0.037	0.022	0.017	0.014	0.008	0.005	0.003	0.002	0.002	0.001	0.001	0.001				
30	0.742	0.552	0.308	0.174	0.099	0.057	0.033	0.020	0.015	0.012	0.007	0.004	0.003	0.002	0.001	0.001	0.001					
40	0.672	0.453	0.208	0.097	0.046	0.022	0.011	0.005	0.004	0.003	0.001	0.001										
50	0.608	0.372	0.141	0.054	0.021	0.009	0.003	0.001	0.001	0.001												

Table C

Mantissas for Four-Place Common Logarithms

N	0	1	2	3	4	5	6	7	8	9
10	0000	0043	0086	0128	0170	0212	0253	0294	0334	0374
11	0414	0453	0492	0531	0569	0607	0645	0682	0719	0755
12	0792	0828	0864	0899	0934	0969	1004	1038	1072	1106
13	1139	1173	1206	1239	1271	1303	1335	1367	1399	1430
14	1461	1492	1523	1553	1584	1614	1644	1673	1703	1732
15	1761	1790	1818	1847	1875	1903	1931	1959	1987	2014
16	2041	2068	2095	2122	2148	2175	2201	2227	2253	2279
17	2304	2330	2355	2380	2405	2430	2455	2480	2504	2529
18	2553	2577	2601	2625	2648	2672	2695	2718	2742	2765
19	2788	2810	2833	2856	2878	2900	2923	2945	2967	2989
20	3010	3032	3054	3075	3096	3118	3139	3160	3181	3201
21	3222	3243	3263	3284	3304	3324	3345	3365	3385	3404
22	3424	3444	3464	3483	3502	3522	3541	3560	3579	3598
23	3617	3636	3655	3674	3692	3711	3729	3747	3766	3784
24	3802	3820	3838	3856	3874	3892	3909	3927	3945	3962
25	3979	3997	4014	4031	4048	4065	4082	4099	4116	4133
26	4150	4166	4183	4200	4216	4232	4249	4265	4281	4298
27	4314	4330	4346	4362	4378	4393	4409	4425	4440	4456
28	4472	4487	4502	4518	4533	4548	4564	4579	4594	4609
29	4624	4639	4654	4669	4683	4698	4713	4728	4742	4757
30	4771	4786	4800	4814	4829	4843	4857	4871	4886	4900
31	4914	4928	4942	4955	4969	4983	4997	5011	5024	5038
32	5051	5065	5079	5092	5105	5119	5132	5145	5159	5172
33	5185	5198	5211	5224	5237	5250	5263	5276	5289	5302
34	5315	5328	5340	5353	5366	5378	5391	5403	5416	5428
35	5441	5453	5465	5478	5490	5502	5514	5527	5539	5551
36	5563	5575	5587	5599	5611	5623	5635	5647	5658	5670
37	5682	5694	5705	5717	5729	5740	5752	5763	5775	5786
38	5798	5809	5821	5832	5843	5855	5866	5877	5888	5899
39	5911	5922	5933	5944	5955	5966	5977	5988	5999	6010
40	6021	6031	6042	6053	6064	6075	6085	6096	6107	6117
41	6128	6138	6149	6160	6170	6180	6191	6201	6212	6222
42	6232	6243	6253	6263	6274	6284	6294	6304	6314	6325
43	6335	6345	6355	6365	6375	6385	6395	6405	6415	6425
44	6435	6444	6454	6464	6474	6484	6493	6503	6513	6522
45	6532	6542	6551	6561	6571	6580	6590	6599	6609	6618
46	6628	6637	6646	6656	6665	6675	6684	6693	6702	6712
47	6721	6730	6739	6749	6758	6767	6776	6785	6794	6803
48	6812	6821	6830	6839	6848	6857	6866	6875	6884	6893
49	6902	6911	6920	6928	6937	6946	6955	6964	6972	6981
50	6990	6998	7007	7016	7024	7033	7042	7050	7059	7067
51	7076	7084	7093	7101	7110	7118	7126	7135	7143	7152
52	7160	7168	7177	7185	7193	7202	7210	7218	7226	7235
53	7243	7251	7259	7267	7275	7284	7292	7300	7308	7316
54	7324	7332	7340	7348	7356	7364	7372	7380	7388	7396

Table C *(concluded)*

N	0	1	2	3	4	5	6	7	8	9
55	7404	7412	7419	7427	7435	7443	7451	7459	7466	7474
56	7482	7490	7497	7505	7513	7520	7528	7536	7543	7551
57	7559	7566	7574	7582	7589	7597	7604	7612	7619	7627
58	7634	7642	7649	7657	7664	7672	7679	7686	7694	7701
59	7709	7716	7723	7731	7738	7745	7752	7760	7767	7774
60	7782	7789	7796	7803	7810	7818	7825	7832	7839	7846
61	7853	7860	7868	7875	7882	7889	7896	7903	7910	7917
62	7924	7931	7938	7945	7952	7959	7966	7973	7980	7987
63	7993	8000	8007	8014	8021	8028	8035	8041	8048	8055
64	8062	8069	8075	8082	8089	8096	8102	8109	8116	8122
65	8129	8136	8142	8149	8156	8162	8169	8176	8182	8189
66	8195	8202	8209	8215	8222	8228	8235	8241	8248	8254
67	8261	8267	8274	8280	8287	8293	8299	8306	8312	8319
68	8325	8331	8338	8344	8351	8357	8363	8370	8376	8382
69	8388	8395	8401	8407	8414	8420	8426	8432	8439	8445
70	8451	8457	8463	8470	8476	8482	8488	8494	8500	8506
71	8513	8519	8525	8531	8537	8543	8549	8555	8561	8567
72	8573	8579	8585	8591	8597	8603	8609	8615	8621	8627
73	8633	8639	8645	8651	8657	8663	8669	8675	8681	8686
74	8692	8698	8704	8710	8716	8722	8727	8733	8739	8745
75	8751	8756	8762	8768	8774	8779	8785	8791	8797	8802
76	8808	8814	8820	8825	8831	8837	8842	8848	8854	8859
77	8865	8871	8876	8882	8887	8893	8899	8904	8910	8915
78	8921	8927	8932	8938	8943	8949	8954	8960	8965	8971
79	8976	8982	8987	8993	8998	9004	9009	9015	9020	9025
80	9031	9036	9042	9047	9053	9058	9063	9069	9074	9079
81	9085	9090	9096	9101	9106	9112	9117	9122	9128	9133
82	9138	9143	9149	9154	9159	9165	9170	9175	9180	9186
83	9191	9196	9201	9206	9212	9217	9222	9227	9232	9238
84	9243	9248	9253	9258	9263	9269	9274	9279	9284	9289
85	9294	9299	9304	9309	9315	9320	9325	9330	9335	9340
86	9345	9350	9355	9360	9365	9370	9375	9380	9385	9390
87	9395	9400	9405	9410	9415	9420	9425	9430	9435	9440
88	9445	9450	9455	9460	9465	9469	9474	9479	9484	9489
89	9494	9499	9504	9509	9513	9518	9523	9528	9533	9538
90	9542	9547	9552	9557	9562	9566	9571	9576	9581	9586
91	9590	9595	9600	9605	9609	9614	9619	9624	9628	9633
92	9638	9643	9647	9652	9657	9661	9666	9671	9675	9680
93	9685	9689	9694	9699	9703	9708	9713	9717	9722	9727
94	9731	9736	9741	9745	9750	9754	9759	9763	9768	9773
95	9777	9782	9786	9791	9795	9800	9805	9809	9814	9818
96	9823	9827	9832	9836	9841	9845	9850	9854	9859	9863
97	9868	9872	9877	9881	9886	9890	9894	9899	9903	9908
98	9912	9917	9921	9926	9930	9934	9939	9943	9948	9952
99	9956	9961	9965	9969	9974	9978	9983	9987	9991	9996

Table D

Binomial Coefficients

n	$\binom{n}{0}$	$\binom{n}{1}$	$\binom{n}{2}$	$\binom{n}{3}$	$\binom{n}{4}$	$\binom{n}{5}$	$\binom{n}{6}$	$\binom{n}{7}$	$\binom{n}{8}$	$\binom{n}{9}$	$\binom{n}{10}$
0	1										
1	1	1									
2	1	2	1								
3	1	3	3	1							
4	1	4	6	4	1						
5	1	5	10	10	5	1					
6	1	6	15	20	15	6	1				
7	1	7	21	35	35	21	7	1			
8	1	8	28	56	70	56	28	8	1		
9	1	9	36	84	126	126	84	36	9	1	
10	1	10	45	120	210	252	210	120	45	10	1
11	1	11	55	165	330	462	462	330	165	55	11
12	1	12	66	220	495	792	924	792	495	220	66
13	1	13	78	286	715	1287	1716	1716	1287	715	286
14	1	14	91	364	1001	2002	3003	3432	3003	2002	1001
15	1	15	105	455	1365	3003	5005	6435	6435	5005	3003
16	1	16	120	560	1820	4368	8008	11440	12870	11440	8008
17	1	17	136	680	2380	6188	12376	19448	24310	24310	19448
18	1	18	153	816	3060	8568	18564	31824	43758	48620	43758
19	1	19	171	969	3876	11628	27132	50388	75582	92378	92378
20	1	20	190	1140	4845	15504	38760	77520	125970	167960	184756

NOTE: $\binom{n}{m} = \dfrac{n(n-1)(n-2)\cdots(n-m+1)}{m(m-1)(m-2)\cdots 3\cdot 2\cdot 1}$; $\binom{n}{0} = 1$; $\binom{n}{1} = n$.

For coefficients missing from the above table, use the relation

$$\binom{n}{m} = \binom{n}{n-m}; \text{ e.g. } \binom{20}{11} = \binom{20}{9} = 167960.$$

Areas under the Standard Normal Curve

This table shows the area between zero (the mean of a standard normal variable) and z. For example, if $z = 1.50$, this is the shaded area shown below which equals .4332.

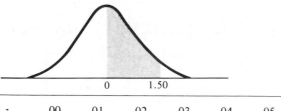

z	.00	.01	.02	.03	.04	.05	.06	.07	.08	.09
0.0	.0000	.0040	.0080	.0120	.0160	.0199	.0239	.0279	.0319	.0359
0.1	.0398	.0438	.0478	.0517	.0557	.0596	.0636	.0675	.0714	.0753
0.2	.0793	.0832	.0871	.0910	.0948	.0987	.1026	.1064	.1103	.1141
0.3	.1179	.1217	.1255	.1293	.1331	.1368	.1406	.1443	.1480	.1517
0.4	.1554	.1591	.1628	.1664	.1700	.1736	.1772	.1808	.1844	.1879
0.5	.1915	.1950	.1985	.2019	.2054	.2088	.2123	.2157	.2190	.2224
0.6	.2257	.2291	.2324	.2357	.2389	.2422	.2454	.2486	.2517	.2549
0.7	.2580	.2611	.2642	.2673	.2704	.2734	.2764	.2794	.2823	.2852
0.8	.2881	.2910	.2939	.2967	.2995	.3023	.3051	.3078	.3106	.3133
0.9	.3159	.3186	.3212	.3238	.3264	.3289	.3315	.3340	.3365	.3389
1.0	.3413	.3438	.3461	.3485	.3508	.3531	.3554	.3577	.3599	.3621
1.1	.3643	.3665	.3686	.3708	.3729	.3749	.3770	.3790	.3810	.3830
1.2	.3849	.3869	.3888	.3907	.3925	.3944	.3962	.3980	.3997	.4015
1.3	.4032	.4049	.4066	.4082	.4099	.4115	.4131	.4147	.4162	.4177
1.4	.4192	.4207	.4222	.4236	.4251	.4265	.4279	.4292	.4306	.4319
1.5	.4332	.4345	.4357	.4370	.4382	.4394	.4406	.4418	.4429	.4441
1.6	.4452	.4463	.4474	.4484	.4495	.4505	.4515	.4525	.4535	.4545
1.7	.4554	.4564	.4573	.4582	.4591	.4599	.4608	.4616	.4625	.4633
1.8	.4641	.4649	.4656	.4664	.4671	.4678	.4686	.4693	.4699	.4706
1.9	.4713	.4719	.4726	.4732	.4738	.4744	.4750	.4756	.4761	.4767
2.0	.4772	.4778	.4783	.4788	.4793	.4798	.4803	.4808	.4812	.4817
2.1	.4821	.4826	.4830	.4834	.4838	.4842	.4846	.4850	.4854	.4857
2.2	.4861	.4864	.4868	.4871	.4875	.4878	.4881	.4884	.4887	.4890
2.3	.4893	.4896	.4898	.4901	.4904	.4906	.4909	.4911	.4913	.4916
2.4	.4918	.4920	.4922	.4925	.4927	.4929	.4931	.4932	.4934	.4936
2.5	.4938	.4940	.4941	.4943	.4945	.4946	.4948	.4949	.4951	.4952
2.6	.4953	.4955	.4956	.4957	.4959	.4960	.4961	.4962	.4963	.4964
2.7	.4965	.4966	.4967	.4968	.4969	.4970	.4971	.4972	.4973	.4974
2.8	.4974	.4975	.4976	.4977	.4977	.4978	.4979	.4979	.4980	.4981
2.9	.4981	.4982	.4982	.4983	.4984	.4984	.4985	.4985	.4986	.4986
3.0	.4987	.4987	.4987	.4988	.4988	.4989	.4989	.4989	.4990	.4990

Source: Adapted from National Bureau of Standards, *Tables of Normal Probability Functions*, Applied Mathematics Series 23 (U.S. Department of Commerce, 1953).

Percentage Points of the *t* Distribution

Example

Pr $(t > 2.086) = 0.025$

Pr $(t > 1.725) = 0.05$ for df $= 20$

Pr $(|t| > 1.725) = 0.10$

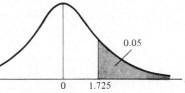

0.05

0   1.725

Pr df	0.25 0.50	0.10 0.20	0.05 0.10	0.025 0.05	0.01 0.02	0.005 0.010	0.001 0.002
1	1.000	3.078	6.314	12.706	31.821	63.657	318.31
2	0.816	1.886	2.920	4.303	6.965	9.925	22.327
3	0.765	1.638	2.353	3.182	4.541	5.841	10.214
4	0.741	1.533	2.132	2.776	3.747	4.604	7.173
5	0.727	1.476	2.015	2.571	3.365	4.032	5.893
6	0.718	1.440	1.943	2.447	3.143	3.707	5.208
7	0.711	1.415	1.895	2.365	2.998	3.499	4.785
8	0.706	1.397	1.860	2.306	2.896	3.355	4.501
9	0.703	1.383	1.833	2.262	2.821	3.250	4.297
10	0.700	1.372	1.812	2.228	2.764	3.169	4.144
11	0.697	1.363	1.796	2.201	2.718	3.106	4.025
12	0.695	1.356	1.782	2.179	2.681	3.055	3.930
13	0.694	1.350	1.771	2.160	2.650	3.012	3.852
14	0.692	1.345	1.761	2.145	2.624	2.977	3.787
15	0.691	1.341	1.753	2.131	2.602	2.947	3.733
16	0.690	1.337	1.746	2.120	2.583	2.921	3.686
17	0.689	1.333	1.740	2.110	2.567	2.898	3.646
18	0.688	1.330	1.734	2.101	2.552	2.878	3.610
19	0.688	1.328	1.729	2.093	2.539	2.861	3.579
20	0.687	1.325	1.725	2.086	2.528	2.845	3.552
21	0.686	1.323	1.721	2.080	2.518	2.831	3.527
22	0.686	1.321	1.717	2.074	2.508	2.819	3.505
23	0.685	1.319	1.714	2.069	2.500	2.807	3.485
24	0.685	1.318	1.711	2.064	2.492	2.797	3.467
25	0.684	1.316	1.708	2.060	2.485	2.787	3.450
26	0.684	1.315	1.706	2.056	2.479	2.779	3.435
27	0.684	1.314	1.703	2.052	2.473	2.771	3.421
28	0.683	1.313	1.701	2.048	2.467	2.763	3.408
29	0.683	1.311	1.699	2.045	2.462	2.756	3.396
30	0.683	1.310	1.697	2.042	2.457	2.750	3.286
40	0.681	1.303	1.684	2.021	2.423	2.704	3.307
60	0.679	1.296	1.671	2.000	2.390	2.660	3.232
120	0.677	1.289	1.658	1.980	2.358	2.167	3.160
∞	0.674	1.282	1.645	1.960	2.326	2.576	3.090

Note: The smaller probability shown at the head of each column is the area in one tail; the larger probability is the area in both tails.

Source: From E. S. Pearson and H. O. Hartley, eds., *Biometrika Tables for Statisticians*, vol. 1, 3d ed., table 12, Cambridge University Press, 1966.

Values of the *F*-Ratio Where the Probability of a Larger Value = to .05

Degrees of freedom for numerator

	1	2	3	4	5	6	7	8	9
1	161.4	199.5	215.7	224.6	230.2	234.0	236.8	238.9	240.5
2	18.51	19.00	19.16	19.25	19.30	19.33	19.35	19.37	19.38
3	10.13	9.55	9.28	9.12	9.01	8.94	8.89	8.85	8.81
4	7.71	6.94	6.59	6.39	6.26	6.16	6.09	6.04	6.00
5	6.61	5.79	5.41	5.19	5.05	4.95	4.88	4.82	4.77
6	5.99	5.14	4.76	4.53	4.39	4.28	4.21	4.15	4.10
7	5.59	4.74	4.35	4.12	3.97	3.87	3.79	3.73	3.68
8	5.32	4.46	4.07	3.84	3.69	3.58	3.50	3.44	3.39
9	5.12	4.26	3.86	3.63	3.48	3.37	3.29	3.23	3.18
10	4.96	4.10	3.71	3.48	3.33	3.22	3.14	3.07	3.02
11	4.84	3.98	3.59	3.36	3.20	3.09	3.01	2.95	2.90
12	4.75	3.89	3.49	3.26	3.11	3.00	2.91	2.85	2.80
13	4.67	3.81	3.41	3.18	3.03	2.92	2.83	2.77	2.71
14	4.60	3.74	3.34	3.11	2.96	2.85	2.76	2.70	2.65
15	4.54	3.68	3.29	3.06	2.90	2.79	2.71	2.64	2.59
16	4.49	3.63	3.24	3.01	2.85	2.74	2.66	2.59	2.54
17	4.45	3.59	3.20	2.96	2.81	2.70	2.61	2.55	2.49
18	4.41	3.55	3.16	2.93	2.77	2.66	2.58	2.51	2.46
19	4.38	3.52	3.13	2.90	2.74	2.63	2.54	2.48	2.42
20	4.35	3.49	3.10	2.87	2.71	2.60	2.51	2.45	2.39
21	4.32	3.47	3.07	2.84	2.68	2.57	2.49	2.42	2.37
22	4.30	3.44	3.05	2.82	2.66	2.55	2.46	2.40	2.34
23	4.28	3.42	3.03	2.80	2.64	2.53	2.44	2.37	2.32
24	4.26	3.40	3.01	2.78	2.62	2.51	2.42	2.36	2.30
25	4.24	3.39	2.99	2.76	2.60	2.49	2.40	2.34	2.28
26	4.23	3.37	2.98	2.74	2.59	2.47	2.39	2.32	2.27
27	4.21	3.35	2.96	2.73	2.57	2.46	2.37	2.31	2.25
28	4.20	3.34	2.95	2.71	2.56	2.45	2.36	2.29	2.24
29	4.18	3.33	2.93	2.70	2.55	2.43	2.35	2.28	2.22
30	4.17	3.32	2.92	2.69	2.53	2.42	2.33	2.27	2.21
40	4.08	3.23	2.84	2.61	2.45	2.34	2.25	2.18	2.12
60	4.00	3.15	2.76	2.53	2.37	2.25	2.17	2.10	2.04
120	3.92	3.07	2.68	2.45	2.29	2.17	2.09	2.02	1.96
∞	3.84	3.00	2.60	2.37	2.21	2.10	2.01	1.94	1.88

Degrees of freedom for denominator

Values of the *F*-Ratio Where the Probability of a Larger Value = to .05

Degrees of freedom for numerator

	10	12	15	20	24	30	40	60	120	∞
1	241.9	243.9	245.9	248.0	249.1	250.1	251.1	252.2	253.3	254.3
2	19.40	19.41	19.43	19.45	19.45	19.46	19.47	19.48	19.49	19.50
3	8.79	8.74	8.70	8.66	8.64	8.62	8.59	8.57	8.55	8.53
4	5.96	5.91	5.86	5.80	5.77	5.75	5.72	5.69	5.66	5.63
5	4.74	4.68	4.62	4.56	4.53	4.50	4.46	4.43	4.40	4.36
6	4.06	4.00	3.94	3.87	3.84	3.81	3.77	3.74	3.70	3.67
7	3.64	3.57	3.51	3.44	3.41	3.38	3.34	3.30	3.27	3.23
8	3.35	3.28	3.22	3.15	3.12	3.08	3.04	3.01	2.97	2.93
9	3.14	3.07	3.01	2.94	2.90	2.86	2.83	2.79	2.75	2.71
10	2.98	2.91	2.85	2.77	2.74	2.70	2.66	2.62	2.58	2.54
11	2.85	2.79	2.72	2.65	2.61	2.57	2.53	2.49	2.45	2.40
12	2.75	2.69	2.62	2.54	2.51	2.47	2.43	2.38	2.34	2.30
13	2.67	2.60	2.53	2.46	2.42	2.38	2.34	2.30	2.25	2.21
14	2.60	2.53	2.46	2.39	2.35	2.31	2.27	2.22	2.18	2.13
15	2.54	2.48	2.40	2.33	2.29	2.25	2.20	2.16	2.11	2.07
16	2.49	2.42	2.35	2.28	2.24	2.19	2.15	2.11	2.06	2.01
17	2.45	2.38	2.31	2.23	2.19	2.15	2.10	2.06	2.01	1.96
18	2.41	2.34	2.27	2.19	2.15	2.11	2.06	2.02	1.97	1.92
19	2.38	2.31	2.23	2.16	2.11	2.07	2.03	1.98	1.93	1.88
20	2.35	2.28	2.20	2.12	2.08	2.04	1.99	1.95	1.90	1.84
21	2.32	2.25	2.18	2.10	2.05	2.01	1.96	1.92	1.87	1.81
22	2.30	2.23	2.15	2.07	2.03	1.98	1.94	1.89	1.84	1.78
23	2.27	2.20	2.13	2.05	2.01	1.96	1.91	1.86	1.81	1.76
24	2.25	2.18	2.11	2.03	1.98	1.94	1.89	1.84	1.79	1.73
25	2.24	2.16	2.09	2.01	1.96	1.92	1.87	1.82	1.77	1.71
26	2.22	2.15	2.07	1.99	1.95	1.90	1.85	1.80	1.75	1.69
27	2.20	2.13	2.06	1.97	1.93	1.88	1.84	1.79	1.73	1.67
28	2.19	2.12	2.04	1.96	1.91	1.87	1.82	1.77	1.71	1.65
29	2.18	2.10	2.03	1.94	1.90	1.85	1.81	1.75	1.70	1.64
30	2.16	2.09	2.01	1.93	1.89	1.84	1.79	1.74	1.68	1.62
40	2.08	2.00	1.92	1.84	1.79	1.74	1.69	1.64	1.58	1.51
60	1.99	1.92	1.84	1.75	1.70	1.65	1.59	1.53	1.47	1.39
120	1.91	1.83	1.75	1.66	1.61	1.55	1.50	1.43	1.35	1.25
∞	1.83	1.75	1.67	1.57	1.52	1.46	1.39	1.32	1.22	1.00

Degrees of freedom for denominator

Values of the *F*-Ratio Where the Probability of a Larger Value = to .01

Degrees of freedom for numerator

		1	2	3	4	5	6	7	8	9
	1	4052	4999.5	5403	5625	5764	5859	5928	5982	6022
	2	98.50	99.00	99.17	99.25	99.30	99.33	99.36	99.37	99.39
	3	34.12	30.82	29.46	28.71	28.24	27.91	27.67	27.49	27.35
	4	21.20	18.00	16.69	15.98	15.52	15.21	14.98	14.80	14.66
	5	16.26	13.27	12.06	11.39	10.97	10.67	10.46	10.29	10.16
	6	13.75	10.92	9.78	9.15	8.75	8.47	8.26	8.10	7.98
	7	12.25	9.55	8.45	7.85	7.46	7.19	6.99	6.84	6.72
	8	11.26	8.65	7.59	7.01	6.63	6.37	6.18	6.03	5.91
	9	10.56	8.02	6.99	6.42	6.06	5.80	5.61	5.47	5.35
	10	10.04	7.56	6.55	5.99	5.64	5.39	5.20	5.06	4.94
	11	9.65	7.21	6.22	5.67	5.32	5.07	4.89	4.74	4.63
	12	9.33	6.93	5.95	5.41	5.06	4.82	4.64	4.50	4.39
	13	9.07	6.70	5.74	5.21	4.86	4.62	4.44	4.30	4.19
	14	8.86	6.51	5.56	5.04	4.69	4.46	4.28	4.14	4.03
	15	8.68	6.36	5.42	4.89	4.56	4.32	4.14	4.00	3.89
	16	8.53	6.23	5.29	4.77	4.44	4.20	4.03	3.89	3.78
	17	8.40	6.11	5.18	4.67	4.34	4.10	3.93	3.79	3.68
	18	8.29	6.01	5.09	4.58	4.25	4.01	3.84	3.71	3.60
	19	8.18	5.93	5.01	4.50	4.17	3.94	3.77	3.63	3.52
	20	8.10	5.85	4.94	4.43	4.10	3.87	3.70	3.56	3.46
	21	8.02	5.78	4.87	4.37	4.04	3.81	3.64	3.51	3.40
	22	7.95	5.72	4.82	4.31	3.99	3.76	3.59	3.45	3.35
	23	7.88	5.66	4.76	4.26	3.94	3.71	3.54	3.41	3.30
	24	7.82	5.61	4.72	4.22	3.90	3.67	3.50	3.36	3.26
	25	7.77	5.57	4.68	4.18	3.85	3.63	3.46	3.32	3.22
	26	7.72	5.53	4.64	4.14	3.82	3.59	3.42	3.29	3.18
	27	7.68	5.49	4.60	4.11	3.78	3.56	3.39	3.26	3.15
	28	7.64	5.45	4.57	4.07	3.75	3.53	3.36	3.23	3.12
	29	7.60	5.42	4.54	4.04	3.73	3.50	3.33	3.20	3.09
	30	7.56	5.39	4.51	4.02	3.70	3.47	3.30	3.17	3.07
	40	7.31	5.18	4.31	3.83	3.51	3.29	3.12	2.99	2.89
	60	7.08	4.98	4.13	3.65	3.34	3.12	2.95	2.82	2.72
	120	6.85	4.79	3.95	3.48	3.17	2.96	2.79	2.66	2.56
	∞	6.63	4.61	3.78	3.32	3.02	2.80	2.64	2.51	2.41

Degrees of freedom for denominator

Values of the *F*-Ratio Where the Probability of a Larger Value = to .01

Degrees of freedom for numerator

	10	12	15	20	24	30	40	60	120	∞
1	6056	6106	6157	6209	6235	6261	6287	6313	6339	6366
2	99.40	99.42	99.43	99.45	99.46	99.47	99.47	99.48	99.49	99.50
3	27.23	27.05	26.87	26.69	26.60	26.50	26.41	26.32	26.22	26.13
4	14.55	14.37	14.20	14.02	13.93	13.84	13.75	13.65	13.56	13.46
5	10.05	9.89	9.72	9.55	9.47	9.38	9.29	9.20	9.11	9.02
6	7.87	7.72	7.56	7.40	7.31	7.23	7.14	7.06	6.97	6.88
7	6.62	6.47	6.31	6.16	6.07	5.99	5.91	5.82	5.74	5.65
8	5.81	5.67	5.52	5.36	5.28	5.20	5.12	5.03	4.95	4.86
9	5.26	5.11	4.96	4.81	4.73	4.65	4.57	4.48	4.40	4.31
10	4.85	4.71	4.56	4.41	4.33	4.25	4.17	4.08	4.00	3.91
11	4.54	4.40	4.25	4.10	4.02	3.94	3.86	3.78	3.69	3.60
12	4.30	4.16	4.01	3.86	3.78	3.70	3.62	3.54	3.45	3.36
13	4.10	3.96	3.82	3.66	3.59	3.51	3.43	3.34	3.25	3.17
14	3.94	3.80	3.66	3.51	3.43	3.35	3.27	3.18	3.09	3.00
15	3.80	3.67	3.52	3.37	3.29	3.21	3.13	3.05	2.96	2.87
16	3.69	3.55	3.41	3.26	3.18	3.10	3.02	2.93	2.84	2.75
17	3.59	3.46	3.31	3.16	3.08	3.00	2.92	2.83	2.75	2.65
18	3.51	3.37	3.23	3.08	3.00	2.92	2.84	2.75	2.66	2.57
19	3.43	3.30	3.15	3.00	2.92	2.84	2.76	2.67	2.58	2.49
20	3.37	3.23	3.09	2.94	2.86	2.78	2.69	2.61	2.52	2.42
21	3.31	3.17	3.03	2.88	2.80	2.72	2.64	2.55	2.46	2.36
22	3.26	3.12	2.98	2.83	2.75	2.67	2.58	2.50	2.40	2.31
23	3.21	3.07	2.93	2.78	2.70	2.62	2.54	2.45	2.35	2.26
24	3.17	3.03	2.89	2.74	2.66	2.58	2.49	2.40	2.31	2.21
25	3.13	2.99	2.85	2.70	2.62	2.54	2.45	2.36	2.27	2.17
26	3.09	2.96	2.81	2.66	2.58	2.50	2.42	2.33	2.23	2.13
27	3.06	2.93	2.78	2.63	2.55	2.47	2.38	2.29	2.20	2.10
28	3.03	2.90	2.75	2.60	2.52	2.44	2.35	2.26	2.17	2.06
29	3.00	2.87	2.73	2.57	2.49	2.41	2.33	2.23	2.14	2.03
30	2.98	2.84	2.70	2.55	2.47	2.39	2.30	2.21	2.11	2.01
40	2.80	2.66	2.52	2.37	2.29	2.20	2.11	2.02	1.92	1.80
60	2.63	2.50	2.35	2.20	2.12	2.03	1.94	1.84	1.73	1.60
120	2.47	2.34	2.19	2.03	1.95	1.86	1.76	1.66	1.53	1.38
∞	2.32	2.18	2.04	1.88	1.79	1.70	1.59	1.47	1.32	1.00

Degrees of freedom for denominator

Source: From E. S. Pearson and H. O., Hartley, eds., *Biometrika Tables for Statisticians,* vol. 1, 3d ed., table 18, Cambridge University Press, 1966.

Table H

Values of d_L and d_U for the Durbin-Watson Test ($\alpha = .05$)

n	$k = 1$		$k = 2$		$k = 3$		$k = 4$		$k = 5$	
	d_L	d_U	d_L	d_U	d_L	d_U	d_L	d_U	d_L	d_U
15	1.08	1.36	0.95	1.54	0.82	1.75	0.69	1.97	0.56	2.21
16	1.10	1.37	0.98	1.54	0.86	1.73	0.74	1.93	0.62	2.15
17	1.13	1.38	1.02	1.54	0.90	1.71	0.78	1.90	0.67	2.10
18	1.16	1.39	1.05	1.53	0.93	1.69	0.82	1.87	0.71	2.06
19	1.18	1.40	1.08	1.53	0.97	1.68	0.86	1.85	0.75	2.02
20	1.20	1.41	1.10	1.54	1.00	1.68	0.90	1.83	0.79	1.99
21	1.22	1.42	1.13	1.54	1.03	1.67	0.93	1.81	0.83	1.96
22	1.24	1.43	1.15	1.54	1.05	1.66	0.96	1.80	0.86	1.94
23	1.26	1.44	1.17	1.54	1.08	1.66	0.99	1.79	0.90	1.92
24	1.27	1.45	1.19	1.55	1.10	1.66	1.01	1.78	0.93	1.90
25	1.29	1.45	1.21	1.55	1.12	1.66	1.04	1.77	0.95	1.89
26	1.30	1.46	1.22	1.55	1.14	1.65	1.06	1.76	0.98	1.88
27	1.32	1.47	1.24	1.56	1.16	1.65	1.08	1.76	1.01	1.86
28	1.33	1.48	1.26	1.56	1.18	1.65	1.10	1.75	1.03	1.85
29	1.34	1.48	1.27	1.56	1.20	1.65	1.12	1.74	1.05	1.84
30	1.35	1.49	1.28	1.57	1.21	1.65	1.14	1.74	1.07	1.83
31	1.36	1.50	1.30	1.57	1.23	1.65	1.16	1.74	1.09	1.83
32	1.37	1.50	1.31	1.57	1.24	1.65	1.18	1.73	1.11	1.82
33	1.38	1.51	1.32	1.58	1.26	1.65	1.19	1.73	1.13	1.81
34	1.39	1.51	1.33	1.58	1.27	1.65	1.21	1.73	1.15	1.81
35	1.40	1.52	1.34	1.58	1.28	1.65	1.22	1.73	1.16	1.80
36	1.41	1.52	1.35	1.59	1.29	1.65	1.24	1.73	1.18	1.80
37	1.42	1.53	1.36	1.59	1.31	1.66	1.25	1.72	1.19	1.80
38	1.43	1.54	1.37	1.59	1.32	1.66	1.26	1.72	1.21	1.79
39	1.43	1.54	1.38	1.60	1.33	1.66	1.27	1.72	1.22	1.79
40	1.44	1.54	1.39	1.60	1.34	1.66	1.29	1.72	1.23	1.79
45	1.48	1.57	1.43	1.62	1.38	1.67	1.34	1.72	1.29	1.78
50	1.50	1.59	1.46	1.63	1.42	1.67	1.38	1.72	1.34	1.77
55	1.53	1.60	1.49	1.64	1.45	1.68	1.41	1.72	1.38	1.77
60	1.55	1.62	1.51	1.65	1.48	1.69	1.44	1.73	1.41	1.77
65	1.57	1.63	1.54	1.66	1.50	1.70	1.47	1.73	1.44	1.77
70	1.58	1.64	1.55	1.67	1.52	1.70	1.49	1.74	1.46	1.77
75	1.60	1.65	1.57	1.68	1.54	1.71	1.51	1.74	1.49	1.77
80	1.61	1.66	1.59	1.69	1.56	1.72	1.53	1.74	1.51	1.77
85	1.62	1.67	1.60	1.70	1.57	1.72	1.55	1.75	1.52	1.77
90	1.63	1.68	1.61	1.70	1.59	1.73	1.57	1.75	1.54	1.78
95	1.64	1.69	1.62	1.71	1.60	1.73	1.58	1.75	1.56	1.78
100	1.65	1.69	1.63	1.72	1.61	1.74	1.59	1.76	1.57	1.78

Table H *(concluded)*

Values of d_L and d_U for the Durbin-Watson Test ($\alpha = .05$)

n	$k = 1$ d_L	d_U	$k = 2$ d_L	d_U	$k = 3$ d_L	d_U	$k = 4$ d_L	d_U	$k = 5$ d_L	d_U
15	0.81	1.07	0.70	1.25	0.59	1.46	0.49	1.70	0.39	1.96
16	0.84	1.09	0.74	1.25	0.63	1.44	0.53	1.66	0.44	1.90
17	0.87	1.10	0.77	1.25	0.67	1.43	0.57	1.63	0.48	1.85
18	0.90	1.12	0.80	1.26	0.71	1.42	0.61	1.60	0.52	1.80
19	0.93	1.13	0.83	1.26	0.74	1.41	0.65	1.58	0.56	1.77
20	0.95	1.15	0.86	1.27	0.77	1.41	0.68	1.57	0.60	1.74
21	0.97	1.16	0.89	1.27	0.80	1.41	0.72	1.55	0.63	1.71
22	1.00	1.17	0.91	1.28	0.83	1.40	0.75	1.54	0.66	1.69
23	1.02	1.19	0.94	1.29	0.86	1.40	0.77	1.53	0.70	1.67
24	1.04	1.20	0.96	1.30	0.88	1.41	0.80	1.53	0.72	1.66
25	1.05	1.21	0.98	1.30	0.90	1.41	0.83	1.52	0.75	1.65
26	1.07	1.22	1.00	1.31	0.93	1.41	0.85	1.52	0.78	1.64
27	1.09	1.23	1.02	1.32	0.95	1.41	0.88	1.51	0.81	1.63
28	1.10	1.24	1.04	1.32	0.97	1.41	0.90	1.51	0.83	1.62
29	1.12	1.25	1.05	1.33	0.99	1.42	0.92	1.51	0.85	1.61
30	1.13	1.26	1.07	1.34	1.01	1.42	0.94	1.51	0.88	1.61
31	1.15	1.27	1.08	1.34	1.02	1.42	0.96	1.51	0.90	1.60
32	1.16	1.28	1.10	1.35	1.04	1.43	0.98	1.51	0.92	1.60
33	1.17	1.29	1.11	1.36	1.05	1.43	1.00	1.51	0.94	1.59
34	1.18	1.30	1.13	1.36	1.07	1.43	1.01	1.51	0.95	1.59
35	1.19	1.31	1.14	1.37	1.08	1.44	1.03	1.51	0.97	1.59
36	1.21	1.32	1.15	1.38	1.10	1.44	1.04	1.51	0.99	1.59
37	1.22	1.32	1.16	1.38	1.11	1.45	1.06	1.51	1.00	1.59
38	1.23	1.33	1.18	1.39	1.12	1.45	1.07	1.52	1.02	1.58
39	1.24	1.34	1.19	1.39	1.14	1.45	1.09	1.52	1.03	1.58
40	1.25	1.34	1.20	1.40	1.15	1.46	1.10	1.52	1.05	1.58
45	1.29	1.38	1.24	1.42	1.20	1.48	1.16	1.53	1.11	1.58
50	1.32	1.40	1.28	1.45	1.24	1.49	1.20	1.54	1.16	1.59
55	1.36	1.43	1.32	1.47	1.28	1.51	1.25	1.55	1.21	1.59
60	1.38	1.45	1.35	1.48	1.32	1.52	1.28	1.56	1.25	1.60
65	1.41	1.47	1.38	1.50	1.35	1.53	1.31	1.57	1.28	1.61
70	1.43	1.49	1.40	1.52	1.37	1.55	1.34	1.58	1.31	1.61
75	1.45	1.50	1.42	1.53	1.39	1.56	1.37	1.59	1.34	1.62
80	1.47	1.52	1.44	1.54	1.42	1.57	1.39	1.60	1.36	1.62
85	1.48	1.53	1.46	1.55	1.43	1.58	1.41	1.60	1.39	1.63
90	1.50	1.54	1.47	1.56	1.45	1.59	1.43	1.61	1.41	1.64
95	1.51	1.55	1.49	1.57	1.47	1.60	1.45	1.62	1.42	1.64
100	1.52	1.56	1.50	1.58	1.48	1.60	1.46	1.63	1.44	1.65

Source: J. Durbin and G. S. Watson, "Testing for Serial Correlation in Least Squares Regression," *Biometrika*, June 1951.

Table I

Formulas for Taking a Derivative

1. The derivative of a constant is zero, and the derivative of x is one.

2. Derivative of a monomial in x:

$$\frac{d(cx^n)}{dx} = cnx^{n-1}$$

Example:

$$\frac{d(2x^3)}{dx} = 2(3)x^{(3-1)} = 6x^2$$

3. Derivative of a power of a polynomial in x where, $u = f(x)$:

$$\frac{d(cu^n)}{dx} = cnu^{n-1}\frac{du}{dx}$$

Example:

$$\frac{d(2x^3 - 4x^2)^3}{dx} = 3(2x^3 - 4x^2)^2(6x^2 - 8x)$$

4. Derivative of a sum of polynomials in x where, $u = f(x)$, $v = g(x)$, . . . , $z = h(x)$:

$$\frac{d(u + v + z)}{dx} = \frac{du}{dx} + \frac{dv}{dx} + \frac{dz}{dx}$$

Example:

$$\frac{d(3x^3 - 6x^2 + 5x - 10)}{dx} = 9x^2 - 12x + 5$$

5. Derivative of a product of two polynomials in x where, $u = f(x)$, $v = g(x)$:

$$\frac{d(uv)}{dx} = u\frac{dv}{dx} + v\frac{du}{dx}$$

Example:

$$\frac{d(x^2 + 2x)(x - 3)}{dx} = (x^2 + 2x)(1) + (x - 3)(2x + 2) = 3x^2 - 2x - 6$$

6. Derivative of a quotient of two polynomials in x where, $u = f(x)$, $v = g(x)$:

$$\frac{d\left(\frac{u}{v}\right)}{dx} = \frac{v\dfrac{du}{dx} - u\dfrac{dv}{dx}}{v^2}$$

Example:

$$\frac{d\left[\dfrac{x^3 - 1}{x^2 + 3}\right]}{dx} = \frac{(x^2 + 3)(3x^2) - (x^3 - 1)(2x)}{(x^2 + 3)^2}$$

$$= \frac{x^4 + 9x^2 + 2x}{(x^2 + 3)^2}$$

7. To take the partial derivative with respect to a particular variable of a multivariate function, $Y = f(X_1, X_2, \ldots, X_n)$, use the formulas above while treating the other independent variables as constants.

Example:

$$w = 3x^2 + 2xy - 3z$$

$$\frac{\partial w}{\partial x} = 6x + 2y$$

$$\frac{\partial w}{\partial y} = 2x$$

$$\frac{\partial w}{\partial z} = 3$$

Author Index

Subject Index

This book has been set Linotron 202, in 10 and 9 point
Palatino, leaded 2 points. Chapter numbers are 1⅛"
height Cheltenham Bold and chapter titles are 20 point
Cheltenham Book Condensed. The size of the type page is
27 by 46 picas.